WOMEN'S SUFFRAGE IN AMERICA

EYEWITNESS HISTORY

WOMEN'S SUFFRAGE IN AMERICA

UPDATED EDITION

Elizabeth Frost-Knappman
and
Kathryn Cullen-DuPont

☑®

Facts On File, Inc.

Women's Suffrage in America, Updated Edition

Copyright © 2005, 1992, by Elizabeth Frost-Knappman and Kathryn Cullen-DuPont
Maps © 2005 by Facts On File, Inc.

Facts On File, Inc.
132 West 31st Street
New York NY 10001

Library of Congress Cataloging-in-Publication Data
Frost-Knappman, Elizabeth.
    Women's suffrage in America : an eyewitness history / Elizabeth Frost-Knappman and Kathryn Cullen-DuPont. — Updated ed.
        p. cm. — (Eyewitness history)
    Includes bibliographical references and index.
    ISBN 0-8160-5693-5
    1. Women—Suffrage—United States—History. 2. Women—Suffrage—United States—History—Sources. 3. Suffragists—United States—History. I. Cullen-DuPont, Kathryn. II. Title. III. Series.
    JK1896.F77 2005
    324.6'23'0973—dc22   2004043339

Facts On File books are available at special discounts when purchased in bulk quantities for businesses, associations, institutions, or sales promotions. Please call our Special Sales Department in New York at (212) 967-8800 or (800) 322-8755.

You can find Facts On File on the World Wide Web at
http://www.factsonfile.com

Text design by Joan M. Toro
Cover design by Cathy Rincon
Maps by Dale Williams

Printed in the United States of America

VB JT 10 9 8 7 6 5 4 3 2

This book is printed on acid-free paper.

There is a word sweeter
than Mother, Home, or Heaven;
that word is Liberty.

—*Gravestone of Matilda Joslyn Gage, 1884*

Grateful acknowledgment is made to the following for permission to reprint previously published material:

Carrie Chapman Catt Papers
Rare Books and Manuscripts Division
The New York Public Library
Astor, Lenox and Tilden Foundations

Challenging Years, by Harriot Stanton Blatch and Alma Lutz, Hyperion Press, Inc.

Ethel Eyre Valentine Dreier Papers
Sophia Smith Collection
Smith College
Northampton, Mass.

Isabel Howland Papers
Sophia Smith Collection
Smith College
Northampton, Mass.

Smith Family Papers
Rare Books and Manuscripts Division
The New York Public Library
Astor, Lenox and Tilden Foundations

We Were There: The Story of Working Women in America, by Barbara Mayer Wertheimer,
copyright © 1977 by Barbara Mayer Wertheimer.
Reprinted by permission of Pantheon Books,
a division of Random House, Inc.

Women in the Campaign to Organize Garment Workers, 1880–1917,
by Carolyn Daniel McCreesh, Garland Publishing Co.

For our daughters,
Amanda Lee Frost Knappman
and
Melissa Cullen-DuPont

NOTE ON PHOTOS

Many of the illustrations and photographs used in this book are old, historical images. The quality of the prints is not always up to modern standards, as in some cases the originals are damaged. The content of the illustrations, however, made their inclusion important despite problems in reproduction.

NOTE ON THE EYEWITNESS TESTIMONY

Many of the letters and diary entries included in this book were written hurriedly by their authors. Others were written by women of strong convictions but limited education. The authors of this book have chosen to let the eyewitnesses' words stand as written, noting errors only when absolutely necessary for comprehension.

CONTENTS

Acknowledgments to the First Edition   xi

Acknowledgments to the Updated Edition   xiii

Authors' Preface to the Updated Edition   xv

1. What Do Women Want? 1800–1834   1
2. Slavery and Suffrage: 1835–1839   21
3. Women Overseas—The World Anti-Slavery Convention: 1840–1847   49
4. Women of Seneca Falls: 1848–1849   72
5. A Wave of Agitation: 1850–1854   84
6. A Whiff of Scandal—Divorce and Reform: 1855–1860   117
7. Civil Wars: 1861–1865   135
8. Bitter Defeats: 1865–1869   165
9. Separate Paths to Suffrage: 1870–1879   202
10. United Once More: 1880–1892   235
11. End of an Era: 1893–1906   265
12. On Strike and On Parade: 1907–1916   292
13. To War and Victory: 1917–1920   325

Epilogue   353

Appendix A: Documents   357

Appendix B: Biographies of Major Personalities   426

Appendix C: Maps   453

Notes   457

Bibliography   463

Index   478

ACKNOWLEDGMENTS TO THE FIRST EDITION

The authors would like to thank Susan Brainard and Jeanne Jimenez for assembling the art and checking the bibliography and footnotes; Cassie Adcock and Mary Jane Meehan for helping to compile the biographies; Cindy Cote, Stephen Athenas, Lillian Rivera, and Jeanne Jimenez for careful keyboarding and organization; Gloria Eustis and the staff of the Chester Public Library, Claudia Funke and the staff of the New York Public Library, Lois Nadel of the Chester Book Company, and Bernard Titowsky of the Austin Bookshop for tracking down books and alerting us to additional sources; Claudianna Mapp for research assistance; Joseph DuPont for taking our picture; Edward Knappman for conceiving the Eyewitness History series; Gerard Helferich for believing in us and commissioning this book; our thoughtful, brainy, and scholarly editors, Nick Bakalar and Traci Cothran, for their guidance and support; Susan Schwartz and Michelle Fellner for keeping this book on schedule; Joan Atwood and Joe Reilly for diligent copyediting; and, finally, our families—our parents and parents-in-law, Lorena Launer Frost, Rena Carpenter Knappman, William Knappman, Arlene Cullen, Martin Cullen, and Barbara DuPont, for their interest and encouragement; our children, Amanda Lee Frost Knappman and Melissa Cullen-DuPont, for providing excellent messenger services; Jesse Cullen-DuPont, for keeping the pencils sharpened; and, in particular, our husbands for help too constant to describe here with anything approaching accuracy.

Acknowledgments to the Updated Edition

The authors would like to thank Victoria Harlow for her conscientious photo research; Nanci A. Young, college archivist for the Smith College Archives, Amy Hague, curator of manuscripts for the Sophia Smith Collection, and the staff of the New York Public Library, for their research assistance; and Cheryl Rivers of the Folk Art Institute of the American Folk Art Museum for sharing her knowledge of suffrage quilts. We also thank Kristine Shiavi for administrative assistance and our editor, Nicole Bowen, and her assistant, Laura Shauger, for their support for a revised and expanded *Women's Suffrage in America*. Finally, thanks to our art director, Cathy Rincon, and copy editor, Laura Magzis.

AUTHORS' PREFACE TO THE UPDATED EDITION

Women's Suffrage in America, published in 1992, was an early book on how women won the vote in the United States. Since that time, mountains of research have appeared on the first wave of the women's movement. While original sources—*History of Women's Suffrage; Life and Work of Susan B. Anthony; William Lloyd Garrison, 1805–1879; Lydia Marie Child Selected Letters, 1817–1880; Democracy in America; Loom and Spindle; Path Breaking, Journal of a Residence on a Georgian Plantation in 1838–1839; Mary Chesnut's Civil War; Women of the War; The Classic Slave Narratives;* and others—remain our most important texts, we have drawn from these and many excellent new works for the revised edition. Of special interest were Joan D. Hendrick's *Harriet Beecher Stowe: A Life;* Barbara Goldsmith's *Other Powers: The Age of Suffrage, Spiritualism, and the Scandalous Victoria Woodhull;* Ellen Chesler's *Woman of Valor: Margaret Sanger and the Birth Control Movement in America;* Elizabeth D. Leonard's *Yankee Women: Gender Battles in the Civil War;* David Von Drehle's *Triangle: The Fire That Changed America;* and Marlene Stein Wortman's *Women in American Law.* Additional collections of archived papers, such as the Isabel Howland Papers and the Ethel Eyre Valentine Dreier Papers housed in the Sofia Smith Collection, have also been consulted.

We have also expanded the revised edition by the addition of approximately 800 dates, which add a broader context to the strictly "movement" events we included in 1992. Women's achievements during the 19th century were exceptional and an inspiration to others. They doubtless encouraged the perception that women were capable and worthy of voting and running for political office.

In the Historical Context sections we have added court decisions regarding property rights, dowry, and divorce; historical background on the women's temperance movement; discussion of women spies during the Civil War; newly discovered information about Clara Barton's work as head of the Missing Soldier's Office; a closer view of Susan B. Anthony's trial on charges of unlawful voting; an examination of Frances Willard's efforts to bring temperance supporters into the suffrage movement; an expanded examination of southern leaders' exploitation of racism in pursuit of women's suffrage, as well as the failure of the movement's national leaders to adequately repond; a survey of the many other countries extending suffrage to women, even as American women remained disenfranchised; and a closer view of the gratitude suffrage workers felt toward their local leaders as the end of the 72-year-long struggle finally approached.

New quotations have been added to the Eyewitness Testimony sections of this book. A number of these newer citations have been added to give a fuller picture of women in the South who lived under slavery. Other letters, such as those to Ethel Dreier, chairman of the Woman Suffrage Party of Brooklyn, have been added to show the deep and personal appreciation many women expressed to those who led the suffrage campaign. Still others, including the October 5, 1897, letter of Susan B. Anthony, and the September 26, 1905, letter of Anna Howard Shaw, throw light on the suffrage leaders' desire to include African-American women in the suffrage movement, their concerns about southern women's opposition to such inclusion, and their ultimate accommodation of the white southerners' views.

More than 20 new photographs and several maps, combined with the updating of each section of the *History of Women's Suffrage in America,* result in a broader, more precise, and, we hope, interesting account of women's journey from the margins to the mainstream of American public life. It presents the essential facts of women's struggle for the vote and acceptance of full citizens in their country in a format designed to appeal equally to student, scholar, and general reader.

We have added almost 20 new biographies to Appendix B. Readers will now find thumbnail histories of figures such as Clara Barton, Myra Bradwell, Lucy Burns, Sara Forten, and Frances Watkins Harper.

We have added a new map appendix C, which did not appear in the original edition. The bibliography has been thoroughly updated and expanded with new sources.

1

What Do Women Want?
1800–1834

THE HISTORICAL CONTEXT

This story begins when women, as Abigail Adams wrote during the American Revolution, were "excluded from honors and offices." The English common law, which regulated the relation of husband and wife in the colonies, gave the "custody" of the wife's person to the husband. It gave him her earnings. It gave him her personal property, which he could will to others. It gave him her real estate, which he could sell or mortgage. Some colonies and states ranked married women, insane persons, and "idiots" together as not fit to make a will. No woman could vote, hold office, or sit on a jury.

English common law stated that, once married, a wife became a *femme coverte* (or *feme covert*), "veiled" or "overshadowed" by her new married status: "When a small brooke or little river incorporatheth with Rhodanus, Humber, or the Thames, the poor rivulet loses its name . . . it beareth no sway, it possesseth nothing . . ." Similarly, a wife looked to her husband as her superior.[1]

After the Treaty of Paris in 1783 brought the final consummation of independence to Americans, the legal position of women did not improve. Women were not even mentioned in the U.S. Constitution that governed the new nation.

The early 19th century cast women in a variety of new roles. These years saw the highest rate of urbanization in American history as people moved to the cities and began producing goods for sale as well as for use at home.[2] In 1787 having earned $150 from the sale of farm products, a farmer in New England wrote: ". . . I never spent more than ten dollars a year which was for salt, nails, and the like. Nothing to eat, drink, or wear was bought, as my farm provided all."[3] Yet from 1825 to 1855 home production of goods dropped sharply. During these years fewer and fewer women made cloth, candles, bread, butter, medicine, or soap for family use; instead, they bought them. As women changed from home-based producers to consumers, their status declined. Factory worker Harriet Robinson wrote, "the law took no cognizance of woman as a moneyspender. She was a ward, an appendage, a relict."[4]

1

European travelers to America commented on the lack of freedom granted to married as compared to single women. On this point writers from Alexis de Tocqueville to Frances Wright and Harriet Martineau agreed. They observed that a married woman gave up all rights of person and property to her husband. A husband owned his wife's wages and labor. Her clothing, household goods, dowry, and inheritance were all his. A husband could sell, lend, mortgage, or give away his wife's material possessions as he chose. However, his wife could not similarly dispose of this same property. He also owned her person in terms of sexual rights. Perhaps "no people, with the exception of chattel slaves, had less proprietary rights over themselves in eighteenth-century and early nineteenth-century America than married women."[5]

Between 1800 and midcentury a woman gave up so many rights when she married that lawyers said she entered a state of "civil death." If a woman's husband died without a will, a wife's right to inherit property was restricted to one-third of his estate. In New York a widow could inherit only a Bible, pictures, books and the like under $50 in value, the spinning wheel, stove, loom, 10 sheep, two pigs and their pork. Along with clothes, bedding and so forth, she also received "one table, six chairs, six knives and forks, six tea cups and saucers, one sugar dish, one milk-pot and six spoons." To some degree a woman's dower rights protected her, giving her a share of the family's joint estate. This meant that no sale, loan, or disposal of a couple's joint property could occur without her authorization. But the courts saw frequent instances of husbands coercing their wives into agreeing with their decisions. Because of this, the laws in some states required wives to be privately examined by judges to determine that they willingly agreed with the disposal of the property. Girls were regularly excluded from their fathers' wills.[6]

Although women were entitled to one-third of their dead husband's property in many of the colonies, men tried to restrict them. "Maryland legislators attempted to prevent a single woman's control over her rightful property by introducing a statute in 1634 declaring that any female inheriting land must marry (or remarry) within seven years of possession or forfeit her claim."[7]

Divorcing was difficult for women in the North, impossible in the South. When the courts did grant a divorce, it was only for extreme cruelty, adultery, desertion, or nonsupport. If divorced, a woman had no right to custody of her own children.[8] Even when a wife had legal reasons for divorcing her husband, her conduct could become an issue, depriving her of property rights. For instance, in 1828 New York law permitted divorce for adultery. That year a Mrs. Peckford went to court to divorce her philandering husband. However, the judge (called Chancellor) disapproved of Mrs. Peckford because she had taken a trip to England without the express permission of her husband, exposing the man to "temptation." In the judge's view, Mrs. Peckford was responsible for her husband's misbehavior. To punish her, he limited Mrs. Peckford's property settlement to the barest minimum. He declared that the couple's property was worth $12,000. Had Mrs. Peckford "been perfectly discreet, prudent and submissive to her husband," he asserted, "I should have allowed her half of this property." However, since she was not "submissive," he granted her only "an annuity equal to the value of one third of the property, at six percent," or about $400 a year for the rest of her life—assuming she lived another 25 years—payable in quarterly installments. So Mrs. Peckford, who was legally the innocent party, found her own conduct penalized by the court. The *Peckford v. Peckford* decision set a precedent, influential through modern times, for making the "proper" conduct of wives a determining factor in divorce settlements.[9]

Married women had no legal right to their own wages, for they were considered incapable of spending their own or other people's money. "In Massachusetts, before 1840, a woman could not, legally, be treasurer of her own sewing society unless some man were responsible for her."[10] Along with dower rights, one of the few legal advantages of marriage for women was that husbands had to provide for their support, including all debts. However, this did not offset the loss of liberty that women faced when they married.

Most state constitutions specifically denied the vote to women. But New Jersey was an exception. On July 2, 1776, the state adopted a constitution that gave the vote to all free inhabitants who met legal age, property, and residency standards. But by 1800 local politicians were condemning the practice of women voting, arguing that soon the legislature would be "filled with petticoats." Men claimed that married women had no independent income and thus should not be allowed to vote. By 1807 the legislature passed a law restricting the right to vote to white propertied males, declaring: "Whereas doubts have been raised and great diversities in practice obtained throughout the state in regard to the admission of aliens, females and persons of color, or negroes to vote in elections . . . it is highly necessary to the safety, quiet, good order and dignity of the state, to clear up said doubts by an act of the representatives of the people . . ."[11]

On top of the legal discrimination they faced, women had few educational opportunities. In 1791 in an "Oration upon Female Education . . ." a Boston speaker explained that as sons were cultivating their minds, preparing them for important employments ahead, daughters should try to become amiable sisters, virtuous children, and mothers. Educators believed women were not bright enough for mathematical or scientific study. Daughters of the wealthy learned only the arts of sewing, painting, and singing. In 1793 the Reverend John Cosens Ogden wrote in *The Female Guide,* that under the Constitution, men were born with an equal right to be elected to the highest office, women, to be the wife of the most eminent man. The Scottish-born Frances Wright, the first woman in America to lecture to "mixed" audiences of men and women,

Women voting in New Jersey before 1800 *(Library of Congress)*

wrote in *Views of Society and Manners in America* (1821), "Hitherto the education of women has been but slightly attended to." There were no advanced educational opportunities for women until Emma Hart Willard opened a seminary for girls in Troy, New York, in 1821. Barred from observing the teaching methods used in men's schools, Willard had to carve cones and pyramids out of turnips and potatoes to teach her girls solid geometry. When she opened Troy Female Seminary, parents were shocked to see their daughters drawing the human circulatory system on the blackboard, so shocked, in fact, that textbook pages depicting human anatomy were then pasted over with cardboard. Nonetheless, a more challenging curriculum was at last being offered to girls, although it in no way equaled

Emma Hart Willard opened the
Troy Female Seminary in Troy,
New York. *(New York Public Library
Picture Collection)*

that of males. Between 1821 and 1872, more than
12,000 women attended the Troy Seminary, and many
of them started their own schools later.[12]

If education for European-American girls was inferior, schooling for African Americans was unavailable.
In the South, it was against the law to teach enslaved
children to read. To do so might undermine the ideology of their inferiority. An enslaved female "faced additional hazards peculiar to her sex. She was used for
breeding purposes to increase her owner's labor force
or his stock of saleable merchandise . . . She had, moreover, no defense against the sexual advances of any
white man, a fact attested to by the widespread presence of mulattoes . . ."[13]

A few freed men and women sent their children to
schools founded by African-American women in South
Carolina, Georgia, and Louisiana, but in the North,
African-American children could not attend public
schools.

The entry of New England women into the labor
market and the need for an educated workforce opened
up education to white girls. In 1814 Francis Cabot
Lowell set up the first power loom in the United States,
uniting spinning and weaving in one factory in
Waltham, Massachusetts. He recruited single farm girls
to tend the power-driven machines as they were disciplined, cheap, and offered no competition for the existing skilled workmen.[14]

The New England textile mills, the first factories in
America, spread rapidly. Large-scale manufacturing saw its full development in
Lowell, Massachusetts. The Merrimack factory in Lowell opened in 1823, two
others started up in 1828, one in 1830, three more in 1831 and another in
1835. Between 1822 and 1839, nine textile companies had opened their doors.
The town's population grew from 200 in 1820 to 17,633 in 1836. The mills
expanded throughout New England.[15]

As a result, the number of women who worked outside the home for
wages during the early part of the 19th century rose dramatically. Concentrated in a few low-paying occupations, most women worked in factories or took
in sewing. By 1831 women constituted 40,000 of all 58,000 textile workers
and were rapidly moving into about 100 other industrial occupations.[16]

In their letters home women wrote that they liked the new work in textiles. They preferred the independence of mill work to farm labor or live-in
domestic service. Further, as more and more young men migrated west,
women needed to fend for themselves. They yearned to escape the isolation of
their fathers' farms to earn their own money in the mills. Most women worked
for only a few years, then married, using their money to pay off debts, to help
fathers pay for their farms, to send brothers or sisters to school, or to have
spending money for current use or for the future. Some left to attend high
school and, a very few, college. Those who worked outside the home married

later in life than those who remained in the home; some became teachers or librarians. More and more joined women's organizations.

Nevertheless, in the cotton and woolen mills, women and children worked long hours, in some places from 12½ to 16 hours a day. Women earned wages lower than men for the same work. Not until the 1830s would a woman operative in Lowell, Massachusetts, take home $1.75 a week, "clear of board" (board was $1.45 a week). The women boarded in dormitories where 50 or 60 slept 10 or 12 in a room, two to a bed. Men's wages were set at the prevailing rate for each trade or skill group, but women had no such going rate. Their pay was just enough to draw women away from farms and domestic labor but not to compete with the unskilled wages of the textile industry in England or to undercut wages paid to men.[17]

Initially, young women away from home for the first time accepted the low pay and conditions. But during the wage cuts and speed-ups of the 1830s they became dissatisfied. Women workers protested early on in the history of the mills. The first female factory workers to strike in America were those in Pawtucket, Rhode Island, in 1824, followed in 1828 by women in Dover, New Hampshire, where 300 to 400 went out on strike. Women in the tailoring trade struck in New York City as early as 1825.

Mill owners required women to attend church. Like many women in New York and New England they organized hundreds of societies around their churches. The earliest of these was the church sewing circle whose aim was to raise money for charity. These groups educated children, fought the liquor business, formed literary clubs, found homes for orphans, and frequently donated money to young seminarians. One young woman, the future suffragist Lucy Stone, rebelled: "Let these men with broader shoulders and stronger arms earn their own education while we use our scantier opportunities to educate ourselves," she said, putting down her needle. Eventually church and charitable work taught women how to run meetings, speak in public, and raise money on their own behalf. Women's later work in the antislavery and women's suffrage movements grew out of these charitable societies.

Traditionally, religion had been a major impediment to the broadening of women's rights. Women could not speak or make decisions in their churches; the clergy lectured them to remain homebound or coarsen their character. Leaders urged women to cultivate the virtues of passivity, silence, obedience, and piety. Except for the more liberal Quaker tradition, the churches taught women inferiority as befitted the daughters of Eve. Yet during the 19th century, religion, paradoxically, enabled women to gain a public voice. Business and politics excluded women, but not charitable groups affiliated with the church. As a result, the positive experiences women felt in their religious lives led to more direct participation in reform politics. Unfortunately, their competence in this area did not win them support when it came to winning the vote.[18]

In the southern cities, women formed organizations, but with a difference. White men ruled the southern family, and plantation wives were too isolated by distance to form community ties. Those women who lived on small farms engaged in subsistence agriculture, not unlike women in colonial times, and had no time for reform associations.[19]

African-American women, however, had formed organizations for mutual aid as far back as the 1790s. These "insurance" societies took money contributed by the members and doled it out to those who were in need. One of the oldest was the Female Benevolent Society of St. Thomas, formed in 1793. Records of the earlier organizations are missing, but reports from two 1821 groups do exist. One, a note from Grace Douglass, states: "Visited Mrs. Jones with the Committee and gave her 50 cts worth of groceries. She has been confined 10 days. Grace Douglass." The other is from the Order Book from 1821 to 1829 belonging to the Daughters of Africa; it records money paid to the sick, loans for funerals, and various expenses. None of the middle-class women whose names would become familiar in the antislavery struggles a decade or two later appear in the Order Book.[20]

Another early group was the African Female Benevolent Society of Newport, Rhode Island. Open to males as well as females, it allowed only men to vote or hold office. So in 1809 the women formed their own group called the Female Society. African-American women also formed temperance and missionary groups around their churches.[21]

Temperance was a major issue for reformers North and South. Women suffered at the hands of drunken husbands, who might abandon their families or squander a whole farm by gambling, so it was logical that temperance was a personal issue for them. The average annual consumption of alcohol in America in 1810 was six to seven gallons; in 1820 it was seven to 10 gallons. Many women felt that drink was ruining their families by triggering violence at home and wasting scarce cash in taverns. Deserted by alcoholic husbands, some women resorted to prostitution. Consequently, women from all classes fought against drinking.[22]

The cash economy, exploitative though it was, brought women into the public sphere. It encouraged their participation in church activities and reform politics. It enabled them to produce greater wealth than ever before. Though they endured unceasing toil, low pay, legal restrictions, and poor education, women's aspirations for equality were rising. Eventually their demand for the vote would be heard.

CHRONICLE OF EVENTS

1800

September 6: Catharine Beecher, writer/educator, is born.

1802

February 11: Lydia Maria Francis (Child), author, is born.

April 4: Dorothea Lynde Dix, army nurse head, is born.

1803

September 3: Teacher/abolitionist Prudence Crandall is born.

1805

The Supreme Court of Massachusetts in *Martin v. Commonwealth* makes the fullest explanation of women's political relationship to the state to date, declaring, in a case involving property rights, that Anna Martin had "no *political* relation to the *state* any more than an *alien.*" For all practical purposes, women did not hold property rights until the passage of the Married Women's Property Acts later in the century.

Mercy Otis Warren publishes a three-volume history of the American Revolution: *The Rise, Progress and Termination of the American Revolution* is the earliest account of the period written by an American.

February 20: Suffragist Angelina Grimké is born.

July 25: Abolitionist Maria Weston (Chapman) is born.

1806

December 25: Women's rights activist Martha Coffin (Pelham Wright) is born.

1807

New Jersey passes bill denying women the vote. Women had been voting in the state since 1787.

Massachusetts incorporates an academy for girls in Pittsfield.

1808

The Pennsylvania Supreme Court, in *Watson v. Bailey,* strengthens the property rights of women by declaring a deed invalid because the wife had not been pri-vately examined by a judge to ensure that she had not been coerced into signing it by her husband.

Maine incorporates an academy for girls in Bath.

October 12: Reformer Francis Dana Barker (Gage) is born.

1809

February 20: Kempe's Lessee v. Kennedy is the first post-Revolutionary married woman's property trial to reach the Supreme Court. To gain ownership of her property, attorneys for Grace Kempe are forced to argue that their client is not a citizen of New Jersey. Chief Justice John Marshall lets the lower decision stand, a revealing commentary on the position of married women at the beginning of the 19th century.

1810

Elizabeth Ann Bayley Seton's Sisters of Charity of St. Joseph establish the first tuition-free girls' parochial school in the United States.

In *Harvey and Wife v. Pecks,* Virginia jurists void a sale of a wife's property, believing the husband forced his wife to make the sale. Proof of a wife's willingness to dispose of her own property was her signature on a deed or private questioning by a judge.

January 13: Reformer Ernestine Siismondi Potowski (Rose) is born.

January 15: Women's rights speaker Abigail Kelley (Foster) is born.

January 25: Women's rights leader Clarina Howard (Nichols) is born.

May 23: Writer Margaret Fuller is born.

1811

In *Ewing v. Smith,* a South Carolina Court of Appeals breaks with tradition and protects a married South Carolina woman selling her own property under threat by her husband.

June 14: Author Harriet Beecher (Stowe) is born.

June 20: In the Virginia case of *Coutts v. Greenhoe* the state supreme court reverses a lower court decision, denying a creditor's claim that a (common-law) widow must pay the debts of her deceased husband out of her marriage settlement. The court thereby strengthens the property rights of widows.

1813

Francis Cabot Lowell's Boston Manufacturing Co. establishes the first textile mill in America (in

Waltham, Massachusetts), which rapidly recruits women as workers.

ca. February 13: Factory worker Harriet Farley is born.

July 10: Pennsylvania v. Addicks introduces the principle of a child's "best interest" into custody cases. After Joseph Lee divorced his wife for adultery, he attempted to secure custody of their young children under common law that assumed the father was the natural guardian of his children, but the court refused to remove them from the home of the mother, because of their "tender age."

August 7: Suffragist Paulina Kellogg (Wright Davis) is born.

1814

The South Carolina Court of Appeals decides in *Johnson v. Thompson* that a father "intended" to bestow a gift of property on his married daughter and therefore her husband had no right to sell it for his own gain. The "doctrine of intentions" reflected a more liberal attitude on the part of southern courts toward the independent property rights of married women.

Emma Hart Willard establishes Middlebury Female Seminary.

First power-driven loom is established in Waltham, Massachusetts, operated by Deborah Skinner.

Catherine Fiske opens a school for girls in Keene, New Hampshire.

1815

November 12: Elizabeth Cady Stanton, suffrage leader, is born.

December 6: Jane Cannon Swisshelm, journalist and women's rights advocate, is born.

1817

Three looms start up in Fall River, Massachusetts, operated by Sallie Winters, Hannah Bordan, and Mary Healey.

1818

Reverend Joseph Emerson opens a female seminary in Byfield, Massachusetts, introducing new teaching techniques such as topical study and discussion instead of rote learning.

Hannah Mather Crocker publishes *Observations on the Real Rights of Women.*

Born in 1818, Lucy Stone focused on women's rights throughout her life. *(Library of Congress)*

In *Gregory v. Paul,* the Massachusetts Supreme Court shows a more liberal attitude toward married women's independent property rights, allowing a woman whose husband had abandoned her to receive an inheritance.

In *Helms v. Franciscus,* Maryland's Chancery Court shows a willingness to support the right of married women to own property independent of their husbands.

May 27: Reformer Amelia Jenks (Bloomer) is born.

August 1: Astronomer Maria Mitchell is born.

August 13: Suffragist Lucy Stone is born.

October 28: Abigail Adams dies.

1819

Emma Willard presents to Governor DeWitt Clinton of New York *An Address to the Public; Particularly to the Members of the Legislature of New York, Proposing a Plan for Improving Female Education*

May 27: Suffragist Julia Ward (Howe) is born.

1820

Rescuer of slaves Harriet Tubman is born.

February 15: Suffrage leader Susan Brownell Anthony is born.

1821

Frances Wright publishes *Views of Society and Manners in America.*

Emma Willard establishes the Troy Female Seminary in New York.

February 3: Elizabeth Blackwell, first woman medical graduate, is born.

June 2: In the New York case of *Kenny v. Udall,* the New York State Court of Chancery returns an estate to an underage married woman. The chancellor does not deny that husbands have the legal right to control the income of a wife's property. But when a husband is guilty of the "prodigal waste of his wife's fortune," leaving her "helpless and destitute," justice demands he be denied the property.

December 25: Clara Barton, president of the American Red Cross, is born.

1822

Mills open in Lowell, Massachusetts. All elements of production are moved under one roof.

Zilpah Grant establishes the Adams Academy for Girls in Derry, New Hampshire, the first school to award diplomas to females.

February 21: First woman receives a military pension. The Pennsylvania Legislature awards Molly Pitcher (Mary Ludwig Hays McCauley) for her wartime actions at the Battle of Monmouth, an annual pension of $40 for the remainder of her life.

May 5: Physician and reformer Lydia Folger (Fowler) is born.

December 5: Elizabeth Cabot (Agassiz), first president of Radcliffe College, in Boston, Massachusetts, is born.

1823

Catharine Beecher founds a school for girls in Hartford, Connecticut, later known as the Hartford Female Seminary.

1824

Earliest known strike by women factory workers takes place in Pawtucket, Rhode Island, where women join men in protesting a wage cut and longer hours.

First public school for girls opens in Worcester, Massachusetts.

Gerrit Smith, cousin of Elizabeth Cady, is caught up in revivalism and experiences conversion. He dedicates himself to reform as a result.

May 5: Mill worker and editor Lucy Larcom is born.

1825

The first woman's labor organization is founded in the United States, the United Tailoresses Society of New York.

February 8: Harriet Hanson Robinson, factory worker and woman's rights leader, is born.

May 20: Minister Antoinette L. Brown (Blackwell) is born.

1826

Second public school for girls opens in New York.

June 23: Anne E. McDowell, founder of the *Woman's Advocate,* is born.

1827

The Maryland case of *Lowry v. Tierman and Williamson* protects a married woman's property, refusing to allow her to sell her stock on command of her husband.

1828

Zilpah Grant and Mary Lyon open a female academy in Ipswich, Massachusetts.

Frances Wright, in the face of great hostility, becomes the first woman to speak in public before audiences of both women and men.

In Dover, Massachusetts, for the first time women participate alone in a labor strike.

April: Sarah Josepha Hale moves to Boston to become editor of *Ladies Magazine,* later *American Ladies Magazine,* an influential periodical for women.

December 2: The New York Court of Chancery in *Peckford v. Peckford* sets a precedent for penalizing wives for conduct that is not "submissive." Mrs. Peckford took a trip to England without permission of her husband, and therefore, when she sued her husband for adultery, the court reduced her property settlement.

1829

Charleston women Sarah and Angelina Grimké leave for the North to become Quakers and champions of women's rights.

Abbot Academy for girls incorporates in Andover, Massachusetts.

In *Tiernan v. Poor,* the Maryland Court of Appeals allows a married woman to mortgage her own property to pay off a husband's debt, a change to the domestic relations law of coverture, which gives the husband absolute title to all property of his wife.

1830

Bradford Academy in Bradford, Massachusetts, restricts its mandate to women's education only.

October 24: Lawyer Belva Lockwood is born.

December 10: Poet Emily Dickinson is born.

1831

Prudence Crandall opens the Canterbury Female Boarding School in Connecticut, which operates peacefully until the daughter of an African-American farmer seeks and is granted admission. It is then forced to close in 1833.

Charles Grandison Finney, revivalist, inspires 15-year-old Elizabeth Cady.

Mrs. Maria W. Stewart, an African-American woman, speaks in Boston for abolition and educational opportunities for women.

February 12: Future lawyer Myra Colby Bradwell is born.

1832

Elizabeth Cady Stanton graduates from Emma Willard's Troy Female Seminary.

In *Garlick v. Strong* New York's Chancery Court decides that women have the right to withhold their consent to the mortgage or sale of their property.

1833

Oberlin College is founded in Ohio, the nation's first coeducational college.

The American Anti-Slavery Society is organized in Philadelphia. Men deny women membership. Lucretia Mott establishes the Philadelphia Female Anti-Slavery Society.

Abigail Goodrich Whittelsey becomes the first editor of a new periodical for women, *Mother's Magazine.*

The Boston Female Anti-Slavery Society is founded.

April: Prudence Crandall reopens the Canterbury Female Boarding School as a boarding and teacher-training school for African-American girls. Crandall is arrested, jailed, and tried for teaching children who, according to the judge, were not citizens. A high court overrules this decision.

1834

The first women's rights petition for a change in the property laws is sent to the New York state legislature by Mary Ayers. It is 10 to 15 feet long when unrolled.

Harriet Martineau sets sail from England to America at the age of 32.

Mary Lyon helps plan the Wheaton Female Seminary (Wheaton College), which opens in 1835.

The young mill women of Lowell, Massachusetts strike.

July 18: A Connecticut court in a 3-1 vote throws out the state's case against Prudence Crandall for operating a school that admits black girls.

September 9: Prudence Crandall closes the Canterbury Female Boarding School for the education of African-American girls due to the violence (arson) of Connecticut citizens.

October 22: Western feminist Abigail Scott (Duniway) is born.

EYEWITNESS TESTIMONY

I long to hear that you have declared an independency—and by the way in the new Code of laws which I suppose it will be necessary for you to make I desire you would Remember the Ladies, and be more generous and favorable to them than your ancestors. Do not put such unlimited power into the hands of the Husbands. Remember all Men would be tyrants if they could. If particular care and attention is not paid to the Ladies we are determined to foment a Rebellion, and will not hold ourselves bound by any Laws in which we have no voice, or Representation.

That your sex are Naturally Tyrannical is a Truth so thoroughly established as to admit of no dispute, but such of you as wish to be happy willingly give up the harsh title of Master for the more tender and endearing one of Friend.

Abigail Adams, letter to John Adams, March 31, 1776, in Butterfield, Friedlander, and Kline, eds., The Book of Abigail and John: Selected Letters of the Adams Family, 1762–1782.

. . . the husband, by the law of this country, and of every well-regulated government, is the head of the family, and the best judge of their finances. A custom for a feme covert [married woman] to surrender her copyhold lands held under a separate estate, without the consent of her husband, is bad; it is said to be contrary to the law and policy of the nation, and tends to make wives independent of their husbands.

Pennsylvania Supreme Court in Torbet v. Twining, *Yeates 438 (1795), in Berkin and Norton,* Women in America, *109.*

Our Constitution gives this right [voting] to maids or widows, black or white.

New Jersey state representative, during debates over who should vote in congressional elections, 1800, in Clinton, The Other Civil War, *15.*

She has . . . too much [intellect] to make her exactly what I wish her to be. I mean only that her thurst for reading, will probably obstruct the attainment of those amiable, condescending, and endearing manners, without which a woman is, in my estimatation, but a poor piece of furniture.

Daniel Davis, letter to James Freeman, April 18, 1801, in Cott, The Bonds of Womanhood, *164.*

Infants, insane, *femes coverts* [married women], all of whom the law considers having no will, cannot act *freely.*

Theopolis Parsons, lawyer for James Martin, winning argument in Martin v. Massachusetts *March 14, 1805, 1 Williams, Mass., 376.*

Election bill met better fate,/On every hand defended,/To check confusion through the State,/The female's voting ended.

A New Jersey newspaper, November 1807, in Clinton, The Other Civil War, *16.*

I am acquainted with a sensible girl who is anxious to improve her mind, but her father, instead of commending her design, endeavours to convince her that all knowledge, except that of domestic affairs, appears unbecoming in a female. An acquaintance with domestic affairs is certainly of the highest importance, but are females in general so totally engaged by the business of the family, as to find no time for cultivating the mind?

Sarah Bradford (Ripley), letter to Abba Allyn, ca. 1809, in Cott, The Bonds of Womanhood, *111.*

We look to you, ladies, to raise the standard of character in our own sex; we look to you, to guard and fortify those barriers, which still exist in society, against the encroachments of impudence and licentiousness. We look to you for the continuance of domestick purity, for the revival of domestick religion, for the increase of our charities, and the support of what remains of religion in our private habits and publick institutions.

Joseph Buckminster, "A Serman Preached before the Members of the Boston Female Asylum, September 1810," in Cott, The Bonds of Womanhood, *148.*

[A] woman's first active duties belong to her own family . . . [in] the ordering of domestic affairs, the regulation of servants, the care & culture of children, the perusal of necessary works in all important concern of education, & of other necessary books, including the Scriptures.

Susan Mansfield Huntington, diary entry, January 5, 1815, in Cott, The Bonds of Womanhood, *45.*

[T]he husband, by marriage, acquires an absolute title to all the personal property of the wife.

The Law of Baron and Femme, Parent and Child, Guardian and Ward, Master and Servant, and of the Powers of the Courts of Chancery, 1816, in Kerber, No Constitutional Right to Be Ladies, *13.*

The right of a husband to the person of his wife . . . is a right guarded by the law with the utmost solicitude; if she could bind herself by her contracts, she would be liable to be arrested, taken in execution, and confined in a prison; and then the husband would be deprived of the company of his wife, which the law will not suffer.

Tapping Reeve, The Law of Baron and Femme, Parent and Child, Guardian and Ward, Master and Servant, and of the Powers of the Courts of Chancery, 1816, in Kerber, No Constitutional Right to Be Ladies, *14.*

With cheerful mind we yield to men
The higher honors of the pen
The needle's our great care
In this we chiefly wish to shine
How far the arts already mine
This sampler does declare.

Message on a sampler, 1817, in Mirra Bank, Anonymous Was a Woman, *30.*

Females may console themselves and feel happy, that by the moral distinction of the sexes they are called to move in a sphere of life remote from those masculine contentions, although they hold equal right with them of studying every branch of science, even jurisprudence. But it would be morally wrong, and physically imprudent, for any woman to attempt pleading at the bar of justice, as no law can give her the right of deviating from the strictest rules of rectitude and decorum.

Hannah Mather Crocker, in her book Observations on the Real Rights of Women, *1818, in Flexner,* Century of Struggle, *24.*

Now you have left your parents wing,/Nor longer ask their care./It is but seldom husbands bring/A lighter yoke to wear.

Lucy Beckley, in journal entry, 1819, in Cott, The Bonds of Womanhood, *77.*

. . . properly fitted by instruction, women would be likely to teach children better than the other sex; they could afford to do it cheaper; and those men who would otherwise be engaged in this employment, might be at liberty to add to the wealth of the nation, by any of those thousand occupations, from which women are necessarily debarred.

Emma Willard, "An Address to the Public Particularly to the Members of the Legislature of New York, Proposing A Plan for Improving Female Education," 1819, in Berkin and Norton, Women in America, *185.*

In no country, where the blessings of the common law are felt and acknowledged, are the interests and estates of married women so entirely at the mercy of their husbands as in *Pennsylvania* . . . The subordinate and dependent condition of the wife, opens the husband such an unbounded field to practise on her nat-

With a charter from New York State and funding from the city of Troy, New York, Emma Hart Willard, a statue of whom is seen in this photograph, opened the Troy Female Seminary in 1821. *(Library of Congress)*

ural timidity, or to abuse a confidence . . . that there is nothing, however unreasonable or unjust, to which he cannot procure her consent. The policy of the law should be, as far as possible, to narrow, rather than widen, the field of this controlling influence. In *England,* the courts of equity will not assist the husband to obtain possession of his wife's personal property, although it becomes his absolutely on the marriage, before he makes an adequate settlement on her: here, he has the power to obtain her personal estate, not only without condition, but in some instances by means of the intestate acts, even to turn her real into personal estate, *against* her consent. In other countries, the wife's dower, that sacred provision which the law makes for her in return for the personal property she brought her husband, and in recompense of a lifetime devoted to him and his children, is put beyond the reach of every effort which selfishness or profligacy can make, to deprive her of it: in this, it may be swept away by his debts, contracted in the gratification of his vices. In the country whence we derive our laws, the wife's land can be alienated only with her assent, deliberately expressed on a fair, full, and careful, separate examination, in a court of record: in this, it is entrusted to a justice of the peace, by whom it is sometimes entirely dispensed with in fact, but often slubbered over, even in the presence of the husband himself . . .

Justice Gibson, opinion in Watson v. Mercer, *6 Serjeant and Rawle 49, (1820) in Berkin and Norton,* Women of America, *111.*

The [marriage] contract is so much more important in its consequences to females than to males for besides leaving everything else to unite themselves to one man they subject themselves to his authority—they depend more upon their husband than he does upon the wife for society & for the happyness & enjoyment of their lives—he is their all—their only relative—their only hope—but as for him—business leads him out of doors, far from the company of his wife . . . & then it is upon his employment that he depends almost entirely for the happiness of his life.

George Younglove Cutler, journal entry, 1820, in Cott, The Bonds of Womanhood, *79.*

The American youth of both sexes are, for the most part, married ere they are two and twenty, and indeed it is usual to see a girl of eighteen a wife and a moth-er. It might doubtless, ere this, be possible, if not to fix them in habits of study, at least to store their minds with useful and general knowledge, and to fit them to be not merely the parents but the judicious guides of their children. Men have necessarily, in all countries, greater facilities than women for the acquirement of knowledge, and particularly for its acquirement in that best of all schools, the world. I mean not the world of fashion, but the world of varied society, where youth loses its presumption, and prejudice its obstinacy, and where self-knowledge is best obtained from the mind being forced to measure itself with other minds, and thus to discover the shallowness of its knowledge and the groundlessness of its opinions. In this country where every man is called to study the national institutions and to examine, not merely into the measures but the principles of government, the very laws become his teachers, and in the exercise of his rights and duties as a citizen he becomes more or less a politician and a philosopher. His education, therefore, goes on through life, and though he should never become familiar with abstract science or ornamental literature, his stock of useful knowledge increases daily, his judgment is continually exercised, and his mind gradually fixed in habits of observation and reflection. Hitherto the education of women has been but slightly attended to. Married without knowing anything of life but its amusements, and then quickly immersed in household affairs and the rearing of children, they command but few of those opportunities by which their husbands are daily improving in sound sense and varied information.

Frances Wright, letter to Mrs. Rabina Craig Millar, February 1819, in Views of Society and Manners in America *(1963), 22.*

The state of Connecticut has appropriated a fund of a million and a half of dollars to the support of public schools. In Vermont, a certain portion of land has been laid off in every township, whose proceeds are devoted to the same purpose. In the other states, every township taxes itself to such amount as is necessary to defray the expense of schools, which teach reading, writing, and arithmetic to the whole population. In larger towns these schools teach geography and the rudiments of Latin. These establishments, supported at the common expense, are open to the whole youth, male and female, of the country. Other seminaries of a higher order are also maintained in the more populous districts, half the expense being discharged by appropriated funds and the remainder by a small charge laid on the scholar. The instruction here given fits the youth for the state colleges, of which there is one or more in every state. The university of Cambridge, in Massachusetts, is the oldest and, I believe, the most distinguised establishment of the kind existing in the Union ...

In the education of women, New England seems hitherto to have been peculiarly liberal. The ladies of the eastern states are frequently possessed of the most solid acquirements, the modern and even the dead languages, and a wide scope of reading; the consequence is that their manners have the character of being more composed than those of my gay young friends in this quarter. I have already stated, in one of my earlier letters, that the public attention is now everywhere turned to the improvement of female education. In some states, colleges for girls are established under the eye of the legislature, in which are taught all those important branches of knowledge that your friend Dr. Rush conceived to be so requisite.

In other countries it may seem of little consequence to inculcate upon the female mind "the principles of government, and the obligations of patriotism," but it was wisely foreseen by that venerable apostle of liberty that in a country where a mother is charged with the formation of an infant mind that is to be called in future to judge of the laws and support the liberties of a republic, the mother herself should well understand those laws and estimate those liberties. Personal accomplishments and the more ornamental branches of knowledge should certainly in America be made subordinate to solid information. This is perfectly the case with respect to the men; as yet the women have been educated too much after the European manner. French, Italian, dancing, drawing engage the hours of the one sex (and this but too commonly in a lax and careless way), while the more appropriate studies of the other are philosophy, history, political economy, and the exact sciences. It follows, consequently, that after the spirits of youth have somewhat subsided, the two sexes have less in common in their pursuits and turn of thinking than is desirable.

Frances Wright, letter to Mrs. Rabina Craig Millar, March 1820, in Views of Society and Manners in America, *215–218.*

If I could for a moment believe the horrible idea, that females have no immortal souls, even at that moment, I would say, Let the female character be raised, that she may elevate her sons.

Joseph Emerson, "Female Education, A Discourse Delivered at the Dedication of the Seminary hall in Saugus [Massachusetts]," January 15, 1822, in Cott, The Bonds of Womanhood, *170.*

... Generally speaking there seems to be no very extensive sphere of usefulness for a single woman but that which can be found in the limits of the school room; but there have been instances, in which women of superior mind and acquirements have risen to a more enlarged and comprehensive boundary of exertion and by their talents and influence have accomplished what in a more circumscribed sphere of action would have been impossible—My employments this winter which have been chiefly mental, and the observations which I have made upon the relative character of the talents which God has given me, have led to the inquiry whether there is not a course which might be pursued, which would lead to a different and more extended field of usefulness, than is attained by the generality of females ...

Catharine Esther Beecher, letter to Lyman Beecher, February 15, 1823, in Boydston, Kelley and Margolis, The Limits of Sisterhood, *35.*

Examine the woman how you will, it is impossible to ascertain with certainty, whether she gives her free consent [to sell her property]; her word must be taken for that; she may, in fact, be under terror, though she be examined in the absence of her husband. But there is a better chance for her speaking her real sentiments, in his absence, than in his presence; and it is difficult for the law to protect her further, than by giving her an opportunity of disclosing her mind to the magistrates, out of the presence of her husband.

Pennsylvania Supreme Court, in Jourdan v. Jourdan, Serjeant and Rawle *(1823), in Berkin and Norton,* Women of America, *102.*

Messrs. Editors:

Will you allow a female to offer a few remarks upon a subject that you must allow to be all-important? I don't know that in any of your papers, you have said sufficient upon the education of females. I hope you are not to be classed with those, who think that our mathematical knowledge should be limited to "fathoming the dish-kettle," and that we have acquired enough of history, if we know that our grandfather's father lived and died. 'Tis true the time has been, when to darn a stocking, and cook a pudding well, was considered the end and aim of a woman's being. But those were days when ignorance blinded men's eyes. The diffusion of knowledge has destroyed those degrading opinions, and men of the present age, allow, that we have minds that are capable and deserving of culture.

Matilda
One of the earliest expressions of women's rights, by an African American, letter to the editor of Freedom's Journal, *August 10, 1827, in Aptheker,* A Documentary History of the Negro People in the United States, *Vol. 1, 89.*

The late strike and grand public march of the female operatives in New Hampshire exhibit the Yankee sex in a new and unexpected light. By and by the governor may have to call out the militia to prevent a gynocracy.
Philadelphia newspaper, December 1828, in Baxandall, Gordon and Reverby, America's Working Women, *58.*

I had rather my daughters would go to school and sit down and do nothing, than to study philosophy, etc. These branches fill young Misses with *vanity* to the degree that they are above attending to the more useful parts of an education.
Editorial writer, Connecticut Courant, *1829, in Cott,* The Bonds of Womanhood, *111.*

We do not, in our country, at least, want . . . those talents and acquirements, which have fitted women to rule empires and manage state intrigues . . . we want patterns of virtue, of intelligence, of piety and usefulness in private life.
Ladies' Magazine, *January 1829, in Cott,* The Bonds of Womanhood, *96.*

Custom and long habit have closed the doors of very many employments against the industry and perseverance of woman. She has been taught to deem so many occupations masculine, and made for men only that, excluded by a mistaken deference to the world's opinion from innumerable labors most happily adapted to her physical constitution, the competition for the few places left open to her has occasioned a reduction in the estimated value of her labour, until it

An early to mid-19th-century Currier & Ives lithograph, titled "Daughters of Temperance: virtue, love, and temperance" *(Library of Congress)*

has fallen below the minimum and is no longer adequate to present comfortable substance, much less to the necessary provision against age and infirmity, of the everyday contingencies of morality.
Boston Courier, *1829, in Flexner,* Century of Struggle, *53.*

Pittsburgh, Dec. 8. Frances Wright. This celebrated female commenced a course of lectures . . . in this city. Her fame and misapplied talents attracted crowded audiences . . . The dogmas inculcated by this fallen and degraded fair one, if acted upon by the community would produce the destruction of religion, morals, law and equity, and result in savage anarchy and confusion.
The Friend, A Religious and Literary Journal, *Vol. III, No. 10, December 19, 1829, in Lerner,* The Grimké Sisters from South Carolina, *95.*

Boarding & Lodging

The subscriber respectfully informs her Friends and the public in general that her House No. 28 Elizabeth street, is still open for the accommodation of genteel persons of colour, with Boarding & Lodging.

P.S. In addition to the above establishment, the subscriber keeps on hand a quantity of best Refreshments, Oysters &c. served up at the shortest notice. Her house is in a healthy and pleasant situation, and she hopes by the unremitted attention that will be paid to all those who may favour her with their patronage, to be entitled to public favour.

Eliza Johnson, Philadelphia Advertisement, June 2, 1828, in Sterling, We Are Your Sisters, *97.*

Leghorn Bonnets
Mrs. Sarah Johnson

No. 551 Pearl-Steet, respectfully informs her Friends and the Public, that she has commenced Bleaching Pressing and Refitting Leghorn and Straw Hats, in the best manner. Ladies Dresses made, and Plain Sewing done on the most reasonable terms.

Mrs. J begs leave to assure her friends and the public that those who patronize her may depend upon having their work done faithfully, and with punctuality and despatch.

New York Advertisement, April 29, 1828, in Sterling, We Are Your Sisters, *98.*

Our men are sufficiently money-making. Let us keep our women and children from the contagion as long as possible.

Sarah Josepha Hale, Ladies' Magazine, *January 1830, in Cott,* The Bonds of Womanhood, *68.*

I attended the annual public exhibition at this school [Dr. Lock's in Cincinnati], and perceived, with some surprise, that the higher branches of science were among the studies of the pretty creatures I saw assembled there. One lovely girl of sixteen *took her degree* in mathematics, and another was examined in moral philosophy. They blushed so sweetly, and looked so beautifully puzzled and confounded, that it might have been difficult for an abler judge than I was, to decide how far they merited the diplomas they received.

This method of letting young ladies graduate, and granting them diplomas on quitting the establishment, was quite new to me; at least, I do not remember to have heard of anything similar elsewhere. I should fear that the time allowed to the fair graduates of Cincinnati for the acquirement of these various branches of education, would seldom be sufficient to permit their reaching the eminence in each which their enlightened instructor anticipates. "A quarter's" mathematics, or "two quarters'" political economy, moral philosophy, algebra and quadratic equations, would seldom, I should think, enable the teacher and the scholar, by their joint efforts, to lay in such a stock of these sciences as would stand the wear and tear of half a score of children, and one help.

Frances Milton Trollope, writing of her observations between 1827 and 1831, in Domestic Manners of the Americans, *68.*

But if the condition of the labourer be not superior to that of the English peasant, that of his wife and daughters is incomparably worse. It is they who are indeed the slaves of the soil. One has but to look at the wife of an American cottager, and ask her age, to be convinced that the life she leads is one of hardship, privation, and labour. It is rare to see a woman in this station who has reached the age of thirty, without losing every trace of youth and beauty. You continually see women with infants on the knee, that you feel sure are their grand-children, till some convincing proof of the contrary is displayed. Even the young girls, though often with lovely features, look pale, thin, and haggard. I do not remember to have seen in any single instance among the poor, a specimen of the plump, rosy, laughing physiognomy so common among our cottage girls. The horror of domestic service, which the reality of slavery, and the fable of equality, have generated, excludes the young women from that sure and most comfortable resource of decent English girls; and the consequence is, that with a most irreverent freedom of manner to the parents, the daughters are, to the full extent of the word, domestic slaves. This condition, which no periodical merry-making, no village *fête,* ever occurs to cheer, is only changed for the still sadder burthens of a teeming wife. They marry very young; in fact, in no rank of life do you meet with young women in that delightful period of existence between childhood and marriage, wherein, if only tolerably well spent, so much useful information is gained, and the character takes a sufficient degree of firmness to support with dignity the more important parts of wife and mother.

The slender childish thing, without vigour of mind or body, is made to stem a sea of troubles that dims her young eye and makes her cheek grow pale, even before nature has given it the last beautiful finish of the full-grown woman.

Frances Milton Trollope, writing of her observations between 1827 and 1831, in Domestic Manners of the Americans, *97–98.*

In America the independence of women is irrecoverably lost in the bonds of matrimony: if an unmarried woman is less constrained there than elsewhere, a wife is subjected to stricter obligations. The former makes her father's house an abode of freedom and of pleasure; the latter lives in the home of her husband as if it were a cloister. Yet these two different conditions of life are perhaps not so contrary as may be supposed, and it is natural that the American women should pass through the one to arrive at the other.

Religious peoples and trading nations entertain peculiarly serious notions of marriage: the former consider the regularity of woman's life as the best pledge and most certain sign of the purity of her morals; the latter regard it as the highest security for the order and prosperity of the household. The Americans are at the same time a puritanical people and a commercial nation: their religious opinions, as well as their trading habits, consequently lead them to require much abnegation on the part of woman, and a constant sacrifice of her pleasure to her duties which is seldom demanded of her in Europe. Thus in the United States the inexorable opinion of the public carefully circumscribes woman within the narrow circle of domestic interests and duties, and forbids her to step beyond it.

Alexis de Tocqueville, visiting America in 1831–32, in Democracy in America, *in Cott,* Roots of Bitterness, *120.*

At a dollar and a quarter a week for board, great care in expenditure was necessary. It was not in my mother's nature closely to calculate costs, and . . . there came to be a continually increasing leak in the family purse. The older members of the family did everything they could, but it was not enough. I heard it said one day, in a distressed tone, "The children will have to leave school and go into the mill." . . . I thought it would be a pleasure to feel that I was not a trouble or burden or expense to anybody. So I went

to my first day's work in the mill with a light heart. The novelty of it made it seem easy, and it really was not hard, just to change the bobbins on the spinning-frames every three quarters of an hour or so, with half a dozen other little girls who were doing the same thing. When I came back at night, the family began to pity me for my long, tiresome day's work, but I laughed and said,—"Why it's nothing but fun. It's just like play . . ."

Lucy Larcom, writing on factory life in the 1830s, in A New England Girlhood, *152–153.*

David has signed my will and I have sealed it up and put it away. It excited my towering indignation to think it was necessary for him to sign it . . . I was not indignant on my own account, for David respects the freedom of all women upon principle, and mine in particular for reason of affection superadded. But I was indignant for womankind made chattel personal from the beginning of time, perpetually insulted by literature, law, and custom. The very phrases used with regard to us are abominable. "Dead in the law." "Femme Couvert" [married woman]. How I detest such language!

Lydia Maria Child, letter from the 1830s, in Flexner, Century of Struggle, *62.*

I had been to school constantly until I was about ten years of age, when my mother, feeling obliged to have help in her work besides what I could give, and also needing the money which I could earn, allowed me, at my urgent request (for I wanted to earn *money* like the other little girls), to go to work in the mill. I worked first in the spinning-room as a "doffer." The doffers were the very youngest girls, whose work was to doff, or take off, the full bobbins, and replace them with the empty ones.

I can see myself now, racing down the alley, between the spinning-frames, carrying in front of me a bobbin-box bigger than I was. These mites had to be very swift in their movements, so as not to keep the spinning-frames stopped long, and they worked only about fifteen minutes in every hour. The rest of the time was their own, and when the overseer was kind they were allowed to read, knit, or even to go outside the mill-yard to play.

Some of us learned to embroider in crewels, and I still have a lamb worked on cloth, a relic of those early days, when I was first taught to improve my time in the good old New England fashion. When not doffing, we were often allowed to go home, for a time, and thus we were able to help our mothers in their housework. We were paid two dollars a week; and how proud I was when my turn came to stand up on the bobbin-box, and write my name in the pay-master's book, and how indignant I was when he asked me if I could "write." "Of course I can," said I, and he smiled as he looked down on me.

The working-hours of all the girls extended from five o'clock in the morning until seven in the evening, with one-half hour for breakfast and for dinner. Even the doffers were forced to be on duty nearly fourteen hours a day, and this was the greatest hardship in the lives of these children. For it was not until 1842 that the hours of labor for children under twelve years of age were limited to ten per day; but the "ten-hour law" itself was not passed until long after some of these little doffers were old enough to appear before the legislative committee on the subject, and plead, by their presence, for a reduction of the hours of labor.

Harriet H. Robinson, writing about factory life in Lowell, Massachusetts, ca. 1832, in Loom and Spindle, *18–19.*

As late as 1840 there were only seven vocations outside the home into which the women of New England had entered. At this time women had no property rights. A widow could be left without her share of her husband's (or the family) property, an "incumbrance" to his estate. A father could make his will without reference to his daughter's share of the inheritance. He usually left her a home on the farm as long as she was single. A woman was not supposed to be capable of spending her own, or of using other people's money. In Massachusetts, before 1840, a woman could not, legally, be treasurer of her own sewing society, unless some man were responsible for her.

Harriet Robinson, writing of mill conditions in the 1830s, Fourteenth Annual Report of the Massachusetts Bureau of Statistics of Labor (1883), in Schneir, Feminism, *52.*

I found that I enjoyed even the familiar, unremitting clatter of the mill, because it indicated that something was going on. I liked to feel the people around me, even those whom I did not know, as a wave may like

Lucy Larcom, mill worker and editor *(Library of Congress)*

to feel the surrounding waves urging it forward, with or against its own will. I felt I belonged to the world, that there was something for me to do in it, though I had not yet found out what. Something to do: it might be very little but still it would be my own work.

Lucy Larcom, writing about factory life in the 1830s, in A New England Girlhood, *193.*

In 1831 Lowell was little more than a factory village. Several corporations were started, and the cotton-mills belonging to them were building. Help was in great demand; and stories were told all over the country of the new factory town, and the high wages that were offered to all classes of work-people—stories that reached the ears of mechanics' and farmers' sons, and gave new life to lonely and dependent women in distant towns and farmhouses. Into this Yankee El Dorado, these needy people began to pour by the various modes of travel known to those slow old days. The stage-coach and the canalboat came every day, always filled with new recruits for this army of useful people. The mechanic and machinist came, each with his home-made chest of tools, and oftentimes his wife and little ones. The widow came with her little flock and her scanty housekeeping goods to open a boarding-house or variety store, and so provided a home for her fatherless children. Many farmers' daughters came to earn money to complete their wedding outfit, or buy the bride's share of housekeeping articles.

Women with past histories came, to hide their griefs and their identity, and to earn an honest living in the "sweat of their brow." Single young men came, full of hope and life, to get money for an education, or to lift the mortgage from the home-farm. Troops of young girls came by stages and baggage-wagons, men often being employed to go to other States and to Canada, to collect them at so much a head, and deliver them at the factories. . . .

These country girls had queer names, which added to the singularity of their appearance. Samantha, Triphena, Plumy, Kezia, Aseneth, Elgardy, Leafy, Ruhamah, Lovey, Almaretta, Sarepta, and Florilla were among them.

Their dialect was also very peculiar. On the broken English and Scotch of their ancestors was ingrafted the nasal Yankee twang; so that many of them, when they had just come *daown,* spoke a language almost unintelligible. But the severe discipline and ridicule which met them was as good as a school education, and they were soon taught the "city way of speaking."

Their dress was also peculiar, and was of the plainest of homespun, cut in such an old-fashioned style that each young girl looked as if she had borrowed her grandmother's gown. Their only head-covering was a shawl, which was pinned under the chin; but after the first payday, a "shaker" (or "scooter") sunbonnet usually replaced this primitive head-gear of their rural life.

But the early factory girls were not all country girls. There were others also, who had been taught that "work is no disgrace." There were some who came to Lowell solely on account of the social or literary advantages to be found there. They lived in secluded parts of New England, where books were scarce, and there was no cultivated society. They had comfortable homes, and did not perhaps need the *money* they would earn; but they longed to see this new "City of Spindles," of which they had heard so much from their neighbors and friends, who had gone there to work.

And the fame of the circulating libraries, that were soon opened, drew them and kept them there, when no other inducement would have been sufficient.

The laws relating to women were such, that a husband could claim his wife wherever he found her, and also the children she was trying to shield from his influence; and I have seen more than one poor woman skulk behind her loom or her frame when visitors were approaching the end of the aisle where she worked. Some of these were known under assumed names, to prevent their husbands from trusteeing their wages. It was a very common thing for a male person of a certain kind to do this, thus depriving his wife of *all* her wages, perhaps, month after month. The wages of minor children could be trusteed, unless the children (being fourteen years of age) were given their time. Women's wages were also trusteed for the debts of their husbands, and children's for the debts of their parents.

Harriet H. Robinson, describing factory life at Lowell, Massachusetts, in 1831, in Loom and Spindle, *38–41.*

Of the unjust right which in virtue of this [wedding] ceremony an iniquitous law tacitly gives me over the person and property of another, I cannot legally, but I can morally, divest myself, and earnestly desire to be considered by others, as utterly divested, now and during the rest of my life, of any such rights, the barbarous relics of a feudal, despotic system.

Robert Dale Owen and Mary Jane Robinson, marriage contract, 1832, in History of Woman Suffrage, *Vol. 1, 294–295.*

[Should] the wife who possesses a mind of superior cultivation and power to her husbands . . . be in subjection to his authority?

Yes, because this is conformable to the general order God has established. Many private citizens may possess minds of powers and gifts superior to those of rulers and magistrates, to whose authority it is their duty to submit. Subordination to principles and laws of order is absolutely essential to the existence of the social state. Break up the order of the social state and woman must become the most abject and helpless of all slaves.

Joseph Richardson, A Sermon on the Duty and Dignity of Woman, Delivered April 22, 1832, in Cott, The Bonds of Womanhood, *59.*

In 1832 the factory population of Lowell was divided into four classes. The agents of the corporations were aristocrats, not because of their wealth, but on account of the office they held, which was one of great responsibility, requiring, as it did not only some knowledge of business, but also a certain tact in managing, or utilizing the great number of operatives so as to secure the best return for their labor. The agent was also something of an autocrat, and there was no appeal from his decision in matters affecting the industrial interests of those who were employed in his corporation.

The agents usually lived in large houses, not too near the boarding houses, surrounded by beautiful gardens which seemed like Paradise to some of the home-sick girls, who, as they came from their work in the noisy mill, could look with longing eyes into the sometimes open gate in the high fence, and be reminded afresh of their pleasant country homes. And a glimpse of one handsome woman, the wife of an agent, reading by an astral lamp in the early evening, has always been remembered by one young girl, who looked forward to the time when she, too, might have a parlor of her own, lighted by an astral lamp!

The second class were the overseers, a sort of gentry, ambitious mill-hands who had worked up from the lowest grade of factory labor; and they usually lived in the end-tenements of the blocks, the short connected rows of houses in which the operatives were boarded. However, on one corporation, at least, there was a block devoted exclusively to the overseers, and one of the wives, who had been a factory girl, put on so many airs that the wittiest of her former work-mates fastened the name of "puk-ersville" to the whole block where the overseers lived. It was related of one of these . . . factory girls, that, with some friends, she once re-visited the room in which she used to work, and, to show her genteel friends her ignorance of her own surroundings, she turned to the overseer, who was with the party, and pointing to some wheels and pulleys over her head, she said, "What's them things up there?"

The third class were the operatives, and were all spoken of as "girls" or "men" . . .

The fourth class, lords of the spade and the shovel, by whose constant labor the building of the great factories was made possible, and whose children soon became valuable operatives, lived at first on what was called the "Acre," a locality near the present site of the North Grammar schoolhouse. Here, clustered around a small stone Catholic Church, were hundreds of little shanties, in which they dwelt with their wives and numerous children . . .

Harriet H. Robinson, describing factory life in Lowell, Massachusetts, 1832, in Loom and Spindle, *8–9.*

Another newspaper estimated in 1833, that women earned only one fourth of men's wages, while still another asserted that three fourths of Philadelphia's working women "did not receive as much wages for entire week's worth of 13 to 14 hours per day, as journeymen receive in the same branches for a single day of 10 hours."

Helen L. Sumner, writing about 1833 in History of Woman in Industry in the United States, *cited in Flexner,* Century of Struggle, *53.*

2 Slavery and Suffrage
1835–1839

THE HISTORICAL CONTEXT

The women's rights movement had its roots in the campaign to end slavery, illustrated by the events of Wednesday, February 21, 1838. On that day, a small, blue-eyed, curly-haired woman stood up before the Massachusetts state legislature and delivered a speech that made history.

Angelina Grimké, called "Devil-ina" by the press, had become the first woman to address a legislative body. She and her sister Sarah were early leaders of the abolitionist movement, and on February 21, they represented the 20,000 Massachusetts women who had signed a petition to end slavery.

The attendance at this speech was extraordinary. Members of the legislature had to fight their way to get to their seats. The aisles and lobby were packed and, after waiting for an hour, many had to be turned away at the doors.

But those who remained were not disappointed, for when Angelina Grimké rose to her feet, this forceful speaker surprised friends and foes alike. Serious by nature and dressed simply in Quaker gray, her words were provocative: ". . . because [slavery] is a political subject, it has often been said, that women had nothing to do with it. Are we aliens because we are women? Are we bereft of citizenship because we are mothers, wives and daughters of a mighty people? Have women *no* country—no interests staked in public weal—no liabilities in common peril—no partnership in a nation's guilt and shame?" "If so," she continued, "then we may well hide our faces in the dust, and cover ourselves with sackcloth and ashes. This dominion of women should be resigned—the sooner the better; in the age which is approaching she should be something more—she should be a citizen."[1]

Angelina Grimké's second appearance was scheduled for Friday, February 23. This time when she rose to speak she was greeted by hisses from the doorway. She was interrupted three times, but when she finished, even the chairman was in tears.

What made this event so remarkable was that in 1838 women could neither vote nor run for office. They were excluded from all colleges except for

Sarah M. Grimké, abolitionist and
women's rights leader *(Library of
Congress)*

Oberlin College, founded in 1833. No church except
that of the Quakers allowed them to speak out or participate in church affairs. In 1828, when Frances
Wright lectured in public, she had been jeered as a
freak. A few years later, an African-American woman,
Mrs. Maria W. Stewart, lectured four times in Boston in
favor of education for girls and the abolition of slavery.
But she quit in despair because so much scorn was
heaped upon her. It was in this social climate that
Angelina and Sarah Grimké, two upper-class Southern
women, became famous for speaking out in public as
the first female antislavery agents in America, and to
"mixed" audiences of men and women at that.

The strangeness of their public protest brought the
wrath of the Congregationalist Church upon the
Grimkés and dragged the sisters into one of the first
public disputes over the rights of women in the history
of the United States. But by then the sisters had experience weathering controversy.

Sarah Grimké was 13 years older than her sister.
Highly intelligent but poorly educated, she had hoped
to become a lawyer. As she watched her brothers go to
college, she remained at home, learned homemaking
skills and secretly studied law, Greek, Latin and philosophy. She also disapproved of slavery. This belief would
eventually alienate her from her slave-holding
Charleston family, and she left the South in 1821, never
to return.

Sarah's younger sister, Angelina, followed her to
Philadelphia in 1829 and promptly took part in abolitionist activities by joining the Philadelphia Female
Anti-Slavery Society. Through it she met women who
sold abolitionist pamphlets and women who painstak-
ingly gathered signatures on petitions to Congress.
These petitions protested the entry of more slave states
to the Union, the presence of slavery in the District of Columbia and the practice of buying and selling enslaved people across state lines.

Four years earlier there had been riots in Philadelphia and New York that
were so violent that the homes of 45 African-American families were
destroyed. The abolitionist leader William Lloyd Garrison ran articles in his
newspaper, the *Liberator,* urging citizens to put a stop to the violence. Angelina
wrote Garrison a supportive letter, which he published without her permission. Three weeks later she found herself at the center of a raging controversy.
The aristocratic Grimké name had been associated with the radical Garrison—
and abolition. Angelina weathered the anger of her Philadelphia Quaker family
and her immediate family in Charleston, South Carolina, as well.

In 1835 more violence erupted, this time directed toward the antislavery
movement itself. Abolitionist speakers were beaten and jeered. In this atmosphere, Angelina wrote *An Appeal to the Christian Women of the South,* published

by the American Anti-Slavery Society in 1836. This document stands alone in the annals of antislavery as the only appeal written by a southern woman for southern women. The Grimkés were not only fighting slavery but also the exclusion of women from reform circles. When copies of the pamphlet reached Charleston, the postmaster publicly burned them. Through her family, policemen warned Angelina not to return to the city. Pouring still more oil on the fire, in 1836 Sarah wrote the *Epistle to the Clergy of the Southern States,* refuting the notion that biblical slavery justified the current injustice.

That year the sisters became agents for the American Anti-Slavery Society, trained by the fearless agitator Theodore Weld, whom Angelina later married. The Grimkés spoke on behalf of the society to small private gatherings in New York. These were called "parlour talks." They became so popular that before long the sisters began speaking to larger groups. Then in 1837, for the first time, they addressed a "mixed" audience of men and women. This was followed with a speaking tour of New England and Angelina's famous address to the committee of the legislature of Massachusetts.

This action was too much for the New England clergy, which had long disapproved of the Grimkés. By the end of July 1837 the Massachusetts clergy issued its *Pastoral Letter of the General Association of Massachusetts to the Congregational Churches under Their Care* with the aim of stopping the Grimkés. It was read in orthodox churches throughout the state. The argument was that when a woman "assumes the place and tone of man as public reformer . . . her character becomes unnatural."

There followed two "Clerical Appeals" that attacked the sisters and their sponsor, William Lloyd Garrison, who financed them and who took the

Angelina E. Grimké, author of *An Appeal to the Christian Women of the South* *(Library of Congress)*

unpopular position that women's rights was as important as abolition. Sarah went on the offensive, writing a series of letters for the *Spectator,* later published as a book called *Letters on the Equality of the Sexes.* In them, she demanded educational reform, equal wages, and an end to other forms of discrimination against women.

She argued that clergymen had misunderstood the Bible when they used it to "prove" women were inferior—this was a theory invented by men to suppress women—and showed that the Bible never taught women to be passive. She wrote that women should not have to ask for equal rights because nature endowed them with such rights already. In her most famous passage, she wrote: "I ask no favors for my sex. I surrender not our claim to equality. All I ask our brethren is, that they will take their feet from off our necks and permit us to stand upright on that ground which God designed us to occupy." This early feminist view was an unpopular one, and even some of Angelina's abolitionist allies, such as John Greenleaf Whittier and Theodore Weld, feared her work on behalf of women would lessen her devotion to the antislavery cause. In her book *The Ladies of Seneca Falls,* Miriam Gurko quotes from a letter by Theodore Weld: "Your woman's rights! You put the cart before the horse . . . in attempting to push *woman's* rights, until human rights have gone ahead and broken the *path.*"

Angelina was also personally attacked for her unfeminine behavior by the educational reformer Catharine Beecher in *An Essay on Slavery and Abolitionism with Reference to the Duty of American Women,* published in 1837. Angelina responded with *Letters to Catharine Beecher* in 1838. Beecher argued that behavior that "throws women into the attitude of a combatant, either for herself or others" was outside the "women's sphere." She believed the Grimkés should not be debating men and speaking in public. God had made men superior and women inferior and under no circumstances should women be petitioning Congress!

This position was popular in Jacksonian America, although it predated it. In 1791, in "Oration upon Female Education . . .", a Boston speaker predicted, "[O]ur young men will be emulous to exceed the geniuses of the east; our daughters will shine as bright constellations in the sphere where nature has placed them." It was during this decade that the "cult of true womanhood" was first romanticized by ministers and magazines alike. "True womanhood," a condition of the middle class, was defined as "domestic, maternal, religious, cultured, idle, and subservient." With production moving from the farm to the factory, women were no longer seen as economic partners who produced goods for family use. They were becoming consumers of cheap factory-made cloth and store-bought goods. Rising professionalism also eliminated traditionally female roles such as midwifery and undertaking.[2]

But Angelina thought it was damaging to women to accept this popular notion of a "woman's sphere." Writing in the *Liberator* in 1838, she argued that women should have the right to speak out on abolition and have a voice in making all laws in the land. Whether women were different from men or equal to them would become the main feminist debate throughout the 19th century.

Angelina now withdrew from public activities. After her marriage to Theodore Weld, it was hard for her to balance the duties of family and public life, as it would be for Elizabeth Cady Stanton and still is for so many other women to this day. Her last speech was given in 1838, two days after her marriage to Theodore Weld, at the Philadelphia Anti-Slavery convention. An angry mob later burned the building to the ground.

A few months later in a letter dated July 13, 1838, the sisters learned that Angelina's marriage to "a person not professing with us," and Sarah's attendance at that ceremony, would cost them their membership in the Society of Friends (Quakers).

But the New England of the 1830s was different from that of the 1820s, and other women were taking a more active role in public life, working in mill towns and publishing political opinions. During 1832–1833 Maria Stewart, an African-American teacher, had given four public speeches in Boston at a time when no woman, save Frances Wright, had ever delivered public addresses. Stewart urged her peers to become educated and fight for their political rights.

In 1833 Lydia Maria Child wrote an early abolitionist book titled *Appeal in Favor of That Class of Americans Called Africans,* which caused many Bostonians to shun her socially and professionally. Ernestine L. Rose began to lecture on behalf of women's rights in 1836, the same year that a bill was introduced to the New York legislature to give married women property rights. The following year New York hosted the National Woman's Anti-Slavery Convention, to which eight states sent delegates. And in 1838 Mary Grove Nichols gave the first public anatomy lectures ever made by a woman.

By participating in the antislavery societies, first formed during the 1830s, women learned to organize, hold public meetings, and gather petitions. Between 1835 and 1837 the number of members of antislavery societies had doubled, to 100,000. The members developed the systematic use of petitions to agitate for change; by 1837 it was the major form of antislavery activity, due largely to the great number of women in the movement and the fact that it was the only method of political expression open to them.[3]

In the North and West, freed women also formed abolitionist organizations. But they met for other purposes as well. In the 1830s, Philadelphia, New York, Boston, and other northeastern cities saw the growth of literary and educational societies. The Ohio Ladies Education Society made a greater contribution at that time to the schooling of African-American children in that state than any other group.[4]

The need to provide better education for their children was a prime motivator of women, black and white. Schooling for African Americans was, of course, illegal in the South, and even in Michigan in 1837, there was not one school that a black child could attend. In the 1840s blacks were taxed in Ohio for schools to which they were not admitted. New England was not immune from racism either. Earlier in the decade Quaker Prudence Crandall had tried to teach children of African descent in her school in Canterbury, Connecticut. First she was jailed. Then her windows were broken and her students stoned. Doctors and shopkeepers denied her their services. Finally, Connecticut passed a law making such teaching illegal. When all else failed, arsonists drove her out of town. Canterbury won the battle, but Crandall won the war. Today a woman's dormitory at Howard University, in Washington, D.C., is named after her.

Gradually, however, the need for female mill workers in the expanding textile industry was changing the way people looked at education for women. Oberlin College, America's first coeducational institution, which was founded in 1833, began admitting both sexes four years later. In 1837 Mary Lyon opened Mount Holyoke Female Seminary in South Hadley, Massachusetts, for the first time making higher education available to girls of middle income. It is today the oldest women's college in the United States. Lyon traveled throughout New England to raise money for her school at a time when such behavior was considered provocative, carrying an infamous green velvet bag for collections.

When Mount Holyoke opened its doors in 1837, there were three women for every two men teaching in the Massachusetts district schools. By 1850 this ratio would become two to one. In 1837 one of every five native-born American white Massachusetts women had at one time taught school; for men, the figure was one in seven. In prerevolutionary New England, the literacy rate for women had been one-half that of men. Such discrimination lessened during the 19th century. By 1850 the federal census "registered equal and universal literacy skills among white native-born New England men and women."[5]

Catharine Beecher was another leader in the female education movement. From 1823 to 1827 she headed the Hartford Female Seminary, which offered broader education for women. Beecher believed that there would soon be a surplus of females in the East because of the westward migrations of so many men and that these women would have to earn their livelihood in dirty factories with long hours and low wages. She believed women should either be educated to teach or else learn domestic skills. She felt education for housewives should be as rigorous as that for doctors or lawyers. Her book *A Treatise on Domestic Economy* (1841) was a reference on home management.[6]

These early pioneers not only helped expand educational opportunities but paved the way for legal and political opportunities as well. European-American men had been accumulating more and more rights since the 1820s, voting by 1835, even if they did not own property. Although this broadening of political participation did not reach women, their new participation in society gave rise to a public debate over their proper role, referred to during the 1830s as the "woman question."[7]

As men were expanding their rights, should not women do likewise? Reformers recognized that Jacksonian equality was rhetoric as far as women and slaves were concerned. Not surprisingly, it was during the 1830s that the first legal changes in the ability of married women to hold property were made. In *Women and the Law of Property in Early America*, legal scholar Marylynn Salmon tells the story of a New York woman, Mrs. Garlick, who went to court against her husband in 1832. She argued that he was breaking a promise he had made to her when he sold some of their property. As this property would have gone to pay for her dowry should her husband die (commonly equal to one-third of their estate), they had agreed that half the selling price ($1,000) be set aside for her. Otherwise, she believed, she and her children would be left destitute when her husband died. When Mr. Garlick refused to put aside this amount, his wife went to a Court of Chancery, which based its decision on what was fair more than on English common law. There Mr. Garlick claimed that, under the English common law, wives could not make contracts with their husbands concerning property, so any statement he had made before the sale was invalid. But the court sided with Mrs. Garlick, declaring their agreement perfectly legal, demonstrating on behalf of the courts of New York a new belief in the property rights of married women.

Such changes, which enabled married women to own property they brought into marriage and the money they earned, eventually undermined male prerogatives. Yet, paradoxically, they developed out of the male-dominated market economy. Men saw that their wives' inability to own or control property under common law could endanger male property as well, as credit and debt became a part of American life. When the debt collector seized a man's assets, he could seize a wife's as well, leaving both penniless. Too, widows increasingly found themselves forced to rely on public alms, leading men as well as women to desire changes in the law.[8]

But for all these advances, there were setbacks. For example, women could sue for divorce more readily during the 17th and 18th centuries, when Puritans were more tolerant of ending marriage, than they could in the early 19th, perhaps because the idea of the home took on a romantic or nostalgic importance in the booming market economy.[9]

This new market economy drew many unmarried women and children (mostly under age eight) into the mills. Although in 1831 women had made up

40,000 of the 58,000 workers in textiles, 20 years later they held 24 percent of all manufacturing jobs. Young men went west while young women stayed in the East—African Americans in the fields, European Americans in the mills—to play an important role in the burgeoning cotton economy.

Factory workers labored from 12 1/2 to 16 hours a day. In many places they started work at 4:30 A.M. and worked until dark. Women earned lower wages than men for the same work, ranging from $1 to $3 a week. In 1834 and again in 1836, female factory workers in Lowell, Massachusetts, went into the streets to oppose salary cuts; these were brave actions at a time when society shunned such unfeminine behavior. Strikes followed in other northeastern cities, and the press jeered. By 1837 America was on the road to economic depression, forcing every textile mill in New England but one to shut down. At North Andover, Nathaniel Stevens increased production, working operatives 76-hour weeks.

Ernestine L. Rose, reformer *(Library of Congress)*

Some women, such as Harriet Farley, writing in the *Lowell Offering,* the Lowell operatives magazine, wrote nostalgically of their years in the mills. Others, like Sarah G. Bagley, tried to expose the low wages and dismal working conditions. Most historians agree that the factories exploited labor, but more recently, some scholars have argued that factory conditions were actually better than the women's earlier lives on the farm. Many were happy to be free of their fathers' controls and to have spending money of their own.

By contrast, freed women had fewer choices than whites. They either took in sewing or worked as washerwomen or cooks. In 1838 5,000 out of 18,000 freed people in Philadelphia worked as live-in servants for whites. Pay was sorry; the going rate for washing shirts in Northern cities was 13 cents per dozen. Overall, a woman's daily average earnings in 1836 were less than 37 cents.

Women in large numbers joined voluntary associations during the 1830s. Middle-class women dominated the benevolent societies while working-class women formed labor unions. Some sought utopian communities like the Shakers', which challenged male prerogatives by advocating female celibacy. Women were twice as likely as men to join these communities, with women between the childbearing ages of 20 and 45 three to five times as likely.[10] By the 1830s there were 18 Shaker communities with 5,000 members.

Angelina Grimké's speeches before the legislature in 1838 occurred 10 years before the historic women's convention at Seneca Falls, New York. Indeed, many of the women who were to lead the women's movement a decade later were inspired by those speeches—Elizabeth Cady Stanton, Lucy Stone, Abby Kelley, and Susan B. Anthony, to name a few. Working in the antislavery movement encouraged the women to fight for their own gender as well. For as Angelina later wrote, when she spoke from the speaker's chair that historic day at the Massachusetts legislature, she was thinking, "We abolitionist women are turning the world upside down."[11]

CHRONICLE OF EVENTS

1835

January 5: Pastor and suffragist Olympia Brown is born.

1836

The Married Woman's Property Act is introduced to the New York state legislature. Ernestine Rose circulates a petition in support of it, but only six people sign.

Angelina Grimké writes "Appeal to the Christian Women of The South."

Angelina Grimké writes *Letters to Catharine Beecher.*

Sarah Grimké writes *Epistle to the Clergy of the Southern States.*

1837

Harriet Martineau publishes *Society in America.*

Lucretia Mott helps organize the Anti-Slavery Convention of American Women.

The first National Anti-Slavery Society convention meets in New York.

Angelina Grimké publishes *Appeal to the Women of the Nominally Free States.*

Economic depression begins in the United States: 39,000 people go bankrupt, and $741 million is lost. Every textile mill in New England except one closes: Nathaniel Stevens' in North Andover increases production and works operatives 76-hour weeks.

The first National Convention of American Antislavery Women is held in New York City.

Angelina and Sarah Grimké give antislavery speeches before mixed audiences of men and women. Angelina Grimké debates two men on the issue of slavery. The women are attacked and called "unchristian" in July by the Congregationalist Church of Massachusetts in the "Pastoral Letter." The letter is followed by two clerical appeals attacking William Lloyd Garrison and female antislavery agents who engage in public speaking.

Sarah Grimké answers the "Pastoral Letter" in a series of letters published in the *New England Spectator,* linking slavery to the position of women in society.

August 17: Educator Charlotte L. Forten (Grimké) is born.

November: Mary Lyon opens Mount Holyoke Female Seminary (now Mount Holyoke College).

Lucy Stone, the "morning star of the women's movement," was the first woman to debate publicly at Oberlin. *(Library of Congress)*

1838

Harriet Martineau publishes *How to Observe Manners and Morals,* the first book on sociological methods.

Reformers start the first National Female Anti-Slavery Society in New York.

Dorothea Dix begins to publicize the conditions in prisons and insane asylums.

Sarah Grimké publishes *Letters on the Equality of the Sexes and the Conditions of Woman,* her 1837 response to the "Pastoral Letter," in pamphlet form.

February 21: Angelina Grimké addresses the Massachusetts state legislature, the first woman ever to make such an appearance before a legislative body.

May 15: The Anti-Slavery Convention of American Women opens in Philadelphia. Lucretia Mott, an organizer of the convention, keeps women calm when mobs attack.

May 17: Pennsylvania Hall is burned down by a mob protesting the women's antislavery convention.

June 26–30: John Quincy Adams defends the right of women to collect signatures and sign petitions in a series of controversial speeches, published in

1838 as *Speech . . . Upon the Rights of the People, Men and Women, to Petition.*

1839

Mississippi passes the first property law for married women. Married women and widows now have rights to retain property and income, earned from their employment, in their own name.

Margaret Fuller begins a series of famous "conversations," or discussion groups, for women in Boston, which were, in Elizabeth Cady Stanton's words "a vindication of woman's right to think." She thus becomes a precursor to the women's rights movement in America.

Ann Winterbotham Stephens becomes the first woman to achieve success as a serial writer, publishing "Maleska," the story of an American Indian woman married to a white man.

September 8: Suffragist Phoebe Wilson Couzins is born.

September 28: Suffragist and temperance worker Frances Willard is born.

EYEWITNESS TESTIMONY

But never in her varied sphere
Is woman to the heart more dear,
Than when her homely task she plies,
With cheerful duty in her eyes;
And every *lowly* path well trod,
Looks meekly upward to her God.
From The Housekeeping Woman, *Caroline Gilman,*
The Ladies Annual Register and Housewife's
Memorandum Book, *1838, 66* History of Women,
Guide to the Microfilm Collection, *1983.*

I sent the first petition to the New York State Legislature to give a married woman the right to hold real estate in her own name, in the winter of 1836 and '37 to which after a good deal of trouble I obtained five signatures. Some of the ladies said the gentlemen would laugh at them; others, that they had rights enough; and the men said the women had too many rights already . . . I continued sending petitions with increased numbers of signatures until 1848 and '49, when the Legislature enacted the law which granted women the right to keep what was their own. But no sooner did it become legal than all the woman said: "Oh! that is right! We ought always to have had that!"
Ernestine Rose, on gathering signatures for the first petition for the Married Woman's Property Law, 1836, in History of Woman Suffrage, *Vol. 1, 99.*

The common law of England, by which the property of married women is taken from them and given to their respective husbands, is *not* and never was constitutional law in this state.
Judge Thomas Hertell, introducing An Act for the Protection and Preservation of the Rights and Property of Married Women, *May 20, 1836, New York State House of Assembly in Remarks Comprising in Substance Judge Hertell's Argument in the House of Assembly of the State of New-York, in the Session of 1837, in Support of the Bill to Restore to Married Women "The Right of Property as Guaranteed by the Constitution of this State," 5–83.*

Resolved, That a select committee be appointed to inquire and report to this house, at the present or succeeding session of the legislature, what provisions, if any, will be proper and necessary to be made by law, the better to protect the rights and property of mar-

ried women from injury and waste by means of improvident, prodigal, intemperate and dissolute habits and practices of their husbands.
Judge Thomas Hertell, introducing An Act for the Protection and Preservation of the Rights and Property of Married Women, *May 20, 1836, New York State House of Assembly in Remarks Comprising in Substance Judge Hertell's Argument in the House of Assembly of the State of New-York, in the Session of 1837, in Support of the Bill to Restore to Married Women "The Right of Property as Guaranteed by the Constitution of this State," 5–83.*

One of the first strikes of cotton-factory operatives that ever took place in this country was that in Lowell [Massachusetts], in October, 1836. When it was announced that the wages were to be cut down, great indignation was felt, and it was decided to strike, en mass. This was done. The mills were shut down, and the girls went in procession from their several corporations to the "grove" on Chapel Hill, and listened to "incendiary" speeches from early labor reformers.

One of the girls stood up on a pump, and gave vent to the feelings of her companions in a neat

Elizabeth Cady Stanton at age 20: She would become the force behind the Seneca Falls convention. *(Brigham Young University Photoarchives)*

speech, declaring that it was their duty to resist all attempts at cutting down the wages. This was the first time a woman had spoken in public in Lowell, and the event caused surprise and consternation among her audience.

Cutting down the wages was not the only grievance, nor the only cause of this strike. Hitherto the corporations had paid twenty-five cents a week towards the board of each operative, and now it was their purpose to have the girls pay this sum; and this, in addition to the cut in wages, would make a difference of at least one dollar a week. It was estimated that as many as twelve or fifteen hundred girls turned out, and walked in procession through the streets. They had neither flags nor music, but sang songs, a favorite (but rather inappropriate) one being a parody on "I won't be a nun."

> "Oh! Isn't it a pity, such a pretty girl as I—
> Should be sent to the factory to pine away and die?
> Oh! I cannot be a slave,
> I will not be a slave,
> For I'm so fond of liberty
> That I cannot be a slave."

My own recollection of this first strike (or "turn out" as it was called) is very vivid. I worked in a lower room, where I had heard the proposed strike fully, if not vehemently, discussed; I had been an ardent listener to what was said against this attempt at "oppression" on the part of the corporation, and naturally I took sides with the strikers. When the day came on which the girls were to turn out, those in the upper room started first, and so many of them left that our mill was at once shut down. Then, when the girls in my room stood irresolute, uncertain what to do, asking each other, "Would you?" or "Shall we turn out?" and not one of them having the courage to lead off, I, who began to think that they would not go out, after all their talk, became impatient, and started on ahead, saying, with childish bravado, "I don't care what you do, *I* am going to turn out, whether any one else does or not;" and I marched out, and was followed by the others.

As I looked back at the long line that followed me, I was more proud than I have ever been since at any success I may have achieved, and more proud than I shall ever be again until my own beloved State gives to its women citizens the right of suffrage.

The agent of the corporation where I then worked took some small revenges on the supposed ringleaders; on the principle of sending the weaker to the wall, my mother was turned away from her boarding house, that functionary saying, "Mrs. Hanson, you could not prevent the older girls from turning out, but your daughter is a child and *her* you could control."

It is hardly necessary to say that so far as results were concerned this strike did no good. The dissatisfaction of the operatives subsided, or burned itself out, and though the authorities did not accede to their demands, the majority returned to their work, and the corporation went on cutting down the wages. After a time, the wages became more and more reduced, the best portion of the girls left and went to their homes, or to the other employments that were fast opening to women, until there were very few of the old guard left; and thus the *status* of the factory population of New England gradually became what we know it to be today.

Harriet H. Robinson, describing an early strike at Lowell, Massachusetts in 1836, in Loom and Spindle, *51–52.*

. . . Since my last we have been mobbed again in the day time. The Mayor and the City officers were with a few exceptions totally inefficient, and pursued such a course as to embolden rather than to intimidate the mob. One of the City officers was openly a leader of the mob. Twice a rush was made up the aisles to drag me from the pulpit. Stones, pieces of bricks, eggs, cents, sticks, etc. were thrown at me while speaking.

As I came out of the house, and while going the whole distance to my lodgings, I was a target for all sorts of missiles—was hit by two stones, tho' not hurt seriously. The mob made desperate efforts to get me into their clutches but were kept at bay by our friends, though often with extreme difficulty. But I have not time to detail. Suffice it to say the Mayor and Common Council declare that they cannot keep the peace of the City, that they cannot protect the Citizens in the exercise of their Constitutional rights!!

Theodore D. Weld, letter to the Reverend Ray Potter, June 11, 1836, in Barnes and Dumond, Letters of Theodore Dwight Weld, Angelina Grimké Weld and Sarah Grimké, *309–310.*

I have thus, I think, clearly proved to you seven propositions, viz.: First, that slavery is contrary to the declaration of our independence. Second, that it is contrary to the first charter of human rights given to Adam, and renewed to Noah. Third, that the fact of slavery having been the subject of prophecy, furnishes *no* excuse whatever to slavedealers. Fourth, that no such system existed under the patriarchal dispensation. Fifth, that *slavery never* existed under the Jewish dispensation; but so far otherwise, that every servant was placed under the *protection of law,* and care taken not only to prevent all *involuntary* servitude, but all *voluntary perpetual* bondage. Sixth, that slavery in America reduces a *man* to a *thing,* a "chattel personal," *robs him of all* his rights as a *human being,* fetters both his mind and body, and protects the *master* in the most unnatural and unreasonable power, whilst it *throws him out* of the protection of law. Seventh, that slavery is contrary to the example and precepts of our holy and merciful Redeemer, and of his apostles.

But perhaps you will be ready to query, why appeal to *women* on this subject? *We* do not make the laws which perpetuate slavery. *No* legislative power is vested in *us; we* can do nothing to overthrow the system, even if we wished to do so. To this I reply, I know you do not make the laws, but I also know that *you are the wives and mothers, the sisters and daughters of those who do;* and if you really suppose *you* can do nothing to overthrow slavery, you are greatly mistaken. You can do much in every way: four things I will name. 1st. You can read on this subject. 2d. You can pray over this subject. 3d. You can speak on this subject. 4th. You can *act* on this subject. I have not placed reading before praying because I regard it more important, but because, in order to pray aright, we must understand what we are praying for; it is only then we can "pray with the understanding and the spirit also."

Angelina Grimké, "Appeal to the Christian Women of
the South," September 1836, in Rossi,
The Feminist Papers, *296–303.*

I have just finished reading your Appeal and not with a dry eye . . . Oh that it could be rained down into every parlor in our land.

Elizur Wright, letter to Angelina Grimké, ca. 1836,
in Lerner, The Grimké Sisters from
South Carolina, *142.*

I felt no more fear. We went to the meeting at three o'clock and found about three hundred women there. It was opened with prayer by Henry Ludlow; we were warmly welcomed by brother Dunbar, and then these two left us. After a moment, I arose and spoke about forty minutes, feeling, I think, entirely unembarrassed. Then dear sister did her part better than I did.

Angelina Grimké, letter to J. Smith, December 17,
1836, in Lerner, The Grimké Sisters of
South Carolina, *153.*

What do I do that is wrong? . . . I ride in the stage coach or cars without an escort. Other ladies do the same. I visit a family where I have been previously invited, and the minister's wife, or some other leading woman, calls the ladies together to see me, and I lay our object before them. Is that wrong? . . . If there is

Mary Lyon, founder of Mount Holyoke *(New York Public Library)*

no harm in doing these things once, what harm is there in doing them twice, thrice, or a dozen times? My heart is sick, my soul is pained with this empty gentility, this genteel nothingness. I am doing great work. I cannot come down.

Mary Lyon, answering critics who thought her
fund-raising was unseemly, ca. January 1837,
in Berkin and Norton, Women of America, *197.*

As I was speaking one day in mtg. [meeting] the Friend who rules in our Yearly Meeting rose in the meeting and desired me to desist in these words: "Perhaps the Fd. [friend] may be satisfied now". I of course instantly resumed my seat and never felt more peaceful, and the conviction then arose that my bonds were broken. The act on the part of this Elder was entirely unprecedented and unsanctioned by our Discipline but his power is undisputed. I cannot give thee any idea of the spiritual bondage I have been in; but notwithstanding this my heart clung to the Society of Friends and the struggle to give them up, to resign the cherished hope of being permitted to preach among them the unsearchable riches of Christ has been very great; but that has past and peaceful resignation clothes my spirit. Still to lift the veil and expose the faults of those to whom I have been so bound is hard work, but I wrote the Address now in thy hands under a sense of duty. It cost me many a tear and many a midnight hour was spent in prayer that god would help me and preserve me from doing wrong. I have not had time to read it over since I asked thee to look at it. Its publication will almost without doubt lead to my disownment, but many precious souls are perishing in our borders and if it is right to print it, I know I ought not to shrink from odium, nor from the trial of alienating almost every friend I have. . . .

Sarah Grimké, letter to Theodore Weld, explaining why
she quit the Society of Friends, New York,
ca. March 10, 1837, in Barnes and Dumond,
Letters of Theodore Weld, Angelina Grimké Weld
and Sarah Grimké, *373.*

. . . I confess that I am wholly indebted to the Abolition cause for arousing me from apathy and indifference, shedding light into a mind which has been too long wrapt in selfish darkness.

In reply to your question—of the "effect of Prejudice" on myself, I must acknowledge that it has often embittered my feelings, particularly when I recollect that we are the innocent victims of it; for you are well aware that it originates from dislike to the color of the skin, as much as from the degradation of Slavery. I am peculiarly sensitive on this point, and consequently seek to avoid as much as possible mingling with those who exist under its influence. I must also own that *it* has often engendered feelings of discontent and mortification in my breast when I saw that many were preferred before me, who by education, birth, or wholly circumstances were no better than myself, THEIR sole claim to notice depending on the superior advantage of being *White;* but I am striving to live above such heart burnings, and will learn to "bear and forbear" believing that a spirit of forbearance under such evils is all that we as a people can well exert . . .

Sarah Forten, letter to Angelina Grimké, April 15,
1837, in Barnes and Dumond, Letters of Theodore
Dwight Weld, Angelina Grimké Weld
and Sarah Grimké, *379–380.*

As I do not know dear brother Weld when I shall have an opportunity of verbally delivering a message I received for thee, from one of our convention Secretaries, I will write it now. "Tell Mr. Weld said she, that when the women got together, they found they had minds of their own, and could transact their business without his directions". The Boston and Phila. women were so well versed in business that they were quite mortified to have Mr. Weld quoted as authority for doing or not doing so and so—as they frequently did. We had some noble spirits among us.

Angelina Grimké, letter to Theodore Weld, New York,
May 18, 1837, in Barnes and Dumond, Letters of
Theodore Dwight Weld, Angelina Grimké Weld
and Sarah Grimké, *388.*

. . . Will the general cause [slavery] be best promoted by your *joint* or *seperate* action? JOINT say I, for the following reasons: 1. "Two are better than one *for* they have a good reward for their labor" Eccl. 7:9. 2. In the mouth of *two* or three witnesses shall every word be established. Slavery is *on trial.* The people of the north are the court. *You* are summoned as *witnesses* to sustain the prosecution. True it is incumbent on you to appear also as *advocates* arguing upon the evidence and as *examiners* cross questioning and sifting counter testimony; but the *great* reason why *you* should operate upon the public mind far and wide at the north rather than Mrs. Child, Mrs. Chapman, Lucretia Mott, etc. is that you are *southern* women, *once in law* slave-holders, your friends all slave holders, etc., hence your testimony; *testimony* TESTIMONY is the great desideratum.

> *Theodore Weld, letter to Sarah and Angelina Grimké, May 22, 1837, in Barnes and Dumond,* Letters of Theodore Dwight Weld, Angelina Grimké Weld and Sarah Grimké, *389.*

It is the grand feature of the Divine Economy, that there should be different stations of superiority and subordination . . . and it is impossible to annihilate this beneficent and immutable law . . . Heaven has appointed to one sex the superior, and to the other the subordinate station . . . but while a woman holds a subordinate relation in society to the other sex, it is not because it was designed that her duties or her influence should be any less important, or all-pervading.

> *Catharine Beecher,* Essay on Slavery and Abolitionism with Reference to the Duty of American Females, *1837, in Sklar,* Catharine Beecher: A Study in American Domesticity, *135.*

Let every woman become so cultivated and refined in intellect, that her taste and judgement will be respected; so benevolent in feeling and action, that her motives will be reverenced; so unassuming and unambitious, that collision and competition will be banished; so "gentle and easy to be entreated," that every heart will repose in her presence; then, the fathers, the husbands, and the sons, will find an influence thrown around them, to which they will yield not only willingly but proudly.

> *Catharine Beecher,* Essay on Slavery and Abolitionism with Reference to the Duty of American Females, *1837, in Sklar,* Catharine Beecher: A Study in American Domesticity, *136.*

Let us help one another to refute the idea, that while the chief end of *man* is to glorify God and enjoy him forever, woman is sharer of the like glorious destiny "but as it were in sort, or limitation."

> *Maria Chapman, letter to female antislavery societies throughout New England, June 7, 1837, in Barnes and Dumond,* Letters of Theodore Dwight Weld, Angelina Grimké Weld and Sarah Grimké, *395–397.*

Catharine E. Beecher, sister of Harriet Beecher Stowe, wrote best-selling books on home management. *(New York Public Library Picture Collection)*

Angelina sends her love and says until thou writes her a letter in ink she shall not answer it, as she considers it [i.e., a letter in pencil] very disrespectful, and as a consistent assertor of the rights of woman she cannot submit to such indignities. She also says she is very lazy about answering C. E. Beechers book until she gets comfortably housed for the winter. She wishes to know if she may not be excused and whether thou knowest what impression the book is making.

> *Sarah Grimké, letter to Theodore Weld, June 11, 1837, in* Letters of Theodore Dwight Weld, Angelina Grimké Weld and Sarah Grimké, *403.*

It is wonderful how the way has been opened for us to address mixed audiences, for most sects here are greatly opposed to public speaking for women, but curiosity and real interest in the antislavery cause . . . induce the attendance at our meetings . . . Our compass of voice has astonished us, for we can fill a house containing 1000 present with ease. We feel that the Lord is with us.

Angelina Grimké, letter to Theodore Weld, June 26, 1837, in Barnes and Dumond, Letters of Theodore Dwight Weld, Angelina Grimké Weld and Sarah Grimké, *402.*

. . . We have had one [antislavery] meeting nearly every day, and I feel some fears least Angelina sh'd be doing more than is best; she seems much exhausted after a Mtg. and I think cannot continue to labor much longer. Altho I only pick up the chips for her, I have some intimations that the flesh is weak, tho' the spirit is willing; but as brother Renshaw says, our cause is worth dying for . . . What will Brother and sister Smith say to our holding mtgs. irrespective of sex? One brother wanted to come and another thought he had a right and now the door is wide open. Whosoever will come and hear our testimony may come.

Sarah Grimké, letter to Gerrit Smith, June 28, 1837, in Barnes and Dumond, Letters of Theodore Dwight Weld, Angelina Grimké Weld and Sarah Grimké, *410.*

My Dear Sister,—. . . Even admitting that Eve was the great sinner, it seems to me man might be satisfied with the dominion he has claimed and exercised for nearly six thousand years, and that more true nobility would be manifested by endeavoring to raise the fallen and invigorate the weak, than by keeping woman in subjection. But I ask no favors for my sex. I surrender not our claim to equality. All I ask of our brethren is, that they will take their feet off our necks and permit us to stand upright on that ground which God designed us to occupy. If he has not given us the rights which have, as I conceive, been wrested from us, we shall soon give evidence of our inferiority, and shrink back into that obscurity, which the high souled magnanimity of man has assigned us as our appropriate sphere.

Sarah M. Grimké, in Letters on the Equality of the Sexes and the Condition of Woman, *July 17, 1837, in Schneir,* Feminism.

. . . We invite your attention to the dangers which at present seem to threaten the female character with widespread and permanent injury.

The appropriate duties and influence of woman are clearly stated in the New Testament. Those duties and that influence are unobtrusive and private, but the source of mighty power. When the mild, dependent, softening influence of woman upon the sternness of man's opinions is fully exercised, society feels the effects of it in a thousand forms. The power of woman is her dependence, flowing from the consciousness of that weakness which God has given her for her protection, and which keeps her in those departments of life that form the character of individuals, and of the nation. There are social influences which females use in promoting piety and the great objects of Christian benevolence which we can not too highly commend.

We appreciate the unostentatious prayers and efforts of woman in advancing the cause of religion at home and abroad; in Sabbath-schools; in leading religious inquirers to the pastors for instruction; and in all such associated effort as becomes the modesty of her sex; and earnestly hope that she may abound more and more in these labors of piety and love. But when she assumes the place and tone of man as a public reformer, our care and protection of her seem unnecessary; we put ourselves in self-defence against her; she yields the power which God has given her for her protection, and her character becomes unnatural. If the vine, whose strength and beauty is to lean upon the trellis-work, and half conceal its clusters, thinks to assume the independence and the overshadowing nature of the elm, it will not only cease to bear fruit, but fall in shame and dishonor into the dust. We can not, therefore, but regret the mistaken conduct of those who encourage females to bear an obtrusive and ostentatious part in measures of reform, and countenance any of that sex who so far forget themselves as to itinerate in the character of public lecturers and teachers. We especially deplore the intimate acquaintance and promiscuous conversation of females with regard to things which ought not to be named; by which that modesty and delicacy which is the charm of domestic life, and which constitutes the true influence of woman in society, is consumed, and the way opened, as we apprehend, for degeneracy and ruin.

We say these things not to discourage proper influences against sin, but to secure such reformation as we believe is Scriptural, and will be permanent.

Congregationalist Church of Massachusetts, "Pastoral Letter," July 1837, in History of Woman Suffrage, *Vol. 1, 305.*

Dear Friend,—When I last addressed thee, I had not seen the Pastoral Letter of the General Association [of Congregational Ministers of Massachusetts]. It has since fallen into my hands, and I must digress from my intention of exhibiting the condition of women in different parts of the world, in order to make some remarks on this extraordinary document . . .

It says, "We invite your attention to the dangers which at present seem to threaten the FEMALE CHARACTER with widespread and permanent injury." I rejoice that they have called the attention of my sex to this subject, because I believe if woman investigates it, she will soon discover that danger is impending, though from a totally different source from that which the Association apprehends,—danger from those who, having long held the reins of *usurped* authority, are unwilling to permit us to fill that sphere which God created us to move in, and who have entered into league to crush the immortal mind of woman. I rejoice, because I am persuaded that the rights of woman, like the rights of slaves, need only be examined to be understood and asserted, even by some of those, who are now endeavoring to smother the irrepressible desire for mental and spiritual freedom which glows in the breast of many, who hardly dare to speak their sentiments.

"The appropriate duties and influence of women are clearly stated in the New Testament. Those duties are unobtrusive and private, but the sources of *mighty power*. When the mild, *dependent,* softening influence of woman upon the sternness of man's opinions is fully exercised, society feels the effects of it in a thousand ways." No one can desire more earnestly than I do, that woman may move exactly in the sphere which her Creator has assigned her; and I believe her having been displaced from that sphere has introduced confusion into the world. It is, therefore, of vast importance to herself and to all the rational creation, that she should ascertain what are her duties and her privileges as a responsible and immortal being . . .

The Lord Jesus defines the duties of his followers in his Sermon on the Mount. He lays down grand principles by which they should be governed, without any reference to sex or condition . . . Men and women were CREATED EQUAL; they are both moral and accountable beings, and whatever is *right* for man to do, is *right* for woman.

But the influence of woman, says the Association, is to be private and unobtrusive; her light is not to shine before man like that of her brethren; but she is passively to let the lords of the creation, as they call themselves, put the bushel over it, lest peradventure it might appear that the world has been benefited by the rays of *her* candle. So that her quenched light, according to their judgment, will be of more use than if it were set on the candlestick. "Her influence is the source of mighty power." This has ever been the flattering language of man since he laid aside the whip as a means to keep woman in subjection. He spares her body; but the war he has waged against her mind, her heart, and her soul, has been no less destructive to her as a moral being . . . "rule by obedience and by submission sway," or in other words, study to be a hypocrite, pretend to submit, but gain your point, has been the code of household morality which woman has been taught . . .

But we are told, "the power of woman is in her dependence, flowing from a consciousness of that weakness which God has given her for her protection." If physical weakness is alluded to, I cheerfully concede the superiority; if brute force is what my brethren are claiming, I am willing to let them have all the honor they desire; but if they mean to intimate, that mental or moral weakness belongs to woman, more than to man, I utterly disclaim the charge. Our powers of mind have been crushed, as far as man could do it, our sense of morality has been impaired by his interpretation of our duties; but no where does God say that he made any distinction between us, as moral and intelligent beings.

"We appreciate," says the Association, "the *unostentatious* prayers and efforts of woman in advancing the cause of religion at home and abroad, in leading religious inquirers TO THE PASTOR for instruction." . . . Then, the whole association of Congregational ministers are ostentatious, in the efforts they are making in preaching and praying to convert souls.

But woman may be permitted to lead religious inquirers to the PASTORS for instruction. Now this is assuming that all pastors are better qualified to give instruction than woman. This I utterly deny. I have suffered too keenly from the teaching of man, to lead any one to him for instruction . . .

The General Association say, that "when woman assumes the place and tone of man as a public reformer, our care and protection of her seem unnecessary; we put ourselves in self-defence against her, and her character becomes unnatural." Here again the unscriptural notion is held up, that there is a distinction between the duties of men and women as moral beings; that what is virtue in man, is vice in woman; and women who dare to obey the command of Jehovah, "Cry aloud, spare not, lift up thy voice like a trumpet, and show my people their transgression," are threatened with having the protection of the brethren withdrawn . . . As to the pretty simile, introduced into the "Pastoral Letter," "If the vine whose strength and beauty is to lean upon the trellis work, and half conceal its clusters, thinks to assume the independence and the overshadowing nature of the elm," etc. I shall only remark that it might well suit the poet's fancy, who sings of sparkling eyes and coral lips, and knights in armor clad; but it seems to me utterly inconsistent with the dignity of a Christian body, to endeavor to draw such an anti-scriptural distinction between men and women. Ah! how many of our sex feel in the dominion, thus unrighteously exercised over them, under the gentle appellation of *protection,* that what they have leaned upon has proved a broken reed at best, and oft a spear.

Thine in the bounds of womanhood . . .

Sarah M. Grimké, in Letters on the Equality of the Sexes and the Condition of Woman, *July 17, 1837, in Schneir,* Feminism, *38–42.*

My Dear Sister . . . During the early part of my life, my lot was cast among the butterflies of the *fashionable* world; and of this cast of women, I am constrained to say, both from my experience and observation, that their education is miserably deficient; that they are taught to regard marriage as the one thing needful, the only avenue to distinction; hence to attract the notice and win the attentions of men, by their external charms, is the chief business of fashionable girls . . .

There is another and much more numerous class in this country, who are withdrawn by education or circumstances from the circle of fashionable amusements, but who are brought up with the dangerous and absurd idea, that *marriage* is a kind of preferment; and that to be able to keep their husband's house, and render his situation comfortable, is the end of her being. Much that she does and says and thinks is done in reference to this situation; and to be married is too often held up to the view of girls as the *sine qua non* of human happiness and human existence. For this purpose more than for any other, I verily believe the majority of girls are trained. This is demonstrated by the imperfect education which is bestowed upon them, and the little pains taken to cultivate their minds, after they leave school, by the little time allowed them for reading, and by the idea being constantly inculcated, that although all household concerns should be attended to with scrupulous punctuality at particular seasons, the improvement of their intellectual capacities is only a secondary consideration, and may serve as an occupation to fill up the odds and ends of time. In most families, it is considered a matter of far more consequence to call a girl off from making a pie, or a pudding, than to interrupt her whilst engaged in her studies. This mode of training necessarily exalts, in their view, the animal above the intellectual and spiritual nature, and teaches women to regard themselves as a kind of machinery, necessary to keep the domestic engine in order, but of little value as the *intelligent* companions of men . . .

There is another way in which the general opinion, that women are inferior to men, is manifested, that bears with tremendous effect on the laboring class, and indeed on almost all who are obliged to earn a subsistence, whether it be by mental or physical exertion—I allude to the disproportionate value set on the time and labor of men and of women. A man who is engaged in teaching, can always, I believe, command a higher price for tuition than a woman—even when he teaches the same branches; and is not in any respect superior to the woman. This I know is the case in boarding and other schools with which I have been acquainted, and it is so in every occupation in which the sexes engage indiscriminately . . . The low remuneration which women receive for their work, has claimed the attention of a few philanthropists, and I hope will continue to do so until some remedy is applied for this enormous evil. I have known a widow, left with four or five children, to provide for, unable to leave home because her helpless babes demand her attention, compelled to earn a scanty subsistence, by making coarse shirts at 12½ cents a piece, or by taking in washing, for which she was paid by some wealthy person 12½ cents per dozen. All these things evince the low estimation in which woman is held . . .

There is another class of women in this country, to whom I cannot refer, without feelings of deepest shame and sorrow. I allude to our female slaves. Our southern cities are whelmed beneath a tide of pollution; the virtue of female slaves is wholly at the mercy of irresponsible tyrants, and women are bought and sold in slave markets, to gratify the brutal lust of those who bear the name of Christians.

> *Sarah M. Grimké,* Letters on the Equality of the
> Sexes and the Condition of Woman, *1837,*
> *in Schneir,* Feminism, *43–46.*

Why! folks talk about women's preaching as tho' it was next to highway robbery—eyes astare and mouth agape. Pity women were not born with a split stick on their tongues! Ghostly dictums have fairly beaten it into the heads of the whole world save a fraction, that *mind* is *sexed,* and *Human rights* are *sex'd, moral obligation sex'd . . .*

> *Theodore Weld, letter to Angelina and Sarah Grimké,*
> *July 22, 1837, in Barnes and Dumond,* Letters of
> Theodore Dwight Weld, Angelina Grimké Weld
> and Sarah Grimké, *411–412.*

We have given great offense on account of our womanhood, which seems to be as objectionable as our abolitionism. The whole land seems aroused to discussion on the province of woman, and I am glad of it. We are willing to bear the brunt of the storm, if we can only be the means of making a break in that wall of public opinion which lies right in the way of woman's rights, true dignity, honor and usefulness.

> *Angelina Grimké, July 25, 1837, in Lerner,*
> The Grimké Sisters from South Carolina, *183.*

The character of the white ladies of the South, as well as of the ladies of color, seems to have been discussed, and the editor of the Courier was of the opinion that the reputation of his paper, and the morals of its readers, might be injuriously affected by publishing the debate.

> *The* Boston Morning Post, *July 27, 1837, in Lerner,*
> The Grimké Sisters from South Carolina, *180.*

She [Angelina Grimké] was calm, modest, and dignified in her manor; and with the utmost ease brushed away the cobwebs, which her puny antagonist had thrown in her way. Her conduct throughout was admirable and her triumph complete.

> *The* Liberator, *describing Grimké's debate over slavery*
> *in Amesbury, Massachusetts, August 4, 1837, in Lerner,*
> The Grimké Sisters from South Carolina, *179.*

In regard to another subject, *'the rights of woman,'* you are now doing much and nobly to vindicate and assert the rights of woman. Your lectures to crowded and promiscuous audiences are a subject manifestly, in many of its aspects, *political,* interwoven with the framework of the government, are practical and powerful assertions of the right and the duty of woman to labor side by side with her brother for the welfare and redemption of the world. Why, then, let me ask, is it necessary for you to enter the lists as controversial writers in this question? Does it not *look,* dear sisters, like abandoning in some degree the cause of the poor and miserable slave, sighing from the cotton plantation of the Mississippi, and whose cries and groans are forever sounding in our ears, for the purpose of arguing and disputing about some trifling oppression, political or social, which we may ourselves suffer? Is it not forgetting the great and dreadful wrongs of the slave in a selfish crusade against some paltry grievance of our own? Forgive me if I have stated the case too strongly. I would not for the world interfere with you in matters of conscientious duty, but I wish you would weigh candidly the whole subject, and see if it does not *seem* an abandonment of your first love. Oh let us try to forget everything but our duty to God and our fellow beings; to dethrone the selfish principle, and to strive to win over the hard heart of the oppressor by truth kindly spoken. The Massachusetts Congregational Association can do you no harm if you do not allow its splenetic and idle manifesto to divert your attention from the great and holy purpose of your souls.

> *John Greenleaf Whittier, letter to Sarah and Angelina*
> *Grimké, August 8, 1837, in Barnes and Dumond,*
> Letters of Theodore Dwight Weld, Angelina
> Grimké Weld and Sarah Grimké, *424.*

. . . we are placed very unexpectedly in a very trying situation, in the forefront of an entirely new contest— a contest for the *rights* of *woman* as a moral, intelligent and responsible being. Harriet Martineau says "God and man know that the time has not come for women to make their injuries even heard of": but it seems as tho' it had come *now* and that the exigency must be met with the firmness and faith of woman in by gone ages. I cannot help feeling some regret that this sh'ld have come up *before* the Anti Slavery question was settled, so fearful am I that it may injure that blessed cause, and then again I think this must be the

Lord's time and therefore the *best* time, for it seems to have been brought about by a concatenation of circumstances over which we had no control.

Angelina Grimké, letter to Theodore Weld, August 12, 1837, in Barnes and Dumond, Letters of Theodore Dwight Weld, Angelina Grimké Weld and Sarah Grimké, *415.*

... 1. As to the *rights* and *wrongs* of women, it is an old theme with me. It was the *first* subject I ever *discussed.* In a little debating society when a boy, I took the ground that *sex* neither *qualified* nor *disqualified* for the discharge of any functions mental, moral or spiritual; that there is no reason why *woman* should not make laws, administer justice, sit in the chair of state, plead at the bar or in the pulpit, if she has the qualifications, just as much as tho she belonged to the other sex. Further, that the proposition of marriage may with just the same propriety be made by the *woman* as the *man,* and that the *existing usage* on that subject, pronouncing it *alone* the province of the *man,* and *indelicacy* and almost, if not quite *immoral* for *woman* to make the first advances, overlooks or rather *perverts* the sacred design of the institution and debases it into the mire of earthliness and gross sensuality, smothering the spirit under the flesh. Now as I have never found man, woman or child who agreed with me in the "ultraism" of womans rights, I take it for granted even *you* will cry out "oh shocking"!! at the *courting* part of the doctrine. Very well, let that pass. What I advocated in boyhood I advocate now, that woman in EVERY *particular* shares equally with man rights and responsibilities. Now I have made this statement of my *creed* on this point to show you that we *fully agree in principle* except that I probably go much farther than you do in a *single* particular. Now notwithstanding this, I do most deeply regret that you have begun a series of articles in the Papers on the rights of woman. Why, my dear sisters, the best possible advocacy which you can make is just what you *are* making day by day. Thousands hear you every week who have all their lives held that woman must not speak in public. Such a practical refutation of the dogma as your speaking furnishes has already converted multitudes. Leading abolitionists, male and female, everywhere are under responsibilities that cover *all* their time, powers and opportunities. How much new good to be explored—facts, principles processes, relations innumerable yet untraced. How few must do the work! How much to be done! How very

short the "*accepted* time" in which to do it. Besides you are *Southerners,* have been slaveholders; your dearest friends are all in the sin and shame and peril. All these things give you great access to northern mind, great *sway* over it. You can do ten times as much on the subject of *slavery* as Mrs. Child or Mrs. Chapman. Why? Not because your powers are superior to theirs, but because you are *southerners.* You can do more at convincing the north than twenty *northern* females, tho' they could speak as well as you. Now this peculiar advantage you *lose* the moment you take *another* subject. You come down from your vantage ground. *Any* women of your powers will produce as much effect as you on the north in advocating the rights of *free* women (I mean in contradistinction to *slave* women). Further, almost any other woman of your capacities and station could produce a greater effect on the public mind on that subject than *you,* because you are quakers and that is a *quaker* doctrine, and all sects are expected to try for proselytes. A Quaker doctrine of any kind would gain more proselytes if advocated by one *not* a Quaker in general belief. Now *you two* are the ONLY FEMALES in the free states who combine all these facilities for anti slavery effort: 1. Are *southerners.* 2. Have been slaveholders. 3. For a long time most widely known by the eminence of friends. 4. Speaking and writing power and practice. 5. Ultra Abolitionists. 6. Acquaintance with the whole subject, argumentative, historical, legal and biblical. Now what unspeakable responsibilities rest on *you*—on YOU! Oh my soul! that you but *felt* them as they are. Now can't you leave the *lesser* work to others who can do it *better* than you, and devote, consecrate your whole bodies, souls and spirits to the *greater* work which you can do far better and to far better purpose than any body else. Again, the abolition question is most powerfully preparative and introductory to the *other* question. By pushing the former with all our might we are most effectually advancing the latter. By absorbing the public mind in the greatest of all violations of rights, we are purging its vision to detect other violations. Rights! Rights! Their value, their sacredness, their changeless nature, all these will be made familiar as house hold words. When you get the tide raised to the summit [?] level, you can pour it over all below it. Mind gravitates from a general principle to its *collaterals.* It *begins* with a case self evidently clear and strong, and then takes up its ramifications. What was it that carried the reform bill thro parliament, will carry thro another next session, and will carry thro a dozen more till Englishmen have restored to them their plundered rights? Answer—it was the momentum given to English mind by the discussion of *Human rights* in parliament and out and *every where.* It was the great slavery question. Let us all *first* wake up the nation to lift millions of slaves of both sexes from the dust, and turn them into MEN and then when we all have our hand in, it will be an easy matter to take millions of females from their knees and set them on their feet, or in other words transform them from *babies* into *women.* One word more. All our opposers . . . will chuckle if only a part of your energies can be directed into *another* chanell, especially if they can be diverted into one which will make you so obnoxious as to cripple your influence on the subject of slavery. I pray our dear Lord to give you wisdom and grace and help and bless you forever.

> *Theodore Weld, letter to Sarah and Angelina Grimké,*
> *August 15, 1837, in Barnes and Dumond,* Letters of
> Theodore Dwight Weld, Angelina Grimké Weld
> and Sarah Grimké, *427.*

. . . can you not see that women *could* do, and *would* do a hundred times more for the slave if she were not fettered? Why! we are gravely told that we are out of our sphere even when we circulate petitions; out of our "appropriate sphere" when we speak to women only; and out of them when we *sing* in the churches. Silence is *our* province, submission *our* duty. If then we "give *no reason* for the hope that is in us", that we have *equal rights* with our brethren, how can we expect to be permitted *much longer to exercise those rights?* IF I know my own heart, I am NOT actuated by any selfish considerations (but I do sincerely thank our dear brother J. G. W[hittier] for the suggestion) but we are actuated by the full conviction that if we are to do any good in the Anti Slavery cause, our *right* to labor in it *must* be firmly established; *not* on the ground of Quakerism, but on the only firm bases of human rights, the Bible . . .

. . . Why, my dear brothers can you not see the deep laid scheme of the clergy against us as lecturers? . . . If we surrender the right to *speak* to the public this year, we must surrender the right to petition next year and the right to *write* the year after and so on. What *then* can *woman* do for the slave when she is herself under the feet of man and shamed into *silence?* . . .

With regard to brother Welds ultraism on the subject of marriage, he is quite mistaken if he fancies he has got far *ahead of us* in the human rights reform. We do *not* think his doctrine at all shocking: it is *altogether right.* But I am afraid I am *too proud* ever to exercise the right. The fact is we are living in such an artificial state of society that there are some things about which we dare not speak out, or act out the most natural and best feelings of our hearts. O! *when* shall we be "delivered from the *bondage of corruption* into the glorious liberty of the sons of God"! By the bye it will be very important to establish this right, for the men of Mass. stoutly declare that women who hold such sentiments of *equality* can never expect to be courted. They seem to hold out this as a kind of threat to deter us from asserting our rights, not *knowing wherunto this will grow.* But jesting is inconvenient says the Apostle: to business then . . .

> *Angelina Grimké, letter to John Greenleaf Whittier and*
> *Theodore Weld, August 20, 1837, in Barnes and*
> *Dumond,* Letters of Theodore Dwight Weld,
> Angelina Grimké Weld and
> Sarah Grimké, *427–432.*

Why are all the old hens abolitionists? Because not being able to obtain husbands they think they may stand some chance for a negro, if they can only make amalgamation fashionable.

> *Reprint from the* New Hampshire Patriot *in the*
> Boston Morning Post, *August 15, 1837, in Lerner,*
> The Grimké Sisters from South Carolina, *146.*

The Misses Grimké have made speeches, wrote pamphlets, exhibited themselves in public, etc. for a long time, but have not found husbands yet. We suspect that they would prefer white children to black under certain circumstances, after all.

> *The* Boston Morning Post, *August 25, 1837,*
> *in Lerner,* The Grimké Sisters from
> South Carolina, *205.*

. . . the very week that I was converted to Christ in the city of Utica during a powerful revival of religion under brother Finney—and the first time I ever spoke in a religious meeting—I urged females both to pray and speak if they felt deeply enough to do it, and not to be restrained from it by the fact that they were *females.* I made these remarks at a meeting when not less than two hundred persons were present of both sexes, and *five* ministers of the gospel at least, and I think more. The result was that seven females, a number of them the most influential female christians in the city, confessed their sin in being restrained by their sex, and prayed publickly in succession at that very meeting. It made a great deal of talk and discussion, and the subject of female praying and female speaking in public was discussed throughout western New York. As I was extensively acquainted west of Utica I had opportunity to feel the pulse of the ministry and church generally, and I did not find one in ten who *believed* it was unscriptural, fully. They grieved and said perhaps, and they didnt know, and they *were opposed to it,* and that it [was] not best; but yet the practice of female praying in promiscuous meetings grew every day and now all over that region nothing is more common in revivals of religion. I found wherever the *practice* commenced *first* it always held its own and gained over crowds; but where it was *first* laid down as a *doctrine* and pushed, it always went hard and generally forestalled the practice and *shut it out.* 2. The feeling of opposition to female praying, speaking, etc., which *men* generally have is from a stereotyped notion or persuasion that they are not competent for it. It arises from habitually regarding them as *inferior* beings. I know that the majority of men regard women as *silly.* The proposition that woman can reason and analyze closely is to them an absurdity. They are surprised [?] greatly if a woman speaks or prays to edification, and in this state of mind it is not strange that they stumble at *Paul.* But let intelligent woman begin to pray or speak and men begin to be converted to the true doctrine, and when they get familiar with it they like it and lose all their scruples. True there is a pretty large class of ministers who are fierce about it and will fight, but a still larger class that will come over if they first witness the successful *practice* rather than meet it in the shape of a doctrine to be swallowed. Now if instead of blowing a blast thro' the newspapers, sounding the onset and summoning the ministers and churches to surrender, you had without any introductory flourish just gone right among them and lectured *when* and *where* and *as* you could find opportunity and paid no attention to criticism, but pushed right on without making any ado about *"attacks"* and *"invasions"* and *"opposition"* and have let the barkers bark their bark out, within one year you might have practically brought over 50,000 persons of the very moral elite of New England. You may rely upon it, your *specimens* of female speaking and praying will do fifty times as much to bring over to womans rights the community as your *indoctrinating* under your own name thro' the newspapers those who never saw you.

Theodore Weld, letter to Sarah and Angelina Grimké, August 26, 1837, in Barnes and Dumond, Letters of Theodore Dwight Weld, Angelina Grimké Weld and Sarah Grimké, *432–433.*

Perhaps some persons may wonder that I should attempt to throw out my views on the important subject of marriage, and may conclude that I am altogether disqualified for the task, because I lack experience. However, I shall not undertake to settle the specific duties of husbands and wives, but only to exhibit opinions based on the word of God, and formed from a little knowledge of human nature, and close observation of the working of generally received notions respecting the dominion of man over woman . . .

Woman, instead of being elevated by her union with man, which might be expected from an alliance with a superior being, is in reality lowered. She generally loses her individuality, her independent character, her moral being. She becomes absorbed by him, and henceforth is looked at, and acts through the medium of her husband . . .

Duty as well as inclination has led me, for many years, into the abodes of poverty and sorrow, and I have been amazed at the treatment which women receive at the hands of those, who arrogate themselves the epithet of *protectors.* Brute force, the law of violence, rules to a great extent in the poor man's domicile; and woman is little more than his drudge. They are less under the supervision of public opinion, less under the restraints of education, and unaided or unbiased by the refinements of polished society. Religion, wherever it exists, supplies the place of all these; but the real cause of woman's degradation and suffering in married life is to be found in the erroneous notion of her inferiority to man; and never will she be rightly regarded by herself, or others, until this opinion, so derogatory to the wisdom and mercy of God, is exploded, and woman arises in all the majesty of her womanhood, to claim those rights which are inseparable from her existence as an immortal, intelligent and responsible being . . .

Sarah M. Grimké in Letters on the Equality of the Sexes and the Condition of Woman, *September 1837, in Schneir,* Feminism, *47.*

... Thou takes it for granted that our heads are so full of *womans rights, womans rights* that our hearts have grown cold in the cause of the slave, that we have started aside like broken bows. Now we think thou hast verily misjudged us. . . . Thou seems to overlook the fact that before a word was written on the subject of womans rights, the Pastoral letter had been issued and that in every place that we lectured the subject of our speaking in public was up for discussion. My reason for giving my views with my name was simply because I wished to be answerable for those views.

Sarah and Angelina Grimké, letter to Theodore Weld, September 20, 1837, in Barnes and Dumond, Letters of Theodore Dwight Weld, Angelina Grimké Weld and Sarah Grimké, 448–452.

As we are frequently asked, what relation we have in past years sustained to the system of slavery, and as we feel that individuals have a *perfect right to know*, we have thought it best to publish the following facts.

When S. M. G. [Sarah Moore Grimké] was quite young, her father gave her a little African girl to wait upon her; but after a few years, she died. This was the only slave she ever owned. It must have been 30 years ago.

In the year 1827, our mother gave A. E. G. [Angelina Emily Grimké] a young woman. She soon became uneasy with holding her a slave, and in a few months returned her to the donor. NO money transactions ever passed about it—NONE was paid, and NONE was received. S[t]ill, she at that time only saw men as trees walking, and was not sensible of the sin she was committing in returning a fellow creature into bondage. She only felt that she did not want the responsibility of such an ownership, but had no clear conception of the intrinsic principles of slavery.

In 1835, she began to read anti-slavery publications, and for the first time saw that slavery, under all circumstances, was sinful; she had always mourned over the ignorance, degradation, and cruelty, of slavery, but never understood the chattel principle, out of which all these abominations grew as naturally as the trunk and branches from the root of the tree. During the eight years which had elapsed since the time of her being a slaveholder, the slave had been sold, and had become the mother of three or four children. A. E. G. felt conscience-stricken at what she had done, and wrote to the then owner of the woman and her children, offering to *redeem* them from slavery at any price that might be named; and at the same time stating the change in her views, and the reasons why she could not offer to *buy* them, as that would be a recogni-

Lowell, Massachusetts *(Library of Congress)*

tion of the right of one man to hold another as property. The owner would not accede to this proposition, so that this slave is still in bondage. This is the only slave she ever owned.

We have been induced to state these facts because many persons have heard that we had slaves and liberated them; and we do not wish the credit of doing that which we had no opportunity of doing.

Sarah and Angelina Grimké, letter to the editor,
National Enquirer, *October 26, 1837, in Barnes and Dumond,* Letters of Theodore Dwight Weld, Angelina Grimké Weld and Sarah Grimké, *471–472.*

. . . my sister Emilie became acquainted with a family of bright girls, near neighbors of ours, who proposed that we should join with them, and form a little society for writing and discussion, to meet fortnightly at their house. We met—I think I was the youngest of the group,—prepared a Constitution and By-Laws, and named ourselves "The Improvement Circle." If I remember it rightly, my sister was our first president. The older ones talked and wrote on many subjects quite above me. I was shrinkingly bashful, as half-grown girls usually are, but I wrote my little essays and read them, and listened to the rest, and enjoyed it all exceedingly. Out of this little "Improvement Circle" grew the larger one whence issued the "Lowell Offering," a year or two later [1840] . . . The printed regulations forbade us to bring books into the mill, so I made my window seat into a small library of poetry, pasting its side all over with newspaper clippings . . . The overseer, caring more for law than gospel, confiscated all he found. He had his desk full of Bibles. It sounded oddly to hear him say to the most religious girl in the room, when he took hers away, "I think you had more conscience than to bring that book in here."

Lucy Larcom, writing on factory life, ca. 1838, in A New England Girlhood, *174–175.*

Why does it follow that women are fitted for nothing but the cares of domestic life, for bearing children and cooking the food of a family, devotion all their time to the domestic circle—to promoting the immediate personal comfort of their husbands, brothers and sons? . . . The mere departure of women from the duties of the domestic circle, far from being a reproach to her, is a virtue of the highest order, when it is done from purity of motive, by appropriate means, and the purpose good.

John Quincy Adams, "Speech . . . Upon the Rights of the People, Men and Women to Petition," 1838, in Flexner, Century of Struggle, *51.*

Now I believe it is woman's right to have a voice in all the laws and regulations by which she is to be governed, whether in Church or State: and that the present arrangements of society, on these points, are a *violation of human rights, a rank usurpation of power,* a violent seizure and confiscation of what is sacredly and inalienably hers.

Angelina Grimké, letter to Catharine Beecher, 1838, in Sklar, Catharine Beecher: A Study in American Domesticity, *34.*

I was so near fainting under the tremendous pressure of feeling, my heart almost died within me. The novelty of the scene, the weight of responsibility, the ceaseless exercise of mind thro' which I had passed for almost a week—all together sunk me to the earth. I well nigh despaired, but our Lord and Master gave me his arm to lean upon and in great weakness, my limbs trembling under me, I stood up and spoke for nearly two hours . . .

Angelina Grimké, letter describing her speech before the committee of the Massachusetts state legislature, February 21, 1838, in Barnes and Dumond, Letters of Theodore Dwight Weld, Angelina Grimké Weld and Sarah Grimké, *546.*

. . . and the hall was jambed to such excess that it was with great difficulty we were squeezed in, and then [we] were compelled to walk over the seats in order to reach the place assigned us. As soon as we entered we were received by clapping. O! Sarah do you know—can you imagine—how I felt? My heart did not sink in prospect of this meeting as it [had] done before. After the bustle was over I rose to speak and was greeted by hisses from the doorway, tho' profound silence reigned thro' the crowd within. The noise in that direction increased and I was requested by the Chairman to suspend my remarks until order could be restored. Three times was I thus interrupted, until at last one of the Committee came to me and requested I would stand near the Speakers desk. I crossed the Hall and stood on the platform in front of it, but was immediately requested to occupy the

Secretaries desk on one side. I had just fixed my papers on two gentlemen's hats when at last I was invited to stand in the Speaker's desk. This was in the middle, more elevated and far more convenient in every respect.

Angelina Grimké, letter to Sarah Douglass, on her speech to the Massachusetts legislature, February 25, 1838, in Barnes and Dumond, Letters of Theodore Dwight Weld, Angelina Grimké Weld and Sarah Grimké, *572–573.*

She exhibited considerable talent for a female, as an orator; appeared not at all abashed in exhibiting herself in a position so unsuitable to her sex, totally disregarding the doctrine of St. Paul, who says "Is it not a shame for a woman to speak in public?" She belabored the slaveholders, and beat the air like all possessed. Her address occupied about 2 hours and a half in delivery, when she gave out, stating that she had a sister who was desirous to speak upon the same subject but was prevented by ill health. She, however, intimated, that after taking a breath for a day, she would like to continue the subject and the meeting was accordingly adjourned to Friday afternoon, at 3 o'clock, when she will conclude her speech.

Boston Gazette, *March 9, 1838, in Lerner,* The Grimké Sisters from South Carolina, *10.*

I thought of you several times while Angelina was addressing the committee of the Legislature. I knew you would have enjoyed it so much. I think it was a spectacle of the greatest moral sublimity I ever witnessed. The house was full to overflowing. For a moment a sense of the immense responsibility resting on her seemed almost to overwhelm her. She trembled and grew pale. But this passed quickly, and she went on to speak gloriously, strong in utter forgetfulness of herself, and in her own earnest faith in every word she uttered "Whatsoever comes from the heart goes to the heart." I believe she made a very powerful impression upon the audience . . . The Boston members of the legislature tried hard to prevent her having a hearing on the same day. Among other things, they said that such a crowd were attracted by curiosity the galleries were in danger of being broken down; though in fact they are constructed with remarkable strength. A member from Salem, perceiving their drift, wittily proposed that a

"committee be appointed to examine the foundations of the State House of Massachusetts, to see whether it will bear another lecture from Miss Grimké."

One sign that her influence is felt is that the "sound part of the community" (as they consider themselves) seek to give vent to their vexation by calling her "Devil-ina" instead of Angel-ina, and Miss Grimalkin instead of Miss Grimké. Another sign is that we have succeeded in obtaining the Odeon, one of the largest and most central halls, for her to speak in; and it is the first time such a place has been obtained for antislavery in this city.

Lydia Maria Child, letter to E. Carpenter, March 20, 1838, in Letters of Lydia Maria Child, *26–27.*

. . . Your being so generally known as a public lecturer to promiscuous assemblies, and especially as having addressed the legislature, all eyes are upon you and almost all mouths filled with cavil. Nine tenths of the community verily believe that you are utterly spoiled for domestic life. A man of whom I hoped better things and who really had great respect for your *principle* and *character* said he did not believe it possible for a woman of your *sentiments* and *practice* as to the sphere of woman to be anything but "an obtrusive noisy clamorer" in the domestic circle "repelled and repelling". He said he could admire your talents and your principles for he did believe you honest, but it was *impossible* for a man of high and pure feeling ever to *marry* you. He said that *nature* recoiled at it.

Theodore Weld, letter to Angeline Grimké, April 15, 1838, in Barnes and Dumond, Letters of Theodore Dwight Weld, Angelina Grimké Weld and Sarah Grimké, *630–640.*

It was a noble day when for the first time in civilized America, a Woman stood up in a Legislative Hall, vindicating the rights of woman . . . This noble woman gave our legislators . . . one of those beautiful appeals for which she alone, as an American female, has been so justly distinguished.

Boston Mercantile Journal, *reprinted in the* Liberator, *April 29, 1838, in Lerner,* The Grimké Sisters from South Carolina, *11.*

Now as to the jeopardy of character, I do very humbly conceive that however it may be with *others, our* marriage is such a matter altogether *extraordinary* and of such marked notoriety, that the fact [that it] will ever be denied is not to be set down among possibilities. And as it respects *"property"*, it will quite rejoice me that there will be no legal record proving my legal right as your husband to what you have.

So I am quite thankful for this unexpected opportunity to give a *little* testimony against a vandal law which prostrates a woman at the feet of her husband the moment after marriage, suing for the *favor* of a pittance of the property just plundered from her by the law, and put at his *sole disposal.* If you WISH Dearest to have a public record made of our marriage, I will most cheerfully consent to the presence of a justice. I leave the question entirely with *you.*

Theodore Weld, letter to Angelina Grimké, May 7, 1838, in Barnes and Dumond, Letters of Theodore Dwight Weld, Angelina Grimké Weld and Sarah Grimké, *667–668.*

Miss Grimké, a pretty Quakeress . . . is a woman of splendid eloquence and has made me 19/20 of an abolitionist.

Detroit Morning Post, reprinted in the Liberator, *May 11, 1838, in Lerner,* The Grimké Sisters from South Carolina, *12.*

Miss Grimké, a North Carolinian [!], we believe, is delivering abolition lectures to the members of the Massachusetts Legislature. Miss Grimké is very likely in search of a lawful protector, who will take her for better or worse for life, and she has thus made a bold dash among Yankee lawmakers.

Pittsburgh Manufacturer, reprinted in the Liberator, *May 11, 1838, in Lerner,* The Grimké Sisters of South Carolina, *11.*

Not merely is your marriage one which sustains and enhances the esteem felt for you individually, but it seems to me the *only* one which could have done justice to either. Who but Angelina E. Grimké could

Power loom weaving *(Library of Congress)*

have arrested the solitary eagle in his sun-high aims and brought him arrow-pierced and fluttering down to Hymen's altar, owning that "marriage *is* honourable"? And who but Theodore D. Weld could ever have satisfied the aspiring champion of woman's rights (forgive my pleasantry, sister) that *after all* "the husband is the head of the wife"?

J. A. Thome, letter to Angelina and Theodore Weld, May 15, 1838, in Barnes and Dumond, Letters of Theodore Dwight Weld, Angelina Grimké Weld and Sarah Grimké, *681.*

. . . I must now give thee some account of my dear sister's marriage, which probably thou hast already heard of . . . Theodore addressed Angelina in a solemn and tender manner. He alluded to the unrighteous power vested in a husband by the laws of the United States over the person and property of his wife, and he abjured all authority, all government, save the influence which love would give to them over each other as moral and immortal beings.

Sarah M. Grimké, letter to Elizabeth Pease, May 20(?), 1838, in Barnes and Dumond, Letters of Theodore Dwight Weld, Angelina Grimké Weld and Sarah Grimké, *679.*

Next morning, attended the Peace Convention, not knowing what to anticipate as to its complexion or numbers, and hardly attempting to imagine what would be the result of its deliberations. (I ought to have said, that we attended bro. May's lecture at the [Marlboro] Chapel, the evening of our arrival. It was delivered in the large hall, but there were very few present, and they were nearly all abolitionists. It was a good lecture). A respectable number of delegates were in attendance. Hon. Sidney Willard, of Cambridge, was elected President, and E. L. Capron and Amasa Walker Vice-Presidents. When the roll of members was about being made out, I rose and suggested, that, as mistakes often occur in procuring signatures, each individual should write his or *her* name on a slip of paper, &c.; thus mooting the vexed "woman question" at the very outset. There was a smile on the countenances of many abolition friends, while others in the Convention looked very grave. Several of the clergy were present, but no one rose to object. Of course, women became members, and were thus entitled to speak and vote. A business committee was then appointed, upon which Abby

Lydia Maria Francis Child, writer and abolitionist
(Library of Congress)

Kelley and a Miss [Susan] Sisson were placed. Mrs. Chapman was added to another committee. In the course of the forenoon, Rev. Mr. Beckwith was called to order by Abby K. Endurance now passed its bounds on the part of the women-contemners, and accordingly several persons (clergymen and laymen) requested their names to be erased from the roll of the Convention, because women were to be allowed to participate in the proceedings! They were gratified in their request. . .

William Lloyd Garrison, letter to his wife, Helen, September 21, 1838, in Garrison and Garrison, William Lloyd Garrison, *227–228.*

Your questions about matrimony chime in with my frequent thoughts. I know not when one will rise up to purify the domestic altar, now so polluted and defiled. It is a subject on which I think almost with despair; for if pure doctrine should be preached, even with an angel's eloquence, how can it be received, or even understood, when the entire public sentiment is so perverted? Deeply, deeply do I feel the degradation of being a woman—not the degradation of being what *God* made woman, but what *man* has made her . . .

Lydia Maria Child, letter to Angelina and Theodore Weld, December 26, 1838, in Barnes and Dumond, Letters of Theodore Dwight Weld, Angelina Grimké Weld and Sarah Grimké, *731.*

[T]his [prejudice] does not prevent Southern women from hanging their infants at the breasts of Negresses, nor almost every planter's wife and daughter from having one or more little pet blacks sleeping like puppy dogs in their very bedchamber, nor almost every planter from admitting one or several of his female slaves to the still closer intimacy of his bed . . .

Fanny Anne Kemble, January 1839, letter to Elizabeth Dwight Sedgwick from Butler Island, Georgia, in Kemble, Journal of a Residence on a Georgian Plantation in 1838–1839, *61.*

With regard to the Woman Question, as it is termed, . . . the Massachusetts [Anti-Slavery] Society have simply refused to take action upon it when the minority have urged them to do it. In the beginning, we were brought together by strong sympathy for the slave, without stopping to inquire about each other's religious opinions, or appropriate [male-female] spheres. Then, women were hailed by acclamation as helpers in the great work. They joined societies, they labored diligently, and they stood against a scoffing world bravely. When the two Grimkes [Sarah and Angelina] came among us, impediments in the way of their lecturing straightway arose, particularly among the clergy. The old theological argument from St. Paul was urged, and the Grimkes replied in their own defense. A strong feeling of hostility to women's speaking in public had always been latent in the clergy, and this incident aroused it all over the country. The sisters found obstacles so multiplied in their path, that they considered the establishment of women's freedom of vital importance to the anti-slavery cause. "Little can be done for the slave," said they, "while this prejudice blocks up the way." They urged me to say and do more about women's rights, nay, at times they gently rebuked me for my want of zeal. I replied, "It's best not to *talk* about our rights, but simply go forward and *do* whatsoever we deem a duty. In toiling for the freedom of others, we shall find our own." On

this ground I have ever stood; and so have my anti-slavery sisters.

Lydia Maria Child, letter to William Lloyd Garrison, September 2, 1839, in Meltzer and Holland, Lydia Marie Child, Selected Letters, 1817–1880, *122–23.*

[A]nd to Mr. [Butler]'s assertion of the justice of poor Teresa's punishment, I retorted the manifest injustice of unpaid and enforced labor; the brutal inhumanity of allowing a man to strip and lash a woman, the mother of ten children; to exact from her, toil, which was to maintain in luxury two idle young men, the owners of the plantation. I said I thought female labor of the sort exacted from these slaves, and corporal chastisement such as they endure, must be abhorrent to any manly or humane man. Mr. [Butler] said he thought it was *disagreeable,* and left me to my reflections with that concession.

Fanny Anne Kemble, Letter from Butler Island, Georgia, February 1839, in Kemble, Journal of a Residence on a Georgian Plantation in 1838–1839, *160–61.*

Judge from the details I now send you; and never forget, while reading them, that the people on this plantation are well off, and consider themselves well off, in comparison with the slaves on some of the neighboring estates.

Fanny has had six children; all dead but one. She came to beg to have her work in the field lightened.

Nanny has had three children; two of them are dead. She came to implore that the rule of sending them into the field three weeks after their confinement might be altered.

Leah, Caesar's wife, has had six children; three are dead.
Sophy, Lewis's wife, came to beg for some old linen. She is suffering fearfully has had ten children; five of them are dead. The principal favor she asked was a piece of meat, which I gave her.

Sally, Scipio's wife, has had two miscarriages and three children born, one of whom is dead. She came complaining of incessant pain and weakness in her back. This woman was a mulatto daughter of a slave called Sophy, by a white man of the name of Walker, who visited the plantation.

Charlotte, Renty's wife, had had two miscarriages, and was with child again. She was almost crippled with rheumatism, and showed me a pair of poor swollen knees that made my heart ache. I have promised her a pair of flannel trousers, which I must forthwith set about making.

Sarah, Stephen's wife; this woman's case and history were alike deplorable. She had had four miscarriages, had brought seven children into the world, five of whom were dead, and was again with child. She complained of dreadful pains in the back, and an internal tumor which swells with the exertion of working in the fields; probably, I think, she is ruptured.

Fanny Anne Kemble, letter from Butler Island, Georgia, February 28–March 2, 1839, in Kemble, Journal of a Residence on a Georgian Plantation in 1838–1839, *230.*

3

Women Overseas— The World Anti-Slavery Convention
1840–1847

THE HISTORICAL CONTEXT

According to Elizabeth Cady Stanton, "The movement for woman's suffrage in England and America may be dated from [the] World's Anti-Slavery Convention." In 1840 a chance meeting between Elizabeth Cady Stanton and Lucretia Mott took place in London. Mott at 47 was a petite woman with straight brown hair and dark eyes. A Quaker, she usually wore a white kerchief across her shoulders and a white cap and plain bonnet on her head. This was customary dress for members of the Society of Friends. Her friends thought Mott soft-spoken, sensitive to the needs of others, and a good listener. Yet this manner masked a will of steel.[1]

Born Lucretia Coffin in 1793 on Nantucket, the young woman recalled in her diary: "I always loved the good in childhood, and desired to do the right. In those early years I was actively useful to my mother, who, in the absence of my father on his long voyages, was engaged in the mercantile business, often going to Boston to purchase goods in exchange for oil and candles, the staple of the island. The exercise of women's talents in this line, as well as the general care which devolved upon them, in the absence of their husbands, tended to develop and strengthen them mentally and physically."[2]

Many Nantucket men were away at sea for much of the time, so their wives not only ran the families but managed the businesses as well. Lucretia's mother ran a shop and did her own bookkeeping, skills that women were thought unable to master. Too, the Quakers were unique in America because generally they treated women and men equally. Women could speak freely in meetings and even become ministers. Mott became a minister in 1821 when she was only 28. Later, as the mother of six, she became a public speaker when such behavior in women was scandalous and even opened her home to the underground railroad.

When she met Lucretia Mott, Elizabeth Cady Stanton was 25. She was short, about five feet, three inches, tall, with blue eyes and "coal black ringlets falling about a rather full face."[3] A friend once described her as the girl with "the joyous laugh, the merry joke, the smile, the kind word." She was lively, social, and a bit of a prankster.[4]

Born in Johnstown, New York, in 1815, Elizabeth was one of the five daughters of the tall, "queenly" horsewoman Margaret Livingston and her lawyer husband, Daniel Cady. Elizabeth thought that Judge Cady's hopes and ambitions rested with his son, Eleaser, "a fine, manly fellow, the very apple of my father's eye."[5]

When Eleaser died at age 20, Elizabeth threw her arms around her father's neck and vowed to be "all my brother was."[6] She studied Greek, learned to ride a horse, and became the only girl in a class of boys studying Latin and math at Johnstown Academy. For all this, she still believed that her father did not value her accomplishments. Years later she would write that Eleaser "filled a larger place in his affections and future plans than the five girls altogether." Until she died she remembered the day that she ran home to show him a top prize she had earned in Greek, only to hear him sigh, "Ah, you should have been a boy!"[7]

At 15 Elizabeth wanted to accompany her male classmates to Union College in Schenectady, New York. But in 1831 no college in America admitted girls, so she was forced to attend the Troy Female Seminary, founded in 1821 by Emma Willard. Although it was the most advanced school for girls of its day, the Troy Seminary could not match the standards of the men's colleges. Elizabeth was unhappy with her education. When she graduated in 1832 she continued to study law and politics at home, and for the rest of her life she championed coeducation.

In 1839 Elizabeth met Henry Stanton, a 24-year-old antislavery leader, at the home of her cousin, the reformer Gerrit Smith. One month later, Henry proposed. However, because of her father's opposition, Elizabeth postponed her decision. But one day Henry told Elizabeth that he was going to London as a delegate to the World Anti-Slavery Convention. Elizabeth immediately decided to marry him, and their wedding was held on May 10, 1840. By May 12 they had boarded the ship *Montreal* and were off to England.

At sea Stanton formed her first impression of Lucretia Mott. Strolling on the deck with the Liberty Party candidate for president, James G. Birney, she listened to him ridicule Mott and other women delegates who had "demoralized" the antislavery ranks by presuming to attend the World Anti-Slavery Convention. In October 1836 the British and Foreign Anti-Slavery Society had invited all "friends of the slave" to the London meeting. But in February 1840, realizing that "friends" might be interpreted to include "women," it revised its invitation to include only "gentlemen." Then, one month before the convention, the American Anti-Slavery Society split in two—partly because of the "insane innovation" of letting women serve as speakers and officers, partly because of the animosity felt toward the society's progressive leader, William Lloyd Garrison.

Garrison, with Lucretia Mott, wanted an immediate end to slavery and full equality for women. Distrustful of politics, he wanted these reforms to come about through moral persuasion alone. His opponents, led by James Birney, advocated the gradual emancipation of slaves through political action. They objected to equal rights for women, opposing women's right to vote and hold office within the organization. These men left the American Anti-Slavery Society to form a new organization, the American and Foreign Anti-Slavery Society. Their group was favored by the British and Foreign Anti-Slavery Society that hosted the London meeting.[8]

When they arrived at their hotel on Great Queen Street, Elizabeth and Henry Stanton found themselves in an awkward situation. As members of the anti-Garrison group, Henry's colleagues were against seating the females at the convention, but Stanton himself favored it. Elizabeth sided wholeheartedly with the pro-Garrisonites. Both of these groups were staying at the same hotel, and when Elizabeth was introduced to Mott, she felt embarrassed, as she was the only woman there associated with the "Birney faction."

At dinner, with "the viands fairly dispenced," Elizabeth wrote, several Baptist ministers began to "rally the ladies on having set the Abolitionists all by the ears in America," aiming at doing the same in England. "I soon found that the pending battle was on women's rights, and that unwittingly, I was by marriage on the wrong side," She agreed with the women who were "battling" the men on this issue, but their only champion was George Bradford, who was too deaf to hear a word. Despite nudgings by Henry under the table, she could not keep silent and jumped in on the side of Lucretia Mott. "I shall never forget the look of recognition she gave me when she saw by my remarks that I fully comprehended the problem of woman's rights and wrongs."[9]

Early on a bright and clear June 12, the Americans arrived at the convention at Freemasons' Hall. They immediately became embattled with clergymen and other delegates over the seating of the women. William Lloyd Garrison's American Anti-Slavery Society had sent five delegates, including one woman, Lucretia Mott, who represented the Philadelphia Anti-Slavery Society. She was accompanied by other women from the Massachusetts Anti-Slavery Society and the Boston Female Society. Garrison had anticipated trouble, writing to his wife: "It is, perhaps, quite probable that we shall be foiled in our purpose; but the subject cannot be agitated without doing good . . ." In another letter he wrote, "With a young woman placed on the throne of Great Britain, will the philanthropists of that country presume to object to the female delegates from the United States, as members of the Convention, on the ground of their sex? In what assembly, however august or select, is that almost peerless woman, LUCRETIA MOTT, not qualified to take an equal part?"[10]

Wendell Phillips moved that a committee prepare a roster of all delegates from any accredited antislavery society. The discussion lasted for many hours. Most delegates were loath to seat the women. The clergymen claimed that women were "constitutionally unfit for public or business meetings." Others believed that to try to settle "the woman question" would weaken the force of a convention dedicated to abolishing slavery. When it was proposed that all accredited delegates be seated regardless of sex, there were shouts of, "Turn out the women!" The debate lasted for hours.

Finally, the gauntlet was thrown by the Reverend C. Stout, who cried, "[s]hall we be divided on this *paltry question* and suffer the whole tide of benevolence to be stopped by *a straw?* No! You talk of being men, then be men!"[11]

The vote went against the women, and they were led to a curtained-off gallery to observe the goings-on.

William Lloyd Garrison, arriving on the fourth day of the convention, joined them there, declaring: "After battling so many long years for the liberation of African slaves, I can take no part in a convention that strikes down the most sacred rights of all women." For 10 days the women watched the convention from their quarters. Indignation burned, but a women's movement was born. Henry's old enemy was now Elizabeth's friend, and a new circle of reformers was about to be formed.[12]

Stanton later wrote, "[T]he crucifixion of their pride and self-respect, the humiliation of the spirit," was treated by the men as a "most trifling matter." It was a radicalizing experience. Between sessions she "took possession of Lucretia, much to Henry's annoyance." Stanton would later recall that one day at the British Museum she and Mott left the others in their group to tour the halls and sat for hours on a bench talking about a women's rights convention they would hold when they returned to America.[13]

Stanton and Mott were not sure where to begin their reform. But Stanton felt compelled to take action anyway. "I could not see what to do or where to begin—my only thought was a public meeting for protest and discussion." Yet when they returned to America, the two women drifted apart; the convention they envisioned was forgotten for eight years.[14]

Back in America, Elizabeth and Henry Stanton went to live with Elizabeth's family. There Henry studied law under Judge Cady, and Elizabeth read law, history, and political economy as she began to raise her family. In 1843 and 1845 she lobbied the New York State legislature for the New York Married Woman's Property Act, which had met defeat in 1836 and 1840. Meanwhile, Lucretia Mott continued her preaching, abolition work, and family duties.

Though the women went their separate ways upon their return to the United States, they must have shared the recognition that the country, New England in particular, was changing. The 1840s was a period of intense urbanization. The "golden age" of the working girl of the 1830s had come to an end. After 1840 factories could get away with speeding up machines and paying lower wages since new waves of poor immigrants desperately needed these jobs. Gradually, conditions worsened for all. Consequently, the discontent felt by Stanton and Mott as a result of their trip to London dovetailed with a rising militancy on the part of the female labor force.

Initially there seemed to be little dissatisfaction with the way the factories were run. The *Lowell Offering,* the literary magazine founded by the female operatives of Lowell, Massachusetts, (printed between October 1840 and March 1841), published essays and sketches by and for women workers. The magazine attracted international attention for the literary accomplishments of its unschooled writers. By April 1841 a rival publication, the *Operatives' Magazine,* was started by another group of Lowell workers. By August 1842 still another magazine made its appearance, the *Olive Leaf, and Factory Girl's Repository,* published in Cobotville, Massachusetts. All of these magazines published articles uncritical of factory life. Perhaps the early experience of working in the factories, as opposed to farm life, was a liberating one. Many young women postponed marriage and child-bearing as the result of their factory work and went on to attain further schooling and better work as teachers, librarians, and the like.

By 1845, however, labor leaders were criticizing such publications as the *Lowell Offering* for being blind to deteriorating factory conditions. That year Sarah Bagley, America's first female labor leader, assailed the *Lowell Offering* publicly at the Independence Day festivities in Woburn, Massachusetts. Before a crowd of 2,000 working people, she criticized the magazine for rejecting her articles. A debate ensued with the paper's editor, Harriet Farley. In the *Lowell Express* on August 7, 1845, Bagley accused her of being a management "mouthpiece." By the end of the year, the *Lowell Offering* had stopped publication. Bagley then helped launch the more militant paper *Voice of Industry,* which appeared in October. Bagley also served as the first president of the Lowell Female Labor Reform Association, soliciting 2,000 signatures to a petition presented to the Massachusetts legislature for a shorter working day.

In September 1845 Allegheny and Pittsburgh cotton mill workers, having launched a campaign against the corporations the previous year, united with women from mills in Manchester to fight the 10-hour day. And on October 20, workers rioted in Pittsburgh to protest scab labor. Through their actions and writings, these young women were waging a battle not dissimilar to the one that Elizabeth Cady Stanton was about to initiate at Seneca Falls. At the same time, reformers such as Dorothea Dix were conducting humanitarian crusades for the weak and helpless of society, establishing mental hospitals, improving prisons, and helping the poor and uneducated.

Also during these years, thousands of men and women migrated to the Pacific Northwest in search of a better life—milder climates, richer soil, and free land. From 1840 to 1860, 250,000 people traveled between 2,000 and 3,000 miles to claim free land. Before the discovery of gold at Sutter's Mill, south of Sacramento, in 1841, California's population was 14,000; after 1849, when news of the gold find had spread around the world, it grew to more than 100,000.[15]

The westward migration drew so many young men away from eastern farms that marriage and family life were not possible for many women. This demographic imbalance may have helped create new opportunities for single women as schoolteachers or librarians. And, educationally, more women were able to take advantage of these opportunities. By 1840, 38 percent of European Americans between the ages of five and 20 attended school, and by 1850 most white women were literate, in contrast to the 18th century, when half could not sign their names. The climate was right for a women's movement.[16]

In 1847 the Stantons moved from Boston to Seneca Falls, New York. This was either due to Henry's desire for a milder climate for health reasons (he suffered from lung congestion and migraines) or to his hope for a more advantageous political base from which to run for office. In any case, as Henry became more content, Elizabeth's spirits plummeted. She was 31, with three wild boys to mother and a husband away on business much of the time. At 32 Washington Street in Seneca Falls, running the household was more difficult than it had been in Boston. Elizabeth began writing of feeling isolated from "lectures, churches, theaters, concerts, and temperance"; she felt reduced to an endless series of household chores. As Seneca Falls was a malarial region, she found herself continually nursing children and servants. Her house was on the outskirts of town, served by muddy roads and no sidewalks. Physically overworked, she craved intellectual stimulation. "My duties were too numerous and varied and none sufficiently exhilarating or intellectual to bring into play my higher faculties. I suffered with mental hunger, which, like an empty stomach, is very depressing."[17]

Soon her personal dissatisfaction would develop into political action. But before it could, Stanton needed, once again, the reassuring and inspiring presence of Lucretia Mott.

CHRONICLE OF EVENTS

1840

Margaret Fuller joins Ralph Waldo Emerson in producing and editing *The Dial,* a transcendentalist journal.

Ernestine Rose is the author of the first petition to grant married women the right to own property. The petition, which in 1848 will become law in New York State, aims to protect the property of married women.

March 3: Lucretia Mott is elected to serve as a delegate from the American Anti-Slavery Society to the World Anti-Slavery Convention in London.

May: The American Anti-Slavery Association splits over the issue of allowing women to speak and vote in the organization. The association's leader, William Lloyd Garrison, is upheld in his support for equal rights for women. A formal vote is taken on the appointment of Abby Kelley to a business committee and is sustained by a majority in favor. Two of the men on the committee ask to be excused from serving. The anti-Garrison minority walks out and later forms the American and Foreign Anti-Slavery Society. Henry Stanton becomes executive secretary of the new group.

May 10: Elizabeth Cady marries Henry Brewster Stanton.

May 12: Elizabeth and Henry Stanton set sail for England to attend the World Anti-Slavery Convention.

June 12–20: A World Anti-Slavery Convention opens in London. Female delegates are denied recognition by majority vote.

October: Lowell Offering begins publication.

Henry Brewster Stanton, husband of Elizabeth Cady Stanton *(New York Public Library Picture Collection)*

April: Operatives' Magazine begins publication.

1841

The first women to receive their baccalaureate degrees, all from Oberlin College, are Mary Hosford, Elizabeth Smith Prall, and Caroline Mary Rudd.

Catharine Beecher writes *A Treatise on Domestic Economy,* later published as *The American Woman's Home* (1869), giving housewives practical information to better fulfill their domestic obligations. Many editions will be published.

March: Dorothea Dix teaches Sunday school for women in the East Cambridge jail and discovers many cold, disheveled inmates whose only crime is mental illness. It is a turning point in her life.

1842

Catharine Beecher writes *Letters to Persons Who Are Engaged in Domestic Service.*

May 27: Massillon, Ohio, hosts a women's rights convention.

August: Olive Leaf, and Factory Girls Repository begins publication.

1843

July: Margaret Fuller publishes "The Great Lawsuit. Man Versus Men, Woman Versus Women" in *The Dial;* it is later published as *Woman in the Nineteenth Century.*

1843–1847

Women turn out for shorter working hours in a succession of strikes in the Allegheny mills near Pittsburgh, Pennsylvania. The one in 1845 is violent.

1844

December: Margaret Fuller becomes the first woman to join the staff of the *New York Tribune.*

December 12: Sarah G. Bagley founds the 600-member Lowell Female Labor Reform Association.

1845

Margaret Fuller publishes *Woman in the Nineteenth Century.*

In *Prince v. Prince* the state of South Carolina decides that a husband who has deserted his wife has the duty to pay her alimony and child support, whether or not he has property or a fixed income.

Dorothea Dix writes *Remarks on Prisons and Prison Discipline in the United States,* which paves the way for reforms in the prison system.

Catharine Beecher writes *The Duty of Women to Their Country,* which argues the need to educate the nation's 2 million children. This leads to 500 New England teachers being sent west under the auspices of the Boston Mount Vernon Board of National Popular Education in Cleveland, Ohio.

July 4: Sarah G. Bagley attacks the *Lowell Offering* under Harriet Farley and conditions in the Lowell mills, in an Independence Day address.

December: Lowell Offering collapses in competition with more radical papers.

1846

Three members of the Lowell Female Labor Reform Association, along with five men, become directors of the New England Labor Reform League.

Catharine Beecher publishes *The Evils of Suffered by American Women and American Children: The Causes and the Remedy.*

Gerrit Smith, cousin of Elizabeth Cady Stanton
(Library of Congress)

1847

Lucy Stone becomes the first Massachusetts woman to earn a college degree (from Oberlin College).

Elizabeth and Henry Stanton move to Seneca Falls, New York.

Lucy Stone gives her first lecture on women's rights in Gardner, Massachusetts.

Clarina Howard Nichols, newspaper editor, begins to write on the need to reform women's legal rights. Her work leads to the married woman's property law in Vermont.

The *Lowell Offering* returns as the *New England Offering.*

Woman's rights advocate Mathilde Anneke publishes *Woman in Conflict with Social Conditions.*

February 14: Anna Howard Shaw, minister and suffragist, is born.

EYEWITNESS TESTIMONY

Your note of yesterday, requesting letters of introduction to anti-slavery friends in England, has just come. As you intimate that you may leave to-morrow, and Francis Jackson informs me that he has a bundle for you, you see I have scarcely a moment to comply with your request. But George Thompson will be sufficient to obtain for you an introduction to a host of noble men and women across the Atlantic. How glad, how very glad, I am that Lucretia Mott and her husband are going to the [World Anti-Slavery] Convention! And how sorry, how *very* sorry, I am that I cannot go with them and with you! My dear Bradburn, it is not probable that I shall arrive in season to be at the opening of the Convention; but, I beseech you, *fail not to have women recognized as equal beings in it.* Interchange thoughts with dear Thompson about it. I know he will go for humanity, irrespective of sex.

God speed you!

William Lloyd Garrison, letter to George Bradburn,
April 24, 1840, in Garrison and Garrison,
William Lloyd Garrison, *354.*

Our [anti-slavery] organization is a stench in the nostrils of the nation, and the approaching meeting will increase it. May the Lord mercifully preserve the cause!

Lewis Tappan, letter to Theodore Weld, May 4, 1840, in
Barnes and Dumond, Letters of Theodore Dwight
Weld, Angelina Grimké Weld
and Sarah Grimké, *834.*

[We] set sail from New York 5 mo. 7th. 1840 . . . Third day out, great storm; everything novel and of deep interest. Tremendous sea, sublime view,—highly enjoyed by those who were not too sick.

Lucretia Mott, en route to World Anti-Slavery
Convention, diary entry, May 7, 1840, in Tolles,
Slavery and "The Woman Question," *13.*

I want you to consider the following things—

1. The *split* [in the anti-slavery ranks] was not *solely* on account of the claim that women shall vote, speak, be on committees, be officers, etc.
2. It was not [at] all because [of] opposition to their being *members* of the Society.

3. But it was chiefly because Garrison and his party (for although he and a few others profess *not* to speak the sentiments of the major part of the old M[assachusett]s Soc. yet it is evident they follow W. L. G.'s beck in everything) foisted upon the Amer. Anti[-Slavery] Soc. the woman question, no government question, etc., and the bad spirit shown by the Liberator, etc.
4. When the Constitution of the A[merican] Anti S[lavery] Soc. was formed in 1833, and the word "person" introduced, *all concerned* considered that it was to be understood as it is usually understood in our benevolent Societies. All have a right to be *members,* but the *business* to be conducted by the men. This understanding continued for 6 years. W. L. G. so understood it. See Phelps's remark in M's. Abolitionist.
5. W. L. G. introduced the question into the Anti S. Soc. to make an experiment upon the public. He had avowed before that there were subjects paramount to the Anti S. cause. And he was using the Society as an instrument to establish these notions. Since he introduced this question the slave has been lost sight of mainly. I add no more. See the Reporter.

L.T.

Women have equal rights with men, and therefore they have a right to form societies of women only. Men have the same right. *Men* formed the Amer. Anti S. Society.

Lewis Tappan, letter to Theodore Weld, May 26, 1840,
in Barnes and Dumond, Letters of Theodore
Dwight Weld, Angelina Grimké Weld
and Sarah Grimké, *836.*

In June, 1840, I met Mrs. Mott for the first time, in London. Crossing the Atlantic in Company with James G. Birney, then the Liberty Party candidate for President, soon after the bitter schism in the anti-slavery ranks; he described to me as we walked the deck day after day, the women who had fanned the flames of dissension, and had completely demoralized the anti-slavery ranks. As my first view of Mrs. Mott was through his prejudices, no prepossessions in her favor biased my judgement.

Elizabeth Cady Stanton, recalling her trip to London
for the World Anti-Slavery Convention in June 1840,
at the eulogy of Lucretia Mott, January 19, 1881,
in History of Woman Suffrage, *Vol. 1, 419.*

In 1840, a World's Anti-Slavery Convention was called in London. Women from Boston, New York, and Philadelphia, were delegates to that Convention. I was one of the number; but on our arrival in England, our credentials were not accepted, because we were women.

Lucretia Mott, diary entry, recalling World Anti-Slavery Convention held in June 1840, in History of Woman Suffrage, *Vol. 1, 418.*

When first introduced to her [Lucretia Mott] at our hotel in Great Queen Street, with the other ladies from Boston and Philadelphia who were delegates to the World's Convention, I felt somewhat embarrassed, as I was the only lady present who represented the "Birney faction" . . . However, Mrs. Mott, in her sweet, gentle way, received me with great cordiality and courtesy, and I was seated by her side at dinner.

Elizabeth Cady Stanton, recalling the World Anti-Slavery Convention held in June 1840, at the eulogy for Lucretia Mott, January 19, 1881, in History of Woman Suffrage, *Vol. 1, 419.*

Joseph Sturge breakfasted with us—begged submission of us to the London Committee . . . acknowledged that he had received letters from America on the same subject—made great professions—invited us to tea at the Anti-Slavery rooms with such of the Delegates as had arrived. We endeavored to shew him the inconstency of excluding Women Delegates—but soon found he had prejudged & made up his mind . . . therefore all reasoning was lost upon him, and our appeals made in vain . . .

Lucretia Mott, diary entry, June 6, 1840, in Tolles, Slavery and "The Woman Question," *22.*

Evening. Several sent to us to persuade us not to offer ourselves to the Convention—Colver rather bold in his suggestions—answered & of course offended him. W. Morgan & Scales informed us "it wasn't designed as a World Convention—that was a mere Poetical licence and that all power would rest with the "London Committee of Arrangements. Prescod of Jamaica (colored) thought it would lower the dignity of the Convention and bring ridicule on the whole thing if ladies were admitted—he was told that similar reasons were urged in Pennsylvania for the exclusion of colored people from our meetings—but had we yielded on such flimsy arguments we might as well have abandoned our enterprise. Colver thought Women

constitutionally unfit for public or business meetings—he was told that the colored man too was said to be constitutionally unfit to mingle with the white man. He left the room angry.

Lucretia Mott, diary entry, June 11, 1840, in Tolles, Slavery and "The Woman Question," *29.*

A letter having been read, addressed to the Secretary, dated Boston, 24th April, signed by Francis Jackson, President, and W. L. Garrison, Corresponding Secretary, of the Massachusetts Anti-Slavery Society, stating that several ladies have been appointed as delegates to the approaching Convention, it was unanimously

"Resolved, That the Committee, in the original summons of the Convention, did not contemplate, collectively or individually, the admission of ladies.

"That at a subsequent period, in the letter of the 15th of February, extensively circulated on both sides of the Atlantic, the invitation is addressed to gentlemen exclusively.

"That the subject having been brought seriously and deliberately before this Committee on the 15th of May, it was unanimously determined that ladies were inadmissible as delegates, and it is now again resolved, without a single dissentient voice, that this opinion be confirmed and respectfully communicated to the parties in question.

W. D. Crewdson, chairman of executive committee of the British and Foreign Anti-Slavery Committee, official refusal to issue tickets to the women delegates on the Massachusetts list, ca. June 12, 1840, in Garrison and Garrison, William Lloyd Garrison, *368.*

The world's Convention—*alias* the "Conference of the British and Foreign Anti-Slavery Society," with such guests as they chose to invite, assembled. We were kindly admitted behind the bar—politely conducted to our seats, and introduced to many, whom we had not met before . . .

Lucretia Mott, diary entry, June 12, 1840, in Tolles, Slavery and "The Woman Question," *29.*

The reception of women as a part of this Convention would, in the view of many, be not only a violation of the customs of England, but of the ordinance of Almighty God, who has a right to appoint our services to His sovereign will.

The Reverend Henry Grew, at the World Anti-Slavery Convention, June 12, 1840, in History of Woman Suffrage, *Vol. 1, 55.*

My vote is that we confirm the list of delegates, that we take votes on that as an amendment, and that we henceforth entertain this question no more. Are we not met here pledged to sacrifice all but everything in order that we may do something against slavery, and shall we be divided on this *paltry question* and suffer the whole tide of benevolence to be stopped by a *straw?* No! You talk of being men, then be men. Consider what is worthy of your attention.

> *The Reverend C. Stout, at World Anti-Slavery Convention, June 12, 1840, in* History of Woman Suffrage, *Vol. 1, 59.*

I entreat the ladies not to push this question too far. I wish to know whether our friends from America are to cast off England altogether.

> *Captain Wanchope, at World Anti-Slavery Convention, June 12, 1840, in* History of Woman Suffrage, *Vol. 1, 59.*

We have been unanimous against the common foe, but we are this day in danger of creating division among heartfelt friends. Will our American brethren put us in this position? Will they keep up a discussion in which the delicacy, the honor, the respectability of those excellent females who have come from the Western world are concerned? I tremble at the thought of discussing the question in the presence of these ladies—for whom I entertain the most profound respect—and I am bold to say, that but for the introduction of the question of woman's rights, it would be impossible for the shrinking nature of woman to subject itself to the infliction of such a discussion as this.

> *The Reverend Dr. Morrison, at World Anti-Slavery Convention, June 12, 1840, in* History of Woman Suffrage, *Vol. 1, 60.*

I have no objection to woman's being the neck to turn the head aright, but do not wish to see her assume the place of the head.

> *The Reverend Eben Galusha, at World Anti-Slavery Convention, June 12, 1840, in* History of Woman Suffrage, *Vol. 1, 56.*

After battling so many long years for the liberties of African slaves, I can take no part in a convention that strikes down the most sacred rights of a woman.

> *William Lloyd Garrison, comment to Elizabeth Cady Stanton, June 17, 1840, in Stanton,* Eighty Years and More, *81.*

William Lloyd Garrison worked for the rights of African Americans, women, and American Indians. *(Library of Congress)*

"Mrs. Mott, our Heavenly Father believes in bright colors. How much it would take from our pleasure if all the birds were dressed in drab." "Yes," said she, "but immortal beings do not depend on their feathers for their attractions. With the infinite variety of the human face and form, of thought, feeling, and affection, we do not need gorgeous apparel to distinguish us. Moreover, if it is fitting that woman should dress in every color of the rainbow, why not man also? Clergymen, with their black clothes and white cravats, are quite as monotonous as the Quakers.

> *Elizabeth Cady Stanton, recalling World Anti-Slavery Convention held in London in June 1840, during eulogy for Lucretia Mott, January 19, 1881, in* History of Woman Suffrage, *Vol. 1, 421.*

Elizabeth Stanton gaining daily in our affections . . .

> *Lucretia Mott, diary entry, June 20, 1840, in Tolles,* Slavery and "The Woman Question," *41.*

While in London a rich young Quaker of bigoted tendencies, who made several breakfast and tea parties for the American delegates, always omitted to invite Mrs. Mott. He very politely said to her on one occasion when he was inviting others in her presence,

"Thou must excuse men, Lucretia, for not inviting thee with the rest, but I fear thy influence on my children!"

Elizabeth Cady Stanton, recalling World Anti-Slavery convention held in London in June 1840, during eulogy for Lucretia Mott, January 19, 1881, in History of Woman Suffrage, *Vol. 1, 423.*

Could no longer have the use of Free Mason's Hall— met in Friends' Meeting house Grace Church St.—front seat upstairs appropriated to "rejected delegates"—didn't like being so shut out from the members.

Lucretia Mott, diary entry, June 22, 1840, in Tolles, Slavery and "The Woman Question," *42.*

Visiting in many Quaker families during our travels in England, I was amazed to hear Mrs. Mott spoken of as a most dangerous woman. Again and again I was warned against her influence. She was spoken of as an infidel, a heretic, a disturber, who had destroyed the peace in the Friends Society in Pennsylvania, and thrown a firebrand into the World's Convention, and that in a recent speech in London she quoted sentiments from Mary Wollstonecraft and Thomas Paine.

Elizabeth Cady Stanton, recalling World Anti-Slavery Convention held in London in June 1840, during eulogy for Lucretia Mott, January 19, 1881, in History of Woman Suffrage, *Vol. 1, 423.*

Last day of the Convention . . . Since we left America, the *man* question has, it seems, split the National Anti-Slavery society; therefore it has a tremendous significancy in our country . . .

Lucretia Mott, diary entry, June 23, 1840, in Tolles, Slavery and "The Woman Question," *43.*

. . . I have had much conversation with Lucretia Mott and I think her a peerless woman. She has a clear head and a warm heart. Her views are many of them so new and strange that my [illegible] finds great delight in her society. The quakers here have not all received her cordially; they fear her heretical notions. I am often asked if you have not changed your opinions on woman's rights and I have invariably taken the liberty to say no, though John Scoble has always contradicted me. Who is right? I heard a very interesting discussion between him and Elizabeth Peas[e] last evening on woman's rights. She fairly vanquished him

I thought for he took refuge under man's strongest weapon in contest with woman—flattery . . .

Elizabeth Cady Stanton, letter to Angelina and Sarah Grimké, June 25, 1840, in Barnes and Dumond, Letters of Theodore Dwight Weld, Angelina Grimké Weld and Sarah Grimké, *846–850.*

DEAR FRIEND:—". . . I regret that I was prevented from making a part of the Convention, as nothing should have hindered me from stating there in the plainest terms my opinion of the *real grounds* on which you were rejected. It is a pity that you were excluded on the plea of being women; but it is disgusting that under that plea you were actually excluded as heretics. That is the real ground, and it ought to have been at once proclaimed and exposed by the liberal members of the Convention; but I believe they were not aware of the fact. I heard of the circumstance of your exclusion at a distance, and immediately said: "Excluded on the ground that they are women?" No, that is not the real cause; there is something behind. And what are these female delegates? Are they orthodox in religion? The answer was "No, they are considered to be of the Hicksite party of Friends." My reply was, "That is enough; *there* lies the real cause, and there needs no other. The influential Friends in the Convention would never for a moment tolerate their presence there if they could prevent it. They hate them because they have dared to call in question their sectarian dogmas and assumed authority; and they have taken care to brand them in the eyes of the Calvinistic Dissenters, who form another large and influential portion of the Convention, as Unitarians; in their eyes the most odious of heretics."

William Howitt, letter to Lucretia Mott, June 27, 1840, in History of Woman Suffrage, *Vol. 1, 434.*

It was decided in our Literary Society the other day that ladies ought to mingle in politics, go to Congress, etc., etc. What do you think of that?

Lucy Stone, letter to her brother, 1840, in Flexner, Century of Struggle, *42.*

I have now been in London eleven days, and, for the first time since my arrival, take up my pen to send you a hasty epistle by the *British Queen*—having been too busy to despatch any letters home until now . . .

The first thing which you and the household, and all our anti-slavery friends, will wish to hear about, is the Convention. On the score of respectability, talent and numbers, it deserves much consideration; but it was sadly deficient in freedom of thought, speech and action, having been under the exclusive management of the London Committee, whose dominion was recognized as absolute . . .

I am quite certain, from all that has transpired, that, had we arrived a few days before the opening of the Convention, we could have carried our point triumphantly. As it is, we have not visited this country in vain. The "woman question" has been fairly started, and will be canvassed from the Land's End to John o' Groat's house. Already, many excellent and noble minds are highly displeased at the decision of the Convention, and denounce it strongly. The new organizers have done what they could to injure us, and have succeeded in creating some prejudice against us, especially on the part of the clergy; but the effect will be temporary. We have all been treated with the utmost respect and hospitality, and invitations to go here and there are pouring in upon us from all quarters.

An excellent Protest against the exclusion of women was drawn up by Prof. Adam, and signed by himself, Phillips, Bradburn, Mott, Col. Miller, etc., and presented to the Convention, which, on motion of Colver, seconded by Scoble, was laid on the table, and refused a place among the printed proceedings! We, who refused to connect ourselves with the Convention, shall have a separate Protest of our own, which we shall publish in some one of the London newspapers. Rely upon it, we have acted most wisely in this matter; but I cannot now go into particulars.

For the proceedings of the Convention, I refer you to the papers accompanying this. It was in session only ten days, but disposed of a considerable amount of business. On Wednesday, a public meeting was held in Exeter Hall, and went off with great éclat. The assembly was immense, and the various speakers were received in the most enthusiastic manner. When O'Connell made his appearance, the applause was absolutely deafening. He made a speech of great power, and denounced American slaveholders in blistering language—at the same time paying the highest compliments to American abolitionists. No invitation was given to Thompson, Phillips, or myself, to speak;

but Birney was assigned a part, and so was Stanton. Remond stepped forward of his own accord, and was repeatedly cheered by the audience. He took them by surprise and acquitted himself very creditably. Prejudice against color is unknown here . . .

Dear Thompson has not been strengthened to do battle for us, as I had confidently hoped he would be. He is placed in a difficult position, and seems disposed to take the ground of non-committal, publicly, respecting the controversy which is going on in the United States. Yet I trust he will soon see his way clear to speak out in our behalf.

Perhaps I may conclude to return home in the *Great Western,* which is to sail from Bristol on the 25th July. If not, I shall aim to take the steamer *Acadia,* for Boston via Halifax, 4th August.

I am waiting, with all a husband's and a parent's anxiety, to hear from you. May the intelligence prove pleasurable to my soul! Dearest, I am

Your loving Husband.
William Lloyd Garrison, letter to his wife, June 29, 1840, in Garrison and Garrison, William Lloyd Garrison, *Vol. 2, 381–385.*

I think it best to avoid giving a judgement upon other matters [the woman question] while we are desirous of simply labouring for the Abolition of Slavery.
Joseph Sturge, letter to James G. Birney, November 6, 1840, in Tolles, Slavery and "The Woman Question," *2.*

It is truly dear Elizabeth a subject of regret with us that thou hast not a correspondent who could more frequently reciprocate thy letters, and who could give thee more general intelligence on the great subject which engrosses so much of thy time and attention; but we have lived so retired since Angelina's marriage and our time has been so occupied in a different way in the service of the slave, and in domestic duties, that we are comparatively ignorant of the movements of abolitionists, and of the measures which are now in operation; yet our hearts are true to the slave if we know ourselves, and we are doing those things which in the ordering of providence we believe it is our duty to do, and if ever He who called us forth to plead the cause of the oppressed again requires us publicly to advocate their cause, we shall I trust be found ready joyfully to leave all that we have to obey the call. Elizabeth

Stanton wrote us word that John Scoble said we had changed our views on the subject of womens rights. I am at a loss to imagine on what he grounded such an assumption. We thought we should have written to E. S. and told her that no one had any just reason for saying so. I do not know any thing about thy views on this subject, but judging from thy letter conclude we do not agree.

Sarah Grimké and Theodore Weld, letter to Elizabeth Pease, November 14, 1840, in Barnes and Dumond, Letters of Theodore Dwight Weld, Angelina Grimké Weld and Sarah Grimké, *852–853.*

It seemed to me at first view that it was cause of regret that the woman question as it is called was introduced, as it has I fear carried with it some of those unchristian feelings which characterize the controversy in this country, but I forbear to judge; it may induce an examination of this subject which may be a blessing to the women of G. B. Certain it is that we are under bondage to man and that our rights and privileges as human beings are little understood, and less appreciated, by our own, as well as the other sex. I apprehended injury to the cause of the slave, the cause which called the Convention together, but it may be the means of extending the usefulness of woman in that very cause. One thing is very clear I think, viz. that the Convention had no right to reject the female delegates; as members of A. S. S. they were entitled to a seat unless it could be proved that they were not persons, the 2d call issued by the Committee to the contrary notwithstanding.

Sarah Grimké and Theodore Weld, letter to Elizabeth Pease, December 20, 1840, in Barnes and Dumond, Letters of Theodore Dwight Weld, Angelina Grimké Weld and Sarah Grimké, *853–854.*

Your error lies in a false idea which you have entertained, that your happiness was to come somewhere from out[side] of your domestic duties, instead of in the performance of them—that they were not part of a wife's obligations, but something that she could put aside if she were able to hire enough servants. I cannot, thus, delegate my business duties to any one; without my governing mind and constant attention, every thing would soon be in disorder, and an utter failure, instead of prosperity, be the result of my efforts. By my carefulness and constant devotion to my business, I am enabled to provide you with every comfort; surely, then, you should be willing also to give careful attention to your department, that I may feel home to be a pleasant place.

T. S. Arthur, "Sweethearts and Wives," article in Godey's Lady's Book, *December 1841, in Cott,* The Bonds of Womanhood, *73.*

The bustle and heartburning created by my former correspondence having nearly subsided in New Market [New Hampshire], I shall venture to address you a short note respecting our condition in the mill. What are we coming to? I can hardly clear my way, having saved from four weeks steady work, but three hundred and ninety-one cents! And yet the time I give to the corporation, amounts to about fourteen or fifteen hours. We are obliged to rise at six, and it is about eight before we get our tea, making fourteen hours. What a glorious privilege we enjoy in this boasted republican land, don't we? Here am I, a healthy New England Girl, quite well-behaved bestowing just half of all my hours including Sundays, upon a company, for less than two cents an hour, and out of the other half of my time, I am obliged to wash, mend, read, reflect, go to church!!! &c. I repeat it, what are we coming to? What is to make the manufacturing interest any better? Our overseer says America will never be able to sell any more cottons than she does now; then how are we to have any better times? I have been studying some new writers on Manufacturers, and shall ask this question often.

Octavia, letter to the editor, of The Factory Girl, *March 1, 1843, in Foner,* The Factory Girls, *76.*

May 2—Great turnout among the girls . . . after breakfast this morning a procession preceded by a painted window curtain for a banner went round the square, the number sixteen. They soon came past again Mr.——, they then numbered forty-four. They marched around awhile and the dispersed. After dinner they sallied forth to the number of forty-two and marched around the Cabot under the direction of Mr.——. They marched around the streets doing themselves no credit. Messrs. Mills and Dwight are up from Boston.

May 4—Girls on the turnout. They had a meeting at the Cabot last night and were ably addressed by

New England Factory Life, by Winslow Homer, in *Harper's Weekly,* 1868 *(Library of Congress)*

Hosea Kenny. This morning after breakfast they came out and marched around the square numbering twenty-two . . . They marched to Cabot but it did no good.

 May 5—The girls had no turnout today.

 May 6—The girls have got over their excitement in some degree.

> *Citizen of Chicopee, Massachusetts, journal entries, in*
> *Flexner,* Century of Struggle, *55–56.*

You will probely want to know the cause of our moveing here which are many. I will menshion a few of them. One of them is the hard times to get a living off the farm for so large a famely so we have devided our famely for this year. We have left Plummer and Luther to care for the farm and grandmarm and Aunt Polly. The rest of us have moved to Nashvill [in Nashua] thinking the girls and Charles they would probely work in the Mill. But we have had bad luck in gitting them in only Jane has got in yet. Ann has the promis of going to the mill next week. Hannah is going to school. We are in hopes to take a few borders but have not got any yet.

> *Jemima Sanborn, letter to Richard and Ruth Bennett,*
> *May 14, 1843, in Dublin,* Farm to Factory, *25.*

It is with pleasure I sit myself to write to you informing you of my good helth &c. I feel as well contented as could be expected. Concidering all things, I think it would be best for me to work in the mill a year and then I should be better prepared to learn a traid. I should like to have gone [to Haverhill] but our folks moving to Nashville I thought I should like to try the Mill and see how I like it. I think I shall like very mutch for I go in all moast every day to see Jane . . . I think I shall go in to work next weak. It is imposable . . . for eny one to get in to the Mill [;] they do not engage only half the help they did before they reduced the spead . . . [To save money, management reduced the speed of the machines.]

> *Ann M. B[lake], letter to Sabrina Bennett,*
> *May 14, 1843, in Dublin,* Farm to Factory, *80.*

It so happened that I was born in New Hampshire, where my mother still resides, with a large family of young children, dependent on her for support, and hard does she have to struggle to gain a living for herself and offspring; and but for the charity of several friends and kind harted neightbors, she would have to put them out before they knew the first rudiments taught in our common schools. Sensible that she had a heavy weight to be borne, to lighten the load, I left home and came into one of the factories in Cabotville. When I came here I could not read, except by spelling out the words like a child of very few years. I had not commenced learning to write, and all the learning I now have has been gained without instruction, having obtained it alone, and that after I had labored in the mill twelve hours a day on the average through the year.

I have often murmured and repined at my lot, thought my case a solitary and hard one, to be thus constantly confined in the factory, and after all could hardly gain a subsistence, while so many were enjoying high life, and "faring sumptuously every day," without labor. But the views I had embraced in this respect, are now entirely changed; and I have begun to think that idleness is the parent of nearly all the sins that have been committed since the morn of creation.

Mary Jane, letter to the editor of the Olive Leaf and Factory Girl's Repository, *September 16, 1843, in Foner,* The Factory Girls, *53.*

. . . perhaps I ought to call your attention to what you may not know—viz., that some years ago Tom Moore—whom I saw twice and chatted with a few minutes once, one of the reasons why I like to sing his songs (I only wish I could do it as well as he does!) wrote a witty rhyme entitled "Proposals for a Gynaecocracy," from which I take these lines:

As Whig reform has its range,
And none of us are yet content,
Suppose, my friends, by way of change,
We try a Female Parliament;
And since, of late, with he M.P.'s
We've fared so badly, take to she's.

. . . Henry says that he has read somewhere that an old Scotch philosopher once said to a troublesome

lady that "idea is the feminine of idiot." And now I am as ever thine, dear friend of us both.

Elizabeth Cady Stanton, letter to John Greenleaf Whittier, October 10, 1843, in Stanton and Blatch, Elizabeth Cady Stanton, *Vol. 2, 9–10.*

The question of reforming our female attire is not new to me. When, for instance, I was in London three or four years ago, I saw much of a person who had known intimately Lady Stanhope, who had died only the year before I was there. She lived for some twenty years in Syria, and used to go about dressed in the costume of an Arabian chieftain. But just what this costume was like, I could not learn. I was further told that she got many of her radical ideas from her father—another instance of a favorite belief of mine that daughters take after their father mentally. This father, so I learned in London, advocated throughout his long career a number of important reforms, most of which failed of adoption during his life because both he and his isms were pronounced visionary by a narrow public opinion. But since his death, which occurred some years ago, one after another of his pet schemes have been put on the English statute book. So the example of Earl Stanhope should be an encouragement to you and the younger generation of us in our dream for the amelioration of the condition of mankind and womankind.

Elizabeth Cady Stanton, letter to Lydia Maria Child, March 24, 1844, in Stanton and Blatch, Elizabeth Cady Stanton, *Vol. 2, 10–11.*

My return to mill-work involved making acquaintance with a new kind a machinery. The spinning-room was the only one I had hitherto known anything about. Now my sister Emilie found a place for me in the dressing-room, beside herself. It was more airy, and fewer girls were in the room, for the dressing-frame itself was a large, clumsy affair, that occupied a great deal of space. Mine seemed to me as unmanageable as an overgrown spoilt child. It had to be watched in a dozen directions every minute, and even then it was getting itself and me into trouble. I felt as if the half-live creature, with its great, groaning joints and whizzing fans, was aware of my incapacity to manage it, and had a fiendish spite against me. I contracted an unconquerable dislike to it; indeed, I had never liked, and never could learn to like, any kind of machinery. And this machine finally conquered me.

Lucy Larcom, writing ca. 1845, in
A New England Girlhood, *226.*

The paymaster asked, when I left, "Going where you can earn more money?"

"No," I answered, "I am going where I can have more time."

"Ah, yes!" he said sententiously, "time is money." But that was not my thought about it. "Time is education," I said to myself; for that was what I meant it should be to me . . . There were only half a dozen girls of us, who measured the cloth, and kept an account of the pieces baled, and their length in yards. It pleased me much to have something to do which required the use of pen and ink, and I think there must be a good many scraps of verse buried among the blank pages of those old account-books of mine, that found their way there during the frequent half-hours of waiting for the cloth to be brought in from the mills.

Lucy Larcom, writing about ca. 1845, in
A New England Girlhood, *228.*

The years between 1835 and 1845, which nearly cover the time I lived at Lowell, seem to me, as I look back at them, singularly interesting years . . . The movement of New England girls toward Lowell was only an impulse of a larger movement which about that time sent so many people from the Eastern States into the West. The needs of the West were constantly kept before us in the churches. We were asked for contributions for Home Missions, which were willingly given; and some of us were appointed collectors of funds for the education of indigent young men to become Western Home Missionary preachers. There was something almost pathetic in the readiness with which this was done by young girls who were longing to fit themselves for teachers, but had not the means. Many a girl at Lowell was working to send her brother to college, who had far more talent and character than he; but a man could preach, and it was not "orthodox" to think a woman could. And in her devotion to him, and her zeal for the spread of Christian truth, she was hardly conscious of her own sacrifice . . .

Lucy Larcom, writing about ca. 1845, in
A New England Girlhood, *248.*

An opportunity now presents itself which I improve in writing to you. I started for this place at the time I talked of which was Thursday. I left Whitneys at nine o'clock stopped at Windsor at 12 and staid till 3 and started again. Did not stop again for any length of time till we arrived at Lowell. Went to a bording house and staid until Monday night. On Saturday after I got here Luthera Griffith went around with me to find a place but we were unsuccessful. On Monday we started again and were more successful. We found a place in a spinning room and the next morning I went to work. I like very well have 50 cts first payment increasing every payment as I get along in work have a first rate overseer and a very good boarding school. I work on the Lawrence Corporation. Mill is No 2 spinning room. I was very sorry that you did not come to see me start. I wanted to see you and Henry but I supposed that your were otherways engaged . . . Stage fare was $3.00 and lodging at Windsor, 25 cts. Had to pay only 25cts for board for 9 days after I got here before I went into the mill. Had 2.50 left with which I got a bonnet and some other small articles.

excuse bad writing and mistakes

This from your own daughter

Mary S. Paul, letter to her father, November 20, 1845,
in Dublin, Farm to Factory, *101.*

I received your letter on Thursday the 14th with much pleasure. I am well which is one comfort. My life and health are spared while others are cut off. Last Thursday one girl fell down and broke her neck which caused instant death. She was going in or coming out of the mill and slipped down it being very icy. The same day a man was killed by the [railroad] cars. Another had all his ribs broken. Another was nearly killed by falling down and having a bale of cotton fall on him. Last Tuesday we were paid. In all I had six dollars and sixty cents paid $4.68 for board. With the rest I got me a pair of rubbers and a pair of 10 cents shoes. Next payment I am to have a dollar a week beside my board . . . Perhaps you would like something about our regulations about going in and coming out of the mill. At 5'o'clock in the morning the bell rings for the folks to get up and get breakfast. At half past six it rings for the girls to get up and at seven they are called into the mill. At half past 12 we have dinner are called back again at one and stay till half past seven [in winter]. I get along very well with my work. I can doff as fast as any girl in our room. I think I shall have frames before I have been in three as I get along so fast. I think that the factory is the best place for me and if any girl wants employment I advise them to come to Lowell.

Mary S. Paul, letter to her father, December 21, 1845, in Dublin, Farm to Factory, *103.*

We are told by gentlemen both in this country and abroad that the Lovell factory operatives are exceedingly well off. Good wages, sure pay, not very hard work, comfortable food and lodgings, and such unparalleled opportunities for intellectual cultivation, (why, they even publish a Magazine there!!) what more can one desire? Really gentlemen! When in the tender transports of true love, you paint for the fairest and fondest of mortal maidens a whole life of uninterrupted joy, do you hope for her as the surpremest facility, the lot of the factory girl? The operatives are well enough off!—Indeed! Do you receive them in your parlors, are they admitted to visit your families, do you raise your hats to them in the street, in a word, are they your equals?

Olivia, letter to the editor of the Voice of Industry, *September 18, 1845, in Foner,* The Factory Girls, *84.*

We are moved to write this by erroneous reports concerning the hours of work under which we operatives in Lowell labor.

The operatives are allowed ten minutes in morning and ten at noon in going from their boarding house to the mills, which deducted from the time the wheels are in operation, leaves twelve hours and ten minutes, the actual amount of time the operatives are required to labor for day's work, the shortest days in December, exclusive of the time required in going to and from their daily task.

Many who board near the mills, commence work as soon as the gates are raised, consequently make out twelve and a half hours of real service during the shortest days in the year.

We are informed by those engaged upon Middlesex, (Woollen) that the mills on that corporation run still longer, and the goods finding a ready market at great profits, every means is resorted to by the manufacturers to produce the largest possible amount. On no corporation in Lowell, do the mills operate less than twelve hours per day, at this season and in the longest days of Summer they run thus:

Commence in the morning 10 minutes before 5, gates shut down for breakfast, at 7 o'clock, commence again 20 minutes past 7. Gates shut down for supper at 7; making thirteen hours and fifteen minutes between the ringing of the bells, thirty minutes of which is allowed the operatives in going to and from their meals, leaving twelve hours and forty-five minutes, of actual service in the mills.

During the month of April, the factories run more hours than in any other month of the year, which is, according to Mr. Miles, thirteen hours and thirty-one minutes. On Saturdays from the 20th of September till about the 20th of March the operatives are released soon after dark, which will take time off upon the average, about one hour per week, during that time.

From the foregoing facts, it will be seen that much deception has been used in reporting the hours of factory labor by self-interested men who wish to aggrandize themselves by courting the favor of the manufactoring power of this country. It will be seen, that, at no season of the year, less than twelve hours is considered a regular days work in the Lowell factories and that they range from about twelve hours and ten minutes up to thirteen hours and thirty-one minutes, and should the time spent in going to and from the mills be taken into account, as it ought, the longest days labor, would exceed fourteen and a half hours, and the shortest, never fall below twelve and a half.

A committee of Lowell factory girls, in Voice of Industry, *December 26, 1845, in Foner,* The Factory Girls, *220.*

TURN-OUTS. There are symptoms of rebellion among the operators in all quarters. At Lowell, Pittsburgh, Philadelphia, Chicopee, and elsewhere, outbreaks follow each other among different classes of mechanics. They are attended by processions, that are in imitation, if not "as terrible as any army with banners." The evils of which they complain, are, the order system, by which they are subjected to extortionate prices for articles of necessity, or to ruinous discounts of cash, which is indispensible for many purchases; and in some cases, they are oppressed by a decrease of wages and an increase of labor. This was the cause which led to the glorious turnout of the fair operatives in the factories at Chicopee. They formed in solemn column, arrayed in their best bibs and tuckers, and waved their kerchiefs to the girls in the other mills to join them. Failing to enlist reinforcements, they returned to their places. A few days later they mustered their forces again, with as little success as before, and to add to their discomfiture, when desirous of turning in a second time, they were turned out by their employers. Processions and martial music are now the usual accompaniments of strikes.

New York State Mechanic *newspaper, May 18, 1843, in Foner,* The Factory Girls, *233.*

When all the mothers, teachers, nurses and domestics are taken from our sex, which the best interests of society demand, and when all these employments are deemed respectable and are filled by well-educated women, there will be no supernumeraries found to put into shops and mills or to draw into the arena of public and political life.

Catharine Beecher, The Evils Suffered by American Women and Children, *1846, in Flexner,* Century of Struggle, *31.*

I know, Mother, you feel badly about the plans I have proposed to myself [to be a speaker for the Anti-Slavery Society], and that you would prefer to have me take some other course, if I could in conscience. Yet, Mother, I know you too well to suppose that you would wish me to turn away from what I think is my duty, and go all my days in opposition to my convictions of right, lashed by a reproaching conscience . . . But, Mother, there are no trials so great as they suffer who neglect or refuse to do what they believe is their duty. I expect to plead not for the slave only, but for suffering humanity everywhere. ESPECIALLY DO I MEAN TO LABOR FOR THE ELEVATION OF MY SEX.

Lucy Stone, letter to her mother, 1846, in Payne, Between Ourselves, *99.*

When I was in Edinburgh I bought one day a little volume because of its title, *Records of Woman.* It was by Mrs. Hemans. I took it up by chance this morning and read it for the first time. It is a charming series of poems all in honor of our sex . . . this little collection is a worthy contribution to high-minded womanhood from the pen of a brilliant poetess. How proud I am when I see one of my sex doing anything well; and I know you are too, which is the reason I called

your attention to this book. Henry's best wishes with this, and mine too.

Elizabeth Cady Stanton, letter to John Greenleaf Whittier, April 11, 1846, in Stanton and Blatch, Elizabeth Cady Stanton, *Vol. 2, 14.*

Last Friday I received a letter from you. You wanted to know what I am doing. I am at work in a spinning room and tending four sides of warp which is one girl's work. The overseer tells me that he never had a girl get along better than I do and that he will do the best he can by me. I stand it well, though they tell me that I am growing very poor. I was paid nine shillings [$1.50] a week last payment and am to have more this one though we have been out considerable for backwater which will take off a good deal. The Agent promises to pay us nearly as much as we should have made but I do not think that he will. The payment was up last night and we are to be paid this week. I have a very good boarding place[,] have enough to eat and that which is good enough. The girls are all kind and obliging. The girls that I room with are all from Vermont and good girls too. Now I will tell you about our rules at the boarding house. We have none in particular except that we have to go to bed at about 10 o'clock. At half past 4 in the morning the bell rings for us to get up and at five for us to go into the mill. At seven we are called out to breakfast and are allowed half an hour between bells and the same at noon till the first of May when we have three quarters [of an hour] till the first of September. We have dinner at half past 12 and supper at seven.

Mary S. Paul, letter to her father, April 12, 1846, in Dublin, Farm to Factory, *104.*

The numerous class of females who are operatives in mills, are required to devote *fifteen twenty-fourths* of every working day to the laborious task incumbent upon them, being thirteen hours of incessant toil, and two hours devoted to meals &c. Is not this fact a painful one? Is it not degrading to the age in which we live? It indicates that barbarism still exists among us, and it would be well for some people to take moral and humane lessons from savage life even. It is not a matter of marvel, that the Lowell girls should rebel against such treatment and petition the legislature of Massachusetts to establish a ten hour system; neither is it surprising that the federal *wise-acres,* who constituted that body, considered it expedient to legislate upon the subject—*they* do not legislate for the protection of the *poor*, but for the protection of the rich; the *gold* that lies within their grasp benumbs their sensibilities; and prevents the administration of that *justice* which humanity demands. We begin to doubt the utility or justice of any legislation for the protection of capital; indeed, if *barbarism* is to be the result of *protection*, we trust that the enlightened and philanthropic inhabitants of this country will cheerfully dispose with such *aid,* and, (as experience teaches it,) consider that legislation for the benefit of the *few*, is inimical to the best interest of the *whole*.

Think of girls being obliged to labor *thirteen* hours each working day, for a net compensation of *two cents per hour,* which is above the average net wages, being $1.56 per week. Two cents per hour for severe labor! Is not such a lesson enough to make an American curse the hour, when in an evil mood our lawmakers first granted a charter to enable the *few* to wield the wealth and power of *hundreds?* Is it not necessary to the maintenance of our rights, that some change be speedily effected in those laws by which our corporations are governed. We trust the friends of *equal rights,* will petition our legislature to make such a revision of these laws, as will cause the more general distribution of those benefits which were designed for all. If such a course is taken, let the tyrants tremble.

Factory Girls' Album, *Exeter, New Hampshire, June 20, 1846, in Foner,* The Factory Girls, *80.*

It is a subject of comment and general complaint, among the operatives, that while they tend three or four looms, where they used to tend but two, making nearly twice the number of yards of cloth, the pay is not increased to them, while the increase, to the owners, is very great. Is this just? Twenty-five cents per week for each week, additional pay, would not increase the cost of the cloth, one mill a yard; no, not the half of a mill.

Now while I am penning this paragraph, a young lady enters my room with "Oh dear! Jane, I am sick and what shall I do? I have worked for three years, and never gave out, before. I stuck to my work, until I fainted at my loom. The Doctor says I must quit work and run about and amuse myself; but I have nowhere to go, and do not know what to do with myself." I have given the language, as it stuck my ear; the conversation going on behind me. It is but the feelings of a thousand homeless, suffering females,

this moment chanting "the Voice of Industry in this wilderness of sin."

"One of the Vast Army of Sufferers," letter to the editor of Voice of Industry, *March 13, 1846, in Foner,* The Factory Girls, *85.*

I have a story to tell you Mr. Voice—it is a sad one—it is about a young girl who came to work in the mills; her mother was dead, and her father used to drink strong drinks which made him cross; and then he treated her ill, and folks thought she had better go and work in the factory, and she did. When she went in, her cheeks were red as roses, and her eyes bright and beautiful, and she would laugh and romp like a little mad thing. I used to follow her sometimes on the "hill side;" for it used to make me feel glad, to see her so very happy. She had not worked there but a short time when she left the Mill looking very pale; and she coughed dreadfully. I used to see her every little while, and she kept growing poorer and weaker, and at last I missed her altogether. Then I used to linger near the house where she lived, and listen to hear some sound that would tell me she was there; for I loved the little girl that was so good and kind, and knew she would soon be an Angel, in Heaven. One day, they lifted her up to the window, where I could see her, it made me weep to look at her, for though she smiled as sweetly as ever, I knew she was dying. I thought she was praying, to, for she clasped her little thin hands, and turned her eyes toward Heaven—her lips moved—then there came a strange look across her face—she didn't move again. They took her away and I knew I should never see her more. In two days after, they buried her in the cemetary, near "my home;" and after they had all gone, I went and gathered some of the flowers I knew she loved best, and laid them on her grave, and as fast as they wilt I get fresh ones for I love to do it, Mr. Voice, altho' it maked me feel sorrowful; and I think she would thank me, if she could. There are a great many who die just as she died; and I wish the folks would not make the girls work so long in the factories; for I think that it the reason why so many die! Perhaps Mr. Voice, you can convince the rich folks, that it is not right to oppress the poor; if you can I think it will make you feel happy. But I must say good-bye for the present.

"The Child of the Hills," letter to the editor of Voice of Industry, *November 13, 1846, in Foner,* The Factory Girls, *154.*

I was about to head this article Corporation Sharing, but when I come to reflect that females are not accustomed to that troublesome operation, and that it was their wrongs which I was about to set forth, I at once discovered its inapplicability . . . It is an old maxim that if the cents are looked after the dollars will take care of themselves; this I believe is universally admitted to be true, so much so, that the son who has not been taught this lesson by his father, would be considered ill fitted to set up for himself, amid the ups and downs of life. Now sir, I see not why the same principle may not with propriety be applied to Hours and Minutes, in connection with "our labor" in our mills.

You are laboring hard to show the injustice of compelling the operatives to labor the unreasonable number of hours which they now do. I rejoice to see it, and bid you God Speed; but the thought struck me, that there are Minutes also to be looked after. I know sir, that it will be said we are dabbling in small matters, but when I reflect that many littles make a great whole, and that these littles are daily being wrenched from the operative, particle by particle, I am contrained to speak out, that this ever grasping, tyrannizing spirit may be rebuked and receive the contempt which it so richly deserves. Perhaps those that are accustomed to reflect and morn over the fact that thousands of hard working females are allowed but thirty minutes to lave themselves, go down three flights of stairs, travel one fourth of a mile to their boarding house, eat their meal and return the same distance to their work; I say perhaps those who are acquainted with these facts are not aware that it is even worse; *it is so.* On some of the Corporations in this city, two of which I will name, the Boot and Massachusetts [Lowell mills], it is, and has been since 1841, an established rule to hoist the gate twenty-eight minutes from the time it shuts down for meals, and on commencing in the morning it is to be hoisted eight minutes from the time that the Merrimack [a Lowell cotton mill] bell strikes, which is two minutes earlier at each time of hoisting, than is practiced on that Corporation. Thus you see by tightening the screws in this way, the operatives lose from four to six minutes per day, under the pretence of allowing them thirty minutes for meals. A little calculation would show how it would stand at the end of five years; and it will be recollected that many of the operatives have worked in the same mill for more than five years. Four to six minutes per day, say average five min-utes—thirty minutes per week, two hours per month, two days of thirteen hours each per year, and ten days for five years. This is the practical effect of this irresponsible, over-working, oppressive system.

Now Mr. Editor is it right? Ought these things so to be? I do hope that the former agent of the Boot, and the present agent of the Massachusetts Corporation, will examine this matter candidly and use their official influence to undo the wrong which themselves have (unauthorized) inflicted on hundreds and thousands of the laboring poor of this city, and restore to them that which is just and honest in the sight of God.

Lowell operative, letter to the editor of Voice of Industry, *January 8, 1847, in Foner,* The Factory Girls, *87.*

Since I was between seven and eight years old, I have been employed almost without intermission in a factory, which is almost 18 years. During this time I have not attended school more than one year. Probably not that. So whatever you may think of my composition, you must acknowledge I ought to be a judge of factory life. I should like to give you my whole experience, but this would take too much room. And beside, you would hardly believe what I should state, although it would be true, so I will confine myself to Lowell, the place where operatives are used as well, I think as any place in New England. I do not wonder at your surprise that the operatives were worked in the summer season, from five in the morning till seven in the evening. Especially when you had been previously informed that we worked but ten hours per day. But 'tis true, we do all this, and against our wishes too. I know scarcely an operative, who would not have it otherwise if they could. But they do not wish their wages cut down, for they have [barely] enough to live on now. The time we are required to labor is altogether too long. It is more than our constitutions can bear. If anyone doubts it, let them come into the mills of a summer's day, at four or five o'clock, in the afternoon, and see the drooping, weary persons moving about, as though their legs were hardly able to support their bodies. If this does not convince then, let them try their hand at it a while, nothing more common amongst operatives, than the remark that "their legs ache so, it seems as though they would drop off." Now if they desired to work so long, they would not complain in this way. I have been an overseer myself, and many times have I had girls faint in the morning, in consequence of the air being so impure in the mill. This is quite a common thing. Especially when girls have worked in the factory for considerable length of time. We commence as soon and work as long as we can see almost the year round, and for nearly half the year we work by lamp light, at both ends of the day lighting up both morning and evening. And besides this, from November till March our time is from twenty minutes to half an hour too slow. So you see instead of getting out of the factory at half past seven in the evening, it is really eight. And more than this some of the clocks are so fixed as to lose ten minutes during the day and gain ten minutes during the night, thereby getting us into the mill five minutes before five in the morning and working us five minutes after seven at night. As to wages, the proprietors do not calculate the average wages of females, to exceed one dollar fifty cents per week, exclusive of board. Notwithstanding those "stray Yankees," state to the contrary. But I am taking too much room, perhaps you may hear from me again in time.

Yours for the right, R.
Letter to the editor of Voice of Industry,
March 26, 1847, in Foner, The Factory Girls, *88.*

Strictly confidential
Dr. Cameron's Patent Family Regulator
Or, Wife's Protector
A New Invention, at once safe, sure and easy application.

In Introducing this novel invention, the writer feels he is broaching a delicate subject. These few explanatory remarks are not therefore, designed for the public eye, but addressed to those only, who have entered the married state, whom, I trust would not be likely to misconstrue the motives of the author, or convert his invention to an evil purpose; and for that class of females is this invention particularly designed, who have entered the married state, with such enfeebled constitutions, inherited either from their ancestors, by sickness, or by having indulged so far in the fashionable follies of our age, as to render them incapable of becoming mothers, without endangering their own lives, or imparting to their offspring, imbecility of mind, or sickly constitution, which would render existence anything but a blessing.

There are those also, whose families are already too numerous for their means of support, and to this class the writer thinks his invention cannot but prove a welcome agent in exonerating them from some of the most cruel sufferings of life, and thus smooth the future pathway of their present existence.

Besides these, there are too, those in the bloom of womanhood, the very picture of health, who having just entered the married state, tremble in constant fear of the awful wreck so often produced by the first born, when,

If not her life upon the altar sacrifice expire,
The rosy cheek, the ruby lip it will require.

To such, therefore, I trust this invention will prove a welcome minister of mercy . . .

This instrument . . . is easily introduced by women, and would not be discovered by the male, were he not apprised of it. It is easily withdrawn, bringing with it every particle of semen, rendering its effects positive; and as it absorbs nothing, can be cleansed in a moment, without even wetting the fingers—can never get out of order, and will last for life . . .

Dr. Walter Scott Tarbox, circular advertising a contraceptive device, 1847, in Berkin and Norton,
Women of America, *266.*

Juliann Jane Tillman, a preacher in the African Methodist Episcopal Church, from an 1844 lithograph by A. Hoffy *(Library of Congress)*

Last evening we spoke of the propriety of women being called by the names which are used to designate their sex, and not by those assigned to males. You differed with me on the ground that custom had established the rule that a woman must take the whole of her husband's name particularly when public mention is made of her. But you are mistaken about this. It is the custom now, since women have commenced forming themselves into independent societies, to use names of the feminine gender. I have looked over several newspapers and asked several persons, and all agree that the tyrant custom does allow every woman to have a name. If you will glance through the public prints containing accounts of the formation of female societies, you will find no titles such as Miss and Mrs., and no Joseph or Ichabod, but Elizabeth and Rebecca; therefore, if you follow custom, let us all appear in the Report as women, or else mention no names at all. I have very serious objections, dear Rebecca, to being called Henry. There is a great deal in a name. It often signifies much, and may involve great principle. Ask our colored brethren if there is nothing in a name. Why are the slaves nameless unless they take that of their master? Simple because they have no independent existence. They are mere chattles, with no civil or social rights. Our colored friends in the country who have education and family ties take to themselves names. Even so with women. The custom of calling women Mrs. John This and Mrs. Tom That, and colored men Sambo and Zip Coon, is founded on the principle that white men are lords of all. I cannot acknowledge this principle as just; therefore, I cannot bear the name of another. But I must stop lest I weary your patience.

Elizabeth Cady Stanton, letter to Rebecca R. Eyster,
May 1, 1847, in Stanton and Blatch,
Elizabeth Cady Stanton, *Vol. 2, 15–16.*

4

Women of Seneca Falls
1848–1849

At age 32, during a particularly sad time in her life, Elizabeth Cady Stanton received an invitation to tea from Jane Hunt of the nearby town of Waterloo. There, on July 13, 1848, she was greeted by Lucretia Mott, Martha C. Wright, and Mary Ann McClintock. She told the Quakers that she was depressed since her move to Seneca Falls. The discussion led to women's rights, and "[b]efore twilight deepened into night," they had written an announcement and sent it to the *Seneca County Courier,* to be published the next day, calling a meeting of women to be held July 19 and 20 at the Wesleyan Methodist chapel in Seneca Falls.[1]

Next morning the women met at the home of Mary Ann McClintock to draw up an agenda for the meeting, feeling "as helpless and hopeless as if they had been suddenly asked to construct a steam engine." None of the women save Lucretia Mott had done any public speaking, and the only political work Stanton had done was to lobby for the Married Woman's Property Act, passed in April of that year, giving married women the right to own real and personal property. Therefore, the women hurriedly read numerous "masculine productions," such as the reports of the peace, temperance, and abolition conventions, to learn how to plan their program. But it "all seemed too tame and pacific for the inauguration of a rebellion such as the world had never before seen." Finally, one of the women picked up the Declaration of Independence and read it aloud. Instantly the group decided to pattern its Declaration of Sentiments on the historic document of 1776. First, they changed "King George" to "all men." Then, seeing that the Declaration listed 18 grievances, they listed 18 injuries experienced by women. Demanding that the rights enumerated in the Declaration of Independence apply to women as well as men, they reworded the document to include women. "We hold these truths to be self-evident: that all men are created equal . . ." became "We hold these truths to be self-evident: that all men and women are created equal . . ." The Declaration of Sentiments was followed by a list of resolutions, demanding that women be allowed to speak in public, be accorded equal treatment under the law, and—at the insistence of Stanton—be granted the vote. Henry Stanton, who helped his wife write some of these resolutions, could not agree with her insistence on including voting rights as a plank; he left town the day of the convention to avoid ridicule. Lucretia Mott also opposed the suffrage resolution, giving in reluctantly to the younger woman. In all, the declaration and resolutions demanded equal education, equal access to trades and professions, equality in marriage, and the rights to make contracts, to own property, to sue and be sued, to testify in court, and to have guardianship over children.[2]

On July 19 "crowds in carriages and on foot, wended their way to the Wesleyan church." But when the leaders arrived—carrying the Declaration of Sentiments, the resolutions and several volumes of the New York State statute books—they found the door locked and had to send Stanton's nephew through an open window to unlock it. Originally it was planned that no men would attend on the first day. But the women who had no experience with running a meeting or leading discussions "shrank from doing either," and hastily decided, with 40 men at their doorstep, that this was "an occasion when men might make themselves preeminently useful." So James Mott, "tall and dignified in Quaker costume," chaired the meeting, and Mary Ann McClintock acted as secretary.[3]

Lucretia Mott introduced the convention. She was followed by Elizabeth Cady Stanton who, terrified, gave her first speech. And quite a speech it was: Passionate, scholarly, exhilarating, it held the attention of everyone in the chapel. Then followed resolutions and discussions, particularly over resolution number nine, "That it is the duty of women of this country to secure to themselves their sacred right to the elective franchise." This resolution passed by a small margin, and the others were approved unanimously. Many feared that the demand for the vote would work against demands "they deemed more rational, and make the whole movement ridiculous." But Stanton and abolitionist Frederick Douglass argued persistently until it was at last approved. At the end of the convention, 68 women and 32 men signed the declaration.

The convention lasted for two days, late into the nights with 300 people in attendance. When it was over, the women faced a "storm of ridicule" from the press. One editorial called the meetings "the most shocking and unnatural incident ever recorded in the history of womanity."[4] The *Worcester Telegraph* in Massachusetts opined, "The list of grievances which the *Amazons* exhibit, concludes by expressing a determination to insist that women shall have 'immediate admission to all rights and privileges which belong to them as citizens of the United States' . . . This is *bolting* with a vengeance." Only a few papers did not condemn the women. They included Douglass's *The North Star* and Horace Greeley's *Tribune.* As a result of this treatment, many of the 100 people who had signed the declaration eventually withdrew their names.[5]

Consequently, it was with "fear and trembling" that Stanton agreed to participate in a convention to be held two weeks later at Rochester, New York, organized by Amy Post, Sarah D. Fish, Sarah C. Owen and Mary H. Hallowell.

Martha C. Wright helped to organize the first women's rights convention. *(Library of Congress)*

On August 2, 1848, the meeting began, and almost immediately a debate broke out about the wisdom of letting a woman chair the meeting. Stanton vividly described the decision to let a woman preside: "[N]ow, with such feeble voices and timid manners, without the slightest knowledge of Cushing's Manual, or the least experience in public meetings, how could a woman preside? [Lucretia Mott, Elizabeth Cady Stanton, and Mary Ann McClintock] were on the verge of leaving the Convention in disgust, but Amy Post and Rhoda De Garmo assured them that by the same power by which they had resolved, declared, discussed, debated, they could also preside at a public meeting, if they would but make the experiment. And as the vote of the majority settled the question on the side of woman, Abigail Bush took the chair, and the calm way she assumed the duties of the office, and the admirable manner in which she discharged them, soon reconciled the opposition to the seemingly ridiculous experiment."[6]

Having so little experience in public speaking, the women spoke quietly, causing cries of "Louder, Louder!" Finally, president Abigail Bush had to rise and quiet the audience: "Friends, we present ourselves here before you, as an oppressed class, with trembling frames and faltering tongues, and we do not expect to be heard by all at first . . ." The group again debated the suffrage resolution, adopting it by a wider margin than at Seneca Falls. Also adopted was a resolution urging women to help raise the wages of the laboring class, "beginning with their own household servants," and one calling for the equality of all women of "whatever . . . complexion." Afterward, Bush recalled, "My strength seemed to leave me and I cried like a baby."[7]

The women held no formal meetings for the next 18 months, but as news spread of Seneca Falls, preparations began for conventions in other states, including Massachusetts, Indiana, Pennsylvania, and Ohio. The struggle toward women's rights that had begun at the beginning of the century had taken a new turn. A program had been put forth and a leadership established. The women's rights movement in America had officially begun.

CHRONICLE OF EVENTS

1848

Honoring her discovery of a comet on October 1, 1847, the Academy of Arts and Sciences elects Maria Mitchell its first woman member.

Susan B. Anthony joins the Daughters of Temperance to work against the sale of liquor.

Elizabeth Blackwell, first woman medical graduate, is admitted to practice at Philadelphia Hospital.

Jane Swisshelm starts an antislavery, women's rights newspaper in Pittsburgh, the *Saturday Visiter.*

Swisshelm's editorials influence the governor of Pennsylvania to reform married women's property rights in a bill that passes the legislature.

Women's rights leader Hannah Conant Tracy completes her studies at Oberlin College, forming close ties with Lucy Stone and Frances Dana Barker. Soon after, she begins her work in the temperance, peace, and suffrage movements.

Dorothea Dix, hoping to secure 5 million acres of public land to use as a trust for the supervision and care of the insane, has her idea presented to Congress by Senator John A. Dix of New York.

spring: Women's rights advocate Mary Upton Ferrin consults a lawyer about divorce and learns that under common law all of a married woman's property belongs to her husband. She petitions the state of Massachusetts to change the law, the first woman to do so on behalf of her gender. Every year from 1848 to 1853, she collects signatures on petitions to deliver to the legislature.

Women turn out in violent strikes in the Allegheny mills near Pittsburgh, Pennsylvania.

April 6: The Married Woman's Property Act is passed in New York.

July 13: Lucretia Mott, Elizabeth Cady Stanton, Mary Ann McClintock, Jane Hunt, and Martha Wright call the first women's rights convention in America.

July 19–20: The Seneca Falls Convention, often regarded as the birth of the movement for women's rights, meets in Seneca Falls, New York; 68 women and 32 men sign the Declaration of Rights and Sentiments.

August 2: The Rochester, New York, convention is held.

August 29: Suffragist and writer Sarah Barnwell (Elliott) is born.

1849

Female doctors are officially allowed to practice in the United States.

German-American women's rights advocate Mathilde Anneke moves to the United States.

Future suffragist Clara Bewick Colby arrives in the United States from England.

Harriet Tubman escapes slavery for freedom in Philadelphia, where she becomes active in the Underground Railroad and the women's suffrage movement.

January: Amelia Bloomer begins publishing the *Lily,* a six-page monthly magazine devoted to temperance. Elizabeth Cady Stanton writes for it under the pseudonym "Sunflower."

January 23: Elizabeth Blackwell becomes the first woman to receive a medical degree in the United States, from Geneva College in New York.

February 9: Women's rights leader Laura Clay is born.

August 13: Working women's leader Leonora Kearney is born.

November: Reformer Lydia Folger Fowler gains admission to Central Medical College in Syracuse, New York, the first medical school to admit women, where she will become the second woman in America to earn a medical degree.

EYEWITNESS TESTIMONY

My husband is very poorly, and it is not likely I shall be able to go to Seneca Falls before the morning of the convention. I hope however, that he will be able to be present the second day. My sister Martha will accompany me, and we will with pleasure accept thy kind invite to your house that night if you should not be too much crowded with company. James says thy great speech thou must reserve for the second day, so that he and others may be able to hear it. The convention will not be so large as it otherwise might be, owing to the busy time with the farmers, harvest, etc. But it will be a beginning, and we may hope it will be followed in due time by one of a more general character.

Lucretia Mott, letter to Elizabeth Cady Stanton,
July 16, 1848, in Stanton and Blatch,
Elizabeth Cady Stanton, *Vol. 2, 17–18.*

I was much gratified at the receipt of your letter of the 22d inst., making inquiries into the history of the law of 1848 in regard to married women holding property independently of their husbands. That the "truth of history" may be made plain, I have looked over the journals of the Senate and Assembly, and taken full notes, which I request you to publish, if you put any part of this letter in print.

I have very distinct recollections of the whole history of this very radical measure. Judge Fine, of St. Lawrence, was its originator, and he gave me his reasons for introducing the bill. He said that he married a lady who had some property of her own, which he had, all his life, tried to keep distinct from his, that she might have the benefit of her own, in the event of any disaster happening to him in pecuniary matters. He had found much difficulty, growing out of the old laws, in this effort to protect his wife's interests.

Judge Fine was a stately man, and of general conservative tendencies, just the one to hold onto the past, but he was a just man, and did not allow his practice as a lawyer, or his experience on the bench, to obscure his sense of right. I followed him, glad of such a leader.

I, too, had special reasons for desiring this change in the law. I had a young daughter, who, in the then condition of my health, was quite likely to be left in tender years without a father, and I very much desired to protect her in the little property I might be able to leave. I had an elaborate will drawn by my old law preceptor, Vice-Chancellor Lewis H. Sanford, creating a trust with all the care and learning he could bring to my aid. But when the elaborate paper was finished, neither he or I felt satisfied with it. When the law of 1848 was passed, all I had to do was to burn this will . . .

We had in the Senate a man of matured years, who had never had a wife. He was a lawyer well-read in the old books, and versed in the adjudications which had determined that husband and wife were but one person, and the husband that person; and he expressed great fears in regard to meddling with this well-settled condition of domestic happiness. This champion of the past made long and very able arguments to show the ruin this law must work, but he voted for the bill in the final decision . . .

In reply to your inquires in regard to debates that preceded the action of 1848, I must say I know of none, and am quite sure that in our long discussions no allusion was made to anything of the kind. Great measures often occupy the thoughts of men and women, long before they take substantial form and

Matilda Joslyn Gage led both the national and New York State suffrage groups. *(New York Public Library Picture Collection)*

become things of life, and I shall not dispute any one who says that this reform had been thought of before 1848. But I do insist the record shows that Judge Fine is the author of the law which opened the way to clothe woman with full rights, in regard to holding, using, and enjoying in every way her own property, independently of any husband ...

George Geddes, senator from 22nd District of New York, letter to Matilda Joslyn Gage, writing about the law in 1848, November 25, 1880, in History of Woman Suffrage, *Vol. 1, 64–66.*

When I undertook my solitary battle for woman's rights, outside the little circle of abolitionists I knew nobody who sympathized with my ideas. I had some hand-bills printed, 12 x 10 inches. I bought a paper of tacks, and, as I could not pay for posting, I put up my bills myself, using a stone as a hammer. I did not take a fee at the door. But there was always the expense of hall and hotel. To cover this, at the close of my speech, I ask help for the great work, by a collection for expenses. Then I took a hat and went through the audience for the collection, for all were strangers to me. I always got enough to pay what was due, and sometimes more.

Lucy Stone, writing about her work in the late 1840s, in Flexner, Century of Struggle, *70.*

Lucretia Mott, Quaker minister *(Friends Historical Library, Swarthmore College)*

WOMANS RIGHTS CONVENTION—A convention to discuss the social, civil, and religious condition and rights of woman, will be held in the Wesleyan Chapel, at Seneca Falls, N.Y., on Wednesday and Thursday, the 19th and 20th of July, current; commencing at 10 o'clock A.M. During the first day the meeting will be exclusively for women, who are earnestly invited to attend. The public generally are invited to be present on the second day, when Lucretia Mott, of Philadelphia, and other ladies and gentlemen, will address the convention.

Seneca County Courier, July 14, 1848, in History of Woman Suffrage, *Vol. 1, 67.*

Insurrection among the Women

A female Convention has just been held at Seneca Falls, N.Y., at which was adopted a "declaration of rights," setting forth, among other things, that "all men and *women* are created equal, and endowed by their Creator with certain inalienable rights." The list of grievances which the *Amazons* exhibit, concludes

by expressing a determination to insist that woman shall have "immediate admission to all the rights and privileges which belong to them as citizens of the United States." It is stated that they design, in spite of all misrepresentations and ridicule, to employ agents, circulate tracts, petition the State and National Legislatures, and endeavor to enlist the pulpit and the press in their behalf. This is *bolting* with a vengeance.

Worcester Telegraph, Massachusetts, July 1848, in History of Woman Suffrage, *Vol. 1, 803.*

To us they appear extremely dull and uninteresting, and, aside from their novelty, hardly worth notice.

Rochester Advertiser, July 1848, in History of Woman Suffrage, *Vol. 1, 804.*

The Women of Philadelphia

Our Philadelphia ladies not only possess beauty, but they are celebrated for discretion, modesty, and unfeigned diffidence, as well as wit, vivacity, and good nature. Whoever heard of a Philadelphia lady setting up for a reformer, or standing out for woman's rights, or assisting to *man* the election grounds, raise a regiment, command a legion, or address a jury? Our ladies glow with a higher ambition. They soar to rule the hearts of their worshipers, and secure obedience by the sceptre of affection. The tenure of their power is a law of nature, not a law of man, and hence they fear no insurrection, and never experience the shock of a revolution in their dominions. But all women are not as reasonable as ours of Philadelphia. The Boston ladies contend for the rights of women. The New York girls aspire to mount the rostrum, to do all the voting, and, we suppose, all the fighting too . . . Our Philadelphia girls object to fighting and holding office. They prefer the baby-jumper to the study of Coke and Lyttleton, and the ball-room to the Palo Alto battle. They object to having a George Sand for President of the United States; a Corinna for Governor; a Fanny Wright for Mayor; or a Mrs. Partington for Postmaster . . . Women have enough influence over human affairs without being politicians. Is not everything managed by female influence? Mothers, grandmothers, aunts, and sweethearts manage everything. Men have nothing to do but to listen and obey to the "of course, my dear, you will, and of course, my dear, you won't." Their rule is absolute; their power unbounded. Under such a system men have no claim to rights, especially "equal rights."

A woman is nobody. A wife is everything. A pretty girl is equal to ten thousand men, and a mother is, next to God, all powerful . . . The ladies of Philadelphia, therefore, under the influence of the most serious "sober second thoughts," are resolved to maintain their rights as Wives, Belles, Virgins, and Mothers, and not as Women.

Public Ledger and Daily Transcript, *July–August 1848, in* History of Woman Suffrage, *Vol. 1, 804.*

One of the most interesting events of the past week, was the holding of what is technically styled a Woman's Rights Convention at Seneca Falls. The speaking, addresses, and resolutions of this extraordinary meeting was wholly conducted by women; and although they evidently felt themselves in a novel position, it is but simple justice to say that their whole proceedings were characterized by marked ability and dignity. No one present, we think, however much he might be disposed to differ from the views advanced by the leading speakers on that occasion, will fail to give them credit for brilliant talents and excellent dispositions. In this meetings, as in other deliberative assemblies, there were frequent differences of opinion and animated discussion; but in no case was there the slightest absence of good feeling and decorum. Several interesting documents setting forth the rights as well as the grievances of women were read. Among these was a Declaration of Sentiments, to be regarded as the basis of a grand movement for attaining the civil, social, political, and religious rights of women. We should not do justice to our own convictions, or to the excellent persons connected with this infant movement, if we did not in this connection offer a few remarks on the general subject which the Convention met to consider and the objects they seek to attain. In doing so, we are not insensible that the bare mention of this truly important subject in any other than terms of contemptuous ridicule and scornful disfavor, is likely to excite against us the fury of bigotry and the folly of prejudice. A discussion of the rights of animals would be regarded with far more complacency by many of what are called the "wise" and the "good" of our land, than would a discussion of the rights of women. It is, in their estimation to be guilty of evil thoughts, to think that woman is entitled to equal rights with man. Many who have at last made the discovery that the negroes have some rights as well as other members of the human family, have yet to be convinced that women are entitled to any. Eight years ago a number of persons of this description actually abandoned the anti-slavery cause, lest by giving their influence in that direction they might possibly be giving countenance to the dangerous heresy that woman, in respect to rights, stands on an equal footing with man. In the judgment of such persons the American slave system, with all its concomitant horrors, is less to be deplored than this "wicked" idea. It is perhaps needless to say, that we cherish little sympathy for such sentiments or respect for such prejudices. Standing as we do up on the watchtower of human freedom, we cannot be deterred from an expression of our approbation of any movement, however humble, to improve and elevate the character of any members of the human family. While it is impossible for us to go into this subject at length, and dispose of the various objections which are often urged against such a doctrine as that of female equality, we are free to say that in respect to political rights, we hold woman to be justly entitled to all we claim for man. We go farther, and express our conviction that all political rights which it is expedient for man to exercise, it is equally so for woman. All that distinguishes man as an intelligent and accountable being, is equally true of woman, and if that government only is just which governs by the free consent of the governed, there can be no reason in the world for denying to woman the exercise of the elective franchise, or a hand in making and administering the laws of the land. Our doctrine is that "right is of no sex." We therefore bid the women engaged in this movement our humble Godspeed.

Frederick Douglass, the North Star, *July 28, 1848, in* Foner, Frederick Douglass, *49.*

Frederick Douglass was the first African American to publish a newspaper in the United States. *(Library of Congress)*

"PROGRESS," is the grand bubble which is now blown up to balloon bulk by the windy philosophers of the age. The women folks have just held a Convention up in New York State, and passed a sort of "bill of rights," affirming it their right to vote, to become teachers, legislators, lawyers, divines, and do all and sundries the "lords" may, and of right now do. They should have resolved at the same time, that it was obligatory also upon the "lords" aforesaid, to wash dishes, scour up, be put to the tub, handle the broom, darn stockings, patch breeches, scold the servants, dress in the latest fashion, wear trinkets, look beautiful, and be as fascinating as those blessed morsels of humanity whom God gave to preserve that rough animal man, in something like a reasonable civilization. "Progress!" Progress, forever!

Lowell Courier, *Massachusetts, July 1848, in* History of Woman Suffrage, *Vol. 1, 804.*

This has been a remarkable Convention. It was composed of those holding to some one of the various *isms* of the day, and some, we should think, who embraced them all. The only practical good proposed—the adoption of measures for the relief and amelioration of the condition of indigent, industrious, laboring females—was almost scouted by the leading ones composing the meeting. The great effort seemed to be to bring out some new, impracticable, absurd, and ridiculous proposition, and the greater its absurdity the better. In short, it was a regular *emeute* of a congregation of females gathered from various quarters, who seem to be really in earnest in their aim at revolution, and who evince entire confidence that "the day of their deliverance is at hand." Verily, this is a progressive era!

Rochester Democrat, *July 1848, in* History of Woman Suffrage, *Vol. 1, 804.*

Women Out of their Latitude

We are sorry to see that the women in several parts of this State are holding what they call "Woman's Rights Conventions," and setting forth a formidable list of those Rights in a parody upon the Declaration of American Independence.

The papers of the day contain extended notices of these Conventions. Some of them fall in with their objects and praise the meetings highly; but the majority either deprecate or ridicule both.

The women who attend these meetings, no doubt at the expense of their more appropriate duties, act as committees, write resolutions and addresses, hold much correspondence, make speeches, etc., etc. They affirm, as among their rights, that of unrestricted franchise, and assert that it is wrong to deprive them of the privilege to become legislators, lawyers, doctors, divines, etc., etc.; and they are holding Conventions and making an agitatory movement, with the object in view of revolutionizing public opinion and the laws of the land, and changing their relative position in society in such a way as to divide with the male sex the labors and responsibilities of active life in every branch of art, science, trades, and professions.

Now, it requires no argument to prove that this is all wrong. Every true hearted female will instantly feel that this is unwomanly, and that to be practically carried out, the males must change their position in society to the same extent in an opposite direction, in order to enable them to discharge an equal share of the domestic duties which now appertain to females, and which must be neglected, to a great extent, if women are allowed to exercise all the "rights" that are claimed by these Convention-holders. Society would have to be radically remodelled in order to accommodate itself to so great a change in the most vital part of the compact of the social relations of life; and the order of things established at the creation of mankind, and continued *six thousand years,* would be completely broken up. The organic laws of our country, and of each State, would have to be licked into new shapes, in order to admit of the introduction of the vast change that it contemplated. In a thousand other ways that might be mentioned, if we had room to make, and our readers had patience to hear them, would this sweeping reform be attended by fundamental changes in the public and private, civil and religious, moral and social relations of the sexes, of life, and of the Government.

But this change is impracticable, uncalled for, and unnecessary. *If effected,* it would set the world by the ears, make "confusion worse confounded," demoralize and degrade from their high sphere and noble destiny, women of all respectable and useful classes, and prove a monstrous injury to all mankind. It would be productive of no positive good, that would not be outweighed tenfold by positive evil. It would alter the relations of females without bettering their condition. Besides all, and above all, it presents no remedy for

the *real* evils that the millions of the industrious, hardworking, and much suffering women of our country groan under and seek to redress.

Mechanic's Advocate, *Albany, New York, July–August 1848, in* History of Woman Suffrage, *Vol. 1, 802.*

The Reign of Petticoats

The women in various parts of the State have taken the field in favor of a petticoat empire, with a zeal and energy which show that their hearts are in the cause, and that they are resolved no longer to submit to the tyrannical rule of the *heartless* "lords of creation," but have solemnly determined to demand their "natural and inalienable right" to attend the polls, and assist in electing our Presidents, and Governors, and Members of Congress, and State Representatives, and Sheriffs, and County Clerks, and Supervisors, and Constables, etc., etc., and to unite in the general scramble for office. This is right and proper. It is but just that they should participate in the beautiful and feminine business of politics, and enjoy their proportion of the "spoils of victory." Nature never designed that they should be confined exclusively to the drudgery of raising children, and superintending the kitchens, and to the performance of the various other household duties which the cruelty of men and the customs of society have so long assigned to them. This is emphatically the age of "democratic progression," of *equality* and *fraternization*—the age when all colors and sexes, the bond and free, black and white, male and female, are, as they by right ought to be, all tending downward and upward toward the common level of equality.

The harmony of this great movement in the cause of freedom would not be perfect if women were still to be confined to petticoats, and men to breeches. There must be an "interchange" of these "commodities" to complete the system. Why should it not be so? Can not women fill an office, or cast a vote, or conduct a campaign, as judiciously and vigorously as men? And, on the other hand, can not men "nurse" the babies, or preside at the wash-tub, or boil a pot as safely and as well as women? If they can not, the evil is in that arbitrary organization of society which has excluded them from the practice of these pursuits. It is time these false notions and practices were changed, or, rather, removed, and for the political millennium foreshadowed by this petticoat movement to be ushered in. Let the women keep the ball moving, so bravely started by those who have become tired of the restraints imposed upon them by the antediluvian notions of a Paul or the tyranny of man.

> Rochester Democrat, *New York, July 1848, in* History of Woman Suffrage, *Vol. 1, 803.*

Place woman unbonneted and unshawled before the public gaze, and what becomes of her modesty and her virtue?

> *The Reverend Henry Bellows,* Christian Inquirer, *ca. 1849, in* History of Woman Suffrage, *Vol. 1, 245.*

A NOVEL CIRCUMSTANCE—Our readers will perhaps remember that some time ago a lady, Miss Elizabeth Blackwell, applied for admission as a student in one of the medical colleges of Philadelphia, her purpose being to go through an entire course of the study of medicine. The application was denied, and the lady subsequently entered the Geneva Medical College, where, at the Annual Commencement on the 23d instant, she graduated with high honors and received the degree of M.D., the subject of her thesis being "ship fever." On receiving her diploma she thus addressed the President: "With the help of the Most High, it shall be the effort of my life to shed honor on this diploma." Professor Lee, who delivered the customary oration, complimented the lady by saying that she had won the distinction of her class by attending faithfully to every duty required of candidates striving for the honor. Eighteen young gentlemen received the degree of M.D. at the same time.

> *The* American, *Rochester, New York, July 1849, in* History of Woman Suffrage, *Vol. 1, 94.*

There is no danger of the Woman Question dying for want of notice. Every paper you take up has something to say about it, and in proportion to the refinement and intelligence of the editor has this movement been favorably noticed. But one might suppose from the articles that you find in some papers, that there are editors so ignorant as to believe that the chief object of these recent conventions was to seat every lord at the foot of the cradle, and to clothe every woman in her lord's attire. Now neither of these points, however important they be considered by humble minds, was touched upon in the conventions. We did not meet to discuss fashions, customs, or dress, the rights of man or the propriety of the sexes changing positions, but simply our own inalienable rights, our duties, our true sphere. If God has assigned a sphere to man and one to woman, we claim the right ourselves to judge of His design in reference to us, and we accord to man the same privilege. We think that a man has quite enough to do to find out his own individual calling, without being taxed to find out also where every woman belongs. The fact that so many men fail in the business they undertake, calls loudly for their concentrating more thought on their own faculties, capabilities, and sphere of action. We have all seen a man making a failure in the pulpit, at the bar, or in our legislative halls, when he might have shone as a general in our Mexican war, as a captain of our canal boat or as a tailor on the bench. Now, is it to be wondered at that woman has doubts about the present position assigned her being the true one, when everyday experience shows us that man makes such fatal mistakes in regard to himself? There is no such thing as a sphere for sex. Every man has a different sphere, in which he may or may not shine, and it is the same with every woman, and the same woman may have a different sphere at different times. For example, the highly gifted Quakeress, Lucretia Mott, married early in life and brought up a large family of children. All who have seen her at home agree that she was a pattern as a wife, mother, and housekeeper. No one ever fulfilled all the duties of that sphere more perfectly than did she. Her children settled in their own homes, Lucretia Mott has now no domestic cares. She has a talent for public speaking. Her mind is of a high order, her moral perceptions remarkably clear, her religious fervor deep and intense; and who shall tell us that this divinely inspired woman is out of her sphere in her public endeavors to rouse this wicked nation to a sense of its awful guilt, to its great sins of war, slavery, injustice to woman, and to the laboring poor?

> *Elizabeth Cady Stanton, letter to George G. Cooper, editor of the* National Reformer *of Rochester, New York, September 14, 1848, in Stanton and Blatch,* Elizabeth Cady Stanton, *Vol. 2, 18–20.*

Thanks for the copy of the Philadelphia *Public Ledger* of the 26th inst., containing a leading editorial article devoted to our recent convention. I see that the editor is especially agitated over my ninth resolution, for he says: "The New York girls desire to mount the rostrum—to do all the voting." No; not all, but our part; and that we will do some day, mark my word, through probably after our death and that of the editor of the *Public Ledger,* unless he is "going in for the hundred."

On the whole, the Philadelphia editorial is better written than that of the New York *Herald,* which you ask to see, though both show men of brains holding the pens, brains in rather narrow heads. The *Herald* writer, whom I am told is Bennett himself, devotes special attention to you, who are mentioned by the name three of four times as "Miss (sic) Lucretia Mott." My humble village is also made famous in the columns of this metropolitan daily. Seneca Falls is printed in full at least twice along with such world-known cities as Paris, Philadelphia, and Baltimore. Buffalo and Utica will be jealous of our little berg. I learn from the editorial that Bennett published *in extenso,* in a previous issue, our "Declaration." That is just what I wanted. Imagine the publicity given to our ideas by thus appearing in a widely circulated sheet like the *Herald.* It will start women thinking, and men too; and when men and women think about a new question, the first step in progress is taken. The great fault of mankind is that it will not think. In this editorial too my "elective franchise" claim seems particularly "to stick on the crop" of this conservative editor. The very fact that this happens shows conclusively that I hit the nail on the head when I made that claim. I fully agree with Mr. Bennett's closing lines, even if you may not. Here they are: "We are much mistaken if Lucretia would not make a better President than some of those who have lately tenanted the White House." Of course you would. Sincerely as ever, Author of the Ninth Resolution.

> *Elizabeth Cady Stanton, letter to Lucretia Mott,*
> *September 30, 1848, in Stanton and Blatch,*
> Elizabeth Cady Stanton, *Vol. 2, 20–22.*

Harriet Tubman escaped slavery to become the "Moses of her people." *(Library of Congress)*

I was born and lived almost forty years in South Bristol, Ontario County—one of the most secluded spots in Western New York; but from the earliest dawn of reason I pined for that freedom of thought and action that was then denied to all womankind. I revolted in spirit against the customs of society and the laws of the State that crushed my aspirations and debarred me from the pursuit of almost every object worthy of an intelligent, rational mind. But not until that meeting at Seneca Falls in 1848, of the pioneers in the cause, gave this feeling of unrest form and voice, did I take action. Then I summoned a few women in our neighborhood together and formed an Equal Suffrage Society, and sent petitions to our Legislature; but our efforts were little known beyond our circle, as we were in communication with no person or newspaper. Yet there was enough of wrong in our narrow horizon to rouse some thought in the minds of all.

In those early days a husband's supremacy was often enforced in the rural districts by corporeal chastisement, and it was considered by most people as quite right and proper—as much so as the correction of refractory children in like manner. I remember in my own neighborhood a man who was a methodist class-leader and exhorter, and one who was esteemed a worthy citizen, who, every few weeks, gave his wife a beating with his horsewhip. He said it was necessary, in order to keep her in subjection, and because she scolded so much. Now this wife, surrounded by six or seven little children, whom she must wash, dress, feed, and attend to day and night, was obliged to spin and weave cloth for all the garments of the family. She had to milk the cows, make butter and cheese, do all the cooking, washing, making, and mending for the family, and, with the pains of maternity forced upon her every eighteen months, was whipped by her pious husband, "because she scolded." And pray, why should he not have chastised her? The laws made it his privilege—and the Bible, as interpreted, made it his duty. It is true, women repined at their hard lot; but it was thought to be fixed by a divine decree, for "The man shall rule over thee," and "Wives, be subject to your husbands," and "Wives, submit yourselves unto your husbands as unto the Lord," caused them to consider their fate inevitable, and to feel that it would be contravening God's law to resist it. It is ever thus; where Theology enchains the soul, the Tyrant enslaves the body. But can any one, who has any knowledge of the laws that govern our being—of heredity and pre-natal influences—be astonished that our jails and prisons are filled with criminals, and our hospitals with sickly specimens of humanity? As long as the mothers of the race are subject to such unhappy conditions, it can never be materially improved. Men exhibit some common sense in breeding all animals except those of their own species . . .

Emily Collins, reminiscence, 1848, in History of Woman Suffrage, *Vol. 1, 88–89.*

AN AMERICAN DOCTRESS—The medical community of Paris is all agog by the arrival of the celebrated American doctor, Miss Blackwell. She has quite bewildered the learned faculty by her diploma, all in due form, authorizing her to dose and bleed and amputate with the best of them. Some of them think Miss Blackwell must be a socialist of the most rabid class, and that her undertaking is the entering wedge to a systematic attack on society by the whole sex. Others, who have seen her, say that there is nothing very alarming in her manner; that, on the contrary, she is modest and unassuming, and talks reasonably on other subjects. The ladies attack her in turn. One said to me a few days since, "Oh, it is too horrid! I'm sure I never could touch her hand! Only to think that those long fingers of hers had been cutting up dead people." I have seen the doctor in question, and must say in fairness, that her appearance is quite prepossessing. She is young, and rather good-looking; her manner indicates great energy of character, and she seems to have entered on her sin-

gular career from motives of duty, and encouraged by respectable ladies of Cincinnati. After about ten days' hesitation, on the part of the directors of the Hospital of Maternity, she has at last received permission to enter the institution as a pupil.

New York Journal of Commerce, ca. 1849, in History of Woman Suffrage, *Vol. 1, 94.*

In a letter just received from my Dublin friends, the Webbs, is a clipping from a newspaper that might be made the starting point of a good sermon. It is an account of a man summoned before the police court in London for deserting his wife. When the prisoner was asked by the judge why he had taken up his residence in a certain little hotel, he answered, because of his wife's "nagging" him. Then the warrant officer spoke up and said: "Your Honor, I have arrested several husbands at this same hotel and they all offered as an excuse that they had more comfort there than in their own homes." And don't overlook the reply of the culprit, when the judge asked him if he meant to return to his wife—"As Ovid has well said, 'Nec sine te nec tecum vivere possum,'" which I take to mean, "Whether I am with thee or absent from thee, I cannot live"—a rather noncommittal and even somewhat cryptic answer. I do not know what was done with the forlorn husband; the item and the Webbs are all silent on this point, important to him, though not so interesting to us. But if I had been the judge, I should have been very lenient, for there is no doubt of it that too many wives worry their husbands in petty ways. My chief explanation of this fact is that most women the world over have no really absorbing interest in life, nothing to take their minds off of the little domestic troubles, real or imaginary, generally the latter. If women took part in public affairs, I am sure that there would be far less nagging at the family hearth. I sometimes wish I were a clergyman for this very reason, for then I could easily reach the ear of slumbering womanhood. So do give us one of your good strong sermons, perhaps from the text, "She that is married careth for the things of the world." (I Cor. 7:34) If you do, please send on the sermon and I will have it published in the Lily, the reform paper we started here in Seneca Falls at the beginning of the present year. Your anti-nagging friend.

Elizabeth Cady Stanton, letter to John Pierpont, September 30, 1849, in Stanton and Blatch, Elizabeth Cady Stanton, *Vol. 2, 22–23.*

5

A Wave of Agitation
1850–1854

THE HISTORICAL CONTEXT

The 1850s saw a burst of grassroots activism across America. Some women refused to pay taxes, others demanded that schools begin to admit women, and still others wrote feminist journals. Even fashion became political with the arrival of the Bloomer outfit.

The country was in a state of optimism and turmoil. In 1849, 300,000 immigrants entered the United States in search of work. Young girls abandoned

Women working in a Pennsylvania brickyard *(National Archives)*

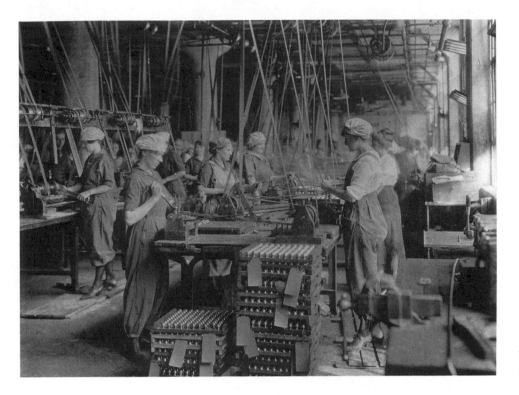

Women slotting fuses in Cambridge, Massachusetts *(National Archives)*

farms for the cities; married women traveled west on wagon trains. That year more than 80,000 people followed the wagon trains to California in search of gold. Susan B. Anthony read of their voyages and wrote, "Oh, if I were but a man so that I could go!"[1]

The admission of Texas to the Union gave a new dimension to the political debate surrounding slavery: Should the new territories that wanted admission into the Union be slave or free? Both North and South threatened secession.

Telegraphs and railroads were under rapid construction. Industry was booming. By 1850 the manufacturing industry employed 1 million people, 250,000 of them women. Women worked in textiles, shoemaking, hatmaking, printing, and even cigar-making industries.[2]

Reform was in the air, and yet it took a full year after the Rochester convention for women to hold another meeting. But when they did, it was more notorious than the first in Seneca Falls. This meeting was held in Salem, Ohio, on April 19 and 20, 1850, at the Second Baptist Church, and the women refused men the right to speak, vote, or even sit on the platform.

The men took this insult with resignation. Not only did they endorse what the women said at the meeting, but later that year Wendell Phillips, William Lloyd Garrison, Gerrit Smith, and others joined a call for the first national women's convention. It was held in 1850 in Worcester, Massachusetts, and was followed by another in 1851; conferences followed every year through 1860, except 1857.

The Worcester convention brought together the most famous feminist leaders in America: Paulina Wright Davis, Ernestine Rose, Angelina Grimké, Abby Kelley Foster, Lucretia Mott; it also attracted new faces such as Antoinette Brown and Sojourner Truth. Most important, it introduced Lucy Stone—the "morning star of the woman's movement"—to the leaders of Seneca Falls.

Lucy Stone was a brilliant speaker. The first woman to debate and speak publicly at Oberlin, newspapers called her a loud, brassy female—a "she hyena," who smoked cigars and wore boots. In reality, she was a petite, soft-spoken, neatly dressed woman whose unassuming manner won her many admirers.[3]

On her father's farm in West Brookfield, Massachusetts, the women were responsible for weaving cloth, nursing children, cooking and laundering for family and field hands alike, making shoes for sale (Lucy made nine pairs a day), and working the farm itself. Lucy's mother was so used to hard work that she milked eight cows the night before giving birth to Lucy.[4]

Lucy wanted a better life than her mother's, but unlike the parents of Elizabeth Cady Stanton and Lucretia Mott, Lucy's father believed girls did not need an education. His response to hearing that she wanted to go to college was to ask, "Is the child crazy?" Although he paid all expenses for his sons' schooling, he reluctantly allowed Lucy to borrow money from him for college. Still, Lucy would have to work off and on until she was nearly 30 before she could finish her degree. Among her many jobs, she worked in the kitchen at Oberlin for three cents an hour and taught in the preparatory school for 12½ cents an hour—earning much less than men doing the same work. She spent only 50 cents a week for food and was too poor to travel home to visit her family. When her father died, he willed all of his money and property to his sons except for $200 to be divided between his two daughters.[5]

Not surprisingly, Lucy Stone sounded like a revolutionary to some. Antoinette Brown, who would become the first woman ordained as a minister in America, was warned by an Oberlin trustee to avoid her because of her dangerous opinions. Yet Brown went out of her way to meet Stone at the earliest opportunity.

Paulina Kellogg Wright Davis planned the first national women's rights convention. *(Library of Congress)*

She and Stone worked together for equality at Oberlin. One of their courses was rhetoric. There the boys would debate for the edification of the girls; the girls were required to listen. When Stone and Brown demanded that the girls be allowed to debate as well, their professor compromised by allowing them to debate each other. This was quickly overruled by the enraged officials, who forbade all future debates by women.

Stone began lecturing for the Massachusetts Anti-Slavery Society in 1848 but publicized the rights of women as well. In spring 1850 she attended an anti-slavery convention in Boston, where she heard an announcement asking those who wanted to hold a women's rights convention to meet afterward. Stone attended, and her name later appeared on a list of prominent people calling for a national convention of women to be held at Worcester.

The newspapers ridiculed the first National Women's Rights Convention. However, Horace Greeley's *Tribune* tried to print both sides. One of the *Tribune*'s subscribers was Susan B. Anthony and she and her family, read of the convention with interest. The

Anthony home was a magnet for liberals where reformers met every Sunday. Each knew where at least one Underground Railroad station could be found. Although Anthony read the reports of the women's rights convention at Worcester in October, she did not immediately embrace feminism.

Anthony's first interest was the temperance movement. In the 1850s a woman could not divorce her husband on the grounds of drunkenness. The wife of an alcoholic who squandered the family's money was helpless. He had custody of her children and full control over her earnings. Anthony became a member, and later president, of the Rochester Daughters of Temperance, traveling as a delegate to various temperance meetings in New York State. In 1852 the Sons of Temperance held a meeting in Albany to which they invited the Daughters. The Rochester group appointed Anthony as its representative. The convention accepted her credentials and seated her, but when she tried to "speak to a motion," the president told her "the sisters were not invited to speak but to listen and learn."[6] Anthony and three or four other women left the conference at once. Most of the women remained, calling Anthony and her three or four supporters "bold, meddlesome disturbers." Anthony sought the advice of Lydia Mott, who said the proper thing was to hold a meeting of their own. So Anthony found a lecture room of her own at the Hudson Street Presbyterian Church. She then went to see Thurlow Weed, editor of the *Evening Journal,* who publicized her treatment by the Sons of Temperance. Anthony soon started her own organization in the Hudson Street Presbyterian Church. Their lecture room was dark and smoky, and the stovepipe collapsed during the meeting.

At the first meeting, Mary Vaughan was elected president, Susan B. Anthony the secretary, and Lydia Mott the chair of the business committee. Anthony said the time had come to form a group of their own, and the women supported this, appointing her president of the Woman's State Temperance Convention. Anthony immediately set to work writing to unions throughout New York, urging them to send representatives to the newly formed group. Horace Greeley, editor of the *New York Herald Tribune* became an unofficial adviser, promising to print out their typewritten speeches, which had been delivered to him the night before, along with telegraphed reports of the meeting. After weeks of preparation, on April 20, 1852, the group met at Corinthian Hall in Rochester, New York. On the first day, 500 women attended. Anthony opened the session, announcing that the purpose of the meeting was to devise action necessary for the protection of women's interests and of society at large. The group elected Elizabeth Cady Stanton as president, even though her speech angered many of those in attendance for its then-radical assertions. In a period when drunkenness was not a legal basis for divorce, she argued that no woman should remain married to a drunkard and that the new organization should petition the New York state legislature to change the marriage laws so that drunkards forfeited custodial rights to their children. She urged that women should not contribute to Christian charities abroad, one of their principal charitable occupations, because the money went to the exclusive education of men. An uproar followed, with only Susan B. Anthony, Ernestine L. Rose, Lucretia Mott, Lucy Stone, Frances D. Gage, and Martha C. Wright supporting Stanton. It was clear that the new organization would push for broader reforms than temperance. The next month the executive committee appointed Susan B. Anthony "state agent" to organize similar societies.

Meanwhile Anthony had become friends with Amelia Bloomer, founder of the first feminist journal, the *Lily*, and popularizer of the Bloomer costume—loose-fitting "Turkish" pants under a knee-length skirt. Bloomer had invited Anthony to her home in Seneca Falls in 1852. During her visit, Anthony met the woman who would be her friend and ally for the next 50 years, Elizabeth Cady Stanton. They met on a street corner one March evening, Anthony rushing to a temperance meeting, Stanton dressed in her Bloomer outfit. They liked each other immediately.

Susan B. Anthony was a tall, slim woman with brown hair. A slightly off-focused eye made her self-conscious about her looks. Although she received several proposals of marriage, she declined them all. The opposition press pictured her as a touchy, plain, humorless spinster, yet friends appreciated her warmth and humor. Unlike the fathers of Lucy Stone and Elizabeth Cady Stanton, Anthony's father was a progressive Quaker who gave Susan a fine education. He wrote to a friend, "What an absurd notion that women have no intellectual and moral faculties sufficient for anything but domestic concerns."[7]

Although Susan B. Anthony had not experienced discrimination at the hands of her father, she did see the results of women's inequality under the law firsthand. As a teenager in 1838, she had seen the collapse of her father's cotton mill. Everything her parents owned was sold to pay his debts—including Susan's clothes and gifts her grandmother had given to her mother. In 1845 Daniel Anthony lost still another mill. Because the Married Woman's Property Act would not be passed for three years, the law allowed his wife's inheritance to be claimed by his creditors. To avoid this, Anthony's parents left their estate to her brother Joshua. In this way, Susan B. Anthony fell into the same precarious legal position as married women.

Amelia Bloomer, founder of the *Lily* and champion of "pantellets"
(Library of Congress)

In 1851 Elizabeth Cady Stanton invited Susan B. Anthony and Lucy Stone to her home. They would become and remain close friends until after the Civil War, when Stone would take a more conservative path from her friends. For now, the radicals planned a new series of meetings to publicize their demands. On May 28 and 29, 1851, they gathered in Akron, Ohio. A greater number of men attended this convention than before but, in the eyes of Sojourner Truth, it seems that many of these were clergymen who had come to heckle the women.

Sojourner Truth was nearly six feet tall, with a proud carriage and a gaze that made her seem to Frances D. Gage "like one in a dream." Enslaved until 1827 in New York State, she could neither read nor write; her back was covered with scars from the beatings she had received from plantation owners. She was forced to marry a man chosen by her master rather than the one she loved and lived to see most of her 13 children sold into slavery. At the Akron convention, when none of the women could quiet the heckling they were receiving from the clergy, Sojourner Truth came forward and sat on the steps to the pulpit in the church that housed the meeting. She wore a gray dress and white turban covered by a bonnet. The leaders trembled on seeing her walk up the aisle. Whispers were heard: "Woman's rights and niggers!"; "I told you so!"; "Go it, darky!"[8]

Susan B. Anthony *(Library of Congress)*

She sat crouched against the wall on the corner of the pulpit stairs while embarrassed members of the audience begged President Frances D. Gage not to let her address the group. The next day, despite hissing opposition, Gage rose to present the next speaker, Sojourner Truth.

There was a hush when Truth went to the pulpit, moving slowly and solemnly. She laid her bonnet at her feet. Then, she turned her attention to a clergyman who had just mocked women as being too helpless to be entrusted with the vote. She said, "The man over there says women need to be helped into carriages and lifted over ditches, and to have the best place everywhere. Nobody ever helps me into carriages or over puddles, or gives me the best place—and ain't I a woman?" By the time she was finished, the ridicule had turned to a roar of approval, with many in the audience in tears. Sojourner Truth would go on to become one of the well-known and best-loved champions of the rights of women.

By midcentury, women who had participated in or read of the Worcester convention were organizing reform groups across New England, in the Middle Atlantic, and in the Midwest. Theirs was a leaderless grassroots movement, yet they did band together for one great political drive: the New York reform campaign of 1853–54.

The drive was led by Susan B. Anthony, who in 1854, along with Elizabeth Cady Stanton, flooded the New York State legislature with petitions urging that custody of children go to the mother in the event of divorce, that women's wages be protected from seizure by their husbands and that women be granted the vote. In 10 weeks 60 women collected 6,000 signatures, which they presented to the New York legislature. The campaign was topped off by a speech by Elizabeth Cady Stanton to a joint judiciary committee of both legislative houses—the first ever made by a woman. In the face of family pressure to stay home, she spoke to the legislature in Albany. On February 14, 1854, in a forceful, lawyer-like speech, she announced, "We are moral, virtuous, and intelligent, and in all respects equal to the proud white man himself, and yet by your laws we are classed with idiots, lunatics and negroes . . ." Once again, the press heaped abuse on the reformers, castigating the "husbands in petticoats" and the "emasculation" of the male sympathizers. And despite Stanton's powers of persuasion and Susan B. Anthony's 6,000 signatures, the legislature refused to reform the law and extend the Married Woman's Property Act that year.

CHRONICLE OF EVENTS

1850

As of 1850 women begin to be accepted as teachers.

Antoinette Brown (Blackwell) completes theological course at Oberlin but is not permitted to graduate because of her gender.

Sojourner Truth's autobiography, *Narrative of Sojourner Truth* (with Olive Gilbert), is published.

The *New England Offering* collapses.

April 19–20: Women's rights convention is held in Salem, Ohio, the first in this state. Women bar men from any vocal participation.

October 23–24: First National Woman's Rights Convention held in Worcester, Massachusetts, followed by another in 1851. Women's movement leaders are brought into national prominence.

1850–1860

National Woman's Rights Conventions are held every year except 1857.

1851

Indiana is one of the first states in the union to form a women's suffrage association.

Hannah E. Meyers Longshore is the first woman to be named to a faculty position at a U.S. medical school and also becomes Philadelphia's first woman doctor.

Harriet Beecher Stowe begins serial publication of *Uncle Tom's Cabin* in *National Era*.

First school to train African-American girls as teachers opens in Washington, D.C. It will close in 1859.

Susan Warner's "The Wide, Wide World" appears, becoming the first American novel to reach the 1 million mark in sales.

winter: Bloomer costume first appears, created by Libby Smith Miller. It is first known as the "Turkish dress."

May: First meeting of Susan B. Anthony and Elizabeth Cady Stanton.

May 28–29: Women's rights convention is held in Akron, Ohio. Sojourner Truth electrifies audience with her "Ain't I A Woman?" speech.

October 15–16: The Second National Woman's Rights Convention is held in Worcester, Massachusetts.

Harriet Beecher Stowe, author of *Uncle Tom's Cabin* (*New York Public Library Picture Collection*)

1852

Susan B. Anthony is turned out of a Sons of Temperance meeting for trying to speak; she organizes a women's meeting where Elizabeth Cady Stanton speaks.

The Woman's State Temperance Society elects Elizabeth Cady Stanton as president and Susan B. Anthony as secretary.

Catharine Beecher establishes the American Woman's Educational Association, which begins schools in Milwaukee, Wisconsin, Dubuque, Iowa, and Illinois.

April 20–21: Woman's State Temperance Convention is held in Rochester.

Clarina Howard Nichols petitions the Vermont legislature for women's right to vote in school meetings.

May 27: A women's rights convention is held in Massillon, Ohio.

June: Amelia Bloomer publishes a sketch of Libby Smith Miller's "Turkish dress" in the *Lily,* and thereafter "the shorts" are called "bloomers."

June 2: The first women's rights convention to take place in Pennsylvania is held in West Chester.

September: Third National Woman's Rights Convention held in Syracuse. In her presidential address, Elizabeth Cady Stanton advocates adding habitual drunkenness as legal grounds for divorce by women.

1853

Amelia Bloomer moves to Ohio.

The *Una,* edited by Paulina Wright Davis, begins publication. Elizabeth Cady Stanton writes monthly essays for the magazine.

January 21: For the first time in the history of New York State a body of women appear before the legislature. In Albany Susan B. Anthony, Antoinette Brown, and other members of the state temperance organizations petition the legislature to either give women the vote on the sale of liquor or pass a law prohibiting it.

May 28–29: A woman's rights convention is held in Akron, Ohio.

September 15: Antoinette L. Brown (Blackwell) becomes the first ordained female minister of a recognized U.S. denomination at the First Congregationalist Church in Wayne County, New York.

October 6–8: Fourth National Woman's Rights Convention held in Cleveland, Ohio.

December 24: Laura Keene is the first woman to work as a theater manager. She holds this position at the Charles Street Theater in Baltimore, Maryland.

1854

Throughout American history wives suffered economically when married to alcoholics. In 1854 Ohio passes the Adair Act, giving mothers and wives of drunks the right to sue alcohol distributors for damages.

From this date Susan B. Anthony travels door to door, sometimes in the freezing cold, to obtain signatures needed to expand New York's Married Woman's Property Law, a goal finally achieved in 1860. Her petitions urge that women be allowed to assume custody of their children in case of divorce, control their own earnings, and have the right to vote.

In Washington Territory a Maine legislator introduces a female suffrage bill in the first session. It is defeated, and the legislature will not bring up the issue up again until 1869. The measure attracted only five yes votes. In 1869 an act will be passed specifically denying women suffrage until a woman suffrage federal amendment is passed.

Married Woman's Property Bill passes in Massachusetts.

Mary Ann Shadd Cary is the first black woman to publish a newspaper, the *Provincial Freeman,* in Windsor, Ontario.

February 14–15: A women's rights convention is held in Albany, New York.

September 19–20: A New England women's rights convention is held in Boston, Massachusetts.

October 18: Fifth National Woman's Rights Convention is held in Philadelphia.

EYEWITNESS TESTIMONY

It will be thirteen years next winter, since I reported from a seat just over the way, a change in the then existing law of descent. At that time the widow of an intestate dying without children, was entitled, under ordinary circumstances, to dower in her husband's real estate, and one-third of his personal property. The change proposed was to give her one-third of the real estate of her husband absolutely, and two-thirds of his personal property—far too little, indeed; but yet as great an innovation as we thought we could carry. This law remained in force until 1841. How stands it now? The widow of an intestate, in case there be no children, and in case there be father, or mother, or brother, or sister of the husband, is heir to no part whatever of her deceased husband's real estate; she is entitled to dower only, of one-third of his estate. I ask you whether your hearts do not revolt at the idea, that when the husband is carried to his long home, his widow shall see snatched from her, by an inhuman law, the very property her watchful care had mainly contributed to increase and keep together?

Robert Dale Owen, chairman, revision committee of the convention to amend the Indiana state constitution to allow women the vote, 1850, in History of Woman Suffrage, *Vol. 1, 297.*

"I am of opinion that to adopt the proposition of the gentleman from Posey (Mr. Owen), will not ameliorate the condition of married women."

"I can not see the propriety of establishing for women a distinct and separate interest, the consideration of which would, of necessity, withdraw their attention from that sacred duty which nature has, in its wisdom, assigned to their peculiar care. I think the law which unites in one common bond the pecuniary interests of husband and wife should remain. The sacred ordinance of marriage, and the relations growing out of it, should not be disturbed. The common law does seem to me to afford sufficient protection."

"If the law is changed, I believe that a most essential injury would result to the endearing relations of married life. Controversies would arise, husbands and wives would become armed against each other, to the utter destruction of true felicity in married life."

"To adopt it would be to throw a whole population morally and politically into confusion. Is it nec-essary to explode a volcano under the foundation of the family union?"

"I object to the gentleman's proposition, because it is in contravention of one of the great fundamental principles of the Christian religion. The common law only embodies the divine law."

"Give to the wife a separate interest in law, and all those high motives to restrain the husband from wrong-doing will be, in a great degree, removed."

"I firmly believe that it would diminish, if it did not totally annihilate woman's influence."

"Woman's power comes through a self-sacrificing spirit, ready to offer up all her hopes upon the shrine of her husband's wishes."

"Sir, we have got along for eighteen hundred years, and shall we change now? Our fathers have for many generations maintained the principle of the common law in this regard, for some good and weighty reasons."

"The immortal Jefferson, writing in reference to the then state of society in France, and the debauched condition thereof, attributes the whole to the effects of the civil law then in force in France, permitting the wife to hold, acquire, and own property, separate and distinct from the husband."

"The females of this State are about as happy and contented with their present position in relation to this right (suffrage), as it is necessary they should be, and I do not favor the proposition (of Woman's Suffrage), which my friend from Posey, Mr. Owen, appears to countenance."

"It is not because I love justice less, but woman more, that I oppose this section."

"This doctrine of separate estate will stifle all the finer feelings, blast the brightest, fairest, happiest hopes of the human family, and go in direct contravention of that law which bears the everlasting impress of the Almighty Hand. Sir, I consider such a scheme not only as wild, but as wicked, if not in its intentions, at least in its results."

Legislator debating the right of women to vote at the Indiana convention, 1850, in History of Woman Suffrage, *Vol. 1, 298.*

And here we come to the cause of the ill-treatment of women in all ranks of society. We underestimate the character of woman, and keep her in a state of forced submission to man; who, in all his transactions with her, treats her as an inferior. She has no legal rights. She is not supposed to exist as a citizen. Her personality is merged in that of a man. She is always a minor, never reaching majority. She still takes rank, in the eye of the law, among man's goods and chattels, and is classified with "his ox and his ass." The law defines her, in a state of marriage, as belonging to and the property of man: the husband and wife are characterized by "baron and femme," the commentator on Blackstone averring that "the word baron or lord attributes to the husband no very courageous superiority."

A man marries a woman possessed of property, and by fact of marriage at once becomes its owner; He is the absolute master of her, her property and her children. The dress she wears ceases to be hers; it is her husband's, and she wears it, as the law phrases it, 'suitably to his quality and to do him honour.' The presents he has made to her before marriage become his again so soon as the ceremony is over. Even the marriage-ring is not hers, but can be devised [willed] away, with all her other jewels and dresses, by her husband. The American State of Pennsylvania has remedied this monstrous injustice, and conferred on married women the power over their own fortunes."

Eliza Cook's Journal, No. 119, August 9, 1851.
History of Women, Guide to the Microfilm Collection, 1983, 1.

This convention [Salem, Ohio] had one peculiar characteristic. It was officered entirely by women; not a man was allowed to sit on the platform, to speak, or to vote. *Never did men so suffer.* They implored just to say one word; but no; the President was inflexible— no man should be heard. If one meekly arose to make a suggestion he was at once ruled out of order. For the first time in the world's history men learned how it felt to sit in silence when questions in which they were interested were under discussion.

Elizabeth Cady Stanton, recalling the Salem, Ohio, women's rights convention, held April 19, 1850, in History of Woman's Suffrage, *Vol. 1, 103.*

Woman's offices, are those of wife, mother, daughter, sister, friend—Good God can they not be content with these?

New York Mirror, *October 23, 1850, in Foner,*
Frederick Douglass, *16.*

We have no hesitation in acknowledging ourselves to be among those who have regarded this movement with decided distrust and distaste. If we have been more free than others to express this disgust, we have perhaps rendered some service, by representing a common sentiment with which this reform has to contend. We would be among the first to acknowledge that our objections have not grown out of any deliberate consideration of the principles involved in the question. They have been founded on instinctive aversion, on an habitual respect for public sentiment, on an irresistible feeling of the ludicrousness of the proposed reform in its details.

The Reverend Henry Bellows, New York Christian Inquirer, October 1850, in History of Woman Suffrage, *Vol. 1, 244.*

It was decided at the Worcester convention that eight states of the Union would petition for woman's right to exercise the elective franchise. The western part of this state is left to me to organize. I must ask each district to see that its senator carries with him a petition to the coming session at Albany. Will you attend to your district? A hundred and fifty names are sufficient to make a petition very respectable.

Elizabeth Cady Stanton, letter to Amy Post, December 4, 1850, in Stanton and Blatch, Elizabeth Cady Stanton, *Vol. 2, 24–25.*

I received this morning the public documents and shall inform myself on this free school question. As the legislators at the Capitol are undoubtedly trembling in their shoes at the prospect of an encounter with me, do relieve your particular friends from their state of suspense. Tell them they have one more year to live, as I shall not be there to annihilate them this season.

Elizabeth Cady Stanton, letter to Henry B. Stanton, February 13, 1851, in Stanton and Blatch, Elizabeth Cady Stanton, *Vol. 2, 26.*

How well I remember the day! George Thompson and William Lloyd Garrison having announced an anti-slavery meeting in Seneca Falls, Miss Anthony came to attend it. These gentlemen were my guests. Walking home after the adjournment, we met Mrs. Bloomer and Miss Anthony, on the corner of the street, waiting to greet us. There she stood, with her good earnest face and genial smile, dressed in gray delaine, hat and all the same color, relieved with pale blue ribbons, the perfection of neatness and sobriety. I liked her thoroughly, and why I did not at once invite her home with me to dinner I do not know. She accuses me of that neglect, and has never forgiven me.

Elizabeth Cady Stanton, recalling her earliest meeting with Susan B. Anthony in March 1851, in Griffith, In Her Own Right, *73.*

Chief among matters of interest and importance in our city this week, are the proceedings of Woman's Temperance Convention, at Corinthian Hall (Rochester). The circumstance of women coming together, not as idle spectators, but as real actors in the scenes of a grand public demonstration in behalf of Temperance, would have, of itself in the present instance, aroused a clamor. But there was additional cause of excitement. It has been adroitly announced

Sojourner Truth subdued jeering men at the Akron, Ohio, convention with her speech. *(Courtesy of The National Portrait Gallery, Smithsonian Institution)*

that the speakers on the occasion would appear in Bloomer Costume, and doubtless, this had its effect in three ways, to attract, to repel, and to make the Convention notorious.

Frederick Douglass, the North Star, *April 22, 1851, in Foner,* Frederick Douglass, *48.*

The leaders of the movement trembled on seeing a tall, gaunt black woman in a gray dress and white turban, surmounted with an uncouth sun-bonnet, march deliberately into the church, walk with the air of a queen up the aisle, and take her seat upon the pulpit steps. A buzz of disapprobation was heard all over the house, and there fell on the listening ear, "An abolition affair!" "Woman's rights and niggers!" "I told you so!" "Go it, darkey!"

I chanced on that occasion to wear my first laurels in public life as president of the meeting. At my request order was restored, and the business of the Convention went on. Morning, afternoon, and evening exercises came and went. Through all these sessions old Sojourner, quiet and reticent as the "Lybian Statue," sat crouched against the wall on the corner of the pulpit stairs, her sun-bonnet shading her eyes, her elbows on her knees, her chin resting upon her broad, hard palms. At intermission she was busy selling the "Life of Sojourner Truth," a narrative of her own strange and adventurous life. Again and again, timorous and trembling ones came to me and said, with earnestness, "Don't let her speak, Mrs. Gage, it will ruin us. Every newspaper in the land will have our cause mixed up with abolition and niggers, and we shall be utterly denounced." My only answer was, "We shall see when the time comes."

The second day the work waxed warm. Methodist, Baptist, Episcopal, Presbyterian, and Universalist ministers came in to hear and discuss the resolutions presented. One claimed superior rights and privileges for man, on the ground of "superior intellect"; another, because of the "manhood of Christ; if God had desired the equality of woman, He would have given some token of His will through the birth, life, and death of the Savior." Another gave us a theological view of the "sin of our first mother."

There were very few women in those days who dared to "speak in meeting"; and the august teachers of the people were seemingly getting the better of us, while the boys in the galleries, and the sneerers among the pews, were hugely enjoying the discomfiture, as they supposed, of the "strong-minded." Some of the tender-skinned friends were on the point of losing dignity, and the atmosphere betokened a storm. When, slowly from her seat in the corner rose Sojourner Truth, who, till now, had scarcely lifted her head. "Don't let her speak!" gasped half a dozen in my ear. She moved slowly and solemnly to the front, laid her old bonnet at her feet, and turned her great speaking eyes to me. There was a hissing sound of disapprobation above and below. I rose and announced "Sojourner Truth," and begged the audience to keep silence for a few moments.

The tumult subsided at once, and every eye was fixed on this almost Amazon form, which stood nearly six feet high, head erect, and eyes piercing the upper air like one in a dream. At her first word there was a profound hush. She spoke in deep tones, which, though not loud, reached every ear in the house, and away through the throng at the doors and windows.

"Wall, chilern, whar dar is so much racket dar must be somethin' out o' kilter. I tink dat 'twixt de niggers of de Souf and de womin at de Norf, all talkin' 'bout rights, de white men will be in a fix pretty soon. But what's all dis here talkin' 'bout?

"Dat man ober dar say dat womin needs to be helped into carriages, and lifted ober ditches, and to hab de best place everywhar. Nobody eber helps me into carriages, or ober mud-puddles, or gibs me any best place!" And raising herself to her full height, and her voice to a pitch like rolling thunder, she asked, "And a'n't I a woman? Look at me! Look at my arm! (and she bared her right arm to the shoulder, showing her tremendous muscular power). I have ploughed, and planted, and gathered into barns, and no man could head me! And a'n't I a woman? I could work as much and eat as much as a man—when I could get it—and bear de lash as well! And a'n't I a woman? I have borne thirteen chilern, and seen 'em mos' all sold off to slavery, and when I cried out with my mother's grief, none but Jesus heard me! And a'n't I a woman?

"Den dey talks 'bout dis ting in de head; what dis dey call it?" ("Intellect," whispered some one near.) "Dat's it, honey. What's dat got to do wid womin's rights or nigger's rights? If my cup won't hold but a pint, and yourn holds a quart, wouldn't ye be mean not to let me have my little half-measure full?" And she pointed her significant finger, and sent a keen glance at the minister who had made the argument. The cheering was long and loud.

"Den dat little man in black dar, he say women can't have as much rights as men, 'cause Christ wan't a woman! Whar did your Christ come from?" Rolling thunder couldn't have stilled that crowd, as did those deep, wonderful tones, as she stood there with outstretched arms and eyes of fire. Raising her voice still louder, she repeated, "Whar did your Christ come from? From God and a woman! Man had nothin' to do wid Him." Oh, what a rebuke that was to that little man.

Turning again to another objector, she took up the defense of Mother Eve. I can not follow her through it all. It was pointed, and witty, and solemn; eliciting at almost every sentence deafening applause; and she ended by asserting: "If de fust woman God ever made was strong enough to turn de world upside down all alone, dese women togedder (and she glanced her eye over the platform) ought to be able to turn it back, and get it right side up again! And now dey is asking to do it, de men better let 'em." Long-continued cheering greeted this. "'Bleeged to

Frances D. Gage in 1875 became the leader of the national and New York State suffrage organizations. *(Library of Congress)*

ye for hearin' on me, and now ole Sojourner han't got nothin' more to say"

Amid roars of applause, she returned to her corner, leaving more than one of us with streaming eyes, and hearts beating with gratitude. She had taken us up in her strong arms and carried us safely over the slough of difficulty turning the whole tide in our favor. I have never in my life seen anything like the magical influence that subdued the mobbish spirit of the day, and turned the sneers and jeers of an excited crowd into notes of respect and admiration. Hundreds rushed up to shake hands with her, and congratulate the glorious old mother, and bid her God-speed on her mission of "testifyin' agin concerning the wickedness of this 'ere people."

> *Frances D. Gage, recalling the Akron, Ohio women's rights convention, May 28–29, 1851, in* History of Woman Suffrage, *Vol. 1, 115–117.*

Your father's tour through this district turned out a more bitter pill for me than for the one for whom it was intended. My going to hear Cousin Gerrit speak and walking out with him flew like wildfire, and all the Whigs had it that Mr Stanton's family and friends were against him [his reelection to the New York State Senate], even his wife disapproving of his course [his opposition to the enlargement of the Erie Canal]. My name was hawked about the streets and in all the public meetings. Two men had a fight in one meeting about my hat. My dress was a subject of the severest animadversions. Some good Democrats said they would not vote for a man whose wife wore the Bloomers. Then the Whigs and procanal Democrats—you know the party was not united on the question—got up all kinds of stories about me. Some said I was bribed by Cousin Gerrit to go against Henry. The truth is I felt no interest whatever in the canal question *per se,* but desired Henry's reelection. But as no one seemed satisfied with my neutral position, after posting myself on the subject, and the Constitution's bearing thereon, I came out an unterrified Democrat, defending resignation and abhorring debt. This seemed to increase the activity of the street urchins, who hissed and sung and screamed "breeches" with the greatest vim throughout the whole campaign. The night after the election—just a week ago this evening—when it was reported that Henry was defeated, they shouted in chorus all through the streets:

Heigh! Ho! the carrion crow,
Mrs. Stanton's all the go;
Twenty tailors take the stitches,
Mrs. Stanton wears the breeches.

> *Elizabeth Cady Stanton, letter to Elizabeth Smith Miller, June 4, 1851, in Stanton and Blatch,* Elizabeth Cady Stanton, *Vol. 2, 29–30.*

You will have read the *Lily* before you get this, and seen your claims set up for the glory of having been the first American woman to wear "the shorts" as a constant dress. The article signed J.V.N. is by your beloved Massa Johnson. But do not mention it, or Mrs. Bloomer would tear my eyes out. In this num-

Bloomers were pioneered by Fannie Kemble (1849) and Amelia Bloomer (1850). *(Library of Congress)*

ber, by the way, are six editorials written by me. The whole column where your name is mentioned is mine, and the "Detroit Tribune," the "Lowell Girls" and the "Man in Petticoats" are also from my pen. My baby is very good and grows finely. I continue to be his wet as well as his dry nurse. It is easier to look after him myself than to train an ignorant girl to do so. I have invented a variety of ways to keep him quiet—that is, ways for him to keep himself quiet.

Elizabeth Cady Stanton, letter to Elizabeth Smith Miller, August 5, 1851, in Stanton and Blatch, Elizabeth Cady Stanton, *Vol. 2, 32.*

Now I have something to tell [you] that will cheer [your] sad heart. Well, you heard of the proposed festival at Glen Haven. I went to it and had a most pleasent time. I took Amelia [Willard], who was in "shorts", and Theodore. There I saw ten ladies in costume—three from Syracuse, four in our party, and the rest residents of Glen Haven. Theodosia Gilbert's get-up pleased me very much. She was dressed in a short green tunic not reaching to the knee, and white linen drilling trousers made *à la masculine.* They all wore white trousers with dresses of various colors. In a word, the "shorts" were the theme of conversation, tracts and addresses. Oh, that you had been there! We dined in the open air and had a great many agreeable people at the table, so that the conversation was quite brilliant and interesting. At dessert, William Burleigh spoke in high praise of the "shorts" and with great disgust of the "longs." "The long dress is now an offense to my eyes," he said; "and I cannot help exclaiming to my self whenever I see a woman trailing bedraggled petticoats through the dust, 'Oh, the dirty creature!'" Warm applause from the delighted listeners. But Mr. Burleigh had with him a Miss B., whom he treated with too great attention. I like fun and frolic, romps and jokes, but sentimental pawings are excessively disgusting to me. Returning from Glen Haven, we reached Skeneateles [sic] at seven, and lo and behold, all the town had come to see us! We had left our carriage and coachman there, and the news had spread through the village that four ladies in "shorts" were to come down in the evening boat; so there the multitude stood—men, women, and children. Ossian Dodge with his guitar in a green baize bag and I with my baby in blue merino cloak took the lead, the three other ladies and two or three odd-looking gentlemen in long hair following. What a spectacle for men and angels as we solemnly proceeded from the boat to our carriages. What would the venerable judge have said could he have witnessed the scene!! I expected to be insulted, but not one word was said. The people had evidently been impelled by an honest curiosity to see—nothing more . . . As we have performed this surgical operation on our entire wardrobe, nothing remains for us to do but to induce as many as possible to follow our example. We can have no peace in traveling until we cut off the great national petticoat. God grant that we may be more successful than the fox.

Elizabeth Cady Stanton, letter to Elizabeth Smith Miller, August 5, 1851, in Stanton and Blatch, Elizabeth Cady Stanton, *Vol. 2, 32–34.*

You do not wish me to visit you in a short dress! Why, my dear child, I have no other. Now, suppose you and I were taking a long walk in the fields and I had on long petticoats. Then suppose a bull should take after us. Why, you, with your long legs and arms free, could run like a shot; but I, alas! should fall a victim to my graceful flowing drapery. Like the deer, you remember, in the fable, my glory would be destruction. My petticoats would be caught by the stumps and the briars, and what could I do at the fences? Then you in your agony, when you saw the bull gaining on me, would say: "Oh! how I wish mother could use her legs as I can." Now why do you wish me to wear what is uncomfortable, inconvenient, and many times dangerous? I'll tell you why. You want me to be like other people. You do not like to have me laughed at. You must learn not to care for what foolish people say. Such good men as cousin Gerrit and Mr. [Theodore] Weld will tell you that a short dress is the right kind. So no matter if ignorant silly persons do laugh. Good night to both of my dear boys.

Your Mother.

Elizabeth Cady Stanton, letter to Daniel C. Stanton, October 14, 1851, in Stanton and Blatch, Elizabeth Cady Stanton, *Vol. 2, 35–36.*

Dear Sisters,
Your courageous declaration of woman's rights has resounded even to our prison, and has filled our souls with inexplicable joy.

Letter read October 15–16, 1851, at the second National Woman's Rights Convention, from Jeanne Deroine and Pauline Roland in a Paris prison, written June 15, 1851, in Stanton, Anthony, and Gage, History of Woman Suffrage, *Vol. 1, 234.*

The executive committee of the Philadelphia Anti-Slavery Society, 1851. Lucretia and James Mott are seated in the front row, right. *(Courtesy of the Sophia Smith Collection, Smith College)*

Only see how they are all coming round. Mama and sister Mag, who are now making me a visit, do not seem to dislike the short dress. Mama even says that when Papa returned from here, he was quite pleased with his visit and his daughter, and declared that he would never have noticed the "shorts" if he had not heard so much about them. He thought them "well enough." I suppose he expected to see me looking just like a man. Well, the ball went off finely. Henry and I danced until four o'clock. Massa Johnson dressed in white, as the black satin waist was tight and I could not sacrifice the most glorious part of our reform—a loose waist—to the becoming. Everybody said I looked well, and I thought I did.

Elizabeth Cady Stanton, letter to Elizabeth Smith Miller, October 18, 1851, in Stanton and Blatch, Elizabeth Cady Stanton, *Vol. 2, 36–37.*

If the lady wants to make herself ridiculous, let her come and make herself as ridiculous as possible and as soon as possible, but I don't believe in this scramble for the breeches!

Chairman, educational committee, Vermont House of Representatives, on casting the dissenting vote to invite Clarina Howard Nichols to speak on her petition to allow women to vote in district school meetings, 1852, in History of Woman Suffrage, *Vol. 1, 173.*

In the winter of 1852 I went as often as twice a week—late P.M. and returned early A.M.—from six to twenty miles. I was sent for where there was no railroad. I often heard of "ready-made pants," and once of a "rail," but the greater the opposition, the greater the victory.

On a clear, cold morning of January, 1852, I found myself some six miles from home at a station on the Vermont side of the Massachusetts State line, on my way to Templeton, Mass., whither I had been invited by a Lyceum Committee to lecture upon the subject of "Woman's Rights," I had scarcely settled myself in the rear of the saloon for a restful, careless two hours' ride, when two men entered the car. In the younger man I recognized the sheriff of our county. Having given a searching glance around the car, the older man, with a significant nod to his companion, laid his hand upon the saloon door an instant, and every person in the car had risen to his feet, electrified by the wail of a "Rachel mourning for her children," "O, father! she's *my* child! *she's my child!*" I reached the door, which was guarded by the sheriff, in a condition of mental exaltation (or concentration), which to this day reflects itself at the recollection of that agonizing cry of the beautiful young mother, set upon by the myrmidons of the law whose base inhumanity shames the brute! "Who is it?" "What is it?" "What does it all mean?" were the anxious queries put up on all sides. I answered: "It means, my friends, that a woman has no legal right to her own babies; that the law-makers of this *Christian country* (!) have given the custody of the babies to the father, drunken or sober, and he may send the sheriff—as in this case—to arrest and rob her of her little ones! You have heard sneers at 'Woman's Rights.' This is one of the rights—a mother's right to the care and custody of her helpless little ones!"

From that excited crowd—all young and grown boys, I being the only woman among them—rose thick and fast—*"They've no business with the woman's babies!"* "Pitch 'em overboard!" "I'll help." "Good for you; so'll I!" "All aboard." (The conductor had come upon the scene). *"All aboard."* "Wait a minute till he gets the other child," cries the old man, rushing out of the saloon with a little three-year-old girl in his arms, while the sheriff rushed in. Standing behind the old man, I beckoned to the conductor, who knew me, to *"go on,"* and in five minutes we were across the Massachusetts line, and I was in the saloon. With his hand on her child, the sheriff was urging the mother to let go her hold. "Hold on to your baby," I cried, "he has no right to take it from you and is liable to fine and imprisonment for attempting it. Tell me, Mr. C——, are you helping the other party as a favor, or in your official capacity? In the latter case you might have

taken her child in Vermont, but we are in Massachusetts now, quite out of your sheriff's beat." "The grandfather made legal custodian by the father, was he? That would do in Vermont, sir, but under the recent decision of a Massachusetts Court, given in a case like this, *only the father* can take the child from its mother, and in attempting it you have made yourselves liable to fine and imprisonment." Thus the "sheriffalty" was extinguished, and mother and child took their seat beside me in the car.

Meantime the conductor had made the old gentleman understand that they could get off at the next station, where they might take the "up train," and get back to their "team" on the Vermont side of the "line." As they could get no carriage at the bare little station, and with the encumbrance of the child, could not foot it six miles in the cold and snow, they must wait some three or four hours for the train, which suggested the possibility of a rescue. I could not stop over a train, but I could take the baby along with me, if some one could be found—The conductor calls. The car stops. As the child robbers step out (the little girl, clutched in the old grandfather's arms) 'mid the frantic cries of the mother and the execrations of the passengers, two middle-aged gentlemen of fine matter-of-fact presence, entered. I at once met their questioning faces with a hurried statement of facts, and the need of some intelligent, humane gentleman to aid the young mother in the recovery of her little girl. Having spoken together aside, the younger man introduced "Dr. B——, who lives in the next town, where papers can be made out, and a sheriff be sent back to bring the men and child; the lady can go with the doctor, and the baby with Mrs. Nichols. I would stop, but I must be in my seat in the Legislature." "I have no money, only my ticket to take me to my friends," exclaimed the anxious mother. "I will take care of that," said the good doctor; "you won't need any." "They will have to pay," I whispered . . .

I gave my lecture at Templeton to a fine audience; accepted an invitation to return and give a second on the same subject, and having left the dear little toddler happy and amply protected, at noon next day found myself back at Orange, where I had left the mother. Here the conductor, who by previous arrangement, left a note from me telling her where to go for her baby, reported that the party had been brought to Orange for trial, spent the night in care of the sheriff, and were released on giving up the little girl and paying a handsome sum of the needful to the mother. He had scarcely ended his report when the pair entered the car, like myself, homeward bound. The old gentleman, care-worn and anxious, probably thinking of his team left standing at the Vermont station, looked straight ahead, but the kind-hearted sheriff caught my eye and smiled. In my happiness I could not do otherwise than give smile for smile.

Arrived at home, I found the affair, reported by the conductor of the evening train, had created quite an excitement, sympathy decidedly with the mother. I was credited with being privy to the escapade and the pursuit, and as having gone purposely to the rescue. Had this been true, I could not have managed it better, for a good Providence went with me. I received several memorial "hanks" of yarn, with messages from the donors that "they would keep me in knitting-work while preaching woman's rights on the railroad"—a reference to my practice of knitting on the cars and the report that I gave a lecture on the occasion to my audience there.

And thus was the seed of woman's educational, industrial, and political rights sown in Vermont, through infinite labor, but in the faith and perseverance which bring their courage to all workers for the right.

Clarina Howard Nichols, recalling events of January 1852, in History of Woman Suffrage, *Vol. 1, 176–178.*

I think you are doing up the temperance business just right. But do not let the conservative element control. For instance, you must take Mrs. Bloomer's suggestions with great caution, for she has not the spirit of the true reformer. At the first woman's rights convention, but four years ago, she stood aloof and laughed at us. It was only with great effort and patience that she has been brought up to her present position. In her paper, she will not speak against the fugitive slave law, nor in her work to put down intemperance will she criticize the equivocal position of the Church. She trusts to numbers to build up a cause rather than to principals, to the truth and the right. Fatal error! The history of the antislavery agitation is, on this point, a lesson to thinking minds. Among the abolitionists, the discussion began by some insisting on compromises in order to draw in numbers and bring over to them a large and respectable body of priests and rabbis. They also decided to turn the cold shoulder on woman's co-operation, as well as let the Church go unrebuked. Where now is that brilliant host in panoply so scared and so respected? Gone back to learn anew the a, b, c, of the reformer. All this I say to you and to no one else, and you will understand why. I would not speak aught to injure Mrs. Bloomer. Yes, I repeat, beware of her conservative suggestions. We are utterly unconscious of his brutality to woman. In the good time coming, what a cause of wonder it will be to recall the fact that the champions of freedom, the most progressive men of the nineteenth century, denied women the right of free speech in an antislavery convention, when, at the same time, they would have received with the greatest *eclat* the most degraded man from a rice plantation. If Sambo had been cast out of the convention for any reason, I wonder if Wendell Phillips and George Thompson would have cooly remarked on his discomfiture, "Well, he is as happy outside as in!" Men and angels give me patience! I am at the boiling point! If I do not find some day the use of my tongue on this question, I shall die of an intellectual repression, a woman's rights convulsion! Oh, Susan! Oh, Susan! Oh, Susan! You must manage to spend a week with me before the Rochester [Woman's New York State Temperance] Convention, for I am afraid I cannot attend it; I have so much care with all these boys on my hands. But I will write a letter. How much I do long to be free from housekeeping and children, so as to have some time to read and think and write. But it may be well for me to understand all the trials of woman's lot, that I may more eloquently proclaim them when the time comes. Good night.

Elizabeth Cady Stanton, letter to Susan B. Anthony, April 2, 1852, in Stanton and Blatch, Elizabeth Cady Stanton, *Vol. 2, 38–42.*

1. Let no woman remain in the relation of wife with a confirmed drunkard. Let no drunkard be the father of her children. . . .

2. Let us petition our State government so to modify the laws affecting marriage, and the custody of children, that the drunkard shall have no claims on wife or child.

And lastly, inasmuch as charity begins at home, let us withdraw our mite from all associations for sending the Gospel to the heathen across the ocean, for the education of young men for the ministry, for the building up of a theological aristocracy and gorgeous temples to the unknown God, and devote ourselves to the poor and suffering around us. Let us feed and clothe the hungry and naked, gather children into schools and provide reading-rooms and decent homes for young men and women thrown alone upon the world. Good schools and homes, where the young could ever be surrounded by an atmosphere of purity and virture, would do much more to prevent immorality and crime in our cities than all the churches in the land could ever possibly do toward the regeneration of the multitude sunk in poverty, ignorance and vice.

Elizabeth Cady Stanton, accepting the presidency of the Woman's State Temperance Convention, in Rochester, New York, April 20, 1852, in Stanton, Anthony, and Gage, History of Woman Suffrage, *Vol. 1, 482.*

The third Woman's Rights Convention of [Massillon] Ohio has just closed its session. It was held in the Baptist church, in this place, and was numerously attended, there being a fair representation of men, as well as women; for though the obect of these, and similar meetings, is to secure woman her rights, as an equal member of the human family, neither speaking nor membership was here confined to the one sex, but all who had sentiments to utter in reference to the object of the Convention—whether for or against it—were invited to speak with freedom, and those who wished to aid the movement to sit as members, without distinction of sex. All honorable classes were represented, from the so-called highest to the so-called lowest—the seamstress who works for twenty-five cents a day; the daughters of the farmer, fresh from the dairy and the kitchen; the wives of the laborer, the physician, the lawyer, and the banker, the legislator, and the minister, were all there—all interested in one common cause, and desirous that every right God gave to woman should be fully recognized by the laws and usages of society, that every faculty he has bestowed upon her should have ample room for its proper development. Is this asking too much? And yet this is the sum and substance of the Woman's Rights Reform—a movement which fools ridicule, and find easier to sneer at then meet with argument.

New York Tribune, *May 27, 1852, in* History of Woman Suffrage *Vol. 1, 123.*

I am glad you are to be at the state temperance meeting [the Men's State Temperance Society, which met at Syracuse in June]. I send you for this convention four resolutions, [including one calling drunkenness grounds for divorce] which I wish you would present to the assemblage as coming from our Woman's State Temperance Society. I do wish you would also speak there on divorce, people have such false, low views on what constitutes true marriage. If woman knew their duty on this point, it would tell in the temperance cause. Man has never begun to appreciate the wrongs of woman.

Elizabeth Cady Stanton, letter to Gerrit Smith, May 25, 1852, in Stanton and Blatch, Elizabeth Cady Stanton *Vol. 2, 43.*

Woman has so long been accustomed to non-intervention with law-making, so long considered it a man's business to regulate the liquor traffic, that it is with much cautiousness she received the new doctrine which we preach; the doctrine that it is her right and duty to speak out against the traffic and all men and institutions that in any way sanction, sustain or countenance it; and, since she can not vote, to duly instruct her husband, son, father or brother how she would have him vote, and, if he longer continues to misrepresent her, take the right to march to the ballot-box and deposit a vote indicative of her highest ideas of practical temperance.

Susan B. Anthony, July 28, 1852 petition for a temperance law, Letter from the "Carson League," in Stanton, Anthony, and Gage, History of Woman Suffrage, *Vol. 1, 488.*

When a woman dies, leaving behind her a husband and children, no appraisers come into the desolated home to examine the effects; the father is the guardian of his offspring; the family relation is not invaded by law. But when a man dies the case is entirely different; in the hour of the widow's deep distress strangers come into the house to take an inventory of the effects, strangers are appointed to be the guardians of her children, and she, their natural caretaker, thenceforth has no legal direction of their interests; strangers decide upon the propriety of the sale of the property—earned, perhaps, by her own and her husband's mutual efforts—and her interest in the estate is coolly designated as the "widow's incumbrance!" In the extremity of her bereavement there is piled upon her, not only the dread of separation from her children, but that of being sent homeless from the spot where every object has been consecrated by her tenderest affections.

Ann Preston, at West Chester, Pennsylvania, women's rights convention, June 2, 1852, in History of Woman Suffrage, *Vol. 1, 361.*

Society is clearly unjust to woman in according her but four to eight dollars per month for labor equally repugnant with, and more protracted than that of men of equal intelligence and relative efficiency, whose services command from ten to twenty dollars per month. If, then, the friends of Woman's Rights could set the world an example of paying for female service, not the lowest pittance which stern Necessity may compel the defenceless to accept, but as approximately fair and liberal compensation for the work actually done, as determined by careful comparison with the recompense of other labor, I believe they would give their cause an impulse which could not be permanently resisted.

Horace Greeley, letter to Mrs. Paulina W. Davis, September 1, 1852, in History of Woman Suffrage, *Vol. 1, 521.*

Should not all women, living in States where they have the right to hold property, refuse to pay taxes so long as they are unrepresented in the government? . . . Man has pre-empted the most profitable branches of industry, and we demand a place at his side; to this end we need the same advantages of education, and we therefore claim that the best colleges of the country be opened to us. . . . In her present ignorance, woman's religion, instead of making her noble and free, by the wrong application of great principles of right and justice, has made her bondage but more certain and lasting, her degradation more helpless and complete.

Elizabeth Cady Stanton, letter to the Woman's Rights Convention in Syracuse, New York, September 8, 1852, in Harper, The Life and Work of Susan B. Anthony, *Vol. 1, 73.*

[T]he common law, which regulates the relation of husband and wife, and is modified only in a few instances by the statutes, gives the "custody" of the wife's person to the husband, so that he has a right to her even against herself. It gives him her earnings, no matter with what weariness they have been acquired, or how greatly she may need them for herself or for her children. It gives him a right to her personal property, which he may will entirely away from her, also the use of her real estate, and in some of the States married women, insane persons and idiots are ranked together as not fit to make a will; so that she is left with only one right, which she enjoys in common with the pauper, the right of maintenance. Indeed, when she has taken the sacred marriage vows, her legal existence ceases. And what is our position politically? The foreigner, the negro, the drunkard, are all entrusted with the ballot, all placed by men politically higher than their own mothers, wives, sisters and daughters! The woman who, seeing this, dares not maintain her rights is the one to hang her head and blush. We ask only for justice and equal rights—the right to vote, the right to our own earnings, equality before the law; these are the Gibraltar of our cause.

Lucy Stone, at the Woman's Rights Convention in Syracuse, New York, September 8, 1852, in Harper, The Life and Work of Susan B. Anthony, *Vol. 1, 73–74.*

If a wife is compelled to get a divorce on account of the infidelity of the husband, she forfeits all right to the property which they have earned together, while the husband, who is the offender, still retains the sole possession and control of the estate. She, the innocent party, goes out childless and portionless by decree of law, and he, the criminal, retains the home and children by favor of the same law. A drunkard takes his wife's clothing to pay his rum bills, and the court declares that the action is legal because the wife belongs to the husband.

Clarina Howard Nichols, at the Woman's Rights Convention in Syracuse, New York, September 8, 1852, in Harper, The Life and Work of Susan B. Anthony, *Vol. 1, 74.*

When woman is tried for crime, her jury, her judges, her advocates, all are men; and yet there may have been temptation and various palliating circumstances connected to her particular nature as woman, such as man cannot appreciate. Common justice demands that a part of the law-makers and law-executors should be of her own sex. In questions of marriage and divorce, affecting interests dearer than life, both parties in the compact are entitled to an equal voice.

Antoinette Brown, at the Woman's Rights Convention in Syracuse, New York, September 8, 1852, in Harper, The Life and Work of Susan B. Anthony, *Vol. 1, 74.*

The women are coming! They flock in upon us from every quarter, all to hear and talk about Woman's rights. The blue stockings are as thick as grasshoppers in hay-time, and mighty will be the force of "jaw-logic" and "broom-stick ethics" preached by the females of both sexes.

Daily Star, *discussing the Syracuse national convention, September 8, 1852, in* History of Woman Suffrage, *Vol. 1, 517.*

What do the leaders of the Woman's Rights Convention want? They want to vote, and to hustle with the rowdies at the polls. They want to be members of Congress, and in the heat of debate to subject themselves to coarse jests and indecent language, like that of Rev. Mr. Hatch. They want to fill all other posts which men are ambitious to occupy—to be lawyers, doctors, captains of vessels, and generals in the field. How funny it would sound in the newspapers, that Lucy Stone, pleading a cause, took suddenly ill in the pains of parturition, and perhaps gave birth to a fine bouncing boy in court! Or that Rev. Antoinette Brown was arrested in the middle of her sermon in the pulpit from the same cause, and presented a "pledge" to her husband and the congregation; or, that Dr. Harriot K. Hunt, while attending a gentleman patient for a fit of the gout or *fistula in ano*, found it necessary to send for a doctor, there and then, and to be delivered of a man or woman child—perhaps twins. A similar event might happen on the floor of Congress, in a storm at sea, or in the raging tempest of battle, and then what is to become of the woman legislator?

New York Herald, *September 12, 1852, in* History of Woman Suffrage, *Vol. 1, 854.*

I am at length the happy mother of a daughter. I never felt such sacredness in carrying a child as I have in the case of this one. She is the largest and most vigorous baby I have ever had, weighing twelve pounds. And yet my labor was short and easy. I laid down about fifteen minutes, and alone with my nurse and one female friend brought forth this big girl. I sat up immediately, changed my own clothes, put on a wet bandage, and, after a few hours' repose, sat up again. Am I not almost a savage? For what refined, delicate, genteel, civilized woman would get well in so indecently short time? Dear me, how much cruel bondage of mind and suffering of body poor woman will

escape when she takes the liberty of being her own physician of both body and soul! I have been wishing to write you ever since the convention to say how pleased I was with the whole proceedings. As to the presidency, it is a matter of congratulation, and argues a great advance in our movement that we now have competitors for the office, when at our first convention no woman could be found with the moral hardihood to take that post of honor. I was greatly pleased too that a bloomer was the pet of the meeting. Depend upon it, Lucretia, that woman can never develop in her present drapery. She is a slave to her rags. But I cannot prove that to you now, for I must write about my daughter to about a dozen other friends.

A Happy Mother
Elizabeth Cady Stanton, letter to Lucretia Mott, October 22, 1852, in Stanton and Blatch, Elizabeth Cady Stanton, *Vol. 2, 44–45.*

The woman shall not wear that which pertaineth unto man; neither shall a man put on a woman's garment; for all that do so are an abomination to the Lord thy God.

The Reverend Byron Sunderland, sermon at Plymouth Congregational Church of Syracuse, New York, September 17, 1852, in History of Woman Suffrage, *Vol. 1, 543.*

I do not know whether the world is quite willing or ready to discuss the question of marriage. I feel in my innermost soul that the thoughts I sent in convention are true. It is in vain to look for the elevation of woman so long as she is degraded in marriage. I hold that it is a sin, an outrage on our holiest feelings, to pretend that anything but deep, fervent love and sympathy constitute marriage. The right idea of marriage is at their foundation of all reforms. How strange it is that man will apply all the improvements in the arts and sciences to everything about him, animate or inanimate, but himself. If we properly understood the science of life, it would be far easier to give to the world harmonious, beautiful, noble, virtuous children, than it is to bring grown-up discord into harmony with the great divine soul of all. I ask for no laws on marriage. I say with Father Chipman, remove law and a false public sentiment, and woman will no more live as wife with a cruel, bestial drunkard than a servant, in this free country, will stay with a pettish, unjust mistress. If lawmakers insist upon exercising their prerogative in some way on this question, let then forbid any woman to marry until she is twenty-one; let them fine a woman $50 for every child she conceives by a drunkard. Women have no right to saddle the state with idiots who must be supported by the public. You know that the statistics of our idiot asylums show that nearly all are the offspring of drunkards. Woman must be made to feel that the transmitting of immortal life is a solemn, responsible act, and should never be allowed except when the parents are in the highest condition of mind and body. Man in his lust has regulated long enough this whole question of sexual intercourse. Now let the mother of mankind, whose prerogative it is to set bounds to his indulgence, rouse up and give this whole matter a thorough, fearless examination. I am glad that Catholic priest said of my letter what he did. It will call attention to the subject; and if by martyrdom I can advance my race one step, I am ready for it. I feel, as never before, that this whole question of woman's rights turns on the pivot of the marriage relation, and, mark my word, sooner or later it will be the topic for discussion. I would not hurry it on, nor would I avoid it.

Elizabeth Cady Stanton, letter to Susan B. Anthony, March 1, 1853, in Stanton and Blatch, Elizabeth Cady Stanton, *Vol. 2, 48–49.*

I send you the Rochester *Journal*. Well, doesn't the editor pitch into me without mercy? I would answer him, but he wouldn't publish what I might say; so there is no use. For the present we must let these narrow-minded and unfair critics rage. They cannot put down our ideas, and we will have our day in the end. I have finished Charley's "cracks." I hesitate about sewing on the soles. My boots would furnish a model which is too small, while Henry's would be too large. You ask me what I wear. Just what I wore last winter; all but the brilliant jewel I now bear in my arms—my lovely daughter. You see, by the way, that the Emperor of France has proposed the short dress for court dress. Stand firm a little longer, dear Liz, and we shall be a respectable majority—respectable and respected. I love what I suffer for, and I have suffered a good deal for this dress. The *Home Journal* speaks in high praise of the short dress. It has been such a boon to me this past winter, which has been the hardest of my life. I have two good girls, but still I have been confined to

the baby, for I fear to trust her in other hands. But this dress [The Bloomer outfit] makes it easier to do all these things—running from cradle to writing-desk, from kitchen to drawing-room, singing lullabies at one moment in the nursery and dear old Tom Moore's ditties the next moment on the piano-stool. If I had on long skirts, how could I accomplish all this? God only knows.

Elizabeth Cady Stanton, letter to Elizabeth Smith Miller, May 1, 1853, in Stanton and Blatch, Elizabeth Cady Stanton, *Vol. 2, 49–50.*

We conceived a very unfavorable opinion of this *Miss* Anthony when she performed in this city on a former occasion, but we confess that, after listening Attentively to her discourse last evening, we were inexpressibly disgusted with the impudence and impiety evinced in her lecture. Personally repulsive, she seems to be laboring under feelings of strong hatred towards male men, the effect, we presume, of jealousy and neglect.

The Utica Evening Telegraph, *March–April, 1853, in Harper,* The Life and Work of Susan B. Anthony, *Vol. 1, 83–84.*

Say not one word to me about another convention. I forbid you to ask me to send one thought or line to any convention, any paper, or any individual; for I swear by all the saints that whilst I am nursing this baby I will not be tormented with suffering humanity. I am determined to make no effort to do anything beyond my imperative home duties until I can bring about the following conditions: 1st, Relieve myself of housekeeping altogether; 2nd, Secure some capable teacher for my children; 3rd, See my present baby on her feet. My ceaseless cares begin to wear upon my spirit. I feel it in my innermost soul and am resolved to seek some relief. Therefore, I say adieu to the public for a time, for I must give all my moments and my thoughts to my children. But above all this I am so full of dreams of the true associative life that all the reforms of the day beside that seem to me superficial and fragmentary. You ask me if I am not plunged in grief at my defeat at the recent convention for the presidency of our society. Not at all. I am only too happy in the relief I feel from this additional care. I accomplished at Rochester all I desired by having the divorce question brought up and so eloquently supported by dear little Lucy Stone. How proud I felt of her that night! We have no woman who compares with her. Now, Susan, I do beg of you to let the past be past, and to waste no powder on the Woman's State Temperance Society. We have other and bigger fish to fry.

Elizabeth Cady Stanton, letter to Susan B. Anthony, June 20, 1853, in Stanton and Blatch, Elizabeth Cady Stanton, Vol. 2, 52–53.

Anniversary week has the effect of bringing to New York many strange specimens of humanity, masculine and feminine. Antiquated and very homely females made themselves ridiculous by parading the streets in company with hen-pecked husbands, attenuated vegetarians, intemperate Abolitionists and sucking clergymen, who are afraid to say "no" to a strong-minded woman for fear of infringing upon her rights. Shameless as these females—we suppose they *were* females—looked, we should really have thought they would have blushed as they walked the streets to hear the half-suppressed laughter of their own sex and the remarks of men and boys. The Bloomers figured extensively in the anti-slavery amalgamation convention, and were rather looked up to, but their intemperate ideas would not be tolerated in the temperance meeting at the Brick Chapel.

New York Courier, September 1853, in Harper, The Life and Work of Susan B. Anthony, Vol. 1, 91.

This [World's Temperance] convention has completed three of its four business sessions, and the results may be summed up as follows:

First Day—Crowding a woman off the platform.
Second Day—Gagging her.
Third Day—Voting that she shall stay gagged. Having thus disposed of the main question, we presume the incidentals will be finished this morning.

Horace Greeley, New York Tribune, September 7, 1853, in History of Woman Suffrage, Vol. 1, 507.

Mrs. President and Ladies: I do not come here with the slightest intention of offering to the ladies any opposition for mere opposition's sake. If they are proved to have more knowledge and intelligence than men, let them govern! My purpose, ladies, is to try and attain truth, which, I think, will not be found favorable to the views you express. I come, rather, as a matter of intelligence than opposition. I do not come here for the purpose of opposing the

ladies too much; but as the question was not only open yesterday, but still is for discussion, I maintain that if the ladies have more intelligence, and more energy, and science than the male sex, they should rule. I think I can give three reasons why men should vote, and one why woman should not vote. (Cheers).

My first reason is, because there was an original command from God that man should rule. It may be supposed that we are in the garden of Eden now, as in the days of Adam and Eve. Now, it will be remembered, when Adam and Eve fell, Adam, because Eve tempted him, was placed in the garden as its keeper, and it was necessary in those days, as it is now, that woman should be a helpmeet for him; but you recollect that by the eating of the forbidden fruit original sin came into the world. What was the expression of God to Adam. He says in the third chapter of Genesis, 17th verse: "Because thou hast hearkened unto the voice of thy wife, and hast eaten of the tree of which I commanded thee, saying, thou shalt not eat of it: cursed is the ground for thy sake; in sorrow shalt thou eat of it all the days of thy life." Now, permit us to be in the relation that Adam and Eve were originally. It behooves the male sex to answer the objections of the female sex—not that we wish to combat them in public; but it behooves us, as a matter of justice, to put the question on a right foundation. It may be necessary, in ninety-nine cases out of a hundred, that the ladies should be here, but in the hundredth it may be necessary that man should say, "Thus far shalt thou go, and no farther." You see the original cause of sin was because man, being placed in the garden, gave way to woman, and the curse fell upon him; the original cause of sin was because man gave up his judgment to woman; and it may be, if we now give up our rights to woman, some great calamity may fall upon us. Had woman only sinned, perhaps we might still have been in Eden. (Great applause).

My second reason why man should vote is the law of physical force over the woman—because man's strength is greater than woman's.

The third reason is, because if women enter the field of competition with men, it may lead not only to domestic unhappiness, but a great many other ill feelings. And I will give another reason why men should be dictators. If woman says she shall vote, and man says she sha'n't, he is in duty bound to maintain what he says. If he says she sha'n't, that is reason enough why she should not. (Cheers and laughter).

Dr. H. K. Root, Woman's Rights Convention, Broadway Tabernacle, New York City, September 7, 1853, in History of Woman Suffrage, *Vol. 1, 560.*

In September and October, 1853, I traveled 900 miles in Wisconsin, as agent of the Woman's State Temperance Society, speaking in forty-three towns to audiences estimated at 30,000 in the aggregate, people coming in their own conveyances from five to twenty miles. . . .

But arrived at Milwaukee, I found that the popular prejudice against women as public speakers, and especially the advocacy of Woman's Rights, with which I had for years been identified, had been stirred to its most disgusting depths by a reverend gentleman who had preceded us, and who had for years been a salaried "agent at large," of the New York State Temperance Society . . .

The chairman and his deacon led off in a long-drawn debate on sundry matters of no importance, and of less interest to the audience, members of which attempted in vain, by motions and votes, to cut it short. When it had become sufficiently apparent that the gentlemen were "talking against time" to prevent speaking, there were calls for speakers. The chairman replied that it was a "business meeting, but Rev. Mr. ——, from Illinois, would lecture in the evening." Several gentlemen rose to protest. One said he "had walked seven miles that his wife and daughters might ride, to hear the ladies speak." Another had "ridden horseback twelve miles to hear them." A storm was impending; the chairman was prepared; he declared the meeting adjourned and with his deacon left the house.

There was a hurried consultation in the ante-room, which resulted in an urgent request for "Mrs. Nichols to remain and speak in the evening." The speaker noticed for the evening, joined heartily in the request; "half an hour was all the time he wanted." But when the evening came, he insisted that I should speak first, and when I should have given way for him, assured me that he "had made arrangements to speak the next evening," and joined in the "go on, go on!" of the audience. So it was decided that I should remain over the Sabbath, and Mrs. F. return with the friends to Milwaukee. . . .

I had achieved a grateful success; license to "plead the cause of the poor and needy," where, how to do so, without offending oldtime ideas of woman's sphere, had seemed to the women under whose direction I had taken the field, the real question at issue. In consideration of existing prejudices, they had suggested the prudence of silence on the subject of Woman's Rights. And here, on the very threshold of the campaign, I had been compelled to vindicate my right to speak for woman; as a woman, to speak for her from any stand-point of life to which nature, custom, or law had assigned her. I had no choice, no hope of success, but in presenting her case as it stood before God and my own soul. To neither could I turn traitor, and do the work, or satisfy the aspirations of a true and loving woman.

Clarina I. Howard Nichols, recalling events of September–October 1853, in History of Woman Suffrage, *Vol. 1, 178–182.*

The assemblage of rampant women which convened at the Tabernacle yesterday was an interesting phase in the comic history of the nineteenth century.

We saw, in broad daylight, in a public hall in the city of New York, a gathering of unsexed women—unsexed in mind all of them, and many in habiliments—publicly propounding the doctrine that they should be allowed to step out of their appropriate sphere, and mingle in the busy walks of every-day life, to the neglect of those duties which both human and divine law have assigned to them. We do not stop to argue against so ridiculous a set of ideas. We will only inquire who are to perform those duties which we and our fathers before us have imagined belonged solely to women. Is the world to be depopulated? Are there to be no more children? Or are we to adopt the French mode, which is too well known to need explanation?

Another reason why we will not answer the logic which is poured out from the lips of such persons as Lucy Stone, Mrs. Mott, Mrs. Amelia Bloomer, and their male coadjutors, Greeley, Garrison, Oliver, Johnson, Burleigh, and others, is because they themselves do not believe in the truth or feasibility of the doctrines they utter. In some cases eccentricity is a harmless disease; but the idiosyncrasies of these people spring from another source. They admit the principle that fame and infamy are synonymous terms. Disappointed in their struggle for the first, they grasp the last, and at the same time pocket all the money they can wring from the "barren fools" who can be found in any community eager to grasp at any doctrine which is novel, no matter how outrageous it may be. They are continually advertising from their platforms some "Thrilling Narrative," or "Account of the Adventures of a Fugitive," which may be had at the low price of one shilling each, or eight dollars per hundred. Recently they have discovered that the great body of their audiences came only to be amused, and they have therefore imposed an admission fee. Lucy Stone, who is a shrewd Yankee, has gone a step further, and in her management of the business of the "Woman's Rights Convention," has provided for season tickets, to be had at "the extremely low price of two shillings."

It is almost needless for us to say that these women are entirely devoid of personal attractions. They are generally thin maiden ladies, or women who perhaps have been disappointed in their endeavors to appropriate the breeches and the rights of their unlucky lords; the first class having found it utterly impossible to induce any young or old man into the matrimonial noose, have turned out upon the world, and are now endeavoring to revenge themselves upon the sex who have slighted them. The second, having been dethroned from their empire over the hearts of their husbands, for reasons which may easily be imagined, go vagabondizing over the country, boring unfortunate audiences with long essays lacking point or meaning, and amusing only from the impudence displayed by the speakers in putting them forth in a civilized country. They violate the rules of decency and taste by attiring themselves in eccentric habiliments, which hang loosely and inelegantly upon their forms, making that which we have been educated to respect, to love, and to admire, only an object of aversion and disgust. A few of these unfortunate women have awoke from their momentary trance, and quickly returned to the dress of decent society; but we saw yesterday many disciples of the Bloomer school at the Tabernacle. There was yesterday, and there will be to-day, a wide field for all such at the Tabernacle.

The "compliments" showered upon *The Herald* by the wretched Garrison yesterday afternoon, at the Woman's Wrong Convention, fully show that he and his coadjutors, Greeley and the rest, are beginning to feel the truth of our remarks during the time they have been amusing our citizens. His insane attack shows that our course has been the true one.

New York Herald, *September 7, 1853 in* History of Woman Suffrage, *Vol. 1, 557.*

Mr Greeley was among the audience, and in passing through the gallery, it was supposed he remonstrated with the sibillating gentlemen, and a great rumpus was raised. Some cheered the peace-maker, others hissed, the rush collected about the scene of the disturbance, and all proceedings were interrupted. Mrs. Rose suspended her remarks for a few moments, but presently said: "Friends, be seated, and I will continue." The audience would not listen, however. The uproar still continued. Cries of "Order," "Mrs. President," "Put him out," "Hurrah!" hisses, groans, and cheers. Mr. Greeley and a policeman presently succeeded in stilling the tumult, the officer collaring several men and compelling them to keep quiet. Mrs. Rose resumed and continued her remarks.

William Lloyd Garrison, founder of the *Liberator* *(Library of Congress)*

Second Day, Morning Session, Opened at 10 A.M. Mrs. Mott: The uproar and confusion which attended the close of our proceedings of last night, although much to be regretted, as indicating an unreasonable and unreasoning disposition on the part of some, to close their ears against the truth, or rather, to drown its voice by vulgar clamor, yet, when viewed aright, and in some phases, present to us matter of congratulation. I do suppose that never, at any meeting, was public propriety more outraged, than at ours of last evening. I suppose no transactions of a body assembled to deliberate, were ever more outrageously invaded by an attempt to turn them into a mere tumult; yet, though voices were loud and angry, and the evil passions exhibited themselves with much of that quality to affright, which usually, if not always, attends their exhibition, not a scream was heard from any woman, nor did any of the "weaker sex" exhibit the slightest terror, or even alarm at the violent manifestations which invaded the peace of our assemblage.

New York Times, *September 8, 1853, in* History of Woman Suffrage, *Vol. 1, 557.*

The Row of Yesterday—Row No. 3 was a very jolly affair, a regular break-down, at the Woman's Convention. The women had their rights, and more beside. The cause was simply that the rowdyish diathesis is just now prevalent. True, a colored woman made a speech, but there was nothing in that to excite a multitude; she did not speak too low to be heard; she did not insult them with improper language; nor did the audience respond at all insultingly. They did not curse, they only called for "half a dozen on the shell." They did not swear, they only "hurried up that stew." They did wrong, however.

If we had our own way every rascally rowdy among them should have Bloomers of all colors preaching at them by the year—a year for every naughty word they uttered, a score of them for every hiss. Out upon the villains who go to any meeting to disturb it. Let anybody who can hire a house and pay for it have his way, and let none be disturbed; the opposers can stay away. But for us, let us be thankful that in such hot weather there is something to amuse us, something to season our insipid dishes, something to spice our dull days with.

New York Times, *September 9, 1853, in* History of Woman Suffrage, *Vol. 1, 568.*

We do not know whether any of the *gentlemen* who have succeeded in breaking up the Woman's Rights Convention, or of the other *gentlemen* who have succeeded in three sessions at Metropolitan Hall in silencing a regularly appointed and admitted delegate, will ever be ashamed of their passion and hostility, but we have little doubt that some of them will live to understand their own folly. At any rate, they have accomplished a very different thing from what they now suppose. For if it had been their earnest desire to strengthen the cause of Woman's Rights, they could not have done the work half so effectively. Nothing is so good for a weak and unpopular movement as this sort of opposition. Had Antoinette Brown been allowed to speak at Metropolitan Hall, her observations would certainly have occupied but a fraction of the time now wasted, and would have had just the weight proper to their sense and appropriateness, and no more. But instead of this the World's Convention was disturbed and its orators silenced. The consequences will be the mass of the people throughout the country who might otherwise not know of its existence, will have their attention called and their sympathies enlisted in its behalf. So too when Antoinette Brown is put down by Rev. John Chambers and his colleagues, and denied what is her clear right as a member of the Temperance Convention by a vociferous mob, composed, we are sorry to say, very largely of clergymen, every impartial person sees that she is surrounded with a prestige and importance which, whatever her talents as a speaker, she could hardly hope to have attained. Many who question the propriety of woman's appearing in public, will revolt at the gagging of one who had a rights to speak and claimed simply to use it on a proper occasion. There is in the public mind of this country an intuitive love of fair play and free speech, and those who outrage it for any purpose of their own merely reinforce their opponents, and bestow a mighty power on the ideas they hate and fain would suppress.

Daily Tribune, *September 9, 1853, in* History of Woman Suffrage, *Vol. 1, 574–575.*

I can go back forty years; and forty years ago, when most of my present audience were not in, but behind, their cradles, passing a stranger, through the neighboring State of New Jersey, and stopping for dinner at an inn, where the coach stopped, I saw at the bar where I went to pay, a list of the voters of the town stuck up.

My eye ran over it, and I read to my astonishment the names of several women. "What!" I said, "do women vote here?" "Certainly," was the answer, "when they have real estate." Then the question arose in my mind, why should not women vote: Laws are made regulating the tenure of real estate, and the essence of all republicanism is, that they who feel the pressure of the law should have a voice in its enactment.

The Reverend John Pierpont, speech to women's rights convention, New York, 1853, in History of Woman Suffrage, *Vol. 1, 451.*

I once addressed an assemblage of men, and did so without giving previous notice, because I feared the opposition of prejudice. A lady who was among the audience said to me afterward, "How could you do it? My blood ran cold when I saw you up there among those men!" "Why," I asked, "are they bad men?" "Oh, no! my own husband is one of them; but to see a woman mixing among men in promiscuous meetings, it was horrible!"

Lucy Stone, women's rights convention, New York, September 6, 1853, in History of Woman Suffrage, *Vol. 1, 555.*

I have received yours of the 26th, this moment. I do not see that my presence in Cleveland could be of any service. The question to be considered concerns principally woman, and women should mostly consider it. I recognize most thoroughly the right of woman to choose her own sphere of activity and usefulness, and to evoke its proper limitations. If she sees fit to navigate vessels, print newspapers, frame laws, select rulers—any or all of these—I know no principle that justifies man in interposing any impediment to her doing so. The only argument entitled to any weight against the fullest concession of the rights you demand, rests in the assumption that woman does not claim any such rights, but chooses to be ruled, guided, impelled, and have her sphere prescribed for her by man.

I think the present state of our laws respecting property and inheritance, as respects married women, show very clearly that woman ought not to be satisfied with her present position; yet it may be that she is so. If all those who have never given this matter a serious thought are to be considered on the side of conservatism, of course that side must preponderate. Be this as it may, woman alone can, in the present state of the controversy, speak effectively for woman, since none others can speak with authority, or from the depths of a personal experience.

Horace Greeley, letter to C. M. Severance, October 2, 1853, in History of Woman Suffrage, *Vol. 1, 125–126.*

Attended a woman's rights convention which has met here. Never saw anything of the kind before. A Mr. Barker spent most of the morning trying to prove that woman's rights and the Bible cannot agree. The Rev. Antoinette L. Brown replied in the afternoon in defense of the Bible. She says the Bible favors woman's rights. Miss Brown is the best-looking woman in the convention. They appear to have a number of original and pleasing characters upon their platform, among them Miss Lucy Stone—hair short and rolled under like a man's; a tight-fitting velvet waist and linen collar at the throat; bombazine skirt just reaching the knees, and trousers of the same. She is independent in manner and advocates woman's rights in the strongest terms:—scorns the idea of woman asking rights of man, but says she must boldly assert her own rights, and take them in her own strength. Mrs. Ernestine L. Rose, a Polish lady with black eyes and curls, and rosy cheeks, manifests the independent spirit also. She is graceful and witty, and is ready with sharp replies on all occasions. Mrs. Lucretia Mott, a Philadelphia Quaker, is meek in dress but not in spirit. She gets up and hammers away at woman's rights, politics and the Bible, with much vigor, then quietly resumes her knitting, to which she industriously applies herself when not speaking to the audience. She wears the plain Quaker dress and close-fitting white cap. Mrs. Frances D. Gage, the president, is a woman of sound sense and a good writer of prose and poetry. Mrs. Caroline Severance has an easy, pleasing way of speaking. Mr. Charles Burleigh, a Quaker, appears to be an original character. He has long hair, parted in the middle like a woman's, and hanging down his back. He and Miss Stone seem to reverse the usual order of things.

Frances Ellen Burr, fragment of diary entry in a letter to Susan B. Anthony, writing about events of October 7, 1853, in History of Woman Suffrage, *Vol. 3, 335.*

I have been asked by several persons, why no provisions have been made for women to speak, and vote, and act on committees, in these assemblies?" My answer is, "Behold yonder beautiful pilaster of this superb hall! contemplate its pedestal, its shaft, its rich entablature, the crowning glory of the whole. Each and all the parts in their appropriate place contribute to the strength, symmetry, and beauty of the whole. Could I aid in taking down that magnificent entablature from its proud elevation, and placing it in the dust and dirt that surround the pedestal? Neither could I drag down the mother, wife, and daughter, whom we worship as beings of a higher order, on the common plane of life with ourselves.

Professor Davies, Rochester, New York, convention, December 1853, in History of Woman Suffrage, *Vol. 1, 515.*

Can you get any acute lawyer—perhaps judge Hay is the man—sufficiently interested in our movement to look up just eight laws concerning us the very worst in all the code? I can generalize and philosophize easily enough of myself; but the details of the particular laws I need, I have not time to look up. You see, while I am about the house, surrounded by my children, washing dishes, baking, sewing, etc., I can think up many points, but I cannot search books, for my hands as well as my brains would be necessary for that work. If I can, I shall go to Rochester as soon as I have finished my Address and submit it—and the Appeal too for that matter—to Channing's criticism. But prepare yourself to be disappointed in its merits, for I seldom have one hour undisturbed in which to sit down and write. Men who can, when they wish to write a document, shut themselves up for days with their thoughts and their books, know little of what difficulties a woman must surmount to get off a tolerable production.

Elizabeth Cady Stanton, letter to Susan B. Anthony, December 1, 1853, in Stanton and Blatch, Elizabeth Cady Stanton, *Vol. 2, 54–55.*

Woman's Rights.—Mr. Channing and Mrs. Rose pleaded the cause of woman's rights before the Senate Committee of bachelors yesterday [N.Y. state legislature]. The only effect produced was a determination more fixed than ever in the minds of the committee, to remain bachelors in the event of the success of the movement. And who would blame them?

Evening Journal, February 15, 1854, in History of Woman Suffrage, *Vol. 1, 606.*

We were not prepared to see Miss Stone called to account for anything, looking like an abandonment of the cause of the colored people, as was the case in our last week's number; though we know how hard it is for abolitionists to comply, in all cases, with the obvious demands of the principles they have espoused. Circumstances do often arise in this negro-hating age and land, which almost compel them to shut the door in the faces of their sable brothers and sisters, and leave them outside to the buffetings of their enemies. It is not easy for any white abolitionist to stand with, and to share the bitter cup commended to the lips of our outcast race. The wonder is that any are found able to stand this trial of their anti-slavery faith. To do this, the heart must be strong, the eye single, and the whole body full of light. Our friend, Lucy Stone, for whom we cherish sentiments of high esteem, to say nothing of gratitude, has had such a trial, and we wish we could say, she has come out of it with credit to herself and honor to her cause; but facts say otherwise, and so must we . . .

When she learned that colored people were to be excluded from her lecture at Musical Fund hall, it is plain that Miss Stone should have felt herself excluded. The public were invited to attend her lecture; and when she found that to gratify a malignant prejudice, and to brand with inferiority, a people already heartbroken, a hateful proscription was to be observed; the course of duty was plain. As an abolitionist and an honorable woman, she should have said, that neither by word or deed, will I sanction this outrage. But it was too late. Ah! there is the mistake. It would not have been too late had the report of this wrong come to her ear while she was yet speaking. An opportunity would have even then been given her, to have dealt a blow for freedom, upon the hoary head of the monster prejudice, far more stunning and destructive than any which by speech or letter she can now give. Had she left the platform, saying, take your money at the door; I cannot lecture under such proscription, she would have won the respect of everyone whose respect is worth having . . .

It seems to us that one outburst of her noble and womanly eloquence in favor of freedom, such as we have heard from her lips in Corinthian Hall, would have scattered the admiring multitudes that thronged to hear her, quicker than they assembled. But she did not go there to speak for the slave—only for woman. Granted. Still, to speak for woman in a slave State where woman is made merchandise of, sold for the basest of purposes, robbed of all that makes woman honorable, without specifying these abominations, is to preach about the exceeding sinfulness of sin, without defining what sin is. The question as to whether a man or woman can consistently withhold for any purpose his or her convictions on the subject of slavery, has been discussed at much length, and with much ability by the anti-slavery journals of the land, in connection with such names as Cox and Hoby, Kossuth and Father Mathew, to say nothing of the Irish transport, John Mitchel, and the free church deputation.—Kossuth went South to plead for woman; and so far as we know, both pursued the same course, both practically acted on the doctrine of non-intervention. May it not be, that having come, so recently from the South, where she had to say to her anti-slavery principles, stand aside, while I deal out truth, less offensive than anti-slavery.—She was the less disposed to adhere to her principles at Musical Fund Hall.

But whatever may have been the cause, Miss Stone has failed to embrace a good opportunity for testifying against a most unnatural and brutal prejudice; and thus to vindicate the principles of freedom and humanity, by the advocacy of which she has won the esteem and admiration of the noble and good, wherever her name and her deeds are known. This failure, and the insults to which such gentlemen as Chas. L. Reason were subjected, may seem light, and quite unimportant in the eyes of some abolitionists; but we who have to endure the cuffs of pro-slavery, can ill bear to be deserted by our friends.

Frederick Douglass' Paper, *February 17, 1854, in Foner, Frederick Douglass, 67–70.*

... it is well known that the object of these unsexed women is to overthrow the most sacred of our institutions, to set at defiance the Divine law which declares man and wife to be one, and establish on its ruins what will be in fact and in principle but a species of legalized adultery.

Mr. Burnett, speaking to the New York legislature in response to petition of 5,931 people asking that the right to vote be given to women, February 20, 1854, in History of Woman Suffrage, *Vol. 1, 613.*

Amongst the notorieties of the United States, regarded with more than ordinary curiosity by visitors from the Old country, are the Emancipated Women ... ladies who are actively, and we have no doubt earnestly, engaged in battling with men for a professional position and standing in the world. Miss Bremer found them lecturing on platforms, making speeches at crowded public meetings, practicing as physicians and even as barristers, and claiming ... to have votes for representatives in the legislature. The *Una,* which is one of the special organs of this movement, advertises schools of design for women, including lithography and wood-engraving; it advertises female doctors, who may be professionally consulted in their own houses, or called out to visit patients as required; it advertises newspapers and periodicals, written and printed by women; it advertises books, lectures, letters, and speeches, written or delivered by women, on various occasions. The *Una* also contains reports of lectures and addresses by women, which are highly credible compositions ... in one number, Miss Harriet K. Hunt, physician, who seems to be the political leader of the women, publishes a protest, addressed to the authorities of the city of Boston, against being called upon to pay taxes without her right to be represented in the legislature being conceded she holds by the old English dogma, that "Taxation without representation is tyranny." We have also the accounts of the addresses delivered by Lucretia Mott, at Maysville, in Kentucky, a slave state, in which she denounced slavery in strong terms, speaking eloquently for an hour and a half without interruption, except for the cheers of her audience. She also delivered before them another lecture on Women's Rights—her favorite topic. Lucy Stone, it appears, was at the same time delivering lectures on the same subjects at Louisville, and other female lecturers were at work in different parts of the Union. In short, a regular propaganda on the subject of Women's Rights seems to be fairly at work. We have already, in a previous article, spoken of the political view of this question, and need not here repeat our remarks. Suffice it to say, that we believe those American women greatly overestimate the advantages derivable from mere political privileges conferred on their sex, such as the right of voting for members of Congress.

Eliza Cook's Journal, *No. 252, February 25, 1854, 1.*

Thus has ended the first Convention of women designed to influence political action. On Monday the 6,000 petitions will be presented in the Legislature, and the address be placed on the members' tables. Whatever may be the final disposition of the matter, it is well to make a note of this first effort to influence the Legislature. It was originated by Miss Susan B. Anthony, and has been managed financially by her.

Albany Transcript, *March 4, 1854, in* History of Woman Suffrage, *Vol. 1, 606.*

WOMEN IN THE SENATE CHAMBER.—The Senate was alarmed yesterday afternoon. It surrendered to progress. The Select Committee to whom women's rights petitions had been referred, took their seats on the president's platform, looking as grave as possible. Never had Senators Robertson, Yost and Field been in such responsible circumstances. They were calm, but evidently felt themselves in great peril. In the circle of the Senate, ranged in invincible row, sat seven ladies, from quite pretty, to quite plain.

Albany Register, *March 4, 1854, in* History of Woman Suffrage, *Vol. 1, 606–607.*

THE RIGHTS OF WOMEN DEFINED BY THEMSELVES.—Miss Anthony and Mrs. Rose before the House Committee, March 3d. The Committee took their seats in the clerks desk, and the ladies took possession of the members seats, filling the chamber, many members of the legislature being present. Miss Anthony presented a paper prepared by Judge William Hay, of Saratoga, asking that husband and wife should be tenants in common property without survivorship, but with a partition on the death of one; that a wife shall be competent to discharge trusts and power the same as a single woman: that the statute in respect to a married woman's property descend as though she had been unmarried; that married women shall be entitled to execute letters testamentary, and of administration; that married women shall have power to make contracts and transact business as though unmarried; that they shall be entitled to their own earnings, subject to their proportional liability for support of children; that postnuptial acquisition shall belong equally to husband and wife; that married women shall stand on the same footing with single women, as parties or witnesses in legal proceedings; that they shall be sole quardians of their minor children; that the homestead shall be inviolable and inalienable for widows and children; that

the laws in relation to divorce shall be revised, and drunkenness made cause for absolute divorce; that better care shall be taken of single women's property, that their rights may not be lost through ignorance, that the preference of males in descent of reat estate shall be abolished; that women shall exercise "the right of suffrage," and be eligible to all offices, occupations, and professions; entitled to act as jurors; eligible to all public offices; that courts of conciliation shall be organized as peace-makers; that a law shall be enacted extending the masculine designation in all statues of the State to females.

Albany Argus, *March 4, 1854, in* History of Woman Suffrage, *Vol. 1, 607.*

Woman's Rights in the Legislature.—While the feminine propagandists of women's rights confined themselves to the exhibition of short petticoats and long-legged boots and to the holding of Conventions, and speech-making in concert-rooms, the people were disposed to be amused by them, as they are by the wit of the clown in the circus, or the performances of Punch and Judy on fair days, or the minstrelsy of gentlemen with blackened faces, on banjos, the tambourine, and bones. But the joke is becoming stale. People are getting cloyed with these performances, and are looking for some healthier and more intellectual amusement. The ludicrous is wearing away, and disgust is taking the place of pleasurable sensations, arising from the novelty of this new phase of hypocrisy and infidel fanaticism. People are beginning to inquire how far public sentiment should sanction or tolerate these unsexed women, who make a scoff of religion, who repudiate the Bible and blaspheme God; who would step out from the true sphere of the mother, the wife, and the daughter, and taking upon themselves the duties and the business of men, stalk into the public gaze, and by engaging in the politics, the rough controversies, and trafficking of the world, upheave existing institutions, and overturn all the social relations of life.

It is a melancholy reflection, that among our American women who have been educated to better things, there should be found any who are willing to follow the lead of such foreign propagandists as the ringleted, glove-handed exotic, Ernestine L. Rose. We can understand how such men as the Rev. Mr. May, or the sleek-headed Dr. Channing may be deluded by her to becoming her disciples. They are not the first instances of infatuation that may overtake weak-minded men, if they are honest in their devotion to her and her doctrines. Nor would they be the first examples of a low ambition that seeks notoriety as a substitute for true fame, if they are dishonest. Such men there are always, and honest or dishonest, their true position is that of being tied to the apron-strings of some "strong-minded woman," and to be exhibited as rare specimens of human wickedness, or human weakness and folly. But, that one educated American woman should become her disciple and follow her infidel and insane teachings, is a marvel.

Ernestine L. Rose came to this country, as she says, from Poland, whence she was compelled to fly in pursuit of freedom. Seeing her course here, we can well imagine this to be true. In no other country in the world, save possibly one, would her infidel propagandism and preachings in regard to the social relations of life be tolerated. She would be prohibited by the powers of government from her efforts to obliterate from the world the religion of the Cross—to banish the Bible as a text-book of faith, and to overturn social institutions that have existed through all political and governmental revolutions from the remotest time. The strong hand of the law would be laid upon her, and she would be compelled back to her woman's sphere. But in this country, such is the freedom of our institutions, and we rejoice that it should be so, that she, and such as she, can give their genius for intrigue full sway. They can exhibit their flowing ringlets and beautiful hands, their winning smiles and charming stage attitudes to admiring audiences, who, while they are willing to be amused, are in the main safe from their corrupting theories and demoralizing propagandism.

The laws and the theory of our government suppose that the people are capable of taking care of themselves, and hence need no protection against the wiles of domestic or foreign mountebanks, whether in petticoats or in breeches and boots. But it never was contemplated that these exotic agitators would come up to our legislators and ask for the passage of laws upholding and sanctioning their wild and foolish doctrines. That was a stretch of folly, a flight of impudence which was hardly regarded as possible. It was to be imagined, of course, that they would enlist as their followers, here and there one among the restless old maids and visionary wives who chanced to be unevenly tempered, as well as unevenly yoked. It was

also to be assumed, as within the range of possibility, that they might bring within the sphere of their attractions, weak-minded, restless men, who think in their vanity that they have been marked out for great things, and failed to be appreciated by the world, men who comb their hair smoothly back, and with fingers locked across their stomachs, speak in a soft voice, and with upturned eyes. But no man supposed they would abandon their "private theatricals" and walk up to the Capitol, and insist that the performances shall be held in legislative halls. And yet so it is.

This Mrs. Ernestine L. Rose, with a train of followers, like a great kite with a very long tail, has, for a week, been amusing Senatorial and Assembly Committees, with her woman's rights performances, free of charge, unless the waste of time that might be better employed in the necessary and legitimate business of legislation, may be regarded as a charge. Those committees have sat for hours, grave and solemn as owls, listening to the outpourings of fanaticism and folly of this Polish propagandist, Mrs. Ernestine L. Rose, and her followers in pantalets and short gowns. The people outside, and especially those interested in the progress of legislation, are beginning to ask one another how long this farce is to continue. How long this most egregious and ridiculous humbug is to be permitted to obstruct the progress of business before the Committees and the Houses, and whether Mrs. Ernestine L. Rose and her followers ought not to be satisfied with the notoriety they have already attained. The great body of the people regard Mrs. Rose and her followers as making themselves simply ridiculous, and there is some danger that these legislative committees will make themselves so too.

Albany Register, *March 7, 1854, in* History of Woman Suffrage, *Vol. 1, 609.*

Going it Blind.—The editor of *The State Register* is going it blind on woman's rights matters. He was out on Monday with a half column leader that touched everything except the matter in dispute. We quote a paragraph:

"People are beginning to inquire how far public sentiment should sanction or tolerate these unsexed women, who make a scoff at religion, who repudiate the Bible, and blaspheme God; who would step out from the true sphere of the mother, the wife, and the daughter, and take upon themselves the duties and the business of men; stalk into the public gaze, and by engaging in the politics, the rough controversies, and trafficking of the world, upheave existing institutions, and overturn all the social relations of life."

Albany Knickerbocker, *March 8, 1854, in* History of Woman Suffrage, *Vol. 1, 611.*

I have read your article in relation to Lucy Stone, and her course at Musical Fund Hall, and also Charles L. Reason's letter on the same subject. I heartily endorse every word, both of the article and the letter. Having thus unqualifiedly endorsed your doctrine, allow me to say a few words in regard to its application . . ."But suppose ye that" Lucy Stone "is a sinner above other" reformers? "I tell you *nay.*" Did you, my brother, ever take part in a meeting or convention, in which one class of community (the class who do not usually dress in "male costume") were not expected to take a part, from whose committees &c., they were carefully excluded? Did you ever speak in a church, on any subject, from which any other person wishing to speak on another subject would be excluded? I take it for granted that it is no worse to shut a man out of your house, than to admit him and then thrust a gag in his mouth! I presume you frequently lecture on anti-slavery in houses that would be closed against an avowed Infidel or Spiritualist. I do not know that you would do any of these things but if you would not, you are more consistent than a great many other very good men.

Francis Bary, letter to Frederick Douglass, March 17, 1854, in Foner, Frederick Douglass, *70.*

The Select Committee, to whom was referred the various petitions requesting "the Senate and Assembly of the State of New York to appoint a joint committee to revise the Statutes of New York, and to propose such amendments as will fully establish the legal equality of women with men," report: That they have examined the said petition, and have heard and considered the suggestions of persons who have appeared before them on behalf of the petitioners . . .

A higher power than that from which emanates legislative enactments has given forth the mandate that man and woman shall not be equal; that there shall be inequalities by which each in their own appropriate sphere shall have precedence to the other; and each alike shall be superior or inferior as they well or ill act the part assigned them. Both alike are the subjects of Government, equally entitled to its protection; and civil power must, in its enactments, recognize this inequality. We can not obliterate it if we would, and legal inequalities must follow.

The education of woman has not been the result of statutes, but of civilization and Christianity; and her elevation, great as it has been, has only corresponded with that of man under the same influences. She owes no more to these causes than he does. The true elevation of the sexes will always correspond. But elevation, instead of destroying, shows more palpably those inherent inequalities, and makes more apparent the harmony and happiness which the Creator designed to accomplish by them.

Your Committee will not attempt to prescribe, or, rather, they will not attempt to define the province and peculiar sphere which a power that we can not overrule has prescribed for the different sexes. Every well-regulated home and household in the land affords an example illustrative of what is woman's proper sphere, as also that of man. Government has its miniature as well as its foundation in the homes of our country; and as in governments there must be some recognized head to control and direct, so must there also be a controlling and directing power in every smaller association; there must be some one to act and to be acted with as the embodiment of the persons associated. In the formation of governments, the manner in which the common interest shall be embodied and represented is a matter of conventional arrangement; but in the family an influence more potent than that of contracts and conventionalities, and which everywhere underlies humanity, has indicated that the husband shall fill the necessity which exists for a head. Dissension and distraction quickly arise when this necessity is not answered. The harmony of life, the real interest of both husband and wife, and of all dependent upon them, require it. In obedience to that requirement and necessity, the husband is the head—the representative of the family . . .

In conclusion, your Committee recommend that the prayer of the petitioners be denied; and they ask leave to introduce a bill corresponding with the suggestions hereinbefore contained.

Report of the Select Committee, Assembly of the State of New York, March 27, 1854, in History of Woman Suffrage, *Vol. 1, 616–618.*

Mrs. Matilda Joslyn Gage, a medium-sized, lady-like looking woman, dressed in a tasty plum-colored silk with two flounces, made the first address upon some of the defects in the marriage laws, quoting Story, Kent, and Blackstone.

Daily Saratogian, *August 19, 1854, in* History of Woman Suffrage, *Vol. 1, 622.*

In October, 1854, with my two eldest sons, I joined a company of two hundred and twenty-five men, women, and children, emigrants from the East to Kansas. In our passage up the Missouri River I gave two lectures by invitation of a committee of emigrants and Captain Choteau and brother, owners of the boat. A pious M.D. was terribly shocked at the prospect, and hurried his young wife to bed, but returned to the cabin himself in good time to hear. As the position was quite central, and I wished to be heard distinctly by the crowd which occupied all the standing room around the cabin, I took my stand opposite the Doctor's berth. Next morning, poor man! his wife was an outspoken advocate of woman's rights. The next evening she punched his ribs vigorously, at every point made for suffrage, which was the subject of my second lecture.

The 1st of November, 1854—a day never to be forgotten—heaven and earth clasped hands in silent benedictions on that band of immigrants, some on foot, some on horseback, women and children, seventy-five in number, with the company's baggage, in ox-carts and wagons drawn by the fat, the broken-down, and the indifferent "hacks" of wondering, scowling Missouri, scattered all along the prairie road from Kansas City to Lawrence, the Mecca of their pilgrimage.

Clarina Howard Nichols, recalling events of October—November 1854, in History of Woman Suffrage, *Vol. 1, 185.*

It was my privilege to celebrate May day by officiating at a wedding in a farm-house among the hills of West Brookfield. The bridegroom was a man of tried worth, a leader in the Western Anti-Slavery Movement; and the bride was one whose fair name is known throughout the nation; one whose rare intellectual qualities are excelled by the private beauty of her heart and life.

I never perform the marriage ceremony without a renewed sense of the iniquity of our present system of laws in respect to marriage; a system by which "man and wife are one, and that one is the husband."

It was with my hearty concurrence, therefore, that the following protest was read and signed, as a part of the nuptial ceremony; and I send it to you, that others may be induced to do likewise . . .

Protest

While acknowledging our mutual affection by publicly assuming the relationship of husband and wife, yet in justice to ourselves and a great principle, we deem it a duty to declare that this act on our part implies no sanction of, nor promise of voluntary obedience to such of the present laws of marriage, as refuse to recognize the wife as an independent, rational being, while they confer upon the husband an injurious and unnatural superiority, investing him with legal powers which no honorable man would exercise, and which no man should possess. We protest especially against the laws which give to the husband:

1. The custody of the wife's person.
2. The exclusive control and guardianship of their children.
3. The sole ownership of her personal, and use of her real estate, unless previously settled upon her, or placed in the hands of trustees, as in the case of minors, lunatics, and idiots.
4. The absolute right to the product of her industry.
5. Also against laws which give to the widower so much larger and more permanent an interest in the property of his deceased wife, than they give to the widow in that of the deceased husband.
6. Finally, against the whole system by which "the legal existence of the wife is suspended during marriage," so that in most States, she neither has a legal part in the choice of her residence, nor can she make a will, nor sue or be sued in her own name, nor inherit property. We believe that personal independence and equal human rights can never be forfeited, except for crime; that marriage should be an equal and permanent partnership, and so recognized by law; that until it is so recognized, married partners should provide against the radical injustice of present laws, by every means in their power.

We believe that where domestic difficulties arise, no appeal should be made to legal tribunals under existing laws, but that all difficulties should be submitted to the equitable adjustment of arbitrators mutually chosen.

Thus reverencing the law, we enter our protest against rules and customs which are unworthy of the name, since they violate justice, the essence of law.

Signed, Henry B. Blackwell,
Lucy Stone
Rev. Thomas Wentworth Higginson, in History of Woman Suffrage, *Vol. 1, 260–261.*

[Paulina Wright Davis] was roused to thought on woman's position by a discussion in the church as to whether women should be permitted to speak and pray in promiscuous assemblies. Some of the deacons protested against a practice, in ordinary times, that might be tolerated during seasons of revival. But those who had discovered their gifts in times of excitement were not so easily remanded to silence; and thus the Church was distracted than as now with troublesome woman's rights....

When her husband was elected to Congress, in 1853, she accompanied him to Washington and made many valuable acquaintances. As she had already called the first National Woman Suffrage Convention, and started *The Una,* the first distinctively woman's rights journal ever published, and was supposed to be a fair representative of the odious, strong-minded "Bloomer," the ladies at their hotel, after some consultation, decided to ignore her, as far as possible. But a lady of her fine appearance, attractive manners, and general intelligence, whose society was sought by the most cultivated gentlemen in the house, could not be very long ostracised by the ladies....

For nearly three years Mrs. Davis continued *The Una,* publishing it entirely at her own expense. It took the broadest ground claimed to-day: individual

"Shake Hands?" a painting by Lily M. Spencer, shows the unrationalized kitchen that Beecher wanted to reform. *(Library of Congress)*

freedom in the State, the Church, and the home; woman's equality and suffrage a natural right . . .

Elizabeth Cady Stanton, recalling events in the 1850s in the life of Paulina Wright Davis, 1873, in History of Woman Suffrage, *Vol. 1, 284–287.*

6

A Whiff of Scandal—
Divorce and Reform
1855–1860

THE HISTORICAL CONTEXT

The years preceding the Civil War were as divisive for the women's movement as for the United States as a whole. Marriages and pregnancies drained the energies of the leaders, leaving most of the work to Susan B. Anthony. In 1856 Elizabeth Cady Stanton, now in her forties, gave birth to her sixth child, Harriot Eaton Stanton. In 1857 Lucy Stone, married to abolitionist Henry Blackwell, gave birth to Alice Stone Blackwell. And that same year, Antoinette Brown, wife of Samuel Blackwell, delivered the first of her seven children.

So it was a lonely Susan B. Anthony who traveled New York State in 1855 to gather petitions for the state legislature to extend the Married Woman's Property Act. Her petitions urged that women be allowed to assume custody of their children in case of divorce, control their own earnings, and have the right to vote. Traveling the country alone was something few women in America would have dared to do at that time, yet Anthony left home on Christmas Day 1854 with only $50 in her pocket. She made all her own arrangements at a time when women who traveled alone might be refused service in a dining room. In the 1850s couples traveling by train ate separately. Men would leave the train and go into the station to eat, while women remained in the car to eat a meal brought from home. Anthony was one of the few women who would leave the train and walk up and down the platform for exercise, a brave action for a woman of her day.

It was one of the snowiest winters on record. Snow blocked the roads and chilled her feet. At times she had to be helped to the stage. Many towns were some distance from the railroad, and Anthony could only reach them by sleigh. Holding her first meeting in Mayville, Chautauqua County, she noted in her expense journal: "56 cents for four pounds of candles to light the courthouse."[1]

After a long trip, Anthony would arrive in an unheated room and have to break the ice in a pitcher in order to bathe. Despite this, she held a meeting every other day. In the afternoons she would read part of her speech, then begin organizing. In the evenings she read the other half. Usually there would be no woman willing to take on a leadership role when she left a community.

When she reached Rochester, Anthony had a pair of snow boots made. She had been suffering from the deep snows and was in pain. So she adopted a "water cure"; she let cold water run over her foot to numb it, then wrapped it up. One night this treatment left her with pain that traveled all the way up her back. The next day she could not move. But having promised to speak in Canton, she rode 17 miles to the town by sleigh, doubled up in agony. She held two meetings and had to wake up the next day at 4:00 A.M. to take a stage to Watertown. From there she took a train into the city and went to a hotel, where she took an ice cold bath and went to bed, ready to speak the next day.

Most towns had never heard a woman speak before, and people turned out by the wagonload to see Anthony. But elsewhere the audience was small. One day Anthony spoke at Riverhead, Long Island (New York). After a long wait, about 12 men joined her. As she spoke, she noticed a woman peeping in, then quickly withdrawing. This went on for the remainder of the speech. The men liked her speech and signed her tracts. After this nod of approval, their wives attended the evening session.

By May 1 Anthony had visited 54 counties and sold 20,000 pamphlets. She received $2,367 in income but spent $2,291 for a balance of $76.

In February 1856 Anthony presented her petitions to the state legislature in Albany. They were referred to the Senate Judiciary Committee, chaired by the distinguished lawyer Samuel G. Foote. Despite the hard work they represented, Foote made light of the petitions. In a notorious statement received with "roars of laughter," according to the *Albany Register,* he quipped: "The Committee is composed of married and single gentlemen. The bachelors, with becoming diffidence, have left the subject pretty much to the married gentlemen. They have considered it with the aid of the light they have before them and the experience married life has given them. Thus aided, they are enabled to state that the ladies always have the best place and choicest tidbit at the table. They have the best seat in the cars, carriages and sleighs; the warmest place in winter and the coolest in summer. They have their choice on which side of the bed they will lie, front or back. A lady's dress costs three times as much as that of a gentleman; and at the present time, with the prevailing fashion, one lady occupies three times as much space in the world as a gentleman. It has thus appeared to the married gentlemen of your committee . . . that if there is an inequality of oppression in this case, the gentlemen are the sufferers."[2]

This blow made Anthony more determined. In May 1856 she asked Stanton to write a speech on the need for coeducation that Anthony would give at the State Teachers' Association meeting in August. At the Stanton home, the two took turns baby-sitting and writing until the speech was done. To prove herself equal to a male speaker, Anthony walked the house for hours memorizing her talk.

In fall 1856 Anthony threw herself into finding speakers for the next annual women's rights convention. But the country was distracted by the looming war, and help was hard to find. Motherhood kept many of the leaders from attending. Horace Greeley refused to speak because he thought the women had become too radical. He wrote to Anthony that he could not publish her notices in the *Tribune* because his political enemies would take advantage of the "anti-Bible, anti-union" doctrines that the women's conventions put forth. Yet

Stanton's cousin Gerrit Smith believed the women were not radical enough. He would neither speak nor write a letter to be read at the conference because he knew his views would be "offensive." He believed that women should go to work to gain equality. But to work, they needed to give up their feminine graces and dresses, and this they would not do. Despite these difficulties, on November 25 and 26, 1856, the Seventh National Woman's Convention met in the Broadway Tabernacle in New York. Wendell Phillips presided.

Throughout the late 1850s the antislavery fight heated up, draining energy from other reform work. Gerrit Smith withheld his usual generous contribution, as did other potential contributors during the economic downturn of 1857. The public was not in a generous mood so the women chose not to hold their annual convention.

Among the other distractions in 1857 and 1858 was the emerging Republican Party, a coalition of the loosely-knit antislavery forces. The *Dred Scott* decision, which declared that enslaved people were "not persons but property" and that the Missouri Compromise was unconstitutional, stirred up anger and resentment as it placed those who opposed the extension of slavery into the territories in the position of being outside the Constitution. Yet the Republicans were not ready to support immediate emancipation even if it meant sacrificing the Union. This is what Susan B. Anthony and the Garrisonians championed, and because of their radicalism, they faced the hatred of the proslavery people and the newly emerging Republicans everywhere they spoke. Thus 1857 was perhaps the worst time to promote the Garrisonian slogan "No Union with Slaveholders."

After 1857, contributions and momentum increased to enable the movement to hold an eighth national convention in 1858. Significantly, it was held in New York City at the same time as the American Anti-Slavery Society meetings, and the leaderships decided to pool their budgets and energies on behalf of both causes.

Unhappy with her increased "domestic bondage," Stanton nevertheless gave birth in 1859, at the age of 43, to the last of her children. She envied her husband's travel and public activities; he could not have been happy with her stepped-up campaign for divorce reform. Lucy Stone and Susan B. Anthony were less extreme on this issue. Still divorce was becoming a topic of debate during the late 1850s. By 1859 Indiana passed a bill, introduced by Robert Dale Owen, that broadened the grounds for divorce beyond adultery. Now drunkenness, cruelty, and abandonment could be reasons for divorce.

New York followed suit with the introduction of a similar bill in 1860. Stanton addressed the legislature and drew a good deal of criticism for her efforts. The bill was defeated in the Senate by four votes.

For many years Stanton was the only woman in America who wrote and spoke on the subject of divorce. But through midcentury the courts viewed grounds for divorce very strictly. The 1845 case of *Shaw v. Shaw* in nearby Connecticut provides one example. Connecticut law held that if a wife were in physical danger in her own home—meaning if she were threatened by injury or death—her husband had to support her somewhere else. Daniel Shaw threatened and intimidated his wife Emeline, so in 1844 she left him to live with her mother and later sued him in court for divorce. In 1845 at the superior court in Litchfield, she claimed that Daniel was violently jealous and would not allow her to visit her friends or family—particularly her mother or his. Daniel turned away her relatives when they came to visit, locking his wife in her room to keep them apart. He forced Emeline to have intercourse with him when she did not wish to do so. And he used obscene language to her in front of her children and falsely accused her of infidelity. Daniel's lawyers argued that he was not guilty of "cruelty" because this word meant "personal violence resulting in extreme suffering or death." Chief Justice Williams read the opinion of the court, raising the question of what constituted intolerable cruelty:

> The first thing to be considered . . . is the language made use of, by this defendant, towards his wife. It is vulgar, obscene, harsh. . . . [It was], however, accompanied by no act or menace indicating violence to her person . . . but when we look further, and find that he was jealous of his wife, it is not so much to be wondered at, as we have been told by authority, that "jealousy is the rage of man." The unfortunate victim of this passion is indeed to be pitied; but the law furnishes no remedy for conduct like this.

Refusing to let Emeline visit her own mother and relatives, was "harsh, if not cruel," Williams said, but patriarchy must be upheld:

> [A]s the husband must have the right to say who shall be admitted to his house, and in some measure to regulate the intercourse of his wife, the court cannot draw a line by which his authority can be restrained.

The chief justice added that even *unreasonable* exercise of a husband's authority was not the kind of cruelty that would warrant a separation. He attributed Daniel's rape of his wife to his ignorance of Emeline's health. Daniel did not *know* he was hurting her, and besides, she suffered no "real" harm. In conclusion, the court refused to allow Emeline either to divorce or separate from Daniel.[3]

In 1860 Stanton decided that divorce would be the theme of her speech before the Tenth National Woman's Rights Convention in New York. Hearing this, Lucy Stone immediately sent word she would not appear with her on the program. Speaking for more than an hour, Stanton compared the status of women with that of slaves and urged the legislature to make marriage more difficult and divorce easier. Most shocking, Stanton demanded divorce for reasons of simple incompatibility. This triggered a fight that lasted for the entire session. Horace Greeley and Wendell Phillips joined the majority against Stanton, arguing that her speech and resolutions should not be recorded. So provocative was the topic that Lucy Stone preferred to see it treated separately along with infanticide, abortion, and similar subjects. Stanton was seated next to Rev. Samuel Longfellow, brother of Henry Wadsworth Longfellow, who whispered, "Nevertheless you are right, and the convention will sustain you." Ernestine Rose and Susan B. Anthony eventually supported her, yet the resolutions were tabled and recorded.[4]

Stanton was universally criticized by the public. Both the press and her friends ridiculed the session. But Stanton fought this issue publicly until the Republican National Convention of 1860, which overshadowed all other news by choosing moderate Abraham Lincoln as its candidate for president.

The Republicans opposed the extension of slavery into the territories, thereby attracting most abolitionists to their party. But Susan B. Anthony, who had lectured for the American Anti-Slavery Society since 1856, as well as the Garrisonians, wanted immediate emancipation. They thought Lincoln had favored the Fugitive Slave Law and did not support black citizenship. But Henry and Elizabeth Stanton supported the Republicans, and Henry joined their campaign. Both welcomed the idea of southern secession. Only Susan B. Anthony foresaw the setback to the organized struggle for woman's rights that war would bring.

CHRONICLE OF EVENTS

1855

The first hospital to treat women's diseases is established by a group of 30 women in New York City. Known as the "birthplace of gynecology," Women's Hospital is now part of St. Luke's Complex.

January: Anne E. McDowell starts the *Woman's Advocate,* the first newspaper staffed by women, who worked as typesetters and printers.

January–May: Susan B. Anthony canvasses 54 counties in New York to gather petitions favoring the extension of the Married Woman's Property Act.

Clarina Howard Nichols of Vermont speaks in Wisconsin and Kansas.

February 14: Elizabeth Cady Stanton appears before a joint judicial committee of both legislative houses in New York, the first woman to do so. Her petitions for an expanded Married Woman's Property Act fail to move lawmakers.

February 14–15: The Albany convention is held by feminists in New York.

May 1: Lucy Stone and Henry Blackwell are married. Stone keeps her own name, inspiring the term "Lucy Stoner" for married women who use their own names. They read a protest at their wedding against marriage laws.

October 17–18: Sixth National Woman's Rights Convention is held in Cincinnati, Ohio.

1856

Mary Ann Patten becomes the first woman to maneuver a clipper ship, the *Neptune's Car,* a 216-foot, 1,616-ton vessel.

Charlotte L. Forten becomes the first black teacher of white children in Salem, Massachusetts.

January 24: Antoinette Brown marries Samuel Blackwell, brother of Dr. Elizabeth Blackwell.

February: Susan B. Anthony sets out to present her petitions to the state legislature.

November 15–26: Seventh National Woman's Rights Convention meets at Broadway Tabernacle in New York. Elizabeth Cady Stanton sends her annual letter to the convention in which she condemns marriage and defends divorce. Lucy Stone presides.

1857

Clarina Howard Nichols moves to Kansas; she speaks in Missouri and later in California.

Dr. Elizabeth Blackwell opens the New York University Infirmary for Women and Children, staffed entirely by women.

The New York Married Woman's Property Act is amended.

Annual national convention is not held, the only year missed from 1850 to 1860.

September 14: Alice Stone Blackwell, daughter of Lucy Stone, is born.

October 28: Martha Carey Thomas, feminist, is born.

1858

Lucy Stone allows the auction of her household goods in lieu of taxes to protest her lack of the vote. She is the first woman arrested for civil disobedience.

Women leaders organize the eighth national convention to coincide with an annual meeting of the American Anti-Slavery Society in New York City.

Elizabeth Cady Stanton with her daughter Harriot in 1856 *(Library of Congress)*

1859

Susan B. Anthony spends six weeks in Albany, lobbying members of the New York state senate for the measure further enlarging the Married Woman's Property Act.

Elizabeth Cady Stanton's cousin, Gerrit Smith, buys arms for John Brown's raid on Harpers Ferry and is known as one of the "Secret Six."

John Brown, hero to abolitionists, is sentenced to die for his raid in October on Harpers Ferry. Gerrit Smith is implicated because of his donations to Brown. He has himself briefly committed to an insane asylum.

The Indiana legislature passes a controversial divorce reform bill, adding desertion, drunkenness, and cruelty as grounds for divorce.

Feminists Clarina Nichols, Mother Armstrong, and Mary Tenney Gray attend the Wyandotte, Kansas, constitutional convention representing Shawnee County and Douglass County women's groups. They try to have the vote for women included in the state constitution. They succeed in getting women's right to equal custody of their children and ownership of property protected under the constitution.

Twenty-five Kansas men and women meet to form the first association to gain political freedom for women.

May 27: New England women's rights convention is held in Mercantile Hall in Boston.

October 31: Judge Daniel Cady, Elizabeth Cady Stanton's father, dies, leaving her a considerable amount of cash and real estate after earlier disinheriting her for her suffrage work.

1860

Mary (Rice) Livermore is the first woman to attain the position of news reporter at a major political convention, the Republican National Convention in Chicago, Illinois, which nominates Abraham Lincoln for president.

Indiana University becomes the first to permit equal rights for women by enrolling Sarah Parke Morrison and later granting her a degree.

The New York legislature introduces a divorce bill similar to Indiana's; it loses by four votes in the senate.

March 19: Elizabeth Cady Stanton addresses the judiciary committee of both houses of the New York legislature in Albany.

March 20: New York State passes an expansion of the Married Woman's Property Act of 1848, called "An Act Concerning the Rights and Liabilities of Husband and Wife." The act is a major reform in the law concerning the property rights of married women and demonstrates the willingness of the state houses to pass reform legislation that corrected some of the inequities of the common law toward wives as interpreted by the courts. The new law improves inheritance laws for wives and gives mothers joint guardianship over their children.

May 8: Elizabeth Cady Stanton addresses opening session of annual American Anti-Slavery Society meetings.

May 10: Elizabeth Cady Stanton, in Tenth Annual Woman's Rights Convention, held in New York City, shocks the audience by recommending liberalized divorce laws.

September 6: Jane Addams, social worker and pacifist, is born in Cedarville, Illinois.

EYEWITNESS TESTIMONY

At the appointed hour a lady, unattended and unheralded, quietly glided in and ascended the platform. She was as easy and self-possessed as a lady should always be when performing a plain duty, even under 600 curious eyes. Her situation would have been trying to a non-self-reliant woman, for there was no volunteer co-operator. The custodian of the hall, with his stereotyped stupidity, had dumped some tracts and papers on the platform. The unfriended Miss Anthony gathered them up composedly, placed them on a table disposedly, put her decorous shawl on one chair and a very exemplary bonnet on another, sat a moment, smoothed her hair discreetly, and then deliberately walked to the table and addressed the audience. She wore a becoming black silk dress, gracefully draped and made with a basque waist. She appears to be somewhere about the confines of the fourth luster in age, of pleasing rather than pretty features, decidedly expressive countenance, rich brown hair very effectively and not at all elaborately arranged, neither too tall nor too short, too plump nor too thin—in brief one of those juste milieu persons, the perfection of common sense physically exhibited. Miss Anthony's oratory is in keeping with all her belongings, her voice well modulated and musical, her enunciation distinct, her style earnest and impressive, her language pure and unexaggerated.

> Rondout Courier, *winter ca. January 1855, in Harper,* Life and Work of Susan B. Anthony, *Vol. 1, 124.*

At Olean, not a church or schoolhouse could be obtained for the lecture and it would have had to be abandoned had not the landlord, Mr. Comstock, given the use of his dining room. . . .

At Angelica, nine towns represented; crowded house, courtroom carpeted with sawdust. A young Methodist minister gave his name for the petition, but one of his wealthy parishioners told him he should leave the church unless it was withdrawn. . . .

At Corning, none of the ministers would give the notice of our meeting, which so incensed some of the men that they went to the printing office, struck off handbills and had boys standing at the door of the churches as the people passed out. Who was responsible for the Sabbath breaking? . . .

At Elmira, took tea at Mrs. Holbrook's with Rev. Thomas K. Beecher. His theology, as set forth that evening, is a dark and hopeless one . . . I find great apathy wherever the clergy are opposed to the advancement of women.

> *Susan B. Anthony, diary entry, winter 1855, in Harper,* Life and Work of Susan B. Anthony, *Vol. 1, 125.*

When, after reading your letter, I asked my husband if I might go to Saratoga [for the woman's rights convention in 1855], only think of it! He did not give me permission, but told me to ask Lucy Stone. I can't get him to govern me at all . . . The Washington Union, noticing our marriage, said "We understand that Mr. Blackwell, who last fall assaulted a southern lady and stole her slave, has lately married Miss Lucy Stone. Justice, though sometimes tardy, never fails to overtake her victim." They evidently think him well punished . . .

> *Lucy Stone, letter to Susan B. Anthony, summer 1855, in Harper,* Life and Work of Susan B. Anthony, *Vol. 1, 130.*

I wish that I were as free as you and I would stump the state in a twinkling. But I am not, and what is more, I passed through a terrible scourging when last at my father's. I cannot tell you how deep the iron entered my soul. I never felt more keenly the degradation of my sex. To think that all in me of which my father would have felt a proper pride had I been a man, is deeply mortifying to him because I am a woman. That thought has stung me to a fierce decision—to speak as soon as I can do myself credit. But the pressure on me just now is too great. Henry sides with my friends, who oppose me in all that is dearest to my heart. They are not willing that I should write even on the woman question. But I will both write and speak. I wish you to consider this letter strictly confidential. Sometimes, Susan, I struggle in deep waters . . .

> *Elizabeth Cady Stanton, letter to Susan B. Anthony, September 20, 1855, in Stanton and Blatch,* Elizabeth Cady Stanton, *Vol. 2, 59–76.*

Your letter full of plans reaches me here. I wish I lived near enough to catch some of your magnetism. For the first time in my life I feel, day after day, completely discouraged. When my Harry sent your letter to me he said, "Susan wants you to write a tract, and I say, Amen." When I go home I will see whether I have any faith in my power to do it . . . Susan, don't you lecture this winter on pain of my everlasting displeasure. I am going to retire from the field; and if you go to work too soon and kill yourself, the two wheel-horses will be gone and then the chariot will stop.

Lucy Stone, letter to Susan B. Anthony,
November 1855, in Harper, Life and Work of
Susan B. Anthony, *Vol. 1, 135–136.*

You said you have but little faith in this reform—the Woman's Rights Movement—because the changes we propose are so great, so radical, so comprehensive; whilst they who have commenced the work are so puny, feeble, and undeveloped. The mass of woman are developed at least to the point of discontent, and that, in the dawn of this nation, was considered a most dangerous point in the British Parliment, and is now deemed equally so on a Southern plantation. In the human soul, the steps between discontent and action are few and short indeed. As to the general cause of woman, I see no signs of failure. We already have a property law, which in its legitimate effects must evaluate the *femme covert* into a living, breathing woman—a wife into a property holder, who can make contracts, buy and sell. In a few years, we shall see how well it works. It needs but little forethought to perceive that in due time these property holders must be represented in the government; and when the mass of women see that there is hope of becoming voters and lawmakers, they will take to their rights as naturally as the negro to his heels when he is sure of escape. Their present seeming content is very much like Sambo's on the plantation. If you truly believe that all the burning indigestion that fires your soul at the sight of injustice and oppression, if suffered in your own person, would nerve you to a lifelong struggle for liberty and independence, then know that what you feel, the mass of women feel also. We need not wait for one more generation to pass away in order to find a race of woman worthy to assert the humanity of woman; and that is all we claim to do.

Elizabeth Cady Stanton, letter to her cousin Gerrit
Smith, January 3, 1856, in Stanton and Blatch,
Elizabeth Cady Stanton, *Vol. 2, 63–64.*

Terribly cold and windy; only a dozen people in the hall; had a social chat with them and returned to

Oberlin's women graduates, including one black woman, Ann Maria Hazle, 1855 *(Oberlin College Archives, Oberlin, Ohio)*

our hotel. Lost more here at Dansville than we gained at Mount Morris. So goes the world.

Susan B. Anthony, canvassing New York State, diary entry, January 8, 1856, in Harper, Life and Work of Susan B. Anthony, *Vol. 1, 138.*

Mercury 12 [degrees] below zero but we took a sleigh for Nunda. Trains all blocked by snow and no mail for several days, yet we had a full house and good meeting.

Susan B. Anthony, canvassing New York State, diary entry, January 9, 1856, in Harper, Life and Work of Susan B. Anthony, *Vol. 1, 133.*

Just emerged from a long line of snowdrifts and stopped at this little country tavern, supped and am now roasting over a hot stove. Oh, oh, what an experience! No trains running and we have had a thirty-six mile ride in a sleigh. Once we seemed lost in a drift full fifteen feet deep. The driver went on ahead to a house, and there we sat shivering. When he returned we found he had gone over a fence into a field, so we had to dismount and plough through the snow after the sleigh; then we reseated ourselves, but oh, the poor horses!

Susan B. Anthony, letter to family, January 11, 1856, in Harper, Life and Work of Susan B. Anthony, *Vol. 1, 138.*

Well, well, good folks at home, these surely are the times that try women's souls. After writing you last, the snows fell and the winds blew and the cars failed to go and come at their appointed hours. We could have reached Warsaw if the omnibus had had the energy to come for us. The train, however, got no farther than Warsaw, where it stuck in a snowdrift eleven feet deep and a hundred long, but we might have kept that engagement at least. Friday morning we went to the station; no trains and no hope of any, but a man said he could get us to Attica in time for an evening meeting, so we agreed to pay him $5. He had a noble pair of greys and we floundered through the deepest snowbanks I ever saw, but at 7 o'clock were still fourteen miles from Attica.

We stopped at a little tavern where the landlady was not yet twenty and had a baby fifteen months old. Her supper dishes were not washed and her baby was crying, but she was equal to the occasion. She rocked the little thing to sleep, washed the dishes and got our

supper; beautiful white bread, butter, cheese, pickles, apples and mince pie, and excellent peach preserves. She gave us her warm bedroom to sleep in, and on a row of pegs hung the loveliest embroidered petticoats and baby clothes, all the work of that young woman's fingers, while on a rack was her ironing perfectly done, wrought undersleeves, babydresses, embroidered underwear, etc. She prepared a 6 o'clock breakfast for us, fried pork, mashed potatoes, mince pie, and for me, at my especial request, a plate of delicious baked apples and a pitcher of rich milk. Now for the moral of this story: When we came to pay our bill, the dolt of a husband took the money and put it in his pocket. He had not lifted a hand to lighten that woman's burdens, but had sat and talked with the men in the bar room, not even caring for the baby, yet the law gives him the right to every dollar she earns, and when she needs two cents to buy a darning needle she has to ask him and explain what she wants it for.

Here where I am writing is a similar case. The baby is very sick with the whooping cough; the wife has dinner to get for all the boarders, and no help; husband standing around with his hands in his pockets. She begs him to hold the baby for just ten minutes, but before the time is up he hands it back to her, saying, "Here, take this child, I'm tired." Yet when we left he was on hand to receive the money and we had to give it to him. We paid a man a dollar to take us to the station, and saw the train pull out while we were stuck in a snowdrift ten feet deep. In spite of this terrible weather, people drive eight and ten miles to our meetings.

Susan B. Anthony, letter to family, January 14, 1856, in Harper, Life and Work of Susan B. Anthony, *Vol. 1, 138–139.*

On the whole, the committee have concluded to recommend no measure, except that they have observed several instances in which husband and wife have both signed the same petition. In such case, they would recommend the parties to apply for a law authorizing them to change dresses, so that the husband may wear petticoats, and the wife breeches, and thus indicate to their neighbors and the public the true relation in which they stand to each other.

Samuel G. Foote, chairman, senate judiciary committee, New York state legislature, on receiving petitions from Susan B. Anthony, February 1856, in History of Woman Suffrage, *Vol. 1, 629.*

[T]hat was a splendid production and well delivered. I could not have asked for a single thing different either in matter or manner; but I would rather have followed my wife or daughter to Greenwood cemetery than to have had her stand here before this promiscuous audience and deliver that address.

Father L. Hazeltine, president of State Teachers' Association, comment to Susan B. Anthony after her lecture at Rand's Hall, Troy, New York, August 1856, in Harper, Life and Work of Susan B. Anthony, *Vol. 1, 143.*

I fully agree with the first part of your remark but dissent entirely from the latter. I should be proud if I had a wife or daughter capable of either writing or reading that paper as Miss Anthony has done.

Superintendent of New York City Schools Randall, letter to Father Hazeltine, August 1856, in Harper, Life and Work of Susan B. Anthony, *Vol. 1, 143.*

. . . And Mrs. Stanton, not a word on that Address for the Teacher's Convention. This week was to be leisure to me, and the Mercy only knows when I can get a moment; and what is worse, as the Lord knows full well, if I get all the time in the world has, I can't get up a decent document. Oh, dear, dear! There is so much to say and I am so without constructive power to put in symmetrical order. So, for the love of me and for the saving of the reputation of womanhood, I beg you, with one baby on your knee and another at your feet, and four boys whistling, buzzing, hallooing "Ma, Ma," set yourself about the work. It is of but small moment who writes the Address, but of vast moment that it be well done. Ah! Mrs. Stanton, don't say No, nor don't delay it a moment; for I must have it all done and almost commit to memory. During July, I want to speak certainly twice at Avon, Clifton, Sharon, and Ballston Springs, and at Lake George. Now will you load my gun, leaving me to pull the trigger and let fly the powder and ball? Don't delay one mail to tell me what you will do, for I must not and will not allow these schoolmasters to say: "See, these woman can't or won't do anything when we give them a chance." No, they sha'n't say that, even if I have to get a man to write it! But no man can write from my standpoint, nor no woman but you; for all, all would base their strongest argument on the unlikeness of the sexes. Antoinette Brown wrote me that she should

do so were she to make the address. And yet, in the schoolroom more than any other place, does the difference of sex, if there is any, need to be forgotten. Now do, I pray you, give heed to my prayer. Those of you who have the talent to do honor to poor—oh! how poor—womanhood, have all given yourself over to baby-making; and left poor brainless me to do the battle alone. It is a shame. Such a body as I might be spared to rock cradles. But it is a crime for you Lucy Stone and Antoinette Brown to be doing it. I have just engaged to attend a progressive meeting in Erie Country, the first of September, just because there is no other woman to be had, but because I feel in the least competent. Oh, dear, dear! If the spirits would only just make me a trance medium and put the right thing into my mouth. You can't think how earnestly I have prayed to be made a speaking medium for a whole week. If they would only come to me thus, I'd give them a hearty welcome. How do I wish I could step in to see you and make you feel my infirmities—mental, I mean. Do get all on fire and be as cross as you please. You remember, Mr. Stanton told how cross you always get over a speech.

Susan B. Anthony, letter to Elizabeth Cady Stanton, June 5, 1856, in Stanton and Blatch, Elizabeth Cady Stanton, *Vol. 2, 64–66.*

Your servant is not dead but liveth. Imagine me, day in and day out, watching, bathing, dressing, nursing and promenading the precious contents of a little crib in the corner of my room. I pace up and down these two chambers of mine like a caged lioness, longing to bring nursing and housekeeping cares to a close. Come here and I will do what I can to help you with your Address, if you will hold the baby and make the puddings. Let Antoinette and Lucy rest in peace and quietness thinking great thoughts. It is not well to be in the excitement of public life all the time, so do not keep stirring them up or mourning over their repose. You, too, must rest, Susan; let the world alone a while. We can not bring about a moral revolution in a day or a year. Now that I have two daughters, I feel fresh strength to work for women. It is not in vain that in myself I feel all the wearisome care to which woman even in her best estate is subject.

Elizabeth Cady Stanton, letter to Susan B. Anthony, June 1856, in Harper, Life and Work of Susan B. Anthony, *Vol. 1, 143.*

Now that I occupy a legal position in which I can not even draw in my own name the money I have earned or give a valid receipt for it when it is drawn or make any contract, but am rated with fools, minors and madmen, and can not sign a legal document without being examined separately to see if it is by my own free will, and even the right to my own name questioned, do you think that, in the grip of such pincers, I am likely to grow amiss? . . . I am not at all sanguine of the success of the convention. However much I hope, or try to hope, the old doubt comes back. My only hope is in your great, indomitable perseverance and your power of work.

Lucy Stone, letter to Susan B. Anthony,
September/October 1856, in Harper, Life and
Work of Susan B. Anthony, *Vol. 1, 146.*

The only reason why I can not publish your notices [about the Seventh National Woman's Rights Convention] in our news columns is that my political antagonists take advantage of such publications to make the Tribune responsible for the anti-Bible, anti-Union, etc., doctrines, which your conventions generally put forth. I do not desire to interfere with your "free speech." I desire only to secure for myself the liberty of treating public questions in accordance with my own convictions, and not being made responsible for the adverse convictions of others. I can not, therefore, print this programme without being held responsible for it. If you advertise it, that is not in my department, nor under my control.

Horace Greeley, letter to Susan B. Anthony,
September/October 1856, in Harper, Life and Work of
Susan B. Anthony, *Vol. 1, 147.*

You invite me to attend the woman's convention in New York. It will not be in my power to do so. You suggest that I write a letter in case I can not attend, but so peculiar and offensive are my views of the remedy for woman's wrongs, that a letter inculcating them would not be well received. Hence, I must not write it. I believe that poverty is the great curse of woman, and that she is powerless to assert her rights, because she is poor. Woman must go to work to get rid of her poverty, but that she can not do in her present disabling dress, and she seems determined not to cast it aside. She is unwilling to sacrifice grace and fashion, even to gain her rights; albeit, too, that this grace is an absurd coventionalism and that this fashion

is infinite folly. Were woman to adopt a rational dress, a dress that would not hinder her from any employment, how quickly would she rise from her present degrading dependence on man! How quickly would the marriage contract be modified and made to recognize the equal rights of the parties to it!

Gerrit Smith, letter to Susan B. Anthony,
September/October 1856, in Harper, Life and Work of
Susan B. Anthony, *Vol. 1, 147.*

The Representatives Hall [Massachusetts legislature] yesterday afternoon was completely filled, galleries and all, to hear the arguments before the Judiciary Committee, to whom was referred the petition of Lucy Stone and others for equal rights for "females" in the administration of government, for the right of suffrage, etc.

Rev. James Freeman Clarke was the first speaker. He said: Gentlemen, the question before you is, Shall the women of Massachusetts have equal rights with the men? The fundamental principles of the Constitution set forth equal rights to all. A large portion of the property of Massachusetts is owned by women, probably one-third of the whole amount, and yet they are not represented, though compelled to pay taxes. It has been said they are represented by their husbands. So it was said that the American colonies were represented in the British Parliament, but the colonies were not contented with such representation, neither are women contented to be represented by men. As long as we put woman's name on the tax-list we should put it in the ballot-box.

Wendell Phillips said: Self-government was the foundation of our institutions. July 4, 1776, sent the message round the world that every man can take care of himself better than any one else can do it for him. If you tax me, consult me. If you hang me, first try me by a jury of my own peers. What I ask for myself, I ask for woman. In the banks a woman, as a stockholder, is allowed to vote. In the Bank of England, in the East India Company, in State Street, her power is felt, her voice controls millions.

Three hundred years ago it was said woman had no right to profess any religion, as it would make discord in the family if she differed from her husband. The same conservatism warns us of the danger of allowing her any political opinions.

Lucy Stone said: The argument that the wife, having the right of suffrage, would cause discord in the family, is entirely incorrect. When men wish to procure the vote of a neighbor, do they not approach them with the utmost suavity, and would not the husband who wished to influence the wife's vote be far more gracious than usual? She instanced the heroic conduct of Mrs. Patton, who navigated her husband's ship into the harbor of San Francisco, as an argument in favor of woman's power of command and of government. The captain and mate lying ill with a fever, she had the absolute control of both vessel and crew. Mrs. Stone's speech was comprehensive and pointed, and called forth frequent applause.

Boston Traveller, March 1857, in History of
Woman Suffrage, Vol. 1, 258.

I was glad to hear of Lucy Stone. I think a vast deal of her and Antoinette Brown. I regret so much that you and Lucy should have had even the slightest interruption to your friendship. I was much interested in the extract from her letter; although I agree with her that

man, too, suffers in a false marriage relation, yet what can his suffering be compared with what every woman experiences whether happy or unhappy? I do not know that the laws and religion of our country even now are behind the public sentiment which makes woman the mere tool of man. He has made the laws and proclaimed the religion; so we have this exact idea of the niche he thinks God intended woman to fill. A man in marrying gives up no right; but a woman, every right, even the most sacred of all—the right to her own person. There will be no response among women to our demands until we have first aroused in them a sense of personal dignity and independence; and so long as our present false marriage relation continues, which in our cases is nothing more nor less than legalized prostitution, woman can have no self-respect, and of course man will have none for her; for the world estimates us according to the value we put upon ourselves. Personal freedom is the first right to be proclaimed, and that does not and cannot now belong to the relation

A typical hospital ward, 1856 (Library of Congress)

of wife, to the mistress of the isolated home, to the financial dependent.

Elizabeth Cady Stanton, letter to Susan B. Anthony, July 20, 1857, in Stanton and Blatch, Elizabeth Cady Stanton, *Vol. 2, 69–70.*

Do you mean to say you want the boys and girls to room side by side in dormitories? To educate them together can have but one result!

Henry H. Van Dyck, state superintendent of public instruction, arguing against resolution by Susan B. Anthony for equal college education of women at the state teachers' convention at Binghamton, New York, August 1857, in Harper, Life and Work of Susan B. Anthony, *Vol. 1, 156.*

Shall an oak and a rose tree receive the same culture? Better to us the clear, steady, softened, silvery moonlight of woman's quiet, unobstrusive influence, than the flashes of electricity showing that the true balance of nature is destroyed.

Unidentified speaker at state teachers' convention at Binghamton, New York, arguing against co-equal education, August 1857, in Harper, Life and Work of Susan B. Anthony, *Vol. 1, 156.*

Miss Anthony vindicated her resolutions with eloquence, force, spirit and dignity, and showed herself a match, at least, in debate for any member of the convention. She was equal if not identical. Whatever may be thought of her notions or sense of propriety in her bold and conspicuous position, personally, intellectually and socially speaking, there can be but one opinion as to her superior energy, ability and moral courage; and she may well be regarded as an evangel and heroine by her own sex.

Birmingham Daily Republican, *August 1857, in* Harper, Life and Work of Susan B. Anthony, *Vol. 1, 156.*

I did indeed see by the papers that you had once more stirred that part of intellectual stagnation, the educational convention. The *Times* was really quite complimentary. Henry brought me every item he could see about you. "Well," he would say, "another notice about Susan. You stir up Susan, and she stirs the world." What a set of fools those schoolmarms must be! Well, if in order to please men they wish to

live on air, let them. I was glad you went to torment them. I will do anything to help you on. If I do nothing else this fall I am bound to aid you to get up an antislavery address. You must come here for a week or two and we will accomplish wonders. You and I have a prospect of a good long life. We shall be good for twenty years at least. If we do not make old Davies shake in his shoes we will make him turn in his grave.

Elizabeth Cady Stanton, letter to Susan B. Anthony, August 20, 1857, in Stanton and Blatch, Elizabeth Cady Stanton, *Vol. 2, 70–71.*

As I look back over those weary years, the most lingering of my many regrets is the fact that I was often compelled to neglect my little children, while spending my time in the kitchen, or at the churn or wash tub doing heavy work for hale and hearty men— work for which I was poorly fitted, chiefly because my faithful mother had worn both me and herself to a frazzle with just such drudgery . . .

Abigail Scott Duniway, on the years 1857–1862, Path Breaking: An Autobiographical History of the Equal Suffrage Movement in Pacific Coast States, *10.*

[A] man came up from the village to our woodpile, where my husband was at work, and asked him to become surety for a considerable sum [endorse the man's loan], with interest at two percent per month, to become compounded semi-annually until paid. The two men parleyed for a while and then went into the house. It dawned on me suddenly, as I was picking a duck, that it would ruin us financially if these notes were signed. I tried hard to be silent, being a nonentity in law, but my hands trembled, my heart beat hard, and I laid the pinioned duck on its back and repaired to the living room to investigate. My husband had already signed two notes and was in the act of signing the third, when I leaned over his shoulder and said tremulously, "My dear, are you quite certain about what you are doing?" The other fellow looked daggers at me but said nothing, and my husband answered, as he signed the last note: "Mama, you needn't worry; you'll always be protected and provided for!" I wanted to say, "I guess I'll always earn all the protection I get," but I remembered that I was nothing but a woman; so I bit my lips to keep silent and rushed back to my work, where for several minutes I fear that duckflesh suffered, for I didn't pluck the feathers tenderly.

Abigail Scott Duniway, ca. 1858, (The loans went unpaid, losing the Duniways their farm in 1862.), Path Breaking: An Autobiographical History of the Equal Suffrage Movement in Pacific Coast States, *13–14.*

I went to Junius and read my address on suffrage, which was pronounced very fine. I feel that two or three such meetings would put me on my feet. But, oh, Susan, my hopes of leisure were soon blasted. The cook's brother was taken sick with fever a few days after you left, and she was obliged to go home. So I have done my work aided by a little girl ever since. But I went to Junius in spite of it all. I see that Mr. Higgians belongs to the Jeremy Bentham school, that law makes right. I am a disciple of the new philosophy that man's wants make his rights. I consider my right to property, to suffrage, etc., as natural and inalienable as my right to life and to liberty. Man is above all law. The province of law is simply to protect me in what is mine.

Elizabeth Cady Stanton, letter to Susan B. Anthony, July 4, 1858, in Stanton and Blatch, Elizabeth Cady Stanton, *Vol. 2, 72–73.*

. . . It was not because the three-penny tax on tea was so exhorbitant that our Revolutionary fathers fought and died, but to establish the principle that such taxation was unjust. It is the same with the woman's revolution; though every law was as just to woman as to man, the principle that one class may usurp the power to legislate for another is unjust, and all who are now in the struggle from love of principle would still work on until the establishment of the grand and immutable truth, "All governments derive their just powers from the consent of the governed."

Susan B. Anthony, letter to her brother, Daniel R., 1859, in Harper, Life and Work of Susan B. Anthony, *Vol. 1, 169.*

The new encyclopedia is just out and I notice in regard to Antoinette Brown Blackwell that it gives a full description of her work up to the time of her marriage, then says: "She married Samuel Blackwell and lives near New York." Thus does every married woman sink her individuality.

Susan B. Anthony, letter to Lydia Mott, 1859, in Harper, Life and Work of Susan B. Anthony, *Vol. 1, 170.*

There is not one woman left who may be relied on, all have "first to please their husband," after which there is but little time or energy left to spend in any other direction. I am not complaining or despairing, but facts are stern realities. The twain become one flesh, the woman "we"; henceforth she has no separate work, and how soon the laststanding monuments (yourself and myself, Lydia), will lay down the individual "shovel and de hoe" and with proper zeal and spirit grasp those of some masculine hand, the mercies and the spirits only know. I declare to you that I distrust the power of any woman, even of myself, to withstand the mighty matrimonial maelstrom!

Susan B. Anthony, letter to Lydia Mott, 1859, in Harper, Life and Work of Susan B. Anthony, *Vol. 1, 171.*

I think our friend's tirades on men are just in some respects and unjust in others. Theodore Parker, Garrison, Phillips, Gerrit Smith, and men of that kidney inspire me with love and respect for the son of Adam. But alas! when we read the view of the average men, their laws, the literature which they father; and when we listen to their every-day talk, to their decisions in the courts, to their sermons in the pulpit, and witness their actions at the fireside, then we feel that they richly deserve all that she says. So if that is her mission, let her attack Mrs. Craik and the door-mat theory. We need some one at that point, while our milder spirited supporters can occupy the middle ground, and go making tender appeals to man's chivalry and sense of justice, while you and I run up and down the scale, always having a royal encounter on "the doormat," singing with due asperity in the chorus hallelujas to single woman, rebukes for spaniel wives, and reasonable denunciations for all flesh in male form. I may add in closing that I think if woman would indulge more freely in vituperation, they would enjoy ten times the health they do. It seems to me that they are suffering from repression. Yours as ever, and with renewed admiration for your championship of my sex.

Elizabeth Cady Stanton, letter to T. W. Higginson, May 1, 1859, in Stanton and Blatch, Elizabeth Cady Stanton, *Vol. 2, 73–74.*

I have had given me $5,000.00 for the woman's rights cause; to procure tracts on that subject, publish and circulate them, pay for lectures and secure such other agitation of the question as we deem fit and best to obtain equal civil and political position for women. The name of the giver of this generous fund [Frances Jackson] I am not allowed to tell you. The only condition of the gift is that it is to remain in my keeping. You, Lucy Stone and myself are a committee of trustees to spend it wisely and efficiently.

Wendell Phillips, letter to Susan B. Anthony, winter 1858, in Harper, Life and Work of Susan B. Anthony, *Vol. 1, 171.*

I shall always recollect our journey on the boat with two or three dozen teachers, and your walking the deck with one and another, talking about women and their rights, in school and out of school, in the most matter-of-fact way, although it was plainly evident that most of them would sooner have listened to a discussion on the rights of the Hottentots.

Antoinette Blackwell, letter to Susan B. Anthony, summer 1859, in Harper, Life and Work of Susan B. Anthony, *Vol. 1, 176.*

I remember a rich scene at the breakfast table. Aaron Powell was with us and the colored waiter pointedly offered him the bill of fare. Miss Anthony glanced at it and began to give her order, not to Powell in ladylike modesty, but promptly and energetically to the waiter. He turned a grandiloquent, deaf ear; Powell fidgeted and studied his newspaper; she persisted, determined that no man should come between her and her own order for coffee, cornbread and beefsteak. "What do I understand is the full order, sir, for your party?" demanded the waiter, doggedly and suggestively. Powell tried to repeat her wishes, but stumbled and stammered and grew red in the face. I put in a working oar to cover the undercurrent of laughter, while she, coolly unconscious of everything except that there was no occasion for a "middleman," since she was entirely competent to look after her own breakfast, repeated her order, and the waiter, looking intensely disgusted, concluded to bring something, right or wrong.

Antoinette Blackwell, recalling an incident in the Fort William Henry Hotel, fall 1859, in Harper, Life and Work of Susan B. Anthony, *Vol. 1, 176–77.*

I'm sorry I can not help you, but pity a poor married woman and forgive. The ordeal that I have been going through, four sewingwomen each giving about two days, no end of little garments to alter and to make, with a husband whose clothes as well as himself have been neglected for three months, the garden to be covered up from the frost, shrubs to transplant, winter provisions to lay in and only one good-natured, stupid servant to help with it all. This Susan is "woman's sphere."

Antoinette Brown, letter to Susan B. Anthony, fall 1859, in Harper, Life and Work of Susan B. Anthony, *Vol. 1, 178.*

I have the honor to acknowledge the receipt of your letter of the 2d inst., with the papers enclosed. The petition to the Legislature will be presented by the senator from this county and I will apprise you of the action had upon it. My daughters are obliged to you for the interest you take in them. To a certain extent I agree with you as to the duties of woman. I am greatly in favor of her elevation to her proper sphere as the equal of man as to her civil rights, the security of her person, the right to her property and, where there is a separation after marriage, her equal right with the father to the custody and education of the children. All this as a legislator I have endeavored to accomplish, making large innovations upon the ancient common law. If I differ from you as to her political rights, it is because I think that, from political as well as moral considerations, she is unfit for, indeed incapacitated from, the performance of most of the duties which are now performed by men as members of the body politic; but there are many avocations and professions now exclusively occupied by men which women are as well, perhaps better fitted to fill. I hope these will soon be thrown open to an active competition of both sexes.

Judge John J. Ormand, letter to Susan B. Anthony, October 17, 1859, in Harper, Life and Work of Susan B. Anthony, *Vol. 1, 183–184.*

In redemption of my promise to tell you the fate of the woman's rights petition to our Legislature, I have the honor to inform you that it was virtually rejected, being laid on the table. I interested a distinguished member of our Senate in its presentation and, in addition, wrote a letter which under ordinary circumstances would have insured its respectful consideration. But after your petition was forwarded came the treasonable and murderous invasion of John Brown. The atrocity of this act, countenanced as it manifestly was by a great party at the North, has extinguished our last spark of fraternal feeling. Whilst we are all living under a Constitution which secures to us our rights to our slaves, the results of which are in truth more beneficial to the whole North, and especially to the New England States, than to us, you are secretly plotting murderous inroads into our peaceful country and endeavoring to incite our slaves to cut the throats of our wives and children. Can you believe that this state of things can last? We now look upon you as our worst enemies and are ready to separate from you. Measures are in progress as far as practicable to establish non-intercourse with you and to proscribe all articles of northern manufacture or origin, including New England teachers. We can live without you; it remains to be seen how you will get along without us. You will probably find that fanaticism is not an element of national wealth or conducive to the happiness or comfort of the people.

In conclusion, let me assure you this is written more in sorrow than in anger. I am not a politician and have always been a strenuous friend of the Union. I am now in favor of a separation, unless you immediately retrace your steps and give the necessary guarantees by the passage of appropriate laws that you will faithfully abide by the compromises of the Constitution, by which alone the slaveholding States can with honor or safety remain in the Union. But that this will be done, I have very little hope, as "madness seems to rule the hour;" and as you have thus constituted yourselves our enemies, you must not be surprised at finding that we are yours.

John J. Ormond, letter to Susan B. Anthony about her support of abolitionism, December 1859, in Harper, Life and Work of Susan B. Anthony, *Vol. 1, 184.*

Where are you? Since a week ago last Monday, I have looked for you every day. I had the washing put off, we cooked a turkey, I made a pie in the morning, sent

The Singer company office in New York City, from *Frank Leslie's Illustrated Newspaper,* 1857 *(Library of Congress)*

my first-born to the depot and put clean aprons on the children, but lo! you did not come. Nor did you soften the rough angles of our disappointment by one solitary line of excuse. And it would do me such great good to see some reformers just now. The death of my father, the worse than death of my dear Cousin Gerrit, the martyrdom of that grand and glorious John Brown—all this conspires to make me regret more than ever my dwarfed womanhood. In times like these, everyone should do the work of a full-grown man. When I pass the gate of the celestial city and good Peter asks me where I would sit, I shall say, "Anywhere, so that I am neither a negro nor a woman. Confer on me, good angel, the glory of white manhood so that henceforth, sitting or standing, rising up or lying down, I may enjoy the most unlimited freedom."

Elizabeth Cady Stanton, letter to Susan B. Anthony, December 23, 1859, in Stanton and Blatch, Elizabeth Cady Stanton, *Vol. 2, 74–75.*

7

Civil Wars
1861–1865

THE HISTORICAL CONTEXT

When the Civil War began in spring 1861, Elizabeth Cady Stanton and Susan B. Anthony had to make a decision: How should members of the women's movement respond? Stanton thought that their activities should be discontinued during the war. She viewed this as a tactical move. It was a detour—but also a chance for women to prove their worth as citizens. The war to preserve the Union would become, she thought, a war to end slavery. The women's rights activists, many of whom had strong abolitionist backgrounds, would involve themselves in the Union cause, and their contributions as citizens would make it clear they were entitled to the vote. Stanton was sure of this.

Susan B. Anthony disagreed. If women, for whatever reason, stopped pressing their claim, their claim would be ignored. Women would get the vote, Anthony believed, only if they continued to demand it. It would not be granted as a reward for patriotism, valor, or sacrifice. Anthony was equally sure of her position.

Virtually all of the women's rights leaders shared Stanton's viewpoint. Less-well-known suffragists agreed with her as well. Moreover, as letters written a few years into the war illustrate, these women remained firm in their position that the war, and what they perceived as its aims, should come first. As E. M. Wilkinson of Laporte County, Indiana, wrote in 1863, "We will labor with all our might, mind, and strength for a free country, where there shall be neither slavery nor involuntary servitude. . . . We believe the sin of slavery to be the cause of this horrid war."[1] Amelia Bloomer agreed, writing, "There are many women . . . who are willing to incur any loss, and make almost any sacrifice, rather than the rebellion should succeed and the chains of the bondman be more firmly rivetted."[2] A general sense of patriotism also informed their priorities. Wilkinson also explained, "As our mothers stood by the Government in the Revolution, we will stand by the present Administration."[3] Mary F. Thomas, of Richmond, Indiana, inspired by the same example, urged contemporary women to remember "the mothers of the Revolution, [who] did not shrink from whatever of trial, of sacrifice, and of toil was theirs to endure."[4]

These women agreed with Stanton that if women redirected their energies during the war, they would, at its conclusion, find a greater recognition of their claims. Thomas may have been bolstered by the example of her Revolutionary War foremothers, but she also looked to the future. She concluded her letter with a thought many suffragists shared, saying, "As the war is working out for women a higher and nobler life, while it is destined in the providence of God to free the slave, it will also bring about in great measure the enfranchisement of women."[5] Finally, when it became clear that not one prominent woman would align herself with Anthony, she acquiesced. The Albany women's rights convention of February 1861 would be the last for a while. Until the war ended, Anthony would put aside women's rights work as such and urge others to do the same. She would do what she could to aid the Union.[6]

The efforts of women—on both sides of the war—began almost immediately. Women in Cleveland, Ohio, met on April 17, 1861, only five days after the attack on Fort Sumter, to create a soldier's aid society. Women all across the Union followed suit. When New York City women held a similar meeting on April 29, they suggested that all the women's aid societies join together as one large association. The Women's Central Association of Relief was then formed to care for the Union's wounded. In May its representatives, together with the members of two New York medical associations, approached the secretary of war. They requested that civilians, "medical men," and military officers be commissioned to advise the Union on the "subject of the prevention of sickness and suffering among the troops" and informed the secretary that the Women's Central Association had already chosen 100 women to train as nurses. On June 13 President Lincoln approved what became known as the Sanitary Commission.[7]

Dorothea Dix, who was 60 years old at the beginning of the Civil War, was appointed the War Department's superintendent of female nurses. The women who served under her, and those who volunteered informally, worked on hospital ships, in camps, and on battlefields. They worked tirelessly to prevent disease by supplementing the soldiers' diets, instituting standards of cleanliness, and providing hospital supplies and quick medical attention to the wounded. In earlier wars, four soldiers died of disease for every one soldier who died in battle or of wounds received there. The Sanitary Commission and other nursing endeavors "by reducing the mortality of our troops by disease . . . to two to one, saved more than one hundred and eighty thousand lives."[8]

Nursing efforts in the Confederacy were not so well organized. They were, however, every bit as intense. The new female heads of households turned their homes into hospitals as needed and shared whatever provisions they had with the wounded. They traveled north to their endangered, imprisoned, or wounded relatives, and there assumed responsibility for any necessary nursing.[9] On both sides, nurses risked their own lives to save the lives of soldiers. As John Adams, national commander of the Grand Army of the Republic, would later comment, these women were "sacrificing and suffering as much as any soldier in the ranks. . . . Many died of exposure and disease contracted in the service. Many returned with health impaired; and some, let it be said with shame and sorrow, died in poverty."[10]

Clara Barton, one of the most famous Civil War nurses, would continue to have a major impact after the war's end. During the war, she nursed Confeder-

Nurses and officers of the U.S. Sanitary Commission in Fredericksburg, Virginia *(Library of Congress)*

ate and Union soldiers alike. After the war, she set out to identify the 13,000 Union soldiers who died in Georgia's Andersonville Confederate prison camp. She began her work with a list kept by a survivor of that camp and was ultimately able to mark several thousand of the Andersonville graves. Many surviving soldiers remained separated from home after the war, and Barton also worked to reunite them with their families. She became the first woman to head a U.S. government bureau when she became head of the federal government's Missing Soldier's Office, overseeing a small staff and managing a congressionally appropriated budget of $15,000. Papers discovered in 1997 document that the Missing Soldier's Office located 22,000 missing soldiers between 1865 and 1869. In 1869 Barton traveled to Switzerland, where she became acquainted with the International Red Cross, which had been founded five years earlier. She returned to the United States determined that her own country should sign the 1864 Geneva Convention and thus join the International Red Cross. The American Red Cross would finally be established in 1900, and Clara Barton—then almost 80 years old—would serve as its first president.[11]

Neither side's nursing effort was governmentally funded.[12] The contributions women made as skilled fund-raisers and as tireless manufacturers of clothing and bandages—at a time when every household responsibility was suddenly theirs—is amazing. In the North, women put their organizational skills to work. There, the New York Women's Central Association of Relief and the Brooklyn Relief Association together "collected supplies and contributions to the amount of several million dollars"; the Soldier's Aid Society of Northern

Ohio received $1,133,405.09 in money and supplies; and the New England Women's Auxiliary Society (including Maine, New Hampshire, Vermont, and Massachusetts) solicited "$315,000 in money and $1,200,000 in stores and supplies."[13] In 1864 even these monies and supplies were insufficient to fund the work of the Sanitary Commission. Union women promptly increased their efforts. In one year, conducting "sanitary fairs" throughout the North, women raised an additional $5,000,000. Including the contributions of the Christian and Western Sanitary Commission and other, similar organizations, approximately $500,000,000 was raised and distributed "for the benefit of the soldier during the Civil War."[14]

In the South, blockades, the frequent presence of enemy soldiers, and the attacks on cities made the furnishing of supplies much more difficult. Still, the women managed. They ran Yankee blockades.[15] They taught their daughters textile-working skills not routinely needed in the years just past, skills that had begun to be replaced, even outside the industrial North, by the workings of machinery.[16] Women young and old, individually and in small groups, knitted socks, scarves, hats, and blankets; sewed uniforms and underclothes; and picked lint for bandages.[17] And, in a reverse economic contribution to their side of the war, they defiantly burned their cotton when Union armies approached so the enemies could not seize it.[18]

Women participated as spies and scouts. Among the Confederacy's most famous spies was Rose O'Neal Greenhow. Born in Maryland, Greenhow was an established political hostess in Washington, D.C., when the Civil War began. She quickly became a member of a Washington-based espionage ring formed by Confederate general Pierre G. T. Beauregard's adjutant general, colonel Thomas Jordan. Information she passed along in July 1861 permitted Confederate preparations in advance of the First Battle of Bull Run. She was confined to her home by the Union army soon after but managed to continue her activities nonetheless. Next jailed in the Old Capitol Prison with other spies

Prior to the Civil War, home-sewn items had begun to be replaced by goods made from factories such as this one, pictured in *Harper's Weekly,* 1859. During the Civil War, many women turned once again to home sewing. *(Library of Congress)*

(including her namesake daughter, Rose) she brandished a Confederate flag from the jailhouse window and managed, again, to thwart those who tried to keep her from gathering and transmitting information. Finally brought before the War Department's Political Prisoners Commission, Greenhow was asked to sign an oath that she would no longer aid the Confederacy; she refused the offer but agreed to return to the South and remain there until the war's end. She was awarded $2,500 by order of Jefferson Davis, for what Confederate secretary of state Judah P. Benjamin said was "an acknowledgment of the valuable and patriotic service rendered by you to our cause."[19]

Belle Boyd was another of the South's famous spies. Born in Martinsburg, Virginia (now West Virginia), Boyd shot and killed a Union soldier who behaved abusively toward her during the Union occupation of her hometown. Thereafter, she began her espionage career with the flirtatious teasing out of information from young occupying Union soldiers. By fall 1861, Boyd was a member of the Confederate intelligence service and a courier, riding her horse "Fleeter" to deliver messages to Generals Stonewall Jackson and Pierre G. T. Beauregard. On May 23, 1863, she dodged Union gunfire to deliver information to Jackson's staff officer Henry Kyd Douglas; the information was instrumental to the Confederate victory at the Battle of Front Royal and the thwarting of Union plans to destroy bridges in the Shenandoah Valley. She was arrested twice—once on the specific orders of U.S. Secretary of War Edwin M. Stanton—and spent two periods of confinement in Old Capitol Prison.[20]

Harriet Tubman was perhaps the North's best-known spy. Born enslaved in Maryland, she made about 19 trips back to the South to rescue other slaves after her own escape from slavery. Before long, a $40,000 reward was offered to anyone who could capture her. During the Civil War, she was a nurse, scout, and spy for the Union army. Issued a pass to travel without restriction on all Union transports, she carried a musket and crossed Confederate lines to gather information from Southern blacks. In June 1863 she led Colonel James Montgomery of the Second South Carolina Volunteers on a successful raid up the Combahee River, earning praise on the front page of the *Boston Commonwealth*. At the war's end, she became the matron of the Colored Hospital at Fortress Monroe.[21]

A number of women were also soldiers: Among the dead and wounded were 400 women disguised as men.[22] "Elizabeth Compton served over a year in the 25th Michigan cavalry; was wounded at the engagement of Greenbrier Bridge, Tennessee, her sex being discovered . . . she was discharged . . . Ellen Goodridge . . . was in every great battle fought in Virginia . . . Sophia Thompson served three years in the 59th O.V.I. . . . Josephine Davidson also served three years in the same company. Her father was killed fighting by her side at Chickamauga . . ."[23]

Frances Hook of Illinois had a particularly colorful military career. She originally enlisted in the 65th Home Guards with her brother, calling herself "Frank Miller." She served the required three months without anyone realizing she was a woman. Mustered out, she then joined the 90th Illinois. She was taken prisoner and shot while trying to escape. Once her sex was discovered by her captors, she was imprisoned separately from the other Union soldiers. Confederate president Jefferson Davis then wrote to her and offered "a lieutenant's commission if she would enlist in the rebel army . . ." Hook declined and joined the Second East Tennessee Cavalry upon her release.[24] Of such women in the war, the *Albany Evening Journal* would later say, "Several hundred fought in the late war, but when their sex was discovered, they were dismissed in disgrace; and to the shame of the Government be it said, they were never paid for their services."[25]

According to report number 386 of the committee on military affairs, Anna Ella Carroll also played a significant role in the fighting of the Civil War: "In the autumn of 1861, the great question as to whether the Union could be saved . . . depended on the ability of the Government to open the Mississippi and deliver a fatal blow upon the resources of the Confederate power. The original plan was to reduce the formidable fortifications by descending this river, aided by the gunboat fleet, then in preparation for that object." The report describes how President Abraham Lincoln himself supervised the plans for this expedition and finally abandoned it when "he became convinced that the obstacles to be encountered were too grave and serious." Thomas A. Scott, writing afterward to the Honorable Jacob M. Howard, U.S. Senate, described what happened then: "On or about the 30th of November, 1861, Miss Carroll . . . called on me as Assistant Secretary of War, and suggested . . . to adopt instead the Tennessee River, and handed me the plan of the campaign . . . which plan I submitted to the Secretary of War, and its general ideas were adopted . . . In 1862, I informed Miss Carroll . . . that through the adoption of this plan, the country had been saved millions, and that it entitled her to the kind consideration of Congress."

Although some historians have since raised questions about the validity of this and other supporting letters, the House of Representatives' committee on military affairs in 1881 found that the evidence before it "completely establishe[d] that Miss Anna Carroll was the author of this change of plan . . ."[26] Despite this conclusion, Anna Ella Carroll died alone, forgotten, and in poverty.[27]

As the war progressed, many former slaves traveled north. Called "contrabands," they were placed under the official jurisdiction of the army. They were now free from bondage, but many were without education and most lacked worldly goods as basic as a change of clothing. Josephine S. Griffing, a veteran of the American and Western Anti-Slavery societies, immediately began to work on behalf of the refugees in Washington, D.C. She approached President Lincoln and Secretary of War Edwin M. Stanton with plans to organize aid. With the approval of the secretary of war, she distributed army blankets and wood from army wagons. She then set up "ration-houses" to feed the former slaves and created shelters in old barracks. Her efforts continued, and she became the general agent of "The National Freedman's Relief Association of the District of Columbia." In 1863, at her instigation, a bill was introduced in the House of Representatives. It finally passed in March 1865 and resulted in the creation of "that great national charity," the Freedmen's Bureau.[28]

Elizabeth Keckley was also distressed about the enormous difficulties faced by the formerly enslaved people. Once enslaved herself, she was now employed by Mary Todd Lincoln as a dressmaker. She addressed the congregation of an African-American church and suggested that blacks already established in the Union join together on behalf of the newly free. The "Contraband Relief Association," of which Keckley became president, raised large amounts of money through various means: African-American women in New York held a charity ball, while those in Boston staged dramatic readings. Fund-raisers received contributions from prominent and successful African Americans and from sympathetic whites. The organization thrived. When African Americans were finally admitted into the army, members of the Contraband Relief Association wanted to provide for their needs as well; in recognition of its expanded mission, the association became the Freedmen and Soldiers' Relief Association of Washington.[29]

Other women, both black and white, traveled south to assist the former slaves who remained there. Most went as teachers with the financial support of northern organizations such as the American Missionary Association and various Friends' Associations. Even so, the hardship was at times acute—especially for women with dependents. One teacher wrote: "[T]en dollars [a month] with board is the salary allowed by the A.M. Asso. for female teachers. This, I would consider a liberal remuneration if it were not that I have a mother, towards whose support I am obliged to contribute . . . I am compelled to ask an increase of 2 dollars."[30] (Male teachers were paid $25 a month.)

Finally, in 1863 the leadership of the women's rights movement again stepped forward. The Emancipation Proclamation had freed slaves only in the Confederate states. Those in states loyal to the Union were still in bondage. When Charles Sumner introduced a bill outlawing slavery in every state, Susan B. Anthony and Elizabeth Cady Stanton acted on a suggestion of Henry Stanton.[31] They published a letter to the "loyal women of the nation," asking them to attend a conference on May 14, 1863, in New York City. The National Woman's Loyal League was then founded and its principal goal declared: the collection of 1 million signatures to a petition in favor of Sumner's bill.[32]

Lucy Stone, Elizabeth Cady Stanton, Susan B. Anthony, Angelina Grimké Weld, Ernestine L. Rose, and Antoinette Blackwell were among the officers. Under their guidance, women of the league collected nearly 400,000 petitions in about 15 months.[33] By February 1864 the first 100,000 of the petitions were tallied, rolled, and ready for presentation. It was a dramatic moment. The rolls, too heavy for the young Senate pages, were carried by two freed African-American men and landed with a thud on Sumner's desk. He stood and described the contents: "They ask nothing less than universal emancipation; and this they ask directly at the hands of Congress. No reason is assigned. The prayer speaks for itself." And then, underscoring the fact that women had only one means of registering their opinion with the government, he added: "So far as it proceeds from the women of the country, it is naturally a petition, and not an argument."[34]

Exercising the right of petition was one way for women to influence government, but Anna E. Dickinson knew another. Still in her teens and an accomplished orator, she campaigned throughout the Northeast for the candidates of her choice. She herself could not vote for abolitionist Republicans, but she could persuade others to do so. Vice President Hamlin and Speaker of the House Schuyler Colfax were convinced she had helped in the 1863 campaigns. In appreciation, they and 100 other members of Congress invited her to give a special address in Washington.[35] President and Mrs. Lincoln attended, as did Supreme Court justices, senators, and congressmen, and the event drew national attention.

Anna E. Dickinson, Civil War
speaker *(Library of Congress)*

Women certainly wished for more direct political
input. After issuing the call for the league's first meeting, Susan B. Anthony began to receive letters from
women all across the Union. Women from large cities
and small towns alike offered their own analysis of the
political situation. Some blamed the current crisis on
women's inability to vote, believing that women would
earlier have eliminated slavery and hence the need for a
war. Others saw a parallel between their own subservient position and that of the slave.[36] Despite this
realization of their own powerlessness, Union women
supported their government. They did so with faith
that their lot would improve. As a woman from Illinois
explained, "[N]otwithstanding the mean position that
we are compelled to occupy, I feel like upholding the
Government as the best there is, feeling quite sure that
the kindness and good sense of our rulers will give us
something a little more like justice after a while."[37] In
the meantime, both the example of Anna Dickinson
and the process of urging a constitutional amendment
involved many women for the first time in national politics.[38]

American women were heroic in the war. Whether sewing for soldiers
while raising children and crops alone, serving as nurses, spies, or soldiers,
working as fund-raisers or teachers, planning military campaigns or relief for
the suddenly free, or petitioning Congress for total emancipation, these women
sacrificed and triumphed. Individual women certainly believed their contributions were important, and their leadership certainly believed women's efforts
would be rewarded.

Susan B. Anthony's 1861 objection to the suspension of the women's
movement was largely forgotten. And yet, something less than rewarding had
already happened: In 1862, as American women were becoming widowed in
unprecedented numbers, the New York State legislature replaced key portions
of the state's Married Woman's Property Act of 1860. A mother's hard-won
right to equal custody of her children and her right to use a deceased husband's estate for the benefit of her children were abolished. "Well, well,"
Anthony wrote to her friend Lydia Mott, "while the old guard sleep the young
'devils' are wide-awake, and we deserve to suffer for our confidence in 'man's
sense of justice,' and to have all we have gained thus snatched from us." It was
only the first sign that Susan B. Anthony might have been right.

CHRONICLE OF EVENTS

1861

Women in Kansas are granted "school suffrage."

Harriet Jacobs, with the help of Lydia Marie Child, publishes *Incidents in the Life of a Slave Girl*.

Ella Trader organizes hospitals throughout the Southern states.

January 18: Vassar Female College (later, Vassar College) is chartered by the state of New York. It will not open until after the Civil War ends.

February: The last Women's Rights Convention until after the Civil War takes place in Albany, New York.

February 27: Anna Dickinson, at age 17, addresses her first major audience in Concert Hall, Philadelphia, saying, "The Constitution of the United States recognizes human slavery, and makes the souls of men articles of purchase and of sale."

April 12: Southerners attack federal Fort Sumter in Charleston Harbor, South Carolina.

April 13: Fort Sumter surrenders.

April 15: The Rhode Island infantry organizes, one of the first regiments to respond after the surrender of Fort Sumter. It makes Kady Brownell the color-bearer of the 11th regiment, a company of sharpshooters. She became one of the quickest and most accurate marksmen of the regiment.

April 17: Women in Cleveland, Ohio, create the Soldier's Aid Society.

April 25: The Ladies' Central Relief, which will become the U.S. Sanitary Commission, is inaugurated at the New York Infirmary at the suggestion of Dr. Elizabeth Blackwell.

June 9: The Sanitary Commission is established with the approval of President Lincoln; its expenses will be paid by Union women.

June 10: The War Department appoints Dorothea Dix the government superintendent of women nurses, the first military job awarded to a female.

July: Senator John C. Breckenridge (Kentucky) delivers a secession speech to Congress, which Anna Ella Carroll soon repudiates so convincingly that the War Department prints and circulates her arguments.

August 10: Belle Reynolds lands at Cairo, Illinois, joining her husband's regiment at Bird's Point, Missouri. From this time until 1865 she keeps a journal of her army life, which includes reminiscences of marching with the soldiers, a musketoon on her shoulder.

September: Anna Carroll writes a paper on the constitutional power of the president to make arrests and to suspend the writ of habeas corpus, a controversial issue of the time.

December: Anna Carroll writes the pamphlet "The War Powers of the General Government" at the request of President Lincoln's War Department.

1862

New York state legislature repeals those sections of the Married Woman's Property Act of 1860 that gave mothers joint guardianship of their children and some property rights to widows.

Mary Jane Patterson is the first African-American woman to earn her baccalaureate degree, awarded by Oberlin College.

President Lincoln signs the Morrill Act, establishing land grant offices in rural areas to aid agricultural and mechanical arts colleges. Millions of women will earn their college degrees under the act.

January: Mrs. A. H. Hoge volunteers to keep the shelves and treasury of the Chicago branch of the U.S. Sanitary Commission filled.

February: Julia Ward Howe publishes "Battle Hymn of the Republic" in the *Atlantic Monthly*.

March 24: Charlotte McKay arrives in Frederick City, Maryland, where she nurses wounded Union troops that the day before had fought Stonewall Jackson in the Battle of Winchester.

April: Margaret Breckinridge leaves her home in Princeton, New Jersey, and heads west to nurse Union soldiers.

May 20: President Abraham Lincoln signs the Homestead Law, which gives free land to "any person who is the head of a family, or who has arrived at the age of twenty-one years, and is a citizen of the United States, or who shall have filed his declaration of intention to become such," so long as he or she lives on it for five years. Single women, especially teachers, are among the many who take advantage of the new law.

summer: Clara Barton hauls medical supplies by mule to battlefields and hospitals. For four years she will nurse soldiers at Cedar Mountain, Bull Run, Chantilly, Antietam, Falmouth, Fredericksburg, Charleston, Spotsylvania, Petersburg, Richmond, and other battles.

President Abraham Lincoln led the Union to victory during the Civil War. *(Library of Congress)*

July: Anna Dickinson joins Frederick Douglass in Philadelphia, appealing to citizens to enlist colored troops in the state militia. Their efforts are successful and a regiment is raised.

July 16: Ida B. Wells (later, Wells–Barnett), journalist, is born.

August: Mary Morris Husband, a Philadelphia volunteer, takes temporary charge of the National Hospital at Baltimore, nursing the mutilated soldiers from the Second Battle of Bull Run, Chantilly, and South Mountain. For three years she will work in field hospitals.

August 8: Elizabeth Keckley organizes the Contraband Relief Association.

fall: Anna Dickinson, age 18, gives a public address in Concord, New Hampshire, convincing many that slavery is the cause of war. The secretary of the State Central Committee remarks at the end of her speech, "If we can get this girl to make that speech all through New Hampshire we can carry the Republican ticket in the coming election." Through his intervention Dickinson gives regular campaign speeches on behalf of the Republican Party.

September 22: President Lincoln issues the Emancipation Proclamation.

1863

Wisconsin State University admits women to its normal school training course.

Fanny Kemble publishes *Journal of a Residence on a Georgia Plantation,* which helps to turn British opinion against the South during the Civil War.

Olympia Brown becomes the first woman ordained as a minister by full authority of her denomination, the Northern Universalists, in Malone, New York.

New Orleans actress Pauline Cushman decides to enter the Secret Service of the United States. Her spying and bravery when wounded and imprisoned earn her the rank of major.

Mary Walker becomes the highest-ranking female in the Union army when she is appointed assistant surgeon.

March: Anna Dickinson begins regular campaign speeches on behalf of the Republicans, eventually bringing several border states to the party.

March: The *New York Tribune* publishes an appeal to the "loyal women of the nation" to join a national convention in New York to discuss how northern women can help the war effort.

May 2: Mary W. Lee helps staff Lacey Hospital in Fredericksburg, Virginia, during the storming of Mayre's Heights by Union troops.

May 14: The "loyal women of the nation" meet in New York City; the National Woman's Loyal League is formed.

August: Emily W. Dana arrives with a large contingent of Maine and Massachusetts women at the General Hospital of the Naval Academy in Annapolis, Maryland, where she will nurse terminal prisoners just released from Belle Isle and Libby Prisons.

August: Louisa May Alcott publishes the book *Hospital Sketches,* which grew out of her work as a nurse during the Civil War.

fall: Mary Morris Husband begins helping young men found guilty of desertion and sentenced to death. She appeals their cases to their commanding officers and up to Abraham Lincoln himself, securing pardons from the president for most of her cases.

November 24–25: Mary Ann Bickerdyke is the only woman to nurse Union forces at the battles of Lookout Mountain and Missionary Ridge in Tennessee.

1864

In *Packard v. Packard* Elizabeth Ware Packard challenges the law that permits husbands to institutionalize their wives. The challenge will prompt the passage of the married women's property law in Illinois (1869) and reform in the commitment laws in other states.

Coeducational Swarthmore College is founded.

Charlotte Forten publishes "Life on the Sea Islands" in the *Atlantic Monthly,* recounting her experiences as a nurse and teacher to freed people in South Carolina.

January 16: Anna E. Dickinson addresses President and Mrs. Lincoln, justices of the Supreme Court and members of Congress in the Senate chamber.

February 9: National Woman's Loyal League petitions Congress to outlaw slavery in all states.

April 8: The Thirteenth Amendment of the U.S. Constitution is passed by the Senate.

June: Mary Putnam-Jacobi receives her medical degree.

June 6: Republican party platform includes call for an amendment to the Constitution, outlawing slavery in all states.

1865

Vassar College opens.

Belle Boyd in Camp and Prison is published, recounting the adventures of the Confederate spy.

Hundreds of white women move to the South to teach at freemen's schools run by various philanthropic organizations.

Physician Mary Walker is the only woman awarded the Congressional Medal of Honor for her work in the Civil War.

Lydia Maria Child publishes *The Freedman's Book.*

January 31: House of Representatives passes the Thirteenth Amendment.

March: Josephine Griffing helps to establish the Freedmen's Bureau.

April 9: Lee surrenders at Appomattox.

July: Clara Barton travels to the concentration camp at Andersonville, Georgia, where she organizes the identification of 13,000 graves of Union prisoners of war. Before the end of the year, she will become the head of the Missing Soldier's Office and first woman to head a U.S. government bureau.

July 7: Mary E. Jenkins Surratt is hanged in Washington, D.C., as an accomplice in the assassination of President Abraham Lincoln.

December 6: The Thirteenth Amendment is ratified, abolishing slavery.

December 18: Secretary of State William H. Seward announces the ratification of the Thirteenth Amendment, abolishing slavery.

EYEWITNESS TESTIMONY

At the time the war broke out my home was in Coldwater, Mich. I entered the service with my husband sometime in May, 1861, as a volunteer nurse, and was not under authority of any one except the surgeon. Later I was appointed matron of Hospital No. 13, Nashville, Tenn., and remained there from September, 1862, until January, 1863. This hospital was in charge of H. J. Herrick, M.D., of the 17th Regiment Ohio Volunteers. I then went to No. 20, Nashville, and stayed until May, as matron under J. R. Goodwin, M.D., surgeon in charge.

I was also in a hospital at Murfreesboro, Tenn., and at Huntsville, Ala.

In all, I was in hospitals about a year; the remainder of the time I was in camp or on the march with my husband, Capt. George W. Van Pelt, and I always found plenty of work to do there. My husband fell in the battle of Chickamauga, in September, 1863, and in November I left the service.

Mary A. Loomis, about her participation in the Civil War, in Holland, Our Army Nurses, *86.*

When the war broke out I was living in a little town called Greencastle, about eleven miles from Chambersburg, Penn. My father was a great Union man, and threw our house open as headquarters for the officers. The generals quartered there were Dana, Smith, and Fitshugh, and they had their staffs. We did all we could for the comfort of the soldiers, and when the call came for nurses, I was one to volunteer. I served three years; first in the hospital at Hagerstown, Md., then at Greencastle . . .

During my hospital service I was on the battlefields of Antietam and Gettysburg, after the fight, helping the wounded and caring for the dying. Many of the injured men were carried to our little town of Greencastle, and we sisters did what we could for them, picking lint, knitting stockings, etc. I was then Mary Alice Smith, and but eighteen years of age. I served under Gen. David Detrich, in Greencastle, but do not remember who was surgeon in charge at Hagerstown. When I was not engaged in the hospitals I was out with an ambulance, gathering provisions for the soldiers.

M. Alice Frusch, about her participation in the Civil War, in Holland, Our Army Nurses, *101.*

Midnight on the Battlefield *(engraved by J. J. Code, New York; published by A. D. Washington & Co. Publishers, Hartford, Conn., 1887)*

Dr. Gibbes says he was at a country house near Manassas when a Federal soldier who had lost his way came in, exhausted. He asked for brandy, which the lady of the house gave him. Upon second thought he declined it. She brought it to him so promptly, he said he thought it might be poisoned. His mind was.

She was enraged.

"Sir, I am a Virginia woman. Do you think I could be as base as that? Here—Bill, Tom, disarm this man. He is our prisoner." The negroes came running, and the man surrendered without more ado. Another Federal was drinking at the well. A negro girl said, "You go in and see Missis." The man went in, and she followed crying triumphantly, "Look here—Missis, I got a prisoner too!" . . .

This lady sent in her two prisoners, and Beauregard complimented her on her pluck and patriotism and presence of mind.

Mary Boykin Chesnut, diary entry, July 24, 1861, in Mary Chesnut's Civil War, *113.*

Mrs. Randolph proposed to divide everything sent to us equally with the Yankee wounded and sick prisoners. Some were enthusiastic from a Christian point of view. Some shrieked in wrath at the bare idea of putting our noble soldiers on a par with Yankees—living, dying, or dead. Shrill and long and loud it was. Fierce dames some of them . . .

Mary Boykin Chesnut, diary entry, August 18, 1861, in Mary Chesnut's Civil War, *156.*

As he came through North Carolina, a woman came aboard the cars. She surveyed the Yankee prisoners curiously.

She told them solemnly, "If you kill all of our men, remember: here are the women, and they will run you out with broomsticks."

Mary Boykin Chesnut, diary entry, August 26, 1861,
in Mary Chesnut's Civil War, *163.*

Women who came before the public are in a bad box now. False hair is taken off and searched for papers. Pistols are sought for [under] "cotillons renversés." Bustles are "suspect." All manner of things, they say, come over the border under the huge hoops now worn. So they are ruthlessly torn off. Not legs but arms are looked for under hoops. And sad to say, found. Then women are used as detectives and searchers to see that no men come over in petticoats.

So the poor creatures coming this way are humiliated to the deepest degree.

I think *these* times make all women feel their humiliation in the affairs of the world . . . Women can only stay at home, and every paper reminds us that women are to be violated, ravished, and all manner of humiliation.

To men—glory, honor, praise, and power—if they are patriots.

To women—daughters of Eve—punishment comes still in some shape, do what they will.

Mary Boykin Chesnut, diary entry, August 29, 1861,
in Mary Chesnut's Civil War, *172.*

Went to the Ladies Aid Society. My initiation fee was ten dollars. Someone said they were in debt. Mrs. Lee (Jersey woman) dolorous. Louisa Salmond active and efficient.

Everybody knitting. Quantities of things were being packed and baled up to send off. I sat with poor Milly Trimlin and the likes of her, who came for work. So this society does good in more ways than one—gives work and aid to the poor soldiers' wives.

They got into debt making underclothes for Tom Warren's company.

Mary Boykin Chesnut, diary entry, October 1, 1861,
in Mary Chesnut's Civil War, *203.*

I can not take leave of my public life without expressing my deep sense of your services to the country during the whole period of our National troubles.

Although a citizen of a State almost unanimously disloyal and deeply sympathizing with secession, especially the wealthy and aristocratic class of her people, to which you belonged, yet, in the midst of such surroundings, you emancipated your own slaves at a great sacrifice of personal interest, and with your powerful pen defended the cause of the Union and loyalty as ably and effectively as it has never yet been defended.

From my position on the Committee on the Conduct of the War, I know that some of the most successful expeditions of the war were suggested by you, among which I might instance the expedition up the Tennessee River.

The powerful support you gave Governor Hicks during the darkest hour of your State's history, prompted him to take and maintain the stand he did, and thereby saved your State from secession and consequent ruin.

All those things, as well as your unremitted labors in the cause of reconstruction I doubt not, are well

Mary Walker, M.D., was the first woman surgeon to serve in the Union army, perhaps any army. *(National Archives)*

known and remembered by the members of Congress at that period.

I also well know in what high estimation your services were held by President Lincoln and I can not leave the subject without sincerely hoping that the Government may yet confer on you some token of acknowledgment for all these services and sacrifices.

The Honorable Benjamin F. Wade, chairman of the committee on the conduct of the war during the Civil War, letter to Anna Ella Carroll, March 1, 1869, regarding the Tennessee River campaign of 1861, in History of Woman Suffrage, *Vol. 2, 866.*

At the end of September Colonel Howard was promoted to brigadier-general, and Dr. Palmer to a brigade surgeon. Dr. Brickett was made surgeon of the Fifth Maine volunteers, and I was transferred with him. I had been two weeks with the regiment, and had got the hospital in fine condition, the Maine people having sent us some two or three dozen of bed-cots; and I, availing myself of an offer in a note Mr. F. N. Knapp wrote me . . . had drawn bedding, pillows, dressing-gowns, jellies, &c., from the Sanitary Commission, when General Slocum came to visit the hospital. "How is this, Dr. Brickett," said he, "that your boys are so much more comfortable than those of the other regiments in the brigade?" "O," said the doctor, "we have got a Maine woman here who understands how to take care of the sick. She has drawn these things form the Sanitary Commission, and has arranged the whole with some of the nurses' assistance." "I can't have any partiality in my brigade," said the general. "Give my compliments to Miss Bradley, doctor, and tell her I should be happy to have her take charge of the sick of the brigade. I will take the Powell House and the Octagon House, that are empty, a short distance from here, where we will move them all; and tell her I would like to have her go there . . .

Of course I accepted . . . The surgeons immediately made requisitions for iron bedsteads, straw bedticks,—about seventy-five, the number our two houses would hold,—and I made another requisition, on the United States Sanitary Commission, for quilts, blankets, sheets, pillow-cases, shirts, drawers, towels, &c. As the government had made no arrangements for brigade hospitals, supposing the sick from the various regiments would be sent to general hospitals, these things could not be obtained in sufficient quantities to supply a hospital like ours; and here I learned,

as early as November, 1861, that a Commission like this was necessary as an auxiliary to government, and could be the means of mitigating a vast amount of suffering, and saving very many valuable lives.

Amy M. Bradley, hospital journal, 1861, in Moore, Women of the War, *417–418.*

We are indebted to the *Richmond Whig* for the pungent letter which we publish today of Mrs. Rose Greenhow to Mr. Seward, touching her late imprisonment in her own house in Washington, as a secession emissary. Having been released and sent over into Secessia, she doubtless furnished a copy of the letter in question to the journal from which it is extracted. It is just a phillipe as one would expect, under the circumstances, from a spirited, dashing, active and fearless female politician of the South Carolina School of Secession Malignants. She complains bitterly of the rude and offensive behavior of her jailers; but she forgets that men thus employed are very seldom remarkable in the refinements and accomplishments, graces and gallantry of the fashionable circles of Washington. She discourses fluently; but flippantly upon the freedom of speech, and the right to exercise it, and upon the cruel tyranny of her imprisonment; but she forgets that while at large in Washington she was a dangerous agent of a hostile army besieging our capital. Grant all the personal rights of freedom of speech which Mrs. Greenhow demands, in the midst of this great rebellion, and we may as well abolish our armies . . .

New York Herald, *December 17, 1861, in* Civil War: Clippings.

She seemed to be nineteen, or perhaps, twenty— rather young, I thought, to be traveling alone. True, I was not older, but then I was married, which made all the difference in the world. What made her an object of special interest to every woman present, was that she was exceedingly well dressed. It had been a long time since we had seen a new dress! She was a brilliant talker, and soon everybody in the room was attracted to her, especially the men. . . . we found that she was devoted to The Cause . . . She soon let us know that she had come directly from Washington, where she had been a prisoner of the United States. She showed us her watch and told us how the prisoners in Washington had made the money up among themselves and presented it to her just before she left . . . The next morning when the maid came in to make the fire, we woke up face to face in the same bed, and then she told me that her name was Belle Boyd, and I knew for the first time that my bedfellow was the South's famous female spy. When we got up she took a large bottle of cologne and poured it into the basin in which she was going to bathe. It was the first cologne I had seen for more than a year, and it was the last I saw until I ran the blockade.

Myrta Lockett Avary, writing of 1861,
in A Virginia Girl, *52.*

Mothers and grandmothers, who in the days of their youth had learned the valuable use of knitting-needles, gave lessons to the younger women of our country, who, through the triumph of mechanical skill in the manufacture of hosiery, had been left untutored in this branch of domestic female industry.

It was delightful to watch the busy fingers of our dear old matrons . . .

Sallie Brock, writing of December 1861, in Richmond
During the War, *85–86.*

Tents were torn in shreds, and the enemy, in solid column, was seen coming over the hill in the distance. Mrs. N. and I . . . passed the large parade ground, close by our camp, where the cavalry was forming. Balls were flying and shells bursting among the terrified horses and fearless riders . . . When within about a half mile from the river, we came upon a number of ambulances, from which the wounded were being taken and laid upon the ground for the surgeons' attention. We stopped, took off our bonnets, and prepared to assist in dressing their wounds; but in less than ten minutes, an orderly came dashing up, with orders to move the wounded immediately to the river, as the rebels were pressing so closely, they were not safe where they were. The surgeon said we had better go to some of the boats, as we should find plenty to do. So we made our way to the steamer Emerald, Captain Norton's headquarters; and just as we were going aboard, General Grant and staff came up from Savannah. Anxious faces they all wore . . . We were rejoiced to find that Mrs. C., one of our nurses, had arrived from Illinois, with quite a large supply of hospital stores, for they came not an hour too soon . . .

Soon the wounded came pouring in upon us, and for thirty-six hours we found no rest. At night we had three hundred and fifty wounded on board our boat . . .

Through the day the thunder of artillery had almost deafened us; the air seemed filled with leaden hail, and the spent balls would patter upon the deck like a summer shower . . .

That night we rested, though the storm was still raging. Wednesday morning the sun came forth upon such a scene of blood and carnage such as our fair land had never known. The roads were almost impassable; yet we felt it our duty to go out, and do all we could for those who were in the hospital. At nine o'clock we left the boat—Mrs. C., Mrs. N., and myself. We . . . came to an old cabin, where the wounded were being brought. Outside lay the bodies of more than a hundred, brought in for recognition and burial . . . We passed on, and entered the house, which contained three rooms. In one were some fifty wounded; in another (smaller) the surgeons were amputating . . .

. . . one by one, they would take from different parts of the hospital a poor fellow, lay him out on those bloody boards, and administer chloroform; but before insensibility, the operation would begin, and in the midst of shrieks, curses, and wild laughs, the surgeon would wield over his wretched victim the glittering knife and saw; and soon the severed limb, white as snow and splattered with blood, would fall upon the floor—one more added to the ghastly pile.

Until three o'clock I had no idle moments . . .

The following day we visited the boats near us. On one the surgeon objected to our coming on board, as he "wanted no women around." But nothing daunted, we went in search of any who might belong to our regiment. We found some of the boys with their wounds undressed, many of them having been wounded on Sunday; and, though there were three or four hundred men on the boat, there were but two or three surgeons, and they unwilling to have us relieve what suffering we could. No hospital stores were allowed us; so, drawing from the small supply on the Emerald, and from the boat of the United States Sanitary Commission, in charge of Dr. Warriner, we removed the heavy flannels, stiff with blood, bathed their burning wounds and powder-stained faces, gave them food, and they sank to sleep like weary children.

Belle Reynolds, diary entry, April 17, 1862, in Moore,
Women of the War, *260–268.*

As a natural consequence of her [New Orleans's] surrender, the forts also gave up, and fair Louisiana with her fertile fields of cane and cotton, her many bayous and dark old forests, lies powerless at the feet of the enemy. Though the Yankees have gained the land, the people are determined they shall not have its wealth, and from every plantation rises the smoke of burning cotton. The order from Beauregard advising the destruction of cotton met with a ready response from the people, most of them agreeing that it is the only thing to do. As far as we can see are ascending wreaths of smoke, and we hear that all the cotton of the Mississippi Valley from Memphis to New Orleans is going up in smoke. We have found it is hard to burn bales of cotton. They will smoulder for days. So the huge bales are cut open before they are lighted and the old cottons burns slowly. It has to be stirred and turned over but the light cotton from the lint room goes like a flash. We should know, for Mamma has $20,000 worth burning on the gin ridge now; it was set on fire yesterday and is still blazing.

Though agreeing on the necessity of destroying the cotton, all regret it. And it has thrown a gloom over the country that nothing but news of a great victory could lighten. We are watching and praying for that. The planters look upon the burning of the cotton as almost ruin to their fortunes, but all realize its stern necessity and we have not heard of one trying to evade it.

The Yankee gunboats are expected to appear before Vicksburg today, and every effort is being made to "welcome them with bloody hands to hospitable graves." It seems hopeless to make a stand at Vicksburg. We only hope they may burn the city if they meet with any resistance. How much better to burn our cities than let them fall into the enemy's hands.

Kate Stone, journal entry, May 9, 1862, in Anderson,
Brokenburn, *100–101.*

. . . a boy from Carolina . . . had been shot through the body, and could not lie down . . . he begged me to write to his mother "a very long letter, sending a lock of my hair . . ." He lingered till Monday; and, after a painful operation, sank away most unexpectedly, and when I got there was in the dead-house. So I went into that dismal place, full of corpses, and cut a lock from the dead boy's head, and enclosed it to the mother, adding some words of comfort . . .

Mrs. John Harris, letter to the president of the
Philadelphia Ladies' Aid Society, May 21, 1862, in
Moore, Women of the War, *182–183.*

Wednesday, May 28, was ashore all day . . . Returned to the boat towards evening, when, as I went aboard, I met Mr. [Frederick Law] Olmstead [the Sanitary Commission's general secretary], who told me he wished me to take charge of the Knickerbocker, and put her in order to receive wounded men from the battle of Fair Oaks . . .

The Knickerbocker was in a very filthy condition, and there were several state-rooms filled with soiled clothes, that were exceedingly offensive. The surgeon in charge, Dr. Swan, requested me to arrange matters to suit myself, furnishing me with all aid necessary. First, then, these clothes must be counted and sent ashore to be washed; four girls (colored) to be hired to wash on board the boat, so that no more should accumulate. Done. Second, see the captain of the boat, and have the crew, with the assistance of the attendants, clean the boat. *They went to work with a will.* Mr. Knapp promised me bedcots to fill the saloon on the main deck and lower one; promptly they were sent. There was a large quantity of clothing on board: this I arranged myself, so that I could know where to find each article needed. Meantime Mrs. Balustier left for home, sick, and Mrs. Annie Etheridge, of the Third Michigan, reported for duty. How faithfully she labored! We divided a little saloon at the forward part of the boat, leaving six berths on one side, and six on the other, making two rooms, the one occupied by the surgeon and his staff, the other by us.

Sunday, June 1, found us nearly ready, our boat clean, our beds set up, and clothing arranged in order. About four P.M the wounded began to arrive.

Amy M. Bradley, journal entry, June 1862, in Moore,
Women of the War, *426–427.*

The [Soldiers'] Home is for all soldiers discharged from the service and awaiting the settlement of their accounts with government; for those who fall sick on their marches, and those of the new regiments who are taken sick while passing through the city. A great number of those admitted must remain each a few days, and we can accommodate about one hundred and twenty comfortably. When these poor veterans come in, weary and ragged, shirtless and with soiled raiment, Amy has the privilege of giving them clean, warm clothing for theirs, so torn and dirty; of feeding them and sending them on their way. Mrs. Murphy has the charge of the culinary department, and occupies, with her help, the first floor. I have charge of the rest. Mr. J. B. Abbott, a very efficient and just man, is the superintendent. I have two colored girls, who do the chamber-work, and an Irish girl for the washing and ironing. I find leisure to visit other hospitals, and do a great deal of good, I hope.

Amy M. Bradley, letter to her sister, autumn 1862, in Moore, Women of the War, *433–434.*

What were the state of things to which the woman order applied?

We were twenty-five hundred men [Union soldiers] in a [Southern] city . . . of one hundred fifty thousand inhabitants, all hostile, bitter, defiant, explosive, standing literally on a magazine, a spark only needed for destruction. The devil had entered the hearts of the women of this town . . . to stir up strife in every way possible. Every opprobrious epithet, every insulting gesture was made by these bejeweled, becrinolined and laced creatures, calling themselves ladies, towards my soldiers and officers, from the windows of the house and in the streets. How long do you suppose our flesh and blood could have stood this without retort. That would lead to disturbances and riot, from which we must clear the streets with artillery—and then a howl that we murdered these fine women. I had arrested the men who had hurrahed Beauregard. Could I arrest the women? No. What was to be done? No order could be made except one that would execute itself. With anxious, careful thought I hit upon this: "Women who insult my soldiers are to be regarded as common women plying their vocation."

Pray how do you treat a common woman plying her vocation in the streets? You pass her by unheeded. She cannot insult you! As a gentleman you can and will take no notice of her . . .

Major General Benjamin F. Butler, commander of occupying forces, letter to a friend in Boston, July 2, 1862, in Civil War: Clippings from various newspapers, 1860–1863, *unpaginated scrapbook.*

I went to Duff Green's Row, Government headquarters for the contrabands here. I found men, women and children all huddled together without any distinction or regard to age or sex. Some of them were in the most pitiable condition. Many were sick with measles, diptheria, scarlet and typhoid fever. Some had a few filthy rags to lie on, others had nothing but the bare floor for a couch. They were coming in at all times, often through the night and the Superintendent had enough to occupy his time in taking the names of those who came in and those who were sent out. His office was thronged through the day by persons who came to hire the poor creatures. Single women hire at four dollars a month, a woman with one child two and a half or three dollars a month. Men's wages are ten dollars per month . . .

Hoping to help a little in the good work I wrote to a lady in New York, a true and tried friend of the slave, to ask for such articles as would make comfortable the sick and dying in the hospital. On the Saturday following an immense box was received from New York. Before the sun went down, I had the satisfaction of seeing every man, woman and child with clean garments, lying in a clean bed. What a contrast! They seemed different beings.

Harriet Jacobs, letter to William Lloyd Garrison, August 1862, in Sterling, We Are Your Sisters, *245–246.*

MRS. JOSEPHINE S. GRIFFING THE ORIGINATOR OF THE FREEDMEN'S BUREAU: The truly excellent and noble woman was fitly spoken of in the *New National Era* just after her death, but at that early date it was not possible to obtain the facts to prove the statement at the head of this article, which is but simple truth and historic justice.

Mrs. Griffing was engaged in an arduous work for the Loyal League in the Northwest in 1862, and foresaw the need of a comprehensive system of protection, help, and education, for the slaves in the trying transition of freedom. She sought counsel and aid from fit persons in Ohio and Michigan and came here only in 1863 to begin her work of urging the plan of a Bureau for that purpose. Nothing daunted by coldness or indifference she nobly persisted, until in December, 1863, a bill for a Bureau of Emancipation was introduced in the House of Representatives by Hon T. D. Elliott, of Massachusetts. After some changes in the bill, and a committee of conference of the House and Senate, and the valuable aid of

Sumner, Wilson, and other Senators, the bill for the Freedman's Bureau finally passed in March, 1865, and was signed by President Lincoln just before his assassination.

The original idea was Mrs. Griffing's; her untiring efforts gave it life, and it is but just that the colored people, of the South especially, should bear in grateful remembrance this able and gentle woman, whose life and strength were spent for their poor sufferers, and who called into useful existence that great national charity, the Freedman's Bureau.

New National Era, *some years after Josephine Griffing,*
death, about her activities during the Civil War,
in History of Woman Suffrage, *Vol. 2, 37.*

I reported to Governor Yeates, who ordered me to go South with the 113th, or Board of Trade Regiment, Colonel Hoge. The colonel put my name on the muster roll as matron for three years, or to the close of the war. I went to Memphis with the regiment, and we encamped at Camp Peabody, about two miles from the city. When they went on the Tulahoma raid I accompanied them, by particular request of Colonel Hoge. The fourth day, was sent with all the sick to Holly Springs, Mississippi. Was there a number of weeks, and before Bragg took the place was ordered to Memphis; on the way was told the troops had gone down the river, and General Wright advised me to keep on down to the fleet. I did so.

While with the Vicksburg fleet, one day I noticed the boat I was on was dragging her hawser from the tree where she had been fastened. I reported to the captain. He said, "I know it." There was no steam on, and we were drifting down the river. The captain said we were going to Vicksburg, and were only a half mile from the line between the two armies. Among the sick was a captain of one of the companies of the 113th Illinois Regiment. I immediately went to him and reported the treachery on board of the boat. He could do nothing, as he was too ill to raise his head. He swore me, and gave me the necessary signal. I went on the hurricane deck; no one was there, no one on the pilot house. I gave the signal as he told me. In a moment I saw it answered. Immediately the "Von Pool" came down and towed the boat to the upper end of the fleet, and put a stop to our going to Vicksburg. All of the crew, from the captain to the chamber-maid, were so very angry they would have killed me had they known I was responsible for the change of programme.

Ruth Helena Sinnotte, about her participation in
the Civil War, in Holland, Our Army Nurses,
125–126.

MUSTERED OUT.—"Frank Miller," the young lady soldier, now at Barracks No. 1, will be mustered out of the service in accordance with the army regulations which prohibit the enlistment of females in the army, and sent to her parents in Pennsylvania. This will be sad news to Frances, who had cherished the fond hope that she would be permitted to serve the Union cause during the war. She has been of great service as a scout to the army of Cumberland, and her place will not be easily filled. She is a true patriot and a gallant soldier.

Louisville Journal, *some time during the Civil War,*
in History of Woman Suffrage,
Vol. 2, 19.

[In August 1862] I made a suggestion in the colored church, that a society of colored people be formed to labor for the benefit of the unfortunate freedmen. The idea proved popular, and in two weeks "the Contraband Relief Association" was organized with forty working members . . .

I told Mrs. Lincoln of my project; and she immediately headed my list with a subscription of $200. I circulated among the colored people, and got them thoroughly interested in the subject, when I was called to Boston . . .

I met Mr. Wendell Phillips, and other Boston philanthropists, who gave me all the assistance in their power. We held a mass meeting at the Colored Baptist Church, Rev. Mr. Grimes, in Boston, raised a sum of money, and organized there a branch society . . .

This branch was able to send us over eighty large boxes of goods, contributed exclusively by the colored people of Boston. Returning to New York, we held a successful meeting at the Shiloh Church. The Metropolitan Hotel, at that time as now, employed colored help. I suggested the object of my mission to Robert Thompson, Steward of the Hotel, who immediately raised quite a sum of money among the dining-room waiters. Mr. Frederick Douglass contributed $200, besides lecturing for us. Other prominent colored men sent in liberal contributions . . .

I was re-elected President of the Association, which office I continue.

Elizabeth Keckley, writing in her autobiography about her services during the Civil War, 1868, in Sterling, We Are Your Sisters, *249–250.*

We done heared dat Lincum gonna turn de niggers free. Ole missus say dey warn't nothin' to it. Den a Yankee soldier tole someone in Williamsburg dat Marse Lincum done signed de mancipation. Was winter time an' moughty cold dat night, but ev'ybody commence gittin' ready to leave, Didn't care nothin' 'bout Missus—was goin' to Union lines. An' all dat night de niggers danced an' sang right out in de cold. Nex' mornin' at day-break we all started out wid blankets an' clothes an' pots an' pans an' chickens piled on our backs, 'cause Missus said we couldn't take no horses or carts.

An enslaved woman's recollection of the Emancipation Proclamation of September 22, 1862, in Sterling, We Are Your Sisters, *244.*

Each Sunday morning we were roused by the drum calling to battle. The men responded promptly, leaving me with only one attendant, to care for the helpless sick. I gave them some coffee and hard-tack, with a smile and the assurance that I would get them out of the way of the flying lead. The camp was in range of the battle, and I knew the regiment had no ammunition, and must soon fall back, perhaps before I could even get the men ready to go. Several balls came tearing through the tent, creating almost a panic. We had gone there in the dark, and had not taken the trouble to find out our position, and what to do we did not know. Suddenly I thought of a lieutenant who had been sick the day before. I sought among tents and found him, and he gave me the points of the compass, and told me of a ravine nearby where we must try to get the men. Those who were unable to walk we carried on poles, and thus all were transported but one old man, who was delirious and would neither go nor be carried.

A captain came in, wounded in the left shoulder, and so once more I went to the camp and returned with what I could carry, then bound up the wound to stop the blood. By that time an orderly came with the command to get the men as far down the ravine as

we could, and an ambulance would meet us there. As soon as all was in order I took a rifle and started for the battlefield . . . When I reached the line I found our men in great numbers, and worked as long as I could find anything to do with. After using my own handkerchief and skirt, and everything I could get at, I went down to the river. There I saw such sights as I never want to see again: wounded men, mules and horses, tents and blankets, in the wildest disorder. The surgeon was attending to putting the men on a boat. He sent me aboard to do what I could. There were men wounded in all imaginable ways. Soon an amputation table was set up . . . I was so exhausted that I paid little attention to anything during the trip. On our arrival I reported to General Grant, who gave me an order to remain on a boat in the harbor until the hospital boat arrived.

Lucy L. C. Kaiser, about her participation in the Civil War, in Holland, Our Army Nurses, *183–185.*

We write to assure you that we appreciate the address of Elizabeth Cady Stanton, published in *The Tribune* of the 18th [regarding the formation of the Woman's National Loyal League]. We have long expected such a call, and regard it as the external manifestation of a wide-spread demand among women.

Mary Dean and seven other women, letter to Susan B. Anthony, April 19, 1863, in History of Woman Suffrage, *Vol. 2, 877.*

That the disenfranchisement of the women of '76 destroyed the moral guarantee of a pure republic, or that their enfranchisement would early have broken the chains of the slave, I may not now discuss. Yet it may be well to note that ever since freedom and slavery joined issue in this Government, the women of the free States have been a conceded majority, almost a unit, against slavery . . . Every legal invasion of rights, forming a precedent and source of infinite series of resultant wrongs, makes it the duty of woman to persist in demanding the right, that she may abate the wrong—and first her own enfranchisement. The national life is in peril, and woman is constitutionally disabled from rushing to her country's rescue . . .

This war is adding a vast army of widows and orphans to this already large class of unrepresented humanity. Shall the women who have been judged worthy and capable to discharge the duties of both parents to their children, be longer denied the legal and political rights held necessary to the successful discharge of a part even of these duties by men?

Clarina Nichols, letter to Susan B. Anthony,
May 4, 1863, in History of Woman Suffrage,
Vol. 2, 887–888.

I read with pleasure the "Call for a meeting of the Loyal Women of the nation." I thing such a gathering can not fail of great and good results. I hope you will have a correct and full report of the proceedings for the benefit of those who can not be present to see and hear for themselves.

Phebe B. Dean, letter May 4, 1863,
in History of Woman Suffrage,
Vol. 2, 878.

I do not wonder that woman lacks enthusiasm in matters of Government, for our laws though they may be nearly just to white men, are very oppressive to women, particularly those that deprive married women of the right to hold property and do business themselves. I think that man and woman both would live more happily if the laws were more equal; but as they are, they are a shame to this enlightened age. They make a married woman a beggar all her life, although she may have a rich husband, and a most pitiable one, if he is poor. Wipe out the law entirely that gives us a third of our husband's property; we can make better bargains than that ourselves with our husbands. The one-third law does us not a mite good, unless our husband dies, and we do not all of us want to part with them, although the laws do make them our oppressors. But notwithstanding the mean position that we are compelled to occupy, I feel like upholding the Government as the best that is, feeling quite sure that the kindness and good sense of our rulers will give us something a little more like justice after a while.

Miriam H. Fish, of LaSalle County, Illinois, letter to
Susan B. Anthony, May 8, 1863, in History of
Woman Suffrage, *Vol. 2, 884–885.*

I thank you for myself, and for thousands of women in Our State [New Hampshire], who may perhaps remain silent, for the clarion call you have rung through the land for a convention of loyal women of the nation, to be held at New York on the 14th of the present month. God bless you for the rallying cry . . .

Mary J. Tappan, letter to Elizabeth Cady Stanton,
May 10, 1863, in History of Woman Suffrage,
Vol. 2, 876.

The women of the League have shown practical wisdom in restricting their efforts to one object, the most important, perhaps, which any Society can aim at; and great courage in undertaking to do what, so far as we remember, has never been done in the world before, namely, to obtain ONE MILLION of names to a petition. If they succeed, the moral influence on Congress ought and can not fail to be great. The passage by the next Congress of an act of general emancipation would do more than any one thing for the suppression of the rebellion. As things now stand with slaves declared free in eight States of the Union, with two more States (Virginia and Louisiana) partly free and partly slave, and with the Border States still slave, we have a state of affairs resulting in interminable confusion, and which, in the very nature of things, can not continue to exist. Congress may find a way out of such confusion by an act of Compensated Emancipation, with the consent of these States and parts of States. God speed the circulation and signatures of the women's petition!

New York Tribune, *May 30, 1863, in* History of
Woman Suffrage, *Vol. 2, 893.*

. . . the extent to which impressment [of food supplies for Confederate soldiers] was carried on in the vicinity of principal depots left a scanty supply for the people, and especially for women and children whose natural protectors were in the army. Famine cursed the large cities, and the instances were not a few in which women marched through the streets with arms [weapons] in the hands, and compelled the satisfaction of their hunger . . .

Harper's, *May 1865, reviewing the conduct of*
the war, in Guernsey and Alden,
Harper's Pictorial History, *792.*

The rioters were represented in a heterogeneous crowd of Dutch, Irish, and free negroes—of men, women, and children—armed with pistols, knives, hammers, hatchets, axes, and every other weapon which could be made useful in their defence, or might subserve their designs in breaking into stores for the purpose of thieving. More impudent and defiant robberies were never committed, than disgraced, in the open light of day, on a bright morning in spring, the city of Richmond. The cry for bread with which this violence commenced was soon subdued, and instead of articles of food, the rioters directed their efforts to stores containing dry-goods, shoes, etc. Women were seen bending under loads of sole-leather, or dragging after them heavy cavalry boots, brandishing their huge knives, and swearing, though apparently well fed, that they were dying from starvation—yet it was difficult to imagine how they could masticate or digest the edibles under the weight of which they were bending. Men carried immense loads of cotton cloth, woolen goods, and other articles, and but few were seen to attack the stores where flour, groceries, and other provisions were kept.

This disgraceful mob was put to flight by the military. Cannon were planted in the street, and the order to disperse or be fired upon drove the rioters from the commercial portion of the city to the Capitol Square, where they menaced the Governor, until, by the continued threatenings of the State Guards and the efforts of the police in arresting the ring-leaders, a stop was put to these lawless and violent proceedings.

It cannot be denied that *want of bread* was at this time too fatally true, but the sufferers for food were not to be found in this mob of vicious men and lawless viragoes who, inhabiting quarters of the city where reigned riot and depravity, when followed to their homes after this demonstration, were discovered to be well supplied with articles of food. Some of them were the keepers of stores, to which they purposed adding the stock stolen in their raid on wholesale houses.

Sallie Brock, remembering "The Bread
Riot of Richmond," 1863,
in Richmond During the War, *208–209.*

It was during the spring of 1863 that one Webster, a clerk in the War Department, and his wife, were suspected, brought to trial, and found guilty of the charge of espionage for the Federal government.

He had undertaken the difficult and dangerous part of a double spy, and was in the pay of both governments, and had also been guilty of murder. The facts being fully made manifest, he was condemned to die upon the gallows, and his wife, not less guilty of treachery, was sent through the lines to Washington.

Sallie Brock, remembering the spring of 1863,
in Richmond During the War, *211.*

I have a great desire to go and labor among the Freedmen of the South. I think it is our duty as a people to spend our lives in trying to elevate our own race. Who can feel for us if we do not feel for ourselves? And who can feel the sympathy that we can who are identified with them? I would have gone upon my own responsibility but I am not able. I thought it would be safer for me to be employed by some Society. Then, I shall not be troubled about my livelihood, for it cramps ones energies to have to think about the means of living.

I suppose I must tell you something of myself. I teach the common English branches, viz. Reading, Writing, Arithmetic, Geography and Grammar. Should there be an opportunity for me to be employed will you please to inform me what the Salary will be and all the particulars. I shall be ready to leave Newport as soon as I can settle my present business. I have a Select School but I believe I can do more good among the Freedmen.

E. Garrison Jackson, an African-American woman from
Rhode Island, letter to Reverend S. S. Jocelyn on
applying to teach in the South, June 13, 1863, in
Sterling, We Are Your Sisters, *263–264.*

Col. Montgomery and his gallant band of 800 black soldiers, under the guidance of a black woman, dashed into the enemies' country, struck a bold and effective blow, destroying millions of dollars worth of commissary stores, cotton and lordly dwellings, and striking terror to the heart of rebeldom, brought off near 800 slaves and thousands of dollars worth of property, without losing a man or receiving a scratch!

Boston Commonwealth, article about Harriet
Tubman's assistance to the Union Army, July 10, 1863,
in Sterling, We Are Your Sisters, *259.*

The summer of 1863 in Richmond was made memorable by the apprehension and arrest of the wife of a wealthy and respectable citizen, for treasonable correspondence with enemies of the Confederacy. The circumstance were of an aggravating character. She was the confidential friend and at the time the guest of the wife of a prominent Presbyterian minister, who was then absent in Europe on a benevolent mission for the Confederacy. Having the unsuspecting confidence of the family under his roof, she acquired the information disclosed in the intercepted correspondence, and basely suggested the plans and time for his arrest, as a person who, from his talents and influence, was dangerous to the Union, and particularly useful to the Confederate cause. At the same time, a child of the minister was dying in the absence of his father, and in simulated sympathy with them in affliction the family were deceived, and unsuspectingly harbored an enemy whose treachery to them was more fiendish than that to the government which she had affected to sustain by her sympathy, her wealth and her influence. The indignation against her was universal . . .

Sallie Brock, describing events in the summer of 1863, in Richmond During the War, *249.*

She applied to both Surgeon-Generals Finlay and Hammond for commission as assistant surgeon. Her competence was attested and approved, yet as the Army Regulations did not authorize the employment of women as surgeons, her petition was denied. A Senator from New York, with an enlightenment which did him honor, urged her appointment to the Secretary of War, but without success.

New York Tribune, *of Dr. Mary Walker, September 15, 1863, in* History of Woman Suffrage, *Vol. 2, 20.*

Forgive your dying daughter. I have but a few moments to live. My native soil drinks my blood. I expected to deliver my country, but the Fates would not have it so. I am content to die. Pray, pa, forgive me. Tell ma to kiss my daguerrotype. P.S. Give my old watch to little Eph.

"Emily," letter to her father, before dying of wounds received in the Battle of Chickamauga River, September 19, 1863, in Moore, Women of the War, *531.*

It is with feelings of deep and heartfelt sorrow that I resume my pen to give you the particulars of the death of your noble son Coleman Stone. He breathed his last at a quarter before ten Tuesday morning, Sept. 22nd. I wrote you a week before his death giving you full particulars up to that time. Then fever set in which with his previous bad health and reduced state and wound combined soon brought him down. The injury, as I stated in my letter, was very serious from the first and never healed as it would have done on a strong, healthy person. Ten days or more before his death I had him moved from the hospital to an office in the yard next to me so I could give him constant care. Mrs. Moore was on the other side so some female was with him all the time . . .

Mary T. Bonham, letter to Mrs. Stone, September 25, 1863, in Anderson, Brokenburn, *260–261.*

Heartily appreciating the value of your services in the campaigns in New Hampshire, Connecticut, Pennsylvania, and New York, and the qualities that have combined to give you the deservedly high reputation you enjoy; and desiring as well to testify that appreciation, as to secure to ourselves the pleasure of hearing you, we unite in cordially inviting you to deliver an address at the capital this winter, at some time suited to your own convenience.

Vice President Hannibal Hamlin, 23 senators, Speaker of the House Schuyler Colfax, and 77 other representatives, inviting Anna E. Dickinson to speak, December 16, 1863, in History of Woman Suffrage, *Vol. 2, 47.*

Miss Dickinson's lecture in the Hall of the House of Representatives last night was a gratifying success, and a splendid personal triumph. She can hardly fail to regard it the most flattering ovation—for such it was—of her life. At precisely half-past seven Miss Dickinson came in, escorted by Vice-President Hamlin and Speaker Colfax. A platform had been built directly over the desk of the official reporters and in front of the clerk's desk, from which she spoke. She was greeted with loud cheers as she entered. Mr. Hamlin introduced her in a neat speech, in which he happily compared her to the Maid of Orleans. The scene was one to test severely the powers of a most accomplished orator, for the audience was not composed of the enthusiastic masses of the people, but rather of loungers, office-holders, orators, critics, and men of the fashionable world. At eight o'clock Mr. and Mrs. Lincoln entered and not even the utterance of a fervid passage in the lecture could repress the enthusiasm of the audience. Just as the President entered the hall Miss Dickinson was criticising with some sharpness [the applicability of] his Amnesty Proclamation [to slaves only in rebel states] and the Supreme Court, and the audience, as if feeling it to be their duty to applaud a just sentiment, even at the expense of courtesy, sustained the criticism with a round of deafening cheers. Mr. Lincoln sat meekly through it, not in the least displeased. Perhaps he knew there was sweets to come, and they did come, for Miss Dickinson soon alluded to him and his course as President, and nominated him as his own successor in 1865. The popularity of the President in Washington was duly attested by volleys of cheers. The proceeds of the lecture—over a thousand dollars—were appropriated at Miss Dickinson's request to the National Freedman's Relief Society.

New York Evening Post, describing
Anna E. Dickinson's lecture of January 16, 1864,
in History of Woman Suffrage,
Vol. 2, 48.

I am a colored woman, having a slight admixture of negro blood in my veins; and have been for several years a teacher in the public schools of Ohio. Since the providence of God has opened in the South, so vast a field for earnest and self-abnegating missionary labor, I have felt a strong conviction of duty, an irresistible desire to engage in teaching the freed people; to aid, to the extent of what ability God has given me, in bringing the poor outcast from the pale of humanity, into the family of man.

Possessing no wealth and having nothing to give but my life to the work, I therefore make this application to you. Can I become a teacher under the auspices of the American Missionary Association? I should be very glad and happy if it might be so.

No thought of suffering, and privation, nor even death, should deter me from making every effort possible, for the moral and intellectual elevation of these ignorant and degraded people. I know that the efforts of a single individual seem small and insignificant but to me this is of the most vital importance.

Sara G. Stanley, of Ohio, letter to the Reverend George
Whipple on applying to teach in the South, January 19,
1864, in Sterling, We Are Your Sisters, *265.*

We ask you to sign and circulate this petition for the entire abolition of slavery. We have now one hundred thousand signatures, but we want a million before Congress adjourns. Remember the President's proclamation reaches only the slaves of rebels. The jails of loyal Kentucky are today "crammed" with Georgia, Mississippi, and Alabama slaves, advertised to be sold

for their jail fees "according to law," precisely as before the war! While slavery exists anywhere there can be freedom nowhere. There must be a law abolishing slavery. We have undertaken to canvass the nation for freedom. Women, you can not vote or fight for your country. Your only way to be a power in the Government is through the exercise of this, one, sacred, constitutional "right of petition"; we ask you now to use it to the utmost.

Elizabeth Cady Stanton and Susan B. Anthony, letter to
"The Women of the Republic," January 25, 1864,
in History of Woman Suffrage, *Vol. 2, 895.*

I was with the regiment the first day at the battle of Shiloh, and we did up wounds until eleven o'clock. Then went to River Landing and aboard the steamer, on which were four hundred wounded. Here, too, I was the only woman. They had no food, so I first sent for coffee, sugar, and hard-tack. Tuesday the boat was ordered to Savannah, where we occupied an unfinished building. After we had been there a few days we received some supplies; then we did very well.

About the first of May four lady nurses were sent to us, and as soon as possible the wounded were removed. The sanitary stores were sent to Farrington. We found twenty-two hundred wounded, and some fever cases; all were in tents. We stayed until September; then the patients were sent North, the hospital was broken up, and the supplies sent to Corinth. Three other nurses and myself were sent to Jackson, where we remained until March, 1863. Then, all patients having been removed, the nurses, twenty-two in number, were ordered to report at Memphis, Tenn. From there we went to Washington. All this time I was a volunteer nurse, without pay.

Modenia R. McColl Weston, about her participation in
the Civil War, in Holland, Our Army Nurses, *164.*

I Lucie Stanton Day am over thirty years of age. Have for the last two or three years supported myself by dress-making. My health has been uniformly good. I am married though myself and child are entirely dependent upon my exertions for support. I hold a diploma as a graduate from the Ladies Department of Oberlin College. Have taught District School in Columbus Ohio some years since, also Select School. Have been a member of the Presbyterian Church for years. I wish to engage in this work because I desire the elevation of my race.

Lucie Stanton Day, an African-American woman from Ohio, letter to Reverend George Whipple on applying to teach in the South, April 26, 1864, in Sterling, We Are Your Sisters, *266–267.*

I hear frequently from Mama, as she writes nearly every day . . . She has many trials and burdens at home; the care of a plantation is a new onus and not properly belonging to her department, but under necessity she assumes it bravely, and right ably and skillfully does she direct. Little one, you may well be proud of your Mother.

Edgeworth Bird, letter to his daughter Sallie (Saida) Bird, August 10, 1864, in The Granite Farm Letters, *184.*

The Yankee raids are no joke, though we laugh at each other for being frightened. Last week 200 of the Corps D'Afrique, officered by six big white men (wretches they are), came out and laid the two little villages of Floyd and Pin Hook in ashes, not allowing the people to remove any of their possessions from their houses and thus leaving them utterly destitute. They were very rough and insulting in their language to the ladies, tore the pockets from their dresses and the rings from their fingers, cursing and swearing, and frightening the helpless folks nearly into fits. The Paternal Government at Washington has done all in its power to incite a general insurrection throughout the South, in the hopes of thus getting rid of the women and children in one grand holocaust. We would be practically helpless should the Negroes rise, since there are so few men left at home. It is only because the Negroes do not want to kill us that we are still alive.

Kate Stone, journal entry, September 5, 1864, in Anderson, Brokenburn, *297–298.*

This lady is a historical character, having served over two years in the Federal army during the war; fifteen months as a private in the Illinois cavalry, and over nine months as a teamster in the noted Lead Mine regiment, which was raised in Washburne district from the countries of Jo Daviess and Carrol. She was at the siege of Corinth, and was on duty during most of the campaign against Vicksburg. At Lookout Mountain she formed one of the party of eighteen selected to make a scout and report on the position of General Bragg's forces. She was an *attache* of General Blair's seventeenth corps during most of the campaign of the Tennessee, and did good service in the reconnoitering operations around the Chattahochie River, at which time she was connected with General Davis' fourteenth corps. She went through her army life under the cognomen of "Soldier Tom."

St. Louis Times, sometime after the Civil War, about a female soldier's participation, in History of Woman Suffrage, *Vol. 2, 20.*

For the first time my spirits gave way, and as Metta was too ill to notice what I was doing, I hid my face in my hands and took a good cry. Then the captain came over and did his best to cheer me up by talking about other things. He showed me photographs of his sisters, nice, stylish-looking girls, as one would expect the sisters of such a man to be, and I quite fell in love with one of them, who had followed him to a Yankee Prison and died there of typhoid fever, contracted while nursing him.

Eliza Frances Andrews, diary entry, December 24, 1864, in The War-Time Journal, *50.*

After our regiment had gone to Stockade Camp, my husband and I had to stay nearly two weeks with nine sick men. The only facilities we had for cooking were a coffee-pot, one mess pan, a spider, and a fireplace. But we got along some way, and the time came when I started an ambulance to join the regiment. I found a great many sick, but we got them into a hospital tent as soon as we could, and soon felt more at home . . .

Soon there were many sick with typhoid fever and other maladies, and I have passed through scenes that I shall never forget. Often and often have I stood by a dying soldier to hear his last words. I had a habit of going through the ward to say goodnight and speak a cheerful word, for I often knew that some would die before another day.

One morning as I was about to enter the hospital the doctor met me with the dreadful news that the small-pox had broken out, but through the providence of God I was spared. There were eighteen cases, and only one died.

Elizabeth B. Nichols, about her participation in the Civil War, in Holland, Our Army Nurses, *97–98.*

Union soldiers and a nurse at an army hospital in Fredericksburg, Virginia *(Library of Congress)*

Among the army nurses with whom I was associated, I recall the names of two most excellent women who are numbered with the dead,—Mrs. Underwood of Brown, and Mrs. Alling of Crittenden Hospital.

The war for the preservation of our Union evidently did much to advance the best interests of woman. It created a necessity for her labor in new and untried ways. It gave her an opportunity to prove her ability, and also to cultivate that true courage without which the most capable person may utterly fail of success. No women appreciate these facts so well as do the active workers of those days, among whom are the army nurses.

Vesta M. W. Swartz, M.D., about her participation in
the Civil War, in Our Army Nurses, *146.*

I have been in luck this year. My book [*Looking Toward Sunset*] sold with wonderful rapidity. The whole edition of 4000 were gone before New Year's Day, and they might have sold 2000 more if they had been in readiness. I had vowed the proceeds of the book to the Freedmen, whether more or less. I received $450 on New Year's Day, and immediately sent every cent every dollar to the poor suffering creatures, in different departments. *That* is something worth living for; to comfort thousands of old people with the book, and pay over the proceeds to

those whom the nation has so long wronged. It made me very happy, and I am humbly thankful to God, who had given me the power to do it. As soon as the poor creatures can have a little land to cultivate, or can get regular employment, they will take care of themselves; but *now* there is imperious need to help. Nor will it do to diminish our care for the wounded soldiers. I remembered them, too, on New Year's Day . . .

Lydia Maria Child, letter to Lydia B. Child,
February 11, 1865, in Selected Letters, *451.*

One cannot conceive of anything which would or could make a grander fire than this one, excepting a larger city than Columbia. The city was built entirely of wood, and was in most excellent condition to burn. The space on fire at midnight was not less than one mile square, and one week before, sheltered from 25,000 to 30,000 people. The flames rolled and heaved like the waves of the ocean; the road was like a cataract. The whole air was filled with burning cinders, and fragments of fire as thick as the flakes of snow in a storm. The scene was splendid—magnificently grand.

The scene of pillaging, the suffering and terror of the citizens, the arresting of and shooting negroes, and our frantic and drunken soldiers, is the other side of the picture, and this I will leave for the present for the imagination of those who choose to dwell upon it. It has for all these been sad indeed. I have in this war, seen too much suffering by far, and choose rather to remember the magnificent splendor of this burning city . . .

While the enemy held the city, a magazine exploded killing twenty rebel soldiers and one hundred women and children. The magazine was near the depot where these people were plundering, and dropped a spark among the powder scattered about.

Thomas Ward Osborn, diary entry, February 17, 1865,
in The Fiery Trail, *129–132.*

We find here a few citizens who have assisted our prisoners confined here among them, and most prominent are three Irish girls [Mrs. Amelia Feaster and two of her daughters]; they have been most faithful, and, indeed have done everything possible for the cause. They will go north with us.

Thomas Ward Osborn, diary entry, February 18, 1865,
in The Fiery Trail, *135.*

Cousin Bessie had brought quantities of beautiful things from beyond the blockade, that make us poor Rebs look like ragamuffins beside her. She has crossed the lines by special permit, and will be obliged to return to Memphis by the 2nd of April, when her pass will be out. It seems funny for a white woman to have to get a pass to see her husband, just like the negro men here do when their wives live on another plantation. The times have brought about some strange upturnings.

Eliza Frances Andrews, diary entry, March 8, 1865,
in The War-Time Journal, *111.*

We were then offered a position [teaching the freed slaves] on one of the islands where several thousand negroes were sent after Sherman's march. That suited us, and we were ordered to leave in two days.

Mary Ames, diary entry, spring 1865, in From a New
England Woman's Diary, *5.*

The wards are filled with the wounded. It is estimated that there are ten thousand patients in the hospitals here, and our Maine regiments have suffered severely. We are very busy, doing all in our power to alleviate suffering. Eleven hundred badly wounded were brought in on one day. In the evening the wards are dismal enough—long and narrow, without floors, dimly lighted with lanterns, and resounding with the groans of the sick and dying. Mrs. Mayhew and Mrs. Sampson go to the front to-morrow. One of us will work here all the time now.

Rebecca R. Usher, letter to "E," April 7, 1865, in
Moore, Women of the War, *461.*

I was in the kitchen getting breakfast. The word came—"All darkies are free". I never finished that breakfast! I ran 'round and 'round the kitchen, hitting my head against the wall, clapping my hands and crying, "Freedom! freedom! freedom! Rejoice, freedom has come!" Oh, how we sang and shouted that day!

Matilda Dunbar (mother of poet Paul Dunbar),
remembering April 1865, in Sterling,
We Are Your Sisters, *243.*

I used to think if I could be free I should be the happiest of anybody in the world. But when my master come to me, and says—Lizzie, you is free! it seems like I was in a kind of daze. And when I would wake up in the morning I would think to myself, is I free!

Hasn't I got to get up before daylight and go into the field to work?

Lizzie, an enslaved woman from Mississippi,
remembering the end of the Civil War, April 9, 1865, in
We Are Your Sisters, *244.*

Caddie had been sold to a man in Goodman, Mississippi. It was terrible to be sold in Mississippi. In fact, it was terrible to be sold anywhere. She had been put to work in the fields for running away again. She was hoeing a crop when she heard that General Lee had surrendered. When General Lee surrendered that meant that all the colored people were free! Caddy threw down that hoe, she marched herself up to the big house, then, she looked around and found the mistress. She went over to the mistress, she flipped up her dress and told the white woman to do something. She said it mean and ugly. This is what she said: "Kiss my ass!"

Maggie Lawson, remembering her grandmother's account
of the Civil War's end, April 9, 1865, in Sterling,
We Are Your Sisters, *244.*

Oh, baby! Dem Freedom Days! Never was no time like 'em befo' or since. Niggers shoutin' an' clappin' hands an' singin'! Chillun runnin' all over de place beatin' tins an' yellin'. Ev'ybody happy. Sho' did some celebratin'. Run to de kitchen an' shout in de winder:

> Mammy don't you cook no mo'
> You's free! You's free!

Run to de henhouse an shout:

> Rooster don't you crow no mo'
> You's free! You's free!

Go to de pigpen an' tell de pig:

> Ol' pig, don't you grunt no mo'
> You's free! You's free!

An' some smart alec boys sneaked up under Miss Sara Ann's window an shouted:

> Ain't got to slave no mo'
> We's free! We's free!

An enslaved woman, remembering the end of the
Civil War, April 9, 1865, in Sterling,
We Are Your Sisters, *243.*

Member de fust Sunday of freedom. We was all sittin' roun' restin' an' tryin' to think what freedom meant an' ev'ybody was quiet an' peaceful. All at once ole Sister Carrie who was near 'bout a hundred started in to talkin':

Tain't no mo' sellin' today,
Tain't no mo' hirin' today,
Tain't no pullin' off shirts today
Its stomp down freedom today.
Stomp it down!

An' when she says "Stomp it down," all de slaves commence to shoutin' wid her:

Stomp down Freedom today—Stomp it down!
Stomp dow Freedom today.
*A Virginia slave, remembering Sunday, April 12, 1865,
in Sterling,* We Are Your Sisters, *244.*

About noon, two brigades of our cavalry passed going west, and at the same time a body of Yankees went by going east. There were several companies of negroes among them, and their hateful old striped rag was floating in triumph over their heads. Cousin Liza turned her back on it, Cora shook her fist at it, and I was so enraged that I said I wished the wind would tear it to flinders and roll it in the dirt till it was black all over, as the colors of such a crew ought to be. Then father took me by the shoulder and said that if I didn't change my way of talking about the flag of my country he would send me to my room and keep me there a week. We had never known anything but peace and security and protection under that flag, he said, as long as we remained true to it. I wanted to ask him what sort of peace and protection the people along Sherman's line of march had found under it, but I didn't dare. Father don't often say much, but when he does flare up like that, we all know we have got to hold our tongues or get out of the way. It made me think of that night when Georgia seceded. What would father have done if he had known that that secession flag was made in his house? It pinches my conscience, sometimes, when I think about it. What a dreadful thing it is for a household to be so divided in politics as we are!
Eliza Frances Andrews, diary entry, May 6, 1865, in
The War-Time Journal, *219–220.*

You know that over nine thousand of our prisoners were delivered to us here; and no human tongue or pen can describe the terrible condition they were in . . .

Three out of the five lady nurses sent by Mrs. Dix have been very ill, and one, Miss Kimball, died this morning . . .

Thank God! the vessel that the Sanitary Commission sent came soon, with nine thousand shirts and drawers, so that when I first saw them, they had at least so much in the way of clothing.

We got possession of twelve hundred yards of cotton cloth and a bale of cotton. I called a meeting of the benevolent ladies of the place. The Sanitary Commission gave us thread, and in a week's time the materials were made up: one hundred and thirty-eight pillow-cases, one hundred and fifty-three pillows, eighty-four bed sacks, and as many sheets. And now the hospitals are all tolerably well supplied.
Harriet W. F. Hawley, May 1865, in Moore,
Women of the War, *392–393.*

We paid Sarah her wages; the first money she ever earned or handled.
*Mary Ames, writing of a formerly enslaved woman,
diary entry, May 25, 1865, in*
From A New England
Woman's Diary, *40.*

. . . I have been exceedingly occupied this summer making "The Freedman's Book." It is intended to encourage, stimulate, and instruct them, and I hope it will perform its mission. I have taken pains to rewrite all the biographies of colored people, that I made use of; in order to have everything very simple, clear, and condensed for them. I shall not take a cent of the proceeds myself, and shall furnish it to them at the cost of paper and printing, which will be immediately used as a fund to print more, if the freedmen manifest a disposition to have the book.

Perhaps you will be pleased to hear that I made $1000 by my Sunset Book. I have paid $750 of it over to the Freedmen, in different sections, for books, clothes, tools, &c; and the remaining $250 will be used for their benefit as soon as I have settled in my mind what is the best way to use it. I vowed the proceeds to the Freedmen, and the popularity of the book has been a prodigious satisfaction to me, on that account.
*Lydia Maria Child, letter to Sarah Shaw,
August 11, 1865, in* Selected Letters, *457.*

I cannot say that I am enjoying my vacation as much as might be expected for my heart and wishes are constantly straying toward my brethren and sisters in the South. It seems to me to be wrong to be away from those dear ones so long & to be wasting time that might be used in working for them. I feel that I cannot do too much or work too constantly for the elevation of my race and for the banishment of those prejudices which have so long formed a barrier to our rise and progress in the world.

S. L. Daffin, missionary teacher, letter to the Rev. George Whipple, August 12, 1865, in Sterling,
We Are Your Sisters, *269–270.*

Our circumstances are so reduced that it is necessary to reduce our establishment and retrench our expensive manner of living. We have not even an errand boy now, for George, the only child left on the place, besides Emily's gang, is going to school! Sister and I do most of the housework while Mammy and Charity are laid up. Sister attended to the bedrooms this morning, while Mett and I cleaned up downstairs and mother washed the dishes. It is very different from having a servant always at hand to attend to your smallest need, but I can't say that I altogether regret the change; in fact, I had a very merry time over my work.

Eliza Frances Andrews, diary entry, August 22, 1865, in
The War-Time Journal, *373.*

On the 13th . . . I had occasion to go for blackberry wine, and other necessities for the patients in the Freedmen's Hospital where I have been *doing* and advising for a number of months. I thought now I would get a ride without trouble as I was in company with another Friend Laura S. Haviland of Michigan. As I assended the platform of the car, the conductor pushed me, saying "go back—get off here." I told him I was not going off, then "I'll put you off" said he furiously, clenching my right arm with both hands, using such violence that he seemed about to succeed, when Mrs. Haviland told him, he was not going to put me off. "Does she belong to you? Said he in a hurried angry tone. She replied "She does not belong to me, but she belongs to Humanity." The number of the car was noted, and conductor dismissed at once upon the report to the president who advised his arrest for assault and battery as my shoulder was sprained by his effort to put me off. Accordingly I had

him arrested and the case tried before Justice Thompson. My shoulder was very lame and swolen but is better. It is hard for the old slaveholding spirit to die. But *die it must.*

Sojourner Truth, letter (dictated to Laura S. Haviland) to Amy Post, October 1, 1865, in
We Are Your Sisters, *254.*

The Contrast.—"Look on this picture and on that." While President James A. Garfield lay dying, another American citizen, one to whom the country owes far more than it did to him, was stricken with an incurable disease. But in this case no telegram heralded the fact; no messages were cabled abroad; few newspapers made comment, and yet had it not been for the wisdom of this person whom the country forgets, we should have possessed no country to-day.

Anna Ella Carroll lies at her home near Baltimore, stricken with paralysis—perhaps already beyond the river. As the readers of the *National Citizen* well know, when the nation was in its hour of extreme peril, with a nearly depleted treasury, with England and France waiting with large fleets for a few more evil days in order to raise the blockade, with President, Congress, and people nearly helpless and despairing, there arose this woman, who with strategic science far in advance of any military or naval officer on land or sea, pointed out the way to Victory, sending her plans and maps to the War Department, which adopted them. Thus the tide of battle was turned, victory perched on the Union banner, and in accordance with the President's proclamation, the country united in a day of public thanksgiving.

But that woman never received recognition from the country for her services. The Military Committee of various Congresses has reported in her favor, but no bill securing her even a pension has ever been passed, and now she is dying or dead.

In another column will be found the report of the Military Committee of the Forty-sixth Congress, in her favor, March, 1881, which as a matter of important history we give in full, hoping no reader will pass it by. Under the circumstances we shall be pardoned for giving an extract from a letter of Miss Carroll to the editor of the *National Citizen*, accompanied by a copy of this report.

Miss Carroll says: "I am sure you retain your kind interest in the matter, and will be gratified by the last action of Congress, which is a complete recognition of my public service, on the part of military men; both Confederate and Union brigadiers belonging to the Military Committee."

While this bill was in no sense commensurable with the services rendered by Miss Carroll to the country, yet as the main point was conceded, it was believed it would secure one more consonant with justice at the next session of Congress.

The nation is mourning Garfield with the adulation generally given monarchs; General Grant is decorating his New York "palace" with countless costly gifts from home and abroad; yet a greater than both has fallen, and *because she was a woman,* she has gone to her great reward on high, unrecognized and unrewarded by the country she saved. Had it not been for her work, the names of James A. Garfield and of Ulysses S. Grant would never have emerged from obscurity. Women, remember that to one of your own sex the salvation of the country is due, and never forget to hold deep in your hearts, and to train your children to hold with reverance the name of Anna Ella Carroll.

National Citizen *(Syracuse, New York), editorial, referring to Anna Ella Carroll's participation in the Civil War, September 1881, in* History of Woman Suffrage, *Vol. 2, 868–869.*

"The Women Who Went to the Field"

The women who went to the field, you say,
The *women* who went to the field; and pray
What did they go for?—just to be in the way?
They'd not know the difference betwixt work and
    play.
And what did they know about *war,* anyway?
What could they *do?*—of what *use* could they be?
They would scream at the sight of a gun, don't you
    see?
Just fancy them round where the bugle-notes play,
And the long roll is bidding us on to the fray.
Imagine their skirts 'mong artillery wheels,
And watch for their flutter as they flee 'cross the
    fields
When the charge is rammed home and the fire
    belches hot;
They never will wait for the answering shot.
They would faint at the first drop of blood in their
    sight.
What fun for us boys,—(ere we enter the fight);

They might pick some lint, and tear up some sheets,
And make us jellies, and send on their sweets,
And knit some soft socks for Uncle's Sam's shoes.
And write us some letters, and tell us the news.
And thus it was settled, by common consent,
That husbands, or brothers, or whoever went,
That the place for the women was in their own
    homes,
There to patiently wait until victory comes.
But later it chanced—just how, no one knew—
That the lines slipped a bit, and some 'gan to crowd
    through;
And they went,—where did they go?—Ah! where
    did they not?
Show us the battle,—the field,—or the spot
Where the groans of the wounded rang out on the
    air
That her ear caught it not, and her hand was not
    there;
Who wiped the death sweat from the cold, clammy
    brow,
And sent home the message:—"'Tis well with him
    now;"
Who watched in the tents whilst the fever fire
    burned,
And the pain-tossing limbs in agony turned,
And wet the parched tongue, calmed delirium's
    strife
Till the dying lips murmured, "My mother" "My
    wife?"
And who were they all?—There were many, my
    men;
Their records were kept by no tabular pen;
They exist in traditions form father to son,
Who recalls, in dim memory, now here and there
    one.
A few names were writ, and by chance live to-day;
But's perishing record, fast fading away.
Of those we recall, there are scarcely a score,
Dix, Dame, Bickerdyke,—Edson, Harvey and
    Moore,
Fales, Wittemeyer, Gilson, Safford and Lee,
And poor Cutter dead in the sands of the sea;
And Frances D. Gage, our "Aunt Fanny" of old,
Whose voice rang for freedom when freedom was
    sold.
And Husband, and Etheridge, and Harlan and Case,
Livermore, Alcott, Hancock and Chase,
And Turner, and Hawley, and Potter and Hall.

Ah! the list grows apace, as they come at the call:
Did these women quail at the sight of a gun?
Will some soldier tell us of one he saw run?
Will he glance at the boats on the great western
    flood,
At Pittsburgh and Shiloh, did they faint at the
    blood?
And the brave wife of Grant stood there with them
    then,
And her calm stately presence gave strength to his
    men. . . .
And these were the women who went to the war:
The women of question; what *did* they go for?
  Because in their hearts God had planted the seed

Of pity for woe, and help for its need;
They saw, in high purpose, a duty to do,
And the armor of right broke the barriers through.
Uninvited, unaided, unsanctioned ofttimes,
With pass, or without it, they pressed on the lines;
They pressed, they implored, 'til they ran the lines
    through,
And *that* was the "running" the men saw them
    do. . . .

Poem written by Clara Barton, commemorating
Civil War nurses, among others, and read aloud
by her in Willard's Hotel, Washington D.C.,
November 1892, in Barton,
The Red Cross, *509–513.*

8

Bitter Defeats
1865–1869

THE HISTORICAL CONTEXT

Soon after the war, Susan B. Anthony's worst fears were realized. The Fourteenth amendment to the Constitution, which would not be officially proposed until April of 1866, was already being discussed in the summer of 1865. Congressman Robert Dale Owen of Indiana sent copies of a draft to the former officers of the National Woman's Loyal League.[1] The amendment would in effect grant suffrage to African Americans, a goal Stanton, Anthony, and their female colleagues had long supported. But it would do so in a manner that pointedly excluded women. Penalizing states when "the right to vote . . . is denied to any of the male inhabitants," the Fourteenth amendment would introduce gender restriction into the Constitution for the first time.[2]

To Anthony and Stanton, this was not "negro suffrage," but male suffrage expanded. They immediately opposed it. Anthony traveled throughout the Northeast, trying to convince other women's rights leaders to oppose it as well.[3] From New York, Stanton argued with abolitionist males who had been instrumental in pressing for the amendment. She wanted them to withdraw support unless the amendment was modified to include women.[4] Her former allies refused. They would support the amendment, they explained, because the former slaves needed the power of the ballot to protect their freedom, rights, and dignity.[5] Cady Stanton did not disagree with that analysis but demanded, "Do you believe the African race is composed entirely of males?"[6]

As soon as Anthony returned to New York, she and Stanton prepared a petition. It requested a constitutional amendment prohibiting states "from disfranchising any of their citizens on the ground of sex."[7] Cady Stanton was now sorry she had not agreed with her friend in 1861. She realized it had been "a blunder" to suspend the women's rights movement during the war and that Anthony had been right to resist that step.[8] As Anthony had predicted, the placing of women's interests beneath those of the abolitionists and the Union army had been perceived as an outright forfeiture of women's claim to their rights. Abolitionist men now seemed surprised, even indignant, that any woman would object to the wording of the Fourteenth Amendment. Most of these men refused to sign the women's petition.[9]

Even worse, in Stanton's view, was the fact that women themselves were torn. Anthony had returned from her trip without the support she had expected to enlist. Few women's rights leaders were willing to oppose the possible enfranchisement of another disfranchised group, even if that enfranchisement came at a cost to women themselves.[10] Women were not only unwilling to oppose the Fourteenth Amendment but also hesitant to press their own claim during what had been declared "the Negro's hour." To Stanton's and Anthony's dismay, the very mention of women's rights while black male suffrage was under consideration was perceived by Republican and abolitionist males—and many females—as too upstaging. As Anthony complained to the writer Caroline Dall, "The real fact is that we have so long held woman's claims in abeyance to the Negro's that to name them now is received as impertinence."[11]

When she realized that women, too, would refuse to sign the petition, Stanton "scolded with tongue and pen."[12] In letter after letter she outlined to one woman at a time what females would face if "male" were inserted into the Constitution. The Constitution had never limited its guarantees of rights to men. It began, "WE THE PEOPLE of the United States" and then discussed the citizenship rights of its "People" and "Persons." The president, and only the president, was referred to as "he." Otherwise, no mention of sex appeared in the document. It was Section Four of the Constitution that stated "The Times, Places, and Manner of holding Elections for Senators and Representatives, shall be prescribed in each State by the Legislature thereof . . ." And it was in the various state constitutions that the word *male* appeared, limiting the franchise— and other rights of citizenship—to men. Thus, although women were not presently considered voters by their respective states, there was, in 1865, no constitutional barrier to state-granted suffrage. (Women in New Jersey, for example, had held franchise from 1776 to 1807.) With the insertion of the word *male* to define a voting citizen under the U.S. Constitution, the situation would change. Women would no longer be able to claim that state constitutions, by limiting suffrage and other rights to men, violated the terms of the Constitution. Moreover, the use of the word *male* to define a citizen raised the question of whether women were actually citizens.[13] "When your granddaughters hear that against such insults you made no protest," Elizabeth Cady Stanton promised Martha Coffin Wright, a fellow organizer of the Seneca Falls convention, "they will blush for their ancestry."[14]

Soon, petitions were being returned with signatures, and supportive editorials began to appear in at least some newspapers. Relieved, Stanton declared, "the skies begin to clear."[15] But if some reformers were now willing to support Anthony's and Stanton's position, they continued to want the women's support for the goals addressed in the proposed amendment. In December 1865 Theodore Tilton suggested that the proponents of women's and black male suffrage merge into one organization, the American Equal Rights Association, to press for "universal or impartial" suffrage.[16]

There had been no national women's rights convention since February 1861. In the first months of 1866, Anthony and Cady Stanton began planning the eleventh such convention[17] and placed Tilton's suggestion on the agenda. Women from around the country sent letters of support. Some, noting the educational and professional advances made since 1861, were optimistic about women's futures. Others, alarmed by the jocular reception their most recent suffrage petition had received in Congress, were less so.[18] Though many favored the impending motion to declare women's suffrage a component of universal or impartial suffrage, others questioned its wisdom—one writer, prophetically, called the idea "that sham."[19]

When the convention was finally held in May 1866, the proposal to merge the movements was fully discussed.[20] Anthony spoke in place of Lucretia Mott, whose voice was impaired by a cold. She recalled the first 10 National Woman's Rights conventions, pointing out that each one had been held in a free state and that women had always "looked to State action only for the recognition of [their] rights." A change in course would be required, she said, now that a war had been fought and concluded. The need for a reconstruction of the union meant that Congress was, now and of necessity, involved in questions concerning the basis of representation. "[T]he whole question of suffrage reverts back to Congress and the U.S. Constitution," she emphasized.

"There is, there can be," Anthony continued, "but one true basis . . . it must extend to the farthest bound of the principle of the 'consent of the governed' . . . We, therefore, wish to broaden our Woman's Rights platform, and make it in *name*—what it has ever been in *spirit*—a Human Rights platform." Anthony reviewed the enormous amount of work involved in the past winter's petition drive and concluded for those assembled: "As women, we can no longer *seem* to claim for ourselves what we do not for others—nor can we work in two separate movements to get the ballot for the two disfranchised classes—the negro and the woman—since to do so must be at double the cost of time, energy, and money."[21]

When the vote was taken, the 11th National Woman's Rights Convention had resolved itself into the American Equal Rights Association (AERA). At Mott's urging, Stanton wrote a preamble for the new organization's constitution. In it, she declared, "[W]e, to-day . . . bury the woman in the citizen, and our organization in that of the American Equal Rights Association." In good faith, she and Anthony placed themselves and their followers in an umbrella organization whose stated object was to "secure Equal Rights to all American citizens, especially the right of suffrage, irrespective of race, color, or sex."[22] Lucretia Mott was elected president; Elizabeth Cady Stanton, first vice president; and Susan B. Anthony, one of three corresponding secretaries. Eleven others, in addition to Stanton and Anthony (Mott's service, due to what she described as her "age and feebleness," was to be titular only), comprised the executive committee.[23] One of the 11 was Wendell Phillips.

Stanton and Anthony thought the prewar coalition was in agreement again, but they were mistaken. Twenty-one days later, at a public meeting of the AERA, Wendell Phillips declared that the African Americans' claim came first.[24] Formerly supportive newspapers, Gerrit Smith and Wendell Phillips' *Anti-Slavery Standard* among them, immediately reduced their coverage of the women's suffrage movement.[25]

That autumn, Stanton decided to take individual action. On October 10, 1866, she declared herself the first woman candidate for Congress. Although women were disfranchised, there appeared to be no legal restriction of a woman's right to hold office. In her letter to the electors of the Eighth

Congressional District, Cady Stanton declared, "as an Independent Candidate, I desire an election at this time, as a rebuke to the dominant party for its retrogressive legislation in so amending the National Constitution as to make invidious distinctions on the ground of sex." The *New York Herald* endorsed her (without sincerity, Stanton later claimed), saying: "A lady of fine presence and accomplishments in the House of Representatives would wield a wholesome influence over the rough and disorderly elements of that body." Even the *Anti-Slavery Standard* recommended "giving her a triumphant election." She was not challenged on her right to run but received only 24 votes from the 22,026 men casting ballots in November.[26]

One month later the Senate voted on a women's rights question. Senator Thomas Cowan, a Republican from Pennsylvania, tried to change the wording of the bill that would extend suffrage to the male portion of the District of Columbia's African-American community. The unabashed ridicule he received for moving to include women by striking the word *male* from the bill made it clear just how far from suffrage women were. Cowan's amendment received nine votes in favor but 37 against.[27]

It was in this climate that women's rights leaders began working in 1867. They had several battles to fight that year, the first of which would take place in Stanton's home state. In January the New York state legislature called a constitutional convention. Stanton addressed the Senate's judiciary committee on January 23, 1867, and insisted that women were among the citizens governed by the state constitution, and, therefore, they had a right to vote for delegates empowered to change that document. Nine members agreed with her, but the motion favoring her stance, introduced by the Honorable Charles Folger, was defeated. She then asked for, and received, permission for women to address the convention when it convened the following summer.[28]

The convention assembled in Albany on June 4, 1867. Stanton and Anthony addressed its suffrage subcommittee on June 27, and Lucy Stone addressed it on July 10. Each of the women asked that women's suffrage be granted during the revision of the state constitution. Horace Greeley of the *New York Tribune* was chairperson of the suffrage subcommittee, and the women anticipated a negative report on their question. They had come prepared, though, to win a point if they could not win the battle. George William Curtis, son-in-law of suffragist Sarah B. Shaw, was enlisted to carry out their plan.

In the months prior to the convention, the women's rights leaders had begun yet another petition drive; by the time Greeley was due to give his report, they had amassed 20,000 signatures. On that morning, below galleries filled with women, members of the legislature presented the petitions to the suffrage subcommittee. They were presented in separate groups, with one or several names for identification: "From Charles J. Seymour, Mrs. Mary Newman and 500 others from Broome County, for equal suffrage . . . Jane E. Turner, Rev. C. H. Bebee, and 56 others, Bridgewater, Oneida County. Another from Julia M. Sherwood and 22 others, Westchester County, asking for woman suffrage." On and on the presentations went until, at last, only one petition remained.

Curtis stood up and said: "Mr. President, I hold in my hand a petition from Mrs. Horace Greeley and three hundred other women citizens of Westchester, asking that the word 'male' be stricken from the Constitution." Greeley's own report followed his wife's petition. What she heard him say was that the "committee does not recommend an extension of the elective franchise to women . . . we are satisfied that public sentiment does not demand and would not sustain an innovation so revolutionary and sweeping . . ." Although the women were disappointed in the report, they—and the reporters of the day's news—were amused by the juxtaposition of Mrs. Greeley's request and Mr. Greeley's refusal.[29] (Horace Greeley was furious.)

The antisuffrage arguments had changed little since 1848. Those opposed to the enfranchisement of women still spoke as if every woman were married; as if every married woman were tenderly treated and as if tender treatment should negate the desire for selfhood. Antisuffragists also claimed that no mother of a well-raised son had any reason to fear government by that son. And all men, they insisted, had an innate desire to make life comfortable for women. But these statements were disproved by the experiences of many women, black and white, young and old, married and single, in every state of the Union.

These experiences, less amusing than the Greeley's opposing opinions, were not noticed by news reporters. Newly free African-American women faced enormous struggles. Many who hired out their services to their former masters realized that nothing had changed in that person's assessment of their status. The complaints filed during this time with the Freedmen's Bureau make it clear that many of these new employers still considered African-American women and their children property. Women were beaten if they took the time to care for a sick child. If a child's behavior displeased a mother's employer, the mother might again be beaten. Even a mother's struggle to educate her child for a better life might be interpreted as confrontational and punishable. One employer explained his attitude: "I acknowledge her freedom, but I do not acknowledge her right to do as she wishes."[30] Against this background, prominent African-American women took opposing views on whether to support the enfranchisement of black men without black women: Sojourner Truth, for example, argued for the necessity to immediately enfranchise women, while Frances Watkins Harper ultimately agreed to press first for black male suffrage.

Both black and white women remained the legal inferiors of males. "In New Jersey a negro father is legally entitled to his children," Lucy Stone explained, "but no mother in New Jersey, black or white, has a legal right to her children. In New Jersey a widow may live forty days in the house of her deceased husband without paying rent, but the negro widower, just like the white widower, may remain in undisturbed possession of house and property."[31] (A widower, but not a widow, continued to own the marital residence.)

Though abolitionists opposed to woman suffrage omitted black women from their discussions, they described the political and legal situation of black men in terms no activist woman could ignore. Increasingly, these women compared their status to that of a slave. Told that very few women wished to vote, Frances Gage said of former slaves, "I never found one who dared in the presence of white men to say he wanted freedom." And the situation of wives and daughters in a household was, she said, similar.[32] Sojourner Truth was particularly convinced of the analogy's soundness: "You have been having our rights so long, that you think, like a slave-holder, that you own us."[33]

Lucy Stone supported the Fifteenth Amendment. *(Library of Congress)*

By the end of 1867 these points were being raised far from the Northeast. The legislature of Kansas announced that the state's white male voters could decide for themselves in November whether or not to enfranchise women and/or blacks. Lucy Stone and Henry Blackwell traveled west at the end of March.

In order to address people all across the state, they had to "climb hills and dash down ravines, ford creeks, and ferry over rivers, rattle across limestone ledges, struggle through muddy bottoms, [and] fight the high winds on the high rolling upland prairies."[34] Woman suffrage supporters transported them all across Kansas, and they spoke to large, enthusiastic audiences. "We have crowded meetings everywhere," Stone wrote to Anthony, elated. "I speak as well as ever, thank God! The audiences move to tears or laughter, just as in the old time."[35]

The Kansas campaign was exciting, but it was also the point at which the women's suffrage movement began to divide internally. Stone and Blackwell returned to New York in time for Stone to address the New York State Constitutional Convention on July 10, 1867. When the convention ended, Stanton and Anthony traveled to Kansas. Arriving in September, they found that Republicans were reinterpreting the American Equal Rights Association's "universal suffrage" to mean universal suffrage for men only and that they had formed an Anti-Female Suffrage Committee.[36] Women's suffrage in Kansas seemed doomed. Suddenly, "at this auspicious moment," as Stanton and Anthony later recalled it, George Train, a Democrat, offered to travel across Kansas and speak on behalf of women's suffrage. A Republican outcry followed the acceptance of that offer. The Republicans objected not only because Train was a Democrat but also because he held racist views and was opposed to black suffrage under any circumstances. When Lucy Stone found out that his appearances with Anthony were represented as American Equal Rights Association events, she printed cards "stating the fact that the Association was in no wise responsible."[37]

But a member of the association close to Stone had, in fact, been responsible for Train's unexpected offer of help. In 1899 Henry Blackwell would describe the reaction of the association's officers to Train's participation in the campaign: "[T]hey could not believe it, and thought it must be some monstrous hoax invented by the enemy."[38] However, Kathleen Barry, while writing her 1988 biography of Susan B. Anthony, discovered an earlier, more confidential record—one that flatly contradicts Blackwell's public statement on the matter. In December 1869 Isabella Beecher Hooker was trying to decide which faction of the women's movement to join. In order to understand what was by then a bitter split, she spoke to all the parties in turn. The most enlightening of these conversations was with Henry Blackwell. Her notes of that meeting and a confidential letter to Susan Howard, both uncovered by Barry, indicate that Republican Sam Wood invited Train to Kansas and that Blackwell and several others suggested the association with Anthony.

Isabella Beecher Hooker was shocked to hear Blackwell say that he had encouraged the racist Democrat Train to campaign on behalf of women's suffrage. Blackwell explained that he and his fellow Republicans had hoped Train might attract Democratic votes for women's suffrage and that Anthony "could perhaps keep him [Train] straight on the negro question." But Train, arguing against black male suffrage and for women's suffrage, Blackwell told Hooker, "lost more republican votes for W[oman's] Suffrage . . . than . . . gained democratic." Blackwell then shrugged off as an "experiment" the alliance he and his colleagues had arranged and then so publicly condemned.[39]

Although they were not responsible for Train's arrival at their headquarters, Stanton and Anthony consciously chose to accept his help. They were accused of racism, a charge they denied. By the time both female and African-American male suffrage were defeated in Kansas, however, Stanton and Anthony had alienated Republicans across the country and many of their own close friends and colleagues in the East. The split in the women's movement widened when Train gave Anthony the funds necessary to begin a newspaper.

The first issue of the *Revolution* was published on January 8, 1868. Susan B. Anthony was its proprietor; Elizabeth Cady Stanton and Parker Pillsbury were its editors. Its uncompromising motto was, "Men, their rights, and nothing more; women their rights and nothing less." In successive issues of the *Revolution,* they unapologetically used only one criterion in their evaluation of proposed legislation and other issues: whether the measure under consideration would have a positive or negative impact upon women. Thus, when the Fifteenth Amendment, guaranteeing the voting rights of all men regardless of "race, color, or previous condition of servitude," was proposed in February 1869, the *Revolution* responded with an article entitled, "That Infamous Fifteenth Amendment." That article prompted a heated discussion of Stanton's and Anthony's views on black male and women's suffrage at the May 1869 meeting of the American Equal Rights Association. Right after that meeting, Stanton

George Francis Train made common cause with Anthony and Stanton. *(Library of Congress)*

and Anthony founded an organization devoted to the women's cause only—the National Woman Suffrage Association (NWSA). Although Lucy Stone, at the AERA meeting, had shown some sympathy for Anthony's and Stanton's views—and had gone so far as to tell Frederick Douglass that "woman suffrage is more imperative than his own"—she had ultimately concluded, "There are two great oceans; in one is the black man, and in the other is the woman. But I thank God for that XV. Amendment, and . . . will be thankful in my soul if *any* body can get out of the terrible pit."[40] She did not join Stanton and Anthony in their new organization.

One of that organization's first concerns was the Fifteenth Amendment. The Fourteenth Amendment, which was finally adopted in July 1868, had penalized states if African-American men were barred from voting. The Fifteenth Amendment would prohibit absolutely any such denial. Just as Stanton, Anthony, and others had wanted a one-word change in the

Fourteenth Amendment—"male citizen" changed to "citizen"—they now wanted a one-word change in the Fifteenth: "on account of race, color, *sex,* or previous condition of servitude."[41] Instead, a separate amendment extending the franchise to women was proposed.

Stanton hoped the proposed Sixteenth Amendment would be "a definite, constructive rallying point."[42] But the uniform support of women's rights leaders for the amendment was not enough to stop the widening split. Lucy Stone had emerged as the leader of suffragists opposed to Stanton's and Anthony's separatist views and confrontational methods. The two sides disagreed about more than whether or not to support the Fifteenth Amendment. Stone and her supporters insisted that men be prominently included in the woman suffrage movement[43] and that woman suffrage be the only women's question addressed. Stanton and Anthony insisted on addressing all questions concerning women, especially through the *Revolution.* They advocated divorce reform, championed a poor, ill-educated woman charged with infanticide,[44] and freely criticized what they saw as the thwarting effect of religion on women's lives. On October 19, 1869, Stone wrote to Stanton. "I *hope* you will see it as I do," she said.[45] She had finally decided to form her own women's rights organization, the American Woman Suffrage Association. It was the beginning of a 20-year split.

CHRONICLE OF EVENTS

1866

Ann Preston becomes the first dean of the Female Medical College of Pennsylvania, first women's medical college in the United States.

Women delegates attend the General Assembly of the Knights of Labor.

St. Lawrence University graduates its first female student.

Congress debates women's suffrage.

Lucy B. Hobbs graduates from the Cincinnati Dental College and becomes the first female dentist in America.

May 10–31: Eleventh National Woman's Rights Convention resolves itself into the American Equal Rights Association in New York City. Lucretia Mott is its first president.

June 18: Fourteenth Amendment to the Constitution proposed.

October 10: Elizabeth Cady Stanton declares herself the first woman candidate for Congress, running as an Independent from New York City.

1867

Lucy Stone, a resident of New Jersey, organizes a state suffrage society, one of the first in the country.

Harriet Burbank Rogers becomes the first woman to teach deaf people solely by speech and lip reading.

Cigar makers are the first national union to welcome women workers.

Kansas holds state referendum; women's suffrage is defeated.

Wisconsin passes first protective labor law in United States, limiting work hours of employed women.

June 4–25: New York State Constitutional Convention is held in Albany; efforts on behalf of women's suffrage fail.

1868

A women's suffrage association is organized in New Hampshire.

Myra Bradwell launches the *Chicago Legal News.*

Women found the Working Women's Protective Union in New York, which gives free legal aid to workers and lobbies for laws to protect women workers, the first of many such groups in America.

Mary Livermore, formerly head of the Sanitary Commission, founds the Illinois Suffrage Association.

The National Labor Union supports equal pay for equal work.

The African Methodist Episcopal Church establishes women's first official office within organized Christianity.

Harriet Beecher Stowe publishes *Men of Our Time* and *The Chimney Corner.*

Susan B. Anthony is appointed delegate to the Democratic presidential convention.

Journalist Jennie C. Croly is refused admission to New York Press Club dinner for Charles Dickens and founds the women's club Sorosis.

New England Women's Club is founded by Julia Ward Howe, Caroline Severance, and others.

Rhode Island Suffrage Association is formed.

January 8: First issue of the *Revolution* is published.

July 2: Hester Vaughan is convicted of murder. Elizabeth Cady Stanton and other women's rights leaders protest her conviction without a woman on the jury ("trial by her peers").

July 28: The Fourteenth Amendment, granting citizenship to African Americans, is adopted.

September: A call is issued for the first Woman Suffrage Convention ever held in Washington, D.C.

September 30: Louisa May Alcott publishes the first part of *Little Women* in two parts for Roberts Brothers publishing company. It will become one of the most popular books in American literature.

1869

Francis Minor submits resolutions to Congress claiming that women are voting citizens under the U.S. Constitution's Fourteenth Amendment according to section I, which says "All persons born or naturalized in the United States . . . are citizens of the United States" and "No state shall make or enforce any law which shall abridge the privileges or immunities of the citizens of the United States."

Catharine Beecher publishes *American Woman's Home.*

The Massachusetts legislature begins to grant hearings to women asking for the franchise and will continue to do so every year after. The hearings generally fill the largest room in the State House, the throng usually extending out into the hall.

Myra Bradwell helps win the passage of a bill giving wives the right to own their wages and protecting widows' rights.

The Illinois Equal Suffrage Association is founded, determined to win the vote for women.

The United States licenses the first female lawyers.

Iowa judiciary is the first to allow a woman to join the bar, admitting Arabella Mansfield Babb, despite the fact that the Iowa statutes specifically state that only males can qualify.

St. Louis Law School, of St. Louis, Missouri, is the first law school to admit women as students in 1869. Phoebe W. Couzins graduates from the college in 1871.

Margaret Van Cott is the first woman granted a license to preach in the Methodist Episcopal Church.

Mary Livermore launches *The Agitator.*

Women of the Laundryworkers Union strike.

Women's suffrage is granted in Wyoming and Utah territories.

The American Woman's Educational Association is founded.

January 14: In *The Revolution* Elizabeth Cady Stanton condemns Gerrit Smith for putting abolition ahead of women's suffrage.

January 21: First National Woman's Suffrage Convention ever held in Washington, D.C., opens.

February 26: Fifteenth Amendment to the United States Constitution is proposed.

March 15: Congress proposes Federal Woman Suffrage Amendment as the Sixteenth Amendment, moving it to committee.

April 14: Louisa May Alcott publishes the second part of *Little Women* for Roberts Brothers publishing company.

May: National Woman Suffrage Association founded.

July 28: Daughters of St. Crispin, a union of female shoe workers, is founded.

September: Myra Bradwell, editor of the *Chicago Legal News,* having passed her bar exam and received the required certificate of qualification, applies for admission to the bar of Illinois.

October 6: Myra Bradwell is refused admission to the Illinois Bar by the State Supreme Court on the grounds that she is a married woman ("by reason of the disability imposed by your married condition—it being assumed you are a woman.").

November: American Woman Suffrage Association is founded.

EYEWITNESS TESTIMONY

When they asked us to be silent on our question during the War, and labor for the emancipation of the slave, we did so, and gave five years to his emancipation and enfranchisement. To this proposition my friend, Susan B. Anthony, never consented, but was compelled to yield because no one stood with her. I was convinced, at the time, that it was the true policy. I am now equally sure that it was a blunder, and, ever since, I have taken my beloved Susan's judgment against the world. I have always found that, when we see eye to eye, we are sure to be right, and when we pull together we are strong. After we discuss any point together and fully agree, our faith in our united judgment is immovable and no amount of ridicule and opposition has the slightest influence, come from what quarter it may.

Elizabeth Cady Stanton, about the Civil War and postwar years, in Eighty Years and More, *254.*

While I could continue, just as heretofore, arguing for woman's rights, just as I do for temperance every day, still I would not mix the movements. That in my view is where, and the only point where, you and I differ, i.e., in a matter of method, of expedient action. I think such mixture would lose for the negro far more than we should gain for the woman. I am now engaged in abolishing slavery in a land where abolition of slavery means conferring or recognizing citizenship, and where citizenship supposes the ballot for all men.

Wendell Phillips, letter to Elizabeth Cady Stanton, May 10, 1865, in Stanton and Blatch, Elizabeth Cady Stanton, Vol. 2, 104.

May I ask in reply to your fallacious letter just one question based on the apparent opposition in which you place the negro and woman. My question is this: Do you believe the African race is composed entirely of males?

Elizabeth Cady Stanton, letter to Wendell Phillips, May 25, 1865, in Stanton and Blatch, Elizabeth Cady Stanton, Vol. 2, 104–105.

I have argued constantly with Phillips and the whole fraternity, but I fear one and all will favor enfranchising the negro without us. Woman's cause is in deep water. With the [Woman's National Loyal] League disbanded, there is pressing need of our Woman's Rights Convention. Come back and help. There will be a room for you. I seem to stand alone.

Elizabeth Cady Stanton, letter to Susan B. Anthony, August 11, 1865, in Stanton and Blatch, Elizabeth Cady Stanton, Vol. 2, 105.

Went to Tilton's office to express regrets at not being able to attend their tin wedding [10-year anniversary, traditionally acknowledged with gifts made of tin]. He read us his editorial on Seward and Beecher. Splendid! . . . Went to hear Beecher, morning and evening. There is no one like him . . . Spent the day at Mrs. Tilton's and went her to Mrs. Bowen's . . . Listened to O. B. Frothingham, "Justice the Mother of Wisdom" . . . Put some new buttons on my cloak. This is its third winter . . . Excellent audience in Friend's meeting house, at Milton-on-the-Hudson. Visited the grave of Eliza W. Farnham . . . Went over to New Jersey to confer with Lucy Stone and Antoinette Blackwell . . . Called at Dr. Cheever's, and also had an interview with Robert Dale Owen . . . Went to Worcester to see Abby Kelly Foster and from there to Boston . . . Found Dr. Harriot K. Hunt ready for woman suffrage work. Took dinner at Garrison's. Saw Whipple and May, then went to Wendell Phillips' . . . Spent the day with Caroline M. Severance, at West Newton. She is earnest in the cause of women . . . Returned to New York and commenced work in earnest. Spent nearly all the Christmas holidays addressing and sending off petitions.

Susan B. Anthony, diary excerpts, last months of 1865, in Harper, The Life and Work of Susan B. Anthony, *Vol. 1, 252.*

For the last thirty years the representative women of the nation have done their uttermost to secure freedom for the negro, and so long as he was lowest in the scale of being we were willing to press his claims. We are asking ourselves whether it would not be wiser when the constitutional door is open, to push in by the negro's side, and thus make the gap so wide that no privileged class could ever again close it against the humblest citizen of the Republic. You say, "This is the negro's hour." I will not insist that there are women of that race, but ask, Is there not danger that he, once intrenched in all his inalienable rights, may be added power to hold us at bay? Why should the African prove more just the generous than his Saxon compeers?

Again, if the two millions of southern black women are not to be secured in their rights of person, property, wages, and children, then their emancipation is but another form of slavery. In fact, it is better to be the slave of an educated white man, than that of a degraded, ignorant black one. We who know what absolute power is given to man, in all his civil, political, and social relations, by the statute laws of most of the states, demand that in changing the status of four millions of Africans, the women as well as the men shall be secured in all the rights, privileges, and immunities of citizens. If our prayer involved a new set of measures, or a new train of thought, it might be cruel to tax white male citizens with even two simple questions at a time. But the disfranchised all make the same demand, and the same logic and justice which secures suffrage for one class gives it to all . . .

If our rulers have the justice to give the black man suffrage, woman should avail herself to this new-born virtue and secure her rights. If not, she should begin with renewed earnestness to educate the people into the idea of true universal suffrage.

Elizabeth Cady Stanton, letter to Wendell Phillips,
December 26, 1865, in Stanton and Blatch,
Elizabeth Cady Stanton, *Vol. 2, 109–111.*

I have just read your letter, and it would have been a wet blanket to Susan and me were we not sure that we are right. With three bills before Congress to exclude us from all hope of representation in the future by so amending the United States Constitution as to limit suffrage to "males," I thank God that *two* women of the nation felt the insult and decided to do their uttermost to rouse the rest to avail themselves of the only right we have in the government—the right of petition. If the petition goes with two names only, ours be the glory, and shame to all the rest. We have had a thousand petitions printed, and when they are filled they will be sent to Democratic members who will present them to the House. But if they come back to us empty, Susan and I will sign every one, so that every Democratic member may have one with which to shame those hypocritical Republicans. Martha, what are you all thinking about that you propose to rest on your oars in such a crisis? I conjure you and Lucretia to be a power at this moment in taking the onward step.

Elizabeth Cady Stanton, letter to Martha C. Wright,
January 6, 1866, in Stanton and Blatch,
Elizabeth Cady Stanton, *Vol. 2, 111.*

Who told you that Mrs. Wendell Phillips (how you scolded me once for writing to Mrs. Henry B. Stanton!) would not sign a petition for women's voting? No, no, child; she will sign a petition whenever she hears of one, and your note is the first hint of one. I know of no antislavery "priesthood" that wishes to prevent it. I'm fully willing to ask for women's vote *now*, and will never *so* ask for negro voting as to put one single obstacle in the way of *her* getting it.

Wendell Phillips, letter to Elizabeth Cady Stanton,
January 14, 1866, in Stanton and Blatch,
Elizabeth Cady Stanton, *Vol. 2, 112–115.*

A quick reaction after a cold shower-bath is the best evidence one can give of a healthy condition! Your letter shows you are sound at the core . . . I have been out of patience with men, women, and fate. Wendell Phillips Garrison informed Susan that his wife would not sign the petition as "it was out of time." I called on Mrs. Fremont to see if she would head a petition. "Oh, no. I do not believe in suffrage for women. I think women in their present position manage men better." . . . I have so scolded with tongue and pen that really the skies begin to clear. See Theodore Tilton's stirring editorial, "A Law Against Women," in the *Independent;* see Martha Wright's last letter, and see Wendell Phillips's last also. These are good signs, and the whole question of "time" is so clear to me that I cannot understand why anyone hesitates. There is now no law favoring slavery, and as it is to the interest of the Republican party to give the black man the suffrage, reformers may as well pass on to some other position a round higher.

Elizabeth Cady Stanton, letter to Martha C. Wright,
January 20, 1866, in Stanton
and Blatch, Elizabeth Cady Stanton,
Vol. 2, 112–113.

The schools of New Orleans have been sustained without aid from northern Associations. But commencing with this month, the government has withdrawn its pecuniary assistance. While the Freedom's Bureau still retains its supervision i.e. regulation of tuition fees, provision of school houses and school property, yet the colored people must compensate the teachers by making an advance installment of $1.50 per mo[nth] for each child they send. This plan was proposed by Maj. Gen. Howard because the Bureau owes an arrearage on teachers salaries of four months standing. Consequently the number of teachers in the city which up to Feb[ruar]y 1st was 150 has been reduced to twenty-eight. I need scarcely inform you that something like 3000 children have been shut out of our schools because their widowed mothers are "too poor to pay." Their fathers being among the numbers "who made way for Liberty and died."

Edmonia G. Highgate, letter to the Reverend M. E. Striebly, February 8, 1866, in Sterling, We Are Your Sisters, *297–298.*

Thank you for your account of the launching of the good ship Equal Rights Association. No vessel like her has been given to the sea since Noah's Ark. Without the presence of woman the ark would have been a failure. I have about made up my mind that if you can forgive me for being negro, I cannot do less than to forgive you for being a woman.

Frederick Douglass, letter to Elizabeth Cady Stanton, February 16, 1866, in Stanton and Blatch, Elizabeth Cady Stanton, *Vol. 2, 106.*

If I should fail to be in New York for the May anniversary of the National Woman's Rights Convention, I will at least send you a letter for the occasion, in which I shall assuredly give my warm approval of your movement for impartial suffrage, without regard to sex; and record my protest against the proposed constitutional amendment, limiting the ballot to males. In this I am with you to the fullest extent.

William Lloyd Garrison, letter to Elizabeth Cady Stanton, April 5, 1866, in Stanton and Blatch, Elizabeth Cady Stanton, *Vol. 2, 106.*

The Freedmen's Industrial School in Richmond, Virginia, 1866 *(Library of Congress)*

I learn by a circular I have received that a Woman's Rights Convention is to be held in New York in May. I can not have the pleasure of attending it, but I would like to take this opportunity of telling you I am with you, heart, and soul, in this cause—of thanking you, and those with whom your are associated, for the noble work you have done, and are doing, in the cause of universal suffrage. There never was a more opportune time for calling a convention of this kind than the present, when it is evident that the United States Constitution is about to undergo some repairs—when all the so-called radicals in Congress are trying to have it so altered as to insure the disfranchisement of one-half the nation. They have so strangely perverted the meaning of the term "universal suffrage," of the suffrage intended, that every one of these special guardians of freedom refused to present Congress a petition for woman's enfranchisement; that the Massachusetts Senator who leads the van of freedom's host, did, finally, most reluctantly present it with one hand, while taking good care to deal it a blow with the other that would prove a most effectual quietus to it; that a representative [Mr. Boutwell], after repeating the self evident truth that "there can be no just government without the consent of the governed," says that "man is endowed by nature with the priority of right to the vote rather than woman or child;" that the two Senators from Massachusetts have each proposed amendments to the Constitution holding out inducements to the States to enfranchise all male inhabitants, but none to enfranchise women when they could have included them by omitting one word; that that light of freedom Mr. Greeley, of the *Tribune,* states that "men express the public sense as fully as if women voted" [speech in Suffield, Conn., last June]. These are a few of the straws pointing to that sham labeled "universal suffrage" . . .

F. Ellen Burr, letter to Susan B. Anthony, April 22, 1866, in History of Woman Suffrage, *Vol. 2, 912.*

What I most wish for women is that they should go right ahead, and do whatever they can do well, without talking about it. But the false position in which they are placed by the laws and customs of society, renders it almost impossible that they should be sufficiently independent to do whatever they can do well, unless the world approves of it. They need a great deal

of talking to, to make them aware that they are in fetters. Therefore I say, success to your Convention, and to all similar ones!

Lydia Maria Child, letter to Elizabeth Cady Stanton, April 28, 1866, in History of Woman Suffrage, *Vol. 2, 910.*

Your letter came into my hands after some delay. I hasten to reply to your inquiries. Our college is young yet. The first class of two graduated last year. Two young ladies are to graduate at the close of this term.

We receive ladies and gentlemen on the same terms and conditions; take them together into the recitation-room where they recite side by side; require them to pursue the same course of study; and, when satisfactorily completed, give them degrees of the same rank and honor—Bachelor of Science and Bachelor of Arts to gentlemen, Laureate of Science and Laureate of Arts to ladies. Both sexes are required to pursue the same course of study, with the exception of civil engineering and political economy, which are merely optional studies with the ladies.

We have two departments—Academical and Collegiate. The sexes are about equal in number in each department. We have only about twenty in the Collegiate Department. Half of these are ladies, among whom are some of our best in Mathematics, Languages, and Natural Sciences.

We have also a Theological Department, to which ladies have access. We have received applications from only two yet. One, Miss Olympia Brown, is pastor of a society in Weymouth, Mass., and is succeeding very well. She is a graduate of Antioch College as well of our Theological department. The other is now here.

Lombard University, Galesburgh, Ill. receives ladies, and takes them through the same course as gentlemen, and gives them equal degrees. I deeply sympathize with you in your efforts to raise the character and improve the condition of woman, though, perhaps, I should not be quite so radical as some in your Convention. Your cause is a good one, and I pray Heaven that it do good.

J. S. Lee, principal of the collegiate department, St. Lawrence University, letter to Susan B. Anthony, May 4, 1866, in History of Woman Suffrage, *Vol. 2, 909.*

. . . I can not agree that this or any hour is 'especially the negro's.' I am an anti-slavery man because I hate tyranny and in my nature revolt against oppression, whatever its form or character. As an Abolitionist, therefore, I am for the equal rights movement, and as one of the confessedly oppressed race, how could I be otherwise? With what grace could I ask the women of this country to labor for my franchisement, and at the same time be unwilling to put forth a hand to remove the tyranny, in some respects greater, to which they are subjected? Again wishing you a successful meeting, I am very gratefully yours.

Robert Purvis, letter to Susan B. Anthony, regarding the 11th Woman's Rights Convention of May 10, 1866, in Harper, The Life and Work of Susan B. Anthony, *Vol. 1, 258.*

A Question of Dress in a San Francisco Court: Mrs. Eliza Hurd De Wolfe, the lady who was arrested by Policeman Moore, on Larkin Street, on Thursday for misdemeanor in violating a city ordinance forbidding a woman to appear in public in male attire, made her appearance in the Police Court at noon today, to answer the charge. She was accompanied by her husband and wore the same dress, according to the testimony of Moore, that she wore when arrested . . . Col. Chapman volunteered a defence of the lady, and claimed her discharge on the ground, first, that there was no State law, nor any decision at common law forbidding the kind of dress worn by Mrs. De Wolfe, and therefore no power in the Board of Supervision to pass an ordinance making the wearing of such a dress a crime; second, that the dress worn by the lady did not contain a single garment belonging to a male attire, and therefore did not come within the provisions of the ordinance, even, if it [the ordinance] were legal. These premises were discussed at length, and at the close of counsel's remarks, Mr. De Wolfe the husband of the prisoner, addressed the Court in a very earnest and well delivered speech in which he discussed the subject of dress generally; in its moral, social, religious, and sanitary bearings, and claimed the constitutional right for himself and his wife to wear such dress as they saw fit, so long as it was decent and becoming, which he claimed his wife's dress to be, far beyond that usually worn by ladies in this city. He requested his wife to stand up in order, as he said, that the people there assembled might behold for once in their lives a suitable and becoming dress for a woman. He called the attention of the Court to the fact that every article of her clothing, with the exception of her pantelettes, or pantaloons, or, as some might choose to call them, breeches, were precisely the same as those ordinarily worn by ladies. There was the hat made precisely like other ladies' hats and after the latest mode; the furs were the same as other furs worn by ladies; the basque was purchased at a fashionable store in this city and was precisely like those generally worn by females in San Francisco. Everything in fact which his wife had on, with the exception of the pantalettes, was in every respect similar to the attire usually worn by persons of her sex. There was no concealment of her sex, for the boys in the street recognized her at once and showed their ill-breeding by shouting, "There goes the woman in man's dress." He wished the question settled whether his wife had a right to wear such attire as she should deem fitting and appropriate, and in accordance with nature, or whether the fashion of her dress was to be dictated by a mob or by the courts of the City . . .

After a few remarks from the District Attorney . . . Judge Rix expressed his views upon the subject. He said that the simple question was whether the conduct of the defendant in wearing such a dress tended to a public disturbance; if it did it must be stopped. He was free to admit that the dress worn by Mrs. De Wolfe, was, in his opinion, intrinsically more appropriate and becoming and healthy than that generally worn by ladies, and could it become the fashion and be generally adopted, it would be better for the female sex; but that was not the question here. If her dress tended to excite a mob and thereby disturb the public peace, it must not be permitted to be worn.

The fault might be in the public and not in the lady—he was inclined to think it was—but so long as public opinion remained as it was now, no person could be permitted to so shock the popular sentiment, even in matters of taste, as to bring on a disturbance of the peace. He did not feel like imposing any fine upon the lady, for she had clearly committed no crime, and he would therefore suggest that she so modify her dress as to make it conform more to the custom and thereby avoid any further difficulty.

Mr. De Wolfe asked the Judge to specify the manner in which the dress should be modified, which the Court declined to do saying that he had no doubt Mrs. De Wolfe would be better able to accomplish the required result than the Court. Mr. De Wolfe then frankly admitted that if his wife were discharged she would be very likely to do the same thing tomorrow for which she was now arraigned in Court.

New York Times, June 11, 1866, 2.

At a meeting of the colored Washerwomen of this city, on the evening of the 18th of June, the subject of raising the wages was considered, and the following preamble and resolution were unanimously adopted:

Whereas, under the influence of the present high prices of all the necessaries of life, and the attendant high rates of rent, we, the washerwomen of the city of Jackson, State of Mississippi, thinking it impossible to live uprightly and honestly in laboring for the present daily and monthly recompense, and hoping to meet with the support of all good citizens, join in adopting unanimously the following resolution:

Be it resolved by the washerwomen of this city and county, That on and after the foregoing date, we join in charging a uniform rate for our labor, and any one belonging to the class of washerwomen, violating this, shall be liable to a fine regulated by the class. We do not wish in the least to charge exorbitant prices, but desire to be able to live comfortably if possible from the fruits of our labor. We present the matter to your Honor, and hope you will not reject it. The prices charged are:

$1.50 per day for washing
$15.00 per month for family washing
$10.00 per month for single individuals

We ask you to consider the matter in our behalf, and should you deem it just and right, your sanction of the movement will be gratefully received.

"The washerwomen of Jackson [Mississippi]," letter to
Mayor Barrows, June 20, 1866, in Sterling,
We Are Your Sisters, 356.

Rhody Ann Hope Col[ored]; Samuel Davison, Beat her with fist and with the trase of an artillery harness. Alledged cause: Daughter of freedwoman was not there at dinner time to keep the flies off the table.

Rhody Ann Hope, complaint registered with Freedman's
Bureau, Baton Rouge, Louisiana, June 26, 1866, in
Sterling, We Are Your Sisters, 333.

Personally appeared before me one Rose Freeman "Freedwoman" who upon oath states that her hus-band (David Freeman "Freedman" to whom she has been married about nine months) has beaten her repeatedly and refuses to support her. We lived at Fernandina Fla about four months—during that time he beat and abused me. I reported it to the Officer in charge of the Freedmans Bureau; he had him arrested & he got out of the *Guard House* & left the place, remaining away until a new officer took charge—he (my husband) then came back & beat me again—I had him arrested—he knocked the officer down & ran away & came here to Savannah. This in May 1866. Since that time he has abused me & refuses to pay for the rent of my room & has not furnished me with any money, food or clothing.

Rose Freeman, complaint registered with the Freedman's
Bureau in Chatham County, Georgia, July 24, 1866,
in Sterling, We Are Your Sisters, 339.

Personally appeared Patsy a freedwoman who being duly sworn deposes and says:—About two months ago, I was delivered of a female child which was begotten by William Harper, he being a white man. Before the child was born he told me that if I had one and it became known that he was the father of it he would kill me. Columbus Harper, a nephew of William Harper told me one day this week that he heard I was going to swear the child to him (William Harper) and that if I did I would certainly be killed.

Patsy, a freedwoman, complaint registered in Anderson
District, South Carolina, August 11, 1866, in Sterling,
We Are Your Sisters, 342.

Although, by the Constitution of the State of New York woman is denied the elective franchise, yet she is eligible to office; therefore, I present myself to you as a candidate for Representative to Congress . . . [A]s an Independent Candidate, I desire an election at this time, as a rebuke to the dominant party for its retrogressive legislation in so amending the National Constitution as to make invidious distinctions on the ground of sex.

Elizabeth Cady Stanton, public letter to the electors of
the Eighth Congressional District, New York, October
10, 1866, in History of Woman Suffrage,
Vol. 2, 180–181.

We cordially hail the movement at this time for your state [New York], in view of the approaching revision of your Constitution. The negro's hour came with his emancipation by law, from cruel bondage. He now has Advocates not a few for his right to the ballot. Intelligent as these advocates are, they must see that this right cannot be consistently withheld from woman.

Lucretia Mott, letter with $50 to Susan B. Anthony,
November 18, 1866, in Barry,
Susan B. Anthony, *171.*

Altogether the ablest, most dignified and best-balanced man in the body is Frederick Douglass, and there is a deep feeling for him for United States senator in spite of the drift of the convention, which is evidently in favor of Susan B. Anthony; notwithstanding which Elizabeth Cady Stanton is likewise a candidate with considerable strength, favoring as she does the Copperheads, the Democratic party and other dead and buried remains of alleged disloyalty. Susan is lean, cadaverous and intellectual, with the proportions of a file and the voice of a hurdy-gurdy. She is the favorite of the convention. Mrs. Stanton is of intellectual stock, impressive in manner and disposed to henpeck the convention which of course calls out resistance and much cackling . . . Susan has a controlling advantage over her in the fact that she is unencumbered with a husband. As male members of Congress rarely have wives in Washington, so female members will be expected to be without husbands at the capital . . .

Parker Pillsbury, one of the notabilities of the body, is a good-looking white man naturally, but has a cowed and sneakish expression stealing over him, as though he regretted he had not been born a nigger or one of these females . . . Lucy Stone, the president of the convention, is what the law terms a "spinster." She is a sad old girl, presides with timidity and hesitation, is wheesy and nasal in her pronunciation and wholly without dignity or command . . . Mummified and fossilated females, void of domestic duties, habits and natural affections; crackbrained, rheumatic, dyspeptic, henpecked men, vainly striving to achieve the liberty of opening their heads in presence of their wives; self-educated, oily-faced, insolent, gabbling negroes, and Theodore Tilton, make up the less than a hundred members of this caravan, called, by themselves, the American Equal Rights Association.

New York World, account of a meeting of the American
Equal Rights Association held November 21, 1866,
in Harper, Life and Work of
Susan B. Anthony, *Vol. 1, 264.*

The Senate devoted yesterday to a discussion of the right of women to vote—a side question, which Mr. Cowan, of Pennsylvania, interjected into the debate on suffrage for the District of Columbia. Mr. Cowan chooses to represent himself as an ardent champion of the claim of woman to the elective franchise. It is not necessary to question his sincerity, but the occasion which he selects for the exhibition of his new-born zeal, subjects him to the suspicion of being considerably more anxious to embarrass the bill for enfranchising the blacks, than to amend it by conferring upon women the enjoyment of the same right . . .

We are not to be suspected of indifference to the question whether woman shall vote. At a proper time we mean to urge her claim, but we object to allowing a measure of urgent necessity, and on which the public has made up its mind, to be retarded and imperilled . . .

We want to see the ballot put in the hands of the black without one day's delay added to long postponement of his just claim. When that is done, we shall be ready to take up the next question.

New York Tribune, December 12, 1866, in
History of Woman Suffrage, *Vol. 2, 103.*

I sit down to write you, with a feeling of despair which never came to me before where a principle is involved.

We have just returned from Philadelphia, where we went to assist in forming an Equal Suffrage Association. Geo. Thompson was there, and said "he did not think it would make any practical difference whether women voted or not." Edward M. Davis said "he sympathized with the Equal suffrage movement but he would take no position in it, that involved work. All his *work,* should be for the Negro." Eight colored men gathered around us during the recess, and said they thought women were well enough represented by their husbands &c. Robert Purvis alone, of them all, said "he should be ashamed to ask suffrage for himself and not at the same time, ask it for women, and he marveled at the patience of women, who were silent as to their own claims, while the great mass of the Negroes for whom they worked, would give their influence like a dead weight against the equality of women with them." Lucretia Mott, clear eyed as ever gave her voice, and her money, for universal justice.

But you, and Phillips, & Garrison, and the brave workers who for thirty years, have said "let justice be done, if the heavens fall," now smitten by a strange blindness, believe that the nation's peril can be averted, if it can be induced to accept the poor half loaf, of justice for the Negro, poisoned by its lack of justice for every woman in the land. As if the application of a *universal* principle to a single class, *could* suffice for the necessity of this hour! . . .

O Abby, it is a terrible mistake you are all making . . . There is no other name given, by which this country *can* be saved, but that of *woman*. The Nation does not know it, and will not learn, Greeley says "*don't* stir your question." Oliver Johnson sits in Theodore Tiltons chair, and snubs Mrs. Stanton and every one of us, not even opening our replies to Tayler Lewis. During a whole year, till very lately, has the Anti Slavery Standard thought it necessary to apologize, if it gave an item looking toward justice for woman. The "World" refuses to publish anything, because "its position would be misunderstood." So we get no access to the public ear. Susan Anthony gets no money from the Hovey fund, for her work in N.Y. . . .

Here is a kiss for the hem of your garment, and all good wishes for you, and yours, but the tears are in my eyes, and a wail goes through my heart akin to that which I should feel, if I saw my little daughter drowning before my eyes with no power to help her.

Lucy Stone, letter to Abby Kelley Foster, January 24, 1867, in Wheeler, Loving Warriors, *215–217.*

We report good news! After half a day's earnest debate, the Convention at Topeka [Kansas], by an almost unanimous vote, refused to separate "the two questions" male and white. A delegation from Lawrence came up specially to get the woman dropped. The good God upset a similar delegation from Leavenworth bent on the same object, and prevented them from reaching Topeka at all. Gov. Robinson, Gov. Root, Col. Wood, Gen. Larimer, Col. Ritchie, and "the old guard" generally were on hand. Our coming out did good. Lucy spoke with all her old force and fire. Mrs. Nichols was there—a strong list of permanent officers was nominated—and a State Impartial Suffrage Association was organized. The right men were put upon the committees, and I do not believe that the Negro Suffrage men can well bolt or back out now.

The effect is wonderful. Papers which have been ridiculing woman suffrage and sneering at "Sam Wood's Convention" are now on our side . . .

[I]f Lucy and I succeed in "getting up steam" as we hope in Lawrence, Wyandotte, Leavenworth, and Atchison, the woman and the negro will rise or fall together, and shrewd politicians say that with proper effort we shall carry both next fall . . .

We are announced to speak every night but Sundays from April 7 to May 5 inclusive. We shall have to travel from twenty to forty miles per day. If our voices and health hold out, Col. Wood says the State is safe . . .

Henry B. Blackwell, letter to Elizabeth Cady Stanton, from Kansas, April 5, 1867, in History of Woman Suffrage, *Vol. 2, 232–233.*

We came here just in the nick of time. The papers were laughing at "Sam Wood's Convention," the call for which was in the papers with the names of Beecher, Tilton, Ben Wade, Gratz Brown, E. C. Stanton, Anna Dickinson, Lucy Stone, etc., as persons expected or invited to be at the convention. The papers said: "This is one of Sam's shabbiest tricks. Not one of these persons will be present, and he knows it," etc. etc. Our arrival set a buzz going, and when I announced you and Susan and Aunt Fanny for the fall, they began to say "they guessed the thing would carry." Gov. Robinson said he could not go to the Topeka Convention, for he had a lawsuit involving $1,000 that was to come off that very day, but we talked the matter over with him, showed him what a glorious hour it was for Kansas, etc. etc., and he soon concluded to get the suit put off and go to the convention . . . When the platform was read, with the names of the officers, and the morning's discussion was over, everybody then felt that the ball was set right. But in the P.M. came a Methodist minister and a lawyer from Lawrence as delegates, "instructed" to use the word "impartial," "as it had been used for the last two years," to make but one issue, and to drop the woman. The lawyer said, "If I was a negro, I would not want the woman hitched on to my skirts," etc. He made a mean speech. Mrs. Nichols and I came down upon him, and the whole convention, except the Methodist, was against him. The vote was taken whether to drop the woman, and only the little lawyer from Lawrence, with a hole in his coat and only one shoe on, voted against the woman . . . The women here are grand, and it will be a shame past all expression if they don't get the right to vote. One woman in Wyandotte said she carried petitions all through the town for female suffrage and not one woman in ten refused to sign. Another in Lawrence said thay sent up two large petitions from there. So they have been at the legislature, like the heroes they really are, and it is not possible for the husbands of such women to back out, though they have sad lack of principle and a terrible desire for office.

Lucy Stone, letter to Elizabeth Cady Stanton from Leavenworth, Kansas, April 10, 1867, in History of Woman Suffrage, *Vol. 2, 134–135.*

I hope not a man will be asked to speak at the convention. If they volunteer, very well, but I have been for the last time on my knees to Phillips or Higginson, or any of them. If they help now, they should ask us, and not we them.

Lucy Stone, letter to Elizabeth Cady Stanton, from Junction City, Kansas, April 20, 1867, in History of Woman Suffrage, *Vol. 2, 235.*

You will be glad to know that Lucy and I are going over the length and breadth of this State speaking every day, and sometimes twice, journeying from twenty-five to forty miles daily, sometimes in a carriage and sometimes in an open wagon, with or without springs. We climb hills and dash down ravines, ford creeks, and ferry over rivers, rattle across limestone ledges, struggle through muddy bottoms, fight the high winds on the high rolling upland prairies, and address the most astonishing (and astonished) audiences in the most extraordinary places. To-night it may be a log school house, tomorrow a stone church; next day a store with planks for seats, and in one place, if it had not rained, we should have held forth in an unfinished court house, with only four stone walls but no roof whatever . . .

One woman told Lucy that no decent woman would be running over the country talking nigger and woman. Her brother told Lucy that "he had had a woman who was under the sod, but that if she had ever said she wanted to vote he would have pounded her to death! . . ."

I think we shall probably succeed in Kansas next fall if the State is thoroughly canvassed, not else. We are fortunate in having Col. Sam N. Wood as an organizer and worker. We owe everything to Wood, and he is really a thoroughly noble, good fellow, and a hero . . . The son of a Quaker mother, he held the baby while his wife acted as one of the officers, and his mother another, in a Woman's Rights Convention seventeen years ago. Wood has helped off more runaway slaves than any man in Kansas. He has always been *true* both to the negro and the woman. But the negroes dislike and distrust him because he has never allowed the word white to be struck out, unless the word male should be struck out also. He takes exactly Mrs. Stanton's ground, that the colored men and women shall enter the Kingdom *together,* if at all . . .

Kansas is to be *the battle ground* for 1867. *It must not be allowed to fail* . . . Do not let anything prevent your being here September 1 *for the Campaign,* which will end in November.

Henry B. Blackwell, letter to Elizabeth Cady Stanton and Susan B. Anthony, from Junction City, Kansas, April 21, 1867, in History of Woman Suffrage, *Vol. 2, 235–237.*

[T]he *Tribune* and the *Independent* alone could, if they would urge *universal* suffrage, as they do negro suffrage, carry this whole nation upon the only just plane of equal human rights. What a power to hold, and not use! I could not sleep the other night, just thinking of it . . .

Lucy Stone, letter to Susan B. Anthony, May 1, 1867, in Wheeler, Loving Warriors, *219.*

Although not permitted to be present with you, yet, in spirit, I join you in all your efforts to secure justice and equality to all the children of God. I have so long felt deeply upon the subjects before you, that I wish to add my word to the voices of those who are more fortunate in being present. Since I was old enough to think upon important subjects, I have constantly felt the pressure of injustice that has borne so heavily upon my sex. At sixteen I earnestly desired to enter some college, that I might have the benefit of those helps to learning which were open to all boys, and I deeply felt the cruelty and injustice that closed the doors of the universities to me, who was longing and thirsting for knowledge, while they were invitingly open to the youth of the other sex, who often only used them to waste their time and give them the name of educated men. I could see no reason for this exclusion, nor could I imagine how it would harm any one to allow girls who desired to learn the privilege of going to the universities.

My next personal experience of the injustice done to women by the laws was, when a widow, I buried one of my little daughters, and found that I, who had borne her and nursed her and provided for all her wants, was not her heir, but her little sister, who had done nothing for her, and was still dependent of me for care, etc. This I felt very keenly, not on account of the property involved, for it was but little, but on account of the great injustice done to my maternal heart. My next personal lesson in the law's iniquity was, when about to marry the second time, both myself and husband desired to secure to me the property I possessed. I employed a great lawyer in Maine, Gov. Fessenden, the father of one of our senators, to make an instrument that would secure that end. After thinking on the subject a week, and doing the best he could, he handed me the paper, saying, "I have done my best; but I can not assure you that this instrument will secure to you your property if your husband should ever become insolvent!" This surely astonished me. The law not only did not protect women in their property rights, but did so much to prevent their getting or keeping them, that an able lawyer could not frame an instrument that would secure them even when signed by their intended husbands before marriage! This was more than thirty years ago, and some improvements have since been made in the laws in reference to women.

The next great wrong that pressed heavily upon me was when I again became a widow. I found myself yearly taxed for State and county, and later for revenue, without a voice in anything that concerned the raising of money, or in any of the elections to office in the great struggle that our country was passing through. With . . . an intensely painful knowledge of the sin of slavery and its concomitant evils, I could not cast a vote in favor of the right, but must look on with folded hands, and give my money to support the Government, without a chance of giving it an impetus, however slight, in the direction of justice and liberty! In view of all these wrongs, I felt that the women of America had as just cause for rebellion against the Government as our Fathers had against the British Government when they resisted, on the ground that taxation and representation were one and inseparable.

Mercy B. Jackson, M.D., letter to the American Equal Rights Association, May 5, 1867, in History of Woman Suffrage, *Vol. 2, 920–921.*

I feel that I must do something for the "Woman's Suffrage" movement in the West. There is much interest here concerning it, but no movement is yet made. Matters are being prepared, and when the movement is made in the West, it will sweep onward majestically. Kansas and Iowa will first give women the right to vote before any other States, East or West. "Man proposes, but God disposes." I have always had a theory of my own concerning this suffrage question. Ever since I began to think of it, and that has been since Dr. Harriot Hunt's first protest against woman being taxed when she had no representation, I have believed that, in my day, woman would vote. But I have thought they would first obtain the right to work and wages, and that the right to vote would naturally follow. For woman's right to work and wages I have labored indefatigably. But I see that my plan is not God's plan. The right to vote is to come first, and work and wages afterwards, and easily. I "stumped" the Northwest during the war. Two women of us, Mrs. Hoge and myself, organized over 1,000 Aid Societies, and raised, in money and supplies, nearly $100,000 for the soldiers; and to do it, we were compelled to get people together in masses, and tell our story and our plans, and make our appeals to hundreds at a time. So I can talk here, and can help you here, when you are ready to lead. In the meanwhile, I have begun to work for the cause through my husband's weekly paper, which has a large circulation in the Northwest. I have announced myself as henceforth committed to the cause of woman suffrage, and have become involved, instanter, in a controversy on the subject. I am associate editor of the paper, and have been these dozen years. I have just completed a reply to an objector to the doctrine, which goes into this week's issue. In my way, I am working with you. I have always believed in the ballot for woman at some future time—always, since reading Margaret Fuller's "Woman in the Nineteenth Century," which set me to thinking a quarter of a century ago.

Mary A. Livermore, letter to Susan B. Anthony, May 5, 1867, in History of Woman Suffrage, *Vol. 2, 921.*

I hope your Convention will not fail to set in its true light the position of those editors in New York who are branding as the "infamous thirteen" the men who, in the New Jersey Legislature, voted against negro suffrage, while they themselves give the whole weight of their journals against woman's right to vote. They use the terms "universal and impartial suffrage," when they mean only negro suffrage; and they do it to hide a dark skin and an unpopular client. They know that a "lie will keep its throne a whole age longer if it skulks behind the shadow of some fair seeming name." In New Jersey a negro father is legally entitled to his children, but no mother in New Jersey, black or white, has a legal right to her children. In New Jersey a widow may live forty days in the house of her deceased husband without paying rent, but the negro widower, just like the white widower, may remain in undisturbed possession of house and property. A negro man can sell his real estate and make a valid deed, but no wife in that State can do so without her husband's consent. A negro man in New Jersey may will all his property as he pleases, but no wife in the State can will her personal property at all, and if she will her real estate with her husband's consent, he may revoke that consent any time before the will is admitted to probate and thus render her will null and void. The women of New Jersey went to the Legislature last winter on their own petition, for the right of suffrage. Twenty-three members voted for them, thirty-two voted against them. But the editors who now find unmeasured words to express their contempt for the "infamous thirteen" who voted against the negro, were as dumb as death when this vote was cast against woman.

Lucy Stone, letter to Susan B. Anthony, May 6, 1867,
in History of Woman Suffrage, *Vol. 2, 919.*

Everywhere we go we have the largest and most enthusiastic meetings, and any one of our audiences would give a majority for woman suffrage. But the negroes are all against us. There has just now left us an ignorant black preacher named Twine, who is very confident that women ought not to vote. These men *ought not be allowed to vote before we do,* because they will be just so much more dead weight to lift.

Lucy Stone, letter to Susan B. Anthony, May 9, 1867,
in History of Woman Suffrage *Vol. 2, 238.*

O, say what thrilling songs of fairies,
Wafted o'er the Kansas prairies,
Charm the ear while zephyrs speed 'em!
Woman's pleading for her freedom.

Chorus—Clear the way, the songs are floating;
Clear the way, the world is noting;

Prepare the way, the right promoting,
And ballots, too, for woman's voting.

We frankly say to fathers, brothers,
Husbands, too, and several others,
We're bound to win our right of voting,
Don't you hear the music floating?

We come to take with you our station,
Brave defenders of the nation,
And aim by noble, just endeavor
To elevate our sex forever.

By this vote we'll rid our nation
Of its vile intoxication.
Can't get rum? Oh, what a pity!
Dram-shops closed in every city.

Fear not, we'll darn each worthy stocking,
Duly keep the cradle rocking,
And beg you heed the words we utter,
The ballot wins our bread and butter.

All hail, brave Kansas! first in duty.
Yours, the meed of praise and beauty,
You'll nobly crown your deeds of daring,
Freedom to our sex declaring.

Song sung by the Hutchinson Family Singers
(lyrics by P. P. Fawler and J. W. Hutchinson),
during the Kansas campaign of 1867, in
History of Woman Suffrage, *Vol. 2, 934.*

Mr. Higginson told us that the slave-master never understood the slave. I know that to be the fact. Neither does man understand woman to-day, because she has always been held subservient to him . . .

It is said that women do not want to vote in this country. I tell you, it is a libel upon womanhood. I care not who says it. I am in earnest. They do want to vote. Fifty-two thousand pulpits in this country have been teaching women the lesson that has been taught them for centuries, that they must not think about voting. But when 52,000 pulpits, or 52,000 politicians, at the beginning of this war, lifted up their voices and asked of women, "Come out and help us," did they stand back? In every hamlet, in every village, in every cabin, and in every palace, in every home in the whole United States, they rose up and went to work. They worked for the Government; they worked for the nation; they worked for their sons, their husbands, their fathers, their brothers, their friends. They worked night and day. Who found women to stand back when this great public opinion that had been crushing them so long and forbidding them to work, at least lift itself up and said, "You may work?"

Frances D. Gage, addressing the American Equal Rights Association, May 10, 1867, in History of Woman Suffrage, *Vol. 2, 198–199.*

My friends, I am rejoiced that you are glad, but I don't know how you will feel when I get through. I come from another field—the country of the slave. They have got their liberty—so much good luck to have slavery partly destroyed; not entirely. I want it root and branch destroyed. Then we will all be free indeed. I feel that if I have to answer for the deeds done in my body just as much as a man, I have a right to have just as much as a man. There is a great stir about colored men getting their rights, but not a word about the colored women; and if colored men get their rights, and not colored women theirs, you see the colored men will be masters over the women, and it will be just as bad as it was before. So I am for keeping the thing going while things are stirring; because if we wait till it is still, it will take a great while to get it going again. White women are a great deal smarter, and know more than colored women, while colored women do not know scarcely anything. They go out washing, which is about as high as a colored woman gets, and their men go about idle, strutting up and down; and when the women come home, they [the men] ask for their money and take it all, and then scold because there is no food. I want you to consider on that, chil'n. I call you chil'n; you are somebody's chil'n, and I am old enough to be mother of all that is here. I want women to have their rights. In the courts women have no right, no voice; nobody speaks for them. I wish woman to have her voice there among the pettifoggers. If it is not a fit place for women, it is unfit for men to be there.

I am above eighty years old; it is about time for me to be going. I have been forty years a slave and forty years free, and would be here forty years more to have equal rights for all. I suppose I am kept here because something remains for me to do; I suppose I am yet to help to break the chain. I have done a great deal of work; as much as a man, but did not get

so much pay. I used to work in the field and bind grain, keeping up with the cradler; but men doing no more, got twice as much pay; so with the German women. They work in the field and do as much work, but do not get the pay. We do as much, we eat as much, we want as much. I suppose I am about the only colored woman that goes about to speak for the rights of the colored women. I want to keep the thing stirring, now that the ice is cracked. What we want is a little money. You men know that you get as much again as women when you write, or for what you do. When we get our rights we shall not have to come to you for money, for then we shall have money enough in our own pockets; and may be you will ask us for money. But help us now until we get it. It is a good consolation to know that when we have got this battle once fought we shall not be coming to you any more. You have been having our rights so long, that you think, like a slave-holder, that you own us. I know that it is hard for one who has held the reins for so long to give up; it cuts like a knife. It will feel all the better when it closes up again. I have been in Washington about three years, seeing about these colored people. Now colored men have the right to vote. There ought to be equal rights now more than ever, since colored people have got their freedom.

Sojourner Truth, addressing the American Equal Rights Association, May 10, 1867, in History of Woman Suffrage, *Vol. 2, 193–194.*

During the last fifteen years, with the utmost industry I could use in ascertaining the public opinion in this country, I have never found one solitary instance of a woman, whom I could meet alone by her fireside, where there was no fear of public opinion, or the minister, or the law-maker, or her father, or her husband, who did not tell me she would like to vote. [Applause]. I never found a slave in my life, who, removed from the eye of the people about him, would not tell me he wanted liberty—never one. I have been in the slave States for years. I have been in the slavepens, and upon the plantations, and have stood beside the slave as he worked in the sugar cane and the cotton-field; and I never found one who dared in the presence of white men to say he wanted freedom. When women and young girls are asked if they want to vote, they are almost always in just that situation where they are afraid to speak what they think; and no wonder they so often say they do not want to vote.

Frances D. Gage, responding to comments at the American Equal Rights Association Meeting, May 10, 1867, in History of Woman Suffrage, *Vol. 2, 200.*

Mr. President, I hold in my hand a petition from Mrs. Horace Greeley and three hundred other women citizens of Westchester, asking that the word 'male' be stricken from the Constitution.

George William Curtis, speaking to the New York State Constitutional Convention, Albany, June 28, 1867, in History of Woman Suffrage, *Vol. 2, 287.*

Your committee does not recommend an extension of the elective franchise to women. However defensible in theory, we are satisfied that public sentiment does not demand and would not sustain an innovation so revolutionary and sweeping, so openly at war with a distribution of duties and functions between the sexes as venerable and pervading as government itself, and involving transformations so radical in social and domestic life.

Horace Greeley, chairman of the committee of the whole, New York State Constitutional Convention, Albany, June 28, 1867, in History of Woman Suffrage, *Vol. 2, 285.*

We should greatly prefer a system like this:

Let the women of our State, after due discussion and consultation, hold a convention composed of delegates from the several counties, equal in number to the members of Assembly. To this Convention let none but women be admitted, whether as officers or spectators. Let this convention, keeping its debates wholly private, decide what department of legislative government may be safely assigned and set apart to woman. We would suggest all that relates to the family: marriage, divorce, separation from bed and board, the control and maintenance of children, education, the property rights of married women, inheritance, dower, etc., etc., as subjects that could wisely and safely be set apart to be legislated upon by woman alone. And we believe that if she (not a few women, but the sex) shall ever suggest and require such an apportionment of legislative powers and duties, man will cheerfully concede it.

"But would you have woman hold elections like ours"? No! we would not! We would have her teach us how to take the sense of the electors far more quietly and cheaply. When a department of legislation shall be assigned to woman, we would have her collect through school-district, or kindred organizations, the names of all female citizens who possess the qualifications, other than the sex, required from male voters at our elections. These being duly, lucidly registered, let, then, women in each Assembly district be designated to collect the votes of its women. Let them simply advertise the address to which votes should be sent and appoint a week wherein to collect them. Now, let every female citizen write her ballot and enclose it, signing her name to the address indicated; and due time having been allowed for votes to arrive by mail or otherwise, let the votes be duly canvassed, and the result ascertained and declared, and certificates of election issued accordingly.

Under this plan, the invalid, the bed-ridden, the bereaved, and even the absent, could vote as well as others, and the cost of holding an election throughout the State need not reach $10,000. Such are the outlines of our views regarding woman in politics . . . A female legislature, a jury of women, we could abide; a legislature of men and women, a jury promiscuously drawn from the sexes we do not believe in.

New York Tribune, editorial, July 26, 1867, in History of Woman Suffrage, *Vol. 2, 304–305.*

I have 60,000 tracts now going to press; all the old editions were gone, and we have to begin new with an empty treasury; but I tell them all, "go ahead;" we must, and will, succeed.

Susan B. Anthony, letter to Lydia Maria Child, August 23, 1867, in History of Woman Suffrage, *Vol. 2, 239–240.*

The other Sunday at Alice Cary's reception, Miss Anthony and I were sitting near a window when we saw Greeley making his way towards us. We had not seen him since the Constitutional Convention, when by our engineering we got [George William] Curtis to present on the floor a petition in favor of woman suffrage, headed by "Mrs. Horace Greeley," just before Greeley presented the adverse report. Well, as he approached us, I said to Miss Anthony, "Prepare for a storm." And sure enough one did burst, and a violent one it was so long as it lasted. To our "Good evening, Mr. Greeley," his reply was rough and curt. Here is about what he said: "You two ladies are

about the best maneuverers among the New York politicians. You tried to bother me at the convention, and I confess that you succeeded. The way Curtis presented Mary's petition showed me that you had prepared the plan." Then turning to me, he continued in a more irritated tone of voice: "You are always so desirous in public to appear under your own rather than your husband's name, why did you in this case substitute 'Mrs. Horace Greeley' for 'Mary Cheney Greeley,' which was really on the petition? You know why. Well, I have given strict orders at the *Tribune* office that you and your cause are to be tabooed in the future, and if it is necessary to mention your name, you will be referred to as 'Mrs. Henry B. Stanton!'" And then he abruptly left us. Of course this will not deter me from speaking my mind in the future as in the past, though I am sorry for our cause that the *Tribune* will henceforth be lukewarm. This may do something to retard our final triumph; but it will take more than Horace Greeley and the New York *Tribune* to prevent the success of the movement which we both have so much at heart. So, more valiant than ever, I am as always,
Your old friend and co-worker,
"Mrs. Henry B. Stanton!"

Elizabeth Cady Stanton, letter to Emily Howland, September 1, 1867, in Stanton and Blatch, Elizabeth Cady Stanton, *Vol. 2, 116–119.*

Elizabeth Bash, Col[ored] complains that she worked last year on the plantation of Brantley Pettigrew, white, about 10 miles from Florence, that she left there last January, and did not get anything but her Share of Potatoes. She says she is entitled to a Share of Cotton, Corn, Peas, Rye and Blades. Laborers were to get one-third of the crop.

Elizabeth Bash, complaint registered with Freedman's Bureau, Monks Corner, South Carolina, September 8, 1867, in Sterling, We Are Your Sisters, *332.*

There is a perfect greed for our tracts. All that great trunk full were sold and given away at our first fourteen meetings, and we in return received $110, which a little more than paid our railroad fare—*eight cents per mile*—and hotel bills. Our collections thus far fully equal those at the East. I have been delightfully disappointed, for everybody said I couldn't raise money in Kansas meetings. I wish you were here to make the

tour of this beautiful State, in which to live fifty years hence will be charming; but now, alas, the women especially see hard times; to come actually in contact with all their discomforts and privations spoils the poetry of pioneer life. The opposition, the "Anti-Female Suffragists," are making a bold push now; but all prophesy a short run for them . . . Their opposition is low and scurrilous, as it used to be fifteen and twenty years ago at the East.

Susan B. Anthony, writing about the Kansas campaign, September 15, 1867, in History of Woman Suffrage, *Vol. 2, 242–243.*

You may be very sure I would have answered Susan's letter sooner if I had been able to inclose any such sum as she hoped to obtain. All that I can do is inclose a draft for $30—ten from our daughter Eliza, ten from William and Ellen, and ten from myself . . . We can only feel grateful for the self-sacrificing labors of those who have gone to Kansas, and hopeful that better success may attend the efforts there, than here or in Michigan . . . I was very glad that Mrs. Stanton could go . . . We shall miss Mrs. Frances D. Gage. I always considered her word as effective as any on our Woman's Rights platform. Her rest [due to a paralytic stroke, which ended her speaking career] has come . . .

Martha C. Wright, letter to Parker Pillsbury, September 17, 1867, in History of Woman Suffrage, *Vol. 2, 240.*

Mrs. Severance desires me to inclose to you this check, $30, and say that it is a contribution by friends at and about Boston, to aid you in the good work of reconstruction on the subject of woman's right to the ballot in Kansas.

T. C. Severance, letter to Susan B. Anthony, September 21, 1867, in History of Woman Suffrage, *Vol. 2, 239.*

In this hour of national reconstruction we appeal to good men of all parties, to Conventions for amending State Constitutions, to the Legislature of every State, and to the Congress of the United States, to apply the principles of the Declaration of Independence to women; "Governments derive their just powers from the consent of the governed." The only form of consent recognized under a Republic is suffrage. Mere tacit acquiescence is not consent; if it were, every despotism might claim that its power is justly held.

rights of every individual. The solution is easy. Base government on the consent of the governed, and each class will protect itself.

James W. Nye, Charles Robinson, S. N. Wood, Samuel C. Pomeroy and others, public letter entitled "To the Voters of the United States," published in the New York Tribune, *October 1, 1867, in* History of Woman Suffrage, *Vol. 2, 247–248.*

It is plain that the experiment of Female Suffrage is to be tried; and, while we regard it with distrust, we are quite willing to see it pioneered by Kansas. She is a young State, and has a memorable history, wherein her women have borne an honorable part. She is preponderantly agricultural, with but one city of any size, and very few of her women are other than pure and intelligent. They have already been authorized to vote on the question of liquor license, and in the choice of school officers, and, we are assured, with decidedly good results. If, then, a majority of them really desire to vote, we, if we lived in Kansas, should vote to give them the opportunity.

Upon a full and fair trial, we believe they would conclude that the right of suffrage for woman was, on the whole, rather a plague than a profit, and vote to resign it into the hands of their husbands and fathers.

New York Tribune, *editorial, October 1, 1867, in* History of Woman Suffrage, *Vol. 2, 248–249.*

There is not a man nor a woman endowed with ordinary common sense who does not know that Kansas is the last State that should be asked to try the dangerous and doubtful experiment. Our society is just forming, our institutions are crude. Ever since the organization of the Territory, we have lived a life of wild excitement, plunging from one trouble into another so fast that we have never had a breathingspell, and we need, more than any other people on the globe, immunity from disturbing experiments on novel questions of doubtful expediency. We can not afford to risk our future prosperity and happiness in making an innovation so questionable. We want peace, and must have it. Let Massachusetts or New York, or some older State, therefore, try this nauseating dose. If it does not kill them, or if it proves healthful and beneficial, we guarantee that Kansas will not be long in swallowing it. But the stomach of our state, if we may be permitted to use the expression, is, as

Caroline M. Severance was founder of the New England Women's Club in 1868. *(Library of Congress)*

Suffrage is the right of every adult citizen, irrespective of sex or color. Women are governed, therefore they are rightly entitled to vote.

The problem of American statesmanship is how to incorporate in our institutions a guarantee of the

yet, too tender and febrific to allow such a fearful deglutition.

John A. Martin, editor of the Atchison, Kansas,
Daily Champion, *responding to the New York*
Tribune *editorial of October 1, 1867,*
in History of Woman Suffrage,
Vol. 2, 249–250.

I have just returned from a trip to [see] S[am] N. Wood at Cottonwood Falls. Things have been as we feared. He [Wood] became discouraged, went home early 1n August & has not done anything since. He was taken sick & nearly died, was in bed three weeks—his wife & children were then sick. He was out of money. The mail to Cottonwood was *robbed* & he never got any letters till a few days ago *for six weeks.* The campaign was left to run itself & of course it ran into the ground. Had not Mrs. S. & Susan come out & Olympia Brown made the most heroic & persevering fight ever known, it would have been a *complete fizzle.* As it is, *we are beat.* It is only a question whether our vote will be large enough to give us respect & bring the case up again hereafter. I predict to *you* a vote of about 5000. It may exceed that. If it reaches 10000 we are *virtually* triumphant. Negro Suffrage is in *great* danger. I think it will carry by a *small vote.* But most people think it is sure to be beat.

Wood is not dishonest, nor without excuse. He is perhaps not be [sic] blamed, yet I confess I am *disappointed.* I got no money from him. He says it is all spent & $150 besides of his own money. Baker of Topeka went down with me, carried me there with his horse & buggy—got no money, but Wood promises to pay him & will probably eventually do so. Baker says that he is sure Wood *expected* strong backing & large pecuniary aid & was disappointed at not receiving them. But I think the disappointment was quite as much due to the fact that the people were not *up to it* & could not be brought up to it in a single campaign, however vigorous. My impression is that whatever may be our vote, the practical steps which I have taken in regard of printing tickets, writing to every County, and getting out circulars will result in *doubling our actual vote.*

And it is really very *important* to get as heavy a vote as possible . . .

Henry Blackwell, letter to Lucy Stone,
October 25, 1867, in Loving Warriors, *221–222.*

Revs. McBurney and Kalloch, C. V. Eskridge and Judge Sears were in the field working with might and main against woman suffrage; while Gov. Crawford was President of the Impartial Suffrage Association of the State, and Judge Wood, Secretary. Such old time radicals as Hon. Chas. Robinson, the first Free State Governor of Kansas, worked hard and well. Prof. John Horner, Senator Ross, Rev. Wm. Starrett, Mr. J. M. Chase, and many others also did good work. Hon. Sidney Clark left his post in the House of Representatives at Washington, and canvassed the State for a re-election, having it in his power to say many things and do much good for the cause of woman, but he did it not. He returned to his own city, Lawrence, to make his last great speech on the eve of election, to find to his great consternation, that the only hall had been engaged by the President of the Woman Suffrage Association of the city for a meeting of their party on that eve. In vain did the honorable gentleman and his friends strive to get possession of that hall. It was paid for and booked to R. S. Tenney. Poor Sidney then sought permission to address their woman suffrage audience, but being refused, he was obliged to betake himself to a dry-goods box in the street, where he tried to interest the rabble, while Col. Horner, Rev. Mr. Starrett, and others, had a fine, large audience in the hall.

R. S. Tenney, formerly of Lawrence, Kansas, letter to
Susan B. Anthony, regarding 1867, in History of
Woman Suffrage, *Vol. 2, 257–258.*

When the question was submitted in 1867, and the men were to decide whether women should be allowed to vote, we felt very anxious about the result. We strongly desired to make Kansas the banner State for Freedom. We did all we could to secure it, and some of the best speakers from the East came to our aid. Their speeches were excellent, and were listened to by large audiences, who seemed to believe what they heard; but when voting day came, they voted according to their prejudices, and our cause was defeated.

Susan E. Wattles, of Mound City, Kansas, letter to
Susan B. Anthony, regarding 1867, in History of
Woman Suffrage, *Vol. 2, 256.*

It is deemed, in certain quarters, wicked heresy to complain of or criticise the republican party, that has done so much in freeing the slaves and in bringing the country victoriously through the war of the rebellion; but if there is to be any truth in history we must set it down, to stand forever a lasting disgrace to the party that in 1867, in Kansas, its leaders selfishly and meanly defeated the woman suffrage amendment.

As the time for the election drew nigh, those political leaders who had been relied upon as friends of the cause were silent, others were active in their opposition. The Central Committee issued a circular for the purpose of preventing loyal Republicans from voting for woman suffrage; not content with this, the notorious I. S. Kalloch, and others of the same stripe, were sent out under the auspices of the Republican party to blackguard and abuse the advocates of woman's cause while professedly speaking upon "manhood suffrage." And Charles Langston, the negro orator, added his mite of bitter words to make the path a little harder for women, who had spent years in pleading the cause of the colored man.

Olympia Brown, letter to Susan B. Anthony, regarding 1867, in History of Woman Suffrage *Vol. 2, 260–261.*

All the old friends, with scarce an exception, are sure we are wrong. Only time can tell, but I believe we are right and hence bound to succeed.

Susan B. Anthony, diary entry, January 1, 1868, in Harper, The Life and Work of Susan B. Anthony, *Vol. 1, 295.*

In all friendliness, and with the highest regard for the woman's rights movement, I cannot refrain from expressing my regret and astonishment that you and Mrs. Stanton should have taken such leave of good sense as to be traveling companions and associate lecturers with that crack-brained harlequin and semilunatic, George Francis Train. . . . You will only subject yourselves to merited ridicule and condemnation, and turn the movement which you aim to promote into unnecessary contempt. . . . The colored people and their advocates have not a more abusive assailant than . . . Train. He is as destitute of principle as he is of sense, and is fast gravitating toward a lunatic asylum. He may be of use in drawing an audience, but so would a kangaroo, a gorilla or a hippopotamus.

William Lloyd Garrison, letter to Susan B. Anthony, January 4, 1868, in Griffith, In Her Own Right, *130.*

Are politicians so pure, politics so exalted, the polls so immaculate, men so moral that women would pollute the ballot and contaminate the voters? Would revolvers, bowie-knives, whisky bottles, profane oaths, brutal towdyism be the feature of elections if women were present? Woman's presence purifies the atmosphere. Enter any Western hotel and what do you see, General? Sitting around the stove you will see dirty, unwashed-looking men, with hats on, and feet on the chairs; huge cuds of tobacco on the floor, spittle in pools all about; filth and dirt, condensed tobacco smoke and a stench of whisky from the bar and the breath on every side. This General is the manhood picture. Now turn to the womanhood picture. She, you think, now will debase and lower the morals of the elections.

George Train, addressing an audience during the Kansas campaign, 1867, in Barry, Susan B. Anthony, *184.*

The Ladies Militant.—It is out at last. If the women as a body have not succeeded in getting up a revolution, Susan B. Anthony, as their representative, has. Her Revolution was issued last Thursday as a sort of New Year's gift to what she considered a yearning public, and it is said to be "charged to the muzzle with literary nitro-glycerine." If Mrs. Stanton would attend a little more to her domestic duties and a little less to those of the great public, perhaps she would exalt her sex quite as much as she does by Quixotically fighting windmills in their gratuitous behalf, and she might possibly set a notable example of domestic felicity. No married woman can convert herself into a feminine Knight of the Rueful Visage and ride about the country attempting to redress imaginary wrongs without leaving her own household in a neglected condition that must be an eloquent witness against her. As for the spinsters, we have always said that every woman has a natural and inalienable right to a good husband and a pretty baby. When, by proper "agitation," she has secured this right, she best honors herself and her sex by leaving public affairs behind her, and endeavoring to show how happy she can make the little world of which she has just become the brilliant center.

New York Sunday Times, upon publication of the Revolution's first issue, January 8, 1868, in Harper, Life and Work of Susan B. Anthony *Vol. 1, 295.*

I know we have shocked our old friends, who were half asleep on the woman question, into new life. Just waking from slumber, they are cross and can't see clearly where we are going. But time will show that Miss Anthony and I are neither idiots nor lunatics. But in starting a paper, the first thing was to advertise it; and that you must admit we have done effectually during the last month. We do care what all good men like you *say*; but just now the men who will *do* something to help us are more important. Garrison, Phillips, and Sumner, in their treatment of our question to-day, prove that we must not trust any of you. All these men, who have pushed us aside for years, saying, "This is the negro's hour," now, when we, dropped by them, find help in other quarters, they turn up the whites of their eye and cry out their curses. No, my dear friend, we are right in our present position.

Elizabeth Cady Stanton, to T. W. Higginson, January 13, 1868, in Stanton and Blatch, Elizabeth Cady Stanton, *Vol. 2, 120.*

The Freedwoman had made a verbal contract to work for Thomas by the day in the absence of her husband who was at work on the R.R. On the last of January 1868 Thomas ordered her to the field very early in the morning before she had had time to properly take care of her child. She refused to go at that time and he cursed and abused her when she told him she was as free as he. On this he kicked her in the head and knocked her down seriously injuring her.

Complaint registered with Freedmen's Bureau, Murray County, Georgia, February 8, 1868, in Sterling, We Are Your Sisters, *333.*

Manervia Anderson States that Harvey Wood (White) of Athens Ga. owes her $1 for washing done by her for him and that he (Wood) Says he dont intend to pay me. I asked him this morning for it and he said I acted damned smart. I said Well I want my money. My child is sick. I asked him why he would not pay me. He said I was too damned saucy for him.

Manervia Anderson, complaint registered with Freedmen's Bureau in Athens, Georgia, April 15, 1868, in Sterling, We Are Your Sisters, *333.*

One view of women's rights, 1869 *(Library of Congress)*

I was sorry you were not present Thursday evening—to see & hear Lucy Stone out do her old self even—It was most delightful I can assure you—to all of us—I felt as if I ought & would overlook her every word and insinuation against me *personally*—Indeed I had done that before—but that speech at the close of that last meeting at 10 o'clock—melted all hearts into a recognition of woman's urgent need of the power of self-protection in her own hands.

> *Susan B. Anthony, letter to Thomas Higginson,*
> *May 20, 1868, in Barry,* Susan B. Anthony, *189.*

I write to inform you that my niece will be to your city this week & also with the expectation of being one of the pupils of your school. I shall start her on Thursday the 19 of this present month. As she is not known in your city—I hope you will see that she is properly cared for as she will be amongst strangers entirely and no one to see to her. If you will do this favor for me I will be under many obligations. You can expect her either Friday or Saturday. I send her to try to learn to be of use to her self & her people who so long have been oppressed . . .

She has no mother. Her father is a labouring man & tries to do for his family. He bought himself & wife and 4 children just before the emancipation & is now trying to give the oldest daughter an education as far as his scanty means will allow. I raised her from a girl of 8 years up to the present.

> *Mrs. E. Cole, letter to Mr. J. Ogden, principal of Fisk*
> *University, November 16, 1868, in Sterling,*
> We Are Your Sisters, *381.*

Yesterday morning the first annual Convention of the State Woman's Suffrage Association of New Jersey took place in Plum-street Hall, in this town. There were about 150 ladies present, several of them in Bloomer costume, and all of the others known as strong minded. Neither Miss Susan B. Anthony nor Mrs. Elizabeth Cady Stanton were present, owing, it is said, to a coolness existing between them and Lucy Stone's organization.

> New York Times, *December 4, 1868, 5.*

I this evening received your earnest letter. It pains me to be obliged to disappoint you. But I can not sign the petition your send me. Cheerfully, gladly can I sign a petition for the enfranchisement of women. But I can not sign a paper against the enfranchise-ment of the negro man, unless at the same time woman shall be enfranchised. The removal of the political disabilities of race is my first desire—of sex, my second. If put on the same level and urged in the same connection neither will be soon accomplished. The former will very soon be, if untrammeled by the other, and its success will prepare the way for the accomplishment of the other.

> *Gerrit Smith, letter to Susan B. Anthony, December 30,*
> *1868, in* History of Woman Suffrage, *Vol. 2, 317.*

In a letter to Susan, your father refuses to sign our petition. I am dissecting him in the next *Revolution*.

> *Elizabeth Cady Stanton, letter to Elizabeth Smith*
> *Miller, January 8, 1869, in Stanton and Blatch,*
> Elizabeth Cady Stanton, *Vol. 2, 121.*

[I]n criticising such good and noble men as Gerrit Smith and Wendell Phillips for their apathy on woman's enfranchisement at this hour, it is not because we think their course at all remarkable, nor that we have the least hope of influencing them, but simply to rouse the women of the country to the fact that they must not look to these men as their champions at this hour . . .

Again; Mr. Smith refuses to sign the petition because he thinks to press the broader question of "universal suffrage" would defeat the partial one of "manhood suffrage"; in other words, to demand protection for woman against her oppressors, would jeopardize the black man's chance of securing protection against his oppressors. If it is a question of precedence merely, on what principle of justice or courtesy should woman yield her right of enfranchisement to the negro? If men can not be trusted to legislate for their own sex, how can they legislate for the opposite sex, of whose wants and needs they know nothing? . . .

He would undoubtedly plead the necessity of the ballot for the negro at the south for his protection, and point us to innumerable acts of cruelty he suffers to-day. But all these things fall as heavily on the women of the black race, yea far more so, for no man can ever know the deep, the damning degradation to which woman is subject in her youth, in helplessness and poverty. The enfranchisement of the men of her race, Mr. Smith would say, is her protection. Our Saxon men have held the ballot in this country for a century, and what honest man can claim that it has been used for woman's protection? Alas! we have given the very hey day of our life to undoing the cruel and unjust laws that the men of New York had made for their own mothers, wives, and daughters.

Elizabeth Cady Stanton, response to Gerrit Smith's December 30, 1868 letter, printed in the Revolution, *January 14, 1869, in* History of Woman Suffrage, *Vol. 2, 318–319.*

The childish argument that all women don't ask for the franchise would hardly deserve notice were it not sometimes used by men of sense . . . Reforms have to be claimed and obtained by the few, who are in advance, for the benefit of the many who lag behind. And when once obtained and almost forced upon them, the mass of the people accept and enjoy their benefits as a matter of course. Look at the petitions now pouring into Congress for the franchise for women, and compare their thousands of signatures with the few isolated names that graced our first petitions to the legislature of New York to secure to the married woman the right to hold in her own name the property that belonged to her, to secure to the poor, forsaken wife the right to her earnings, and to the mother the right to her children. "All" the women did not ask for those rights, but all accepted them with joy and gladness when they were obtained; and so it will be with the franchise.

Ernestine L. Rose, letter to Josephine S. Griffing, January 14, 1869, in History of Woman Suffrage, *Vol. 1, 356.*

At last we shall have a definite, constructive rallying point. We pass from the sphere of vainly endeavoring to broaden the narrow demands of men to an amendment wholly our own. Hon. George W. Julian acceded to our wish, and will propose a XVI Amendment, basing the right of suffrage on citizenship "without any distinction and discrimination whatever founded on sex." I feel an added dignity!

Elizabeth Cady Stanton, letter to Lucretia Mott, January 21, 1869, in Stanton and Blatch, Elizabeth Cady Stanton, *Vol. 2, 121–122.*

Thank you for so promptly sending me the letters of Mr. Sumner.

I herewith return them, and agree with you that there is nothing in them, to make it desirable we should publish them, even if we had not his express wish that they should not be.

I wish he felt moved to give our cause, the great, brave help he rendered to the slave.

Nevertheless we must be forever grateful for what he *has* done for human rights, even tho' it does not tell directly for us. I think God rarely gives to one man, or one set of them, more than *one,* great moral victory to win. Hence we see the old abolitionist generally, shrink from the van of our movement, tho' they are in hearty sympathy with it. If Mr. Sumner "don't want to be in this fight," as he told me, in my heart, I yet say "God bless him"! Our victory is sure to come. And I can endure anything but recreancy to principle.

I think I would send petitions to Geo. W. Julian. He has really *done* more this winter, than any other member for us. And promptly after Grant's inauguration introduced three bills for woman suffrage in the District [of Columbia] in [territories of the U.S.], and an amendment to the constitution, securing woman suffrage . . .

Lucy Stone, letter to Mrs. Field, March 24, 1869, in Wheeler, Loving Warriors, *226–227.*

I have written to the New England friends to let bygones be bygones and come to the May meeting. It seems to me personal feelings should be laid aside and women should all pull together . . .

It seems as if everybody who does not like the *Revolution* is bound to take the *Agitator,* which is very well, since they are detachments of the same corps. We must keep up a good understanding and work together. If you want to let people know there is no rivalry between us, you can announce that I am to send your paper fortnightly letters from the West detailing the progress of affairs here.

Mary A. Livermore, letter to Susan B. Anthony, April 4, 1869, in Harper, The Life and Work of Susan B. Anthony, *Vol. 1, 321.*

We have written every one of the old friends, ignoring the past and urging them to come [to the May Anniversary of the Equal Rights Association]. We do so much desire to sink all petty considerations in the one united effort to secure woman suffrage. Though many unkind acts and words have been administered to us, which we have returned with sarcasm and ridicule, there are really only kind feelings in our souls for all the noble men and women who have fought for freedom during the last thirty years.

Elizabeth Cady Stanton, spring 1869, in Harper, The Life and Work of Susan B. Anthony, *Vol. 1, 321.*

Susan Anthony has us all in the *Revolution.* She called a meeting of the Executive Committee of the American Equal Rights Society while I was absent at the Springfield Convention (tho' I am chairman of the Executive Committee) issued a Call with names of all officers of the Society, and published it in the *Revolution* the next week, as tho' it were the organ of our Association!

Lucy Stone, letter to the Reverend Sam J. May, April 9, 1869, in Wheeler, Loving Warriors, *228.*

Our readers will find Mr. Train's valedictory in another column. Feeling that he has been a source of grief to our numerous friends and, through their constant complaints, an annoyance to us, he magnanimously retires. He has always said that as soon as we were safely launched on the tempestuous sea of journalism, he should leave us "to row our own boat." Our partnership dissolves today. Now we shall look for a harvest of new subscribers, as many have written and said to us again, if you will only drop Train, we will send you patrons by the hundred. We hope the fact that Train has dropped *us* will not vitiate these promises. Our generous friend starts for California on May 7, in the first train over the Pacific road. He takes with him the sincere thanks of those who know what he has done in the cause of woman, and of those who appreciate what a power the *Revolution* has already been in rousing public thought to the importance of her speedy enfranchisement.

The Revolution, *May 1, 1869, in Harper,* The Life and Work of Susan B. Anthony, *Vol. 1, 319.*

. . . I must say that I do not see how any one can pretend that there is the same urgency in giving the ballot to woman as to the negro. With us, the matter is a question of life and death, at least, in fifteen States of the Union. When women, because they are women, are hunted down through the cities of New York and New Orleans; when they are dragged from their houses and hung upon lamp-posts; when their children are torn from their arms, and their brains dashed out upon the pavement; when they are objects of insult and outrage at every turn; when

they are in danger of having their homes burnt down over their heads; when their children are not allowed to enter schools; then they will have an urgency to obtain the ballot equal to our own. (Great applause.)

A Voice:—Is that not all true about black women?

Mr. Douglass:—Yes, yes, yes; it is true of the black woman, but not because she is a woman, but because she is black. (Applause.) . . .

Woman! why, she has 10,000 modes of grappling with her difficulties.

Exchange between Frederick Douglass and another participant in the American Equal Rights Association meeting, May 12, 1869, in History of Woman Suffrage, *Vol. 2, 382–383.*

. . . When Mr. Douglass mentioned the black man first and the woman last, if he had noticed he would have seen that it was the men that clapped and not the women. There is not the woman born who desires to eat the bread of dependence, no matter whether it be from the hand of father, husband, or brother; for any one who does so eat her bread places herself in the power of the person from whom she takes it. (Applause.) Mr. Douglass talks about the wrongs of the negro; but with all the outrages that he to-day suffers, he would not exchange his sex and take the place of Elizabeth Cady Stanton. (Laughter and applause.)

Mr. Douglass:—I want to know if granting you the right of suffrage will change the nature of our sexes? (Great laughter.)

Miss Anthony:—It will change the pecuniary position of woman; it will place her where she can earn her own bread. (Loud applause.) She will not then be driven to such employments only as man chooses for her.

Exchange between Frederick Douglass and Susan B. Anthony at the American Equal Rights Association meeting, May 12, 1869, in History of Woman Suffrage, *Vol. 2, 383.*

The gentleman who addressed you [Frederick Douglass] claimed that the negroes had the first right to the suffrage, and drew a picture which only his great word-power can do. He again in Massachusetts, when it had cast a majority in favor of Grant and negro suffrage, stood upon the platform and said that woman had better wait for the negro; that is, that both could not be carried, and that the negro had better be the one. But I freely forgave him because he felt as he spoke. But woman suffrage is more imperative than his own; and I want to remind the audience that when he says what the Ku-Kluxes did all over the South, the Ku-Kluxes here in the North in the shape of men, take away the children from the mother, and separate them as completely as if done on the block of the auctioneer. Over in New Jersey they have a law which says that *any* father—he might be the most brutal man that ever existed—*any* father, it says, whether he be under age or not, may by his last will and testament dispose of the custody of his child, born or to be born, and that such disposition shall be good against all persons, and that the mother may not recover her child; and that law modified in form exists over ever State in the Union except in Kansas. Woman has an ocean of wrongs too deep for any plummet, and the negro, too, has an ocean of wrong that can not be fathomed. There are two great oceans; in the one is the black man, and in the other is the woman. But I thank God for that XV. Amendment, and hope that it will be adopted in every State. I will be thankful in my soul if *any* body can get out of the terrible pit.

Lucy Stone, speaking at the American Equal Rights Association meeting, May 12, 1869, in History of Woman Suffrage, *Vol. 2, 383–384.*

Mrs. [Frances Watkins] HARPER (colored) [said] . . . When it was a question of race, she let the lesser question of sex go. But the white women go for sex, letting race occupy a minor question. . . . If the nation could only handle one question, she would not have the black women put a single straw in the way, if only the men of the race could obtain what they wanted.

Account of Frances Watkins Harper's comments at the American Equal Rights Association meeting, May 12, 1869, in History of Woman Suffrage, *Vol. 2, 391–392.*

That Equal Rights Association is an awful humbug. I would not have come on to the anniversary, nor would any of us, if we had known what it was. We supposed we were coming to a woman suffrage convention.

Mary A. Livermore, letter to Susan B. Anthony, May 17, 1869, in Harper, The Life and Work of Susan B. Anthony, *Vol. 1, 327–328.*

Mary A. Livermore was the only female reporter at Lincoln's nomination. *(Library of Congress)*

I see by the daily papers that a committee has been appointed by the Working Women's Association to inquire why women are excluded from the "Free College of the City of New York." I am glad that women are taking this matter in hand, for I feel that I and every woman who has a family of sons and daughters to educate, have a right to ask this question and press it to a fair answer.

I am convinced that upon a just knowledge of the facts, no thinking man or woman, who treats the question with candor, can deny that it is absolute injustice that this city is to-day offering a free collegiate course of instruction to hundreds of boys who care so little for it that seldom more than three percent of those who enter the introductory class, stay to graduate, while their sisters or other daughters of taxpayers are dismissed from the public schools with a grade of scholarship only slightly above that required to enter the introductory class of the college . . .

[T]he property of women, as well as men, is taxed to support this institution; also, the property of men whose children are all daughters must contribute to the free education of the children of other and perhaps wealthier men than themselves, while their own family must be instructed in the higher branches—if at all in the notoriously expensive and still more notoriously superficial boarding schools.

Letter of a "Mother" to the editor of the New York Times, June 1, 1869, 2.

Not a little surprise, and some indignation, were expressed by the representatives of upper tendom sojourning here, that strong minded women were not only coming to Saratoga, but actually intending to hold a convention. What next? What place would henceforth be safe from the assaults of these irrepressible amazons of reform? Saratoga has survived the shock, however; Flora McFlimsey has looked in the face of Miss Anthony, and has not been turned to stone. More than that, finding the convention pouring into the parlors of Congress Hall, and escape actually cut off, Flora, after deliberating whether to faint and be carried out, or gratify her curiosity by looking on, finally submitted gracefully to the inevitable and did the latter. From her crimson cushioned arm chair by the window, she saw the meeting called to order, saw one after another of "those horrid women, whose names are in the newspapers," quietly taking their places, doing the thing proper to be done, and carrying forward the business of the meeting. Really, they were not so dreadful after all. They neither wore beards nor pantaloons. There was not even a woman with short hair among them. On the contrary, they seemed to be decidedly appreciative of "good clothes" and if less familiar with the goddess of fashion than Miss Flora they did not walk arm in arm with her, they at least followed at no great distance and were, to a woman, finished off with the regulation back-bow of loops and ends. Spite of herself, Miss McFlimsey became interested, and when Miss Anthony mentioned the fact that the majority of men felt it necessary to talk down to women, instead of sharing with them their best thoughts and most vital interests, Flora looked reflective, as if in that direction might lie the clew to the insufferable stupidity which she often found in the young gentlemen of her acquaintance.

That a Woman Suffrage Convention should have been allowed to organize in the parlors of Congress Hall . . . that such men as Millard Fillmore, Thurlow Weed, George Opdyke, and any number of clergymen from different parts of the country, should have been interested lookers-on, are significant facts that

may well carry dismay to the enemies of the cause. That the whole business of the Convention was transacted by women in a dignified, orderly, and business like manner, is a strong intimation that in spite of all that has been said to the contrary, women are capable of learning how to conduct meetings and manage affairs. Even the least friendly spectator was compelled to admit it, that the delegates to the Convention were as free from eccentricity in dress and manner as the most fastidious taste could demand; that they were remarkable only for the comprehensive range of thought, indicated in their utterances, and the earnestness with which they advocate principles which they evidently believe to be right. Another fact worth noticing is the character of the reports of the Convention furnished to the daily papers. They were, for the most part, full, impartial, and respectful in tone; especially was this the case with the local newspapers. Altogether, the Woman Suffrage Conventions in the State of New York must be regarded as a decided success. The interest manifested shows that thought on the subject is no longer confined to the few, but that it is gradually permeating the whole public mind.

Celia Burleigh, describing the Saratoga Women's Rights Convention, New York, July 16, 1869, in History of Woman Suffrage, Vol. 2, 402–403.

In behalf of the progressive women of this country we would express to you the deep interest we feel in the present movement among the women of Europe, everywhere throwing off the lethargy of ages and asserting their individual dignity and power, showing that the emancipation of woman is one of those great ideas that mark the centuries. While in your circular you specify various subjects for consideration, you make no mention of the right of suffrage . . .

Perhaps in your country, where the right of representation is so limited even among men, women do not feel the degradation of disfranchisement as we do under this Government, where it is now proposed to make sex the only disqualification for citizenship . . .

We are now holding conventions in the chief cities of the several States, and petitioning Congress for a sixteenth amendment to the Federal Constitution that shall forbid the disfranchisement of any citizen on account of sex. In January, soon after the convening of Congress, we shall hold a National Convention in Washington to press our arguments on the representatives of the people. Sooner or later you will be driven to make the same demand; for, from whatever point you start in tracing the wrongs of citizens, you will be logically brought step by step to see that the real difficulty in all cases is the need of representation in the government.

Women of the National Woman Suffrage Association, letter to the Woman's Industrial Congress at Berlin, September 28, 1869, in History of Woman Suffrage, *Vol. 2, 405.*

It is decided to hold the Convention to form an American Woman Suffrage Association at Cleveland on the 17 & 18 of Nov.

Can you not be present to help organize?

Our cause suffers today from the lack of the organizing talent of MEN, in its management. Col. [Thomas Wentworth] Higginson has promised to be there, and we need you to help him.

If we can only organize wisely and well, with half our officers men, of the right kind, there will be no end to the good, that will come of it.

There has been no event of such large significance since the formation of the American Anti Slavery Soc. It is even greater than that, as it concerns not a class, but the race.

It should be organized by men and women whose names will command confidence, & win cooperation and sympathy.

I hope you will not say nay, but if necessary, let other things give away, for this very serious business!

We can only pay expenses. I wish it were possible to do more.

As soon as you can decide, please let me know, as we wish to advertize the names of those who will take part in the convention. The call, carefully drawn up by Col. Higginson, will be out I think on Sat. next.

Lucy Stone, letter to the Reverend James Freeman Clarke, October 6, 1869, in Wheeler, Loving Warriors, *228–229.*

Enclosed I send you a copy of the call for a convention to form an American Woman Suffrage association. I wish I could have had a quiet hour with you, to talk about it. I *hope* you will see it as I do, that with two societies each, in harmony with itself, each having the benefit of national names, each attracting those who naturally belong to it, we shall secure the hearty active cooperation of *all* the friends of the cause, better than either could do alone. People will differ, as to what they consider the best methods & means. The true wisdom is not to ignore, but to provide for the fact. So far as I have influence, this soc. shall never be an enemy or antagonist of yours in any way. It will simply fill a field and combine forces, which yours does not. I shall rejoice when any of the onerous works are carried, no matter who does it.

Your little girls, and mine will reap the easy harvest which it costs so much to sow.

Lucy Stone, letter to Elizabeth Cady Stanton, October 19, 1869, in Wheeler, Loving Warriors, *229.*

All wise women should oppose the Fifteenth Amendment for two reasons: 1st. Because it is invidious to their sex. Look at it from what point you will, and in every aspect, it reflects the old idea of woman's inferiority, her subject condition. And yet the one need to secure an onward step in civilization is a new dignity and self respect in women themselves. No one can think that the pending proposition of "manhood suffrage" exalts woman, either in her own eyes or those of the man by her side, but it does degrade her practically and theoretically, just as black men were more degraded when all other men were enfranchised.

2nd. We should oppose the measure, because men have no right to pass it without our consent. When it is proposed to change the constitution or fundamental law of the State or Nation, all the people have a right to say what that change shall be.

If women understood this pending proposition in all its bearings, theoretically and practically, there would be an overwhelming vote against the admission of another man to the ruling power of this nation, until they themselves were first enfranchised. There is no true patriotism, no true nobility in tamely and silently submitting to this insult. It is mere sycophancy to man; it is licking the hand that forges a new chain for our degradation; it is indorsing the old idea that woman's divinely ordained position is at man's feet, and not on an even platform by his side.

By this edict of the liberal party, the women of this Republic are now to touch the lowest depths of their political degradation.

Elizabeth Cady Stanton, writing for the Revolution, *October 21, 1869, in* History of Woman Suffrage, *Vol. 2, 333–334.*

In the present stage of the Woman's Suffrage movement in this country a division in our ranks is rather to be deplored, for when friends disagree newcomers hesitate as to which side to join; and from fear of being involved in personal bickerings they withhold their names and influence altogether; still more deplorable is the result to the old friends themselves, when instead of fighting the common enemy, prejudice, custom, unjust laws and a false public sentiment, they turn, as the old Abolitionist in their divisions did, and rend each other.

Elizabeth Cady Stanton and Susan B. Anthony, writing in the Revolution, *October 28, 1869, in Barry,* Susan B. Anthony, *205.*

I write especially to ask if the N. Jersey State Soc. will make you a delegate, to the Cleveland Convention. Will you not go? I am afraid we shall not get rid of the N. York host unless those who know the real need of doing so are there.

Col. Higginson, either influenced by Theodore Tilton, or from a feeling [of] (what shall I say), mistaken magnanimity, perhaps, told Mrs. Stanton, and Susan, that he expected to see them at Cleveland.

They neither of them intended to go—I do not know that they will—But it will be so dreadful an incubus, to take them up again! tho' perhaps there will be no help for it if they go. But I do very much wish you could plan to be there, so that we may counsel . . .

Harry will join me at Newburyport, and we shall set to, to raise $10,000 to start a paper. I suppose you know the N.E. Woman Suffrage Association propose to take the "Agitator"—call it the "Woman's Journal," with Mrs. Livermore, Mrs. Howe, T. W. Higginson & Mr. Garrison as editors—*If we can raise the money.* If we do I shall try and work through the paper, for the future, and quit this lecturing field nearly altogether.

Lucy Stone, letter to Antoinette Brown Blackwell, October 31, 1869, in Merrill, Friends and Sisters, *175.*

The *Revolution* is out against us & says that Gerrit Smith, Henry Ward Beecher, Geo. Wm. Curtis, and others would not have signed the call if they had known its real meaning. But Gerrit Smith writes a cordial letter which I bring with me . . .

I am going to see Tilton tomorrow to try to make him see how necessary it is to influence Mrs. S. & Susan to *stay away from Cleveland* & not to fight us, either. I think I have made Mrs. Tilton see it. I had a very pleasant half hour's interview with Mr. G. W. Curtis yesterday afternoon, to try to get him at V[ermont] to address the legislature. He cannot go. I spoke to him about taking the Presidency of the Am As if elected. He has taken it into consideration . . .

I judge from the last *Revolution* that John Neal is planning to get up a Maine Society in the interest of Mrs. Stanton. Can you not head if off & have one formed in connection with the Am. W. S. As.?

Henry Blackwell, letter to Lucy Stone, November 1, 1869, in Wheeler, Loving Warriors, *230–232.*

Please do what you can conscientiously for Susan and Lib. It would seem a foolish thing to form an "*American* Woman's Suffrage association," when there is already a "National Woman's S.A." It would seem a pity to start another paper when those we have can hardly live. And why change when these papers and this society are true as steel to all the interests of women.

Elizabeth Smith Miller, letter to her father, Gerrit Smith, November 13, 1869, in the Smith Family Papers.

. . . several weeks before the election of 1869 I gave out word that I was going to the polls to vote. I had the previous year removed with my family from Olympia, and was living on White River in King County. The announcement that I would attend the election caused a great commotion in White River precinct. A fearful hue and cry was raised. The news reached Olympia and Seattle, and some of the papers deprecated the idea that "a woman should unsex herself by dabbling in the filthy pool of politics." But I was fully committed. The law had been on our statute books for nearly three years. If it was intended for our benefit, it was time we were availing ourselves of it. So, nothing daunted, I determined to repair to the polling place, the district school-house, accompanied by my husband, my daughter (Mrs. Axtell) and her husband—a little band of four—looked upon with pity and contempt for what was called our "fanaticism."

For several days before the election the excitement in the neighborhood and other settlements along the river was intense. Many gentlemen called on me and tried to persuade me to stay at home and save myself from insult. I thanked them for their kindness, and told them I fully appreciated their good intentions, but that I had associated with men all my life, and had always been treated as a lady; that the men I should meet at the polls were the same that I met in church and social gatherings, and I knew they would treat me with respect. Then they begged my husband not to allow me to go; but he told them his wife had as good a right to go as he had; and that no citizen can legally deprive another of the right to vote.

On the morning of the election, just before we reached the school-house, a man met us and said, "Mr. Brown, look here now! If Mrs. Brown goes up to vote she will be insulted! If I was in your place I wouldn't let her go any farther. She had better go back." My husband answered, "Mr. Brannan, my wife has a good a right to vote as I have, and I would not prevent her if I could. She has a mind of her own and will do as she thinks best, and I shall stand by her and see that she is well treated! . . ." "Well," said the man, "If she was my wife she shouldn't go! She'll be sure to be insulted!" I looked him full in the face, and said with decision, "Mr. Brannan, a gentleman will be a gentleman under all circumstances, and will always treat a lady with respect." I said this because I knew the man, and knew that if anyone offered any annoyance, it would be he . . .

As we drove up to the school-house and alighted, a man in an angry voice snapped out, "Well! if the women are coming to vote, I'm going home!" But he did not go; he had too much curiosity; he wanted to see the fun. He stayed and was converted. After watching the sovereign "white male citizen" perform the laborious task of depositing his vote in the ballot-box, I thought if I braced myself up I might be equal to the task. So, summoning all my strength, I walked up to the desk behind which sat the august officers of election, and presented my vote. When behold! I was pompously met with the assertion, "You are not an American citizen; hence not entitled to vote."

. . . My daughter now went up and offered her vote, which was, of course, rejected.

Mrs. Mary Olney Brown, of her attempt to vote in Washington Territory, 1869, in History of Woman Suffrage, *Vol. 3, 781–784.*

The Woman's Suffrage Convention of New Jersey continued its session at the Newark Opera House, in Market Street, yesterday. The morning's proceedings were opened at 10:30 o'clock, Mrs. LUCY STONE (BLACKWELL) presiding . . .

Mrs. Stone then alluded to a petition to the Legislature that would be circulated among the audience. She desired that every woman in the State, if necessary, should sign it.

The venerable Mrs. Lucretia Mott then addressed the audience, after which a preamble and resolutions were read by Mr. BLACKWELL. The preamble recites that as the women of New Jersey prior to the adoption of the present Constitution were legally entitled to vote, and did actually vote, and as they were excluded from taking a part in the election of delegates to the Convention which formed the Constitution, thus disfranchising about one-half of the legal voters of the State, it is therefore resolved that woman's right to vote in New Jersey has never been legally canceled.

New York Times, *December 10, 1869, 2.*

Since your visit here, through which I obtained somewhat of an insight into your struggles and labors, I have been in special sympathy with you. I do admire the liberal and comprehensive spirit which you and Mrs. Stanton show in allowing both sides of a question to be fairly discussed in your paper, and in giving any woman who does good work for her race in any field the credit for it, even though she may not exactly agree with you on all points. The spirit of exclusiveness is not calculated to push any reform among the masses . . . Our house and hearts are always open to you. I want to send you something more than good wishes and so enclose a little New Year's gift to you, with my love and earnest prayers for your success.

Dr. Kate Jackson, letter to Susan B. Anthony, December 1869, in Harper, The Life and Work of Susan B. Anthony, *Vol. 1, 335.*

As to changing the name of the *Revolution,* I should consider it a great mistake. If all these people who for twenty years have been afraid to call their souls their own begin to prune us and the *Revolution,* we shall become the same galvanized mummies they are. There could not be a better name than *Revolution.* The establishing of woman on her rightful throne is the greatest revolution the world has ever known or ever will know. To bring it about is no child's play. You and I have not forgotten the conflict of the last twenty years—the ridicule, persecution, denunciation, detraction, the unmixed bitterness of our cup for the past two years, when even friends crucified us. A journal called the *Rosebud* might answer for those who come with kid gloves and perfumes to lay immortal wreaths on the monuments which in sweat and tears others have hewn and built; but for us and for that great blacksmith of ours [Parker Pillsbury] who forges such red-hot thunderbolts for Pharisees, hypocrites, and sinners, there is no name like *Revolution*.

> *Elizabeth Cady Stanton, letter to Susan B. Anthony,*
> *December 28, 1869, in Stanton and Blatch,*
> Elizabeth Cady Stanton, *Vol. 2, 123–124.*

[Lucy Stone's] husband told me in the course of a long conversation on the "differences"—that Mr. Train went to Kansas on the invitation of one Wood, a republican, to lecture to whomever would hear on Woman Suffrage among other things . . . Mr. Blackwell & Gov. Robinson & two or three others who were conducting the W[oman] S[uffrage] campaign thought it might be well for Susan to accompany Train & so get democratic votes—while at the same time she could perhaps keep him straight on the negro question—Train being there against negro suffrage. *They accordingly advised & promoted her Kansas trips with Train* and she went as General Agent of the Equal Rights Association & with their full approval on that whole Kansas campaign . . . I could hardly believe my ears when Mr. Blackwell quietly told me this, the beginning of the story—& so I waited a while & then asked him if I understood him rightly in saying thus & so—he said I did & then went on to show me that the thing didn't work out well, that they thought they lost more republican votes for W. Suffrage by Train's advocacy than they gained democratic & were disgusted with the experiment.

> *Isabella Beecher Hooker to Susan Howard, describing her*
> *December 1869 conversation with Henry Blackwell,*
> *January 2, 1870, in Barry,* Susan B. Anthony, *181.*

After my wife and I had returned from our campaign work in Kansas, *George Francis Train was invited into the State by Miss Anthony* [emphasis added], at the insistence of friends in Missouri, to speak in behalf of the woman suffrage amendment. While undoubtedly done with the best intentions, this was most unwise. Mr. Train, as everyone knows, was a semi-lunatic . . . He was also a virulent copperhead, and the last person who should have been asked to speak for woman suffrage in a strongly Republican state, like radical Kansas . . .

When the offices of the American Equal Rights Association at the East read in the papers that this fantastic personage was speaking for the suffrage amendment in Kansas, they could not believe it, and thought it must be some monstrous hoax invented by the enemy. When they found his meetings were actually being advertised in Kansas as held under the auspices of the American Equal Rights Association, Lucy Stone, as chairman of its executive committee, published a card stating the fact that the Association was in no wise responsible.

> *Henry Blackwell, about the Kansas campaign of 1867,*
> *in* The Woman's Journal, *March 11, 1899, in Barry,*
> Susan B. Anthony, *182.*

9 Separate Paths to Suffrage
1870–1879

THE HISTORICAL CONTEXT

When Elizabeth Cady Stanton and Susan B. Anthony founded the National Woman Suffrage Association (NWSA) in May 1869, they had wanted to restrict membership to women only. Several of the women present had objected, though, refusing to join unless men were granted admission. Stanton and Anthony then agreed to a mixed membership but insisted on "filling the positions of trust exclusively with women."[1] That policy was abandoned by the membership of the NWSA at its first anniversary meeting.

Theodore Tilton had tried in 1865 to reunite the divided abolitionists and women's rights activists through the American Equal Rights Association. Now, in 1870, he tried to merge the women's rights organizations. Though he did not succeed in uniting the American Woman Suffrage Association and the National Woman Suffrage Association, he was elected president of the NWSA.[2]

The split between activist women was to remain a fact. The AWSA, under the guidance of Lucy Stone and Henry Blackwell, restricted itself to the question of woman suffrage. That demand, the most shocking of all the Seneca Falls demands in 1848, now seemed less threatening to the public than others. The additional questions of marriage and divorce reform, Stone felt, only made women's opponents increasingly eager to keep the vote—and thus influence on these matters—out of female hands. It was essential, she believed, that women desiring the franchise not alarm those holding the power to grant it.[3]

Stanton and Anthony disagreed. During the first months of 1870, they struggled to keep the controversial *Revolution* in existence. Stanton, as editor, maintained the paper as a broad forum for the discussion of everything Stone and Blackwell wished to avoid.[4] Anthony, meanwhile, struggled with the paper's finances. Potential supporters who did not object to the paper's contents did object to its first benefactor, George Train. When he finally disassociated himself from the paper, Stanton and Anthony refused to denounce him and received few substitute contributions. In May 1870 the *Revolution* was sold. By that time it had accrued a debt of $10,000, which Anthony personally assumed and paid over six years.[5] She delivered an unencumbered paper to its new proprietor, Laura Curtis Bullard. Its cherished motto, "Men their rights and nothing more; women their rights and nothing less," became the less revolutionary "What God has joined together, let no man put asunder."[6] The *Revolution,* under its new editor, Theodore Tilton, became similar in tone to the AWSA's less controversial *Woman's Journal.*

By summer 1870 Stanton was no longer an officer of the NWSA or editor of a newspaper. She began what was to become a decade-long journey back and forth across the United States. Now in her fifties, she became a well-paid lecture circuit speaker. She refused to restrict herself to polite topics and had little interest in placating anyone, especially her opponents. As she explained to one friend, "When I think of all the wrongs that have been heaped upon womankind, I am ashamed that I am not forever in a condition of chronic wrath, stark mad, skin and bone, my eyes a fountain of tears, my lips overflowing with curses, and my hand against every man and brother! Ah, how I do repent me of the male faces I have washed, the mittins I have knit, the trousers mended, the cut fingers and broken toes I have bound up!"[7] Lucy Stone called her "utterly indiscreet,"[8] but the crowds loved her. Conversing with women in private parlors before public speeches, or with the women that would "flock"[9] to her side when she stepped down from the podium, Stanton felt sure that she was "stirring up women generally to rebellion."[10] Since she remained closely associated with the NWSA, her remarks were seen as reflecting the NWSA viewpoint.

The "Western World," as the traveling Stanton called the American West, had had successes that the eastern states had not. Wyoming Territory had been organized in 1869; in 1870 its women voted.[11] Women's suffrage made an impact even before the first election, since women were called to serve as jurors as soon as their names appeared on lists of eligible voters. In March 1870 Esther Morris was appointed justice of the peace. Though Morris's cases were decided "so ably that not one of them was appealed to a higher court," not anyone was pleased by such innovations.[12] In 1871 the state's democrats introduced an act to repeal women's suffrage in Wyoming. The act was passed by the legislature but vetoed by Governor John Allen Campbell.[13] When Wyoming entered the Union in 1890, it became the first state since New Jersey (1776–1807) to include women's suffrage in its state constitution.

Utah Territory women, without "battling the usages, prejudices and policy of our nation"[14] as their sisters in the states continued to do, were also granted suffrage in 1870. Though seven signers of one letter thanked God for conferring that right, the granting of suffrage was probably more expediency than miracle. During the winter just passed, the Cullom Bill, prohibiting polygamy, had been introduced in Congress. Male Mormon leaders claimed that Mormon women endorsed polygamy; the franchise appears to have been extended to women in order that they might have a

Women voting in Wyoming Territory, 1888 *(New York Public Library Picture Collection)*

means of demonstrating support to a hostile Congress and thus dissuading Congress from acting against the institution. When the Cullom Bill failed to pass the Senate, the Edmunds-Tucker Bill, also outlawing polygamy, was introduced. This passed in 1887. Among its provisions was one disfranchising the women of Utah. Although this was denounced by women's rights leaders as penalizing the territory's women but not its men, Utah's women remained disfranchised until the Mormon Church's renunciation of polygamy and Utah's entrance into the Union in 1896.[15]

There was indeed a battle going on in the states. Victoria C. Woodhull was one of a new generation of activists whose efforts were reported even in the territories. The first woman stockbroker in America, a former psychic healer, and a self-declared candidate for the presidency, she was as much commented upon for her beauty and home life as for her political actions. The question of whether or not to accept her help became another dividing point between the women's rights organizations. Woodhull herself was undaunted by criticism. "One of the charges made against me is that I lived in the same house with my former husband, Dr. Woodhull, and my present husband, Col. Blood. The fact is a fact," she said, adding that her first husband's illness made this an act of charity, "one of the most virtuous acts of my life."[16]

Woodhull gained notoriety and the attention of Congress. In 1869 the attorney Francis Minor had prepared resolutions claiming that women were, in fact, already voting citizens under the U.S. Constitution as amended. Where Elizabeth Cady Stanton and Susan B. Anthony had emphasized Section 2 of the Fourteenth Amendment, which penalized states that denied suffrage to "male inhabitants," Minor focused on Section 1. That first portion of the Fourteenth Amendment declared that "All persons born or naturalized in the United States . . . are citizens of the United States . . ." and "No state shall make or enforce any law which shall abridge the privileges or immunities of citizens of the United States . . ." Since women were "persons born or naturalized in the United States," and all such persons were now guaranteed citizenship and privileges the states could not abridge, Minor believed that women were aided rather than injured by the Fourteenth Amendment. He stated in his resolutions that the "Constitution . . . nowhere gives them [states] the right to deprive any citizen of the elective franchise which is possessed by any other citizen." His resolutions were adopted by the Missouri Woman Suffrage Association, of which Minor's wife, Virginia Minor, was then president. They were published in the *Revolution* and explored and endorsed by Stanton in one of her speeches.[17] Finally, in 1871 they were set before Congress by Victoria Woodhull.

Woodhull had sent a memorial to the Senate and House of Representatives in December 1870, outlining the argument and asking Congress to declare that women already had the right to vote. She was granted

Victoria C. Woodhull (New York Public Library Picture Collection)

the opportunity to present a fuller argument to the Judiciary Committee of the House of Representatives on January 11, 1871.[18]

The NWSA was to begin its annual convention that morning, also in Washington, D.C. Instead, the officers and many members crowded inside the committee room to hear Woodhull's "bare legal argument."[19] She was mesmerizing. At the conclusion of her address, she was invited to the NWSA convention and treated as the day's hero.

Although the Judiciary Committee issued a negative report,[20] women around the country refused to give up the idea that they might immediately exercise the right to vote. In 1871 and 1872 at least 150 women showed up at the polls. Most were turned away, but some actually voted.[21] Susan B. Anthony was among the successful voters in 1872 and she—along with 14 others—was promptly arrested.[22]

Anthony was charged with unlawfully voting and scheduled to stand trial in 1873. Since women could be ruled incompetent to testify in court, she traveled to each of the postal districts in her county to present her views prior to her trial. In one speech after another, she introduced herself as one who "stands before you under indictment for the alleged crime of having voted at the last presidential election, without having a lawful right to vote" and urged other women to "no longer petition legislatures to give us the right to vote, but . . . to exercise their long neglected 'citizen's right.'"[23] Claiming that Anthony had prejudiced potential jurors, the prosecution had the trial relocated to Ontario County. Anthony just as energetically addressed the citizens in that county, but there was no further change of venue.

When the trial finally took place, Anthony was ruled incompetent to testify and forced to listen to the proceedings in silence. She was convicted of unlawful voting and fined $100. U.S. Associate Justice Ward Hunt then asked, "Has the prisoner anything to say why sentence should not be pronounced?" Indeed, she had. Over the judge's repeated attempts to silence her, Anthony spoke her mind, beginning, "I have many things to say; for in your ordered verdict of guilty, you have trampled underfoot every vital principle of our government. My natural rights, my civil rights, my political rights, are all alike ignored. . . . Your denial of my citizen's right to vote is the denial of my right of consent as one of the governed, the denial of my right of representation as one of the taxed, the denial of my right to a trial by a jury of my peers as an offender of law, therefore, the denial of my sacred rights to life, liberty, property, and—"[24]

Futilely, Judge Hunt tried to silence Anthony with orders such as "The Court can not allow the prisoner to go on," and "The prisoner must sit down." She continued presenting her point of view without acknowledging anything Hunt said, until he told Anthony and all assembled that "[T]he prisoner has been tried to the established forms of law." To that, Anthony responded directly, "Yes, your honor, but by forms of law all made by men, administered by men, in favor of men, and against women; and hence, your honor's ordered verdict of guilty, against a United States citizen for the exercise of 'that citizen's right to vote,' simply because that citizen was a woman and not a man." She also rejected any claim that unjust laws need be obeyed: "But, yesterday, the same man-made forms of law declared it punishable with a $1000 fine and six months' imprisonment, for you, or me, or any one of us, to give a cup of cold water, a crust of bread, or a night's shelter to a panting fugitive as he was tracking his way to Canada. And every man or woman in whose veins coursed a drip of human sympathy violated that wicked law, reckless of consequences, and was justified in so doing." Then she compared her actions to the actions of those fleeing slavery: "As then the slaves who got their freedom must take it over, or under, or through the unjust forms of law, precisely so now must women, to get their right to a voice in this government, take it; and I have taken mine, and mean to take it at every possible moment."[25] Anthony ultimately refused to pay the $100 fine, and Judge Hunt declined to jail her. (Jailed, Anthony could have appealed to the U.S. Supreme Court on a writ of habeas corpus; released, she had no basis for such appeal.)

The question of whether or not women were included in the Fourteenth Amendment's protections would ultimately be settled—for 19th-century women—by two Supreme Court decisions. In Illinois Myra Bradwell, having fulfilled all the necessary requirements, applied for admission to the bar. In its 1873 opinion the Court upheld an Illinois state law that barred women from the practice of law in its state courts. "[T]he right of females to pursue any lawful employment for a livelihood (the practice of law included)" was not, according to the decision, "one of the privileges and immunities of women as citizens."

Meanwhile, in Missouri the Minors pursued what had become known as "the new departure." When Virginia Minor was turned away from the polls in November 1872, she—and her husband, who was required to join any legal action his wife might bring—petitioned the courts of St. Louis for damages in the amount of $10,000.00. They cited section 1 of the Fourteenth Amendment. Their case also went to the Supreme Court. In 1875 that body rendered its decision: Under the U.S. Constitution, women had no right to vote.[26] (The Supreme Court would first find sex discrimination to be a violation of the Fourteenth Amendment's equal protection clause in 1971, in *Reed v. Reed*.)

Women responded to the Anthony and Minor voting decisions, in part, by protesting "taxation without representation." Two sisters, Julia and Abby Smith, allowed their meadows and cows to be sold by the government year after year, rather than pay the tax upon them. By Julia's 83rd year, only two cows remained: Taxey and Votey.[27] (The sisters sued and eventually won the right to buy back part of their property.)

Women also protested their status during the U.S. centennial in 1876. At the focal point of the celebration, at Independence Hall, Philadelphia, the Declaration of Independence was to be read aloud to U.S. citizens and visiting leaders of other countries. Stanton asked for permission to present the Declaration of Rights for Women. "We do not ask to read our declaration . . . only to present it, that it may become a historical part of the proceedings," she wrote. When permission was denied, the NWSA planned an "overt action." The New York *Tribune* reported that "[i]mmediately after the Declaration of Independence had been read by Richard Henry Lee . . . two ladies pushed their way vigorously through the crowd and appeared upon the speaker's platform. They were Susan B. Anthony and Matilda Joslyn Gage. Hustling generals aside, elbowing governors, and almost upsetting Dom Pedro in their charge, they reached Vice-President Ferry, and handed him a scroll about three feet long, tied with ribbons of various colors. He was seen to bow and look bewildered;

but they had retreated in the same vigorous manner before the explanation was whispered about."[28]

Lucy Stone thought the declaration a fine document. Nonetheless, she refused Stanton's invitation to affix her signature, since she had had no part in its writing or presentation.[29] The two women were writing to each other during this time, primarily about the *History of Woman Suffrage* that Anthony, Stanton, and Gage had begun. Other activist women also made overtures across organizational lines, but reunion remained unlikely.

One of the reasons for the tension was a scandal. Henry Ward Beecher and Elizabeth Tilton (wife of Theodore Tilton) had been having an affair. Anthony, who had learned this from Elizabeth Tilton, confided it to Stanton, who in turn relayed the information to Victoria Woodhull.[30] Woodhull eventually grew angry about the criticism she continued to receive and the hypocrisy of Beecher,[31] who was closely allied with the source of much of that criticism—the AWSA. She published an exposé of the affair in *Woodhull and Claflin's Weekly,* a newspaper she owned with her sister, Tennessee ("Tinnie") Claflin.

Tennessee "Tinnie" Claflin was an early stockbroker who supported women's suffrage. *(National Archives)*

Although the women's movement was injured by the highly publicized trial that followed (and the charges of "free love" back and forth), there were partial successes during the decade. Lucy Stone and Henry Blackwell were unable to persuade the Republican Party to support women's suffrage as part of its platform. They did, however, manage to secure a statement that the "Republican party is mindful of its obligations to . . . women . . . and the honest demands of any class of citizens for additional rights should be treated with respectful consideration." And again, in 1878, the Sixteenth Amendment to the Constitution was proposed—this time by Senator A. A. Sargent of California.[32] As had become customary, women sent petitions and their ablest speakers. But when Stanton addressed the Senate Committee on Privileges and Elections, "the chairman, Senator Wadleigh of New Hampshire . . . alternately looked over some manuscripts and newspapers before him, and jumped up to open or close a door or a window. He stretched, yawned, gazed at the ceiling, cut his nails, sharpened his pencil . . ."[33] and more. The committee issued a negative report, but the proposed women's suffrage amendment began to be introduced on a yearly basis.[34]

Near the close of the decade, in July 1878, the still disfranchised women of America celebrated the 30th anniversary of the Seneca Falls Convention. The meeting was held in the Unitarian Church of Fitzhugh Street in Rochester, New York. Women from all across the country—and from abroad as well—sent letters. Amy Post, active in that first convention of 1848 and now 77 years old, helped with the anniversary preparations; Lucretia Mott, now 86, attended what would be her last convention. Although suffrage had not yet been won, Post, Mott, and other leaders of their generation could point to many other gains. The increase in educational opportunity was particularly gratifying. Vassar (1861), Wellesley (1870), Smith (1871), and a number of other private women's colleges had been founded in the years since the Seneca Falls convention, as was the first Catholic women's college in the United States, Ursuline College (1871). Oberlin College, founded as a coeducational institution in 1833, had been followed by the founding of coeducational Antioch College (1852) and Swarthmore College (1869), among others. Some previously all-male colleges, including Colby College in 1871 and Boston University in 1872, had also begun admitting female students into the general population, while others had added separate women's divisions, as Cornell University did in 1874, when it created Sage College. State universities and colleges—beginning with Iowa in 1858 and in increasing numbers after 1862, when states began to build colleges on federal Morrill Land Grant parcels—had also begun to admit women.[35]

Elizabeth Cady Stanton, now 62 years old, referred to these increased educational opportunities when she addressed the members of a younger generation: "I urge the young women especially to prepare themselves to take up the work so soon to fall from our hands. You have had opportunities for education such as we had not. You hold to-day the vantage-ground we have won by argument. Show now your gratitude to us by making the uttermost of yourselves, and by your earnest, exalted lives secure to those who come after you a higher outlook . . . a larger freedom . . ."[36]

She could not have known that young women of 20 in that audience would themselves reach 62 before women's suffrage was won.

CHRONICLE OF EVENTS

1870

Women in Utah Territory, who win the suffrage after Wyoming, are the first to cast their votes in municipal elections.

The Massachusetts Woman Suffrage Association is founded.

Ada Kepley graduates from the Law Department of the University of Chicago; she and her husband lead a campaign to allow women to practice law in Illinois.

Sojourner Truth petitions President Ulysses Grant for freedmen and women to be given western lands on which to live. The migration of formerly enslaved people to Kansas and Missouri resulted from her efforts.

Alice Stone Blackwell was the editor of the *Woman's Journal* for 35 years. *(Library of Congress)*

Mary Harris Thompson becomes the first woman surgeon in the United States.

Daughters of St. Crispin, a Massachusetts union of women shoe workers, pass resolution demanding equal pay for equal work.

First women students (34) enter University of Michigan.

Wellesley College is chartered.

January: Elizabeth Cady Stanton presents Francis Minor's argument in address before a congressional committee in the District of Columbia.

The Michigan Equal Suffrage Association is formed.

January 8: First issue of the *Woman's Journal* is published.

February 3: States ratify the Fifteenth Amendment. It prohibits, rather than penalizes, the withholding of voting from African-American men, but not women.

February 14: Esther Morris becomes the first woman government official: She is a justice of the peace in South Pass City, Wyoming.

March: For the first time women serve on juries (Wyoming Territory).

March: Marilla M. Ricker of Dover, New Hampshire, is the first woman to try to vote. She casts her ballot, but it is refused.

May 10–11: The National Woman Suffrage Association meets in Irving Hall, New York.

1871

Smith College, endowed by Sophia Smith, opens. It is the first college to be endowed by a woman.

Ursuline College, the first Catholic college for women, opens.

Colby College admits women.

Illinois Supreme Court refuses to admit Alta Hulett to the practice of law.

Suffragists believe attorney Francis Minor is correct in his determination that women are entitled to vote under the Fourteenth Amendment. They now make a practical test of this question by registering and voting in the state and presidential elections of 1871–72.

Louisa May Alcott publishes *Little Men*.

The Women's Centenary Association, first organization of church women, forms. The group forms to assist disabled preachers and their families. It aids those in missionary work, and helps to teach women students in the ministry.

Caroline White Soule becomes the first president of the Woman's Centenary Association.

Frances Elizabeth Willard is the first woman to become president of a college. She assumes the post at Evanston College for Ladies in Evanston, Illinois, which later merges with Northwestern University.

Catharine W. Waite of Illinois sues her registrar for denying her the right to vote.

January 11: Victoria Woodhull addresses the Judiciary Committee of the House of Representatives, remarking "With the right to vote sex has nothing to do."

March: Marilla M. Ricker of Dover, New Hampshire, is the first woman to cast her vote under the Fourteenth Amendment. She becomes the first U.S. woman accepted as an official voter.

April 3: Nannette B. Gardner in Detroit, Michigan, is the second woman to vote under the Fourteenth Amendment.

July 21: Ellen Rand Van Valkenburg of Santa Cruz, California, having been denied the right to register to vote, sues the registrar of Brown County. It is the first decision under the Fourteenth Amendment.

September 16: Carrie S. Burnham of Philadelphia, Pennsylvania, sues her registrar for denying her the right to vote, after she has paid taxes and is registered on the canvasser's list of legal voters.

October: Sara Andrews Spencer and Sarah E. Webster and 70 other women of Washington, D.C., having their votes refused, sue the Board of Inspectors in the Supreme Court of the District.

December 12: Emma Abbot, opera singer, makes her first professional appearance in New York.

1872

Virginia and Francis Minor file suit in lower court against Reese Happersett, voter's registrar.

Nine hundred working women of Lynn, Massachusetts, join together to protest pay cuts and changed employment rules in boot and shoe trades.

Abigail Duniway addresses Oregon Legislature.

Victoria Claflin Woodhull is the first woman to become a candidate for president of the United States. At her own convention in May 1872, Woodhull is named as the presidential candidate of her newly established Equal Rights Party. Her running mate is an African-American abolitionist.

Congress passes a law giving women in federal employment equal pay for equal work.

Julia W. Howe wrote the "Battle Hymn of the Republic." *(Library of Congress)*

Charlotte Ray of Washington, D.C., becomes the first African-American woman attorney in the country.

September 1: The New England Hospital for Women and Children, the first school of nursing, is established and is totally run by women.

November 5: Susan B. Anthony votes and is arrested.

1873

The first woman graduates from the Massachusetts Institute of Technology. Ellen Swallow Richards, accepted as a special student in chemistry, receives a B.S. degree.

Eliza Daniel Stewart establishes the first Woman's Temperance League.

Julia and Abigail Smith refuse to pay property taxes because they cannot vote in Glastonbury, Connecticut. Their cows are sold for taxes the following year.

March: Congress passes the Comstock Act, which suppresses the circulation of "obscene" literature and articles for "immoral use." By the 1890s the law also will reduce the dissemination of birth control information and contraceptives.

Emilie Foeking graduates from the Baltimore College of Dental Surgery.

April 15: The Supreme Court decides in *Bradwell v. Illinois* that Myra Bradwell's rights have not been denied because Illinois refused her the right to practice law on the grounds that she is a married woman.

May 29: Julia Ward Howe calls first convention of women preachers in America.

June 17: The trial of Susan B. Anthony begins in Ontario County, New York. She is charged with voting in the presidential election of November 5, because "[a]t that time she was a woman." When she is called to the stand, the U.S. district attorney claims she is "not competent as a witness on her own behalf" because she is a woman.

June 18: Susan B. Anthony is found guilty of voting because, according to Judge Ward Hunt, the Fourteenth Amendment does not protect her right to vote. She refuses to pay the $100 fine.

December 15: Centennial Tea Party is held in Boston to reaffirm that "taxation without representation is tyranny." Three thousand people participate.

1874

Michigan holds state referendum; women's suffrage is defeated.

Cornell University opens Sage College, a separate division for women.

January: The National Woman Suffrage Association holds its fifth convention in Washington, D.C.

June 1: Second convention of women preachers in America is held.

November: Woman's Christian Temperance Union is formed in Cleveland, Ohio.

1875

Michigan and Minnesota grant suffrage, on school issues only, to widowed mothers of schoolchildren.

Mount Hermon Seminary is founded in Mississippi.

Reverend Henry Ward Beecher, brother of Harriet Beecher Stowe and past president of the American Woman Suffrage Association, goes on trial for adultery, embarrassing the suffrage movement.

Reverend Antoinette Brown Blackwell publishes a feminist criticism of Charles Darwin's theory of evolution titled *The Sexes through Nature.*

Mary Baker Eddy publishes *Science and Health,* the handbook for Christian Scientists.

March 29: In *Minor v. Happersett* the Supreme Court rules, for the second time in two years, that the Fourteenth Amendment does not protect a woman's right to vote.

1876

Sarah Stevenson is the first woman to become a member of the American Medical Association (AMA).

July 4: Matilda Joslyn Gage authors the Declaration of Rights for Women.

1877

Helen Magill (White) is the first woman to obtain a Ph.D. degree, from Boston University.

The first state reformatory for women is established in Sherborn, Massachusetts.

Alzina Parsons Stevens becomes the first president of the Working Woman Union Number 1 in Chicago.

Victoria Woodhull and Tennessee Claflin move to England.

Colorado's referendum on granting women the vote is defeated.

1878

Thirtieth anniversary of the Seneca Falls convention is celebrated in Rochester.

Senator A. A. Sargent introduces the Sixteenth Amendment to the U.S. Constitution. Known as the Susan B. Anthony Amendment, it is introduced every year until its passage in 1919.

The Medical Society of New England Hospital is established, the first women's medical society in the world.

September 17: State legislatures from 1873–1900 had begun to pass progressive laws that allowed wives, as well as husbands, to own personal and real property. The New York case of *Birbeck v. Ackroyd* (1878) is a test of New York's law.

May 12: Catharine Beecher dies.

1879

Senate committee issues favorable minority report on women's suffrage amendment.

February 15: Congress allows women to practice law in federal courts.

March: The president of the Illinois Woman's Christian Temperance Union (WCTU), Frances Willard, organizes the presentation of more than 100,000 petitions to the legislature asking that women be given the vote on matters of liquor. Later this year she wins election as president of the national WCTU.

March 3: Belva Lockwood becomes the first woman lawyer admitted by the U.S. Supreme Court to practice at its bar.

November 1: After the Rhode Island decision in *McKim v. McKim,* courts begin awarding custody to mothers during their child's "tender years."

December 20: Women in Cambridge, Massachusetts, exercise municipal suffrage.

EYEWITNESS TESTIMONY

Brothers, when you were weak, and I was strong, I toiled for you. Now you are strong, and I am weak because of my work for you, I ask your aid. I ask the ballot for myself and my sex, and as I stood by you, I pray you stand by me and mine.

Clara Barton, speaking to assembly at the woman suffrage convention, January 19, 1870, in History of Woman Suffrage, *Vol. 2, 418.*

Theodore Tilton is making a great effort to "Consoli-date["] the Equal rights, National and American Woman Suffrage Associations.

There is an *executive Com. meeting of the American Equal* rights soc. on Thursday, next (Mar. 24.) to vote the Equal rights soc. into this plot.—Now, since the 15th amendment is adopted and two National soci-eties for woman are in existence, *we* think it much better to *drop* the Equal rights soc. If *all* the members of the Committee meet next Thursday, at 76 Columbia St. Brooklyn—we can carry this, and save our good old Equal rights soc. from being smirched, by an Alliance with the National soc. which will be done, if we are not there. Now can you not come up, even at some inconvenience, to the meeting on Thursday, to give a last vote?

It will give a good chance too, to talk over many other things of family, and friendly interest—Do come Nettee.

Mr. Tilton has also sent out a circular, asking a "conference meeting"—Three from Mrs. Stanton's soc. Three from our soc. and three, whom the Signers of the Call, for a conference will chose, to unite all the old friends and to unite the National and Cleve-land societies.

We have private advices, that the object is, to make Mrs. Mott Prest. of the soc. which unites both, and Mr. Beecher Vice Prest. of course Mrs. Mott, to resign, and nominate Mrs. Stanton as her successor— Strain a point Nettee, and come on to N. York— Thursday Mar. 24—

Lucy Stone, letter to Antoinette Brown Blackwell, March 22, 1870, in Lasser and Merrill, Friends and Sisters, *177.*

With all my prejudices against the policy, I am under conscientious obligations to say that these women acquitted themselves with such dignity, decorum,

Belva Lockwood, shown here, was the first woman lawyer to practice before the U.S. Supreme Court in 1879. *(Library of Congress)*

propriety of conduct and intelligence as to win the admiration of every fair-minded citizen of Wyoming. They were careful, pains-taking, intelli-gent and conscientious. They were firm and resolute for the right as established by the law and the testi-mony. Their verdicts were right, and, after three or four criminal trials, the lawyers engaged in defend-ing persons accused of crime began to avail them-selves of the right of peremptory challenge to get rid of the female jurors, who were too much in favor of enforcing the laws and punishing crime to suit the interests of their clients. After the grand jury had been in session two days, the dance-house keep-ers, gamblers and *demi-monde* fled out of the city in dismay, to escape the indictment of women grand jurors! In short I have never, in twenty-five years of constant experience in the courts of the country, seen more faithful, intelligent and resolutely honest grand and petit juries than these.

A contemptibly lying and silly dispatch went over the wires to the effect that during the trial of A. W. Howie for homicide (in which the jury consisted of six women and six men) the men and women were kept locked up together all night for four nights. Only two nights intervened during the trial, and on these nights, by my order, the jury was taken to the parlor of the large, commodious and well-furnished hotel of the Union Pacific Railroad, in charge of the sheriff and a woman bailiff, where they were supplied with meals and every comfort, and at 10 o'clock the women were conducted by the bailiff to a large and suitable apartment where beds were prepared for them, and the men to another adjoining, where beds were prepared for them . . .

Nothing occurred to offend the most refined lady (if she was a sensible lady) and the universal judgment of every intelligent and fair-minded man present was and is, that the experiment was a success.

Judge Howe, letter to Myra Bradwell, April 4, 1870, in History of Woman Suffrage, *Vol. 3, 736–737.*

I will first state to what I am not opposed. And, first, I am not opposed to women speaking in public to any who are willing to hear, nor do I object to women's preaching, sanctioned as it is by a prophetic apostle— as one of the millennial results. It is true that no women were appointed among the first twelve, or the seventy disciples sent out by the Lord, nor were women appointed to be apostles or bishops or elders. But they were not forbidden to teach or preach, except in places where it violated a custom that made a woman appear as one of a base and degraded class if she thus violated custom.

Nor am I opposed to a woman earning her own independence in any lawful calling, and wish many more were open to her which are now closed.

Nor am I opposed to the agitation and organization of women, as women, to set forth the wrongs suffered by great multitudes of our sex, which are multiform and most humiliating. Nor am I opposed to women's undertaking to govern both boys and men—they always have done it, and always will. The most absolute and cruel tyrants I have ever known were selfish, obstinate, unreasonable women to whom were chained men of delicacy, honor, and piety, whose only alternatives were helpless submission, or ceaseless and disgraceful broils.

Nor am I opposed to the claim that women have equal rights with men. I rather claim that they have the sacred, superior rights that God and good men accord to the weak and defenseless, by which they have the easiest work, the most safe and comfortable places, and the largest share of all the most agreeable and desirable enjoyments of this life. My main objection to the woman suffrage organizations is mainly this, that a wrong mode is employed to gain a right object.

The "right object" sought is to remedy the wrongs and relieve the sufferings of great multitudes of our sex. The "wrong mode" is that which aims to enforce by law instead of by love. It is one which assumes that man is the author and abetter of all these wrongs, and that he must be restrained and regulated by constitutions and laws, as the chief and most trustworthy method.

In opposition to this, I hold that the fault is as much, or more, with women than with men, inasmuch as that we have all the power we need to remedy all wrongs and sufferings complained of, and yet we do not use it for that end. It is my deep conviction that all reasonable and conscientious men of our age, and especially of our country, are not only willing, but anxious to provide for the best good of our sex, and that they will gladly bestow all that is just, reasonable, and kind, whenever we unite in asking in the proper spirit and manner. It is because we do not ask, or "because we ask amiss," that we do not receive all we need both from God and men. Let me illustrate my meaning by a brief narrative of my own experience. To begin with my earliest: I can not remember a time when I did not find a father's heart so tender that it was always easier for him to give anything I asked than to deny me. Of my seven brothers, I know not one who would not take as much or more care of my interests than I should myself. The brother who presides is here because it is so hard for him to say "No" to any woman seeking his aid.

It is half a century this very spring since I began to work for the education and relief of my sex, and I have succeeded so largely by first convincing intelligent and benevolent women that what I aimed at was right and desirable, and then securing their influence with their fathers, brothers, and husbands; and always with success. American women have only to unite in asking for whatever is just and reasonable, in a proper spirit and manner, in order to secure all that they need.

Here, then, I urge my greatest objections to the plan of female suffrage; for my countrywomen are seeking it only as an instrument for redressing wrongs and relieving wants by laws and civil influences. Now, I ask, why not take a shorter course, and ask to have the men do for us what we might do for ourselves if we had the ballot? Suppose we point out to our State Legislatures and to Congress the evils that it is supposed the ballot would remedy, and draw up petitions for these remedial measures, would not these petitions be granted much sooner and with far less irritation and conflict than must ensue before we gain the ballot? And in such petitions thousands of women would unite who now deem that female suffrage would prove a curse rather than a benefit.

And here I will close with my final objection to woman suffrage, and that is that it will prove a measure of injustice and oppression to the women who oppose it. Most of such women believe that the greatest cause of the evils suffered by our sex is that the true profession of woman, in many of its most important departments, is not respected; that women are not trained either to the science or the practice of domestic duties as they need to be, and that, as the consequence, the chief labors of the family state pass to ignorant foreigners, and by cultivated women are avoided as disgraceful.

They believe the true remedy is to make woman's work honorable and remunerative, and that the suffrage agitation does not tend to this, but rather to drain off the higher classes of cultivated women from those more important duties to take charge of political and civil affairs that are more suitable for men.

Now if women are all made voters, it will be their duty to vote, and also to qualify themselves for this duty. But already women have more than they can do well in all that appropriately belongs to women, and to add the civil and political duties of men would be deemed a measure of injustice and oppression.

Catharine Beecher, statement in opposition to women's suffrage, read on her behalf by Henry Blackwell at the American Woman Suffrage Association Convention of May 11, 1870, in History of Woman Suffrage, *Vol. 2, 787–788.*

I have received letters innumerable. Women respond to this divorce speech as they never did to suffrage. In a word, I have had grand meetings. Oh, how the women flock to me with their sorrows. Such experiences as I listen to, plantation never equaled.

Elizabeth Cady Stanton, letter to Susan B. Anthony, June 27, 1870, in Stanton and Blatch, Elizabeth Cady Stanton, *Vol. 2, 127.*

As Paulina Davis has taken the decade meeting in hand, I hope you will lend her all the aid you possibly can in making it a success. I do wish this approaching coming together might be the means of our reunion. The present divisions in the woman suffrage ranks are frivolous and unworthy of us, while it seems to me most humiliating that both of our associations have men as presidents. There was some excuse for this is 1848, when women were just starting public work. But to-day!

Elizabeth Cady Stanton, letter to Sarah Pugh, August 5, 1870, in Stanton and Blatch, Elizabeth Cady Stanton, *Vol. 2, 129.*

I was early at the polls, but too late to witness the polling of the first female vote—by "Grandma" Swain, a much-esteemed Quaker lady of 75 summers . . .

I saw the rough mountaineers maintaining the most respectful decorum whenever the women approached the polls, and heard the timely warning of one of the leading canvassers as he silenced an incipient quarrel with uplifted finger, saying, "Hist! Be quiet! A woman is coming!"

And I was compelled to allow that in this new country, supposed at that time to be infested by hordes of cut-throats, gamblers and abandoned characters, I had witnessed a more quiet election than it had been my fortune to see in the quiet towns of Vermont. I saw ladies attended by their husbands, brothers, or sweethearts, ride to the places of voting, and alight in the midst of a silent crowd, and pass through an open space to the polls, depositing their votes with no more exposure to insult or injury than they would expect on visiting a grocery store or meat-market. Indeed, they were much safer here, every man of their party was pledged to shield them, while every member of the other party feared the influence of any signs of disrespect.

The Reverend D. J. Pierce, letter to the editor of the Laramie Sentinel, *regarding election day in Wyoming, September 1870, in* History of Woman Suffrage, *Vol. 3, 739.*

Mr. Tilton, Mrs. Stanton, Miss Anthony, and others of the N. York Society are going to Cleveland to try to force us into combination with them. They have been stirring up some of our Western members who are ignorant of the facts to join them there.

It is very *important* that Mass[achusetts] should be represented. Mrs. Howe is trying to see you in order to induce you to go *if possible*.

I am authorized by the Mass[achusetts] Ex. Com to find *delegates* & if you will act in that capacity I will hand you credentials at Cleveland.

It will be best to start Sunday night. But early Monday AM will bring you to Cleveland Tuesday morning.

Mr. Beecher will not be willing to serve another term tho very kind & cordial. We think of electing Mr. Julian in his place if our opponents do not put Mrs. Stanton or Mr. Tilton upon us inspite of ourselves.

If you cannot go, please write a letter to my wife Lucy Stone—care of Mrs. Hannah M. Clarke Cleve-land O. expressing your opinion that we should not merge the American WS As in any other & that we should stick to the question of *Suffrage* & not complicate the cause with marriage, divorce & other outside questions.

By so doing, you will give us material aid & much oblige.

Henry Blackwell, letter to the Reverend Freeman Clark,
November 17, 1870, in Wheeler,
Loving Warriors, *237–238.*

. . . I attended the Cuh. [Cuyahoga] Co. Soc. meeting here yesterday. Susan was there, & John Gage. Susan told how she got money from Train, how I would not work with him, &c &c. I stated the real ground of difference and urged that in any action they took they should make suffrage the main issue.

Lucy Stone, letter to Henry Blackwell, November 27,
1870, in Wheeler, Loving Warriors, *238.*

Women delegates arguing in favor of suffrage in front of the Judiciary Committee of the U.S. House of Representatives, 1871 *(Library of Congress)*

Women's suffrage is an unjust, unreasonable, unspiritual abnormality. It is a hard, undigested, tasteless, devitalized proposition. It is a half-fledged, unmusical promethean abomination. It is a quack bolous to reduce masculinity even by the obliteration of feminity . . . it is the sediment, not the wave of the sex. It is the antithesis of that highest and sweetest mystery—conviction by submission, and conquest by sacrifice.

John Boyle O'Reilly, writing in the Boston Pilot,
January 4, 1871, in Diner,
Erin's Daughters in America, *146.*

I do think the crowing insult to us from the Republican party is Bingham's majority report [of the House Judiciary Committee, opposing woman suffrage]. He declares we are not citizens, but only "members of the state." Well, you remember in my 15th amendment speech I said that in the establishment of an aristocracy of sex on this continent, woman would know deeper depths of degradation under this government than she has ever known before. That night in Washington when you said you had never before seen me so on the rampage, I had a vivid intuition of the dark clouds hanging over us; and now they are breaking. In fact, simultaneously with the 15th amendment comes a generally insulting tone in the press, propositions in several state legislatures to license prostitution and now an open declaration by the most liberal one of the parties that we are "not citizens." Of course, I may add in passing, Mary A. Livermore and those of her kidney can "wait patiently for the suffrage," as she never cared two pins about the right—in fact, laughed at the idea four years ago. But we cannot afford to wait, nor can the nation afford to have us wait. So go ahead and "deal damnation round the land with a high hand," as the *Tribune* says you do; only don't run in debt in order to do it! We will win this battle yet, Susan! With love unchanged, undimmed by time and friction.

Elizabeth Cady Stanton, letter to Susan B. Anthony,
February 6, 1871, in Stanton and Blatch,
Elizabeth Cady Stanton, *Vol. 2, 129–130.*

The truth is my dear friend, I came to the determination about a year ago, never to allow any *man* however excellent to interpret any woman for me . . . I made a silent vow . . . that without wholesale condemnation of man, but with prayer that his eyes might be opened to see himself as he is in the sight of God, and woman as she is I would stand by all suspected women as if they were my own sisters—and when they were proved guilty I would stand by harder than ever . . . [T]his is the battle we are set to fight in the very outset of our last campaign—indeed the reason it is any campaign at all, is that men perceive at last that the little white symbol of power is coming into our hands and begin to realize what we shall do with it. It is by no accident that the question of licensing prostitution appears just when our Constitutional right to the suffrage is about to be acknowledged—but a God sent conjunction—for women are nearly unanimous on the one matter and are simply becoming impatient for an opportunity to vote upon it. If you could have been here [Washington] these two months! . . . [L]et me assure you that Mrs. Woodhull stands in a most enviable position in this city today—and she is there because she . . . worked for womanhood twelve hours out of the twenty four with such quiet dignity and sweetness that not one person who has seen her in private and talked with her for five minutes and I verily believe not one who heard her great speech (for it is truly great—I never saw an audience of fourteen hundred, many standing, listening as this did to a bare legal argument in my life) has wished to utter a word against her or been able to do it . . .

The lips of women are being unsealed a Mr[.] Mill prophesied—all over the world . . .

Isabella Beecher Hooker, letter to Mary Rice Livermore,
March 15, 1871, in Boydston, Kelley, and Margolis,
The Limits of Sisterhood, *309–310.*

You will see by the last No. of the Journal, that Mrs. Livermore's article looks toward an affiliation with Mrs. Hooker, who is the sworn ally of Susan, and Mrs. Stanton and who in connection with Paulina Davis and Josephine Griffing, have done their best to defeat, and undermine, the A.W.S.A.

Now I regret her article, and think it so much better, for us to keep clear of other organizations at least, till they prove, that their work is good.

Now, if you agree with me in this view, will you not write a private, friendly note to Mrs. Livermore, and suggest that it seems best to you, not to strike hands, with those people at Washington. They were our late enemies. We dont know that they are our friends. The attempt to get names to a Declaration, is poor work, as not one woman, in ten thousand, will or can send her name, even if she cares much for suffrage.

Do not mention to *any one* that I suggested this to you. But it is easier to stop a small leak, than a great hole.

Lucy Stone, letter to Rebecca Smith Janney, March 19, 1871, in Wheeler, Loving Warriors, 239.

The National Woman Suffrage Convention met at Apollo Hall, yesterday, and was numerously attended, the majority of those present being ladies.

Mrs. ISABELLA BEECHER HOOKER presided. She urged every woman to vote for or attempt to vote at every State and Federal election under the provisions of the act to enforce the Fifteenth Amendment. She deprecated the fear which some women had of going to the polls.

New York Times, May 12, 1871, 8.

Because I am a woman, and because I conscientiously hold opinions somewhat different from the self-elected orthodoxy which men find their profit in supporting; and because I think it my bounden duty and my absolute right to put forward my opinions and to advocate them with my whole strength, self-elected orthodoxy assails me, villifies me, and endeavors to cover my life with ridicule and dishonor. This has been particularly the case in reference to certain law proceedings into which I was recently drawn by the weakness of one very near relative and the profligate selfishness of other relatives.

One of the charges made against me is that I lived in the same house with my former husband, Dr. Woodhull, and my present husband, Col. Blood. The fact is a fact. Dr. Woodhull, being sick, ailing and incapable of self-support, I felt it my duty to myself and to human nature that he should be cared for, although his incapacity was in no wise attributable to me. My present husband, Col. Blood, not only approves of this charity, but co-operates in it. I esteem it one of the most virtuous acts of my life. But various editors have stigmatized me as a living example of immorality and unchastity.

My opinions and principles are subjects of just criticism. I put myself before the public voluntarily. I know full well that the public will criticise me and my motives and actions, in their own way and at their own time. I accept the position. I except to no fair analysis and examination, even if the scalpel be a little merciless.

But let him who is without sin cast his stone. I do not intend to be made the scape-goat of sacrifice, to be offered up as a victim to society by those who cover over the foulness of their lives and the feculence of their thoughts with hypocritical mouth of fair professions, and by diverting public attention from their own iniquity and pointing the finger at me. I know that many of my self-appointed judges and critics are deeply tainted with the vices they condemn. I live in one house with one who was my husband; I live as the wife with one who is my husband. I believe in Spiritualism; I advocate free love in the highest, purest sense, as the only cure for the immorality, the deep damnation by which men corrupt and disfigure God's most holy institution of sexual relations. My judges preach against "free love" openly, practice it secretly. Their outward seeming is fair; inwardly they are full of "dead men's bones and all manner of uncleanness." For example, I know of one man, a public teacher of eminence, who lives in concubinage with the wife of another public teacher of almost equal eminence. All three concur in denouncing offenses against morality, "Hypocrisy is the tribute paid by vice to virtue." So be it. But I decline to stand up as "the frightful example." I shall make it my business to analyze some of these lines, and will take my chances in the matter of the libel suits.

I have faith in critics, but I believe in public justice.

Victoria C. Woodhull, letter to the editor of the New York Times, May 22, 1871, 5.

I was both surprised and pained to read a communication in your edition of last Monday, from a woman [Victoria Woodhull] who not only lives a life of infamy, but has had the unblushing affrontery to uphold and justify her conduct in the sacred name of "charity," to the admiration (!) of the community of the Metropolis of the Western World. A publication of that kind, although couched in decent language, is so disgusting in its details as to be offensive in the highest degree to the mortal sense of the respectable portion of the public.

She must, indeed, be lost to every sense of virtue and decency who can make the acknowledgement to the world that at the time of all others when a husband most needs a true wife's care, during sickness or incapacity of any kind, he is thrown aside, like so much rubbish, and another, for the nonce, substituted in his place.

Above all, what saith the Redeemer of man kind! "Whoso divorceth his wife and marrieth another comiteth adultery." "And whoso marrieth her that is divorced, commiteth adultery." In the face of this God-given-law, what mortal can dare to offer his or her opinion!

Letter from "A Wife and Mother" to the editor of the New York Times, *May 25, 1871, 2.*

It is not of the individual woman but of the representative woman that I would now speak. In my person various editors and public speakers, of more or less weight, have chosen to attack principles on purely personal grounds. A well-known Joe Miller gives instance of a lawsuit in which there being no defense, the client's instructions were to blackguard the plaintiff's lawyer. This is precisely the disingenuous and cowardly line of practice in which I am the victim. Woman's suffrage and woman's rights being the issue and there being no defense, I am taken as the representative woman, and my personal character being maligned and depreciated, the cause suffers. Let it not be supposed that I assume to myself the character of representative. The assumption is on the part of those who, being anti-suffragists, can neither rise above prejudice nor meet the irrefragable justice of the woman's cause by honest argument. In this strait they blackguard the "plaintiff's lawyer."

I will not ask of you whether such course is manly, is just. The editor of one of the leading journals of America cannot afford to defend such flagrant injustice. Through you I appeal to the public. But, in appealing to the public, I would carry my argument a little further. If I be a "notorious woman," a person with "soiled hands," and so forth, (I need not sully your columns with the filth and impurity of which I have been the target,) if I be all this, and thereby am rendered unfit to present and advocate the woman's cause, how is it with those—my opponents—who are themselves reprobate, and of impure life and conversation! I ask by what equity and justice a woman is to be held accused on the mere imputation of offenses which her accusers may commit without condemnation! . . .

I think you will acquit me of egotism in alluding to *Woodhull & Claflin's Weekly;* the same argument applies to the *Weekly* that applies to its editors. If the *Weekly* happen, in the exercise of its critical functions, to trench on the conduct or management of trading or corporate bodies, a howl resounds through the street, "Those women! those adventuresses!" If, without naming any one, notorious spots or blemishes are alluded to, whispers come round how Sorooze & Dickhoff intend to squelch those women, and drive them out of Broad-Street. Let us see!

Woman suffrage will succeed, despite this miserable guerrilla opposition, and the *Weekly* is strong enough to take care of itself. But I only repeat: Is it fair to treat a woman worse than a man, and then revile her because she is a woman!

Victoria C. Woodhull, letter to the editor of the New York Times, *May 24, 1871, 2.*

You see Susan and I are slowly journeying westward. Since I left you, I have filled twenty engagements, speaking twice in nearly every place, once on suffrage and once to women alone. This idea of mine of addressing women by themselves should produce a rich fruitage in the future. What radical thoughts I then and there put into their heads, and as they feel untrammeled, these thoughts are permanently lodged there! That is all I ask. And what a magnificent chance on these lines is in store for us. We have just received letters from Salt Lake City saying that Brigham consents to let "Miss Susan and Mrs. Elizabeth" speak in the Tabernacle. P.S. Later. This letter got into the pocket of my valise rather than in the mail bag. Since it was written we have been at the Utah capital. There were to have been two sessions of our meeting with the Mormon women; but as Susan and I felt they would never be allowed back again, we decided to say all we had to say at the first session. This meeting began at two P.M., and did not end until seven P.M. Every aspect of the institution of marriage was discussed; then the doors of the Tabernacle were closed to our ministrations.

Elizabeth Cady Stanton, letter to Elizabeth Smith Miller, June 12, 1871, in Stanton and Blatch, Elizabeth Cady Stanton, *Vol. 2, 132–133.*

God, through His servant has conferred on us the right of franchise, for a wise purpose. This privilege has been granted without our solicitation; and in this, as well as in very many other respects, we realize that woman in Utah possesses advantages greatly superior to woman elsewhere.

In the States, a few women have for years been battling the usages, prejudices and policy of our nation, and have not yet succeeded in obtaining for themselves and their sisters what has been . . . conferred upon us.

Eliza B. Snow, Margaret T. Smoot, Rachel Grant, Mary A. Leaver, Mary I. Horne, Sarah M. Kimball, and Priscilla Stainer, addressing their "Dearly Beloved Sisters," June 21, 1871, in the New York Times, *July 6, 1871, 5.*

Excuse the boldness of this communication, as I write to you as to a friend, for you *are* a friend to us all. And without further preliminaries, let me state my case.

I am a farmer's wife—in this little hill-side town, having been here seventeen years. I have no children and have only the dreary routine of household cares to occupy my mind. My husband is an old-fashioned farmer, and plods contentedly on year after year without a mower or reaper, without books or anything to make home pleasant. His amusement is to go to the village store to spend his evenings and rainy days, while I *amuse* myself by mending his old pants, or some other equally agreeable occupation. I have often asked him to allow me to take some child to care for, but this he will not do. It involves expense. Of course, such a man is bitterly opposed to "woman's rights" and loses no opportunity for the usual sneer. I have no money and but few clothes. He forbids my giving anything away, as everything is *his* and nothing mine. In short I am nothing but a housekeeper without wages, doing *all* the work of the family. I have no fondness for this kind of life, but on the contrary have as keen a relish for amusements, concerts, lectures etc. as any woman in the city of Hartford.

Now Mrs. Hooker, please give me a little advice. Is it my duty to spend *all* my life in this way? Would it be wrong for me to go to Hartford this winter for a few weeks or to some other place where people *live?* Have you any friend who would give me a pleasant home, and an opportunity to attend an occasional entertainment in exchange for my services? If you ask what I can do, I reply I can do what women in the country usually do. I can sew, or do anything that is necessary to be done,—can take care of children and teach them, as this was formerly my employment. I must get away from here for a while or go crazy. Perhaps you will say I am *already* deranged.

My husband's father buried his *fourth wife* a few days since. She laid down the burden of life willingly, at sixty-two years of age. He will doubtless marry again soon, as it *costs too much* to hire a housekeeper.

You are my first and *only* confidant in this matter. If this seems worthy of a reply, please address Mrs. S. H. Graves
P.S. I have omitted to say that this husband of mine has bonds[,] stocks, and notes and to these he is wedded.

S. H. Graves, letter to Isabella Beecher Hooker, October 24, 1871, in Boydston, Kelley, and Margolis, The Limits of Sisterhood, *204–205.*

Being a constant reader of your valuable paper, I take the liberty of asking you to explain to me why it is that when respectable women of color answer an advertisement for a dressmaker, either in families or with a dressmaker, [they] are invariably refused, or offered a place to cook or scrub, or to do house work; and when application is made at manufactories immediately after having seen an advertisement for operators or finishers, meet with the same reply, sometimes modified by bidding you "call again," "just suited," "will want more hands in the course of a few weeks," etc.

There are many respectable women of color competent to fill any of the above named positions, and who eke out a scanty livelihood sewing at home, who would gladly take permanent situations, to sew, operate or finish; and some have advertised to that effect, making their color known, and received no answers.

The "brotherly love" for which this city is proverbial should extend to all, irrespective of color, race or creed.

Letter from "A Colored Woman" to the editor of the Philadelphia Post, *November 1, 1871, in Sterling,* We Are Your Sisters, *423–424.*

It is a mistake to call Miss Anthony a reformer, or the movement in which she is engaged a reform; she is a revolutionist, aiming at nothing less than the breaking up of the very foundations of society, and the overthrow of every social institution organized for the protection of the sanctity of the altar, the family circle and the legitimacy of our offspring, recognizing no religion but self-worship, no God but human reason, no motive to human action but lust. Many, undoubtedly, will object that we state the case too strongly; but if they will dispassionately examine the facts and compare them with the character of the leaders and the inevitable tendency of their teachings, they must be convinced that the apparently innocent measure of woman suffrage as a remedy for woman's wrongs in over-crowded populations, is but a pretext or entering wedge by which to open Pandora's box and let loose upon society a pestilential brood to destroy all that is pure and beautiful in human nature, and all that has been achieved by organized associations in religion, morality and refinement; that the whole plan is coarse, sensual and agrarian, the worst phase of French infidelity and communism . . .

She did not directly and positively broach the licentious social theories which she is known to entertain, because she well knew that they would shock the sensibilities of her audience, but confined her discourse to the one subject of woman suffrage as a means to attain equality of competitive labor. This portion of her lecture we have not time to discuss. Our sole purpose now is to enter our protest against the inculcation of doctrines which we believe are calculated to degrade and debauch society by demolishing the dividing lines between virtue and vice. It is true that Miss Anthony did not openly advocate "free love" and a disregard of the sanctity of the marriage relation, but she did worse—under the guise of defending women against manifest wrongs, she attempts to instil into their minds an utter disregard for all that is right and conservative in the present order of society.

Beriah Brown, writing in the Seattle Territorial Dispatch, *November 1871, in Harper,* Life and Work of Susan B. Anthony, *Vol. 1, 401–402.*

I have your letter, & certainly rejoiced that all your delegates are right . . . We *need* every clean soul to help us, now when such a flood of what is fatal to the peace, and purity of the family, is rolled in on our question. Please say to dear good, clear eyed, Mary Grew, that my one wish, in regard to Mrs. Woodhull is, that [neither] she nor her ideas, may be so much as heard of at our meeting.

Lucy Stone, letter to John K. Wildman, November 7, 1871, in Wheeler, Loving Warriors, *239–240.*

As to what Mrs. Woodhull means by that threat [to expose the affairs of her "self-appointed judges"] I do not know and I have no time to ask. I have never talked with her on the social question fifteen minutes and I will not. My ground is that she alone of all the women in the U. States [is] succeeding in getting a hearing and a report out of a dead Congress—a Congress that told Mrs. Stanton and me last winter that they had no *time* to attend to such a question even if they thought it worthy of consideration—to which Susan B. Anthony well replied—"if we had *votes* gentlemen the time would be forthcoming and ever at hand."

Isabella Beecher Hooker, letter to Anna Savery, November 12 and 18, 1871, in Boydston, Kelley, and Margolis, The Limits of Sisterhood, *311.*

The Supreme Court of Illinois has just refused to admit to the bar Miss ALTA HULETT, a law student of Rockford, on account of her sex. The Rockford *Register* says: Miss HULETT is a young lady of superior talents and attainments, and well qualified to enter upon the profession of her choice. Under an appointment of the Circuit Judge here, she was examined for admission to the legal practice by Messers. WRIGHT, MILLER and BRAZEE, of the Rockford Bar, who certified to her ample qualifications. But the Supreme Court has again, as in the late application of the gifted and accomplished editress of the Chicago *Legal News* [Myra Bradwell], decided against the admission of women to the legal profession.

New York Times, *November 15, 1871, 2.*

A final vote was reached in the [Wyoming] House today on the bill No. 4, entitled "An act to repeal the Woman Suffrage law." The bill was indorsed by Hon. C. E. CASTLE, of Anita County. The vote stood: Ayes—Blair, Castle, Dayton, Friend, Kay, Kendall, Sheeks, Pease and Willson, all Democrats. Nays—Brown, Haley and Nickerson, Republicans. The bill will come up in Council in a day or two.

New York Times, *November 21, 1871, 1.*

Gov. CAMPBELL, of Wyoming, in his message to the Territorial Legislature, vetoing the bill repealing woman suffrage, recounts some of the practical results of the experiment there, as follows:

"In this Territory women have manifested for its highest interests a devotion strong, ardent, and intelligent. They have brought to public affairs a clearness of understanding and a soundness of judgment which, considering their exclusion hitherto from practical participation in political agitation and movements, are worthy of the greatest admiration, and above all praise. The conscience of women in all things is more discriminating and sensitive than that of men; their sense of justice not compromising or time-serving, but pure and exacting; their love of order not spasmodic or sentimental merely, but springing from the heart. All these the better conscience, the exalted sense of justice and the abiding love of order have been made by the enfranchisement of women to contribute to the good government and well-being of our Territory. To the plain teachings of these two years I cannot close my eyes."

The Message closes with the constitutional objection that the Repeal act exceeds the limits of legislative power, a Legislature having no power to disfranchise its own constituents. The effort to pass the bill over the veto failed in one branch of the legislature.

New York Times, *December 21, 1871, 2.*

The National Woman Suffrage Association is to hold a three days' convention the present week, in Lincoln Hall, commencing on the morning of Wednesday, the 10th. Nothing would afford the officers and speakers of the convention greater pleasure than to hold a debate, during some session, with yourself and your friends, upon the question of woman suffrage. As you have publicly expressed your opposition to woman's enfranchisement, not only through the papers, but also by a petition against it to Congress, we feel sure you will gladly accept our invitation and let us know your reason for the faith that is within you.

Mrs. Elizabeth Cady Stanton, as president of the association and convention, will afford you every opportunity for argument, and will herself enter the list against you. Not only Mrs. Stanton, but all members of the committee, cordially extend this invitation for debate, to be held at any session most convenient for yourself.

An early answer is desirable.

Matilda Joslyn Gage, letter to Madeline Victor Dahlgren, Januanry 8, 1872, in History of Woman Suffrage, *Vol. 2, 494.*

Mrs. Sherman and myself are this morning in receipt of a note from you in which you invite us, in the name "of the officers and speakers of the National Woman Suffrage Association," to hold a debate upon the question of "woman suffrage," and mention that "Mrs. Elizabeth Cady Stanton, as President of the association and convention, will afford every opportunity for argument, and will herself enter the lists," etc.

In reply to this invitation, for which we thank you, in so far as it may have been extended in a true desire to elicit fair argument, we would remind you that in the very fact of soliciting us to "hold debate" on a public platform, on this or any other question, you entirely ignore the principle that ourselves and our friends seek to defend, viz., the conservation of female modesty.

Madeline Victor Dahlgren response to January 8 invitation of Matilda Joslyn Gage, January 9, 1872, in History of Woman Suffrage, *Vol. 2, 494–495.*

Old golly, come and hear my ditty
As I will sing of Springfield city
The small pox goes like all creation
Since Mrs. Williams goes on vaccinating
When other cities do not but wishin'
Springfield has her "she" physician
Weak-kneed men who did this duty
Must now make way for female beauty
Free love now in all its branches
Judges clear away your benches
Lawyers quit and leave the forum
Before your pants and vest are torn
For women's rights will surely dock us
Of pants and vests as well as office

The Irish World *(a U.S. newspaper), published upon the appointment of a female doctor as a city physician in Springfield, Massachusetts, February 10, 1872, in* Diner, Erin's Daughters in America, *144.*

"My soul is cast down" at the ignorance and mistaken zeal of my poor sister Bell [Isabella Beecher Hooker] and her coagitators—Can you not lend a helping pen to show what mercy it is to woman to *have a head* to take the thousand responsibilities of family life—and how much *moral* power is gained by taking a subordinate place—as the Bible and Nature both teach is her true position . . .

God made woman for her appropriate duties and her health and intellect both will be best developed in these duties. But in these days, young girls, even of the

Women working in a factory making matches *(Library of Congress)*

working classes, are giving up housework and running all to brain and nerve . . .

> *Catharine E. Beecher, to Leonard Bacon, March 9, 1872, in Boydston, Kelley, and Margolis,* The Limits of Sisterhood, *257.*

Aaron Powell says that Mrs. Woodhull & her set of odds & ends are going to hold a grand political convention & make a Presidential nomination. Mrs. Hooker wrote to him to try & engage Steinway Hall for it, but Aaron says the proprietors wont let them have it, as the last meeting held here was very disreputable.

> *Henry Blackwell, letter to Lucy Stone, March 20, 1872, in Wheeler,* Loving Warriors, *240.*

Since leaving you, I have thought much about Mrs. Woodhull and of all the gossip about her past, and have come to the conclusion that it is great impertinence in any of us to pry into her private affairs. To me there is a sacredness in individual experience which it seems like profanation to search into or expose. This woman stands before us to-day as an able speaker and writer. Her face, manners, and conversation all indicate the triumph of the moral, intellectual, and spiritual. The processes and localities of her education are little to us, but the result should be everything. Most women, who, like some tender flower, perish in the first rude blast, think there must be some subtle poison in the hardy plant which grows stronger and more beautiful in poor earth and rough exposure, where they would fall faded, withered, and bleeding to the ground. We have already women enough sacrificed to this sentimental, hypocritical prating about purity, without going out of our way to increase the number. Women have crucified the Mary Wollstonecrafts, the Fanny Wrights and the George Sands of all ages. Men mock us with the fact and say we are ever cruel to each other. Let us end this ignoble record and henceforth stand by womanhood. If this present woman must be crucified, let men drive the spikes.

Elizabeth Cady Stanton, letter to Lucretia Mott, April 1, 1872, in Stanton and Blatch, Elizabeth Cady Stanton, *Vol. 2, 136.*

I do wish that our Suffrage friends who think the cause has lost through the advent of Victoria and our advocacy of her would show us where the money and brains and unceasing energy . . . would have come from if she had not been moved to present her *Memorial* and follow it up with the prodigious outlays of the last year and a half. I verily believe she has sunk a hundred thousand dollars in Woman Suffrage besides enduring tortures of soul innumerable—let us never forget this—let us still overlook her faults, if she has them, remembering that she is human like ourselves.

Isabella Beecher Hooker, letter to Elizabeth Cady Stanton, May 12, 1872, in Boydston, Kelley, and Margolis, The Limits of Sisterhood, *210–211.*

I have done all I can to get our resolution through, but the prospect is not promising. The Committee on Resolutions contains about 40 members, one from each State and Territory. None of these were selected until yesterday PM, and several not until this morning; each State delegation having a right to name its man.

Dr. Loring true to his promise, got a name changed so as to give us a friend on the Committee—Coggeswell of Yarmouth. He has taken the resolution and will urge its adoption, but will not make a minority report in case he is out-voted, as he probably will be. I felt over-joyed when I found that Ex.-Governor R. B. Hayes was the member of the Committee from Ohio. But though he greeted me very cordially and promised to have the resolution brought before the Committee, he said he was acting in a representative capacity, and that while he felt a personal sympathy with the object, he knew that his constituents did not and should not be in favor of putting it in. This has greatly disappointed me. I have seen some 15 or more of the Committee—only one bitterly opposed, and he from Rhode Island. But not

one thoroughly prepared to fight for it, and most afraid of it. I have sent a brief note, enclosing copies of the resolution to each member of the Committee and asking each to urge its adoption. This is all that can be done. If the Committee do not report it, I am trying to get some one in the Convention to move its adoption, but doubt whether I can find a mover, and don't believe it will be carried if I should succeed in finding one.

Hayes asked me if I would rather have the Massachusetts resolution with the last clause left out than nothing. At first I said, "No, that if no allusion was made to suffrage, it would have no value." But on reflection, I said, "Anything is better than nothing, but in case the last clause is omitted, change the phraseology of what precedes."

To-morrow AM I shall know the fate of my attempt. I tried to persuade Gerrit Smith who is here in great glory and honor, to offer our resolution. He could probably carry it through. But he called on the New York member for me and urged him to support the resolution.

Miss Anthony is here in a very reasonable mood. She has addressed a letter to the President of the Convention asking for a recognition of Woman Suffrage. I dont know whether it will be read or not. I attended a meeting of the Radical Club at E. M. Davis' office during the recess of the Convention this PM. Miss Anthony brought a letter to you from Mrs Stanton which I enclose, and am glad of its kindly tone. I shall return to New York to-morrow night, and shall take the Stonnington boat Friday P.M. . . .

Henry Blackwell, letter to Lucy Stone, from the Republican Convention, June 5, 1872, in Wheeler, Loving Warriors, *244–245.*

The Republican party is mindful of its obligations to the loyal women of America for their noble devotion to the cause of freedom; their admission to wider fields of usefulness is viewed with satisfaction; and the honest demands of any class of citizens for additional rights should be treated with respectful consideration.

Resolution adopted by the Republican Party at its convention, June 1872, in Wheeler, Loving Warriors, *245.*

I try to feel that the Philadelphia splinter—it cannot be dignified with the name of plank—is something. But sometimes it makes me intensely bitter to have my rights discussed by popinjays, priests, and politicians; to have woman's work in the church and state decided by striplings of twenty-one; and to have the press of the country on the broad grin because forsooth some American matrons chose to attend a national convention.

Elizabeth Cady Stanton, letter to Lucretia Mott,
July 16, 1872, in Stanton and Blatch,
Elizabeth Cady Stanton, *Vol. 2, 139.*

Why do you talk of giving up the paper *just now?* That would be a miscalculation surely. Beg or borrow but do push on through the year somehow. We feel as poor as church mice, but I pledge 25 dollars and think scores would do likewise rather than see it thrown up just as it is getting started.

Antoinette Brown Blackwell, letter to Lucy Stone,
September 6, 1872, in Lasser and Merrill,
Friends and Sisters, *178–179.*

Well, I have been and gone and done it! positively voted the Republican ticket—straight—this A.M. at seven o'clock, and *swore my vote in, at that,* was registered on Friday and fifteen other women followed suit in this ward, then in sundry other wards some twenty or thirty women *tried to register,* but all save two were refused. All my three sisters voted—Rhoda De Garmo, too. Amy Post was rejected, and she will immediately bring action for that—similar to the Washington action. Hon. Henry R. Selden will be our counsel; he has read up the law and all of our arguments, and is satisfied that we are right, and ditto Judge Samuel Selden, his elder brother. So we are in for a fine agitation in Rochester on this question.

I hope morning telegrams will tell of many women all over the country trying to vote. It is splendid that without any concert of action so many should have moved here . . .

How I wish you were here to write up the funny things said and done. Rhoda De Garmo told them she wouldn't swear nor affirm, "but would tell them the truth," and they accepted that. When the Democrats said that my vote should *not go* in the box, one Republican said to the other, "What do you say, Marsh?" "I say put it in." "So do I," said Jones, "and we'll fight it out on this line if it takes all winter." Mary Hallowell was just here. She and Sarah Willis tried to register, but were refused; also Mrs. Mann, the Unitarian minister's wife, and Mary Curtis, sister of

Catharine Stebbins. Not a jeer, not a word, not a look disrespectful has met a single woman.

If only now *all the Woman Suffrage women* would work to *this* end of *enforcing the existing Constitutional supremacy of National law* over State law, what strides we might make this very winter! But I'm awfully tired; for five days I have been on the constant run, but to splendid purpose; so all right. I hope you voted too.

Susan B. Anthony, letter to Elizabeth Cady Stanton,
November 5, 1872, in History of Woman Suffrage,
Vol. 2, 934–935.

Warrants have been issued by United States Commissioner Sibris for the arrest of Susan B. Anthony and fourteen other females, who voted at the late election. The parties will probably be brought into Court next week.

New York Times, *November 16, 1872, 3.*

After closing up a speech last evening in which I had been as usual rather severe on Horace Greeley, I was dreadfully shocked to hear that he was dead! Poor man, the disappointment of his defeat was too much for him; he was wholly unprepared for such a fiasco. Well, I think he had done his work, and with his departure one of woman's worst enemies has gone from this sphere, leaving our path to enfranchisement the smoother. But I cannot help thinking of his earlier and better days, when he took a broader outlook, when he and his journal aided us materially. Here, as in many other cases, you and I have made enemies of old friends because we stood up first and always for woman's cause and would not agree to have it take second place. Expediency does not belong to our vocabulary.

Elizabeth Cady Stanton, letter to Susan B. Anthony,
November 30, 1872, in Stanton and Blatch,
Elizabeth Cady Stanton, *Vol. 2, 140–141.*

[T]he female "Suffrage Convention" has met in the city and the cackling of the hens is loud and extensive . . .

Correspondent for the Irish World *(a U.S. newspaper),*
January 1873, in Diner, Erin's Daughters in
America, *143.*

The Twenty-fifth Woman Suffrage Anniversary will be held in Apollo Hall, New York, Tuesday, May 6,

1873. Lucretia Mott and Elizabeth Cady Stanton, who called the first Woman's Rights convention at Seneca Falls, 1848, will be present to give their reminiscences. That Convention was scarcely mentioned by the local press; now, over the whole world, equality for woman is demanded. In the United States, woman suffrage is the chief political question of the hour. Great Britain is deeply agitated upon the same topic; Germany has a princess at the head of its National Woman's Rights organization. Portugal, Spain, and Russia have been roused. In Rome an immense meeting, composed of the representatives of Italian democracy, was recently called in the old Coliseum; one of its resolutions demanded a reform in the laws relating to woman and a re-establishment of her natural rights. Turkey, France, England, Switzerland, Italy, sustain papers devoted to woman's enfranchisement. A Grand International Woman's Rights Congress is to be held in Paris in September of this year, to which the whole world is invited to send delegates, and this Congress is to be under the management of the most renowned liberals of Europe. Come up, then, friends, and celebrate the Silver Wedding of the Woman Suffrage movement. Let our Twenty-fifth Anniversary be one of power; our reform is everywhere advancing, let us redouble our energies and our courage.

Matilda Joslyn Gage and Susan B. Anthony, call issued for the annual May convention, May 6, 1873, in History of Woman Suffrage, *Vol. 2, 533.*

Your letter of June 18, inclosing the quarter of the United States Government's fine for my alleged violation of *State law* was most welcome. I have waited this acknowledgement from fact of my absence from home since the judge pronounced that verdict and penalty. What a comedy! Such a *grave offense* and such a paltry punishment!

Now if the United States Government would only demand the payment of the $100 and costs—but it will never do it, because all parties *know* I will never *pay a dime—no, not one.* It is quite enough for me to pay all the *just claims* of the trial; my own counsel, etc. I owe no allegiance to the Government's penalties until I have a voice in it, and shall pay none. What the Government can *exact* it may, whether of cash or imprisonment.

Do you know my *one regret now is* that I am *not possessed of some real estate* here in Rochester so that my name would be on the tax list, and I would *refuse to pay the taxes thereon,* and then I could carry that branch of the question into the courts. *Protests* are no longer worth the paper they are written on. Downright resistance, the actual throwing of the tea overboard, is now the word and work. With many thanks for the $25.

Susan B. Anthony, letter to Dr. E. B. Foote, regarding her fine for voting, July 2, 1873, in History of Woman Suffrage, *Vol. 2, 941.*

I have your letter. So you have not paid your fine; are not able to pay it; and are not willing to pay it! I send you herein the money to pay it. If you shall still decline doing so, then use the money at your own discretion, to promote the cause of woman suffrage.

I trust that you feel kindly toward Judge Hunt. He is an honest man and able judge. He would oppress no person—emphatically, no woman. It was a light fine that he imposed upon you. Moreover, he did not require you to be imprisoned until it was paid. In taking your case out of the hands of the jury, he did what he believed he had a perfect right to do . . . You have not forgotten how frequently in the days of slavery, the Constitution was quoted in behalf of the abomination. As if that paper had been drawn up and agreed upon by both the blacks and the whites, instead of the whites only; and as if slavery protected the rights of the slave instead of annihilating them . . .

[Y]our case, is another wrongful use of the Constitution. The instrument is cited against woman, as if she had united with man in making it, and was, therefore, morally bound by the flagrant usurpation, and legally concluded by it. Moreover, an excuse for turning the Constitution against her is that doing so deprives her of nothing but the pastime of dropping in a box of little piece of paper. Nevertheless, this dropping, inasmuch as it expresses her choice of the guardians of her person and property, is her great natural right to provide for the safety of her life and of the means to sustain it. She has no rights whatever, and she lives upon mere privileges and favors, if others may usurp her rights. In fact she lies at the mercy of men, if men only may choose into whose hands to put the control of her person and property . . .

Gerrit Smith, letter to Susan B. Anthony, August 15, 1873, in History of Woman Suffrage, *Vol. 2, 941.*

I am so busy just now proving "woman's right to labor," that I have no time to help prove "woman's right to vote."

When I read your note aloud to the family, asking "What shall I say to Mrs. Stone?" a voice from the transcendental mist which usually surrounds my honored father instantly replied, "Tell her you are ready to follow her as leader, sure that you could not have a better one." My brave old mother, with the ardor of many unquenchable Mays shining in her face, cried out, "Tell her I am seventy-three, but I mean to go to the polls before I die, even if my three daughters have to carry me."

Louisa May Alcott, letter to Lucy Stone, October 1, 1873, in History of Woman Suffrage, *Vol. 2, 831–832.*

Much as I wish to be with you the 13th and 14th, I can not. My work in the University can not be given to another, and I have no right to leave it undone. I hope your meeting will be profitable and successful. It is said "Interest in woman suffrage is dying out." This is not true, so far as I know. There is more sober, candid talk on the subject in private circles, here in Ohio, than ever before. Our students in the University are asking questions, with a desire for intelligent answers . . . The stir may not be so demonstrative in cities as formerly, but through the country there is general awakening . . . The distance between men and women is lessening every year. Colleges are bringing them on to the same plane, and the agitation of this question of women's right to a voice in the government, has given and is giving men new ideas respecting the strength of woman's intellect and her determination to be more than a doll in this busy world.

Whether we are made voting citizens or not, let no man beguile himself with the thought that the old order of things will be restored. They who step into light and freedom will not retrace their steps. This end is equality, civil, religious and political—there is no stopping-place this side of that.

Miriam M. Coly, Otterbein University, letter to Henry Blackwell, October 4, 1873, in History of Woman Suffrage, *Vol. 2, 832–833.*

There was an election held by the order of the township committee of Landis, to vote on the subject of bonding the town to build shoe and other factories.

The call issued was for all legal voters. I went with some ten or twelve other women, all tax-payers. We offered our votes, claiming that we were citizens of the United States, and of the State of New Jersey, also property-holders in and residents of Landis township, and wished to express our opinion on the subject of having our property bonded. Of course our votes were not accepted, whilst every *tatterdemalion* in town, either black or white, who owned no property, stepped up and very pompously said what he would like to have done with his property. For the first time our claim to vote seemed to most of the voters to be a just one. They gathered together in groups and got quite excited over the injustice of refusing our vote and accepting those of men who paid no taxes.

Mrs. Portia Gage, letter, December 2, 1873, in History of Woman Suffrage, *Vol. 3, 481.*

I hope I have not delayed so long in asking—what you will deny me altogether—But I do very much want you to send me a letter to be read at our Washington Convention next week—Something short and sharp—just what Congress ought to do to protect women in their *political rights,* as well as *civil* rights—not a man of them seems to dream that women suffer the deprivation of their *civil* rights a thousand times more grievously than black men . . .

Susan B. Anthony, letter to Gerrit Smith, January 9, 1874, in the Smith Family Papers, Rare Books and Manuscripts Division, New York Public Library.

The National Woman Suffrage Convention opened in Lincoln Hall this morning with a full house . . .

Miss Anthony stated that the two articles of the woman suffrage creed were: First, That every woman should get her vote into the ballot box whenever she could get a judge of election to take it; and wherever refused, should go just the same again next time. Second, That all women owning property should refuse to pay taxes.

Frances Ellen Burr, writing for the Hartford Times *(Connecticut), January 15, 1874, in* History of Woman Suffrage, *Vol. 2, 538–539.*

I wrote the N. York speech on "Evolution applied to the Woman Question," and gave it in Susan's Convention; first because I had something to say, 2nd because they are anxious now to be respectable and proper, and I am desirous they should; and would like to help them. Some of their elbows were apparently quite ready to give me a poke; but if they did, it was not hard enough to hurt; and it was really a good meeting.

Antoinette Brown Blackwell, letter to "Dear Bostonians" (Lucy Stone, Henry Blackwell, and Alice Stone Blackwell), May 21, 1874, in Lasser and Merrill, Friends and Sisters, 184.

I am ever so sorry about Mrs. Hazelett, Stanton & Michigan! It is a thousand pities that a great cause must be gibbeted by its friends. I see the Michigan papers criticize & blame Mrs. Stanton, but in one case, at least, she explained what she had really said, and that was well enough. But her attacks on the Republican party are making enemies, and there is no need of it. I was sorry when I found that Mrs. S. was to be in Michigan, for she is utterly indiscreet. But it seems to me that, in another way Mrs. Hazelett will do as much harm. Between the two, will *the cause* be ground to powder? I hope not, for if only one State will give suffrage, the rest cannot keep long behind. I was amazed at what you said about the pay of Mrs. Stanton. I read it after having that very day traveled about Boston to rich men, to raise money for Michigan, where I had promised to go for nothing. Somehow, it took away my courage for doing the disagreeable work . . .

Lucy Stone, letter to Mrs. Campbell, June 13, 1874, in Wheeler, Loving Warriors, 250.

Come right down and pull my ears. I shall not attempt a defense. Of course I admit that I have made an awful blunder in not keeping silent so far as you were concerned on this terrible Beecher-Tilton scandal. The whole odium of this *scandalum magnatum* has, in some quarters, been rolled on our suffrage movement, as unjustly as cunningly; hence I feel obliged just now to make extra efforts to keep our ship off the rocks. There was never anything so base and cowardly as that statement of some of Beecher's supporters, building a footstool for him to stand upon out of the life, character, aspirations, and ambition of a large circle of reputable women. This terrible onslaught on the suffrage movement has made me feel like writing for every paper daily. From the silence on all sides, I saw it was for me to fight alone. I have in fact written several articles, *incog.*, in the *Graphic*. But I am too silent when I

know I should be thundering against this wholesale slaughter of womanhood. When Beecher falls, as he must, he will pull all he can down with him. But we must not let the cause of woman go down in the smash. It is innocent.

Elizabeth Cady Stanton, letter to Susan B. Anthony, July 30, 1874, in Stanton and Blatch, Elizabeth Cady Stanton, Vol. 2, 145–146.

I send you by today's mail a lot of newspapers containing an a/c of Beecher's acquittal by Plymouth Church & Society—&c &c—We are all well . . . Several friends have written thanking you for your article on Mrs. Tilton. It has been recopied by several papers . . . This Beecher-Tilton affair is playing the deuce with WS in Michigan. No chance of success this year I fancy! Well—the Lord reigns.

Henry Blackwell, letter to Lucy Stone, September 3, 1874, in Wheeler, Loving Warriors, 250–251.

I feel extremely desirous that some helping hand shall be given to Elisabeth [sic] Tilton so that she shall never get into the grip of Theodore.

She has no money, nor resource of any kind, so far as I know. And her heart, aching for her children, may yield again to the power of her old tormentor if something is not done for her.

I do not mean, charity, but that some plan may be made by which she can support herself, and at least, the younger children, & have them with her. I do not know what to advise, but I feel sure that *you,* with your noble band of coworkers, will know what to do to help her. She needs *occupation* to save her from utter misery.

Pray see her, and find something for her to do that will have a money value.

Tilton has no legal right to the children, since he disclaims being their father, but I fear he will give her all the trouble he can.

Is it asking too much, that you will let me know whether anything, and what, is being done for her?

If I were not overborne with work, and drained of money, I would go to see you about it.

But I hope plans are already made for the poor woman, and that she will come into them.

Lucy Stone, letter to Anna Cromwell Field, September 8, 1874, in Wheeler, Loving Warriors, 251.

I trust that the great plea made at the Convention on the 10th inst. will be for woman suffrage in the new Constitution of Colorado . . .

If it was tyranny to tax the colonists a century ago, and deny them representation, it is tyranny to do the same to women now. If it was wrong then to govern men without their consent, it is wrong now, to govern women without their consent. No part of the new Constitution of Colorado in this Centennial year, can be more appropriate, or have more historic credit a hundred years hence, than that part which shall secure for women the right to a voice in making the laws they will be required to obey, and in the amount and use of the taxes they will have to pay.

The women of Colorado should not cease to remind the Commissioners of their high duty in this respect.

Lucy Stone, letter to Anna Cromwell Field, January 5, 1875, in Wheeler, Loving Warriors, *252–253.*

The New York *Evening Post* has a long article relative to the decision of the Supreme Court regarding the right of women to vote under the Constitution of the United States, coinciding in the decision. It closes by saying: "The advocates of woman suffrage will scarcely be disappointed by this judgment. We do not believe that sincere friends of the proposed reform will regret the failure to secure it by trickery."

There are few who have maintained that the XIV. and XV. Amendments secured suffrage to women as well as to colored men, who would be willing to admit that they desired to obtain suffrage through trickery? Either it is, or is not, conveyed through the Constitution and the Amendments. Certainly if it is, they have a right to avail themselves of it; and even if it is not, it is nevertheless, a right. The woman suffragists believe that the withholdal from women of the right of suffrage is a fraud and an imposition. To secure them what is already their right, can not involve trickery. Every day and every hour that the right of suffrage is withheld from women, a monstrous wrong is practiced upon them. As long as there were no women who demanded the ballot, and by tacit consent it was relinquished, the fraud practiced by debarring them from it was merely of a negative character—but the privilege should have been left open; but from the moment that one woman demanded it, an outrage was practiced upon her by the entire people in denying it her, and the plea that it

is not woman's sphere, which is sometimes made, is the most shallow subterfuge of any, for it is not for men, but for woman alone, to determine what that sphere is, or is not.

The Toledo, Ohio Sunday Journal, *following the Supreme Court decision in* Minor v. Happersett, *March 29, 1875, in* History of Woman Suffrage, *Vol. 2, 952.*

What a fraud is practiced by the administration of this government upon the provisions of the Constitution of the United States! As government is administered, the female portion of the public are defrauded of constitutional right, and made to become political slaves. Since the beginning, all the way down to the present day, woman has been debarred of all political privilege, though reckoned and accounted as one of the people, in matters of census and taxation. Her disabilities in this behalf were removed by the adoption of the National Constitution; but nullification of that Constitution and a high handed usurpation on the part of the States, have ever hindered the enjoyment of her constitutional rights. But so long as she is classed by the Constitution as one of the people—so long as the people are the owners, the proprietors of the government established by the Constitution—so long as it provides for self-government, popular sovereignty—so long must she be *entitled* to take part in administration, though prevented from doing so by fine and imprisonment.

I am awakened to this subject of woman suffrage by a decision of the Supreme Court of the United States, made at Washington this week. I have not seen the text of the opinion read by the Chief Justice, but I find this statement in the Court news of Monday last:

"No. 182.—Virginia L. Minor agt. Reese Happersett: in error to Supreme Court of Missouri—The plaintiff in error instituted an action against Happersett, who was the judge of an election, for denying her the right to vote. She based her right to vote upon the ground that as a citizen of the United States she had that right under the Constitution. Mr. Chief Justice Waite delivered the opinion, holding, first, that women are and always have been citizens of the United States as well as men; second, the Constitution of the United States does not attach the right of voting to the right of citizenship; third, nor does the Constitution of any of the States make the right to vote coextensive with citizenship; fourth, consequently, women are not entitled to vote by virtue of the Constitution of the United States, when the State laws do not give the right. Affirmed."

The great usurpation is now affirmed, legalized, by the decree of the Judicial Department of this government! More than 20,000,000 of the people of this Nation have been declared without the pale of political rights secured to them by the Constitution of the fathers. This decision indorses the defranchisement of every female in the land, so long endured by her. Her citizenship . . . is worthless—is only a name; and does not enable her to exercise the privileges and immunities of our system of self-government which that Constitution declares this government to be—a government by and for its citizens. Woman can not now exercise her constitutional right—. . . the Supreme Court of the United States wink[s] at the wickedness of the States as nullifiers, and allow[s] the masculine usurpation to remain . . .

Perhaps this grave body of learned Justices look upon the question of qualification in a broader or other sense than that taught by Dr. Webster. Their decision, it seems, turns upon the use and meaning of that word. This, then, is the solemn conclusion of the embodied justice of the land—*qualification to vote,* MASCULINE GENDER!—and not things in common belonging to every person of the entire population, no matter what the sex; such as age, residence, etc.

Madam, you have no available political rights—the Constitution intends you shall have and exercise them, and it has made provisions accordingly—but the false interpretations of the courts, and the trespassing State Constitutions have hitherto hindered you. But I believe a day of revolution, call it reckoning if you please, is at hand—fast approaching. President Lincoln liberated by proclamation, three or four millions of chattel slaves. President Grant has the power, Constitutional power, to liberate to-day, twenty millions of political slaves, of which, I am sorry to say, you are one. Let politicians and political parties beware how they treat this question of woman suffrage. What became of the old Whig Party, in consequence of its alliance with chattel slavery.

Horace Dresser, to the president of the Toledo, Ohio Woman's Suffrage Association, reprinted in the Toledo Sunday Journal, April 1875, in History of Woman Suffrage, *Vol. 2, 950–952.*

My poor wandering sister Bell [Isabella Beecher Hooker]—my heart is sad for her. Every disclosure this trial makes of those wretched people the Woodhulls and "omne ͺenus" fills me with pain for her. They got an ascͺꞁdancy over her by producing conviction thro that apology that they wrung from Henry and which they showed to Mrs. Stanton—they *fixed* it in her mind that Henry had indeed fallen and they used it as an argument with her to show that the marriage laws ought to be given up since so *great* a man could not get along under them without falling.

Harriet Beecher Stowe, letter to Anne Seymour Robinson, May 2, 1875, in Boydston, Kelley, and Margolis, The Limits of Sisterhood, *291.*

If you will consider me a member of the Suffrage Association from this time on (I forget what the terms of admission are) I will pay you the admission fee in N. York. Then if I remember right, I can be a speaking member, though perhaps that is a mistake, and if so I must either get appointed as delegate or speak by courtesy.

I never withdrew through intention; but simply from neglect to pay the annual dues at a time when I was not present at an annual meeting; and if any one had dunned me for the fee, as they did in the Congress [of Women], I should have paid it. But finding myself out and dropped, I simply staid there. Now let me in again, as I *have* no desire to be counted out from the suffrage movement when the papers are saying that the women of the Congress are giving up suffrage.

I hate the machinery of both the A. Association and the Congress; but have concluded that those who run societies must have their own way about that. I shall work with them "under protest," not public protest, only to you privately.

I should really like to make a 15 minute suffrage speech if my voice will make itself heard . . . If you can sandwich me in on the first evening, I will try, and if my voice will not make itself heard, I will stop in 8 minutes. Will that do?

Antoinette Brown Blackwell, letter to Lucy Stone, September 13, 1875, in Lasser and Merrill, Friends and Sisters, *186.*

Your letter is here. In reply let me say, our Philadelphia meeting is to pay special honor to the establishment of woman suffrage in New Jersey [from

1776–1807]. It will continue only one day. Those who are there will be very likely to stay over the 4th, or longer. I shall ask for hospitality for some of our speakers and among them, I will ask for you—I don't know how Susan comes to have a meeting. We do not expect to have any clash, i.e. we shall not go to their meeting, and hope they will not come to ours. Susan is in this city today, speaking for the Parker Fraternity on "Woman and Purity"!

Lucy Stone, letter to Antoinette Brown Blackwell, May 21, 1876, in Lasser and Merrill, Friends and Sisters, *188–189.*

I cannot express to you in fitting language the thoughts and feelings which stirred me as I sat on the platform, awaiting the presentation of that document [the Woman's Declaration of Rights].

We were about to commit an overt act. Gen. Hawley, president of the centennial commission and manager of the programme, had peremptorily forbidden its presentation. Yet in the face of this—in the face of the assembled nation and representatives from the crowned heads of Europe, a handful of women actuated by the same high principles as our fathers, stirred by the same desire for freedom, moved by the same impulse for liberty, were to again proclaim the right of self-government; were again to impeach the spirit of King George manifested in our rulers, and declare that taxation without representation is tyranny, that the divine right of one-half of the people to rule the other half is also despotism. As I followed the reading of Richard Henry Lee, and marked the wild enthusiasm of its reception, and remembered that at its close, a document, as noble, as divine, as grand, as historic as that, was to be presented *in silence;* an act, as heroic, as worthy, as sublime, was to be performed in the face of the contemptuous amazement of the assembled world, I trembled with suppressed emotion. When Susan Anthony arose, with a look of intense pain, yet heroic determination in her face, I silently committed her to the Great Father . . . to strengthen and comfort her heroic heart, and then she was lost to view in the sudden uprising caused by the burst of applause instituted by General Hawley in behalf of the Brazilian emperor. And thus at the close of the reading of a document which repudiated kings and declared the right of every person to life, to liberty, and the pursuit of individual happiness, the American people, applauding a crowned monarch, received *in*

silence the immortal document and protest of its discrowned queens!

Phoebe W. Couzins, speaking to group gathered in the First Unitarian Church, Philadelphia, July 4, 1876, in History of Woman Suffrage, *Vol. 3, 36–37.*

Mrs. Livermore was in our office day before yesterday. I had not seen her before, since she returned from California. Among other things she told me, she found you, tired and ill. I suppose it is the result of your hard work, and anxiety. I do most sincerely hope the rest of the summer will restore you. I would not do a bit of public work. If God can wait for Colorado to be just to Women we can. At any rate, so precious a life as yours must be saved to rejoice when the victory is won. So take it easy this summer my dear Mrs. Campbell . . . Nearly every body here has quartered for the summer by the sea, or in the mountains. But if we left the Journal would stop. The money for it, is shorter than usually, and we do not quite see how we are to get through the year. But I suppose we shall some way.

Every body seems to be short of money, but those who have any go to the Centennial with it. It seems a most shameful shame that this hundredth year of our national existence should find women, as we are politically, & legally. You will see by the Woman's Journal, what a cute thing Mrs. Stanton and Susan did on the 4th July. They told John Hutchinson that they "meant to go down to history with doings of the 4th July 1876"—and so they will. By the use of Lucretia Mott's name, they got the use of the church of Dr. Furness, and they made a really good meeting, and good will come of it. I have dreaded the effect of their presence in Philadelphia. But they seem to be on their good behavior. Give my regards to Mr. Campbell, and for yourself a great deal of love, and pray rest, and get strong dear Mrs. Campbell, and let all the work go.

Lucy Stone, letter to Mrs. Campbell, July 19, 1876, in Wheeler, Loving Warriors, *254–255.*

I do not add my name to the "Declaration" because, as I had nothing to do with its presentation, it would be wrong to say so. I think it is an admirable paper and my only regret about it was the sensational manner of presenting it.

In regard to the History of the Woman's Rights Movement, I do not think it *can* be written by any one who is alive today. Your "wing" surely are not competent to write the history of "our wing," nor should we be yours, even if we thought best to take the time while the war goes on; rations, recruits and all are to get as we go.

There will come a time when this greatest of all the world movements will have made history and *then* it can be written. I do not wish to have any hand in the present one.

The complete set of the Woman's Journal can be sent to you for the purpose you desire, at three dollars a volume, The regular price is five dollars. Six volumes would cost eighteen dollars. Do you want them?

Lucy Stone, letter to Elizabeth Cady Stanton, August 3, 1876, in Wheeler, Loving Warriors, *255–256.*

Your postal card asking me for the number of Legislatures I have addressed on Woman's Rights and the dates of those addresses is received. I have never kept a diary, or any record of my work, and so am unable to furnish you the required dates.

I made my first speech in the pulpit of my brother, in Gardner, Mass., in 1847. I commenced my regular public work for Anti Slavery and Woman's Rights in 1848. I have continued it to the best of my ability ever since, except when the care of my child and the War prevented.

Mrs. Stanton[,]

In your postal card you say "must be referred to" in the history you are writing. If you will publish the letter [above], it will be a sufficient reference. I cannot furnish a "biographical sketch" and trust you will not try to make one.

Yours with ceaseless regret that any "Wing" of suffragists should attempt to write the history of the other.

Lucy Stone, letter to Elizabeth Cady Stanton, August 30, 1876, in Wheeler, Loving Warriors, *257.*

I cannot dispose of the furniture to pay N's debts as it is considered *his* personal property, it is *mine* for *housekeeping* purposes but [I] cannot dispose of it, but my piano is my personal property and it can[not] be seized to settle debts contracted by Nathan.

Rosetta Douglass Sprague, to her father, Frederick Douglass, September 17, 1876, in Sterling, We Are Your Sisters, *421–422.*

The Congress [of Women], I think is doing its very best. It has made a great deal of progress. And there has been a great deal to contend with. They began, afraid to say the word suffrage. And in three years, they are ready to have a paper on that subject. Don't let us condemn, but give them time . . .

As to joining the temperance workers, I cannot advise. To *me* the suffrage work seems so immeasurably above, and broader, lifting *all women* up to a plane where they can work for temperance, and every other good thing, at such infinite advantage over their present plane, that I grudge the taking of a straw's weight of help away from it. You have on your shoulders, the suffrage work, the Contagious Diseases Acts, and your family. If you add anything more wont you fail? . . . But you must judge. Miss [Frances] Willard is coming on grandly. I rejoice in her every day. But don't let her take you from your moorings . . .

I wonder if you could be responsible to raise $100 for the Journal for the next year? We *must* have help from somewhere, and the Orange and Newport people if you were to *ask* them might easily make up that sum.

Lucy Stone, letter to Cornelia Collins Hussey, November 29, 1876, in Wheeler, Loving Warriors, *257–258.*

I have just come in, & found your most welcome letter . . . The Suffrage Amendment passed the Senate, and comes today into the House, where municipal suffrage was lost last Friday 83 to 127. The Senate agreed not to discuss it and pushed it to a third reading, and then a Mr. Sleeper moved to reconsider but it could not be done, and passed by a large vote.

Lucy Stone, letter to Henry Blackwell, April 2, 1877, in Wheeler, Loving Warriors, *264–265.*

I am so tired today, body and soul, it seems as though I should never feel fresh again. I have been trying to get advertisements for the Woman's Journal, to eke out its expenses. Yesterday I walked miles to picture stores, crockery stores, grocery stores, book stores, to soap stores, to "special sales" going up flight after flight of stairs, only to find the men out, or not ready to advertise, and for all my day's toil, I did not get a cent. And when I came home at night to find the house cold, the fire nearly out in the furnace, and none on the hearth, &c. &c. it seemed as though the tired of a whole life came into my essence. I don't often complain, or feel like complaining. But I do wish there was some way of carrying on the Woman's Journal without such hard constant tug—and if only the housekeeping would go on without so much looking after! ...

Lucy Stone, letter to Mrs. Campbell, April 12, 1877, in
Wheeler, Loving Warriors, *265–266.*

There are but two of our cows left at present, Taxey and Votey. It is something a little peculiar that Taxey is very obtrusive; why, I can scarcely step out of doors without being confronted by her, while Votey is quiet and shy, but she is growing more docile and domesticated every day, and it is my opinion that in a very short time, wherever you find Taxey there Votey will be also.

Julia Smith, responding to inquiries about her remaining
cows after her other cows and her land had been
sold to pay taxes, January 12, 1878, in
History of Woman Suffrage, *Vol. 3, 98.*

I suppose you are waiting to hear about the convention. It went off well; there were crowded houses as usual and $200 in the treasury after all the bills were paid. I prepared the resolutions a week before and had them in print, so that there was no worry at the last moment over them. I devoted my whole vacation to the speech to be made before the committee. All said, "Very good." The day before, Senator Sargent had presented in the Senate a resolution proposing the following amendment: "Article 16, sec. 1. The right of citizens of the United States to vote shall not be denied or abridged by the United States or by any State on account of sex." The day after the close of the convention, Isabella Beecher Hooker held a regular Moody and Sankey prayer meeting in the ladies' reception room right next to the Senate Chamber. Those present prayed, sang "Hold the Fort," "Guide Us, Oh, Thou Great Jehovah" and "The Battle Hymn of the Republic," and made speeches from tops of tables. In the meantime the Senators were assembling and the corridors were crowded. Senator Sargent told us it was a regular mob. Mrs. Sargent and I did not attend the prayer meeting, for, as Jehovah has never taken a very active part in the suffrage movement, I thought I would stay at home and get ready to implore the committee, having more faith in their power to render us the desired aid. At this same time a debate was precipitated in the Senate, and when a fellow member rallied Senator Sargent on the mob

character of his constituency, he cleverly replied: "This is nothing to what you will see at this Capitol if these women's petitions are not heard." Altogether it was a week of constant agitation and I think the result—prayer meeting, mob and all—is good. I reached home Saturday night and found a telegram asking for my speech as the committee intends to print it. So I sat up last night four o'clock in order to copy it and I sent off this morning 150 pages of manuscript. I was so interested in "National Protection for National Citizens," that the night slipped away and I felt neither tired nor sleepy, though to-day I am like a squeezed sponge and have done nothing.

Elizabeth Cady Stanton, letter to Susan B. Anthony,
January 14, 1878, in Stanton and Blatch,
Elizabeth Cady Stanton, *Vol. 2, 153–154.*

How thankful I am for these bright young women now ready to fill our soon-to-be vacant places. I want to shake hands with them all before I go, and give them a few words of encouragement.

Lucretia Mott, speaking to Elizabeth Cady Stanton on
the 30th anniversary of the Seneca Falls convention,
July 19, 1878, in History of Woman Suffrage,
Vol. 3, 123.

Last week in Washington I sat up two nights until three o'clock in the morning to write a speech and

Lucretia Mott *(Library of Congress)*

the resolutions for the convention which occured on the 8th and the 9th. I presided at all the sessions during two days. The Washington papers were very complimentary to me as a presiding officer, and Susan says I never did so well. I came home by the night train and now have until Monday—this is Saturday—in which to get ready for a five months' trip in the West. Some of my resolutions seemed to hit the nail on the head; especially these, which caused considerable amusement in all circles: Resolved, That we cannot have honest money until we have honest men. Whereas, a Sixteenth Constitutional Amendment for Woman Suffrage is now pending on a tie vote in the House Judiciary Committee—Yeas, Leapham, N.Y.; Lynde, Wis.; Frye, Me.; Butler, Mass.; Conger, Mich.—Nays, Knott, Ky.; Hartridge, Ga.; Stenger, Penn.; McMahon, O.; Culberson, Texas;—Absent, Harris of Va., who declares he has never investigated the subject: Therefore Resolved, That it is the duty of Harris of Va. to remain absent when a vote on this question is taken, unless he has given it as much consideration, as if the rights of all men were therein involved. Whereas, In President Hayes' last message, he makes a truly paternal review of the interests of the Republic, both great and small, from the Army, the Navy and our foreign relations, to the ten little Indians in Hampton, Va., our timber on the Western mountains, and the switches of the Washington railroad; from the Paris Exposition, the postal service and the abundant harvests, to the possible bulldozing of some colored men in various southern districts, cruelty to live animals, and the crowded condition of the mummies, dead ducks and fishes in the Smithsonian Institution, yet forgets to mention twenty million women citizens robbed of their social, civil and political rights; Therefore, Resolved, That a committee of three be appointed from this Convention to wait upon the President and remind him of the existence of one-half of the American people whom he has accidentally overlooked, and of whom it would be wise for him to make some mention in his future messages.

Elizabeth Cady Stanton, letter to her son, Theodore Stanton, January 11, 1879, in Stanton and Blatch, Elizabeth Cady Stanton, Vol. 2, 157–159.

The *Woman's Journal* has, I see, some strictures on us for allowing those Mormon women on our platform. But I think if the Congress of the United States can allow George Q. Cannon to sit for Utah in that body without it being supposed to endorse polygamy, we could permit Mormon women the same privilege in our association without our being accused of embracing their principles. If Congress can stand Cannon with four wives, we might stand the women with only the fourth part of a husband! And, furthermore, when Congress proposes to disfranchise the women of a Territory, where should they go to plead their case but to the National Woman Suffrage Association?

Elizabeth Cady Stanton, letter to Susan B. Anthony, April 5, 1879, in Stanton and Blatch, Elizabeth Cady Stanton, Vol. 2, 160.

10

United Once More
1880–1892

THE HISTORICAL CONTEXT

In 1880, as the Republican and Democratic Parties prepared for their respective conventions, Susan B. Anthony worked especially hard to have support for women's suffrage become part of both party platforms. Rather than collect signatures for yet another petition, she asked that women from all across the country send postcards as evidence of their wish to vote. Thousands of women found the size of a postcard inadequate; young and old, rural and urban, European American and African American, they sent long, personal letters to Anthony. They wanted to vote.[1]

The women's rights leaders were continuing to do all they could to bring this about. Members of the American Woman Suffrage Association, under the guidance of Lucy Stone, worked primarily on a state-by-state basis. Women's suffrage within an individual state could be obtained in one of two ways: Either suffragists could convince the delegates to a constitutional convention to include women's suffrage in the new, revised version of the state constitution, or they could convince members of a state's legislature to present a women's suffrage bill to its male voters, who could then pass or defeat the measure.

Susan B. Anthony thought the state-by-state route unfeasible, and with good reason: ". . . I do not wish to see the women of the thirty-eight States of this Union compelled to leave their homes to canvass each one of these, school district by school district. It is asking too much of a moneyless class. The joint earnings of the marriage co-partnership in all the States belongs legally to the husband," she said, referring to the fact that a housewife, however hard she worked, was entitled to no share of her husband's earnings. A housewife's labor was presumed to belong to her husband. Unlike wages paid to an unrelated housekeeper for identical services, any monies given by an "employed" husband to an "unemployed" wife in recognition of her contributions actually remained the husband's property. (It was subject, for example, to seizure by his creditors.) Anthony continued to explain women's inability to fund state campaigns: "It is only the wife who goes outside the home to work whom the law permits to own and control the money she earns. Therefore, to ask of women, the vast majority of whom are without an independent dollar of their own, to make a thorough canvass of their several States, is an impossibility."[2]

Nevertheless, women and their male supporters did just this. Between the Kansas referendum of 1867 and the adoption of the Nineteenth Amendment in 1920, there would be no less than 480 campaigns made upon various legislatures, asking that male voters be able to decide whether or not to enfranchise women. Of these, 424 would fail.[3]

Each one of the legislative campaigns, and each one of the 56 state referenda that resulted, involved the same amount of work. Suffrage leaders left their homes and traveled to the various states to work beside local suffragists. Countless numbers of women knocked on their neighbors' doors and asked for signatures in support of women's suffrage; speeches were made, tracts passed, legislators and male voters beseeched. The results were not encouraging. In 1884 Anthony said of the four states in which the question had actually reached voters: ". . . with the best campaign possible for us to make, we obtained a vote of only one-third. One man out of every three voted for the enfranchisement of the women of his household, while two out of three voted against it . . ."[4]

Between 1880 and 1892 the question was defeated by voters in Nebraska, Oregon, Rhode Island, Washington, and South Dakota. Suffragists placed much of the blame for these defeats upon what they saw as the undemocratic attitudes of the newest immigrant groups.[5] After several failed state referenda, they began to believe that the "representative men" of the legislatures might be more willing than the general population to enfranchise women.[6] Whenever a state held a constitutional convention, women organized. They requested public hearings, collected signatures for petitions, and lobbied for suffrage under the revised constitution. Before 1920 they would do this 47 times.[7]

Despite the amount of work involved in the state-by-state approach, the hard-won gains, if any, might be only temporary. In 1883 the legislature of Washington Territory granted woman suffrage. This was challenged and repealed by the territorial supreme court in 1887. Two years later, as Washington prepared to apply for statehood, suffragists campaigned for a women's suffrage clause in the new state constitution. Their campaign was unsuccessful.[8] (Washington's women would again achieve state suffrage in 1910.)

The members of the National Woman Suffrage Association, under the leadership of Elizabeth Cady Stanton and Susan B. Anthony, preferred to pressure the members of Congress for passage of the federal women's suffrage amendment, which had first been introduced in 1869. The passage of such an amendment would, of course, necessitate a series of similar state-by-state campaigns, since three-fourths of the state legislatures would have to ratify the amendment before it could become part of the U.S. Constitution. Anthony expected this to be a long and difficult process; in fact, she thought the state campaigns for ratification would not be concluded until 20 years after Congress's passage of such an amendment.[9] Nonetheless, a constitutional amendment offered a distinct advantage: Every American woman could be enfranchised, even if 25 percent of the state legislatures opposed the move.

The pressuring of the major political parties by the NWSA was but one of its strategies on behalf of a federal women's suffrage amendment. The NWSA members held annual conventions in Washington, D.C. There, they presented petitions to the members of Congress and sought hearings before the Judiciary Committees of both houses. The proposed amendment received favorable reports from a majority of the Senate committee in 1882, 1884, 1886, 1890, and 1892. In the House committee it received favorable majorities in 1883 and 1890, but adverse majorities in 1884 and 1886.[10] When the amendment was voted upon for the first time by the full Senate, on January 25, 1887, it was defeated, 34 to 16, with 25 members absent.[11] Perhaps more disheartening, the 17-year-long struggle to disenfranchise Utah Territory's women finally succeeded: The Edmunds–Tucker Act was passed in Congress in 1887; intended to outlaw polygamy, it contained a provision disfranchising the women of Utah Territory.[12]

Yet, on both a state and federal level, there were advances. In several states women were granted a vote in school board elections. School suffrage, as this was called, was passed in Massachusetts in 1879; in his 1880 inaugural address, incoming governor John D. Long advocated a further expansion of voting rights for Massachusetts women. School suffrage was also granted in Vermont and New York in 1880. (Women were, however, only grudgingly accepted at many polls.) "Municipal suffrage," a vote on local matters only, was granted to women in Kansas in 1887.[13]

State battles were not restricted to suffrage. Although many mothers had only a limited legal basis for protecting their daughters, their united efforts did increase the protection offered by the states to female children. Before the Seneca Falls convention, the "age of protection" for girls ("the age when they are declared to have sufficient understanding to consent to intercourse, and above which they can claim no legal protection"[14]) was, in every State, 10 years of age.[15] As women developed greater political acumen, they demanded that state legislatures raise this age. In 1864 Oregon extended protection to girls up to age 14; in 1882 Wyoming became the second state to do so. (Delaware's legislature, however, lowered the age to seven in 1871; it agreed to raise the age to 15 in 1889 but reduced the status of rape to a mere misdemeanor.)[16]

Wisconsin took an especially novel approach to women's demands on this issue. Its legislature first raised the protected age to 14 in 1887. Then, in 1889, it reduced the age to 12, changed the punishment from life imprisonment to imprisonment for five to 35 years, and dictated a more lenient sentence "if the child shall be a common prostitute."[17] New York also raised the age of protection (to 16) in 1887; when its legislature later tried to lower that age to 12, Mary H. Hunt of the Woman's Christian Temperance Union appeared before the judiciary. "I represent 21,000 women," she said, "and any man who dares to vote for this measure will be marked and held up to scorn. We are terribly in earnest." The age of protection remained the same.[18]

Elizabeth Cady Stanton and Susan B. Anthony, president and vice president at-large of the National American Woman Suffrage Association *(Library of Congress)*

The Woman's Christian Temperance Union, under the leadership of its second national president, Frances Willard, was also instrumental in the broader suffrage struggle. Many of the conservative women who joined Willard's organization did so with an interest only in the prohibition of alcohol. Willard persuaded many of these women to support suffrage as well, pointing out that the vote would be the best possible means of securing their agenda. Willard herself acknowledged that some conservatives questioned her alliance with suffrage leaders such as Elizabeth Cady Stanton. During an address in 1891, Willard said, "Our friends have said that, as President of the National American Woman Suffrage Association, Mrs. Stanton leads the largest army of women outside, and I the largest army inside, the realm of a conservative theology. However this may be, I rejoice to the day when, with distinctly avowed loyalty to my Methodist faith, and as distinctly avowed respect for the sincerity with which she holds views quite different, I can clasp hands in loyal comradeship with one whose dauntless voice rang out over the Nation for 'women's rights' when I was but a romping girl upon a prairie farm."[19] She was ultimately able to move her organization from the antisuffrage sentiments of its first president, Anne Wittenmeyer, to one that had an active "franchise department" working to win suffrage. Willard's marshaling of demonstrable support for suffrage by large numbers of conservative women was in many respects a boon to the suffrage movement, but the link she established between prohibitionists and suffragists would ultimately contribute to antisuffrage sentiment among those who opposed the temperance movement and, later, Prohibition.[20]

On the federal level, both the House of Representatives and the Senate appointed Select Committees on Woman Suffrage in 1882.[21] This meant that a particular group of representatives was responsible for receiving "all petitions, bills, and resolves for the extension of suffrage to women."[22] Addressing the chairman of the Senate Select Committee for the first time, Elizabeth Cady Stanton exclaimed, ". . . you cannot imagine the satisfaction that thrilled the hearts of our countrywomen. After fourteen years of constant petitioning, we are grateful for even this slight recognition."[23]

Most important, in 1890 Wyoming was admitted to statehood. Its women had voted since 1870 under a bill passed by the first legislative council of the territory. In 1889 women's suffrage was included in the proposed state constitution, despite fears that such a clause might impede statehood. It turned out that those fears were well founded. The House of Representatives' Committee on Territories issued a favorable report on Wyoming's request for admission. A minority report in opposition was also issued; of its 23 pages, 21 were filled with objections to women's suffrage.[24]

The bill to admit Wyoming then reached the House floor. There was tremendous opposition to its proposed state constitution. As Joseph E. Washington of Tennessee explained, "My chief objection to the admission of Wyoming is the suffrage article in the constitution. I am unalterably opposed to female suffrage in any form. It can only end in unsexing and degrading the womanhood of America. It is emphatically a reform against nature . . . I have no doubt that in Wyoming today women vote in as many [different] precincts as they can reach on horseback or on foot after changing their frocks and bustles . . . Tennessee has not adopted any of these new fangled ideas . . ."[25] Washington was joined with particular enthusiasm by congressmen from Missouri, Georgia,

Illinois, and New Jersey, and by William C. Oates, who complained for the record: "I like a woman who is a woman and appreciates the sphere to which God and the Bible have assigned her. I do not like a man-woman."[26] Nevertheless, after three days' argument, the House passed the bill of admission, 139 to 127.

Opposition to Wyoming's constitution was just as strong in the Senate. George G. Vest of Missouri was emphatic: "I shall never vote to admit into the Union any State that adopts woman suffrage . . . If there were no other reason with me, I would vote against the admission of Wyoming because it has that feature in its constitution. I will not take the responsibility as a senator of endorsing in any way, directly or indirectly, woman suffrage. I repeat that in my judgment it would be not only a calamity but an absolute crime against the institutions of the people of the United States . . ."[27] John Reagon of Texas offered his version of an argument used since Seneca Falls: "But what are we going to do, what are the people of this Territory going to do, by the adoption of this Constitution? They are going to make men of women, and when they do that the correlative must take place that men must become women. So I suppose we are to have women for public officers, women to do military duty, women to work the roads, women to fight the battles of this country, and men to wash the dishes, men to nurse the children, men to stay at home while the ladies go out and make stump speeches in canvasses." The bill to admit Wyoming passed anyway, 29 in favor, 18 opposed.[28] Women now had suffrage in one state of the Union.

The arguments and prejudice against women may have remained constant since 1848, but the lives of individual women had changed. In celebration of the number of women who had graduated college, the Society of Collegiate Alumnae was founded. In recognition of the increasing number of wage-earning women, the Working Girls' Club was also founded. Women had become preachers, doctors, and lawyers. Women paid tribute by gathering on the birthdays of the women's rights leaders. The honored woman's photograph would be displayed, appreciative speeches made, and a telegram composed and sent.

To many of these women, the suffrage movement and its leaders were important. They were the daughters and granddaughters of women legally unable to own or bequeath property. As they themselves now drew up wills, they left property to the women's movement. Some bequests were as small as $500. Eliza Eddy's bequest in 1882 was $40,000. (Later, Mrs. Leslie Frank would leave $2,000,000.) Women without financial reserves contributed salable goods. One farm woman, for example, brought a 60-pound tub of butter to an NWSA convention and asked that proceeds from its sale go into the organization's treasury. Other women made and sold "suffrage quilts" to benefit the cause.

This woman was arrested in the late 1800s for wearing an unacceptable swimsuit. *(National Archives)*

The first International Council of Women. Susan B. Anthony is seated second from the left and Elizabeth Cady Stanton is seated fourth from the left. *(New York Public Library Picture Collection)*

There were also indications that many women were unhappy with the split in the suffrage movement. The women's suffrage organization in Indianapolis steadfastly refused to affiliate with either the National Woman Suffrage Association or the American Woman Suffrage Association and sent delegates to each organization's conventions. In 1887 the Kansas association went so far as to resolve to send delegates to both conventions with instructions to ask for a merger.

The desire for greater unity was not restricted to the movement's rank and file. In 1888 Susan B. Anthony and Elizabeth Cady Stanton were planning a celebration of the 40th anniversary of the Seneca Falls convention. In connection with this, they decided to launch the International Council of Women. Women from many countries were invited, as were Lucy Stone and members of the American Woman Suffrage Association.

To Anthony and Stanton's delight, their invitations were accepted. Women came from England, Ireland, France, Finland, Denmark, Norway, Italy, India, and Canada and from the ASWA; for the first time in many years, Stanton, Anthony, and Stone shared a platform.[29]

Soon after, negotiations for a merger began. In 1890 the National American Woman Suffrage Association was formed. Stanton was elected president; Anthony, vice president; Stone, chairman of the executive committee; and Stone's daughter, Alice Stone Blackwell, corresponding secretary. A 21-year breach had been healed.[30]

CHRONICLE OF EVENTS

1880

Vermont legislature grants school suffrage to women.

February: New York state grants school suffrage to women.

Women permitted to serve, for first time, as U.S. census enumerators.

August 25: James A. Garfield becomes the first presidential candidate to answer Susan B. Anthony's query on his position on women's suffrage. (He declined to support it.)

September: Henry Blackwell lobbies for women's suffrage at Republican state convention, Worcester, Massachusetts.

October: Anna Shaw is ordained as the first woman minister in the Methodist Protestant church.

October 20: Lydia Maria Child dies.

November 11: Lucretia Mott dies.

1881

Clara Barton founds the American Red Cross.

The Minnesota Woman Suffrage Association forms.

Elizabeth Cady Stanton, Susan B. Anthony, and Matilda Joslyn Gage publish Volume 1 of *The History of Woman Suffrage.*

The Knights of Labor admit women.

1882

The Society for the Collegiate Instruction of Women (the "Harvard Annex") is founded.

The Association of Collegiate Alumnae is founded. In 1921 it becomes the American Association of University Women.

Nebraska holds state referendum; women's suffrage is defeated.

U.S. Senate and House of Representatives appoint Select Committees on Woman Suffrage.

Connecticut Supreme Court admits first woman, Mary Hall of Hartford, to the bar.

Eliza F. Eddy dies, leaving $40,000 to be split between Susan B. Anthony and Lucy Stone "to further . . . 'The Woman's Rights Cause.'"

Senate committee issues favorable majority report on federal women's suffrage amendment.

Elizabeth Cabot Agassiz becomes the first president of Radcliffe College.

Elizabeth Cady Stanton, Susan B. Anthony, and Matilda Joslyn Gage publish Volume 2 of *The History of Woman Suffrage.*

June 2: Woman's Ministerial Conference is formed; Julia Ward Howe elected president.

1883

Legislature of Washington Territory grants women's suffrage.

House of Representatives committee issues favorable majority report on federal women's suffrage amendment.

Lucy Stone gives address at Oberlin College.

Nebraska defeats women's suffrage.

September 5: Mary F. Hoyt is the first woman (and second person) named to a federal position under the guidelines of the Civil Service Act.

1884

The first class of women graduates from Radcliffe.

The court decision in the case of *Rosencrantz v. Washington* validates the decision of a jury with women jurors even though most states and territories bar them.

U.S. Congress awards army pension to Sarah Edmonds Seelye, who fought in the Civil War using the name Frank Thompson.

The first state college for women is established in Columbus, Mississippi. It is named Mississippi Industrial Institute and College for the Education of White Girls of the State of Mississippi.

Martha Carey Thomas becomes the first woman on a college faculty to become a dean. Bryn Mawr College names her to the post while she teaches as a professor there.

Belva Lockwood is nominated for president of the United States by the national Equal Rights Party.

First Working Girls' Club is founded in New York City by Grace Dodge and 12 factory workers.

Senate committee issues favorable majority report on federal women's suffrage amendment.

House of Representatives committee issues adverse majority report on federal women's suffrage amendment.

Oregon holds state referendum; women's suffrage is defeated.

First office of police matron is established in Milwaukee.

1885

The Association of Working Girls' Societies is founded to unite Working Girls' Clubs across the country.

Bryn Mawr College opens; it later becomes the first American institution to offer graduate work to women.

The State Woman Suffrage Association is formed in Ohio. It will hold annual conventions for the next 35 years.

The first union for women's work is established in New York, with Leonora Barry its director.

Elizabeth Cochrane writes for the *Pittsburgh Dispatch* under the pen name Nellie Bly.

1886

Anna Howard Shaw receives her medical degree.

Senate committee issues favorable majority report on federal women's suffrage amendment.

House of Representatives committee issues favorable minority report on federal women's suffrage amendment.

Martha Dandridge Custis, the wife of President George Washington, is the first woman to have her portrait printed on U.S. paper currency. Her portrait appears on the one-dollar silver certificate.

The Young Women's Hebrew Association is established as a branch of the Young Men's Hebrew Association (YMHA). Julia Richman is elected as first president.

The Young Women's Christian Association is established.

Louisa May Alcott publishes *Jo's Boys.*

Elizabeth Cady Stanton, Susan B. Anthony, and Matilda Joslyn Gage publish Volume 3 of *The History of Woman Suffrage.*

May 15: Poet Emily Dickinson dies.

November 22: Confederate diarist Mary Chesnut dies.

December 8: "Susan B. Anthony Amendment" (for women's suffrage) is debated on the Senate floor.

1887

Rhode Island holds state referendum; women's suffrage is defeated.

Senate votes on federal women's suffrage amendment; amendment fails.

U.S. Congress passes the Edmunds-Tucker Act, forbidding polygamy and disfranchising women in Utah Territory.

Territorial supreme court repeals women's suffrage in Washington Territory.

"Age of protection" for girls is raised from 10 to 14 in Wisconsin; violation is made punishable by life imprisonment.

The first woman mayor is elected in the United States: At 27 years old, Suzanna Madora Salter wins the election for mayor in Argonia, Kansas.

Congress raises the age of consent to 16 for the District of Columbia and territories. It does so after an intense petition campaign conceived by Aaron Macy Powell and Emily Blackwell, and with the support of the Woman's Christian Temperance Union and the Knights of Labor.

Kansas grants the vote to women.

January 25: "Susan B. Anthony Amendment" (for women's suffrage) is again debated on the Senate floor.

July 18: Dorothea Dix dies.

1888

Fortieth anniversary of the Seneca Falls convention.

International Council of Women founded.

Kentucky's Equal Rights Association is formed. At this time Kentucky, in the words of Madeline McDowell (*History of Woman Suffrage,* Volume 6) is "the only state that did not permit a married woman to make a will; a wife's wages might be collected by her husband; property and inheritance laws between husband and wife were unequal; fathers were sole guardians of their children and at death could appoint one even of a child unborn; the age of consent was 12 years and it was legal for a girl to marry at 12."

The Equal Rights Party again nominates Belva Lockwood as its candidate for president.

March 6: Novelist Louisa May Alcott dies.

November 2: Elizabeth Cady Stanton tries to vote in Tenafly, New Jersey.

1889

Washington holds state referendum; women's suffrage is defeated.

Wisconsin's 1887 law regarding "age of protection for girls" is amended to lower age to 12. Punishment is reduced from life imprisonment to five to 35 years.

A lighter sentence, one to seven years, applies to men having intercourse with a child "if the child shall be a common prostitute."

The Woman's Christian Temperance Union and the Knights of Labor force the U.S. Congress to raise the age of consent to 21 in Washington, D.C., and the territories.

Lucy Larcom writes *A New England Girlhood.*

June 28: Astronomer Maria Mitchell dies.

September: Jane Addams and Ellen Starr move into Chicago's Hull mansion to found the relief organization Hull-House.

1890

New York Consumers League founded.

South Dakota holds state referendum; women's suffrage is defeated.

The first women's suffrage society of Georgia is formed in Columbus.

General Federation of Women's Clubs is founded.

Senate committee issues favorable majority report on federal women's suffrage amendment.

House of Representatives committee issues favorable majority report on federal women's suffrage amendment.

American Federation of Labor declares support for federal women's suffrage amendment.

February 18: National Woman Suffrage Association and American Woman Suffrage Association merge; officers of the new National American Woman Suffrage Association (NAWSA) are Elizabeth Cady Stanton, Susan B. Anthony, Lucy Stone, and Alice Stone Blackwell.

NAWSA decides, on motion made by Alice Stone Blackwell, to hold conventions in Washington only in alternate years and to rotate through other states in the intervening years.

March: Mary McDowell joins social workers Jane Addams and Ellen Gates Starr at Hull-House in Chicago.

July 23: Wyoming is admitted to Union; women's suffrage is included in its constitution.

1891

The medical school of Johns Hopkins University becomes the first in the country to open its doors to men and women together.

Mary McDowell, founder of the Chicago Settlement House *(National Archives)*

Jeannette Thurber establishes the only U.S. nationally chartered music school, the National Conservatory of Music.

The World Woman's Christian Temperance Union organizes in Boston, Massachusetts.

Women of Illinois win suffrage in school elections.

1892

Elizabeth Cady Stanton resigns the presidency of the National American Woman Suffrage Association.

Charlotte Perkins Gilman publishes *The Yellow Wallpaper,* which becomes a feminist classic.

Mary Kenney (O'Sullivan) is the first woman to be an overall organizer for the American Federation of Labor.

The University of Kansas is the first school to offer a women's studies course.

Reverend Olympia Brown and others establish the Federal Suffrage Association.

Susan B. Anthony is elected president of the National American Woman Suffrage Association.

Senate committee issues favorable majority report on federal women's suffrage amendment.

December: "Foremothers' Day" is celebrated by 200 women in New York City.

EYEWITNESS TESTIMONY

I repeat my conviction of the right of woman suffrage. If the commonwealth is not ready to give it in full by a constitutional amendment, I approve of testing it in municipal elections.

Massachusetts Governor John D. Long, in his inaugural address, 1880, in History of Woman Suffrage, *Vol. 3, 287.*

It is discouraging how every state except Wisconsin has just come short of taking an advance step for women. The New York law is almost worse than none. N.J. and Iowa lost all they asked for, and I have not heard from Ohio where they were earnestly trying for school suffrage. Massachusetts crowned herself with added shame. Dear Lavinia Goodell! I am so sorry for her death! I had a letter from her while in N.Y. explaining why she did not write for the Journal. She said she was "flat on her back suffering from sciatica and rheumatism." I wrote her a comforting letter, and asked her to explain to me, or to let me know the exact action Wisconsin had taken. But I never heard from her & saw she went home to Janesville to die.

Lucy Stone, letter to Henry Blackwell, April 9, 1880, in Wheeler, Loving Warriors, *277.*

Women voting in the town election, Cambridge, Massachusetts, 1879 *(Library of Congress)*

I feel with you that, in spite of all minor drawbacks, the union of the suffrage forces would be a move in the right direction. But our cause is too great to be permanently hurt by what any one individual or group of individuals may do. For over thirty years some people have said from time to time that I have injured the suffrage movement beyond redemption; but it still lives. Train killed it, Victoria Woodhull killed it, the *Revolution* killed it. But with each death, it put on new life . . . Reforms are not made of blown glass to be broken to pieces with the first adverse wind.

Elizabeth Cady Stanton, letter to Isabella Beecher Hooker, May 10, 1880, in Stanton and Blatch, Elizabeth Cady Stanton, *Vol. 2, 169.*

Your Call for all women of These United States to sign a petition or postal Card to be sent to you, from Your Mass Meeting to be sent to the Republican Presidential Convention asking them to extend to us Woman some recognition of our rights. We are your Sisters though Colored still we feel in our Bosom and want of Fraternal love from our White Sister of the Country. Our White men of this State of Virginia, who rule us with a rod of iron, and show themselves on every occasion the same Crule Task Master, as ever, have introduce on the Statute books right to wipp woman for any poor Discretion, that she might be guilt of. During the early part of febuary a poor weak colored Woman who was in the Extremes wants, stole a Over skirt Value fifty Cent, for which the presiding Magistrate Named J. Gruchfield, Did order the poor creature 72 lashes to be well laid on. 36 lashes at the time the Other 36 in a week time and the man or brute, went himself and saw the whipping was executed. Captain Scott a Col man became indignant went to the jail to see the poor Creature, was refused admission at first but succeed at Last. O My God, what a sight he then saw. the poor Woman Breast was Cut wide open by the lash, her poor back cut to pieces I call some woman together went to the Governer and stated the Case. he forbid the further lashing of the poor woman because the Dr. Beal said she could not live to receive further whipping. Yet the woman still have to remain in jail 12 month for stealing one over skirt Value fifty Cent and have since then been enable to enroll quite a number of Woman to gather form a Club. Our Object is to petition Lecture and to do all things wich shall so soffen the heart of Mankind that they will see and must grant and respect our rights. Would and pray that the Mass Meeting may endorse or demand of the Republican Convention to be Held in Chicago the rights of Woman to put an Amendment to the Constitution a Cumpulsory Education of Every state of this Union. Pardon me for this long letter i must i feel let my feeling go out, so to you Dear Madam have i address you on Behalf of your Down Trodden Colored Sisters of Virginia.

Live Pryor, of Richmond, Virginia, letter to Susan B. Anthony, 1880, in DuBois, Elizabeth Cady Stanton/Susan B. Anthony, 205–206.

I always come to the same conclusion, namely that our rotten marriage institution is the main obstacle in the way of womans freedom, and just as long as our girls are taught to barter the use of their bodys for a living, must woman remain the degraded thing she is. Of course the Ballot is the great lever to lift her into self esteem and independence. I am more than glad to see the women getting so in dead earnest in the matter.

Mrs. L. M. R. Pool, letter to Susan B. Anthony, 1880, in DuBois, Elizabeth Cady Stanton/Susan B. Anthony, 207.

Withholding from feminine humanity evry natural right from infancy to death, is man's natural propensity. It is so natural that it requires more than ordinary courage in one to favor equal rights legally or morally.

So much has the world been accustomed to subjecting females (human) to all sort of penances that even female children are forced to forego nearly evry pleasure encouraged in the *MALE* sex. Bah! My blood has been brought to boiling heat while reading the contemptable pusilanimious proceedings of the late great Methodist Conference. Even now my cheek burns with contempt and disgust for the foolish virgins who unsuspectingly support them.

Believe me, I cannot sue and plead for my *evry* natural right. But am bitter enough if it comes to that, to fight manfully for our liberty. I would, were it in my power make a destroying Angel of my self, and go from house to house and should I personally receive the treatment that I daily receive in common with other female human beings, *distroy* the man or woman who would utter against equal and unqualified rights and privileges. Words fail to convey the bitter hatred I have for the foul demagogues who would take from me the freedom they claim for themselves.

Mrs. H. Griswold, letter to Susan B. Anthony, 1880, in DuBois, Elizabeth Cady Stanton/Susan B. Anthony, 203.

I thank God, for giving you the *moral courage* to insist, and persist, under such difficulties and discouragements, as you for so many years have, that woman should have some of the rights she for so many centuries has unjustly been deprived of; and may your life be spared, until you see *all women* in possession of the first great right, Suffrage!

A Cleveland woman (signature is illegible), to Susan B. Anthony, 1880, in DuBois, Elizabeth Cady Stanton/Susan B. Anthony, 207.

i have a disire to vote from ms Jane E. Sobers free holder and tax payer when will we have our Rights and Justice in this world. i do not know some times what to think of some of the woman of our city they are a sleep they want to be roused up in Some way i for one have Bin Struggling hard with this world Scince 1874 all Lone By my Self. i have to be man and woman boath i have to be at the helamn and look out for the Brakers i am now 48 years old. have Bin the mother of 9 children and still struggling for my freedom. Are we to have the chinia man to governs us and the colard man it Looks as it was fast approaching.

i feel proud that we have some noble woman to help unnBar the Prison Doors for the Poor Down trodden honst hard working woman of this countery. i have Suffered inJustice from the Law of this my native city. wronged and Robbed of what Did by Rights Belong to me. So good Bye you have my hand and my hart. i only wish i have the power to help you though But I hope the day will come soon . . .

Jane E. Sobers, letter to Susan B. Anthony, 1880, in DuBois, Elizabeth Cady Stanton/Susan B. Anthony, 202–203.

Although only a working woman, I have by hard work and close economy accumulated a small property that I find I have the privilege to pay taxes for, but have not right to vote for men that tax me. I also find that I am taxed for said property as much again as what many men are that have political influence. Last year I appealed against the enormous tax the assessor put on my property. But could get no resolution because I have no political influence . . .

Mrs. Callor, letter to Susan B. Anthony, 1880, in DuBois, Elizabeth Cady Stanton/ Susan B. Anthony, *207.*

. . . in every case where a man ill treats his wife, I want him carried off to the Insane Asylum in Indiana or some other infernal place. I am over 76 years old; have lived in different places; have seen man's cruelty to women many times; just because they delighted to show their power over them. It must be stopped. I should be glad to say something on that great occasion [Woman Suffrage Convention, Chicago, 1880] and hear others; but I am a poor woman and a widow; and could not get money to come to save my life so sent my name and childrens.

Mrs. A. Beaumont, of Illinois City, Illinois, letter to Susan B. Anthony, 1880, in DuBois, Elizabeth Cady Stanton/Susan B. Anthony, *200.*

Do I wish to vote? do the farm-house slaves of the north want to vote? This is a question involving a two sided problem. What has the Womens-rights movement done for us? Just this, if nothing more, raised the wages of women and girls, and opened places in shops and stores where girls may earn more in a month than the farmers wife can command in a year. Well this is good for the girls in some respects but it means death, after a short life of endless toil and care, for the poor Mother at home. Help cannot be had in the farm house, for love nor money . . .

I would not tie any woman down to this life of unpaid toil, but justice means justice to all; and it is an undeniable fact that the condition of the farmers and their poor drudging wives, is every year becoming more intolerable . . .

But do I want to vote; yes, I do . . .

Mrs. Mary Travis, of Fore's Bend, Minnesota, to Susan B. Anthony, 1880, in DuBois, Elizabeth Cady Stanton/Susan B. Anthony, *204–205.*

I cannot be at the meeting although it is my greatest desire to be there. I am an old-lady not able to make the journey . . . What a sham is freedom. My mother, good old lady living yet most one hundred and never wrote her name in her life she said that boys must be educated so they could go out in the world smart men well they are what the world call smart judges

and statesmen while I old lady not capable to do anything for my poor down troden sisters. I am so thankful there is so many capable to do something strike your best blows go to all their great conventions let them know you mean freedom if we never get it keep them stirred up that is some satisfaction if nothing more all this scribbling does not amount to much of course but I have give you my mind on the subject now you can laugh over my composition it will do that much good any way you will find my name in the list [of women demanding suffrage] from Shellsburg Iowa was not able to write when I put it there poor show for a town of 600 inhabitants we had to work hard to get that many . . .

Alzina Rathbun, of Shellsburg, Iowa, letter to Susan B. Anthony, 1880, in DuBois, Elizabeth Cady Stanton/Susan B. Anthony, *203–204.*

As vice-president-at-large of the National Woman Suffrage Association, I am instructed to ask you, if, in the event of your election, you as President of the United States, would recommend to congress, in your message to that body, the submission to the several legislatures of a sixteenth amendment to the national constitution, prohibiting the disfranchisement of United States citizens on account of sex. What we wish to ascertain is whether you, as president, would use your official influence to secure to the women of the several States a national guarantee to their right to a voice in the government on the same terms with men. Neither platform makes any pledge to secure political equality to women—hence we are waiting and hoping that one candidate or the other, or both, will declare favorably, and thereby make it possible for women, with self-respect, to work for the success of one or the other or both nominees.

Susan B. Anthony, letter to presidential candidate James A. Garfield, August 17, 1880, in History of Woman Suffrage, *Vol. 3, 185.*

Your letter of the 17th inst. came duly to hand. I take the liberty of asking your personal advice before I answer your official letter . . . in view of the fact that the Republican convention has not discussed your question, do you not think it would be a violation of the trust they have reposed in me, to speak, "as their nominee"—and add to the present contest an issue that they have not authorized? Again, if I answer your question on the ground of my own private opinion, I shall be compelled to say, that while I am open to the freest discussion and fairest consideration of your question, I have not yet reached the conclusion that it would be best for woman and for the country that she should have the suffrage. I may reach it; but whatever time may do to me, that fruit is not yet ripe on my tree. I ask you, therefore, for the sake of your own question, do you think it wise to pick my apples now? Please answer me in the frankness of personal friendship.

James A. Garfield, letter to Susan B. Anthony, August 25, 1880, in History of Woman Suffrage, *Vol. 3, 185–186.*

Yours of the 25th ult. has waited all these days that I might consider and carefully reply . . . For the candidate of a party to add to the discussions of the contest an issue unauthorized or unnoted in its platform, when that issue was one vital to its very life, would, it seems to me, be the grandest act imaginable . . . I know, if you had in your letter of acceptance, or in your New York speech, declared yourself in favor of "perfect equality of rights for women, civil and political," you would have touched an electric spark that would have fired the heart of the women of the entire nation, and made the triumph of the Republican party more grand and glorious than any it has ever seen . . .

As to picking fruit before it is ripe! Allow me to remind you that very much fruit is *never* picked; some gets nipped in the blossom; some gets worm-eaten and falls to the ground; some rots on the trees before it ripens; some, too slow in ripening, gets bitten by the early frosts of autumn; while some rich, rare, ripe apples hang unpicked, frozen and worthless on the leafless trees of winter! Really, Mr. Garfield, if, after passing through the war of the rebellion and sixteen years in congress;—if, after seeing, and hearing, and repeating, that *no class* ever got justice and equality of chances from any government except it had the power—the ballot—to clutch them for itself;—if, after all your opportunities for growth and development, you cannot yet see the truth of the great principle of individual self-government;—if you have only reached the idea of class-government, and that, too, of the most hateful and cruel form—bounded by sex—there must be some radical defect in the ethics of the party of which you are the chosen leader.

No matter which party administers the government, women will continue to get only subordinate positions and half-pay, not because of the party's or the president's lack of chivalric regard for woman, but because, in the nature of things, it is impossible for any government to protect a disfranchised class in equality of chances. Women, to get justice, must have political freedom. But pardon this long trespass upon your time and patience, and please bear in mind that it is not for the many *good* things the Republican party and its nominee have done in extending the area of liberty, that I criticize them, but because they have failed to place the women of the nation on the plane of political equality with men—alone, without father, brother, husband, son—battling for bread! It is to help the millions of these unfortunate ones that I plead for the ballot in the hands of all women. With great respect for your frank and candid talk with one of the disfranchised . . .

Susan B. Anthony, letter to James A. Garfield, September 9, 1880, in History of Woman Suffrage, *Vol. 3, 186–187.*

We have good audiences, but in this country the foreign population is 9/10 of the whole, and there is not a ghost of a chance to carry the amendment and that too, on account of the Germans, Bohemians, & Irish, and Scandinavians who will all vote against it. We would not have staid if we had known how it was. But all the same we do our best. We tell the truth, scatter leaflets, and collect the names of friends for the use of the Nebraska society—and leave the good seed to grow.

Lucy Stone, letter to Alice Stone Blackwell, September 24, 1880, in Wheeler, Loving Warriors, *283.*

My neighbor and I were proud of the privilege of casting our first vote.

A woman from Poland, New York, after voting at a Poland school meeting, October 12, 1880, in History of Woman Suffrage, *Vol. 3, 428.*

. . . over forty [women] went to the polls on the 13th. Two women were on one of the tickets; the opposition ticket was made up entirely of males. We were supported by the best men in the village. The ticket bearing the names of Mrs. Fidelia J. M. Whitcomb, M.D., Mrs. S. Augusta Herrick, was elected.

A woman from Nunda, New York, after voting at Nunda's school meeting, October 13, 1880, in History of Woman Suffrage, *Vol. 3, 428.*

The ladies had an independent ticket opposing the incumbent clerk and trustee. Seven voted. Four were challenged. They swore their votes in. Boys just turned twenty-one years of age voted unchallenged. The clerk, who is a young sprig of a lawyer, made himself conspicuous by challenging our votes. He first read the opinion of the State superintendent of public instruction, and said that the penalty for illegal voting was not less than six months' imprisonment. My vote was challenged, and although my husband is an owner of much real estate and cannot sell one foot of it without my consent, I could not vote.

A woman from Lowville, Lewis County, New York,
October 16, 1880, in History of Woman Suffrage,
Vol. 3, 427–428.

In Port Jervis, the Board of Education declined a hall that was offered, and had the election in a low, dirty little room. Smoke was puffed in the ladies' faces, challenges were frequent, and all sorts of impudent questions were asked of the voters. In Long Island City many ladies were challenged, and stones were thrown in the street at Mrs. Emma Gates Conkling, the lady who was most active in bringing out the new voters. In New Brighton, the village paper threatened the women with jail if they voted; and when a motion was made in one district that the ladies be invited to attend, a large negative vote was given, one man shouting, "We have enough of women at home; we don't want 'em here!" . . . In Newham a gang of low fellows took possession of the polling place early, filled it with smoke of the worst tobacco, and covered the floor with tobacco juice; and through all this the few ladies who ventured to vote had to pass. In New York [City] a man who claims to be a gentleman said: "If my wife undertook to vote I would trample her under my feet." In New Rochelle the school trustee told the women they were not entitled to vote, and tried to prevent a meeting being held to inform them. Clergymen from the pulpit urged women not to vote, and a mob gathered at the polls and blocked the way.

Account of New York state's board of education elections,
October 1880, in History of Woman Suffrage,
Vol. 3, 430.

Though I could not be at Lucretia Mott's funeral today to say my word, yet I have thought of her, read about her, and written of her all alone here by myself. This Sunday was with me a sacred memorial day to her, and as I consider her repose, self-control, and beautiful spirit . . . I have vowed again, as I have so many times, that I shall in the future try to imitate her noble example.

Elizabeth Cady Stanton, diary entry,
November 14, 1880, in Stanton and Blatch,
Elizabeth Cady Stanton, *Vol. 2, 178.*

I have been shown a form of petition for the suffrage which you enclosed to Rev. Mary J. DeLong, of this place. Will you please inform me if this is to be the form of petition to be presented during the present session of the legislature? We wish the exact words in order that we may have it published in our local paper.

We think it best to call a meeting, even now at this somewhat late day, and send women to Lincoln who will attend personally to this matter. We have left these things neglected too long. Will you call on all women of the State who can do so to assemble at Lincoln during the session of the legislature, appointing the day, etc.? I think we would be surprised at the result. This town contains scarcely a woman who is opposed to woman suffrage. We know we are a power here . . .

Mrs. Lucinda Russell, of Tecumseh, Nebraska, letter to
Mrs. Harriet S. Brooks, December 4, 1880, in
History of Woman Suffrage, *Vol. 3, 682.*

The Equal Suffrage Society of Indianapolis, in behalf of citizens of Indiana who believe that liberty to exercise the right of suffrage should neither be granted nor denied on the ground of sex, would respectfully notify you that during the next session of the State legislature it will invite the attention of that body to the consideration of what is popularly called "The Suffrage Question." The society will petition the legislature to devote a day to hearing, from representative advocates of woman suffrage, appeals and arguments for such legislation as may be necessary to abolish the present unjust restriction of the elective franchise to one sex, and to secure to women the free exercise of the ballot, under the same conditions and such only, as are imposed upon men. To this matter we ask your unprejudiced attention, that when our cause shall be brought before the legislature its advocates may have your cooperation.

Zerelda G. Wallace, president, and May Wright Sewall,
secretary, of the Equal Suffrage Society of Indianapolis, to
every member of the Indiana General Assembly,
December 22, 1880, in History of
Woman Suffrage, *Vol. 3, 537.*

Thanking you for the politeness, the courtesy, the chivalry even, that has been shown me to-day, allow me to make of you the following request: Please sit down at your earliest leisure, and endeavor to realize in imagination how you would feel if you were sued by a woman, and the case was brought before a court composed entirely of women; the judge a woman; every member of the jury a woman; women to read the oath to you, and hold the Bible, and every lawyer a woman. Further, your case to be tried under the laws framed entirely by women, in which neither you nor any man had ever been allowed a voice. Somewhat as you would feel under such circumstances, you may be assured, on reading this, I have felt during the trial to-day. Perhaps the women would be lenient to you (the sexes do favor each other), but would you be satisfied? Would you feel that such an arrangement was exactly the just and fair thing? If you would not, I ask you on the principle of the Golden Rule, to use your influence for the enfranchisement of women.

The Reverend Anna Oliver, pastor of the Willoughby Avenue Methodist Episcopal Church of Brooklyn, New York, "To his Honor, the Judge, the Intelligent Jury, the Lawyers and all who are engaged in the case of Jones vs. Oliver," *1881, in* History of Woman Suffrage, *Vol. 3, 440.*

. . . one day Mrs. Stuart came to me and said: "Now, Mrs. Brown, write out your bill; the speaker of the House sent me word they were ready for it." I sat down and framed a bill to the best of my ability, which was duly presented and respectfully debated. Mrs. Duniway came from Portland to urge its passage, and the day before it came to a vote both Houses adjourned and invited her to speak in the hall of representatives. She made one of her best speeches. The members of both Houses were present, besides a large audience from the city. The next day the House passed the bill by two majority, and on the day following it was lost in the Council by two majority. In the House the vote stood, ayes, 13; nays, 11. In the Council ayes, 5; nays, 7 . . . Mr. White, a lobby member . . . disclosed the cause of the defeat of the bill in the Council. He said, after the bill passed the House the saloon-keepers, alarmed lest their occupation would be gone if women should vote, button-holed the members of the Council, and as many of them as could be bought by drinks pledged themselves to vote against the bill. The members of the Council were

present, and though an urgent invitation was given to all to speak, not one of them denied the charge made by Mr. White.

Mary Olney Brown, of Washington Territory, 1881, in History of Woman Suffrage, *Vol. 3, 787.*

Believing that my wife is entitled to all the rights that I enjoy, I vote aye.

C. B. Slocumb, of the Nebraska House of Representatives, voting in favor of a bill permitting a women's suffrage amendment to his state's constitution, February 21, 1881, in History of Woman Suffrage, *Vol. 3, 684.*

I would like to see the moral influence of women at the polls, but I would not like to see the immoral influence of politics in the home circle. The Almighty has imposed upon woman the highest office to which human nature is subject, that of bearing children. Her life is almost necessarily a home life; it should be largely occupied in rearing and training her children to be good men and pure electors. Therein her influence is all-powerful. Again, I incline to the belief that to strike out the word "male" in the constitution would not change its meaning so as to confer the suffrage upon women. I am not acquainted with half a dozen ladies who would accept the suffrage if it were offered to them. They are not prepared for so radical a change. For these reasons, briefly stated, and others, I vote *No.*

State Senator Church Howe, of Nebraska, voting against a women's suffrage amendment to his state's constitution, February 21, 1881, in History of Woman Suffrage, *Vol. 3, 685–686.*

. . . on the evening of February 15, there were gathered in the spacious parlors of Dr. Carey's hospitable home, one hundred and fifty persons representing the best circles of Indianapolis society. A portrait of Miss Anthony rested upon an easel, conspicuously placed, that all might see the serene face of the woman who for thirty years has preached the gospel of political freedom, and expounded the constitution of the United States in favor of justice for all. The programme was somewhat informal, all but two of the speeches being spontaneous expressions of admiration for Miss Anthony and her fidelity to principle. There were two regrets connected with the programme. These were caused by the absence of

Gov. Porter and Hon. Schuyler Colfax; but the gracious presence of Mrs. Colfax was a reminder of her husband's fidelity to our cause, and Mrs. Porter's sympathetic face was a scarcely less potent support than would have been speech from the governor. Just before the close of the meeting . . . [a] telegram was sent to Miss Anthony . . .

May Wright Sewall, about a celebration in honor of Susan B. Anthony's 62nd birthday, February 15, 1882, in History of Woman Suffrage, *Vol. 3, 538.*

Between ourselves—there is no more hope of carrying woman suffrage in Nebraska than of the millennium coming next year. Both parties have avoided it. The republicans refused to endorse it day before yesterday in their state convention. I had not been in Omaha 48 hours before I saw how the matter stood, but as we don't want to discourage the workers, we keep our opinions to ourselves & talk and work as if we expected to win. But the prospect is not nearly so good as it was in Kansas in 1869. I am confirmed in my opinion that we shall have to get what we can from the State legislatures by statute without going down to the masses—to be beat.

Don't publish my predictions as to Nebraska. I count the days till we can return to relieve you from your cares [as solitary editor of the *Woman's Journal*]. God bless you . . .

Henry Blackwell, letter to Alice Stone Blackwell, September 24, 1882, in Wheeler, Loving Warriors, *282–283.*

Today is the eventful day for Nebraska and for women. I am anxious to know, but I dread to hear the result. As usual, I carried Papa down to vote. My political superiors were standing around quietly. Some smoking, some talking. One fellow said he was waiting to get five dollars for his vote. A ticket was passed to Papa who took it with a polite bow. It was a Butler ticket. People came and went—male people. Our Irish fellow citizens lingered around the polls. At last I asked for a ticket, which was promptly handed to me. I said, "Is it not rather hard that I, who live in this ward, own property, pay taxes, and am an orderly citizen cannot vote?" "But you can vote on School." "Yes," I said, "but why should I not vote this ticket." "Did you ever ask for it?" said he. "Oh, yes many times." "But it has never been brought to the polls?" "No, the Democrats put it in their platform this year."

"Only promises, I suppose," said he. Then Papa came and we left.

Lucy Stone, letter to Alice Stone Blackwell, November 7, 1882, in Wheeler, Loving Warriors, *284.*

I was very glad indeed to receive notice of your midwinter conference in time to send you a few words about the progress of our work in England. I believe our disappointment at the result of the vote in Nebraska must have been greater than yours, as, being on the spot, you saw the difficulties to be surmounted. I had so hoped that the men of a free new State would prove themselves juster and wiser than the men of our older civilizations, whose prejudice and precedents are such formidable barriers. But we cannot, judging from a distance, look upon the work of the campaign as thrown away. Twenty-five thousand votes in favor of woman suffrage in the face of such enormous odds is really a victory . . .

Caroline A. Biggs, of London, England, letter to Susan B. Anthony, January 10, 1883, in History of Woman Suffrage, *Vol. 3, 261.*

When in the call I read that for fourteen consecutive years the National Woman Suffrage Association had held a convention in Washington, I was oppressed by two thoughts; First, how hard it is to overcome prejudice and ignorance when they have been fortified by the usages and customs of ages; and secondly, the sublime faith, courage and perseverance of the advocates of woman's enfranchisement, and their confidence in the ultimate triumph of justice . . . I entirely agree with you that, while agitation in the States is necessary as a means of education, a sixteenth amendment to the national constitution is the quickest, surest and least laborious way to secure the success of this great work for human liberty. Any legislature of Indiana in the last six years would have ratified such an amendment.

Zerelda G. Wallace, former first lady of Indiana, letter to Susan B. Anthony, January 21, 1883, in History of Woman Suffrage, *Vol. 3, 257–258.*

I wish I could show the people who are so wonderfully exercised on the subject of female suffrage just how it works. The women watch the nominating conventions, and if the Republicans put a bad man on their ticket and the Democrats a good one, the Republican women do not hesitate a moment in scratching off the bad and substituting the good. It is just so with the Democratic women. I have seen the effects of female suffrage, and instead of being a means of encouragement to fraud and corruption, it tends greatly to purify elections and give better government.

Former Chief Justice Fisher, of Cheyenne, Wyoming, 1883, in History of Woman Suffrage, *Vol. 4, 1091.*

Last week our new town-house was dedicated. The women accompanied their husbands. One man spoke in favor of woman suffrage—said it was "surely coming." In this town, at the Corners, for several years they tried to get a graded school, but the men voted it down, After the women had the school-suffrage, one lady, who had a large family and did not wish to send her children away from home, rallied all the women of the Corners, carried the vote, and they now have a good graded school. Our village is moving down, that the boys and girls may have the benefit of the good school there. I think the women who have been indifferent and not availed themselves of their small voting privilege, by which we might have established the same class of school in our village will now regret their negligence, at least every time they have to send three miles for a doctor. Thus, stupid people, blind to their own interest punish themselves. I regret not being able to send a fuller report of the good that woman's use of the ballot, in a limited form, has done for us in this State. The voting in the town-hall is the "infant school" for women in the use of the ballot. Thanking the ladies all for meeting at the capital of the nation, and regretting not to be counted among the number.

Mary A. P. Filley, of New Hampshire, letter to her "Dear Friends assembled in the Washington Convention," January 5, 1884, in History of Woman Suffrage, *Vol. 3, 380.*

I think but few women have, as yet, availed themselves of the privilege of voting in school meetings in this State.

Justus Dartt, letter to Lydia Putnam of Brattleboro, Vermont, February 7, 1884, in History of Woman Suffrage, *Vol. 3, 394.*

If I may be pardoned a suggestion, it would be the specification to the public mind of the practical uses and benefits which would result from the exercise of the suffrage by women. Men are not conscious that women lack the practical protection of the laws or the comforts and conveniences of material and social relations more than themselves. The possession of the ballot as a practical means of securing happiness does not appear to the masses to be necessary to women in our country. Men say: "We do the best we can for our wives and children and relatives. They are as well off as we." In a certain sense this appears to be true. The other and higher truth is that women suffrage is necessary in order that society may advance . . . Here it seems to me that the convention may now strike a blow more powerful than for many years. Society has not so labored with the great problems which concern its own salvation for generations.

What would woman do with the ballot if she had it? What good things . . . could woman do in New Hampshire and in New York City . . . which she cannot do as well without as with the suffrage? Would woman by her suffrage even *help* to remove illiteracy from Louisiana, intemperance from New England, and stop society from committing murder by the tenement-house abuses of New York? Let [those attending] the [coming] convention specify what practical good woman will try to achieve with her God-given rights, provided that men will permit her to enjoy them. Show us wherein you will do *us* good if we will rob you no longer. It might influence us greatly . . .

Senator Henry W. Blair, letter to Susan B. Anthony, March 5, 1884, in History of Woman Suffrage, *Vol. 3, 380–382.*

An old gentleman, Aaron Burr Harrison, a resident of East Orange, has just passed on to his long home, full of years—eighty-eight—and with a good record. He told me about his sister's voting in New Jersey, when he was child—probably about 1807. The last time I took a petition for woman suffrage to him, he signed it willingly, and his daughter also.

Mrs. Cornelia Collins Hussey, address to those assembled at the National Woman Suffrage Association Convention, Washington, D.C., March 1884, in History of Woman Suffrage, *Vol. 3, 490.*

We canvassed four localities in the city of Boston, two in smaller cities, two in country districts and made one record also of school teachers in nine schools of one town. The teachers were unanimously in favor of woman suffrage, and in the nine localities we found that the proportion of women in favor was very much larger than of those opposed. The total of women canvassed were 814. Those in favor were 405, those opposed, 44; indifferent, 166; refused to sign, 160; not seen, 39. These canvasses were made by respectable, responsible women, and they swore before a Justice of the Peace as to the truth of their statements. Thus we have in Massachusetts this reliable canvass of women showing those in favor are to those opposed as nine to one . . .

Mrs. Harriet R. Shattuck, to the U.S. Senate Committee on Woman Suffrage, March 7, 1884, in History of Woman Suffrage, *Vol. 4, 36.*

You ask us if we are impatient. Yes; we are impatient. Some of us may die, and I want our grand old standard-bearer, Susan B. Anthony, whose name will go down to history beside those of George Washington, Abraham Lincoln and Wendell Phillips—I want that woman to go to Heaven a free angel from this republic.

Mrs. Helen M. Gougar, of Indiana, to the U.S. Senate Committee on Woman Suffrage, March 7, 1884, in History of Woman Suffrage, *Vol. 4, 38.*

I have been devoting my energies this week to writing for the *North American Review* an article on divorce in answer to Judge Noah Davis, who proposes an amendment to the national Constitution which would make the laws on divorce homogeneous from Maine to Texas. My reply is that there should be no further legislation on the subject until woman has a word to say in the law-making; that when there are uniform laws from the Atlantic to the Pacific on woman suffrage, then women will be in a position to help adjust the marriage relation.

Elizabeth Cady Stanton, diary entry, June 28, 1884, in Stanton and Blatch, Elizabeth Cady Stanton, *Vol. 2, 217–218.*

Miss Anthony and I did missionary work in stirring the women up to vote at the school election, which came off two days ago. We held several preliminary meetings to see how many we could get to vote and if any could be persuaded to stand for trustees. When the day came, the large upper room in the old academy was filled with ladies and gentlemen. The chairman opened the proceedings, welcoming the ladies to their new duties. One of them was appointed teller, and she performed her part creditably. We had one woman candidate and she was elected by seven majority. The announcement called forth loud and hearty cheers with which were mingled a few hisses from the Democrats. Miss Anthony and I enjoyed in silence this little revolution, and thought of what a great step in advance all this meant, happening in our sleepy old Johnstown, where my father once refused to have me visit him because of my radicalism.

Elizabeth Cady Stanton, diary entry, August 28, 1884, in Stanton and Blatch, Elizabeth Cady Stanton, *Vol. 2, 119–120.*

My prejudices were formerly all against woman suffrage, but they have gradually given way since it became an established fact in Wyoming. My observation, extending over a period of fifteen years, satisfies me of its entire justice and propriety.

Attorney General M. C. Brown, of Wyoming, 1884, in History of Woman Suffrage, *Vol. 4, 1091.*

On the Fourth of July of this year a grand celebration was held at Vancouver, on Washington soil, the women of Oregon having resolved in large numbers that they would never again unite in celebrating men's independence-day in a State where they are denied their liberty.

Abigail Scott Duniway, writing about July 4, 1885, in History of Woman Suffrage, *Vol. 3, 779.*

This is Friday morning. You are up at the printing office probably, and busy with the proofs . . . We found a lot of women here [Warsaw, Indiana] who had never heard a suffrage speech. They had written to ask, that there might be a meeting here. One bright woman brought her 4 months old boy, and said, she dedicated him that day to the suffrage cause, and as she nursed him from her own breast, he will probably drink in all his mother's spirit . . . Everybody has sent their love to you. Mrs. Campbell, Mrs. Ripley, whom you know, and others whom you do not know. They praise your editorials and rejoice that my daughter is on the suffrage side.

Lucy Stone, letter to Alice Stone Blackwell, October 27, 1885, in Wheeler, Loving Warriors, *292.*

. . . no active suffrage work was done until December 3, 1879, when Susan B. Anthony was induced to stop over on her way from Frankfort to Ludington

Abigail Scott Duniway *(Library of Congress)*

[Michigan] and give her lecture, "Woman Wants Bread; Not the Ballot." She was our guest, and urged the formation of a society, and through her influence a "Woman's Department" was added to the *Times and Standard,* which is still a feature of the paper. In the following spring (April), Elizabeth Cady Stanton gave her lecture, "Our Girls," with two "conversations," before the temperance women and others, which revived the courage of the few who had been considering the question of organization. A call was issued, to which twenty-three responded, and the society was formed June 8, 1880, adopting the constitution of the National [Woman Suffrage Association] and electing delegates to attend a convention to be held under the auspices of the association the following week at Grand Rapids. The society at once made a thorough canvass of the city, which resulted in the attendance of seventy tax-paying women at the school election in September, when the first woman's vote was cast in Manistee county. Each succeeding year has witnessed more women at the school election, until, in 1883, they outnumbered the men, and would have elected their ticket but for a fraud perpetrated by the school-board, which made the election void.

In August 1881, Mrs. May Wright Sewall delivered two lectures in Manistee. In February 1882, a social, celebrating Miss Anthony's birthday, was given by the association at the residence of Mr. and Mrs. Fowler . . .

During the autumn of 1882, petitions asking for municipal suffrage were circulated. The venerable Josiah R. Holden of Grand Rapids, father of Mrs. Fowler, then in his 88th year, obtained the largest number of signatures to his petition of any one in the State. A bill granting municipal suffrage to women was drawn by Mrs. Fowler, introduced in the legislature by Hon. George J. Robinson, and afterwards tabled. At the session of 1885 a similar bill came within a few votes of being carried.

In Grand Rapids there was no revival of systematic work until 1880, when the National Association held a very successful two days' convention in the city. In response to a petition from the society, the legislature in the winter of 1885 passed a law, giving to the tax-paying women of the city the right to vote on school questions at the charter elections. At the first meeting a hundred women were present, and hundreds availed themselves of their new power and voted at the first election.

Mrs. Fannie Holden Fowler, of Manistee, Michigan, ca.
1885, in History of Woman Suffrage,
Vol. 3, 529–530.

On December 4, 1884, by unanimous consent of our General Assembly the state-house was granted to us for the first time, for a woman suffrage convention. A large number of our best men and women, and some of our ablest speakers [including Susan B. Anthony, Henry Blackwell, Frederick Douglass and Lucy Stone] were present. An immense audience greeted them and listened with eager interest throughout. The occasion was one of the most pleasant and profitable we have enjoyed in a long time. At the following session of our legislature, 1885, an amendment to our State constitution

Alice Stone Blackwell *(Library of Congress)*

Women voting in 1888 *(Library of Congress)*

most limited suffrage of any State, many *men* being debarred from voting by reason of the property qualification still required here of foreign-born citizens. Such a social atmosphere is not favorable to the extension of the franchise, either to men or women, and makes peculiarly necessary with us, the educational process of a very large amount of moral agitation before much can be expected in the way of political changes.

My own residence here dates back only to 1878, though before that from my Massachusetts home I was somewhat familiar with Rhode Island people and laws. Our work has consisted of monthly meetings, made up usually of an afternoon session for address and discussion, followed by a social tea; of an annual State convention in the city of Providence; and of petitioning the legislature each year, with the appointment of the customary committees and hearings. For many years the centre of the woman movement with us has been the State association, and since my own connection with that, the leader about whom we have all rallied, has been your beloved friend and mine, Elizabeth B. Chace . . . By her constant appearance before legislative committees, her model newspaper articles which never fail to command general attention even among those who would not think of agreeing with her, and by her persistent fidelity to her sense of duty in social life, she is the recognized head of our agitation in Rhode Island. But she has not stood alone . . . Elizabeth K. Churchill lived and died a faithful and successful worker. The Woman's Club in this city was her child; temperance, suffrage, and the interests of working-women were dear to her heart. She was independent in her convictions, and true to herself, even when it compelled dissent from the attitude of trusted leaders and friends, but her work on the platform, in the press, and in society, made her life a tower of strength to the woman's rights cause and her death a lamentable loss. Another active leader in the work here, though not a speaker, who has passed on since my residence in Providence, was Susan B. P. Martin. I think those of us accustomed to act with her always respected Mrs. Martin's judgement and felt sure of her fidelity. What more can be said of any one than that? . . .

If final victory seems farther off here than in some of the newer States, as it certainly does, that is only the greater reason for earnest, and ceaseless

was proposed giving the franchise to women, on equal terms with men. It passed both Houses by a large majority vote, but by some technicality, for which no one seemed to blame, it was not legally started on its round to the vote of the people. Hence the proposition to submit the amendment will be again passed upon this year, and with every promise of success. We have strong hopes of making our little commonwealth the banner State in this grand step of progress.

Elizabeth B. Chace, of Rhode Island, September 9, 1885, in History of Woman Suffrage, *Vol. 3, 348–349.*

. . . ours is a very small State—the smallest in the Union—and has a very closely compacted population. With us the manufacturing interest overshadows everything else, representing large investments of capital. On the one hand we have great accumulations of wealth by the few; on the other hand, a large percentage of unskilled foreign labor. For good or ill we feel all those conservative influences which naturally grow out of this two-fold condition. This accounts in the main, for the Rhode Islander's extreme and exceptionally tenacious regard for the institutions of his ancestors. This is why we have the work. We know we are right, and be it short or long I am sure we have all enlisted for the war.

Frederick A. Hinkley, writing of women's suffrage efforts in Rhode Island, September 14, 1885, in History of Woman Suffrage, *Vol. 3, 349–350.*

. . . I have found that the one great obstacle is I have no certificate to prove I am a trained nurse and with [out] one I shall have a hard time to get established. People and doctors both require some proof of ones proficiency, so I have been trying to get into the only training school that there is in Frisco. I cannot enter now but I have a promise [from] the board of directors that in the spring they will admit me on probation and if the term is pass satisfactorily that they will give me [permission] to take the two years course. They were willing to take me this month but the nurse of whom there are eight would not work with a colored person . . .

Paulina Lyons Williamson, letter to her sister, Maritcha Lyons, November 10, 1885, in Sterling, We Are Your Sisters, *438.*

The women avail themselves quite generally of their privilege of voting at the annual and special school district meetings, at which district officers are elected, and all questions of taxes and expenditures are voted on and settled. Women are, in many instances, elected members of the board of school directors, and thus are charged with the duty of employing teachers, with the supervision of the schools, and with the general management of the affairs of the district. Women vote on the question of the issue of school district bonds, and thus they take part in deciding whether new school houses shall be built and the property of the districts be pledged for the future payment of the cost of the same . . . Women do not vote for either city, county, or State superintendents, and it is not considered that under our constitution they have the right to do so.

In 1884, there were 4,915 women teaching in the State, and 1,936 men. The average monthly wages of women was $32.85, and of men $40.70. There are at present twelve women holding the office of county superintendent of public schools in the State. In 72 counties the office is filled by men. Thus, of the 84 organized counties of the State, one-seventh of the school superintendents are women, who generally prove to be competent and efficient, and the number elected is increasing.

In one county, Harper, a woman holds the office of county clerk. A young woman was recently elected to the office of register of deeds, in Davis county. It is conceded that these two offices can very appropriately be filled by women; and now that the movement has begun, no doubt the number of those elected will increase at recurring elections. Already, in numerous instances, women are employed as deputies and assistants in these and other public offices.

. . . the chief influence which is bringing about a growth of opinion in favor of woman suffrage in Kansas, comes from what has now become the actual, and I may say, the popular and salutary practice of woman suffrage at school district meetings. It is seen that the reasons which make it right and expedient for women to vote on questions pertaining to the education of their children, bear with little, if any, less force upon the propriety of their voting upon all questions affecting the public welfare.

F. G. Adams, letter to Susan B. Anthony, November 26, 1885, in History of Woman Suffrage, *Vol. 3, 710–711.*

The other day I had a brief letter from Mrs. Stanton; she said she did wish I could get you to meet with her and Susan & me once more, to have it seem like the old days; before we all go forward "to work or rest." So should I like to be we four together, with all the remembrances not desirable buried; and judgement left where it belongs.

Antoinette Brown Blackwell, letter to Lucy Stone, January 6, 1886, in Lasser and Merrill, Friends and Sisters, *249.*

As to meeting Mrs. Stanton it is out of the question with me. She sent a letter to Mr. Shattuck of this city, which he read to a little group, of which I was one, in which she said I was "the biggest liar and hypocrite she had ever seen." After that, you will see that I cannot with any self respect meet her with a pretence of good fellowship. For yourself, of course, such a letter about me need make no difference. Mrs. Stanton is as bright and as witty as ever, and Susan just as egotistical. When Susan came here to get her share of the Eddy fund, I invited her to come and spend the day with us. I gave her a time table, and told her I would meet her at any train, if she would let me know. Instead, she sent me a hateful note, that made me feel the last plank between us had broken. I am too busy with the work that remains, to take time to mend broken cisterns.

Lucy Stone, letter to Antoinette Brown Blackwell, January 10, 1886, in Wheeler, Loving Warriors, *293.*

Last Friday I went with young Dr. Blake to see an operation performed. There was present two doctors a nurse and myself. It took two hours to do it . . . I tell you I enjoyed it. Everything was so scientifically done and so neatly. One doctor gave the either [ether] and the other performed the operation. The nurse and myself assisted the doctor . . . The either [ether] made me deathly sick and I did not get over it for several days.

Paulina Lyons Williamson, letter to Maritcha Lyons, January 18, 1886, in Sterling, We Are Your Sisters, *438–439.*

I sent to the State House [Massachusetts] for the bill you had in hand for the punishment of rape . . . there is need of a statute to raise the "age of consent" from ten, where it now is, so that a minor girl may have the same protection for her person that she does for her property. She cannot dispose of her property till she is of age. She should not be permitted to dispose of her honor any earlier than she is permitted to dispose of her property . . . Will you kindly let me know whether anything has been done about this, and if not, how it may still be done, and who is the chairman of the proper committee?

Lucy Stone, letter to Dr. Gleason, March 2, 1886, in Wheeler, Loving Warriors, *293–294.*

[T]he baser class of females would rush to the polls, and this would compel the intelligent, virtuous and refined females, including wives and mothers, to relinquish for a time their God-given trust and go, contrary to their wishes, to the polls and vote to counteract the other class . . . the ignorant female voters would be at the polls en masse, while the refined and educated, shrinking from public contact, would remain at home . . . The ballot will not protect females against the tyranny of bad husbands, as the latter will compel them to vote as they dictate . . . [nonetheless, I also fear that] [w]ives will form political alliances antagonistic to the husbands, and the result will be discord and divorce.

U.S. Senator Joseph A. Brown, of Georgia, explaining his objection to a federal women's suffrage amendment, January 25, 1887, in Harper, Life and Work of Susan B. Anthony, *Vol. 2, 618.*

Your telegram telling of the passage of the R[hode]I[sland] amendment by such a handsome vote came just after breakfast. It would be a joy if it could be carried by the voters. I am sorry to have so much of the work of the campaign there devolve on you. The R. Islanders will take the brunt of the planning it, but you will have to go down for speaking. No speech will be so effective as yours . . . I do wish RI would adopt the amendment! I saw the Maine Senate has passed its amendment. The record adds coolly, "but it will be killed in the house."

Lucy Stone, letter to Henry Blackwell, March 5, 1887, in Wheeler, Loving Warriors, *297–298.*

I feel ashamed to write you such short letters but they are better than none. I fear there is very little hope of carrying RI. If we can get even a decent minority I shall feel relieved. More & more I see that it is *premature* to go to the voters. We must stick to the Legislatures, here in the East especially. But we are getting a good hearing & shall do much to break the crust of conservatism & liberalize the little hidebound State.

Henry Blackwell, letter to Lucy Stone, March 15, 1887, in Wheeler, Loving Warriors, *298.*

Well, we are beaten, as I feared, 5,392 to 15,398— only 26 per cent of the votes were cast for Woman Suffrage; 74 per cent against it . . . If placing four leaflets and a copy of "The Amendment" in the hands of every voter in Rhode Island by mail, and about 100 public meetings large and small (mostly small), and active discussion in the papers during the past month—have any educational or converting influence, much good seed has been sown. But a large proportion of the voters will have to die and be born again before they can be converted, and the mass of the population (factory operators of Irish and French Canadian extraction) are as incapable of being reached by reason as Choctaw Indians. I have no hope that Rhode Island will become woman suffrage during Mrs E B Chace's life-time, or that of most of us.

Henry Blackwell, letter to Lucy Stone, April 7, 1887, in Wheeler, Loving Warriors, 302–303.

The undersigned believe that the Creator intended that the sphere of the males and females of our race should be different . . .

First sentence of the Senate Select Committee's minority report in opposition to the proposed 16th Amendment, signed by Senator Joseph E. Brown and others, 1887, in Harper, Life and Work of Susan B. Anthony, Vol. 2, 590.

Miss Anthony intends to have a great celebration of the 40th anniversary of the movement, [and] if after conferring with our auxiliary societies, it was thought best to do so, we might propose to make it a Jubilee Anniversary and union of the two national societies under the name of "the United Suffrage Societies," with an American Branch and a National Branch which should each be responsible for the management of its work, but all meeting upon occasion, and working together as friendly societies, and in this way, escaping for the most part, any indiscretions which the National Branch might run into. I mean escape responsibility for their false moves, or for their indiscreet ones.

They are now doing very good work as an association, and APPARENTLY there is no reason why we should not unite. Besides it would take away the feeling of grievance &c &c &c, and would on the whole perhaps be best. I have about come to the conclusion that this will be the best for the cause.

You will be glad of any real help any of them give to the cause, even the worst of them, if you put the cause FIRST OF ALL. If I were starving or freezing, you would be glad if your worst enemy brought me food or warmth. But this is the cause, not of any one woman, but all women, and of the whole race. Its success and prosperity have always been more to me, than any personal feeling, and any damage to IT far more than any personal ill will, or misunderstanding of myself, so I could always rejoice in good work no matter who did it. Try to look at it in this way dear . . .

Lucy Stone, letter to Alice Stone Blackwell, April 12, 1887, in Wheeler, Loving Warriors, 304.

It is very pleasant that Mrs. Stanton can enjoy her [son] Theodore, *alone,* this summer—but I miss her very much—in the work needing to be done for the International . . .

Susan B. Anthony, letter to Elizabeth Smith Miller, May 17, 1887, in the Smith Family Papers, Rare Books and Manuscripts Division, New York Public Library.

It was splendid of you to think of us, and at this early day, too, when it almost seems hopeless, *financially*— and your good contribution—therefore—is doubly welcome—because it helps bring hope!! Everything looks bright, as to the [International] Council—very many conservative associations have appointed delegates—and Lucy Stone—*and* Mrs. Caroline H. Dall accept the *National's Invitation*—apparently gladly!!

Yes—we are confidently expecting Mrs. Stanton—and I have written her—she will never be forgiven by me, or any of our association—if she fails to come!—She says Harriot is not coming till later—But I hope she'll yet decide to be at the council . . . I hope *you* and *Mr. Miller* will both be with us—for *you both signed* the *Seneca Falls* Declaration in 1848 . . . I want

Mary Elizabeth Lease, public speaker and reformer *(Library of Congress)*

every living Seneta Falls and Rochester man and woman of the 1848 Conventions to be invited—so that we may have at least a letter—if not the actual presence of all who are alive—Won't you scim over the names . . . and tell me if you know of any one now alive—I shall be very sorry to miss any one . . .

P.S.—I enclose your letter to Mrs. Stanton—and do you write her that *every evil fate will persecute* her if she dares be absent!!

Susan B. Anthony, letter to Elizabeth Smith Miller, January 26, 1888, in the Smith Family Papers, Rare Books and Manuscripts Division, New York Public Library.

About Union with S[usan] B. A[nthony] We did suggest Mrs. Livermore for Pres[ident] and also Mrs. Howe. But Susan said neither of them stood distinctively for Woman Suffrage—She so much wishes to be president herself! To bring her to the top at last would be such a vindication she cannot bear to forgo it. I withdraw in my whole soul from all of the set. She (Susan) said you were to be asked to offer prayer . . . Alice dreads these people even more than I do, but wants to have Union, to take the burden of work of the American from me, and to save it from coming on her, when I drop out.

Lucy Stone, letter to Antoinette Brown Blackwell, winter 1888, in Lasser and Merrill, Friends and Sisters, 255.

At this memorable convention a small minority, led by Walter Thomas Mills, did its utmost to defeat the equal suffrage plank, on the plea that "two issues" could not be carried at a time, that this plank alienated the South, in general, and conservatives in the North, in particular, with other minor objections. This minority had agitated the subject vigorously for a year or more, and had thus put leaders, as well as rank and file, so thoroughly on guard, that when the vote came, only about sixty voted to drop the plank which had been in from the first nominating convention of the party in 1872.

Frances Willard, writing of events leading to the Prohibition Party's endorsement of women's suffrage as part of its party platform in 1888, in Willard, Glimpses of Fifty Years, 441.

When our committee filed into the great hall next day, the gentlemen and ladies that composed it marching arm in arm upon the platform, all felt that the hour was come when the manhood of this rising power in American politics [James Black, the Prohibition Party's first nominee for president] was to declare decisively not only in favor of prohibition by law and prohibition by politics, but prohibition by woman's ballot, as the final consummation of the war upon King Alcohol, the most relentless foe of women in the home.

Frances Willard, writing of events leading to the Prohibition Party's endorsement of women's suffrage as part of its party platform in 1888, in Willard, Glimpses of Fifty Years, 442.

These [temperance] women do not seem to see that all this special legislation about faith, Sabbaths, drinking, etc., etc., is the entering wedge to general governmental interference which would eventually subject us to an espionage that would soon become tyrannical in the extreme.

Elizabeth Cady Stanton, diary entry, February 8, 1888, in Stanton and Blatch, Elizabeth Cady Stanton, Vol. 2, 247.

The highest power of organization for women is that it brings them out; it translates them from the passive voice into the active voice; the dear, modest, clinging things didn't think they could do anything, and, lo and behold! they found they could. They come to you with a quiver of the lip, and look at you so hopeful and expectant, and wonder if they could so something; and a year or two after, you hear them with a deep voice and perfect equipose telling their dearest thought to a great audience, or you see them in the silent charities, carrying out their noblest purpose toward humanity.

Frances Willard speaking before the National Council of Women, 1888, in Willard, Glimpses of Fifty Years, 592.

If . . . our brothers answer, "It is not because you women are inferior that we don't want you to vote, but because you are too good and nice and pure to come into politics," then I say to you: "My Friend, we don't expect to leave political affairs as we find them; not at all. You, our brothers, all alone by yourselves and no women with you, have constructed this 'filthy pool' that you talk about so much, and that you don't admire, and that you can't make any worse. You know that into the witch's broth they pour all the ingredients together. Now, you have all the ingredients there are, except women's votes. Turn them in; it may be the branch of sweetness that it needs; and certainly it can't be any worse." So I want to say to my brothers, that we are coming in, as we believe, just as we should go into a bachelor's hall. We should take along broom and dust-brushes and dust-pans, open the windows and ventilate the place and try to have a general "clarin" out, and that is exactly what we want to do . . . if ever a place needed a "clarin" out we think it is the kitchen of Uncle Sam. So we have made up our minds and you will see us coming in, and nothing on this universal earth will keep us out of it.

Frances Willard speaking before the National Council of Women, 1888, in Willard, Glimpses of Fifty Years, *594.*

I wish you were here that we might talk over the matter of union. I have an utter abhorrence of so many of those who are in that society that it seems as tho' it would be impossible to work with them. And to accept Miss Anthony as president seems to be so unjust to the American, or so like giving her a vindication of her past, and saying that the American had had no occasion for its existence that is, it will seem like that, & they and theirs will trumpet it as a surrender—and a vindication. I did think when I proposed a union that Miss Anthony would see the propriety of an agreement with me that we would neither of us, (or Mrs. Stanton) take the presidency. But her old grasping spirit is just as fully alive as ever. I would rather the American would die altogether than to seem to condone Susan's past, and put ourselves in the erring historically . . .

Lucy Stone, letter to Mrs. Campbell, March 17, 1888, in Wheeler, Loving Warriors, *313.*

On Sunday, the 26th ult., the International Council of Women opened and continued for a whole week most successfully, the splendid agitation closing with hearings before the committees of both the House and Senate. There can be no question that Susan and I have been well inspired in always advocating the securing of these hearings, which educate the large public throughout the Union and modify the prejudices of the senators and representatives sitting on these committees, and who there make their first acquaintance with "strong-minded women" and do

not find them "such a bad lot, after all," as a certain prominent congressman once remarked to me.

Elizabeth Cady Stanton, diary entry, April 4, 1888, in Stanton and Blatch, Elizabeth Cady Stanton, *Vol. 2, 250.*

While here [in Cleveland], I have been writing an appeal bringing forward the right of women to vote for members of a constitutional convention. Ohio intending to revise its constitution this fall. Mrs. Southworth is to have 50,000 copies of this document printed and distributed at the State exhibition now under way at Columbus. of course I do not imagine that this paper will get women delegates into the convention, but it will set people thinking on the whole question of woman's political disabilities, and when men and women begin to think on any subject, half the victory is won.

Elizabeth Cady Stanton, diary entry, August 20, 1888, in Stanton and Blatch, Elizabeth Cady Stanton, *Vol. 2, 251.*

. . . the ballot for a woman is as superfluous as a corset for a man.

Brooklyn Times, *editorial, April 26, 1889, in Harper,* Life and Work of Susan B. Anthony, *651.*

In our hearing before the Committee on Constitut[io]n[a]l Amendm[en]ts—which had charge of this Bill on striking out male six were strongly in favor and only two against—and of these two one was a young man who did no[t] attend either of our hearings, and the other was an Irish saloon keeper—but even he was so much impressed that he listened to me with his mouth wide open and in the public debate last Tuesday said that Mrs. Hooker was fit to be President of the U.S. but that she was an exception . . .

I mean to have such a Club in every town in this State in the course of the year—then in parlor meetings women will be reading and talking about the same things and getting ready to manage town affairs as they should be managed. My first and chief proposition is that if the towns and villages are well cared for in sanitary matters, in schools in jails and poor houses, in temperance regulations and in police then the State is safe—and the States being well regulated the republic is safe and can never be brought low, as other republics have been. But masculine wisdom and patriotism cannot be depended on to protect and educate even a village community as experience has shown—so we must compel women to bear their share of burden and responsibility. At Litchfield lately, a young teacher on her way from school through some woods, was seized by a young man of respectable family and violated twice in the same afternoon—being nearly choked to death—so much for our protectors!! . . .

Isabella Beecher Hooker, letter to Alice Hooker Day, May 17, 1889, in Boydston, Kelley and Margolis, The Limits of Sisterhood, *216–217.*

I think it will be utterly impossible to get woman suffrage into the body of the Constitution here [North Dakota]. The opponents would be willing to submit WS as a separate question,—feeling, as they do, quite sure it will be voted down. They will oppose, many of them, the empowering the Legislature to act, but that is all we can hope to carry, & if we do carry that, it will be a great and fruitful victory.

Henry Blackwell, letter to Lucy Stone, July 8, 1889, in Wheeler, Loving Warriors, *317.*

There has never been a woman suffrage meeting held in Montana. The only hope here, as in No[rth] Dakota, is a clause empowering the Legislature. If we get that, we shall have here a woman suffrage state within five years; else not in 20.

Henry Blackwell, letter to Lucy Stone, July 14, 1889, in Wheeler, Loving Warriors, *320.*

. . . I am forever cured of the dream of a prohibition alliance. Miss Willard & her third party associates are the most dangerous enemies of our cause, because just so far as they educate the women, they array them *against the men* as a means of *coercing* the habits of the other sex. And men will not submit to this coercion. I never before realized the necessity of respecting personal *liberty*, even when that liberty takes injurious forms.

Henry Blackwell, letter to Lucy Stone, July 29, 1889, in Wheeler, Loving Warriors, *326.*

. . . bad news from Montana, tho it is really better than I expected—viz. a defeat by a tie vote 33 to 33.

Henry Blackwell, letter to Lucy Stone, July 31, 1889, in Wheeler, & Loving Warriors, *326–328.*

We have saved one of the new States to Liberty! Thanks to Cora E. Smith . . . & our good friends in the Convention, the [North Dakota] State Legislature has been empowered to extend Suffrage to women . . . I shall leave here on Saturday morning for Seattle. Shall go to Tacoma Sunday, to Portland Monday—& to Boise City on Tuesday. If we can only get the Legislature empowered to extend suffrage to women in this State [Washington] . . .

Henry Blackwell, letter to Lucy Stone, August 1, 1889, in Wheeler, Loving Warriors, *327–328.*

You want petitions. Well I have two which I got up some time, ago, but did not send on because I thought the names too few to count much. The one is of *white* women 130 in number. The other contains 110 names of black women. This last is a curiosity, and was gotten up under the following circumstances:

Some ladies were dining with me and we each promised to get what names we could to petitions for woman suffrage. My servant who waited on table was coal-black woman. She became interested and after the ladies went away asked me to explain the matter to her, which I did. She then said if I would give her a paper she could get a thousand names among the black women, that many of them felt that they were as much slaves to their husbands as ever they had been to their white masters. I gave her a petition, and said to her, "Tell the women this is to have a law passed that will not allow the men to *whip their wives,* and will put down drinking saloons." "Every black woman will go for that law!" She took the paper and procured these 110 signatures against the strong opposition of black men who in some cases threatened to whip their wives if they signed. At length the opposition was so great my servant had not courage to face it. She feared some bodily harm would be done her by the black men. You can see this is a genuine negro petition from the odd way the names are written, sometimes the capital letter in the middle of the name, sometimes at the end.

Elizabeth Avery Meriwether, letter to Mrs. Spencer, December 11, 1889, in History of Woman Suffrage, *Vol. 3, 153–154.*

In the matter of the union of our two national woman suffrage societies now on the carpet, I am urging simplicity in everything. I especially do not like article 12 in the proposed constitution, which makes possible the election of a man to the presidency of the organization. I would never vote for a man to any office in our societies, not, however, because I am "down on" men *per se*. Think of an association of black men officered by slave-holders! Having men pray and preside for us at our meetings has always seemed to me a tacit admission that we haven't the brains to do these things ourselves. Perhaps "always" is a little too strong in my case, for I must admit that at our first convention, that of Seneca Falls, I insisted on James Mott being in the chair. But I have outgrown that feeling, I am happy to say . . . I ask Susan what is the matter with our little old constitution, which we simple-minded women drew up back I do not know when? I tell her that I get more radical as I grow older, while she seems to get more conservative.

Elizabeth Cady Stanton, diary entry, January 9, 1890,
in Stanton and Blatch, Elizabeth Cady Stanton,
Vol. 2, 253–254.

I appeal to every woman who has any affection for the old National or for me not to vote for Susan B. Anthony for president. I stand in a delicate position. I have letters which accuse me of having favored the union solely for personal and selfish considerations, and of trying to put Mrs. Stanton out. Now what I have to say is, don't vote for any human being but Mrs. Stanton. There are other reasons why I wish her elected, but I have these personal ones: When the division was made twenty years ago, it was because our platform was too broad, because Mrs. Stanton was too radical; a more conservative organization was wanted. If we Nationals divide now and Mrs. Stanton is deposed from the presidency, we virtually degrade her. If you have any love for our old association, which from the beginning, has stood like a rock in regard to creeds and politics, demanding that every woman should be allowed to come upon our platform to plead for her freedom—vote for Mrs. Stanton.

Susan B. Anthony, addressing members of the National
American Woman Suffrage Association, February 17,
1890, in Barry, Susan B. Anthony, *297.*

I made the opening address at the Washington Convention this morning. It was the first meeting of the united woman suffrage associations, of which I had just been elected president. Ida Husted Harper said it was "one of the best speeches of my life." I opened

with the remark: "I consider it a greater honor to go to England as the president of this association than would be the case if I were sent as minister plenipotentiary to any court in Europe." When I arose to say farewell the entire audience began waving handkerchiefs and the men cheering. Needless to say that I was deeply touched by this hearty demonstration.

Elizabeth Cady Stanton, diary entry,
February 18, 1890, in Stanton and Blatch,
Elizabeth Cady Stanton, *Vol. 2, 261.*

I came from Washtn. on Monday . . . the personal consultations, Committee work, and Convention of four days, all coming after the Susan Anthony banquet which lasted till two o'clock, were enough to disable the strongest, so I am rather triumphant than otherwise . . .

Speaking of Convention Mrs. Stanton gave a magnificent address and then called from the box where I was sitting with her, her daughter Mrs. [Harriet Stanton] Blatch of Basingstoke Eng. and introduced her to the audience—and she spoke for ten minutes with admirable manner and perfect self possession. She is the one whose address I sent you for England and she wishes much to meet you. She has a daughter five yrs. old, is happily married to a well to do Englishman[—]his father a rich brewer who wont let him come to this country so long as he lives[—]Mrs. Stanton sailed with her the day after this and I could almost envy her such a daughter—beautiful and gifted, who will not only take up her work after she is gone but is enthusiastically with her already. She is a college graduate—Studied in the School of Oratory and is already a statesman—yet dresses with exquisite taste and looks not over twenty one—and her husband enjoys seeing her devoted to reform work in England of the most radical sort . . .

Isabella Beecher Hooker, letter to Alice Hooker Day,
February 28, 1890, in Boydston, Kelley, and Margolis,
The Limits of Sisterhood, *218–219.*

The masculine represents judgement, the practicable, the expedient, the possible, while the feminine represents emotion, what ought to be, the dream of excellence, the vision of complete beauty . . . The predominance of sentiment in woman renders her essentially an idealist. She jumps at conclusions . . . She can make no allowance for slowness, for tentative or compromising measures. Her reforms are sweeping. She would close all the bars and liquor saloons, and make it a crime to sell intoxicating drink.

Octavius B. Frothingham, writing in The Arena, *July 1890, in Kraditor,* The Ideas of the Woman Suffrage Movement, *19.*

I have received a letter of twenty-two pages from Susan, which I have duly considered. As to the presidency of our national organization, I have written in reply that I do not want to serve "to keep out any objectionable person" but I will accept what those on the ground think best. I write them that I would prefer to see Susan made president rather than anybody else, and that if I were present I should give my vote for her. I would also be ready to vote for Lucy Stone.

Elizabeth Cady Stanton, in England, diary entry, January 3, 1891, in Stanton and Blatch, Elizabeth Cady Stanton, *Vol. 2, 271.*

I came through Rochester last Friday night and was sorry not to stop, but I was miserable. The lime water of the West always makes me ill, and I had no courage to add even a straw to the situation . . . I happened to be in Chicago at the time of the five-days business meeting of the Women's Department. So many distinguished women were there from all over the Union, and so many of them were fine-looking, noble women . . . They came to me from everywhere to say they were suffragists. Especially the Southern women to whom the question is a fresh gospel. It did my heart good to meet them, and to see and feel their warm enthusiasm. And they are still young, able to fight when we are gone . . .

Yours in good hope of the victory not so far off as it was once . . .

Lucy Stone, letter to Susan B. Anthony, September 6, 1891, in Wheeler, Loving Warriors, *342–343.*

Mr. Washington introduced me as Dr. Dillon who came to take the State Examination. The Supervisor said very politely "any information I give &c". I said that is alright I am ready to begin *immediately* in chemistry. I also showed him my diploma & letters of introduction. The diploma especially excited comment from the Supervisor & another young doctor who was taking the examination. They both said well I have [never] seen a woman doctor before or a diploma from a Woman's Medical College. They treated [me] quite cordially and gave me a

very pleasant desk by the window & I began at once on Chemistry . . . One question in Hygiene occurs to me now & it certainly was to my mind incomprehensible, "Discuss the *hygiene* of the reproductive organs of the female."

. . . It is the first time that there has been a woman physician in Tuskegee [Alabama].

Dr. Halle T. Dillon, letter to Dr. Clara Marshall, October 3, 1891, in Sterling, We Are Your Sisters, *449.*

Mrs. Stanton seemed so bright and splendid at Washington!—and I think *"The Solitude of Self"* is her *crowning speech*—and so thought able minds . . . it made those *ignorant* and *indifferent* [illegible] men on the Com. wipe tears that would moisten their eyes— as she sat and stood there—alternately—and portrayed the *Soul's utter aloneness* in *all the deepest experiences of life!*

Susan B. Anthony, letter to Elizabeth Smith Miller, February 15, 1892, in the Smith Family Papers, Rare Books and Manuscripts Division, New York Public Library.

Writing: Several letters to conventions and an Appeal to the women of this state [New York] to arouse themselves and demand their right to be represented in the coming constitutional convention. Louisa Alcott once told me that it distressed her to see her father in his last years display his waning powers in public. I can still do good work with my pen, and it shall be at the service of our reforms so long as its powers last. But I cannot clamber up and down platforms, mount long staircases into halls and hotels, be squeezed in the crush at receptions, and do all the other things public life involves. That day is passed for me.

Elizabeth Cady Stanton, diary entry, November 1, 1892, in Stanton and Blatch, Elizabeth Cady Stanton, *Vol. 2, 290.*

My father intends to go on to Syracuse with my mother. Privately, we do not think it quite safe for her to travel alone, although I should not say that to her. So, if you can make a place for him on the programme, as you proposed, no doubt he would be glad to speak for you. His heart is very much bound up at present in his plan of the suffrage enrollment, and I know he would be glad of a chance to present it to the convention.

Alice Stone Blackwell writing of her parents, Lucy Stone and Henry Blackwell, to Isabel Howland, November 5, 1892, in the Isabel Howland Papers, Sophia Smith Collection, *Smith College.*

I meant to tell you . . . how delighted I am with all of the results of your splendid work in arranging for & carrying out the Syracuse Convention—they were simply perfect—and I am too proud of you two—to keep still—so here goes my heart full of love and rejoicing over my two new young girls in Syracuse— two more added to my long list of adopted nieces— you are just lovely—and I am very, very glad you are both going to try your oratorical messages in the town of Cayuga [illegible]—before going to the Wash[ington] Con.—for when you are there—I want both of you to let your voices be heard—in state- ments—at least—of work done—Isabel can tell how she has started the enrollment work—how many she has pledged to help her—etc.—and I want both of you to be ready with about a *ten minute's* speech— that can be sandwiched between the two regular speeches of an evening.

Susan B. Anthony to Isabel Howland and Harriet May Mills, November 23, 1892, Isabel Howland Papers, Sophia Smith Collection, *Smith College.*

Senator Hemphill wrote to me a few days ago about the amendment he is intending to introduce. Of course I was delighted. I sent him a letter and some literature. I should be glad to do something more to support and encourage him if I could think of any- thing to do. Can you suggest anything? He has been receiving a free copy of the "Woman's Column" for a good while, and I suspect it was that which put it into his head. Senator Inger, who as also been receiving a free copy for some time, writes me that he is going to introduce a similar amendment in Alabama.

That meeting at Cornell seems to have done a good deal of good. A letter received today from Mrs. Davis of Ithaca says she has already obtained twenty- five subscribers for the "Woman's Column" and expects to get as many more.

Thank you for the item about Mrs. Neymann[?]. We have had the one about her daughter. There has been nothing very recent heard from Iowa, but at last account Mrs. Baily of Dunlap was pushing the work with the greatest energy.

Alice Stone Blackwell to Isabell Howland, December 16, 1892, Isabel Howland Papers, Sophia Smith Collection, *Smith College.*

A day or two ago we celebrated for the first time "Foremothers' Day." For a long time men have been commemorating, as each December rolled round, "Forefathers' Day." Mrs. Davereux Blake had the happy idea of suggesting that we do the same thing for the Pilgrim Mothers. So we did it, and did it with success. Two hundred ladies, many of whom were descendants of old and distinguished families, sat down at the tables in a large dining hall, which was handsomely decorated with evergreens. The speeches were good, Mrs. Beecher-Hooker and Anna Shaw being particularly pointed and humorous. Mrs. Blake, who presided, did well. I also spoke. It is remarkable that nearly three centuries should have passed before women ever thought of celebrating their own landing on the Rock. Henceforth Foremothers' Day should be the feature of this eventful December season. I tried to scatter through my address humor as well as wisdom. Of the former quality, I gave this: "From the *Mayflower* we hear much of Elder Brewster and his eloquence in exhortation, but nothing of Mrs. Brew- ster and her twelve children, shut up in a slow sailing vessel, nursing them, no doubt, through chickenpox, whooping cough, and the measles, for the little ones always choose the most inopportune moments to indulge in these popular infantile diseases. It is safe to assume that while Mother Brewster watched night and day over the young fry, the good Elder sat com- fortably on deck during the waking hours, enjoying his pipe, while at night he slept midst pleasant dreams in his berth." This sally at the expense of the ruling elder was warmly applauded.

Elizabeth Cady Stanton, diary entry, December 25, 1892, in Stanton and Blatch, Elizabeth Cady Stanton, *Vol. 2, 290–291.*

11

End of an Era
1893–1906

THE HISTORICAL CONTEXT

As the 19th century ended and the 20th began, the women's rights leaders could claim progress. In 1848 the signatories of the Declaration of Rights and Sentiments had resolved to change the status of women in specific ways. Their goals for women included an acknowledgment of the rights to speak in public, testify in court, and preach from the pulpit, access to equal education, the continuation of civil existence after marriage, control of personal wages and property, legal

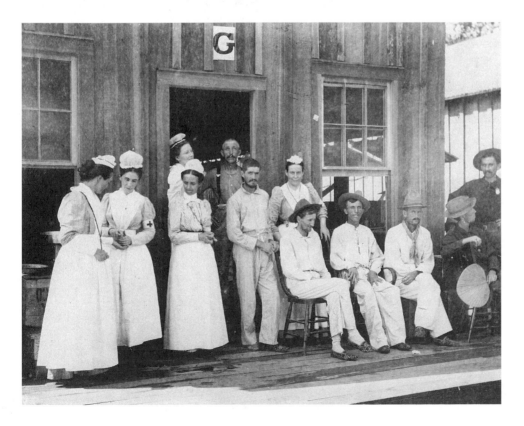

One of the few occupations open to women in the 19th century was nursing. Here Spanish-American War nurses care for their patients at Camp Chickamauga, Georgia, 1898. *(National Archives)*

265

custody of children, entrance into the professions, and suffrage. At that time no state granted any one of these rights to women. In 1900, 52 years later, not one state denied them all.[1]

Educational opportunities had certainly increased. In 1831 young Elizabeth Cady was one of the few girls in her high school class. Now, in 1900, 58.36 percent of the country's high school enrollment was female.[2] No Massachusetts woman graduated from college before Lucy Stone in 1847. Now there were 40,000 U.S. women enrolled in college and 30,000 college alumnae.[3]

Women's hopes for gainful employment and control of their earnings were beginning to be realized as well. In 1900 more than 3 million women worked for wages in positions other than that of domestic servant:[4] 431,153 women had entered the professions; 503,574 had entered the trades; 1,315,890 worked in manufacturing; and 980,025 farmed.[5] In two-thirds of the states, the married of these women now owned their own wages; in three-fourths, they were now able to own and manage property separate from their husbands.[6]

The family, with its "hoary sanction of antiquity," had been particularly resistant to change. In 39 states and territories, fathers still had "sole custody and control of the persons, education, earnings and estates of minor children."[7] When drawing up a will in several of these states, a father could still name someone other than a child's mother as the guardian of that child—and in each of these states he could do so even while the woman was still pregnant.[8] But in nine states—Washington, New York, Nebraska, Massachusetts, Maine, Kansas, Illinois, Connecticut, and Colorado—and in the District of Columbia as well—mothers now shared equal guardianship rights with fathers.[9]

The right of suffrage was proving the most difficult to secure. As of 1900 women had full suffrage in four states—Wyoming, Utah, Colorado, and Idaho.

Women's employment *(Library of Congress)*

Women in Kansas had been able to vote on municipal matters since 1887, and school suffrage existed in 26 other states and territories as well (this last right, however, was constantly challenged in the courts and denied at the polls).[10] Still, it was becoming clear to the women's rights leaders that they themselves would not live to vote legally. In 1893 Elizabeth Cady Stanton finally conceded to her diary, ". . . we are sowing winter wheat, which the coming spring will see sprout and which other hands than ours will reap and enjoy."[11]

A review of these years must also include another fact: A number of Southern women had begun to exploit racism in their pursuit of women's suffrage, and the NAWSA and its leaders, despite reservations expressed in private correspondence, did not intervene. Southern suffragists wished to enfranchise only those women who were literate or educated taxpayers, which they expected would permit many white women to vote, but prevent most African-American women from casting a ballot. Such a strategy, they assured Southern men, would add only white votes to the final tallies and "insure white supremacy."[12]

This was not generally thought to be NAWSA's view; indeed, when NAWSA held its 1903 convention in New Orleans, a newspaper editorial voiced concern at NAWSA's history of open membership and "assailed the association because of its attitude on the race question."[13] NAWSA's national board of officers capitulated. Choosing to accommodate rather than reject racist views, the NAWSA board issued a public response in the same paper and stated that "[t]he doctrine of State's rights is recognized in [NAWSA's] national body."[14] It assured the people of New Orleans that "[l]ike every other national association [NAWSA] is made up of persons of all shades of opinion on the race question and on all other questions except those relating to its particular object. The northern and western members hold the views on the race question that are customary in their sections; the southern members hold the views that are customary in the South . . . and each auxiliary State association arranges its own ideas and in harmony with the customs of its own section."[15] The custom of the Southern section was to exclude African-American women, a practice the national board left unquestioned. The board assured Southerners that "[t]o advise southern women to beware of lending 'sympathy or support' to the National Association because its auxiliary societies in the northern states hold the usual views of northerners on the color question, is as irrelevant as to advise them to beware of the National Woman's Christian Temperance Union because in the northern and western States it draws no color line."[16]

While in New Orleans, Susan B. Anthony, Elizabeth Blackwell, and Elizabeth Smith Miller eagerly accepted an invitation to address the members of the Phillis Wheatley Club, an African-American women's literary and social service club headed by Sylvanie Williams.[17] Letters written by two NAWSA presidents—Susan B. Anthony, writing several years before the New Orleans convention, and Anna Howard Shaw, writing afterward[18]—also indicate that they were not in personal sympathy with the views of the Southern suffragists. That the national leadership may have held different views than the Southern suffragists does nothing, however, to diminish the impact of the board's decisions in New Orleans.

As the century neared its end, the three most prominent early suffrage leaders approached the end of their lives. Lucy Stone suffered illness during

Elizabeth Cady Stanton wrote *The Woman's Bible*. *(Library of Congress)*

much of her last decade. She had been able to campaign with Henry Blackwell throughout Nebraska in 1880 and Rhode Island in 1885, but by the time of the 1889 campaigns in North Dakota and Montana, Henry Blackwell was campaigning alone. Lucy Stone died on October 18, 1893, at the age of 75.

Elizabeth Cady Stanton began to go blind near the end of her life. Her mental abilities were in no way impaired, however, and she never lost her gift for causing controversy.

Although she had hoped for the union of the National and American Woman Suffrage Associations, she had also worried that the merged organization would lack flexibility. When she received the proposed constitution, she wrote, "One would think it was written to hedge in a pack of foxes. I ask Susan what is the matter with our little old constitution, which we simple-minded women drew up back I do not know when?"[19] After 23 years of service as president, first of the National, then of the National American Woman Suffrage Association (NAWSA), she resigned in 1892. "I am a leader of thought rather than of numbers," she wrote to her friend Olympia Brown, ". . . I would rather be a free-lance article . . . than to speak as president of an Association."[20]

In her letter to Brown, she also commented that "The . . . Association has been growing conservative for some time. Lucy and Susan alike see suffrage only. They do not see woman's religious and social bondage, neither do the young women."[21] In 1895 Stanton found out just how correct that assessment had been.

In that year, Stanton published volume 1 of *The Woman's Bible*. She had long been convinced that religious teachings were a root cause of the prejudice against women. She hoped this work—a critical examination of the Bible's depiction of women—would help "exonerate the snake, [and] emancipate the woman."[22] The young suffragists she had left behind in the NAWSA were outraged. Convinced that the radical nature of *The Woman's Bible* would damage the suffrage cause, they demanded that the national association publicly repudiate the book. Susan B. Anthony, who had succeeded Stanton as president, pleaded with the members not to vote for such a resolution. She was unable to sway the younger women, however, and Stanton found herself censured by the very organization she had founded. Angry but undeterred, she began work on volume 2 of *The Woman's Bible*.

The last letter Stanton dictated was to President Theodore Roosevelt, asking him to support the federal woman suffrage amendment. She died on October 26, 1902, at the age of 86.

Susan B. Anthony continued to work for suffrage until the end of her life. In 1895, when 75 years old, she spoke in Santa Monica, San Diego, Pomona, Pasadena, Riverside, Los Angeles, San Jose, Yosemite, Palo Alto, San Francisco, Salt Lake City, Cheyenne, Denver, St. Louis, Washington, D.C., Atlanta, and in parts of Louisiana, Tennessee and Kentucky—all within six months.[23] At the end of this tour, she returned to Rochester to rest briefly and then set out to Lakeside, Ohio. There, standing before a large crowd of her supporters, she collapsed. It was, she said, "the whole of me coming to a sudden stand-still like a clap of thunder under a clear sky."[24]

By the end of the year, Anthony had recovered from what the doctors termed "nervous prostration." She attended Stanton's 80th birthday celebration in November 1895, and then she returned to work. She spent 1896 in California, working for suffrage during that state's referendum. (Women's suffrage was defeated.) She also worked closely with the younger women in the National American Woman Suffrage Association, even after their resolution against *The Woman's Bible;* she was rewarded with the knowledge that, upon her retirement, the organization would be left in the hands of her able "lieutenants" and her devoted, would-be "nieces."

In 1900 Anthony resigned as president of the National American Woman Suffrage Association. She did not wish to die in office, she explained to her disappointed followers; she preferred "to see you all at work while I am alive, so I can scold you if you do not do it well." She also told them: "Give the matter of selecting your officers serious thought. Consider who will do the best work for the political enfranchisement of women and let no personal feelings enter into the question." Carrie Chapman Catt was the woman elected.

Although Catt said she would not be able to be the "leader Miss Anthony has been," but "only an officer of this association," she served ably and well for four years.[25] In 1904, when her husband became ill, Catt resigned in order to care for him. (She would be reelected NAWSA's president in 1915.)

The Reverend Anna Howard Shaw, a gifted orator and one of Anthony's closest friends, became president of the National American Woman Suffrage

Susan Brownell Anthony won adulation late in life.
(Library of Congress)

Association upon Catt's retirement. On March 13, 1906, the day of Anthony's death, Shaw was at her bedside. "Anna," Anthony said, "if there is a continuance of life beyond, and if I have any conscious knowledge of this world and of what you are doing, I shall not be far away from you; and in times of need I will help you all I can."[26]

Anthony, the woman who had been called "Aunt Susan," died at the age of 86. The suffrage movement had come to the end of an era.

CHRONICLE OF EVENTS

1893

Radcliffe (Harvard University's women's college) is chartered.

International Council of Women meets for the second time.

Lillian D. Wald and Mary Brewster found New York City's Henry Street Settlement, which eventually becomes the nation's first visiting nurse organization.

Colorado is the first state to adopt a state referendum giving women the vote.

Congress of the International Council of Women meets for the second time.

Mary Eileen Ahern becomes librarian of the state of Indiana.

Hannah Greencbaum Solomon establishes the first assembly of Jewish women in America.

June 27: Gertrude Hickman Thompson is named as the first woman to lead the board of directors of a U.S. railroad.

October 18: Lucy Stone dies.

October 20: President Grover Cleveland dedicates the first monument to a woman in the United States. The monument is placed over the grave of Martha Ball Washington, the mother of President George Washington.

1894

Kansas holds state referendum; women's suffrage is defeated.

New York State Constitution revised; women's suffrage is not included in new state constitution.

House of Representatives committee issues adverse minority report on federal woman's suffrage amendment.

The Boston *Woman's Era,* a monthly newspaper devoted to publishing the work of "representative colored women" from all parts of the United States, is founded; Josephine St. Pierre Ruffin is editor.

Ohio gives women the right to vote for members of the boards of education.

Mary McDowell is invited by University of Chicago faculty members to direct the University of Chicago Settlement, which assists working-class immigrants.

Dr. Mary Putnam-Jacobi publishes the pamphlet "Common Sense Applied to Woman Suffrage" refuting the "scientific" idea that women's bodies make them unsuitable for voting.

Charlotte Scott is the first woman elected to the council of the American Mathematical Society (AMS).

February 14: Lawyer Myra Bradwell dies.

1895

National Federation of Afro-American Women founded.

An auxiliary of the National American Woman Suffrage Association is formed in Oklahoma.

Hull-House Maps and Papers, about conditions in the 19th Ward of Chicago, is published and becomes a landmark study.

The first request for women's suffrage in Georgia is put before the state legislature. After this date women put before the legislature bills requesting that the age of protection for girls be raised from 10 years; the prevention of employment of children in factories under age 10 or 12; that women be allowed on boards of education; that colleges open their doors to women; and coguardianship of children. These are all defeated by large male majorities.

Elizabeth Cady Stanton publishes the first volume of *The Woman's Bible,* a critical examination of biblical passages that diminish women.

November 5: Utah adopts its state constitution, which includes women's suffrage.

1896

California holds state referendum; at Susan B. Anthony's request, Frances Willard does not hold the Woman's Christian Temperance Union's convention there, but women's suffrage is nonetheless defeated.

Susan B. Anthony constitutional amendment for women's suffrage is introduced; it will not be introduced again until 1913.

Senate committee issues favorable majority report on federal women's suffrage amendment.

Utah is admitted to statehood; its women are enfranchised under the new state's constitution.

National Association of Colored Women is founded, merging the National Federation of Afro-American Women and the Colored Women's League of Washington.

The Louisiana State Suffrage Association is formed by the union of the Portia and Era clubs.

Ida Hyde, working at the Harvard Medical School, is the first woman to perform medical research.

Reverend Anna Howard Shaw secures the passage of a resolution disassociating the National American Woman Suffrage Association from *The Woman's Bible,* published by its former president, Elizabeth Cady Stanton.

May: Mary Eileen Ahern, new editor of *Public Libraries,* supervises its first issue, acquainting new libraries with the Dewey Decimal System.

1897

The first bill for woman suffrage in North Carolina is introduced by Senator James L. Hyatt, Republican, of Yancey County. It is referred to the Committee on Insane Asylums.

Women of New Jersey lose their school suffrage.

Isabel Hampton Robb establishes the American Nurses' Association and is first president of the organization.

February 17: National Congress of Mothers founded in Washington, D.C., which eventually becomes the Parent-Teachers Association.

1898

Elizabeth Cady Stanton publishes the second volume of *The Woman's Bible.*

Anita Newcomb McGee is the first woman named assistant surgeon general in the U.S. Army.

Dorothy Reed (Mendenhall) is one of the first two women hired by a U.S. Navy hospital, working in the Brooklyn (New York) Navy Yard Hospital's operating room and bacteriological laboratories.

Women and Economics—arguing for independence for women—by Charlotte Perkins Gilman is published.

Mrs. Eliza Murphy of New Jersey dies, leaving $500 to the National American Woman Suffrage Association.

Mrs. A. Viola Neblett of South Carolina dies, leaving $500 to the National American Woman Suffrage Association.

February 17: Frances Willard dies.

April: The Spanish-American War breaks out. Clara Barton immediately volunteers to go to Cuba to supervise health services. More than 1,500 other women nurse Americans in Cuba, Puerto Rico, Hawaii, and the Philippines.

1899

The pregnant Mary Kenney braves a blizzard to address striking shoeworkers in Marlboro, Massachusetts.

Frances Willard, president of the National Women's Christian Temperance Union *(Library of Congress)*

Kate Chopin publishes *The Awakening,* an early feminist work about female sexuality.

The establishment of Chicago's first juvenile court is the result of lobbying by Jane Addams's Hull-House.

National Consumers' League is founded. Florence Kelley is president.

The first state convention of the Georgia suffrage society, auxiliary to the National American Woman Suffrage Association, is held. It remains active until one year after the passage of the Nineteenth Amendment.

For the first time, the U.S. Senate confirms the presidential appointment of a woman, Esther Reed, as national superintendent of Indian schools.

1900

Woman Suffrage Group at Radcliffe is founded by Maud Wood (later, Maud Wood Park).

General Federation of Women's Clubs refuses to accept Josephine St. Pierre Ruffin's credentials as delegate of the Era Club, an organization of black women.

Susan B. Anthony resigns the presidency of the National American Woman Suffrage Association, recommending Carrie Chapman Catt as her successor. Catt is elected president.

With the aid of Elizabeth Cady Stanton, Lillie Devereux Blake founds the National Legislative League.

Nannie Helen Burroughs's speech to the National Baptist Convention results in the formation of the Women's Convention, which becomes the largest African-American women's organization.

Carrie Chapman Catt testifies before the Senate Committee on Woman Suffrage, saying, "Ordinary fair play should compel every believer, no matter what are his views, on woman suffrage, to grant to women the easiest process of enfranchisement and that is the submission of a federal amendment."

The Alaska Territorial Legislature convenes in the spring and passes a woman suffrage bill by a two-thirds vote. However, the governor, Alexander O. Brodie, an appointee of President Theodore Roosevelt, vetoes it.

Sister Mary Alphonsa (Lathrop) is the founder of the first U.S. hospice unit for the care of terminally ill patients. Lathrop and an associate, Alice Huber, establish the Dominican Congregation of St. Rose of Lima, the Servants of Relief for Incurable Cancer.

Anna Carroll Moore is the first person to act as chair of the Children's Services Division of the American Library Association (ALA). The organization is first called the Club of Children's Librarians.

Florence R. Sabin is the first woman to graduate from the Johns Hopkins University School of Medicine. The first woman on staff at Johns Hopkins, her studies focus on the lymphatic system, blood cells, and blood vessels.

January 13: The first annual convention of the Alabama Equal Suffrage Association meets in Selma with 25 delegates from Selma, Birmingham, Huntsville, and Montgomery.

June 3: The International Ladies' Garment Workers' Union (ILGWU) is founded in New York City. It brings about new protective legislation for female workers and becomes an early example of the successful unionization of women.

July 5: Elizabeth Cohn, seconding William Jennings Bryan's nomination for president of the United States, becomes the first woman delegate to make a seconding speech at the Democratic National Convention.

September 1: Laura Clay, officer of the National American Woman Suffrage Association, comes to the Alaska Territory at her own expense to help organize women to support a suffrage amendment. Alaskan women do not support her and the women's suffrage bill that she introduces is defeated in both houses.

December 27: Carrying a hatchet, Carrie Nation destroys her first barroom in the Hotel Carey, in Wichita, Kansas, protesting the sale of liquor.

1901

The Boston Equal Suffrage Association for Good Government is founded in Massachusetts to draw support for the vote.

Maud Wood Park founds the College Equal Suffrage League in Massachusetts.

U.S. Army Nurse Corps is formed in the aftermath of the Spanish-American War.

Colorado makes its 1893 woman suffrage law a part of the state constitution.

Margaret Haley is the first woman to speak from the floor of the National Education Association meeting.

Maud Wood Park, founder of the College Equal Suffrage League in Massachusetts, 1901, and first president of the National League of Women Voters, 1920–25 *(National Archives)*

1902

Harriot Stanton Blatch returns to the United States after 20 years in England.

New Hampshire holds state referendum; women's suffrage is defeated.

Jane Addams publishes her first book, *Democracy and Social Ethics.*

Jessie Field (Shambaugh) establishes the organizations that become the 4-H Club.

New Hampshire holds a state referendum, but women's suffrage is defeated.

Ida Tarbell is the first woman "muckraker." She publishes "The Rise of the Standard Oil Company" in *McClure's Magazine.*

Susan B. Anthony and Ida Husted Harper publish Volume 4 of *The History of Woman Suffrage.*

May 28: Massachusetts passes the Equal Guardianship bill, allowing mothers, as well as fathers, to be guardians of their children.

October 26: Elizabeth Cady Stanton dies.

December 6: The first postage stamp with a woman's likeness—that of Martha Washington—is printed.

1903

Reporter Winifred Sweet Black (Bonfils), whose pen name is Annie Laurie, becomes the first woman to cover a prizefight.

Margaret Dreier Robins founds the National Women's Trade Union League. Mary Kimball Kehew is named its first president and remains in the position for one year.

Emily Dunning (Barringer) becomes the first woman ambulance surgeon.

The first women's local of the Jewish Socialist United Cloth Hat and Cap Makers Union is organized by Rose Schneiderman.

July 28: Maggie Lena Walker becomes the nation's first African-American bank president, taking over the St. Luke Penny Savings Bank in Richmond, Virginia.

1904

Carrie Chapman Catt resigns as president of the National American Woman Suffrage Association; she begins to focus on suffrage efforts internationally.

Anna Howard Shaw is elected president of the National American Woman Suffrage Association.

Mary McLeod Bethune establishes what will become Bethune-Cookman College.

The first public trade school for girls is established in Boston, Massachusetts, with Florence M. Marshall serving as its first principal.

June: International Woman Suffrage Alliance meets in Berlin, Germany.

December 16: New York City's Majestic Theater becomes the first theater in the country to hire women ushers.

1905

Maud Malone establishes the Harlem Equal Rights League in New York City.

Mary Whiton Calkins (1863–1930) becomes the first woman to be elected president of the American Psychological Association.

June 21: Oregon meeting of the National American Woman Suffrage Association honors Sacagawea (Sacajawea).

April 17: The Supreme Court in *Locher v. the United States* makes one of the most controversial rulings in its history, postponing minimum wage laws for women. Later in the 20th century wage and price laws for women will be considered discriminatory.

November: At the age of 85, Susan B. Anthony travels to Washington, D.C., to ask President Theodore Roosevelt to support a federal suffrage amendment.

1906

Oregon holds state referendum; women's suffrage is defeated.

Mary Drier becomes president of the Women's Trade Union League.

The General Federation of Women's Clubs achieve a success in the passage of the Pure Food and Drug Act.

March 6: Nora Stanton Blatch (Barney) is the first woman to join the American Society of Civil Engineers.

March 13: Susan B. Anthony dies.

June 13: The first class at Simmons College graduates in Boston, Massachusetts.

August 11: Mary Miller becomes the first woman airship passenger at Franklin, Pennsylvania.

EYEWITNESS TESTIMONY

I wish that you & Alice could call Laura Johns & Mrs. Carrie Lane Chapman into a *Council of War.* If I understand aright Colorado votes *first* on the WS Const Amd. It is *very important* to carry Colorado & if that be impossible (of which I am not at all sure) then it is very important to get the largest possible vote . . . I suggest that Mrs. Johns & Mrs. Chapman confer with Mrs. Louise Tyler of Denver & work up Colorado *first of all.* Not merely by meetings, but by a quiet move on the newspaper press and the Labor Unions & Knights of Labor . . . Don't try to enlist the W.C.T.U. Let the Temperance question quietly alone.

Henry Blackwell, letter to Lucy Stone, May 21, 1893, in Wheeler, Loving Warriors, *350.*

. . . I think my working days are over . . . Be careful of yourself for Alice's sake. She will need you.

Lucy Stone, letter to Henry Blackwell, August 15, 1893, in Wheeler, Loving Warriors, *353.*

Caroline M. Severance called to-day. She is now living in California and says the woman suffrage cause is making slow but sure progress there. "I'm going in for the hundred," she said, smiling, "so as to vote before I die."

Elizabeth Cady Stanton, diary entry, October 6, 1893, in Stanton and Blatch, Elizabeth Cady Stanton, *Vol. 2, 298.*

My birthday. I am seventy-eight. Susan dined with us. She has been here for the past week to get me to write a plan of work for the New York campaign, and to get ready for the constitutional convention to be held in this state next May. We also prepared some resolutions for the Brooklyn convention. This plan of work and the resolutions will be printed as leaflets and other names signed to them, so that it will not be known that they are my composition. I have been doing this sort of thing for half a century.

Elizabeth Cady Stanton, diary entry, November 12, 1893, in Stanton and Blatch, Elizabeth Cady Stanton, *Vol. 2, 300.*

I have just had a long call from Mary Foster Fordham, of England, daughter of Walter Foster, M.P. She is full of enthusiasm about the suffrage. She was delighted at the news from Colorado, where women suffrage has just been carried by six thousand majority. "What a pity we cannot Colorado our English men," she exclaimed. Now we have full suffrage in two states. My soul rejoices. But how slowly the world moves.

Elizabeth Cady Stanton, diary entry, November 21, 1893, in Stanton and Blatch, Elizabeth Cady Stanton, *Vol. 2, 300–301.*

I vote, not because I am intelligent, not because I am moral, but solely and simply because I am a man.

Francis M. Scott, speaking against a proposed New York state women's suffrage amendment, July 1894, in Harper, Life and Work of Susan B. Anthony, *Vol. 2, 769.*

. . . the friends in the [New York State Constitutional] Con[vention] held a private meeting—& among them—they found there were 70 members ready to vote *for* submitting our amendment—The number needed is 88—No—I am not disappointed nor disheartened for myself—but I do feel very sorry for the thousands of new and young women who have had such strong hope of gaining our demand—I am used to having defeat every time—and know how to pick up and push on for another attack upon the enemy—

Susan B. Anthony, letter to Elizabeth Smith Miller, July 25, 1894, in the Smith Family Papers, Rare Books and Manuscripts Division, New York Public Library.

I am only a little school girl, but when I saw your picture in the paper your dear, kind face made me want to send you my best wishes on your birthday, and I hope you will see many more happy birthdays. My papa says you are one of the greatest women in the world and I know it must be so, for all good women and men seem to think so much of you. With best wishes I am your little friend . . .

Olive B. Dorsett, letter to Susan B. Anthony on her 75th birthday, February 15, 1895, in Harper, Life and Work of Susan B. Anthony, *Vol. 3, 1378.*

At my seventy-fifth birthday dinner, Ebbit House, Washington, D.C., February 15th, my loving and loved niece, Rachel Foster Avery, surprised and delighted me by the announcement that she had secured an $800 annuity for me, and now, a month later in her own lovely county home, she has read to me the names of the dear friends who contributed to the generous gift. Among them was yours and I hasten to thank you for this helping to lift me financially above the need of earning the necessary sum to meet my simple home expense.

For myself and my only surviving sister, Mary S. Anthony, who has ever made it possible for me to do and be for our good cause, I am most gratefully yours . . .

Susan B. Anthony, letter to Elizabeth Smith Miller, dictated March 10, 1895, dated and signed April 16, 1895, in the Smith Family Papers.

Your letter enclosing $10.00 is at hand. It will be applied to the May Benefit fund for the Sherwood Club. I thank you most cordially for it.

The news from California is indeed splendid. I really believe they will carry that state and we shall have Idaho too. We are almost sure to get through with our labors before we realize it. With California and Idaho carried, I am sure we shall have five or six states next year, and by the end of this Century I really we believe we shall find ourselves through. Won't that be glorious? Again thanking you for your generosity. . . .

Carrie Chapman Catt to Isabel Howland, May 19, 1895, marked "dictated" and signed in another's handwriting, Isabel Howland Papers, Sophia Smith Collection, Smith College.

Yesterday was my eightieth birthday and the event was widely celebrated. The scene in the Metropolitan Opera House was beautiful. Among those who came was Robert Collyer, who, in the most natural, spontaneous manner, kissed me on my forehead, such a kiss as only babies and grandmothers ever receive, an evanescent holy tribute, love for those supposed to need our protection. Nothing which has happened these past two days, so full of emotion to me, has touched me more deeply. I was particularly pleased with some friendly articles from the pen of Baroness Gripenberg, of Helsingfors, which appeared in the leading Finnish papers, and which I have had translated to me. But nothing caused me more pleasure, perhaps, mixed though it was with regret, than the ballot-box of onyx and silver sent me by the free women of Utah. It will not open, and ballots cannot penetrate to the interior. It is indeed a suggestive gift from the enfranchised of the far West to a political pariah of New York, and this beautiful heavy stone is as heavy as our hearts

Elizabeth Smith Miller was a lifelong financial supporter of the women's rights movement. *(Courtesy of the Seneca Falls Historical Society)*

when we think of our civic degradation. There it stands on my mantlepiece seemingly saying: "You have tried for fifty years to enter these sacred precincts, but may you not be condemned to try for fifty years to come." I have been affected to tears more than once during these days of triumph. Knowing myself, conscious of all my shortcomings, remembering how I have left undone so many things I should have done, I often feel myself unworthy these generous praises, the outpouring of so much love and friendship from so many unexpected sources. All this I cannot forget.

Elizabeth Cady Stanton, diary entry, November 13, 1895, in Stanton and Blatch, Elizabeth Cady Stanton, *Vol. 2, 314–315.*

So far as the operation of the law in this State is concerned, we were so well satisfied, with twenty years experience under the Territorial government, that it went into our constitution with but one dissenting vote, although many thought that such a section might result in its rejection by Congress. If it does nothing else it fulfils the theory of a true representative government, and in this State, at least, has resulted in none of the evils prophesied. It has not been the fruitful source of family disagreements feared. It has not lowered womanhood. Women do generally take advantage of the right to vote, and vote intelligently. It has been years since we have had trouble at the polls—quiet and order, in my opinion, being due to two causes, the presence of women and our efficient election laws. One important feature I might mention, and that is, in view of the woman vote, no party dare nominate notoriously immoral men, for fear of defeat by that vote. Regarding the adoption of the system in other States I see no reason why its operation should not be generally the same elsewhere as it is with us. It is surely true that after many year's experience, Wyoming would not be content to return to the old limits . . .

> *U.S. Senator Clarence D. Clark, of Wyoming, to the constitutional convention of Utah, 1895, in* History of Woman Suffrage, *Vol. 4, 1092.*

. . . the religious part has never been mine—you know I won't take it up—so long as the men who hold me in durance vile—won't care a dime what a Bible says—all they care for is what the saloon says.

> *Susan B. Anthony, letter to Elizabeth Cady Stanton, July 24, 1895, in Barry,* Susan B. Anthony, *309.*

5,000 words if still living, no limit, if dead.

> *Chicago newspaper's telegraphed instructions to its reporter, upon Susan B. Anthony's collapse, July 25, 1895, in Harper,* Life and Work of Susan B. Anthony, *308.*

I never realized how desolate the world would be to me without you until I heard of your sudden illness . . .

> *Elizabeth Cady Stanton, letter to Susan B. Anthony, July 1895, in Barry,* Susan B. Anthony, *308.*

In the necessity of the hour which compels me to use every possible means to raise money with which to complete the year's work, I come to you.

You know I am a crank on the subject of organization. I believe that we must lay everything aside and work to this end. I feel very sure that in two or three years, if we will but keep our shoulders to the wheel, we will have no trouble in raising the necessary money with which to keep our machinery going. I am very anxious that we should raise ten thousand dollars for organization next year, but, before that can be planned, we must raise the necessary amount to cover the expenses of this year. I have, therefore, adopted a suggestion given me of using the "chain" letters which have been so useful in many church and philanthropic societies. This will be a real test of the strength of the suffrage work.

I will ask you to start the chain for Western New York. I know how faithful you have been to this cause, and feel sure that you will render this assistance.

Susan B. Anthony devoted her life to fighting for women's suffrage. *(Library of Congress)*

Elizabeth Cady Stanton, shown here, and Susan B. Anthony met in 1851 and worked together for women's suffrage until their deaths. *(Library of Congress)*

If you can have a little oversight of the chain, it would be well for its interests.

Thanking you for may past favors. . . .

> *Carrie Chapman Catt to Isabel Howland, December 16, 1895, Isabel Howland Papers, Sophia Smith Collection, Smith College.*

Your letter of Dec. 11 is received only this morning, owing to you having accidentally addressed it to Boston, N.Y., instead of Boston, Mass. The notice shall go in next week.

What is the Albany paper most favorable to woman suffrage? Or, if the most widely circulated one is not favorable editorially, but is willing to publish communications on our side, perhaps it will be better for me to write to it about that Wyoming matter. You will observe that the anti-Wyoming leaflet got out by the Albany opponents is made up almost exclusively from people who do not live in Wyoming.

We have had a standing challenge for years inviting them to find two persons in all Wyoming who will assert over their own names and addresses that equal suffrage has had any bad results there. They have thus far failed to respond.

> *Alice Stone Blackwell to Isabel Howland, December 17, 189[5?], Isabel Howland Papers, Sophia Smith Collection, Smith College.*

. . . of [Mrs. Stanton's] Bible Commentaries, I am not proud—either of their spirit or letter.

> *Susan B. Anthony, to Clara Colby, December 18, 1895, in Barry*, Susan B. Anthony, *309.*

Your letter with $1.00 enclosed came in same mail with one from Mrs. Julia D. Sheppard with $1.00 also enclosed. Mrs. Osborne had not yet been heard from. Mrs. Shepperd sent your letter back to me saying she did not believe in the method [chain letters] and would not continue it. Several persons have written in this way. I am at a loss to know why they should object to it, unless it is because it has been used so long as to wear it out. I find it has been run into the ground in several places, and yet in all my experience I never received such a letter from anyone and did not know such things existed until it was suggested to me. Many thanks for your dollar. Our "chain" letters now amount to $16.00 in receipts.

> *Carrie Chapman Catt to Isabel Howland, December 27, 1895, marked "dictated" and signed in another's handwriting, Isabel Howland Papers, Sophia Smith Collection, Smith College.*

What you should do is to say to outsiders that a Christian has neither more nor less rights in our Association than an atheist. When our platform becomes too narrow for people of all creeds and of no creeds, I myself shall not stand upon it. Many things have been said and done by our orthodox friends that I have felt to be extremely harmful to our cause; but I should no more consent to a resolution denouncing them than I shall consent to this. Who is to draw the line? Who can tell now whether Mrs. Stanton's commentaries may not prove a great help to woman's emancipation from old superstitions that have barred her way? Lucretia Mott at first thought Mrs. Stanton had injured the cause of all woman's other rights by insisting upon the demand for suffrage, but she had sense enough not to bring a resolution against it. In 1860, when Mrs. Stanton made a speech before the New York Legislature in favor of a bill making drunkenness a cause for divorce, there was a general cry among the friends that she had killed the woman's cause. I shall be pained beyond expression if the delegates here are so narrow and illiberal as to adopt this resolution. You would better not begin resolving against individual action or you will find no limit. This year it is Mrs. Stanton; next year it may be me or one of yourselves who will be the victim.

. . . I pray you, vote for religious liberty, without censorship or inquisition. This resolution, adopted, will be a vote of censure upon a woman who is without a peer in intellectual and statesmanlike ability; one who has stood for half a century the acknowledged leader of progressive thought and demand in regard to all matters pertaining to the absolute freedom of women.

Susan B. Anthony, to assembly at the National American Woman Suffrage Association convention, January 28, 1896, in appendix to Stanton, The Woman's Bible, *Vol. 2, 216–217.*

A woman's brain evolves emotion rather than intellect; and whilst this feature fits her admirably as a creature burdened with the preservation and happiness of the human species, it painfully disqualifies her for the sterner duties to be performed by the intellectual faculties. The best wife and mother and sister would make the worst legislator, judge and police.

The excessive development of the emotional in her nervous system, ingrafts on the female organization, a neurotic or hysterical condition, which is the source of much of the female charm when it is kept within due restraints. In . . . moments of excitement . . . it is liable to explode in violent paroxysms . . . Every woman, therefore, carries this power of irregular, illogical and incongruous action; and no one can foretell when the explosion will come.

The Reverend Father Walsh, of Troy, New York, speaking at a "Mass Meeting" organized by the Anti-Women's Suffrage Association of Albany, New York, 1896, in Kraditor, The Ideas of the Woman Suffrage Movement, *20–21.*

Well—I am glad I went to Geneva and that we have had another chat over everything& everybody—not excluding Educated Suffrage—and now—while I plod on until my job is done—I do hope you will give your thought to saying your best word—the first session of the 50th Anniversary—of . . . the First organized demand of women for liberty—Seneca Falls July 19, 1848!! . . .

I feel sure you will be *inspired* for this occasion—this rounding out of your half-Century's magnificent utterances for Woman's Emancipation—perfect equality of rights in the State, the church, the home!—And I hope, too, that darling Harriot will be inspired to come over and help make the occasion glorious!

Susan B. Anthony, letter to Elizabeth Cady Stanton, September 7, 1897, in the Smith Family Papers, Rare Books and Manuscripts Division, New York Public Library.

My dear;—To yours of the 28th let me say, I would be delighted to have a representative of the colored race of the South speak at our Fiftieth Anniversary celebration and also before the Congressional committee.

I remember Miss Logan's letter and was very much pleased with it and if I *knew* she was a splendid speaker and would just make every one of the full Anglo-Saxon women feel ashamed of their race, I would hold up both hands for her to come to Washington next February. I would not on any account bring on our platform a woman who had a ten-thousanth part of a drop of African blood in her veins, who would prove an inferior speaker either as to matter or manner, because it would so militate against the colored race. Of course we have women in our society, the [Laura] Clays, Mrs. Young and lots of others who will come up from the south and the Congressmen and their wives in Washington who would be hopping mad if we brought colored women on our platform. We have always had Frederick Douglass and our Mrs. Harper but to bring right from the south a woman who would almost be an ex-slave, would vex them more than either of these they are accustomed to seeing. So I want to leave it to your judgment and knowledge, if you *know* she can write a speech strong in argument, beautiful in rhetoric, and can deliver it in a splendid fashion, then let me know, and bring her to Washington.

You see I do not in the slightest shrink from having a colored woman on the platform, but I do very much shrink from having an incompetent one, so unless you really *know* that Miss Logan is one who would astonish the natives, just let her wait until she is more cultured and can do the colored race the greatest possible credit.

There is another point from which I shrink and that is, it will take just so much more money out of your aunt Emily's pocket and just at this time when it seems impossible for us to get enough to pay our ordinary expenses we cannot promise to pay them and if somebody has to pay her expenses, that somebody will be Aunt Emily, but again I say if you and aunt Emily say Mrs. Logan *is the* woman and this convention is *the time,* let me know at your earliest convenience and we will give her a place on the programme. I have talked this over with Harriet and told her to tell you.

I am to be at the "May" celebration and maybe you, Aunt Emily, your father and mother will be down there so we can all talk this over to our hearts content.

Susan B. Anthony to Isabel Howland, signed "Susan B. Anthony (Per A.)" in another's handwriting, October 5, 1897, Isabel Howland Papers, Sophia Smith Collection, Smith College.

I have read the comments of Miss Putman on my failure to call out the descendants of Frederick Douglass at the Pioneers Session in Washington. We had had his grandson playing the violin for us and he received a most cordial encore, and I failed to discern any of them on the platform or in the audience. I had especially asked the children and grandchildren, nieces and nephews of all pioneers, to come to the platform, but very few of them did so, hence I was obliged to depend on my short sight to catch those whom I knew scattered through the audience. As I began reading Miss Putnam, I supposed she was going to criticise me because I did not give my consent for Mrs. Douglass to have an hour at the evening session to present the horrors of the chain-gangs of the South. I refused her request because I felt that we were not assembled to right the wrongs of the Negroes South, or the white boys and girls of the North, and most of all because no person on the program had over thirty minutes . . .

Miss Putnam, like so many of the women interested in all the different reforms, makes the blunder of supposing that our suffrage associations are to take up and protest against everything wrong in the country and the world, whereas our one business is to demand of our government, State, and National, the right to have their opinions counted at the ballot-box on every one of the different questions brought there.

Susan B. Anthony, letter to Elizabeth Smith Miller, May 30, 1898, in the Smith Family Papers, Rare Books and Manuscripts Division, New York Public Library.

As my eyes grow dimmer from day to day, my intellectual vision grows clearer. But I have written Susan not to lay out any more work for me, but to call on our younger coadjutors to write the letters to senators and congressmen. Say to them, I write, that "it requires no courage now to talk suffrage; they should demand equality everywhere . . ."

Elizabeth Cady Stanton, diary entry, February 4, 1899, in Stanton and Blatch, Elizabeth Cady Stanton, *Vol. 2, 337–338.*

Miss Susan B. Anthony, we are very much more than pleased to observe, is again before the footlights. We had sighed for Susan through the many long and weary moons of her beautiful silence—for of all the beautiful things about Susan her silence is the most artistically and acceptably beautiful—even as the heart panteth after the brook . . . But, behold! she hath arisen, and she returns to the old warpath with a pair of sound lungs and a healthy and well-developed desire to see her name in print, and reengages in the crusade against her hideous former foe, the bifurcated beast, the braggart brute, the miserable and melodramatic monster—Man. Madly she snatches the veil from the face of her maidenly reserve, launches the gunboat of her vengeance, uncorks the bottle of her wrath, and goes after this heinous wretch in a way that would make doughty Aguinaldo himself quake with perceptible fear and arouse a flame of admiration in the breast of Colonel Quixote sufficient to justify the calling of the fire department. Yes, Susan is on tap with a vengeance, and the slight, spare-made tyrant who has lorded it so long over her oppressed and unfortunate sex would do well to take wings and fly to tall timber—for Susan is an avenger worthy of note.

Memphis Scimitar (Tennessee), editorial remarks about Susan B. Anthony, reprinted on the editorial page of the Birmingham News (Alabama), February 11, 1899, in Harper, Life and Work of Susan B. Anthony, *Vol. 3, 1,124–1,125.*

My dear girl—Your note of Sunday is here this morning. The day for the political study question is

Thursday, Nov. 9th, at 3 o'clock P! M., so do not fail to be on hand. Miss Shaw will be here with us and there will be a corner for you if you will put up with the wee bed room. I know you would like to be with her, and still I know that Mrs. Greenleaf will claim you. They are still at the lake, and I hope enjoying this delightful weather. . . .

Your resolution is very much improved from that formed by the Warren lawyer. I am in receipt of a nice letter from Mrs. Osborn this morning. I suppose you will attend the Cayuga County Convention which is to be held at Auburn. She invites me over, but she does not tell me when it is going to be, and I do not see how I can go, although I should like to be present; but it is pleasant to be with them in spirit, and also every other convention as the friends assemble from day to day.

My refractory wisdom tooth is behaving itself quite well, and I trust will not make itself manifest again for a long time, but it does make me feel so mean to have a tooth growling in my jaw bone.

Give your mother my best love, your father also, and your brother, and believe me ever, always, Affectionately yours.

Susan B. Anthony to Harriet May Mills, October 17,
1899, Isabel Howland Papers, Sophia Smith Collection,
Smith College.

Susan writes asking me to put on paper what I think ought to be done by our national association at its next meeting. So I have replied as follows: . . .

1. A resolution should be passed in favor of establishing a new government in Hawaii. It is a disgrace to the civilization of the nineteenth century to make that island a male oligarchy.

2. We should protest in clarion tones against the proposal by railroad kings to turn women out of all the positions which they hold in the North Western Railroad, especially as it is generally admitted that they have given faithful service.

3. We should discuss and pass a resolution against the proposition of the Knights of Labor to remove women from all factories and industries which take them from home. If these gentlemen propose to provide every woman with a strong right arm on which she may lean until she reaches the other side of Jordon; a robust generous man pledged to feed, clothe and shelter the woman and her children to the end of life; a husband or brother sure not to die or default on the

way—why then this proposal might be worthy of woman's consideration. But as long as she is often forced to be the breadwinner for herself, husband, and children, it would be suicidal for her to retire to the privacy of home and with folded hands wait for the salvation of the Lord. There is an immense amount of sentimental nonsense talked about the isolated home. This is evident when we see what it really means for the mass of the human family. For Deacon Jones, a millionaire surrounded with every luxury, no material change may be desireable. But for a poor farmer with wife and child in the solitude of a prairie home, a co-operative household with society would be inestimable blessing. Woman's work can never be properly organized in the isolated home. One woman cannot fill all the duties as housekeeper, cook, laundress, nurse, and educator of her children. Therefore we should oppose all sly moves to chain woman in the home.

4. To my mind, our Association cannot be too broad. Suffrage involves every basic principle of republican government, all our social, civil, religious, educational, and political rights. It is therefore germane to our platform to discuss every invidious distinction of sex in the college, home, trades, and professions, in literature, sacred and profane, in the canon as well as in the civil law. At the inauguration of our movement, we numbered in our Declaration of Rights eighteen grievances covering the whole range of human experience. On none of these did we talk with bated breath. Note the radical claims we made, and think how the world responded. Colleges were built for women, and many of the older male colleges opened their doors to our sex. Laws were modified in our favor. The professions were thrown open to us. In short, in response to our radicalism, the bulwarks of the enemy fell as never since. At that time you gave on many occasions a radical lecture on social purity. I was responsible for an equally advanced one on marriage and divorce. Lucretia Mott was not less outspoken on theological questions. But at present our association has so narrowed its platform for reasons of policy and propriety that our conventions have ceased to point the way . . .

Elizabeth Cady Stanton, diary entry, December 3,
1899, in Stanton and Blatch,
Elizabeth Cady Stanton, Vol. 2, 345–346.

I wish you could realize with what joy and relief I retire from the presidency. I want to say this to you while I am yet alive—and I am good for another decade—as long as my name stands at the head I am Yankee enough to feel that I must watch every potato which goes into the dinner pot and supervise every detail of the work. For the four years since I fixed my date to retire I have constantly been saying to myself, "Let go, let go." I am now going to let go of the machinery but not of the spiritual part. I expect to do more work for woman suffrage in the next decade than ever before. I have not been for nearly fifty years in this movement without gaining a certain "notoriety" at least, and this enables me to get a hearing before the annual conventions of many great national bodies and to urge on them the passage of resolutions asking Congress to submit to the State legislatures a Sixteenth Amendment to the Federal Constitution forbidding disfranchisement on account of sex. This is a part of the work to which I mean to devote myself henceforward. Then you all know about the big fund which I am going to raise so that you young women may have an assured income for the work and not have to spend the most of your time begging money, as I have had to do.

Susan B. Anthony, resignation speech, February 1900, in Harper, Life and Work of Susan B. Anthony, *Vol. 3, 1170–1171.*

Good friends, I should hardly be human if I did not feel gratitude and appreciation for the confidence you have shown me; but I feel the honor of the position much less than its responsibility. I never was an aspirant for it. I consented only six weeks ago to stand. I was not willing to be the next president after Miss Anthony. I have known that there was a general loyalty to her which could not be given to any younger worker. Since Miss Anthony announced her intention to retire, there have been editorials in many leading papers expressing approval of her—but not of the cause. She has been much larger than our association. The papers have spoken of the new president as Miss Anthony's successor. Miss Anthony never will have a successor.

A president chosen from the younger generation is on a level with the association, and it might suffer in consequence of Miss Anthony's retirement if we did not still have her to counsel and advise us. I pledge you whatever ability God has given me, but I can not do this work alone. The cause has got beyond where one woman can do the whole. I shall not be its

leader as Miss Anthony has been; I shall be only an officer of this association. I will do all I can, but I can not do it without the co-operation of each of you. The responsibility much overbalances the honor, and I hope you will all help me bear the burden.

Carrie Chapman Catt, upon her election as president of the National American Woman Suffrage Association, February 1900, in History of Woman Suffrage, *Vol. 4, 388.*

Miss Susan B. Anthony has resigned. The woman who for the greater part of her life has been the star that guided the National Woman Suffrage Association through all of its vicissitudes until it stands today a living monument to her wonderful mental and physical ability, has turned over the leadership to younger minds and hands, not because this great woman feels that she is no longer capable of exercising it, but because she has a still larger work to accomplish before her life's labors are at an end. In a speech which was characteristic of one who has done so much toward the uplifting of her sex, Miss Anthony tendered her resignation during the preliminary meeting of the executive committee, held last night at the headquarters in the parlors of the Riggs House.

Although Miss Anthony had positively stated that she would resign in 1900, there were many of those present who were visibly shocked when she announced that she was about to relinquish her position as president of the association. In the instant hush which followed this statement a sorrow settled over the countenances of the fifty women seated about the room who love and venerate Miss Anthony so much . . . Life-long members of the association, who had toiled and struggled by her side, could not restrain their emotions and wept in spite of their efforts at self-control.

Washington Post, *account of the resignation of Susan B. Anthony from the presidency of the National American Woman Suffrage Association, February 8, 1900, in* Harper, Life and Work of Susan B. Anthony, *Vol. 3, 1170–1171.*

How can you expect me to say a word? And yet I must speak. I have received letters and telegrams from all over the world, but the one that has touched me most is a simple note which came from an old home of slavery, from a woman off whose hands and feet the shackles fell nearly forty years ago. That letter, my

Carrie Chapman Catt *(Library of Congress)*

friends, contained eighty cents—one penny for every year. It was all this aged person had . . .

Susan B. Anthony, speaking to those gathered for her 80th birthday celebration, February 15, 1900, in Harper, Life and Work of Susan B. Anthony, *Vol. 3, 1187–1188.*

It is undeniable that Miss Anthony has missed wifehood and motherhood, and in summing up a woman's life it is only fair that we should count the things she has missed along with the things she has gained. Miss Anthony has gained the love and reverence of millions of people now living and of millions

yet to be, but then she has never known the unspeakable bliss of nursing a family of children through the measles, whooping cough and mumps. She has lived a useful and perfectly unselfish life, but she doesn't know a thing in the world about the supreme happiness that lies in being housekeeper, cook, chambermaid, nurse, seamstress, hostess and half-a-dozen other things every day in the year till nervous prostration puts an end to the complicated business.

She has stood on a thousand platforms and listened to the applause of vast audiences, but she doesn't know the glory and honor there is in picking up a bucket of hot water and climbing a step ladder to wash the doors and windows. All the joy and rapture of housecleaning in the beautiful month of May are as a sealed book to her. She has made the life of womankind broader, deeper and higher than women ever dreamed it could be, but she has no conception of the breadth, depth and height of satisfaction to be found in nursing a baby through "three-months-colic."

She has made the world over but she is ignorant of the abandon of joy a woman feels when she makes over an old dress for the third time and then sees John start off on his summer fishing trip. She has been free and independent always and the women who are happier for her work will see that she never lacks for any good thing, but alas, she has never known the ecstasy of asking John for ten cents to pay street-car fare and she has never experienced the bliss of hearing him growl about the price of her Easter bonnet and groan over the monthly grocery bill. Here the "element of tragedy" looms up very large indeed.

It is said that on Miss Anthony's last birthday anniversary she received 3,000 letters congratulatory of the things she has gained in her eighty years of life. But there are wives and mothers who would cheerfully and heartily write her 300,000 more letters congratulatory of the things she has missed.

Cleveland Leader (Ohio), editorial on the occasion of Susan B. Anthony's 80th birthday, February 15, 1900, in Harper, Life and Work of Susan B. Anthony, *Vol. 3, 1190–1191.*

There is not a political party in the State that will ever dare to insert in its platform an anti-suffrage plank; for it must not be forgotten that upon this question the voting power of the women would equal that of the men. It is no more likely that the women of Colorado will ever be disfranchised than that the men will be.

Horace M. Hale, former president of Colorado State University, 1901, in History of Woman Suffrage, *Vol. 4, 1087.*

Woman suffrage has been in operation in Idaho for over four years and there have been no alarming or disastrous results. I think most people in the State, looking over the past objections to the extension of the right of suffrage, are now somewhat surprised that any were every made.

S. H. Hays, former attorney general of Idaho, in History of Woman Suffrage, *Vol. 4, 1088.*

I write to you because I believe you will listen to my appeal & in some way help me. I am a young Negro woman engaged in the practice of medicine in this city. I have made a pretty good practice, but mostly among the very poor & neglected districts. I have been quite ill for six weeks with La Grippe. I have not been able to make a single dollar. I cannot retain my place of business unless some one will help me. Rent is $12.00 per month & this place is the only one that can be had down town now. There are a great many forces operating against the success of the Negro in business. These, however, I hope someday will be overcome. The only thing that impedes my progress is that I am illy prepared in a financial way to contend when hardships & want come on.

I graduated from the Woman's Coll. of Penn. Phila. Class '97. Please help me in this my time of severe trial.

Dr. Eliza Anna Grier, letter to Susan B. Anthony, March 7, 1901, in Sterling, We Are Your Sisters, *447.*

My sympathies are very strong for all these women, but my purse is not equal to helping them financially. Cannot you suggest some way out of her troubles?

Susan B. Anthony, letter to the Woman's Medical College, enclosing Dr. Eliza A. Grier's letter of March 7, 1901, in Sterling, We Are Your Sisters, *447–448.*

I have promised Mrs. Sewall that I would beg money for her to establish headquarters at the Pan American Exposition next summer. You will receive a pamphlet containing a report of her work during the Paris Exposition, and also of the meeting of the Executive Committee held there.

I know that you will feel that it is a good work, and one that overlaps all others, for the hope of the world lies in the women of the different countries becoming acquainted with each other. I hope you will see that it is a good thing to be done and that you will send the $100 for you to become a patron of the International Council, which is equivalent to a life membership.

Susan B. Anthony, letter to Elizabeth Smith Miller, March 12, 1901, in the Smith Family Papers, Rare Books and Manuscripts Division, New York Public Library.

I shall be 80 next Feby.—but I am going to Rochester next month to Convention of the National Municipal League and hope to get in a few words on Woman in Municipal Government—this is our Bill in Legislature this year.

Isabella Beecher Hooker, letter to Olympia Brown, April 25, 1901, in Boydston, Kelley, and Margolis, The Limits of Sisterhood, *357.*

Rachel Foster Avery was corresponding secretary of the National American Woman Suffrage Association. *(Library of Congress)*

At the Minneapolis convention next month Mrs. Rachel Foster Avery will resign the office of corresponding secretary of our national organization, which she has held for almost twenty one years . . .

When I resigned the office in 1900, she begged to be allowed to retire with me, but I insisted that she should give one year of her experienced service to my successor. Now I have yielded to her appeal that she may devote her time and labors to her home and children . . .

Susan B. Anthony, letter to Elizabeth Smith Miller, May 1, 1901, in the Smith Family Papers, Rare Books and Manuscripts, Division, New York Public Library.

The passage of the Tax-Payers Bill is not altogether a blessing to the women who live in the cities and own property in the villages and towns. For instance; there is a Mrs. Curtis lives in this city whoes [sic] husband is a lawyer here. She spends six months of every year on the old family homestead at Cooksackie, so in order to vote she will have to declare her residence to be at Cooksackie and the law will not allow that her husband and she should have two residences. You will have to look into the law before you praise it too highly.

Susan B. Anthony, letter to Anne F. Miller, May 7, 1901, in the Smith Family Papers, Rare Books and Manuscripts Division, New York Public Library.

For one I am proud of Utah's record in dealing with her female citizens. I take the same pride in it that a good husband would who had treated his wife well, and I look forward with eager hope to the day when woman suffrage shall become universal.

Governor Herbert M. Wells, of Utah, 1902, in History of Woman Suffrage, Vol. 4, 1,089.

It is said that equal suffrage would make family discord. In Colorado our divorce laws are rather easy, though stricter than in the neighboring States, but since 1893, when suffrage was granted, I have never heard of a case where political differences were alleged as a cause for divorce or as the provoking cause of family discord. Equal suffrage, in my judgment, broadens the minds of both men and women. It has certainly given us in Colorado candidates of better character and higher class of officials. It is very true that husband and wife frequently vote alike—as the magnet draws the needle they go to the polls together. But women are not coerced. If a man were known to coerce his wife's vote I believe he would be ridden out of town on a rail with a coat of tar and feathers. Women's legal rights have been improved in Colorado since they obtained the ballot, and there are now no civil distinctions. Equal suffrage tends to make political affairs better, purer and more desirable for all who take part in them.

Senator Thomas M. Patterson, of Colorado, 1902, in History of Woman Suffrage, Vol. 4, 1,088.

I shall indeed be happy to spend with you November 12, the day on which you round out your four-score and seven, over four years ahead of me, but in age as in all else I follow you closely. It is fifty-one years since first we met and we have been busy through every one of them, stirring up the world to recognize the rights of women. The older we grow the more keenly we feel the humiliation of disfranchisement and the more vividly we realize its disadvantages in every department of life and most of all in the labor market.

We little dreamed when we began this contest, optimistic with the hope and buoyancy of youth, that half a century later we would be compelled to leave the finish of the battle to another generation of women. But our hearts are filled with joy to know that they enter upon this task equipped with a college education, with business experience, with the fully admitted right to speak in public—all of which were denied to women fifty years ago. They have practically but one point to gain—the suffrage: we had all. These strong, courageous, capable young women will take our place and complete our work. There is an army of them where we were but a handful. Ancient prejudice has become so softened, public sentiment so liberalized and women have so thoroughly demonstrated their ability to leave not a shadow of doubt that they will carry our cause to victory.

And we, dear, old friend, shall move on to the next sphere of existence—higher and larger, we cannot fail to believe, and one where women will not be placed in an inferior position but will be welcomed on a plane of perfect intellectual and spiritual equality.

Susan B. Anthony, letter to Elizabeth Cady Stanton, a few days before Stanton's death, 1902, in History of Woman Suffrage, Vol. 5, 741.

As you are the first President of the United States who has ever given a public opinion in favor of

During the early 1900s sewing was one of the few occupations open to African-American women. The workers in this garment factory are stitching men's coats, using power-driven sewing machines. *(National Archives)*

woman suffrage, and when Governor of New York State, recommended the measure in a message to the Legislature, the members of the different suffrage associations in the United States urge you to advocate in your coming message to Congress, an amendment to the National Constitution for the enfranchisement of American women, now denied their most sacred right as citizens of a Republic.

In the beginning of our nation, the fathers declared that "no just government can be founded without the consent of the governed," and that "taxation without representation is tyranny." Both of these grand declarations are denied in the present position of woman, who constitutes one-half of the people. If "political power inheres in the people"—and women are surely people—then there is a crying need for an amendment to the National Constitution, making these fundamental principles verities.

In a speech made by you at Fitchburg, on Labor Day, you say that you are "in favor of an amendment to the Constitution of the United States, conferring additional power upon the Federal Government to deal with corporations." To control and restrain giant monopolies for the best interests of all the people is of vast import, but of far vaster importance is the establishment and protection of the rights and liberties of one-half the citizens of the United States. Surely there is no greater monopoly than that of all men in denying to all women a voice in the laws they are compelled to obey.

Abraham Lincoln immortalized himself by the emancipation of four million Southern slaves. Speaking for my suffrage coadjutors, we now desire that you, Mr. President, who are already celebrated for so many honorable deeds and worthy utterances, immortalize yourself by bringing about the complete emancipation of thirty-six million women.

With best wishes for your continued honorable career and re-election as President of the United States.

Elizabeth Cady Stanton, letter to Theodore Roosevelt, dictated October 25, 1902, just 24 hours before her death, in Stanton and Blatch, Elizabeth Cady Stanton, *Vol. 2, 368–369.*

My—how I do miss Mrs. Stanton—to talk to her about everything and everybody—I wonder if Maggie and Hattie and Bob—miss her more and more as time rolls on—But for me time and no letters coming from week to week—no messages—all is silent!—Does Hattie write you now & then?—She hasn't written me but once since her mother's death—I hear that she has told Mrs. Catt that she will not go to the New Orleans Convention—I wrote her setting forth what I thought *good reasons* for her going—among them was that I thought she should be there & *represent her mother*—It will be the first Convention in our fifty years that *Mrs. Stanton* has *not been present either in person* or *by letter* . . .

Susan B. Anthony, letter to Elizabeth Smith Miller, December 29, 1902, in the Smith Family Papers, Rare Books and Manuscripts Division, New York Public Library.

You saw Hattie too, at Albany? How she did speak. She wrote me some time ago that she was not well, that the whole burden of setting up affairs came upon her.

Susan B. Anthony, letter to Elizabeth Smith Miller, February 4, 1903, in the Smith Family Papers, Rare Books and Manuscript Division, New York Public Library.

The association as such has no view on this subject. Like every other national association it is made up of persons of all shades of opinion on the race question and on all other questions except those relating to its particular object. The northern and western members hold the views on the race question that are customary in their sections; the southern members hold the views that are customary in the South. The doctrine of State's rights is recognized in the national body and each auxiliary State association arranges its own affairs in accordance with its own ideas and in harmony with the customs of its own section. Individual members in addresses made outside of the National Association are of course free to express their views on all sorts of extraneous questions but they speak for themselves as individuals and not for the association. . . .

The National American Woman Suffrage Association is seeking to do away with the requirements of a sex qualification for suffrage. What other qualifications shall be asked for it leaves to each State. The southern women most active in it have always in their own State emphasized the fact that granting suffrage to women who can read and write and who pay taxes would insure white supremacy without resorting to any methods of doubtful constitutionality. The Louisiana association asks for the ballot for educated and taxpaying women only and its officers believe that in this lies "the only permanent and honorable solution of the race question." . . .

The suffrage associations of the northern and western States ask for the ballot for all women, though Maine and several other states have lately asked for it with an educational or tax qualification. To advise southern women to beware of lending "sympathy or support" to the National Association because its auxiliary societies in the northern States hold the usual views of northerners on the color question is as irrelevant as to advise them to beware of the National Woman's Christian Temperance Union because in the northern and western States it draws no color line; or to beware of the General Federation of Women's Clubs because the State Federations of the North and West do not draw it; or to beware of Christianity because the churches in the North and West do not draw it.

Statement of the National American Woman Suffrage Association (NAWSA) board of officers, in rebuttal to a New Orleans Times-Democrat *editorial that characterized NAWSA as having "northern" views on race; printed in full in the* Times-Democrat, *March 1903, in* History of Woman Suffrage, *Vol. 5, 59.*

I am home again safe and sound as eighty-three can well be. I suppose Aunt Emily will not be home for some time. I left her and Harriet and Agnes at

Tuskegee. They were going to Mr. Ward's school and then to visit schools in Montgomery.

We had a splendid time at New Orleans. Women's speaking and their appearing in public seemed to be so novel that even men had to come out to gratify their curiosity. Hattie Mills will undoubtedly come up and tell you everything when she comes home. . . .

Tell your father he made a great mistake that he did not take you and go to New Orleans. It was such a splendid eye-opener. It did one good to see them look and listen to the words that were uttered by Miss Shaw, Mrs. Catt and others. We elected all the old officers and moved the headquarters to Warren, Ohio, so as to relieve Mrs. Catt entirely from office business. She is looking very thin and pale but she intends to go to Europe and take a real rest from everything.

Susan B. Anthony to Isabel Howland, April 6, 1903,
Isabel Howland Papers, Sophia Smith Collection,
Smith College.

The *school* suffrage Hearing was a weak affair I reckon—and the tax *paying* hearing ditto!!—The fact is all *fractional* suffrage is *weakness* itself—

Susan B. Anthony, letter to Elizabeth Smith Miller,
March 19, 1904, in the Smith Family Papers,
Rare Books and Manuscripts Division,
New York Public Library.

Your letter follows me to the Cape, where I have been spending ten days recruiting, and I assure you that I feel very much better from my out-door exercise, and the good, fresh air.

In regard to having a colored woman speak at the Convention, I have been intending to try to find one for I am as anxious as you possibly can be to have a representative from the colored woman upon our platform. I am, however, not going to try to get either Mrs. [Mary Church] Terrell or Mrs. Cook, for they have both spoken several times and I must confess that I am disappointed that they come to our Convention, when they are invited to speak, and sit on the platform and never do anything towards organizing the colored women, or in any way trying to help our work along. Both Mrs. Terrell and Mrs. Cook could do a great deal if they would, but neither of them have ever done anything in that direction. They do not feel themselves like joining the colored women,—and I do not blame them,—but that would not prevent them from organizing the colored

women and that would help them and encourage them in joining the Association. I am going to try to get a Miss (or Mrs., I do not know which) Anna Julia Cooper, who is the Principal of the High School in Washington; she is a very pleasant woman, and I think would make a good speech. In addition to her I shall try to get Mrs. Booker Washington, if I can, though I doubt very much if she would come. The fact of it all is, they do not want to do anything which they think would injure their school, and are no more willing to stand up for Suffrage in the South than the Southern women are to stand up for the colored people. I think that each race is a good deal alike, in that neither of them want to hurt themselves in the interest of any other reform; all are willing to suffer for righteousness' sake, provided somebody else besides ourselves is doing the suffering. This cannot be said of you, however, or of other individuals among either the black or white race, but it is true of us as a whole. However, I shall do my best to have the colored woman represented. I wish I could get a Japanese and a Chinese on the platform; I would like to have a representative there from all the races.

Thank you for writing me on the subject. . . .

Anna Howard Shaw to Isabel Howland, September 26,
1905, Isabel Howland Papers, Sophia Smith Collection,
Smith College.

Hattie is a very brilliant women, but she lacks something of being a person to *draw to her the masses of the people.* Just what it is I am not able to discover. With all her ability and seeming wish to help the cause, it is such a pity that we cannot have her utilized in our movement.

Susan B. Anthony, letter to Elizabeth Smith Miller,
October 27, 1904, in the Smith Family Papers,
Rare Books and Manuscripts Division,
New York Public Library.

I have before me your letter of Nov. 12th. You have doubtless heard of my break-down in Philadelphia, so that I did not get home until after Dec. 1st . . .

I am very glad that you are thinking of going to Baltimore. The prospects are that we shall have a good convention.

Susan B. Anthony, letter to Mrs. Eliza Wright Osborn,
December 13, 1905, in the Smith Family Papers,
Rare Books and Manuscripts Division,
New York Public Library.

I remember so well your early meetings in Washington which were all so new to me, a Western girl, ignorant and timid, with a moral courage wavering because undeveloped, but from that time steadily you developed it and gave me a strength invaluable ever since. With every convention, as the years went by; I realized more and more that I owed everything to you and your teachings—everything which helped me to grow, to lift myself to a broader plane of self-support, to a higher sense of the dignity of labor—self-respecting and respected by others. It is due to you that I am what I am—not much perhaps but never lacking in moral courage, in truth, in sense of justice. You know my work in the newspaper world, but you do not know how I turned from the aimless life of fashionable people once a year when you came, and Mrs. Stanton, Lucy Stone and the other great leaders with the convention. It seemed as pure and fresh and strengthening as a mountain stream after a murky pond.

Janet Jennings, journalist, letter to Susan B. Anthony, Winter 1905–6, in Harper, Life and Work of Susan B. Anthony, *Vol. 3, 1454.*

I am glad to tell you that Aunt Susan is better, although she is quite weak and will of course have to be just as careful as it is possible for a sick person to be. She is having the best of care and the Doctor thinks that within a week she will be able to sit up in a chair . . .

Lucy E. Anthony, letter to Elizabeth Smith Miller, March 2, 1906, in the Smith Family Papers, Rare Books and Manuscripts Division, New York Public Library.

No matter what is done or is not done, how you are criticized or misunderstood, or what efforts are made to block your path, remember that the only fear you need have is the fear of not standing by the thing you believe to be right. Take your stand and hold it: then let come what will, and receive the blows like a good soldier.

Susan B. Anthony, speaking on her deathbed to Anna Howard Shaw, March 13, 1906, in Barry, Susan B. Anthony, *355.*

I have none. I owe it to Miss Anthony that I am able to practice medicine. It has been a blessed privilege

to care for her. I could not accept a dollar for that service . . .

Dr. Marcena Sherman-Ricker, response to Mary Anthony, when asked for her statement regarding the care of Susan B. Anthony during her last illness and death, March 13, 1906, in Harper, Life and Work of Susan B. Anthony, *Vol. 3, 1466.*

Susan B. Anthony was an extraordinary woman, who, enveloped in a delusion, pursued a phantom for more than threescore years. She had persuaded herself that her sex was the victim of man's tyranny and man's perfidy, and she became a leader of that circle of masculine womanhood that clamored for "woman's rights," even as Don Quixote set himself to redress woman's wrongs; but the world went jogging along in the same old rut, believing that it was Darby's business to plow the glebe and Joan's work to sweep the room.

Who of us would not prefer Ruth to wife than Jael? Some half-a-dozen centuries ago that was a

Anna Howard Shaw, ca. 1910 *(Library of Congress)*

masculine woman who was possessed of the crown matrimonial of England—Margaret of Anjou. She was a heroine wedded to a weakling, and she ruled her lord and the realm with a rod of iron. Caligula was little more cruel. In that same age lived Chaucer's sweetheart:

> "I saw her dance so comelily,
> Carol and sing so sweetly,
> And laugh and play so womanly,
> And look so debonairly,
> That, certes, I trow that nevermore
> Was seen so blissful a treasure.
> For every hair upon her head
> Sooth to say, it was not red,
> Nor yellow, neither, nor brown it was.
> But, oh! what eyes my lady had,
> Debonair, goode, glad and sad,
> Simple, of good size, not too wide.
> Thereto her look was not aside
> Nor overwart."

Can you imagine her on the stump shrieking politics? On the contrary, she is the home body, fit to wife some good man, or to gird the sword on some brave man, or be the mother of some sturdy boy or lovely lass—that is her mission in life. There are millions and millions of her, and she pesters her mind naught about "rights" and "freedom" and "suffrage" and things foreign to her estate. Her duty is to be a good woman, a faithful wife, a fond mother—to such, rights come in troops. If she only make her husband happy, he will embarrass her with the number of rights he will bestow upon her.

While Napoleon's answer to Madam de Staël was impertinent and disgraceful, yet woman's sphere is not political but domestic. It was a fine compliment great Marcius paid to his mother: "Hadst thou been wife to Hercules, six of his labors thou wouldst have done, and saved your husband so much sweat," but that was poetry; besides, Volumnia was not a womanly woman. She was a Jael, a Margaret of Anjou, a Boadicea. We prefer the gentle Ruth, the lively Rosaline, the lovely sweetheart old Chaucer tells us of.

Man's hand is fitted to grasp the scepter, woman's is fashioned for the distaff.

> Washington Post, *upon Susan B. Anthony's death,*
> *March 13, 1906, in Harper,* Life and Work of
> Susan B. Anthony, *Vol. 3, 1560.*

Women who contend most strenuously for the rights of their sex are as a rule never especially attractive to the masculine half of the world's population. This may be a decidedly uncomplimentary admission with respect to the mental endowments of the latter but nevertheless, it is so. But, above all, do women deliberately run the risk of losing the finer respect of the sterner sex when they don the garments of their brothers. Men admire—every prompting of nature incites them to do so—what is known as womanliness in women, and the least departure from that standard at once lowers their esteem. And the wearing of men's clothes, as Miss Anthony did, is one of the surest methods of impressing upon the male mind a lack of womanliness in the wearer.

Still there can be no doubt but that Miss Anthony by her long life so loyally devoted to the effort to bring the world to agree with her in regard to the social reforms she advocated, has left an indelible mark upon the thought of her time. She made many converts to her peculiar views, and though probably not much nearer to their universal prevalence now than when she first undertook her life's mission, she has not lived or labored in vain.

> Atlanta Chronicle *(Georgia), upon Susan B. Anthony's*
> *death, March 13, 1906, in Harper,* Life and Work of
> Susan B. Anthony, *Vol. 3, 1593.*

Miss Susan B. Anthony is dead. She died at a ripe old age and through her long life she was never pestered by contaminating association with the unspeakable man. She never married. In fact, Miss Anthony seems to have conceived the fancy that the members of the stronger sex had some deep-seated grudge against all women in general and she took upon herself the task of avenging the wrongs and injustices of the sex.

Miss Anthony was one of the best known women in America and her popularity was obtained through her indomitable efforts towards woman suffrage. Although she was fervidly sincere, still, evil fate that it was, she was guided by an evil star. She wore ever the garb of delusion and spent the long years of her life in pursuit of a phantom, which grew none the less phantasmal through her ardent chase of it.

Although she put the best efforts of her life into the task of securing suffrage for the women of America, still when the angel of death called for her she was forced to look back over a life strewn with little but failure. Miss Anthony was sincere and meant well, but she had the wrong idea of the likes and desires of the other members of her sex all over the land. She never realized the fact that the great majority of American women cared not for suffrage. Had she realized this she would have spent her energies in a more profitable and worthy cause.

No, the good women of our country do not want suffrage. They care nothing for "rights" and "franchises." They are happy and content to reign in the happy kingdom of the home. They esteem more highly the work of rearing the children aright and making the home cozy and attractive than they do for the matter of the "ways and means" of getting Bill Jones elected as coroner. They have a work, a calling apart and by far more sacred than that of making good laws and steering the Ship of State.

Our good women have ever been happy in their God-given work, and that they may be content and happy in it forever is our earnest wish.

> Charlotte News *(North Carolina), upon the death of Susan B. Anthony, March 13, 1906, in Harper,* Life and Work of Susan B. Anthony, *Vol. 3, 1593–1594.*

The country has lost one of its most distinguished citizens, and women their best friend. The debt of gratitude I owe Miss Anthony is two-fold for I am a woman and a member of the race for whose freedom she labored so faithfully and so long. The debt which the women of all the world owe her is great indeed, but the debt of colored women is greater than all the rest.

> *Mary Church Terrell, letter to Mary Anthony upon the death of Susan B. Anthony, March 13, 1906, in Harper,* Life and Work of Susan B. Anthony, *Vol. 3, 1452.*

How intelligent men can continue to be thus indifferent to the right and privileges of women is beyond my conceptions—Well. I am persuaded that as much as I would like to remain at home the coming months, it will be for the best for me to go to Oregon and do the little I can (and it will be so little) to help along with the work of trying to bring that state into line—Miss Shaw, and sister Susan felt it was the thing for me to do, and although I am sure Miss Shaw will be very much disappointed in regard to the aid I will be capable of rendering, I will go and do the best I can.

> *Mary S. Anthony, letter to Elizabeth Smith Miller, March 20, 1906, in the Smith Family Papers, Rare Books and Manuscripts Division, New York Public Library.*

I sent you the morning paper items that you may see the magnitude of the suffrage fight that is waging—It is certainly amazing, the energy and bitterness with which the Antis persist in fighting a question, which, if carried, will not make the slightest difference with them about their voting or letting it alone, leaving them as free as they are today to exercise their *womanly qualities* and desires and remaining *uncontaminated* and *spotless* from the common herd . . . Well, before you get this we shall know the result . . . Day before yesterday we had forty-four workers at headquarters, and yesterday, thirty-four, folding, addressing & mailing documents to the *hundred thousand* voters of the state . . .

We shall soon be wending our way homeward, sorrowing or rejoicing, but Sister Susan will not be at 17 Madison Street to sorrow or rejoice with us— What it will mean to me I can hardly realize.

> *Mary S. Anthony, letter to Elizabeth Smith Miller, June 1, 1906, in the Smith Family Papers, Rare Books and Manuscripts Division, New York Public Library.*

My left foot, ankle, and leg are behaving worse then ever before. So it is all I can do to walk to the bathroom & back to my bedroom. I am getting quite discouraged . . . I do hope you and Miss Nannie will keep well & both be able to go to the Convention in Chicago. Which I evidently must give up.

> *Mary S. Anthony, letter to Elizabeth Smith Miller, December 18, 1906, in the Smith Family Papers, Rare Books and Manuscripts Division, New York Public Library.*

12

On Strike and On Parade
1907–1916

THE HISTORICAL CONTEXT

When Lucy Stone, Elizabeth Cady Stanton, and Susan B. Anthony died, their natural rights argument for suffrage was replaced by one stressing its usefulness. Where the earliest leaders had looked for authority to the Declaration of Independence, their successors looked to any number of investigatory reports about the wages and hours of working women. Women's lives had changed, these new leaders argued, and women needed the ballot in order to deal with the consequences. In 1892 Stanton said that "[t]he strongest reason why we ask for woman a voice in the government under which she lives; in the religion she is asked to believe; equality in social life . . . a place in the trades and professions . . . is because of her birthright to self-sovereignty . . ."[1] By the early part of the 20th century, Melinda Scott, a hat trimmer in a New York factory, had found, in her "place in the trades," reasons of her own. "If women had the ballot," she explained, ". . . [they] would have dared to pass the 54-hour bill . . . I do not want to be governor of the State . . . but I do want the ballot to be able to register my protest against the [working] conditions that are killing and maiming . . ."[2]

Working conditions were, indeed, dreadful for many women. Garment workers, for example, frequently worked 11- and 12-hour days, six or seven days a week,[3] in buildings that were poorly maintained, dimly lit, and often in violation of safety codes. They not only were paid meager wages but were also expected to use those funds to purchase their own sewing supplies.[4]

Thousands of women went on strike. As the winter of 1909 began, the employees of the Triangle Shirtwaist Company of New York "left the factories from every side, all of them walking down toward Union Square . . . the spirit of a conqueror led them on."[5] The shirtwaist workers of Philadelphia struck that same winter; the following year, 14 women walked out on Hart, Schaffner and Marx in Chicago, and 8,000 coworkers followed; and in 1912, women were among the 20,000 textile workers to strike in Lawrence, Massachusetts.

There had been strikes before, but none, of men or women, to equal these strikes in size or duration. Women stayed out on strike despite arrests, beatings, and the need for wages with which to feed their children. This last need was real: During the winter of the Chicago strike, 1,250 strikers or wives of strikers gave birth. One newly-delivered woman explained her continued support of the strike: "It is not only bread we give our children . . . We live by freedom, and I will fight till I die to give it to my children."[6]

The members of the Women's Trade Union League (WTUL) worked to ensure that women *didn't* die in this particular fight. The WTUL was an organization that joined women factory workers with women from the middle and upper classes, including such well-known society women as Anne Morgan, Alva Belmont, Mrs. Henry Morgenthau, and Helen Taft (the president's daughter). Those from the monied half of the partnership were called "allies."[7]

Although some of the factory workers found some of their "allies" patronizing, there is no dispute about the amount of aid rendered. In New York, 75 of what some called the "mink brigade" joined the picket lines, and many were arrested along with the strikers. Others raised bail money for the arrested factory workers and secured legal representation for them. They did what they could to end the police brutality taking place daily. Individually, they acted as witnesses, brought charges against abusive foremen and police, and monitored the courts day and night to ensure fair treatment of the arrested strikers. When police brutality continued, the WTUL and 10,000 sympathizers marched in protest to City Hall.[8]

Militant methods found their way into the women's suffrage campaign as well. In 1887 Elizabeth Cady Stanton had written, "If all the heroic deeds of women recorded in history and our daily journals . . . have not yet convinced our opponents that women are possessed of superior fighting qualities, the sex may feel called upon in the near future to give some further illustrations of their prowess. Of one thing they may be assured, that the next generation will not argue the question of woman's rights with the infinite patience we have had for half a century . . ."[9] One younger person notably lacking in patience was Stanton's own daughter Harriot.

Because American graduate schools were largely closed to women, Harriot Stanton Blatch had attended graduate school in England. There, in 1882, she married a British citizen (losing her own U.S. citizenship in the process, since a woman's citizenship followed her husband's) and became involved in the English women's movement. In 1902, the last year of her mother's life, Blatch returned to the United States with her husband and daughter Nora; when Elizabeth Cady Stanton died, Harriot was at her side.

Eight weeks after Stanton's funeral, Susan B. Anthony complained about Blatch's failure to attend a convention in New Orleans. "I thought," Anthony wrote, "she should be there & *represent her mother.*" Gradually, Blatch began to do that and more.

The National American Woman Suffrage Association (NAWSA) Blatch found upon her return to the United States had become, she believed, the staid organization her mother had predicted. Blatch thereupon founded the Equality League of Self-Supporting Women, which was joined by a large number of factory women who wanted

Harriot Stanton Blatch *(Library of Congress)*

suffrage. When it became clear that many other would-be members were not yet self-supporting, the name was changed to the Women's Political Union. (Not all the women active in the labor movement appreciated efforts to link labor rights and women's suffrage. Activist Mary Harris "Mother" Jones, for example, heartily resented it.) In 1910 the Women's Political Union held the first suffrage parade in New York City. A year later there was another one, with "3,000 marchers and perhaps 70,000 onlookers."

The *New York Times's* coverage of the suffragists' parade in New York City, 1913 *(Library of Congress)*

Suffrage parade in Washington, D.C.,
1913 *(Library of Congress)*

There was also a funeral parade in New York City in 1911. It was in memory of 146 victims, mostly female, of the Triangle Shirtwaist Company fire.

The employees of this company had gone on strike two years before, but their working conditions had not changed. The building had inadequate fire escapes and no sprinkler system. Worse, the doors were locked from the outside to prevent the women from leaving during working hours. When the fire broke out, on March 25, 1911, the women were trapped. They clung to the breaking fire escapes on the ninth floor. Firefighters tried to reach them, but their ladders stopped at the sixth floor. Women jumped from the windows and died on the sidewalk. Other women, remaining inside, died of burns or suffocation. That night, the 26th Street pier was filled with 146 corpses and 2,000 people in search of their loved ones' bodies.

It took a week to identify the dead, and seven women could not be identified at all. The outraged members of the New York Women's Trade Union League and the International Ladies' Garment Workers' Union planned a funeral for the unnamed women. When Mayor William J. Gaynor had the bodies buried in a city plot, the women's funeral procession was conducted with an empty hearse. New York's grieving population turned out in full on the rainy, cold day, April 5, 1911. Through the steady downpour, they marched. The Washington Square Arch was the agreed point of merger for marchers from all across the city to become members of the parade. There were so many people at that spot by 3:20 P.M. that the last person had to wait until 6:00 P.M. to pass below the arch. Almost half a million people lined the sidewalks in silence to witness the procession.

Afterward, Max Blanck and Isaac Harris, the owners of the company, were acquitted of manslaughter charges. (Max Blanck was charged two years later for once again locking his female employees in their work room. He was fined $20)[10] Even before the acquittal, female labor leaders such as Leonora O'Reilly demanded woman suffrage with an increased sense of urgency.[11]

When the next New York City suffrage parade was held in 1912, there were 20,000 marchers and another half million people lining the sidewalks. The 1913 New York City suffrage parade was even larger. Then, in Washington, D.C., on March 3, 1913, the day before President Wilson's inauguration, there was another parade. Women were so badly harassed during this parade that a special session of the U.S. Congress conducted hearings to investigate the behavior of the District of Columbia police department, and the chief of police was dismissed. One woman, however, was particularly ill-treated—and by the women's rights activists themselves. That woman was Ida B. Wells-Barnett.

Wells-Barnett, prominent newspaper owner, journalist, and president of the first African-American women's suffrage organization, the Alpha Suffrage Club of Chicago, stood with the Illinois section as preparations for the parade began. When women from the Southern states refused to participate in an integrated event, NAWSA officials asked Wells-Barnett to join a special "Negro women's contingent." Fellow suffragists of European descent argued among themselves about the need to keep as many southern women as possible in the suffrage movement; few of these women spoke up to say that Wells-Barnett should be welcomed regardless of potential southern defection. Wells-Barnett finally said that she would join Illinois's contingent or none at all. Then she left.

When the parade started, Ida B. Wells-Barnett was among the many bystanders. As her state's contingent passed before her, she left the crowd and took her place in the parade. Two European-American women then left their assigned places to march at her side.[12]

The parade Wells-Barnett joined had not been going smoothly. Passage through the streets had been arranged in advance with the police department. Police officers on duty were instructed to "give every attention to protecting those comprising the parade against embarrassments and afford them every security." Those orders were not obeyed.[13]

Instead, as participants in the parade began to walk down Pennsylvania Avenue, hordes of people filled the center of the street. Men, many of them drunk, poked and jeered at the suffragists. Only an occasional police officer tried to control the crowd. As one woman recalled for U.S. senators, "[T]here was no space whatever. There was not 10 inches . . . between us and the crowd . . . I had with me a number of young girls in our division—my daughter and one or two others—and the crowd did hoot and jeer and make the most insulting remarks to these girls. They tried to grab their flowers away from

"Homemakers" Suffrage Pageant, 1913 *(Library of Congress)*

them, and one man stuck his foot out . . . She was tripped but did not fall . . . because the crowd was too dense . . . there were two policemen standing together that were egging the crowd on to jeer, and they themselves were making remarks to us and jeering."

Asked why she did not complain to the police, the witness said, "None of us complained. I simply told the young girls to keep out of their way. I was just as much alarmed at those policemen as I was at the crowd."[14]

Even after this experience, people who were becoming militant suffragists continued to use whatever methods they could to call attention to their cause. Emmeline Pankhurst, the self-described "Hooligan woman" from England, was invited to speak in Carnegie Hall. Mrs. Richard Hornsby and several of her suffragist friends flew an airplane above President Wilson's yacht and dropped petitions on board.

These were strategies of which Carrie Chapman Catt, the reelected president of NAWSA and, by now, a superb tactician, did not approve. Working through a network of state organizations between 1907 and 1916, NAWSA and its affiliates had helped secure suffrage in Washington, California, Arizona, Kansas, Oregon, Montana, Nevada, Illinois, and Alaska Territory. Moreover, by 1916, she had quietly established a rapport with President Wilson.

A young woman exercises her freedom by smoking a cigarette in the smoking car of an early 1900s train. *(National Archives)*

Catt addressed the NAWSA's Executive Council in a private session following the organization's 1916 convention. The convention would "not adjourn, should it sit until Christmas," Catt told her national officers and state chapter presidents, unless it adopted "a logical and sensible policy toward the Federal Amendment . . ." Catt herself had devised such a plan. Using military metaphor, she described a new campaign to secure women's suffrage in at least 36 states, the number needed to ratify a federal amendment. Once this was accomplished, voting women would apply organized pressure to get a federal amendment passed by their representatives and senators and ratified by the members of their state legislatures. In secret, more than 36 state chapter presidents signed a document pledging themselves to the campaign. It would be Carrie Chapman Catt's "Winning Plan."[15]

CHRONICLE OF EVENTS

1907

Harriot Stanton Blatch and others form the Equality League of Self-Supporting Women (later called the Women's Political Union).

Actress and writer Elizabeth Robbins stages a popular play, "Votes for Women," and publishes a novel, *The Convert,* both of which help to persuade many to support suffrage.

Jane Addams publishes *Newer Ideals of Peace.*

Emily Bissell heads first Christmas seal drive for children with TB.

Esther Pohl Clayson Lovejoy is the first woman to act as director of the board of health for a major U.S. city. After becoming a member of Portland, Oregon's Board of Health, she is elected director in 1907.

March 4: Hoffman House Hotel in New York City refuses to serve Harriot Stanton Blatch because she has no male escort. Blatch sues the management.

June 27: Elizabeth Cabot Agassiz, first president of Radcliffe College, dies.

September 26: Yale University, in New Haven, Connecticut, holds the first Woman's Missionary Conference.

December 9: Emily Perkins Bissell designs and prints the first Christmas seal to aid tuberculosis research.

1908

National College Women's Equal Suffrage League is formed. Smith, Radcliffe, Barnard, Bryn Mawr, Mt. Holyoke, and the Universities of Chicago, California, and Wisconsin are represented by faculty and graduates.

President M. Carey Thomas of Bryn Mawr stresses the practical need for women's suffrage over the natural rights arguments used by earlier women's rights leaders.

National Association of Colored Graduate Nurses founded. (In 1950, American Nursing Association will open its membership to both black and white nurses, and this organization is dissolved.)

The U.S. government creates the Navy Nurse Corps.

The National American Woman Suffrage Association sets a goal of 1 million signatures for its suffrage petition but will attain less than half this number.

At the age of 50, Annie Smith Peck becomes the first person to climb Peru's Mt. Huascarán reaching the highest altitude (21,812 feet) ever attained in the Western Hemisphere.

Julia Ward Howe is the first woman elected to the American Academy of Arts and Letters. She remains its only female member until 1930.

January 15: New York City passes the Sullivan Ordinance, criminalizing public smoking by women.

February 24: In *Muller v. Oregon* the Supreme Court upholds the constitutionality of a maximum-hour law ("protective legislation") for women.

March 8: Socialist women march in New York City on behalf of suffrage and labor improvements.

August 13: The National Convention formally adopts the Democratic Party platform, which includes support for women's draft registration, in New York City.

1909

Social worker and feminist Jane Addams publishes *The Spirit of Youth and the City Streets* and becomes the first woman president of the National Conference of Charities and Correction (later National Conference of Social Work).

National Association for the Advancement of Colored People is established, an important voice for the equal rights of African-American women.

October 31: Woman Suffrage Party founded.

November 24: Twenty thousand female garment workers employed by Leisters & Company and the Triangle Shirtwaist Company strike in New York.

December 20: Shirtwaist workers strike in Philadelphia.

1910

Some 404,000 women petition Congress, requesting women's suffrage.

First women's suffrage parade is held in New York City; it is organized by the Women's Political Union.

Oregon holds state referendum; women's suffrage is defeated in this state for the fourth time.

Lyda Burton Conley becomes the first Native American woman lawyer in the United States, passing the bar in Kansas.

Wyoming elects Mary Bellemy to the House of Representatives.

Social worker and feminist Jane Addams publishes her most popular work, *Twenty Years at Hull-House.* In the same year she becomes the first woman to receive an honorary degree from Yale.

New Mexico holds a convention to prepare a constitution for statehood, which becomes the battleground for school suffrage for women. After a stormy debate, the majority votes to give women the right to vote for school trustees, on the issuing of bonds, and in the local administration of public schools but not for county or state superintendents.

The National American Woman Suffrage Association (NAWSA) establishes the Congressional Committee as a liaison group to Congress, headed by Elizabeth Kent.

At a NAWSA conference, Alice Paul, recently returned from imprisonment at England's Halloway Prison, speaks to the delegates' meeting at the Arlington Hotel in Washington, D.C., endorsing the militant tactics of the Pankhursts in England.

NAWSA leader Carrie Chapman Catt testifies before the Senate Committee on Woman Suffrage on behalf of a federal amendment.

Crystal Eastman becomes the first woman to draft workers' compensation legislation.

The first suffragist newsstand is established in New York City.

The Equality League changes its name to the Women's Political Union, organizing the first suffrage foot parade of 400 women. Eighty-seven men from the Men's League for Woman Suffrage take part, marching to jeering crowds in New York.

February 15: Triangle Shirtwaist Company strike ends.

March 17: Charlotte Vetter Gulick, her husband Dr. Luther H. Gulick, and their friends found the Camp Fire Girls, the first national nonsectarian interracial organization for girls.

June 25: Congress passes the Mann Act (also called the White Slave Traffic Act), criminalizing interstate or foreign transportation of women for immoral acts.

August 13: Eleonora R. Sears is the first woman to compete against men in a polo match (Narragansett Pier, Rhode Island).

September: Bessie Abramowitz, Anne Shapiro and 12 other women are first to walk out in what becomes a strike of 8,000 workers against Hart, Schaffner and Marx in Chicago.

September 2: Alice Stebins Wells, America's first female police officer, wins appointment in Los Angeles.

November: The first meeting of the Men's League for Woman Suffrage is held in New York at the New York City Club. Founded by Max Eastman, the group elects George Foster Peabody its president.

November 9: Washington State holds state referendum; women's suffrage passes.

1911

National Council of Women Voters is organized.

California holds state referendum; women's suffrage passes, making California the sixth state to enfranchise women.

National Association Opposed to Woman Suffrage is founded.

Wage Earners League for Woman Suffrage is founded.

Social worker and pacifist Jane Addams becomes the first head of the National Federation of Settlements.

Iowa's monthly suffrage newspaper, the *Woman's Standard* (founded 1886) ends publication, as there is now opportunity for suffrage information to circulate through regular newspapers.

Alice Henry, supporter of suffrage, becomes the first editor of the publication *Life and Labor.*

Virginia Crocheron Gildersleeve becomes dean of Barnard College. She will retain the position for 36 years.

Mary Elizabeth Dreier becomes the sole woman member of the Factory Investigation Commission, which examines the cause of the Triangle Shirtwaist Company Fire.

The first agricultural training school for women is established on 200 acres of land donated by Alva Belmont in Hempstead, Long Island.

Theresa West Elmendorf is the first woman president of the American Library Association.

Clara Dutton Noyes establishes the first U.S. school for midwives, at Bellevue Hospital in New York City.

January: The Equal Franchise Society is formed in Nevada.

March 25: Triangle Shirtwaist Company building burns; 146 of the company's employees die.

April: About 80,000 demonstrators march in New York City protesting the Triangle Shirtwaist Company fire.

June 19: Printers' Association of America campaigns to keep depictions of women's skirts off billboards.

August: A monthly suffrage journal called the *Woman Citizen* begins publication, founded in Indianapolis by the suffrage association there.

August 1: Harriet Quimby becomes the first U.S. woman pilot to receive a license to fly.

1912

Progressive Party supports women's suffrage; Jane Addams seconds the nomination of Theodore Roosevelt.

Michigan holds state referendum; women's suffrage is defeated.

Ohio holds state referendum; women's suffrage is defeated.

Wisconsin holds state referendum; women's suffrage is defeated.

Arizona holds state referendum; women's suffrage passes.

Social worker and feminist Jane Addams publishes *A New Conscience and an Ancient Evil,* encouraging women to fight prostitution.

In *Quong v. Oregon* the Supreme Court rules constitutional a state law that limits women's (but not men's) workday to 10 hours.

The Woman Suffrage League is formed in Atlanta, Georgia.

Georgia passes a bill enabling women to be notaries public.

Gertrude Battles Lane becomes the editor-in-chief of *Woman's Home Companion.*

Katherine Philips Edson is the first woman to become a member of the National Municipal League.

Lucy Burns returns from England, and is immediately visited by her friend Alice Paul. They discuss how to apply the militant tactics of the English suffragists to the American movement and are subsequently appointed to the Congressional Committee of the NAWSA.

Marie Jenny Howe founds *Heterodoxy,* a legendary woman's group of the early 20th-century feminist movement, in New York City.

Ada Comstock becomes the first woman dean of Smith College, in Northampton, Massachusetts.

Julia Clifford Lathrop becomes the first woman to direct a major U.S. government bureau, the Children's Bureau.

Lillian Wald is named to the position of first president of the National Organization for Public Health Nursing.

January 13: 20,000 textile workers strike in Lawrence, Massachusetts.

February: Eleanor H. Porter's book *Pollyanna* is published, coining a new word in the English language.

March 7: A resolution to submit to voters a woman suffrage amendment to the Iowa constitution, submitted every General Assembly since 1870, passes the Senate by a vote of 31 to 15.

March 12: Daisy Gordon and 10 other girls form the first patrol of the Girl Guides, forerunners of the Girl Scouts, on Juliette Low's property in Savannah, Georgia.

May 19: Dora Keen is first woman to climb Mount Blackburn in Alaska.

November 5: Kansas grants suffrage to women by a vote of 175,246 to 159,197. No other state has won by so large a majority.

November 5: In Arizona a woman suffrage amendment receives 13,442 ayes, 6,202 nays, passing by a majority of two to one.

1913

Legislature of the new Alaska Territory, as its first act, passes women's suffrage bill.

Feminist Charlotte Perkins Gilman publishes *Women and Economics: A Study of the Economic Relations between Men and Women as a Factor in Social Evolution.*

Colorado elects its first woman senator, Helen Ring Robinson.

Willa Cather publishes *O Pioneers!,* her first major novel.

Carolyn C. Van Blarcom is the first female nurse to be named a licensed midwife.

The Muncy Act, lengthening prison terms for women, is passed by Congress.

The Congressional Committee of the National American Woman Suffrage Association under the leadership of Alice Paul and Lucy Burns organizes its first delegation to the White House.

Kate Gordon founds the Southern States Suffrage Conference.

Mary Harris "Mother" Jones, 83, enters prison for organizing West Virginia miners, sentenced to 20 years.

January: In New York City 150,000 garment workers go on strike. The strike will spread to Boston in the next month and end in New York City on March 12 and Boston on April 21.

January 2: The Congressional Committee of the National American Woman Suffrage Association (NAWSA), under the leadership of Alice Paul and Lucy Burns, holds its initial meeting to organize, finance, and arrange a massive parade in Washington, D.C. in March, to coincide with the inauguration of president-elect Woodrow Wilson.

January 6: Clara Munson becomes first woman elected mayor of a city west of the Rockies, Warrington, Oregon.

January 23: The New York State Senate votes 40 to 2 for a woman suffrage amendment. Four days later the Assembly concurs with only five dissenting votes.

January 29: A resolution to submit a woman suffrage amendment to the Alabama state constitution to the voters is for the first time introduced by the legislature. It will be voted down.

February 23: Governor Emmet D. Boyle of Nevada signs an "easy divorce" law.

March: Ida B. Wells-Barnett founds the Alpha Club in Chicago, an African-American suffrage organization.

March: Lucy Paul and Dora Lewis of the Congressional Committee of the National American Woman Suffrage Association (NAWSA) meet with Anna Howard Shaw and Mary Ware Dennett of the parent organization in New York City. They propose that their committee work exclusively for a federal suffrage amendment, rather than pursue a state-by-state campaign.

March 3: Alice Paul and Lucy Burns organize suffrage parade of 5,000–8,000 women in Washington, D.C., on the day preceding Woodrow Wilson's inauguration.

March 3: The governor of Nevada signs a resolution to submit to the voters an amendment to the state constitution giving full suffrage to women.

March 6: An investigating committee of the U.S. Senate meets for four days to hear eyewitness testimony that supported Alice Paul's claims of police misconduct at the parade of 8,000 supporters of a federal suffrage amendment.

March 10: Harriet Tubman dies.

April: The Congressional Union for Woman Suffrage is established by Alice Paul and Lucy Burns, existing separately from the Congressional Committee of the National American Woman Suffrage Association (NAWSA).

April 4: A delegation of the College Equal Suffrage League meets with President Woodrow Wilson on behalf of a federal woman suffrage amendment. This is part of a campaign by the Congressional Committee (Congressional Union) under the leadership of Alice Paul to support a bill before both houses of Congress.

April 7: The Congressional Committee (Congressional Union) under the leadership of Alice Paul organizes an assembly of one woman from every congressional district in the nation to coincide with the opening of a special session of Congress set aside to debate Senate Joint Resolution I, advocating a federal suffrage amendment. The women carry petitions and resolutions from their districts advocating a federal suffrage amendment. They meet at the capitol and then proceed to locate representatives and senators to push for the bill.

April 7: Alice Paul reports to her Congressional Committee/Congressional Union that Senator George E. Chamberlain of Oregon and Representative Frank Mondell of Wyoming had introduced Senate Joint Resolution I, calling for the passage of a federal suffrage amendment. The Senate refers the bill to the Senate Woman Suffrage Committee.

May 5: Helen Keller publicly supports women's suffrage.

May 7: A bill granting Illinois women suffrage, first introduced in 1893, passes the state senate, 29-14.

June 6: Representatives of the National Council of Women Voters visit the White House to persuade President Woodrow Wilson to support a federal woman suffrage amendment that is before both houses of congress. This is part of a campaign by the Congressional Committee (Congressional Union) under the leadership of Alice Paul in support of the measure.

June 13: The Senate Woman Suffrage Committee issues a unanimously favorable report on Senate Joint Resolution I, calling for the passage of a federal suffrage amendment.

July 10: For the first time in North Carolina history, a handful of women organize a woman suffrage club, the Morgantown Equal Suffrage Association.

July 31: The U.S. Senate holds a full discussion on Senate Joint Resolution I, which calls for a federal suffrage amendment.

September 18: U.S. Senator Wesley M. Jones of Washington argues on the Senate floor on behalf of Senate Joint Resolution I.

October 18: Emmeline Pankhurst arrives in United States and is ordered deported by the Ellis Island Board. President Wilson admits her to the United States.

November 15: The Congressional Committee (Congressional Union) under the leadership of Alice Paul and Lucy Burns begins publication of *The Suffragist,* a weekly newsmagazine intended to inform a national audience of progress being made on the federal amendment for suffrage now in Congress.

November 17: Seventy-five New Jersey women ask President Woodrow Wilson to advocate a federal women suffrage amendment during the regular session of Congress.

December 6: An editorial by Lucy Burns in the December 6 issue of *The Suffragist* declares that the

Suffragists hanging up posters in New Jersey, ca. 1914 *(Library of Congress)*

Congressional Committee (Congressional Union) will hold the party in power (the Democrats) responsible for the fate of the federal suffrage amendment, a British tactic. The National American Woman Suffrage Association (NAWSA) holds its annual convention, during which the first public clash occurs between the old guard and the new, who are called the "New Suffragists."

December 6: At the adjournment of the NAWSA convention, the leaders of the old guard meet with Alice Paul and other leaders of the Congressional Union and present them with an ultimatum: Alice Paul can retain her chair of the Congressional Committee if she resigns as chair of the Congressional Union. Paul refuses.

December 8: Anna Howard Shaw of NAWSA leads a delegation to the White House to personally advocate a federal suffrage amendment before President Woodrow Wilson.

December 11: NAWSA members meet with Congressional Union leaders, with Lucy Burns representing Alice Paul. The two sides cannot agree on tactics.

1914

National American Woman Suffrage Association and Congressional Union separate.

South Dakota holds state referendum; women's suffrage is defeated.

North Dakota holds state referendum; women's suffrage is defeated.

Nebraska holds state referendum; women's suffrage is defeated.

Missouri holds state referendum; women's suffrage is defeated.

Ohio holds state referendum; women's suffrage is defeated.

Montana holds state referendum; women's suffrage passes.

Nevada holds state referendum; women's suffrage passes.

Debating teams of Yale, Princeton, and Harvard Universities debate the merits of women's suffrage.

U.S. Senate committee issues favorable majority report on federal women's suffrage amendment.

Willa Cather publishes *My Antonia.*

Margaret Sanger calls for the legalization of contraceptives in *Woman Rebel.* The Post Office refuses to distribute the publication through the mails, and Sanger is arrested.

African Americans in Minneapolis, Minnesota, organize the Everywoman Suffrage Club.

The Progressive Party and the Socialist Party introduce suffrage measures. The Democratic Party has a plank in its platform recommending a constitutional amendment giving women the vote.

Harvard denies the use of one of its halls to English suffragist Emmeline Pankhurst. The Harvard Corporation votes that thereafter no woman should be allowed to lecture in the college halls except by its invitation.

Amendments are made in Kentucky's new primary law by the legislature securing the right of women to vote in the primary elections for county superintendent of schools. This right was in doubt the year before and was denied in many counties.

The Equal Suffrage Party of Georgia is founded in Atlanta.

Margaret Anderson, editor of the *Little Review,* is the first person to publish excerpts from James Joyce's *Ulysses* in the United States.

Bessie Abramowitz Hillman and her husband, Sidney, begin the Amalgamated Clothing Workers of America.

Margaret Sanger forms the National Birth Control League.

Delaware, the last state to provide an institution of higher education for women, opens a women's college at the University of Delaware.

Annette Abbott Adams becomes the first woman assistant U.S. attorney. She is named federal prosecutor for the Northern District of California.

January 5: Conflict between NAWSA under Anna Howard Shaw and Alice Paul's Congressional Union becomes public as newspapers carry stories of the clash.

January 12: Belle La Follette, Mrs. John Jay White, Ellen Hale, and others demonstrate their support for Alice Paul in the face of NAWSA charges that the Congressional Union under Paul raised money wrongly using NAWSA's name.

February 2: Under the leadership of Rose Schneiderman (National Women's Trade Union League) and Melinda Scott (New York Women's Trade Union League), 400 working women meet with President Woodrow Wilson to lobby for a federal amendment for women's suffrage.

February 3: The Democratic House Caucus meets to announce its stand on a federal suffrage amendment. It votes 123 to 57 to accept a resolution by Representative J. Thomas Heflin (Alabama) declaring suffrage a states' rights issue, not a federal issue.

February 12: Alice Paul, in the face of great opposition from NAWSA, meets for the final time with NAWSA leaders in Washington, D.C., in an attempt to mend fences. The meeting is a failure and Paul's now-independent Congressional Union for Woman Suffrage breaks from NAWSA.

March 2: Shafroth-Palmer Amendment presented to Congress, requiring states to hold referenda on suffrage if 8 percent of voters in prior election petition for it.

March 2: Demonstrations organized by Alice Paul's Congressional Union are held across the country in support of the Anthony amendment (Mondell Resolution), introduced in the Senate.

March 5: The House Judiciary Committee votes out the Mondell Resolution (Anthony amendment) without recommendation, the first time a suffrage measure had been voted out of committee in the House of Representatives.

March 19: For the first time in 27 years the U.S. Senate votes on a federal suffrage amendment (Anthony amendment). It fails by a vote of 35-34, less than the two-thirds needed.

April 11: Feminist Alliance drafts letter to President Woodrow Wilson for passage of a constitutional amendment prohibiting job discrimination on the basis of sex.

May 14: Illinois holds its first big suffrage parade. Nearly 15,000 women march down Michigan Street, with hundreds of thousands more lining both sides of the street for two miles.

June 2: Alice Paul organizes a delegation from the General Federation of Women's Clubs to meet with President Woodrow Wilson at the White House.

June 22: Doctors Alice Gertrude Bryant and Florence West Duckering are the first women elected to the American College of Surgeons.

June 30: President Woodrow Wilson declares that suffrage for women should be decided by the states.

July 16: Former presidential candidate William Jennings Bryan publicly supports the vote for women.

August 28: The Rules Committee of the U.S. House of Representatives meets to discuss several issues, including the Anthony amendment, recently defeated in the Senate. It fails to act on women's suffrage.

August 29: Representatives of the Congressional Union meet at Alva Vanderbilt Belmont's Rhode Island mansion, Marble House, to plan tactics to oppose Democrats in close elections in 1914 for failure to support a federal amendment for woman suffrage.

September: Mrs. Frank Leslie, publisher of *Leslie's Weekly,* bequeaths legacy of $2 million to Carrie Chapman Catt for the "furtherance of the cause of woman suffrage."

September 28: With the assassination of the Austrian archduke Francis Ferdinand in Sarajevo, World War I breaks out in Europe.

October: The *New Southern Citizen,* a 20-page magazine that supports suffrage, begins publication in Louisiana.

October 23: Some 25,000 supporters of women's suffrage demonstrate in New York City.

November 3: Women's suffrage becomes a national issue on Election Day when the Congressional Union under Alice Paul wages anti–Democratic Party campaigns against those who oppose the federal suffrage amendment.

December: A petition of 500,000 names supporting a women's suffrage amendment is delivered to President Woodrow Wilson.

1915

Carrie Chapman Catt is reelected president of the National American Woman Suffrage Association.

New York holds state referendum; women's suffrage is defeated.

New Jersey holds state referendum; women's suffrage is defeated.

Pennsylvania holds state referendum; women's suffrage is defeated.

Massachusetts holds state referendum; women's suffrage is defeated.

Laura Howe Richards wins the Pulitzer Prize for biography, with her sister, Maude Howe Elliot. They are the first women to achieve this honor. The biography is of their mother, Julia Ward Howe.

Bertha Van Hoosen becomes the first president of and helps to establish the American Medical Women's Association (AMWA).

When Margaret Sanger flees to Europe to avoid prosecution on obscenity charges, Mary Ware Dennett and others lead Sanger's National Birth Control League on a more law-abiding path.

Localities such as Fellsmere, Florida, begin endorsing women's suffrage in their town charters, in spite of inaction by the state legislatures.

The National Advisory Council of the Congressional Union under the leadership of Alice Paul decides to organize in the states where the organization does not already have a branch.

January: Jane Addams and others organize the Woman's Peace Party.

January: A resolution to submit a woman suffrage amendment to the state constitution to the voters for the first time is introduced in the Alaska Territorial Legislature. It is defeated.

January: Mary Roberts Rinehart becomes the first woman correspondent actively reporting from the field in World War I.

January 15: House of Representatives votes on federal women's suffrage amendment; amendment fails.

June: The Equal Suffrage Party of Georgia makes its first effort to sponsor a suffrage bill in the state legislature.

October: The Woman's Political Equality League is formed in Arkansas.

September 23: Approximately 25,000 supporters of women's suffrage march in New York City.

November 11–15: The first suffrage parade in Georgia takes place in Atlanta, led by Eleanor Raoul on horseback.

December: A petition of 500,000 names supporting a women's suffrage amendment is delivered to President Woodrow Wilson. It was carried by Sara B. Field from San Francisco to Washington, D.C.

1916

West Virginia holds state referendum; women's suffrage is defeated.

House of Representatives committee issues report, without recommendation, on federal woman suffrage amendment.

Women's suffrage baseball game is held at Polo Grounds, New York.

Georgia passes a bill enabling women to practice law.

Edna Ferber's feminist play *Our Mrs. McChesney,* about a woman drummer, becomes the hit of the season in New York.

Born in 1862, Catharine W. McCulloch is the first woman to be nominated as a president elector.

Navy Reserve Act calls for the enlistment of qualified "persons." Navy Secretary Josephus Daniels asks, "Is there any law that says a Yeoman must be a man?"

February 11: Emma Goldman is arrested for speaking out on birth control, a crime in New York at the time.

February 29: South Carolina raises the minimum age of children employed in mills, factories, and mines from 12 to 14 years.

June: Alice Paul's Congressional Union becomes the National Woman's Party, formalizing its split with the National American Woman Suffrage Association.

June: In a letter to Carrie Chapman Catt, President Woodrow Wilson promises to recommend to the states that they grant women the vote.

August: Representatives of more than 36 NAWSA state chapters sign Carrie Chapman Catt's "Winning Plan."

September: President Wilson, campaigning for reelection, addresses the National American Woman Suffrage Association; First Lady Edith Galt Wilson attends as well.

October 16: Margaret Sanger, Ethel Burn, and Fania Mindell open America's first birth control clinic in Brooklyn, New York.

November: Jeannette Rankin of Montana is elected to the U.S. Congress.

December 2: Mrs. Richard Hornsby and other suffragists fly an airplane above President Wilson's yacht and drop petitions supporting the Nineteenth Amendment.

December 5: The Congressional Union for Woman Suffrage unfurls a banner in the House of Representatives with the words "Mr. President, What Will You Do for Woman Suffrage?" printed on it, while Woodrow Wilson is speaking.

EYEWITNESS TESTIMONY

I am a workman's daughter, by occupation a dressmaker and school teacher, and during this last twenty-five years an active worker in the organized labor movement . . . In this fight I wept at the grave of nineteen workers shot on the highways of Latterman, Pennsylvania in 1897. In the same place I marched with 5,000 women eighteen miles in the night seeking bread for their children, and halted with the bayonets of the Coal and Iron police who had orders to shoot to kill . . .

The same forces put me, an inoffensive old woman, in jail in West Virginia in 1902. They dragged me out of bed in Colorado in March, 1904, and marched me at the point of fixed bayonets to the border line of Kansas in the night-time. The same force took me from the streets of Price, Utah, in 1904, and put me in jail. They did this to me in my old age, though I never violated the law of the land, never been tried by a court on any charge but once, and that was for speaking to my fellow workers.

> *Mary Harris "Mother" Jones, letter to Mrs. Potter Palmer, January 12, 1907, in Steel,* Correspondence of Mother Jones, *61–62.*

I came to this country some twenty years ago. I had been trained for the tailoring trade . . . My mother was a great politician. Some people think that doesn't do for wives and mothers; they say it makes us neglect the home. Well, my home was always neat and orderly. And my mother is living today, a hale and hearty old lady of over eighty with nine sons and three daughters. Politics and home life seem to me to be a pretty good combination. Perhaps, to think outside themselves makes both men and women more self-reliant . . . My experience teaches me that it is the upright and downright woman that makes the best home and the best worker. The meek woman is ready to knuckle under to anything, for she has no self-respect.

We working women are often told that we should stay at home and then everything would be all right. But we can't stay at home. We have to get out and work. I lost my husband. He was a diamond setter, a fine workman, and he earned good money, but he fell ill and was ailing a long time. I had to go back to my trade to keep the family together. Gentlemen, we need every help to fight the battle of life, and to be left out

by the State just sets up a prejudice against us. Bosses think and women come to think themselves that they don't count for so much as men. I think that the ladies who just asked you not to give them suffrage lack self-respect. I was sorry to hear them speak of women as they did in front of men. They seem to look for all the vices and not the virtues of their sisters . . .

> *Clara Silver, of the Buttonhole Workers Union and member of the Equality League of Self-Supporting Women, speaking in the New York Senate chamber, Albany, February 1907, in Blatch and Lutz,* Challenging Years, *97.*

Trade unionism is not very popular with some of you; but gentlemen, it is the only protector we working women have. . . . We are ruled out in the State, and why shouldn't our trade union get all our feeling of patriotism?

Miss Schneiderman, who wanted to come here today, but could not leave the city, sent you a message by me. Rose Schneiderman is a cap-maker. She is a

Rose Schneiderman, president of the Cloth Hat, Cap, and Millinery Workers' International Union *(National Archives)*

Russian, but has been a long time in America. She told me to tell you how we women who were born in America, or have lived here a long time and have learned to understand the laws in this country, feel when we see some man from Europe who knows nothing of free government and is too old to learn, just put right over our heads. And, gentlemen, this shows in our working life. That man learns his lesson quickly, and thinks himself superior to every woman. He won't take his place in any organization according to his ability, but wants to push in and lead, when he is not up to it . . .

Gentlemen . . . the trade union, has taught me that men and women must stand as equals. The big, strong man doesn't want any advantage over us, and the small man ought not to have any advantage in citizenship, for it only makes him cocky. Two million of the big, strong men, the men in the National Federation of Labor, have declared that they want us working women to be their equals in the State. And I bring you a resolution from the Central Federated Union in New York, asking you to help us get the vote.

Mary Duffy, of the Overall Workers' Union and member of the Equality League of Self-Supporting Women, speaking in the New York Senate chamber, Albany, February 1907, in Blatch and Lutz, Challenging Years, *95–96.*

If women had the ballot they . . . would have dared to pass the 54-hour bill without the cannery exemption, in spite of big business. Yea, and if necessary they would have saved women and children from disease. Not only that, but they would see to it that the laws were enforced which would give them far more than all this sickening sentiment about motherhood and the home.

We working women cannot help wondering when we hear all this gush about the home how many of us would have a home if we did not go out from the home and work for it . . .

I do not want to be governor of the State. I do not want to be a policeman nor an assemblyman, nor yet a senator, but I do want the ballot to be able to register my protest against the conditions that are killing and maiming . . .

Melinda Scott, hat trimmer, to a New York state senator, n.d., in Melinda Scott, Hat Trimmer, *pamphlet, Reprint, Research Publications microfilm, Reel 951, no. 9223.*

You may remember me as being the colored student to whom you gave a scholarship to The Woman's Medical College of Penn. I graduated in the class of 1897 and came South. I have done well and have a very large practice among all classes of people.

It seemed when I came to Columbia [South Carolina] that the harvest was ready and waiting for me. The obstacles I did not consider very much and I have had unlimited success. I was the first woman physician to hang out a shingle in this state. Since I have returned to my native state, others have gone to our beloved College to take degrees. The last case is that of a colored woman, a friend of mine, named Melissa Thompson, in whose behalf I am about to write you.

I have known this young woman for nine years and she has been in my nurse-training department and has helped in the dispensary at the hospital. She would be of great service, if she could get a few years in medicine and surgery. She will not be able to continue her course without some aid being given. Her sisters, who are teachers, are sending her their earnings to help her pursue her studies. I would be greatly pleased, if you can do something for her. I am sure that she will be a great service to the race and to suffering humanity. I need her greatly in my work. The poor people of her race need her.

Thanking you kindly for what you did for me and hoping that you will consider her case . . .

Dr. Matilda A. Evans, letter to philanthropist Alfred Jones, March 13, 1907, in Sterling, We Are Your Sisters, *444–445.*

I went to work for the Triangle Shirtwaist Company in 1901. The corner of a shop would resemble a kindergarten because we were young, eight, nine, ten years old. It was a world of greed; the human being didn't mean anything. The hours were from 7:30 in the morning to 6:30 at night when it wasn't busy. When the season was on we worked until 9 o'clock. No overtime pay, not even supper money. There was a bakery in the garment center that produced little apple pies the size of the ashtray [holding up ashtray for group to see] and that was what we got for our overtime instead of money.

My wages as a youngster were $1.50 for a seven-day week. I know it sounds exaggerated, but it isn't; it's true. If you worked there long enough and you were satisfactory you got 50 cents a week increase every year. So by the time I left the Triangle Waist Company in 1909, my wages went up to $5.50, and that was quite a wage in those days.

All shops were as bad as the Triangle Waist Company. When you were told Saturday afternoon, through a sign on the elevator, "If you don't come in on Sunday, you needn't come in on Monday," what choice did you have? You had no choice.

I worked on the 9th floor with a lot of youngsters like myself. Our work was not difficult. When the operators were through with sewing shirtwaists, there was a little thread left, and we youngsters would get a little scissors and trim the threads off.

And when the inspectors came around, do you know what happened? The supervisors made all the children climb into one of those crates that they ship material in, and they covered us over with finished shirtwaists until the inspectors had left, because of course we were too young to be working in the factory legally.

The Triangle Waist Company was a family affair, all relatives of the owner running the place, watching to see that you did your work, watching when you went into the toilet. And if you were two or three minutes longer than foremen or foreladies thought you should be, it was deducted from your pay. If you came five minutes late in the morning because the freight elevator didn't come down to take you up in time, you were sent home for a half a day without pay.

Rubber heels came into use around that time and our employers were the first to use them; you never knew when they would sneak up on you, spying, to be sure you did not talk to each other during working hours.

Most of the women rarely took more than $6.00 a week home, most less. The early sweatshops were usually so dark that gas jets (for light) burned day and night. There was no insulation in the winter, only a pot-bellied stove in the middle of the factory. If you were a finisher and could take your work with you (finishing is a hand operation) you could sit next to the stove in winter. But if you were an operator or a trimmer it was very cold indeed. Of course in the summer you suffocated with practically no ventilation.

There was no drinking water, maybe a tap in the hall, warm, dirty. What were you going to do? Drink this water or none at all. Well, in those days there were vendors who came in with bottles of pop for 2 cents, and much as you disliked to spend the two pennies you got the pop instead of the filthy water in the hall.

The condition was no better and no worse than the tenements where we lived . . . the facilities were down in the yard . . .

We wore cheap clothes, lived in cheap tenements, ate cheap food. There was nothing to look forward to, nothing to expect the next day to be better.

Someone once asked me: "How did you survive?" And I told him, what alternatives did we have? You stayed and survived, that's all.

Pauline Newman, at Cornell University in 1975, describing conditions in the Triangle Shirtwaist Company, 1901–1909, in Wertheimer, We Were There, 294–295.

I'm tired of your picking my brain and not giving me any credit.

Eva MacDonald Velesh, American Federation of Labor worker, to AFL president, Samuel Gompers, from the Federationist, 1909, in Kenneally's Women and American Trade Unions, 23.

New York has never seen, such a gathering of women as that which was brought together last night at Carnegie Hall to listen to Mrs. Pankhurst, the English suffragette. The big house which seats 3,000 people was packed to the doors . . . A little after 7 o'clock, long before the doors were opened, the crowd had arrived in such numbers that it reached the corner and turned into Seventh Avenue. Eventually the line extended from 57th down to 59th Street, four abreast.

New York Times, report of Emmeline Pankhurst's visit to New York, October 25, 1909, in Blatch and Lutz, Challenging Years, 113.

I do not think I should have come to see you this fall if I had not been invited by the League of Self-Supporting Women, but I know what it is to be a self-supporting woman without a vote. I know you have not all come here tonight because you are interested in suffrage. You have come to see what a militant suffragette looks like and to see what a Hooligan woman is like. But I thank you all, and I know you will come to other meetings when I am gone. I am not going to tell you why we need the vote but how we are going to get it.

Emmeline Pankhurst founded the British Women's Social and Political Union. *(Library of Congress)*

men at Winchester objected to having some historic guns removed a short time ago, they broke every window on the main street, and the guns were put back. I very much exaggerate when I estimate the entire number of stones that have been thrown by suffragettes during this campaign at fifty. Around every one of these flinty messengers was wrapped a piece of paper with a question on it. We only threw them because we were not admitted to Liberal meetings and had no chance to ask our questions any other way.

Emmeline Pankhurst, speaking at Carnegie Hall, New York, October 25, 1909, in Blatch and Lutz, Challenging Years, *114–115.*

Thousands upon thousands left the factories from every side, all of them walking down toward Union Square. It was November, the cold winter was just around the corner, we had no fur coats to keep warm, and yet there was the spirit that led us on out of the cold at least for the time being.

I can see the young people, mostly women, walking down and not caring what might happen. The spirit, I think, the spirit of a conqueror led them on. They didn't know what could happen to them. They just didn't care on that particular day; that was *their* day.

Pauline Newman, recalling the beginning of the Triangle Shirtwaist Company strike, November 22, 1909, in Wertheimer, We Were There, *301.*

You don't have to send out notices. You just take a platform along, put up a banner and begin to talk. While someone is speaking others go around and distribute circulars among the girls and ask questions. These circulars are in Yiddish, Italian and English and we vary them. The last one we got was on getting married . . . It is helpful in time of strike to hold street meetings . . . we . . . talk to the scabs when they come out [of the factories] . . . It gives tremendous courage to the union girls to have us talk there . . . I think these street meetings are something we can all get courage out of. We make great friends with the policemen in New York. Miss O'Reilly has already converted one policeman.

Helen Marot, of the Women's Trade Union League, about street meetings held during the Triangle Shirtwaist Company strike, 1909–1910, in Wertheimer, We Were There, *273.*

It is by going to prison, rather than by any arguments we have employed that we have won the support of the English working man, and it is by going to prison that we will eventually win over all England . . .

It is to women rather than to men that I wish to make my plea. Men, I think, understand the situation better. Have they not had a fight for their liberties? . . . Much has been said about our throwing stones. New I want to tell you that stone throwing is a time-honored British political argument. When the

You uptown scum, keep out of this or you'll find yourself in jail.

> *Police officer, to Helen Marot of the Woman's Trade Union League, during Triangle Shirtwaist Company strike, ca. November 1909, in McCreesh,* Women in the Campaign, *133.*

The officer wouldn't let us girls sit down on the benches because we were strikers . . . One of our girls got so tired she went to crouch down to rest herself, when one of the officers came over and poked her with his club and says, "Here, stand up. Where do you think you are? In Russia?" . . .

Well, when I got before the judge I was so worn out I didn't care what they did to me. I just let the union pay the fine and went home. But I won't let them pay the fine next time! They can send me to jail; they can do what they like with me; but I ain't going to let any more money be paid into the court for me, when benefits are needed by the girls.

> *Esther Lobetkin, about her arrest during the Triangle Shirtwaist Company Strike, 1909—1910, in Wertheimer,* We Were There, *304.*

Fannie [Zinsher] was arrested for speaking to one of these [prostitutes]. The officer pinched her arm black and blue as he dragged [her] to court . . .

The hiring of women thugs [by the company to mingle with the striking women] ended dramatically. Six of them attacked two young pickets, threw them to the ground and beat them until their faces streamed with blood . . . This last incident was too much to endure and the whole street [i.e., all the factories on the block] went on sympathetic strike. In less than two days the prostitutes were removed.

> *Mary Brown Sumner, describing Triangle Shirtwaist Company strike, November or December 1909, in Wertheimer,* We Were There, *303.*

The most of our girls had to walk both ways in order to save their car fare. Many came without dinner, but the collection baskets had more pennies than anything else in them—it was our girls themselves who helped to make it up, and yet there were so many rich women present. And I'm sure the speakers made it plain to them how badly the money was needed, then

how comes it that out of the $300 collected there should be $70 in pennies?

> *Theresa Malkiel, in* Diary of a Shirtwaist Striker, *about Women's Trade Union League rally at the Hippodrome during the Triangle Shirtwaist Company strike, 1909–1910, in Wertheimer,* We Were There, *305–306.*

"You are on strike against God and Nature, whose prime law is that man shall earn his bread with the sweat of his brow. You are on strike against God."

> *Judge Willard Olmsted, to striking female shirtwaistmakers in New York City, February 1910, in McCreesh,* Women in the Campaign, *141.*

In every instance where the woman [poll watchers] were arrested, the Magistrate before whom they were taken after a ride in the patrol wagon, discharged them, and they returned to their posts in the polling places, smiling triumphantly at the crestfallen inspectors on whose complaints they were arrested. Though shoved about by the police, the women bobbed up smiling every time, and at nine o'clock last night, when the polls closed, were still on duty.

> New York Times, *account of election day in New York City, November 2, 1909, in Blatch and Lutz,* Challenging Years, *116–117.*

[Margaret Robins was] appalled at the idea of a child of twelve being involved in a strike. But by her gracious manner she did not let me know, nor did I feel . . . any sign of her being sorry for me. Instead, she gave me an inspiration that I was fighting for my fellow workers and myself, an inspiration that I still follow, an inspiration that through the many years has helped over many a difficult job.

> *Ada Rose, upon learning of Robins's death in 1945, about Robins, encouragement during the Philadelphia shirtwaist strike, 1910, in Payne,* Reform, Labor, and Feminism, *143.*

It is the women of your class, not the actual strikers who have stirred up all this strife. Had you and your kind kept out of this it would have been over long ago.

> *Magistrate, to Martha Gruening, a Bryn Mawr graduate student, arrested for her participation in the Philadelphia strike, ca. January 1910, in McCreesh,* Women in the Campaign, *138–139.*

In both Philadelphia and New York, some of the most devoted members of the Ladies Waist Makers Union are colored girls. In Philadelphia several of the girls going on strike were colored girls and two of these were the best pickets the union had in that city. They were not only able to persuade the girls of their own race and color from acting as strikebreakers, but they were able to keep wavering white girls from going back to work.

In New York, colored girls are not only members of the union but they have been prominent in the union. One . . . has been secretary of her shop organization all through the strike and has been very frequently at the union headquarters doing responsible work . . . meetings were held during the strike at the Fleet Street Methodist Church in Manhattan . . . in both, members of the Ladies Waist Makers Union said definitely and publicly that colored girls were not only eligible but welcome to membership.

Elizabeth Dutcher, letter to the editor of The Horizon, *March 1910, in Wertheimer,* We Were There, *307.*

The National Norwegian Woman Suffrage Association sends to you and Mrs. Roosevelt warm greetings from the enfranchised women of Norway . . . We hope, your visit in Norway will become a help for the American women to obtain justice, to become enfranchised.

F. M. Qvam, president of the Norwegian Woman Suffrage Association, to Theodore Roosevelt, May 4–5, 1910, in the Carrie Chapman Catt Papers, Rare Books and Manuscripts Division, New York Public Library.

Mrs. Roosevelt and I have always believed in the Suffrage for Women, although we have not thought that the question was as yet of great practical importance in America . . .

Theodore Roosevelt, response to F. M. Qvam of the National Norwegian Woman Suffrage Association, May 6, 1910, in the Carrie Chapman Catt Papers.

Flying their banners and wearing yellow Votes-for-Women sashes, the greatest suffrage parade and

Harriot Stanton Blatch (front seat) and other suffragists in a parade, 1913 *(Library of Congress)*

demonstration ever seen in New York moved on Union Square thousands strong this afternoon . . .

> Evening Telegram, *May 21, 1910, in Blatch and Lutz,* Challenging Years, *130.*

My dear young man, I am a grandmother. All my progeny, although I was graduated from college, are bouncing and lusty.

> *Harriot Stanton Blatch, to a male detractor skeptical about the parenting abilities of "suffragettes," May 21, 1910, in Blatch and Lutz,* Challenging Years, *131.*

I have been restraining myself for two weeks, but I can't keep to my resolution to leave you undisturbed. There is a critical turn of affairs down in the Shirt Waist Makers Union which none of us can manage but you. We have been needing you all through the months, and now I fear we must have you. Could you possibly come back next Wednesday and see us at the League on Thursday and be ready for a meeting of the Shirt Waist Makers Thursday night. This leaves your month [of planned vacation] uncompleted . . . but I don't see what we are going to do without you.

P.S. I hope and pray dear that you are rested or have had a chance for rest. The work ahead of you is so appalling! You must—must have strength or what shall we do?

> *Helen Marot, letter to Rose Schneiderman, August 10, 1910, in Wertheimer,* We Were There, *288.*

I hereby promise that:

1. I WILL give what I can and do my share of the work to gain Votes for Women.

Women working in a mending room, 1912 *(Library of Congress)*

2. I WILL NOT give either money or service to any other cause until the women of New York State have been enfranchised.

Pledge prepared by the Women's Political Union, made available for signature December 10, 1910, in Blatch and Lutz, Challenging Years, *137.*

I cannot see that anyone was responsible for the disaster. It seems to me to have been an act of the Almighty . . . I paid great attention to the witnesses while they were on the stand. I think the girls who worked there were not as intelligent as those in other walks of life and were therefore the more susceptible to panic.

Juror H. Houston Hierst, explaining his refusal to convict company owners Max Blank and Isaac Harris on charges of manslaughter in connection with Triangle Shirtwaist fire of March 25, 1911, in Wertheimer, We Were There, *314–315.*

Over and over again we suffragists insist that women are citizens and should be equally responsible with men, but a frightful shock like this makes us know it as we never knew it before. It is enough to silence forever the selfish addleheaded drivel of the anti-suffragists who recently said at a legislative hearing that working women can safely trust their welfare to their "natural protectors." We might perhaps be willing to consign such [anti-suffrage] women to the sort of protection, care and chivalry that is indicated by the men who allow 700 women to sit back to back, wedged in such close rows between machines that quick exit is an impossibility; a ten-story building with no outside fire escapes, and only one rickety inside fire escape, with a jump of 25 feet at the bottom of it, and the exits leading to the fire escape shuttered and locked; with iron gates shutting off the staircase, and cigarette-smoking allowed in the midst of inflammable materials. But we are not willing to consign unwilling women or helpless young girls to any such tender mercies. And we claim in no uncertain voice that the time has come when women should have the one efficient tool with which to make for themselves decent and safe working conditions—the ballot.

Mary Ware Dennett, writing of the Triangle Shirtwaist Company fire in the Woman's Journal, *April 1, 1911, in Kraditor,* The Ideas of the Woman Suffrage Movement, *155.*

Hay wagon ride for suffrage, 1913 *(National Archives)*

The women worked in the mills for lower pay and in addition had all the housework and care of the children. The old-world attitude of man as the "lord and master" was strong. At the end of the day's work—or, now, of strike duty—the man went home and sat at ease while his wife did all the work preparing the meal, cleaning the house, etc. There was considerable male opposition to women going to meetings and marching on the picket line. We resolutely set out to combat these notions. The women wanted to picket. They were strikers as well as wives and were valiant fighters.

Elizabeth Gurley Flynn, writing in 1955 of women during the Lawrence Textile strike, 1912, in Wertheimer, We Were There, *363.*

One cold morning, after the strikers had been drenched on the bridge with the firehose of the mills, the women caught a policeman in the middle of the bridge and stripped off his uniform, pants and all. They were about to throw him in the icy river, when other policemen rushed in and saved him from the chilly ducking.

Bill Haywood, of Industrial Workers of the World, writing in 1929 of the Lawrence Textile strike, 1912, in Wertheimer, We Were There, *364.*

The police killed Anna LaPiza [sic]. The picket line was out that morning 23,000 strong, an endless chain of pickets. And the police began to crowd them . . .

until they were massed in so thick that they could not move back any further. Then the police began to club them. Some of the sympathizers threw coal from the windows. The strikers themselves threw snowballs and chunks of ice at the policemen. And one of the policemen was hit with a chunk of coal or a chunk of ice on the leg. It was the sergeant. He ordered the policemen to pull out the guns. And as they did, they fired. And officer Benoit is said to have fired the shot that killed Anna LaPiza. Nineteen witnesses saw him fire the shot . . .

> *Bill Haywood, of Industrial Workers of the World, recalling the death of Ann LoPizzo during the Lawrence, Massachusetts, strike, 1912, in Wertheimer, We Were There, 362.*

When the time came to depart, the children arranged in a long line, two by two in an orderly procession with the parents near at hand, were about to make their way to the train when the police . . . closed in on us with their clubs, beating right and left with no thought of the children who then were in desperate danger of being trampled to death. The mothers and the children were thus hurled in a mass and bodily dragged to a military truck and even then clubbed . . . We can scarcely find words with which to describe this display of brutality.

> *Volunteer, describing the attempt to take the children of Lawrence's striking workers to Philadelphia for the remainder of the strike, February 24, 1912, in Wertheimer, We Were There, 365–366.*

Your methods are utterly abhorrent to me at all times, but now, after the superb unselfishness and heroism of the men of the Titanic, your march is untimely and pathetically unwise.

> *Annie Nathan Meyer, letter to the offices of the Women's Political Union prior to the New York City suffrage parade, 1912, in Blatch and Lutz, Challenging Years, 181.*

I don't wish you any bad luck, but I hope the sidewalk falls through and you all go to Hell.

> *Anonymous, letter to the office of the Women's Political Union prior to the New York City suffrage parade, 1912, in Blatch and Lutz, Challenging Years, 181.*

We shall be surprised indeed if the suffrage parade this afternoon does not astound those who are not closely

A drawing of Election Day *(Library of Congress)*

in touch with the spread of the demand for votes for women. The growth of this propaganda is one of the remarkable developments of the day and its importance is now indicated by the space of attention given to the parade by the entire press of the city. This week columns and pages have been given to advance notices, and it is realized that here is a movement which must be taken seriously and respectfully. Just how democratic this cause is the parade will show, since women of every position in life will be represented . . .

> *Evening Post, about the New York City suffrage parade, May 4, 1912, in Blatch and Lutz, Challenging Years, 181.*

I had my marching orders, that's
Why I marched today,
For all the women that I loved
Were marching the same way . . .

> *Richard LeGallienne, May 1912, in Blatch and Lutz, Challenging Years, 183.*

A year ago 3000 marchers and perhaps 70,000 onlookers. This year 20,000 marchers and 500,000 watching.

New York Tribune, *about the New York City suffrage parade, 1912, in Blatch and Lutz,* Challenging Years, *183.*

As you ride today in comfort and safety to the Capitol to be inaugurated as President of the people of the United States, we beg that you will not be unmindful that yesterday the Government which is supposed to exist for the good of all, left women while passing in peaceful procession in their demand for political freedom at the mercy of a howling mob on the very streets which are being at this moment efficiently officered for the protection of men.

Harriot Stanton Blatch, letter to President-elect Woodrow Wilson, March 4, 1913, in Blatch and Lutz, Challenging Years, *197.*

When I got to Ninth Street there were two points I want to bring out about the police. When I reached Ninth Street I had had no trouble, but just as I crossed over there was quite a file of young men, black and white, with hands on each other's shoulders, going from side to side. They made the most insulting remarks to the women. They tore a woman's suffrage badge from off my coat and nearly knocked me down. When I managed to get up the crowd was very dense. A woman cried out—she was crying—that they had torn two children away from her.

Mrs. Cordelia Powell Odenheimer, testifying about the 1913 suffrage parade, March 6, 1913, in U.S. Congress. Senate. Committee on the District of Columbia, Suffrage Parade: a report of the Committee on the District of Columbia, *31.*

I noticed a general air of indifference which struck me at the time. There was no endeavor to assist. I wish to speak very conservatively, but at the moment, not realizing what was going on elsewhere, I was impressed with the fact that there was no active interest either in the procession or in maintaining the protection of the people who were passing along in it . . .

Suffragists on parade, 1912 *(Library of Congress)*

Suffragist parade in New York City, 1912 *(Library of Congress)*

My impression was of a very occasional police-man, perhaps. It would be a very rough guess if I should say once in 50 feet or so I saw some one who seemed either like a policeman in uniform or a man with a star.

Julia C. Lathrop, chief of the Children's Bureau, Washington, D.C., testifying about the 1913 suffrage parade, March 6, 1913, in U.S. Congress. Congress. Senate. Committee on the District of Columbia, Suffrage Parade: a report of the Committee on the District of Columbia, *20.*

I got a letter from the Trades Union Women in N.Y. and all of the cold, sentimental documents that ever I read it was one of them, fortunately for me I have never mixed with them and I certainly shall not waste postage or paper in replying to them.

Mary Harris "Mother" Jones, letter to Caroline Lloyd, April 12, 1913, in Steel, Correspondence of Mother Jones, *112.*

. . . I inherit plenty of the spirit of '76. My great-grandmother—so the story goes—loaded guns, and if she did not kill any one in Revolutionary days it was because she was the proverbial bad shot. She aimed to kill her country's enemy. My grandmother . . . taught me to admire the courage, the devotion, the patrio-tism of my maternal ancestors. As a child I honored her, and I frankly admit I honor her still. And I would not honor her the less if she had loaded guns to gain liberty for women instead of merely for the men of her time . . .

My opposition of even a suggestion of militancy in America does not rest, then, upon any abstract theories in regard to physical force, not upon the flattering assertion that American men are different, nor upon the reassuring prophecy that it will never be necessary here. My objection to militancy rests upon the substantial fact that in our time the vote has not been won through violence. To suggest mil-itancy in the United States is singularly inept. In our country the final appeal is to the body of voters . . .

But because I hold such a political philosophy, I see no reason for condemning the conduct of the suffrage movement in another land. Surely a little modesty is demanded on the part of the Americans. The English battle is not ours. To speak of its lead-ers, as some do, as "hysterical," as "viragos," as "insane," is to speak with ignorance of facts, or with desire to deceive. Were they such women their movement could be easily crushed. The militants are women of marked intelligence, of exceptional poise, of self-sacrifice and devotion of the highest order.

Opposed to them stands a government that has shown itself weak, vacillating, and false to every pledge.

Harriot Stanton Blatch, letter to the Evening Sun, *summer 1913, in Blatch and Lutz,* Challenging Years, *200–203.*

I am not a militant, and believe in evolutionary rather than revolutionary methods for obtaining reforms. Consequently, I do not indorse the policy of the militants, but on the contrary, I have much admiration for Mrs. Pankhurst, whose sincerity of purpose and willingness to sacrifice herself no one who knows her can question . . . The United States has long been the haven for political exiles from all lands, and as an American I should be heartily ashamed if it should now make an exception to its honored custom by excluding Mrs. Pankhurst.

Carrie Chapman Catt, letter to the New York Tribune, *summer 1913, Blatch and Lutz,* Challenging Years, *203.*

I feel as if I butted in wher I was not wanted. Miss Hay gave me a badge was very nice to me but you know they had a school teacher represent the Industrial workers if you ever herd her it was like trying to fill a barrel with water that had no bottom not a word of labor spoken at this convention so far. You would have to be a real politician now to be a Suffrage. This convention is a verry quite serious affair after the hole thing was over some people came to me and said I had a right to speak for labor but they kept away until it was over.

Lenora they are all old members in this convention all the young people is gone over to the Congressi[on]al Union and there is a big fight but they have taken a vote to standing together one to back the other I am not goying to wait for sunday meeting I am goying home satturday.

Margaret Hinchey, letter to Leonora O'Reilly, ca. 1913, in Kraditor, The Ideas of the Woman Suffrage Movement, *160.*

Suffrage parade, Washington, D.C., 1913 *(Library of Congress)*

Marchers and spectators at the Washington, D.C. parade, 1913   *(Library of Congress)*

Your letter of April 6th has been referred to me for reply.

I am instructed by the executive committee of the board of trustees to say that the trustees are not empowered to grant any special permission to use the front steps of the museum building as requested, but that the public has the right to occupy the steps to view any parade that may pass the building, avoiding the making of speeches or the putting up of structures.

> *William Henry Fox, director of Museums, for the*
> *Central Museum (the Brooklyn Institute of Arts and*
> *Sciences, Eastern Parkway and Washington Avenue),*
> *to Ethel Dreier, April 10, 1914,*
> *Ethel Eyre Valentine Dreier Papers,*
> *Sophia Smith Collection, Smith College.*

If the women of America start an international women's peace society, I shall do all that lies in my power to assist in Europe or South Africa. It should be a society in which all women of all races on earth should equally find their places. It should overstep the miserable little bonds of nationality and race which lie at the root of the world's evil and war today. Its watchword should be Humanity.

> *Olive Schreiner, letter to Mrs. Petchick Lawrence of En-*
> *gland, read by Lawrence to those assembled at the*
> *"War and Women" meeting, October 30, 1914, in*
> *Blatch and Lutz,* Challenging Years, *252.*

I want woman as my mother was. I would rather have the mild, tender voice of my mother bidding me, as my father did, to vote whenever the Commonwealth gave me the privilege to vote linger in my ears than to hear the high, shrieking voice of woman around the polls dragging her sisters to the ballot box.

> *Senator Martine, of New Jersey, speaking during the 63d*
> *Congress, 2d session, 1914, in Kraditor,* The Ideas of
> the Woman Suffrage Movement, *37.*

I do not wish to see the day come when the women of my race in my state shall trail their skirts in the muck and mire of partisan politics. I prefer to look to the American woman as she always has been, occupying her proud estate as the queen of the American home, instead of regarding her as a ward politician in the cities. As the mother, as the wife, as the sister she exercises a broader and deeper and mightier influence than she can ever exercise or hope to on the stump and in the byways of politics in this land.

Representative Frank Clark, of Florida, speaking to his colleagues in the House of Representatives, 1915, in Kraditor, The Ideas of the Woman Suffrage Movement, *26.*

There will be political night meetings of negro men and negro women . . . Southern Congressmen know, and should protect our women on the farms, without police protection, from the return of those days when the farmer's wife sat in her home with fear and trembling—her vine and fig tree being but the crouching place of the brute ready to pounce upon her and take advantage of her helplessness . . . These flippant city girls, singing airily, "Votes for

Another suffragist *(Library of Congress)*

women," know not the disasters they invite by this reckless movement.

Daily Telegraph (Georgia), editorial included by a Southern congressman in the Congressional Record, 63d Congress, 3d Session, 1915, in Kraditor, The Ideas of the Woman Suffrage Movement, *29–30.*

Good for two drinks if woman suffrage is defeated.

Pink slips handed out in Massachusetts saloons before vote on women's suffrage amendment to that state's constitution, 1915, in History of Woman Suffrage, *Vol. 6, 289.*

Women insist on their "divine rights", "immutable rights", "inalienable rights". These phrases are not so sensible as one might wish. When one comes to think of it, there are no such thing as divine, immutable or inalienable rights. Rights are things we get when we are strong enough to make good our claim to them. Men spent hundreds of years and did much hard fighting to get the rights they now call divine, immutable and inalienable. Today women are demanding rights that tomorrow nobody will be foolhardy enough to question . . .

Helen Keller, in the New York Call, *1915, in Payne,* Between Ourselves, *152.*

I am so glad that you feel confident that Brooklyn will not fail in numbers in the parade, and I join you in hoping that you will have ten thousand marchers. I know it will be much more difficult to get people to come from Brooklyn to march in Manhattan, than it is to have people here. I am beginning to feel that it will be the greatest public demonstration ever held, and I hope it really will sweep us on to victory.

I doubt if you realize the great admiration I have for your work. It always comes easier for me to scold than to do the opposite.

Mrs. Norman deR. Whitehouse to Ethel Dreier, October 18, 1915, Ethel Eyre Valentine Dreier Papers, Sophia Smith Archives, Smith College.

As you know, the Woman Suffrage Amendment will be settled at the polls next Tuesday.

We must carry the Borough of Brooklyn and I believe it is entirely possible to do so if we leave no stone unturned. It may be that the Brooklyn vote will be the deciding factor in the state.

Some 20,000 women marched in New York City's suffrage parade, 1915. *(Library of Congress)*

In these last days we need more money to carry out our plans, and we need your help. May I ask you to share in this great struggle for Justice and Democracy by sending whatever you feel able to give for this last and most important piece of work?

Ethel Dreier to Mrs. Joseph Hendricks, October 29, 1915, Ethel Eyre Valentine Dreier Papers, Sophia Smith Archives, Smith College.

In the Headquarters News Letter, which will be issued the 15th of this month, there will appear a set of the conclusions arrived at by the Board after a week's meetings. This statement contains all that we wish given to the public. I will not repeat here any of that material.

What we did not put in the public statement and what we do not wish to make public at this time is our plan for nation-wide congressional activity. We propose to organize four Congressional Campaign Corps composed of as good speakers as we can secure. We shall offer them to the states with the view of holding, in each and every one which will accept our offer, a Congressional Campaign Conference. One Corps will be offered to New England; one to the South, one to the Middle West, one to the Enfranchised States. A different kind will be offered West Virginia, Iowa and South Dakota (where a referendum is pending) including a school for suffrage workers . . . The National will supply the speakers, the only responsibility for you being their entertainment while in your state . . . If these meetings are worked up well, on a generous, bold plan, they will . . . inform all . . . that your workers are after a Federal Amendment . . .

It is further proposed to have a National Suffrage parade in Chicago in connection with the Republican Convention . . . Some kind of demonstration will be planned for St. Louis and the Democratic Convention . . . Will you kindly see that neither of these plans leaks out to the press now? . . .

Lets make this old world hum with "Suffrage first;" Suffrage by the Federal route, Suffrage by the State route, Suffrage East and Suffrage West, until our dear lawmakers surrender. There are enough of us to give them no rest if we "get together" and pull together. It is worth it.

Carrie Chapman Catt, letter to the NAWSA state presidents, January 7, 1916, in the Carrie Chapman Catt Papers. Rare Books and Manuscripts Division, New York Public Library.

I was away from the city and did not get your telegram of June sixteenth promptly.

I am very glad to make my position about the suffrage plank adopted by the convention clear to you, though I had not thought it necessary to state again a position I have repeatedly stated with entire frankness. The plank received my entire approval before its adoption and I shall support its principle with sincere pleasure. I wish to join with my fellow-Democrats in recommending to the several States that they extend the suffrage to women upon the same terms as men.

Woodrow Wilson, letter to Carrie Chapman Catt, June 19, 1916, in the Carrie Chapman Catt Papers, Rare Books and Manuscripts Division, New York Public Library.

I am chagrinned to note from your letter of July 24th regarding "Questionnaires" that the one sent to us in January has never been returned to you . . . It was given to Miss MacAlarney who was acting as our general Secretary at that time with request that it be completed promptly and returned. As Miss MacAlarney is no longer in our employ I cannot take up the matter with her, but we have made a careful search here and cannot locate the document . . .

Below I am answering the questions . . .

"How many counties are there in your State?" *67*

"How many were there organized in January?" *50*

"How many paid or unpaid regular field workers who were occupied steadily did you have on your staff last January? Who were they and for how long were they engaged?" *2*

Miss Emma L. MacAlarney for six months, Miss Leona Huntzinger for five months—both paid.

Mary Orlady, letter to Carrie Chapman Catt, July 25, 1916, in the Carrie Chapman Catt Papers, Rare Books and Manuscripts Division, New York Public Library.

I fully appreciate the splendid work which the National Association has done in the states. Little could be done toward speedy and universal emancipation through the Federal Amendment until a certain number of the states were won for suffrage.

When, however, that number of states was won, the old non-partisan tactics, as abundantly proved by reference to the history of minorities in American politics, became not only obsolete, but in fact a hindrance to the cause. Non-partisanship is all right when you are dealing with referenda, but when dealing with responsible public bodies dominated by political parties that can be held responsible, non-partisanship is futile. What you say in effect is: 'Please approve woman suffrage but if you do not see fit to do so, we shall ask the women of your party to vote for you just the same.' You may ask any seasoned politician what he thinks of appeals not backed by votes . . .

In my opinion all that was got at [the Republican and Progressive Party Conventions in] Chicago and [the Democratic Convention in] St. Louis was got only because the politicians were afraid of the impending danger created by the Congressional Union and the Woman's Party, namely, that western women would not be non-partisan when the freedom of their sisters was at stake, but would vote for the party that gave the most promising assurances of quick and speedy emancipation . . . What do you suppose won Lodge, Butler, and the other anti-suffrage

Woman suffrage headquarters in Cleveland, Ohio *(Library of Congress)*

leaders in the Republican Convention? The Parade? If so, then you do not know these men as I do . . .

You say that you [and the National American Woman Suffrage Association] represent 97 per cent of the woman suffragists. That may be true, but it would have required only 35 voters in the 1912 Nevada Congressional election to turn the scale. It is not mere numbers that count in war or politics; it is tactics and explosives.

I am sorry to have 'annoyed' you, but I do not believe that I caused you as much distress as you have caused me by informing President Wilson, in effect, that western women will, and ought to, vote for him whether he favors national emancipation or not.

Charles Beard, letter to Carrie Chapman Catt, August 5, 1916, in Blatch and Lutz, Challenging Years, 265–267.

I very much value and appreciate your kind letter of August seventh inviting me to address the National American Woman Suffrage Association on September eighth next during its 48th Annual Convention, and wish to assure you that my desire will be to accept the invitation.

I say "my desire" because I am not sure as yet of my liberty on that date. I am going to Kentucky early in September to accept for the Nation the gift of the Lincoln Birthplace and I have made conditional promises in connection with that journey which make it somewhat uncertain when I shall be again within reach of Atlantic City, but I shall try.

I hope it will not inconvenience you to leave the matter in this shape for the moment, since I sincerely wish to come.

Woodrow Wilson, letter to Carrie Chapman Catt, August 10, 1916, in the Carrie Chapman Catt Papers, Rare Books and Manuscripts Division, New York Public Library.

When thirty-six state associations, or preferably more, enter into a solemn compact to get the [Federal] Amendment submitted by Congress and ratified by their respective legislatures; when they live up to their compact by running a red-hot, never ceasing campaign in their own states designed to create sentiment behind the political leaders of the states and to aim both these forces at the men in Congress as well as the legislatures, we *can* get the Amendment through, and ratified. We cannot do it by any other process. No

such compact has ever been made, and no virile intention exists in the minds of the majority of the Association to back up a Washington lobby. Whether this is due to a prevailing belief that a lobby, assisted now and then by a bombardment of letters and telegrams, can pull the Amendment through, or to a lack of confidence in suffrage by the Federal route, or to sheer, unthinking carelessness, I am not prepared to say. I am inclined to believe that all three of these causes exist. . . .

This Convention must not adjourn should it sit until Christmas, until it creates a logical and sensible policy toward the Federal Amendment . . . If it be decided that we *do* want enfranchisement by the Federal route, then at least thirty-six states must sign a compact to go after it with a will . . .

National Boards must be selected thereafter for one chief qualification—the ability to lead the national fight. There should be a mobilization of at least thirty-six armies, and these armies should move under the direction of the national officers. They should be disciplined and obedient to the national officers in all matters concerning the national campaign. This great army with its thirty-six, and let us hope, forty-eight divisions, should move on Congress with precision, and a will . . . More, those who enter on this task, should go prepared to give their lives and fortunes for success, and any pusillanimous coward among us who dares to call retreat, should be court-martialled . . .

When a general is about to make an attack upon the enemy at a fortified point, he often begins to feint elsewhere in order to draw off attention and forces. If we decide to train up some states into preparedness for campaign, the best help which can be given them is to keep so much "suffrage noise" going all over the country that neither the enemy nor friends will discover where the real battle is . . .

We should win, if it is possible to do so, a few more states before the Federal Amendment gets up to the legislatures . . . A southern state should be selected and made ready for a campaign, and the solid front of the "anti" south broken as soon as possible.

Some break in the solid "anti" East should be made too. If New York wins in 1917 the backbone of the opposition will be largely bent if not broken . . .

By 1920, when the next national party platforms will be adopted, we should have won Iowa, South

Dakota, North Dakota, Nebraska, New York, Maine and a southern state . . .

With these victories to our credit and the tremendous increase of momentum given the whole movement, we should be able to secure planks in all platforms favoring the Federal Amendment (if it has not passed before that time) and to secure its passage in the December term of the 1920 Congress.

It should then go to the legislatures of thirty-nine states which meet in 1921, and the remaining states would have the opportunity to ratify the amendment in 1922. If thirty-six states had ratified in these two years, the end of our struggle would come by April 1, 1922, six years hence . . .

Marching costume for Chicago's suffrage parade, 1916 *(Library of Congress)*

It will require, however, a constructive program of hard, aggressive work for six years, money to support it, and the cooperation of all suffragists. It will demand the elimination of the spirit of criticism, back-biting and narrow-minded clashing of personalities which is always common to a stagnant town, society or movement, and which is beginning to show itself in our midst. Success will depend less on the money we are able to command, than upon our combined ability to lift the campaign above this sordidness of mind, and to elevate it to the position of a crusade for human freedom.

Carrie Chapman Catt, "Report of Survey Committee to National Board of NAWSA" prior to adoption of her "Winning Plan," during national convention, September 4–10, 1916, in Flexner, Century of Struggle, 290–292.

My dear Leader:—

You are receiving so many letters all the time that I hesitate to send another, but it is such a splendid opportunity for the Captains in your District to cover the full list of Registered voters on Election Day by having at each polling place two workers to hand out literature that I hope the opportunity will not be lost. Can you not appoint the Secretary of your District, or some other woman to take charge of the volunteers for that day?

First. She should have a list of polling places.

Second. She should try to get at least four women for each Election District.

Third. They should be instructed to stand 100 ft. from the polls on each side, to wear some Suffrage insignia, to get quiet and dignified in manner, to hand out our special literature to every voter who passes, and if possible to note down the sentiment of individuals towards our Amendment.

As this is the Presidential election, the largest number of Registered voters will be reached, and we want to gain their favor toward our cause and toward our Organization.

The Teachers' Branch of the New York State Suffrage Party has many volunteers who will be free to serve on Election Day. I am sure that the teachers of your District will help you.

Ethel Dreier to Mrs. Norman deR. Whitehouse [?], October 25, 1916, Ethel Eyre Valentine Dreier Papers, Sophia Smith Collection, Smith College.

Mother, this has been a most interesting fight . . . When we called for volunteers to sell papers on the street (women) I told some of the men that I would bet my money on the women providing they did not have to fight the entire family in order to come out. And much to my astonishment Chas. Meyers wife—Secy. of the Central Labor Council, and Mrs. Drake, wife of the editor of the Labor paper joined the rest of us, and it was a good stunt. I am enclosing clipping from last Sunday's Times, so you will please note we have acquired reputations via the Times route. Some of the leading club women came out with us—we had about 100 all told.

Last night the women had a big meeting in the Trinity Auditorium and it was packed to the doors. Mrs. Fremont Older and two other women came from Frisco. Mrs. Older was the best of the three—the other two were about as good as I would be . . . These semi-society ladies are about the limit no matter where you put them. Don't you think so Mother? May find an occasional worth-while one, but generally speaking it is a waste of time to bother with them.

Katherine L. Schmidt, letter to Mary Narris "Mother" Jones, October 29, 1916, in Steel, Correspondence of Mother Jones, *158–159.*

The enclosed resolutions concerning discriminations against women applicants for civil service positions have been passed by the National Board of the National American Woman Suffrage Association.

In compliance with the instructions contained in the resolutions, I beg leave to call the facts set forth to your attention and respectfully urge you to give them your most serious attention.

Carrie Chapman Catt, letter to Woodrow Wilson, November 15, 1916, in the Carrie Chapman Catt Papers, Rare Books and Manuscripts Division, New York Public Library.

13

To War and Victory
1917–1920

THE HISTORICAL CONTEXT

On January 10, 1917, suffragists determined to get the vote stood outside the White House gates. The organization to which this faction belonged was now, after two mergers and a secession, the National Woman's Party. It was led by Alice Paul and Lucy Burns, neither of whom was accustomed to compromise.

Among the organization's members was Harriot Stanton Blatch. When the United States entered World War I, she understood what would happen if women put aside their demand for suffrage. "The suffragists of Civil War days had given up their campaign to work for their country, expecting to be enfranchised in return for all their good services, but when the war was over, they heard on all sides, 'This is the Negro's hour.' They were told they must wait, their turn would come next. My mother and Miss Anthony led the small rebel group who were not willing to wait. But women did not rally behind them. They stepped aside for the Negro. Now in 1917 women were still waiting . . ."[1] The National Woman's Party pickets remained in front of the White House.

Beginning in June, many members of the National Woman's Party were arrested on charges of "obstructing traffic." Found guilty, Alice Paul and 96 other suffragists served sentences of up to six months. Held in the Occoquan workhouse, they were physically abused, put into solitary confinement and, when they refused to eat, subjected to force feeding.[2] The women believed they were jailed for their political beliefs rather than for the obstruction of a sidewalk. On scraps of paper, they composed a document claiming political prisoner status and managed to pass it from woman to woman for signing. It was the first time that a U.S. citizen had made such a claim.[3]

Although the District of Columbia Court of Appeals would ultimately find each of the arrests and imprisonments to have been "invalid,"[4] no response to the demand for political prisoner status was made.

At the same time, women were joining the war in now familiar and even expected ways. They were serving at the front as nurses, filling "male" positions in private industry, and working to make weapons. When Red Cross and other female war volunteers joined the New York City women's suffrage parade on October 27, 1918, the gap between women's rights and responsibilities was truly visible.

There was also a gap of the women's rights leaders' own creation. As the NAWSA continued to seek support for women's suffrage in the South, it backed away from the open membership policies of its past. It allowed its Southern state chapters to decide whether to admit African-American women, and it countenanced prejudiced discussion at national conventions.[5] Kate Gordon and Laura Clay—both Southern women and, for a time, officers of the NAWSA—had for several years actively explored the possibility of enfranchising European-American but not African-American women. By 1916 Laura Clay had come to believe that passage of a federal suffrage amendment would violate states' rights; she left NAWSA to found and lead the Citizens Committee for a State Suffrage Amendment, while simultaneously becoming a fierce opponent of a federal suffrage amendment. By this time, Kate Gordon had also left NAWSA to work for state suffrage amendments and against a federal one. Although Gordon's organization, the Southern States Woman Suffrage Conference, did not significantly drain membership from NAWSA in southern states and was dissolved in 1917,[6] Carrie Chapman Catt would not ignore the threat of Southern defection from the federal suffrage campaign. In 1919 Catt requested that the president of a 6,000-member African-American organization withdraw her group's request to join the NAWSA so that the Southern states would not be alarmed.[7]

Catt's primary concern remained her "Winning Plan." Unlike the movement's leaders during the Civil War, she did not allow her organization to suspend suffrage activities during wartime. Unlike the National Woman's Party's Alice Paul and Lucy Burns, she also refused to publicly challenge a wartime president. Instead, she maintained the course she had set in 1916. As she had outlined then, her first goal was the winning of state suffrage in at least 36 states—the number needed to ratify a federal amendment. Once that was accomplished, she expected the enfranchised women of those 36 states to pressure their legislatures into support for a federal suffrage amendment, enfranchising *all* American women. The work was hard, methodical, and well organized. Women such as Ethel Dreier, chairman of the Woman Suffrage Party of Brooklyn, New York, worked tirelessly to organize and champion suffrage workers in each assembly district of her borough, earning gratitude and affection from both those she led and those to whom she reported.[8] This process was steadfastly and quietly duplicated all across the United States, gaining fewer headlines than the picketing of the White House, but applying pressure that was equally difficult to ignore. Catt herself waged a forceful, unrelenting behind-the-scenes campaign, pressing President Wilson for a federal suffrage amendment. He finally agreed to intervene directly with Congress on behalf of the federal amendment.[9]

President Woodrow Wilson faced Alice Paul's "silent sentinels" at the White House gates.
(Library of Congress)

On September 30, 1918, he did so. Addressing the Senate in person, he said: "We have made partners of the women in this war; shall we admit them only to a partnership of suffering and sacrifice and toil and not to a partnership of privilege and right? This war could not have been fought, either by the other nations engaged or by America, if it had not been for the services of women—services rendered in every sphere—not merely in the fields of effort in which we have been accustomed to see them work, but wherever men have worked, and upon the very skirts and edges of the battle itself . . . I tell you plainly, that this measure which I urge upon you is vital to the winning of the war . . . And not to the winning of the war only. It is vital to the right solution of the great problems which we must settle, and settle immediately, when the war is over."[10]

The measure was nevertheless defeated, securing just two votes less than the two-thirds majority needed. For the first time, the NAWSA campaigned against legislators who had voted against women's suffrage. Two lost their campaigns for re-election—Senator John W. Weeks of Massachusetts and Senator Willard Saulsbury, Jr. of Delaware—and suffragists began to look forward to 1919. In the meantime, American suffragists could take note of the other countries that had already enfranchised women: New Zealand (1893), Australia (1901), Finland (1906), Norway (1913), Denmark (1915), Iceland (1915), Russia (1917), Austria (1918), Canada (1918), Poland (1918), England (1918), Ireland (1918), Scotland (1918), and Wales (1918). (In 1919, women in Germany, Luxembourg, and the Netherlands would also win suffrage.)[11]

On May 21, 1919, the U.S. House of Representatives passed the Federal Woman Suffrage Amendment, originally suggested as a 16th amendment but now, with the passage of time and other amendments, the 19th. On June 4, 1919, it was passed by the Senate and sent to the states for ratification.

A new suffrage campaign began in every state. Women had not won suffrage in Catt's hoped-for 36 states, but they had won it in 30. (In nine of those states, suffrage was restricted to presidential elections.) As Catt had predicted, legislators hoping either to stand for reelection themselves or to court the women's vote for their party could not entirely ignore state-enfranchised women as they demanded a nationwide extension of female suffrage. Where it had taken almost 71 years to win suffrage in the individual 30 states, it took only 15 months to win ratification of the Nineteenth Amendment. Not one state with women voters failed to ratify the amendment.

This is not to say that the final struggle was an easy one. The states that had previously enfranchised women would all ultimately ratify the federal amendment, but many initially resisted calling special sessions to consider the matter. Some state suffrage chapters, not heeding Catt's advice to stand ready for passage of the federal amendment, had allowed members to disperse when suffrage was won in their own state; where suffrage organizations had first to rebuild, legislative response tarried. Meanwhile, those who opposed women's suffrage or, like Laura Clay and Kate Gordon, opposed a federal amendment to secure it, increased their efforts and fought against it until the end. The liquor interests—acting on antisuffrage sentiment that dated back to Frances Willard's presidency of the National Woman's Christian Temperance Union—also tried to prevent ratification of the Nineteenth Amendment, using especially underhanded tactics. They tried to get legislators drunk before a scheduled vote on the amendment, and they even threatened to end the careers of individual leg-islators unless they cast a negative vote.

In Tennessee such threats provided the background for one of the struggle's last acts of courage and integrity. Before Tennessee was to vote and, with its vote, possibly complete ratification of the amendment, Representative Harry Burn was threatened by the liquor interests. They promised an end to his career unless he cast a negative vote. For a few days, he hoped the amendment would pass without his vote in its favor. When it became clear that his vote was required, he decided he had to grant his mother's wish for suffrage. Burn cast the deciding vote, and the Nineteenth Amendment was ratified. The work of 72 years was finally complete.

CHRONICLE OF EVENTS

1917

Indiana, Michigan, Nebraska, Rhode Island and Ohio state legislatures grant women suffrage.

Ohio holds state referendum; women's suffrage, granted by legislature earlier in the year, is rescinded.

Senate committee issues favorable majority report on federal women's suffrage amendment.

House of Representatives issues a report, without recommendation, on federal women's suffrage amendment.

The Athletic Conference of American College Women (ACACW) is established by Blanche Trilling of the University of Wisconsin.

Grace Abbott, social worker, becomes head of the Children's Bureau's Child Labor Division, and eventually champions the need for a constitutional amendment abolishing child labor.

The federal suffrage amendment is tied up in the U.S. Congress when a petition from the California State Federation of Women's Clubs reaches the legislature. Without a nay vote, the following passes both houses in 12 minutes: "Whereas, the women of the United States are being called upon to share the burdens and sacrifices of the present national crisis and they are patriotically responding to that call, be it Resolved by the Senate of California with the Assembly concurring that the denial of the right of women to vote on equal terms with men is an injustice and we do urge upon Congress the submission to the Legislatures of the States for their ratification of an amendment to the U.S. Constitution granting women the right to vote."

Dorothy Jacobs Bellanca becomes the first full-time woman organizer for Amalgamated Clothing Workers.

Mary Frances Lathrop becomes the first woman admitted to the American Bar Association.

Kate Gleason is the first woman to be president of a national bank, the First National Bank of Rochester (New York).

Mrs. W. C. Tyler of Los Angeles, California, is one of three women (with Mrs. Spinks from San Francisco and Mrs. Wylie from Fresno) to be the first to sit in the Electoral College.

Carrie Chapman Catt joins the Woman's Committee of the Council of National Defense. As president of the National American Woman Suffrage Association, she believes that support for World War I will win support for women's suffrage after the conflict.

Loretta Walsh is the first woman to enlist in the U.S. Navy, and is thought to be the first woman to ever sign up for enlistment in a naval armed service.

January: Huge crowds attend meetings of an antiprostitution drive in San Francisco, California.

January 14: National Woman's Party members picket outside the White House.

January 16: The legislature of North Dakota approves both a presidential and municipal suffrage bill and an amendment to the state constitution giving women full suffrage. The governor will sign the bill on January 23. This legislature also adopts a resolution to Congress asking it to submit a federal woman suffrage bill.

February 10: Picketing by suffragists resumes at the White House, although four women have been arrested and given prison sentences. Now 41 women are arrested.

February 22: A presidential suffrage bill is signed by the governor of Indiana.

February 27: The Woman Suffrage League of Maryland is organized in Baltimore.

March 6: Arkansas state legislature grants suffrage to women, restricted to primaries.

March 17: War Labor Board decision permits continued employment of women streetcar conductors in Cleveland.

April 2: President Woodrow Wilson reads his war message to Congress, asking permission to enter World War I.

April 2: Jeannette Pickering Rankin of Montana becomes the first woman sworn in and seated to the House of Representatives.

April 4: Senate approves Wilson's request.

April 6: Representative Jeannette Rankin votes against U.S. entry into World War I.

April 6: House of Representatives approves Wilson's request. United States enters World War I.

May 19: Belva Lockwood dies.

June 22: The first of the National Woman's Party pickets are arrested.

August 28: Ten women picketing for women's suffrage are arrested in front of the White House. Four will receive six-month sentences in the penitentiary.

September: Maine holds state referendum; women's suffrage is defeated.

Jeannette Rankin was the first woman elected to the U.S. House of Representatives. *(Library of Congress)*

September 15: Favorable report on women's suffrage is given by the Senate Committee on Woman Suffrage Issues.

September 24: U.S. House of Representatives appoints a Committee on Woman Suffrage.

October 16–22: Alice Paul and other picketing members of the National Woman's Party are convicted and sentenced to the penitentiary.

October 27: Women's suffrage parade is held in New York City; female Red Cross volunteers and other female wartime volunteers join the march.

November 6: New York holds state referendum; women's suffrage is passed.

November 27 and 28: All National Woman's Party pickets released from prison.

1918

House of Representatives issues favorable majority report on federal women's suffrage amendment.

South Dakota holds state referendum; women's suffrage passes.

Michigan holds state referendum; women's suffrage passes.

Oklahoma holds state referendum; women's suffrage passes.

Louisiana holds state referendum; women's suffrage is defeated.

Texas legislature passes primary election bill giving women a vote in primary elections.

Harriot Stanton Blatch publishes *Mobilizing Woman Power,* with foreword by Theodore Roosevelt.

Representative Jeannette Rankin introduces mother and child welfare bill.

The Massachusetts Woman Suffrage Association, under directions from the National American Woman Suffrage Association, initiates a heavy campaign on behalf of the Federal Suffrage Amendment.

Georgia passes a law raising the age of consent to 14. The Georgia suffrage association had worked for this for 23 years and had always asked that the age be 18.

Pauline M. Newman establishes the first health clinic for the New York International Ladies' Garment Workers' Union (ILGWU).

Caroline Leonetti Ahmanson becomes one of the first two women (with Jean A. Crocket) appointed as chair of a Federal Reserve regional bank, serving for one year at the Federal Reserve Bank of San Francisco.

Anne Henrietta Martin, Nevada suffragist, is the first woman to run for a seat in the U.S. Senate.

The National Birth Control League becomes the Voluntary Parenthood League.

The Red Cross certifies 1,800 African Americans as nurses.

Kathryn Sellers is named as the first woman to act as head judge of a juvenile court.

The American Bar Association admits women as members.

January 8: Margaret Sanger's victory in *New York v. Sanger* allows doctors to advise their married patients about contraception for health purposes.

January 9: President Wilson declares himself in support of the federal women's suffrage amendment.

January 10: House of Representatives votes upon federal women's suffrage amendment; amendment passes.

March 4: District of Columbia Court of Appeals declares the 1917 arresting and sentencing of picketers to have been invalid.

May: In Arkansas, the first statewide primary election in which women can vote is held.

June: Women in Industry Service of the Department of Labor is formed.

August 12: Opha May Johnson becomes the first woman to join the U.S. Marine Corps.

September: President Woodrow Wilson addresses the U.S. Senate in support of the vote for women.

September 30: Disregarding President Wilson's plea, Senate fails to give the necessary two-thirds vote to federal women's suffrage amendment.

November 5: A majority passes a joint resolution to amend the Massachusetts constitution to eliminate the word *male* as a qualification for voters.

November 11: World War I ends.

December 3: Women win suffrage in Oklahoma.

1919

Texas holds state referendum; women's presidential suffrage is defeated.

Senate committee issues unanimously favorable report on federal women's suffrage amendment.

House of Representatives committee issues favorable majority report on federal women's suffrage amendment.

Florence Ellinswood Allen becomes assistant county prosecutor of Cuyahoga County, Ohio, the first woman in American history to hold such office.

Virginia Furman becomes the first woman to act as a bank officer in New York City. She coordinates a women's department at the Columbia Trust Company.

Mabel Edna Gillespie founds the Boston's Trade Union College.

Mary White Ovington becomes chair of the National Association for the Advancement of Colored People (NAACP).

Mary H. Donlon becomes the first woman editor-in-chief of a law review.

Reverend Anna Howard Shaw receives the Distinguished Service Medal, the highest military award given to a civilian.

Suffragist Alice Hamilton is the first woman on staff of the Harvard Medical School.

The Woman's Peace Party becomes the Women's League for Peace and Freedom and elects Jane Addams its president.

January: States ratify the Eighteenth Amendment, which criminalizes the making and sale of liquor, a victory for the Woman's Christian Temperance Union.

January: The U.S. House of Representatives passes the proposed Nineteenth Amendment. The Senate defeats it by one vote.

January 2: Both houses of the Colorado state legislature pass the following resolution in less than one hour: "Whereas, Colorado has long enjoyed the help and counsel of its women in all political matters of citizenship and by these years of experience demonstrated the benefit to be derived from equal suffrage; and whereas, there is now pending in the Senate of the United States a constitutional amendment providing for national woman suffrage; therefore be it Resolved, that we urge the United States Senate to take up and submit this amendment at the earliest possible date in order that all the women of the nation may have the right of suffrage and the nation may have the benefit of their citizenship."

February 10: Senate votes on federal women's suffrage amendment: amendment fails.

February 28: Missouri legislature approves a presidential suffrage bill, 21 to 12.

March: Women win the right to vote in Texas primaries.

March 24: The League of Women Voters (LWV) is established as a successor to the National American Woman Suffrage Association (NAWSA). The National Federation of Business and Professional Women and the Women's International League for Peace and Freedom are also founded this year.

April: A bill allowing women to vote in presidential elections passes both houses of Iowa's legislature.

May: The white women of Atlanta, Georgia, win the vote in city primaries.

May 21: House of Representatives votes on federal women's suffrage amendment; amendment passes.

June 4: Senate votes again on the federal women's suffrage amendment; amendment passes and goes to the states for ratification.

June: Illinois, Wisconsin, Michigan, Kansas, Ohio, New York, Pennsylvania, Massachusetts, and Texas ratify Nineteenth Amendment.

July: Iowa, Missouri, Arkansas, Nebraska, and Montana ratify Nineteenth Amendment.

July 2: Dr. Anna Howard Shaw dies at the age of 72.

August 18–24: Annual Conference of Governors meets in Salt Lake City; National American Woman Suffrage Association sends envoys to request action on behalf of the Nineteenth Amendment.

September: Minnesota, New Hampshire, and Utah ratify Nineteenth Amendment.

November: California and Maine ratify Nineteenth Amendment.

December: North Dakota, South Dakota, and Colorado ratify Nineteenth Amendment.

1920

The Army Reorganization Act improves the status of nurses in U.S. Army to give nurses "relative rank status." Before this, nurses could not become officers.

Florence Ellinwood Allen becomes the first woman to be elected to a judgeship in America. Her triumph comes in the first Ohio general election in which women have the right to vote.

President Woodrow Wilson selects Helen Hamilton Gardener (1853–1925; born Alice Chenoweth) to serve on the Civil Service Commission, the highest government position ever held by a woman. She is the first woman to serve on any federal commission.

The Women's Joint Congressional Committee is founded.

Mary Anderson becomes the first director of the Women's Bureau of the U.S. Department of Labor.

Rose Tyler Barrett becomes the first woman city manager (Warrenton, Oregon).

Women's Bureau is founded as a branch of the Labor Department.

Annette Abbott Adams becomes the first woman to hold office as U.S. assistant attorney general.

Texas holds state referendum; women's presidential suffrage is defeated.

Social worker and pacifist Jane Addams helps to found the American Civil Liberties Union.

January: Rhode Island, Kentucky, Oregon, Indiana, and Wyoming ratify Nineteenth Amendment.

February: New Jersey, Idaho, Arizona, New Mexico, Nevada, and Oklahoma ratify Nineteenth Amendment.

March: West Virginia and Washington ratify Nineteenth Amendment.

April 9: Society of Automotive Engineers elects its first woman member, Marie Luhring.

June 6–12: The Congress of the International Woman Suffrage Alliance meets in Geneva.

August 2: Montana governor Samuel V. Stewart calls a special session of the legislature to meet to ratify the federal suffrage amendment. It passes unanimously in the House and 38 to 1 in the Senate.

August 24: Tennessee is the 36th state to ratify the Nineteenth Amendment; Governor Roberts signs certificate and sends it to the U.S. Secretary of State, Bainbridge Colby.

August 26: Secretary of State Colby receives ratification certificate from Tennessee and signs proclamation; Nineteenth Amendment is adopted. Women of the United States are enfranchised.

September 21: Nebraska voters approve the rewritten state constitution, which carries a clause giving full suffrage to women. Before the constitution went to the voters, the federal amendment was passed and women fully enfranchised. With women voting, the constitution received 65,483 ayes to 15,416 noes.

EYEWITNESS TESTIMONY

No amount of reading or imagination prepares one for the sight of wounded from the front. One cannot describe it; one must see it to feel it.

Katherine Foote, U.S. nurse serving in France, letter to her parents, January 14, 1917, in 88 Bis and V.I.H., *1.*

Mrs. Gardener has been requested by Mrs. Carrie Chapman Catt to invite the President to head a small group of honorary members of the National American Woman Suffrage Association. This group will be made up of leading members of the political parties, who will be asked to affiliate themselves in this way with the Association in order to show their approval of the non partisan policy and the non militant methods of this, the oldest and largest body of suffragists in the United States. As honorary members they will not be expected to render active service in the organization.

Mrs. Catt hopes that the President will consider this an opportunity in accord with the intention he expressed at Atlantic City, of working with our organization, & she would greatly appreciate a statement from the President of his approval of the non partisan attitude which the National American Woman Suffrage Association has steadily maintained in its efforts to secure suffrage for women.

Helen Guthrie Miller (Mrs. Walter McNab Miller), first vice president of the National American Woman Suffrage Association, letter to Joseph P. Tumulty, secretary to President Wilson, January 13, 1917, in the Carrie Chapman Catt Papers.

It is an outrage that you women should have to stand here and beg for your rights. We gave it to our women in Australia long ago.

Male visitor to the United States, bowing to the Washington, D.C., pickets, 1917, in Stevens, Jailed for Freedom, *68.*

During the eighteen years I have been a newspaper correspondent in Washington I have seen no more impressive sight than the spectacle of the pickets surrounding the White House on the afternoon of March fourth. The weather gave this affair its character. Had there been fifteen hundred women carrying banners on a fair day the sight would have been a pretty one. But to see a thousand women—young women, middle-aged women, and old women—and there were women in the line who had passed their three score and ten—marching in a rain that almost froze as it fell; to see them standing and marching and holding their heavy banners, momentarily growing heavier—holding them against a wind that was half a gale—hour after hour, until their gloves were wet and their clothes soaked through . . . was a sight to impress even the jaded senses of one who has seen much . . . A special committee carrying the Resolutions of the Woman's Party Convention went to the west gates leading to the Executive Offices of the White House, but these gates for the first time in two decades were locked . . . Policemen were planted at intervals of fifty feet inside the iron fence and they were almost as numerous as the pickets. By some absurd arrangement there was not even a messenger or watchman to accept the written Resolutions. The delegation parleyed with the policeman and waited in the rain. They waited for a long time—which was typical of the attitude of the Administration on the subject of the Federal Amendment for woman suffrage. Mr. Wilson, from the first, has kept the women waiting. It is a poor business—both for the women and for Wilson.

Gilson Gardner, Washington correspondent for the Scripps newspapers, spring 1917, in Blatch and Lutz, Challenging Years, *279.*

I say, Miss, this *is* the White House, isn't it? . . . We went three times around the place and I told the boys, the big white house in the center was the White House, but they wasn't believing me and I wasn't sure, but as soon as I saw you girls coming with your flags, to stand here, I said, 'This *must* be the White House. This is sure enough where the President lives; here are the pickets with their banners that we read about down home.'

Man from Alabama, to one of the pickets, spring 1917, in Stevens, Jailed for Freedom, *74.*

I feel very strongly that this Party has been brought together for one purpose, the national enfranchisement of women. We are composed of pacifists, militarists, Protestants, Catholics, Jews, Republicans, Democrats, Socialists, Progressives, Populists, and every other following . . . If we for a moment divert our Party from the purpose of its organization we not only weaken it, but we may destroy it.

Suffragists picketing in front of the White House, ca. 1916
(Library of Congress)

It is inconceivable that an organization composed of Americans should be anything but loyal to their country . . . Those of us who want to work for peace, or those of us who want to work for war should do so through other channels than the National Woman's Party. As individuals they can work for these purposes, but the Woman's Party is to work, and should work, and should not cease to work for the enfranchisement of the women of this country. We must be considered an integral part of this country . . .

  Florence Bayard Hills, at assembly of the Woman's Party,
  prior to the United States entry into
  World War I, 1917, in Blatch and Lutz,
  Challenging Years, *278.*

The United States entered the war on April 6, 1917. The Woman's Party continued its picketing, thereby arousing a storm of protest and hostility. But we were convinced, all of us, that we must stick to our program. The suffragists of Civil War days had given up their campaign to work for their country, expecting to be enfranchised in return for all their good services, but when the war was over, they heard on all sides, "This is the Negro's hour." They were told they must wait, their turn would come next. My mother and Miss Anthony led the small rebel group who were not willing to wait. But women did not rally behind them. They stepped aside for the Negro. Now in 1917 women were still

waiting, and we of the Woman's Party would wait no longer.

  Harriot Stanton Blatch, in 1940, recalling 1917, in
  Blatch and Lutz, Challenging Years, *280–281.*

We got eight stretcher cases in about ten last night, and sixteen more came during the night. They are mostly from the Vimy Ridge fighting . . .

  Katherine Foote, while serving with the 76th
  Detachment, Chesire County Division, British Red
  Cross Society, letter to her family, April 18, 1917, in 88
  Bis and V.I.H., *44.*

As you have probably seen by the papers, we all are in the midst of alarms. We have had less than a week's notice to get ready for mobilization for service in France . . . I just wish I had the words to express what I think about this opportunity. Aside from what we think about the causes and principles involved, and the tremendous satisfaction of having a chance to help work them out, to be in the front ranks in this most dramatic event that ever was staged, and to be in the first group of women ever called out for duty with the United States Army, and in the first part of the army ever sent off on an expeditionary affair of this sort, is all too much good fortune for any one person like me.

  Julia C. Stimson, a U.S. nurse, letter to her mother and
  father, May 4, 1917, in Finding Themselves, *1–3.*

You are always thoughtful and considerate, and I greatly value your generous attitude.

In reply to your letter of May Seventh, let me say that I candidly do not think that this is the opportune time to press the claims of our women upon the Congress. The thought of the Congress is so much centered upon the matters immediately connected with the conduct of the war that I think the general feeling would be that the time was not well chosen.

I know how many persons whose judgement I greatly value dissent from this conclusion, but my contact with the gentlemen in Congress convinces me that I am not judging wrongly.

  Woodrow Wilson, letter to Carrie Chapman Catt,
  May 8, 1917, in the Carrie Chapman Catt Papers.

I am sure you will believe that I have as much interest as even you have not only in putting nothing in the way of the women of Russia, but also in aiding them in any way to the full realization of their rights under the new order of things there; but I have had some pretty intimate glimpses of the new situation over there recently and the thing that stands out most clearly to my mind is that they would at the present juncture of affairs not only be very sensitive to any attempt at their political guidance on our part, but would resent it and react from it in a way that would be very detrimental to the interest of the country and to the relations of Russia and the United States.

I am trying to put over on the commission whose popular sympathies and catholic view of human rights will be recognized (at least, in the case of most of them), but they are going, not to offer advice or to attempt guidance, but only to express the deep sympathy of the United States, its readiness to assist Russia in every way that can wisely be planned, and our desire to learn how the cooperation between the two countries can be most intimate and effective in the present war.

> *Woodrow Wilson, letter to Carrie Chapman Catt (marked "Confidential"), May 8, 1917, in the Carrie Chapman Catt Papers, Rare Books and Manuscripts Division, New York Public Library.*

TO THE RUSSIAN ENVOYS

PRESIDENT WILSON AND ENVOY ROOT ARE DECEIVING RUSSIA WHEN THEY SAY "WE ARE A DEMOCRACY, HELP US WIN THE WORLD WAR SO THAT DEMOCRACY MAY SURVIVE."
WE THE WOMEN OF AMERICA TELL YOU THAT AMERICA IS NOT A DEMOCRACY. TWENTY-MILLION AMERICAN WOMEN ARE DENIED THE RIGHT TO VOTE. PRESIDENT WILSON IS THE CHIEF OPPONENT OF THEIR NATIONAL ENFRANCHISEMENT.
HELP US MAKE THIS NATION REALLY FREE. TELL OUR GOVERNMENT IT MUST LIBERATE ITS PEOPLE BEFORE IT CAN CLAIM FREE RUSSIA AS AN ALLY.

> *Banner held outside the White House by Lucy Burns of New York and Mrs. Lawrence of Philadelphia, during meeting of Russian diplomats and President Wilson, spring 1917, in Stevens,* Jailed for Freedom, *92.*

My attention has been called to the question as to whether it was desirable to appoint a Committee on Woman Suffrage in the House of Representatives. Of course, strictly speaking, it is none of my business, and I have not the least desire to intervene in the matter,

but I have a letter written in admirable spirit from Mrs. Helen Gardener, in which she says that she has been told that you said that you would report out a proposal for such a committee if I should approve. On the chance that I may be of some slight service in the matter, which seems to me of very considerable consequence, I am writing this line to say I think it would be a very wise act of public policy, and also an act of fairness to the best women who are engaged in the cause of woman suffrage.

> *Woodrow Wilson, letter to Edward W. Pou, chairman of the Rules committee, U.S. House of Representatives, May 14, 1917, in the Carrie Chapman Catt Papers, Rare Books and Manuscripts Division, New York Public Library.*

We have had a very strenuous morning to-day for six stretcher cases came in from Dover during the night. They are all bad fractures and one poor boy has terrible wounds at the top of his spine. He is in agony; I have turned him and tried to make him comfortable so many times this morning, and every time I went to him the slow tears were rolling down his cheeks. He's a little more at ease since his wounds were dressed, but the dressing was hideous.

> *Katherine Foote, letter to her family, May 19, 1917, in* 88 Bis and V.I.H., *60.*

First night in danger zone safely passed and everything O.K. My bunch all went to bed and slept finely.

> *Julia Stimson, letter to her family, May 26, 1917, in* Finding Themselves, *14.*

I was frightfully tired from my work when I returned from [Women's Rights Convention in Washington, D.C.] but I started right in to secure the vote of Mr. Davidson of this district and of Mr. Classon of the Ninth District after Christmas. I traveled over a good deal of their districts not making public speeches but seeing men who were politically prominent and talking the question out with each one of them, putting my best efforts into making them see the situation from our viewpoint. Some days I got up at 5:30, took an electric train, and did not get home until midnight, talking the question out with from six to eight men and going from office to office all during the day. The day I was in Appleton it was ten below. The day I was in Marinette there was a very bad snow storm. I spent the night there and got to Oconto before any of the walks were clean, so had to wade through snow up to the tops of my shoes. There are no street cars in Oconto. As far as I could see there were no taxis. I worked up until the last moment, until I knew nothing more could reach Washington, and then I gave it up. There is nothing the matter with me except nervous and physical exhaustion. I am not complaining because I would do it all over again to get the result even if I were in bed for six months.

Mrs. Jessie J. Hooper, of Wisconsin, letter to Theodora M. Youmans, June 13, 1917, in Flexner, Century of Struggle, 302–303.

All day yesterday and in the night we heard the booming of guns, and the night nurses say the windows in our surgical hut rattled. It was the loudest I have heard since we have been here.

Julia Stimson, letter to her family, June 16, 1917, in Stimson, Finding Themselves, 71.

We shall fight for the things we have always held nearest our hearts, for democracy, for the right of those who submit to authority to have a voice in their own government.

Banner carried by Katherine Morey, of Boston, and Lucy Burns on the day of their arrest, June 22, 1917, in Stevens, Jailed for Freedom, 94.

Allow me as an intense lover and believer in the democracy of Lincoln, Adams, and Jefferson, and as a plain citizen of the Republic, to beg for justice to the women who are petitioning at your door. They have been misrepresented in the public press and hounded by hoodlums enough . . . If they are violating the law of the land in their manner of presenting their petition, may they not, at least, have a fair and impartial trial on charges that will properly present the issues involved before a court of some degree of respectability which will hear and determine those issues in harmony with the great principles of democracy upon which our Government is founded?

Representative Charles A. Lindbergh, letter to President Wilson after witnessing mob harassment of Women's Party pickets, in Blatch and Lutz, Challenging Years, 281.

Two years ago I had the honor of being received by President Wilson to discuss the then status of woman suffrage. He and our delegation of four women talked for one hour and twenty minutes. The final word of the President was to the effect that those who worked for a reform are apt to be impatient of all delay, and then he added, "You will not get what you want this year, but certainly in four years". Pausing a moment as if considering, he went on, "Yes, I might say, certainly in two years". That interview was in July 1916. The time limit is up. The President's recognition of the importance of our being a democracy and the statement that the Suffrage Amendment is a war measure should lead him forthwith to visit the Capitol and speak on the Amendment to the Senate face to face as he has on so many questions when important legislation was in jeopardy. If he had followed that course, what happened yesterday in the Senate [filibuster threatened by some Democratic Senators in opposition to woman suffrage] would not have occurred.

Harriot Stanton Blatch, letter of protest, June 28, 1918, in Blatch and Lutz, Challenging Years, 283.

It is Bastille Day, July fourteenth. Inspiring scenes and tragic sacrifices for liberty come to our minds. Sixteen women march in single file to take their own "Liberty, Equality, Fraternity" to the White House gates. It is the middle of a hot afternoon. A thin line of curious spectators is seen in the park opposite the suffrage headquarters. The police assemble from obscure spots; some afoot, others on bicycles. They close in on the women and follow them to the gates.

The proud banner is scarcely at the gates when the leader is placed under arrest. Her place is taken by another. She is taken. Another, and still another steps into the breach and is arrested.

Meanwhile the crowd grows, attracted to the spot by the presence of the police and the patrol wagon. Applause is heard. There are cries of "shame" for the police, who, I must say, did not always act as if they relished carrying out what they termed "orders from higher up." An occasional hoot from a small boy served to make the mood of the hostile ones a bit gayer. But for the most part an intense silence fell upon the watchers, as they saw not only younger women, but white-haired grandmothers hoisted before the public gaze into the crowded patrol, their heads erect, their eyes a little

The earliest beginnings of women's participation in government: Five women learn how to use a voting machine in Chicago. *(National Archives)*

moist and their frail hands holding tightly to the banner until wrested from them by superior brute force.

Doris Stevens, recalling arrests on July 14, 1917, in Stevens, Jailed for Freedom, *88.*

There has been a "war measure" plan in mind for some time past. Mrs. Catt hopes to have the opportunity to explain it to you in person.

She is now "booked" in the campaign as speaker in Maine and in New York, so, that except on Saturday of this week (July 21) she has not an open date when she could come to Washington until August 2.

If you think there is reason to believe it wise for her to see you before August second could you see her on Saturday?

If so, I must wire her at once . . .

It may not be unwise for me to say in this connection, that our next annual National Convention is set for Washington this second week in December . . .

Our hope has been to secure your interest and powerful influence at that time—at the opening of the New Congress—for a real drive for the enfranchisement of twenty million of American women, as a "war measure" and to enable our women to throw yet more fully and whole-heartedly, their entire energy into work for their country and for humanity, instead of for their own liberty and independence.

We hope and believe that you will see your way to help us then in the manner we have thought out, if you do not feel that any move is wise sooner.

Therefore we have refrained from forcing the matter to your attention while you have been so overwhelmed, and have been meeting with such splendid courage, the immediate demands of the war, both here and abroad.

Nevertheless, Mr. President, we do not want to be found wanting should you deem the time ripe to act at an earlier date and we think that a conference (wholly without publicity) might be most helpful to us, and we trust not unwelcome to you.

Helen H. Gardener, letter to Woodrow Wilson, July 19, 1917, in the Carrie Chapman Catt Papers.

We are not guilty of any offence, not even of infringing a police regulation. We know full well that we stand here because the President of the United States refuses to give liberty to American women. We believe, your Honor, that the wrong persons are before the bar in this Court . . .

We believe the President is the guilty one and that we are innocent.

Mrs. John Rogers, Jr. (descendant of Declaration of Independence signer Roger Sherman), speaking in her own defense against charges of obstructing traffic ca. July 14, 1917, in Stevens, Jailed for Freedom, *102.*

This is what we are doing with our banners before the White House, petitioning the most powerful representative of the government, the President of the United States, for a redress of grievances; we are asking him to use his great power to secure the passage of the national suffrage amendment.

As long as the government and the representatives of the government prefer to send women to jail on petty and technical charges, we will go to jail. Persecution has always advanced the cause of justice. The

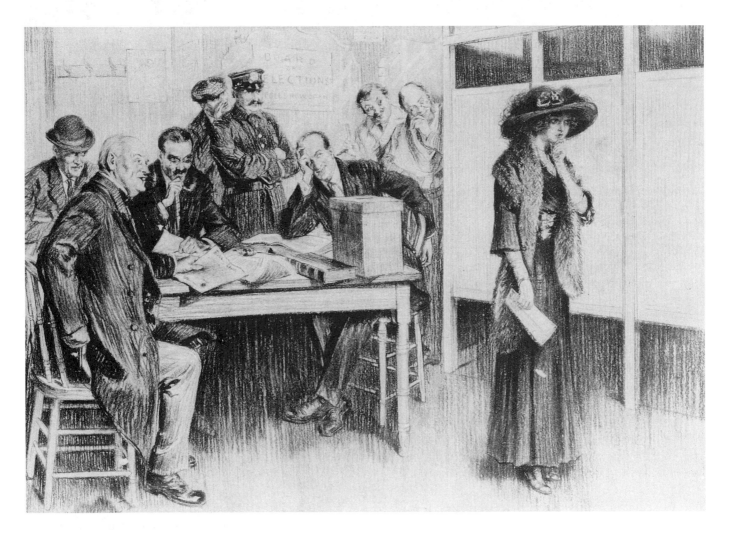

Cartoon of women voting for the first time *(National Archives)*

right of American women to work for democracy must be maintained . . . We would hinder, not help, the whole cause of freedom for women, if we weakly submitted to persecution now. Our work for the passage of the amendment must go on. It *will* go on.

Anne Martin, speaking in her own defense against charges of obstructing traffic ca. July 14, 1917, in Stevens, Jailed for Freedom, *102.*

For generations the men of my family have given their services to their country. For myself, my training from childhood has been with a father who believed in democracy and who belonged to the Democratic Party. By inheritance and connection I am a Democrat, and to a Democratic President I went with my appeal . . . What a spectacle it must be to the thinking people of this country to see us urged to go to war for democracy in a foreign land, and to see women thrown into prison who plead for that same cause at home.

I stand here to affirm my innocence of the charge against me. This court has not proven that I obstructed traffic. My presence at the White House gate was under the constitutional right of petitioning the government for freedom or for any other cause. During the months of January, February, March, April and May picketing was legal. In June it suddenly becomes illegal . . .

Florence Bayard Hills, speaking in her own defense against charges of obstructing traffic ca. July 14, 1917, in Stevens, Jailed for Freedom, *103.*

Not a dollar of your fine will we pay. To pay a fine would be an admission of guilt. We are innocent.

Katherine Morey, Annie Arneil, Mabel Vernon, Lavinia Dock, Maud Jamison, and Virginia Arnold, choosing to spend three days in jail rather than pay $25 fine, 1917, in Stevens, Jailed for Freedom, *95.*

Sixty days in the workhouse in default of a twenty-five dollar fine.

Judge Alexander Mullowny, sentencing Doris Stevens, Anne Martin, Florence Bayard Hills, and Mrs. John Rogers, upon their convictions of obstructing traffic, in Stevens, Jailed for Freedom, *106.*

In the past 24 hours we have admitted more patients than the total capacity of the Barnes and Children's Hospital, not the average number of patients, but the total capacity . . .

We have been receiving patients that have been gassed, and burned in a most mysterious way. Their clothing is not burned at all, but they have bad burns on their bodies, on parts that are covered by clothing. The doctors think it has been done by some chemical that gets its full action on the skin after it is moist, and when the men sweat, it is in these places that are the most moist that the burns are the worst. The Germans have been using a kind of oil in bombs, the men say it is oil of mustard. These bombs explode and the men's eyes, noses, and throats are so irritated they do not detect the poison gas fumes that come from the bombs that follow these oil ones, and so they either inhale it and die like flies, or have a delayed action and are affected by it terribly several hours later. We have had a lot of these delayed-action gassed men, who cough and cough continuously, like children with whooping cough. We had a very bad case the other night who had not slept one hour for four nights or days, and whose coughing paroxysms came every minute and a half by the clock. When finally the nurses got him to sleep, after rigging up a croup tent over him so that he could breathe steam from a croupkettle over a little stove that literally had to be held in the hands to make it burn properly, they said they were ready to get down on their knees in gratitude, his anguish had been so terrible to watch . . .

Julia Stimson, letter to her family, July 25, 1917, in Finding Themselves, *79–80.*

Mrs. Catt now thinks that the proposed conference with the President might better be left to a later date when the war measures and the Congress will bear less heavily upon him.

You and Mr. Tumulty were both good enough to say, in our recent talks, that the exact date might be left open and that if any great stress on suffrage action became imminent we could arrange the date upon application to you.

This is wholly satisfactory to Mrs. Catt and she thanks you, and through you the President, for your always kind appreciation of the situations as they arise.

His [serene] and tactful handling of the recent "picket crisis" cleared the air for the time, at least, and makes a conference unnecessary, we hope, with the close of Congress.

Helen Gardener, letter to T. W. Brahany, member of President Wilson's staff, July 25, 1917, in the Carrie Chapman Catt Papers, Rare Books and Manuscripts Division, New York Public Library.

I beg to acknowledge receipt of your letter of July 25th. I thank you for it.

The fine spirit which prompts it is genuinely appreciated.

T. W. Brahany, response to Helen H. Gardener, July 28, 1917, in the Carrie Chapman Catt Papers, Rare Books and Manuscripts Division, New York Public Library.

My nurses are beginning to show the effect of the emotional strain . . . I have had about a dozen of them weeping . . . I would have given a good deal myself to have had some one like Mother to weep on, last Sunday. You can imagine how I miss my older women friends. Naturally I cannot do any weeping here, since I have to be wept on . . .

Julia Stimson, letter to her family, August 8, 1917, in Finding Themselves, *92.*

Last autumn, as the representative of your Administration, I went into the woman suffrage states to urge your reelection. The most difficult argument to meet among the seven million voters was the failure of the Democratic party, throughout four years of power, to pass the federal suffrage amendment looking toward the enfranchisement of all the women of the country. Throughout those states, and particularly in California, which ultimately decided the election by the votes of women, the women voters were urged to support you, even though Judge Hughes had already declared for the federal suffrage amendment, because you and your party, through liberal leadership, were more likely nationally to enfranchise the rest of the women of the country than were your opponents.

And if the women of the West voted to reelect you, I promised them that I would spend all my energy, at any sacrifice to myself, to get the present Democratic Administration to pass the federal suffrage amendment.

But the present policy of the Administration, in permitting splendid American women to be sent to jail in Washington, not for carrying offensive banners, not for picketing, but on the technical charge of obstructing traffic, is a denial even of their constitutional right to petition for, and demand the passage of, the federal suffrage amendment. It, therefore, now becomes my profound obligation actively to keep my promise to the women of the West.

In more than twenty states it is a practical impossibility to amend the state constitutions; so the women of those States can only be enfranchised by the passage of the federal suffrage amendment . . .

To me, Mr. President, as I urged upon you in Washington two months ago, this is not only a measure of justice and democracy, it is also an urgent war measure . . . It will hearten the mothers of the nation, eliminate a just grievanace, and turn the devoted energies of brilliant women to a more hearty support of the Government in this crisis . . .

I have not approved all the methods recently adopted by women in pursuit of their political liberty; yet, Mr. President, the Committee on Suffrage of the United States Senate was formed in 1883, when I was one year old; this same federal suffrage amendment was first introduced in Congress in 1878, brave women like Susan B. Anthony were petitioning Congress for the suffrage before the Civil War, and at the time of the Civil War men like William Lloyd Garrison, Horace Greeley, and Wendell Phillips assured the suffrage leaders that if they abandoned their fight for suffrage, when the war was ended the men of the nation "out of gratitude" would enfranchise the women of the country . . .

It is no small sacrifice now for me, as a member of your Administration, to sever our political relationship. But I think it is high time that men in this generation, at some cost to themselves, stood up to battle for the national enfranchisement of American women. So in order effectively to keep my promise made in the West . . . I hereby resign my office as Collector of the Port of New York, to take effect at once, or at your earliest convenience.

Dudley Field Malone, letter to Woodrow Wilson, September 7, 1917, in Stevens, Jailed for Freedom, *166–168.*

Then we began in the operating room. Miss Taylor was on duty in the office, so I was free to help in the operating room. The supervisors were each on their side of the hospital, and the nurses were all getting the poor creatures as comfortable as possible. One patient who was too far gone from bloodlessness to stand operation was made as comfortable as possible and the minister sent for; they were all given tea and partially bathed. This was about 4:30 P.M. Then we began in the operating room, taking out foreign bodies and incising and draining. I scrubbed up and helped, not so much because they needed me but because I wanted to be in it. We kept three tables going all the time. The medical students gave ether and even some of the medical men were helping. Out in the little hall there were always three or four patients on stretchers on the floor. My friend, Dr. (Sgt.) Voorsanger, the Rabbi, was in charge of the records and stretcher bearers and worked like a Trojan. We took pieces of shell out of necks, hips, knees, skulls, ankles, shoulders, and out of the spine of my poor paralyzed man.

Julia Stimson, letter to her family, September 28, 1917, in Finding Themselves, *122–123.*

Eight stretcher and four sitting cases came in Thursday evening; I was off duty before they came, but it was quite a rush getting ready for them. Four convalescents were moved into the new ward, others shifted to the gallery, and the usual preparations for a convoy, besides the evening routine made my last hour very busy. The new cases are bad; an amputation, and a man with a terrible leg, and a horrible case of mustard gas and liquid fire burns.

Katherine Foote, letter to her family, October 17, 1917, in 88 Bis *and* V.I.H., *44.*

Dear Madam:—

Thursday and Friday evening suffrage posters were pasted on the outside of the windows of our Annex, 67 Court Street. So many were there on Saturday morning when we arrived for our meeting, and it took considerable time to remove them. We regret that it is necessary to call your attention to this unwarrantable attack upon Anti-suffrage propaganda in Kings County, and ask you to see that such attacks be immediately stopped.

Mrs. George Phillips [first name signed, but illegible], Secretary of the Brooklyn Auxiliary of the New York State Association Opposed to Woman Suffrage, to Mrs. H. Edward [Ethel] Dreier, Chairman of the Woman Suffrage Party, Brooklyn, October 29, 1917, Ethel Eyre Valentine Dreier Papers, Sophia Smith Archives, Smith College.

To the Pastors of Brooklyn—

If you believe that equal suffrage is a moral issue and that giving the vote to women will be a help in maintaining moral conditions in a community, I trust that you will take the opportunity on next Sunday of calling to the attention of your congregation the importance of settling this question on Nov. 6th. The arguments for woman suffrage have frequently been presented to you and I hope that you are ready to join with us in the fight for democracy at home, as a fundamental part of the great cause of democracy in the world.

Yours faithfully,

Ethel Dreier, chairman of the Woman Suffrage Party, Brooklyn, to the Pastors of Brooklyn, November 1, 1917 (an identical letter was also sent "To the Ministers of Brooklyn"), Ethel Eyre Valentine Dreier Papers, Sophia Smith Archives, Smith College.

I am appealing to you to help a young Russian girl imprisoned in the workhouse near Washington. Her name is Nina Samarodin. I have just come from one of the two monthly visits I am allowed to make her, as a member of her family.

The severity and cruelty of the treatment she is receiving at Occoquan are so much greater than she would have to suffer in Russia for the simple political offense she is accused of having committed that I hope you will be able to intercede with the officials of this country for her.

Her offense, aside from the fact that she infringed no law or disturbed the peace, had only a political aim, and was proved to be political by the words of the judge who sentenced her, for he declared that because of the innocent inscription on her banner he would make her sentence light.

Since her imprisonment she has been forced to wear the dress of a criminal, which she would not in Russia; she has had to eat only the coarse and unpalatable food served the criminal inmates, and has not been allowed, as she would in Russia, to have other food brought to her; nor has she, as she would be there been under the daily care of a physician. She is not permitted to write letters, nor to have free access to books and other implements of study. Nina Samarodin has visibly lost in weight and strength since her imprisonment, and she has a constant headache from hunger.

Her motive in holding the banner by the White House, I feel, cannot but appeal to you, Excellency, for she says it was the knowledge that her family were fighting in Russia in this great war for democracy, and that she was cut off from serving with them that made her desire to do what she could to help the women of this nation achieve the freedom her own people have.

Will you, if it is within your power, attempt to have her recognized as a political prisoner, and relieve the severity of the treatment she is receiving for obeying this impulse born of her love of liberty and the dictates of her conscience?

Vera Samarodin, letter to the Russian ambassador, about her imprisoned sister, 1917, in Stevens, Jailed for Freedom, *179–180.*

The Women are all so magnificent, so beautiful. Alice Paul is as thin as ever, pale and large-eyed. We have been in solitary for five weeks. There is nothing to tell but that the days go by somehow. I have felt quite feeble the last few days—faint, so that I could hardly get my hair brushed, my arms ached so. But to-day I am well again.

Rose Winslow, message smuggled out on scrap of paper during her imprisonment, 1917, in Stevens, Jailed for Freedom, *188.*

I was getting frantic because you seemed to think Alice was with me in the hospital. She was in the psychopathic ward. The same doctor feeds us both, and told me. Don't let them tell you we take this well. Miss Paul vomits much. I do, too, except when I'm not nervous, as I have been every time against my will.

Rose Winslow, message to her husband, smuggled out on scrap of paper during her imprisonment, 1917, in Stevens, Jailed for Freedom, *190.*

. . . Asked for Whittaker, who came. He seized Julia Emory by the back of her neck and threw her into the room very brutally. She is a little girl. I asked for counsel to learn the status of the case. I was told to "shut up," and was again threatened with a strait-jacket and a buckle gag. Later I was taken to put on prison clothes, refused and resisted strenuously. I was then put in a room where delirium tremens patients are kept.

Lucy Burns, message smuggled out of prison, November 16, 1917, in Stevens, Jailed for Freedom, *200.*

I was seized and laid on my back, where five people held me, a young colored woman leaping upon my knees, which seemed to break under the weight. Dr. Gannon then forced the tube through my lips and down my throat, I gasping and suffocating with the agony of it. I didn't know where to breathe from and everything turned black when the fluid began pouring in. I was moaning and making the most awful

Alice Paul formed the Congressional Union for Woman Suffrage. *(Library of Congress)*

sounds quite against my will, for I did not wish to disturb my friends in the next room. Finally the tube was withdrawn. I lay motionless. After a while I was dressed and carried in a chair to a waiting automobile, laid on the back seat and driven into Washington to the jail hospital. Previous to the feeding I had been forcibly examined by Dr. Gannon, I struggling and protesting that I wished a woman physician.

Mrs. Lawrence Lewis, about her experience in prison, 1917, in Stevens, Jailed for Freedom, *201.*

Mrs. Lewis and I were asked to go to the operating room. Went there and found our clothes. Told we were to go to Washington. No reason as usual. When we were dressed, Dr. Gannon appeared, and said he wished to examine us. Both refused. Were dragged through halls by force, our clothing partly removed by force, and we were examined, heart tested, blood pressure and pulse taken. Of course such data was of no value after such a struggle. Dr. Gannon told me then I must be fed. Was stretched on bed, two doctors, matron, four colored prisoners present, Whittaker in hall. I was held down by five people at legs, arms and head. I refused to open mouth. Gannon pushed tube up left nostril. I turned and twisted my head all I could, but he managed to push it up. It hurts nose and throat very much and makes nose bleed freely. Tube drawn out covered with blood. Operation leaves one very sick. Food dumped directly into stomach feels like a ball of lead. Left nostril, throat and muscles of neck very sore all night. After this I was brought into the hospital in an ambulance. Mrs. Lewis and I placed in the same room. Slept hardly at all. This morning Dr. Ladd appeared with his tube. Mrs. Lewis and I said we would not be forcibly fed. Said he would call in men guards and force us to submit. Went away and we were not fed at all this morning. We hear them outside now cracking eggs.

Lucy Burns, midnight, November 21, 1917, in Stevens,
Jailed for Freedom, *201.*

It was about half past seven at night when we got to Occoquan workhouse. A woman [Mrs. Herndon] was standing behind a desk when we were brought into this office, and there were five or six men also in the room. Mrs. Lewis, who spoke for all of us . . . said she must speak to Whittaker, the superintendent of the place.

"You'll sit here all night, then," said Mrs. Herndon.

I saw men begin to come upon the porch, but I didn't think anything about it. Mrs. Herndon called my name, but I did not answer . . .

Suddenly the door literally burst open and Whittaker burst in like a tornado; some men followed him. We could see a crowd of them on the porch. They were not in uniform. They looked as much like tramps as anything. They seemed to come in—and in—and in. One had a face that made me think of an ourang-outang. Mrs. Lewis stood up. Some of us had been sitting and lying on the floor, we were so tired. She had hardly begun to speak, saying we demanded

to be treated as political prisoners, when Whittaker said:

"You shut up. I have men here to handle you." Then he shouted, "Seize her!" I turned and saw men spring toward her, and then some one screamed, "They have taken Mrs. Lewis."

A man sprang at me and caught me by the shoulder. I am used to remembering a bad foot, which I have had for years, and I remember saying, "I'll come with you; don't drag me; I have a lame foot." But I was jerked down the steps and away into the dark. I didn't have my feet on the ground. I guess that saved me. I heard Mrs. Cosu, who was being dragged along with me, call, "Be careful of your foot."

Out of doors it was very dark. The building to which they took us was lighted up as we came to it. I only remember the American flag flying above it because it caught the light from a window in the wing. We were rushed into a large room that we found opened on a large hall with stone cells on each side. They were perfectly dark. Punishment cells is what they call them. Mine was filthy. It had no window save a slip at the top and no furniture but an iron bed covered with a thin straw pad, and an open toilet flushed from outside the cell . . .

In the hall outside was a man called Captain Reems. He had on a uniform and was brandishing a thick stick and shouting as we were shoved into the corridor, "Damn you, get in here . . ."

At the end of the corridor they pushed me through a door. Then I lost my balance and fell against the iron bed. Mrs. Cosu struck the wall. Then they threw in two mats and two dirty blankets. There was no light but from the corridor. The door was barred from top to bottom. The walls and floors were brick or stone cemented over. Mrs. Cosu would not let me lie on the floor. She put me on the couch and stretched out on the floor on one of the two pads they threw in. We had only lain there a few minutes, trying to get our breath, when Mrs. Lewis doubled over and handled like a sack of something, was literally thrown in. Her head struck the iron bed. We thought she was dead. She didn't move. We were crying over her as we lifted her to the pad on my bed, when we heard Miss Burns call:

"Where is Mrs. Nolan?"

I replied, "I am here."

Mrs. Cosu called out, "They have just thrown Mrs. Lewis in here, too."

At this Mr. Whittaker came to the door and told us not to dare to speak, or he would put the brace and bit in our mouths and the straitjacket on our bodies. We were so terrified we kept very still. Mrs. Lewis was not unconscious; she was only stunned. But Mrs. Cosu was desperately ill as the night wore on. She had a bad heart attack and was then vomiting. We called and called. We asked them to send for our own doctor, because we thought she was dying . . . They [the guards] paid no attention. A cold wind blew in on us from the outside, and we three lay there shivering and only half conscious until morning.

"One at a time, come out," we heard some one call at the barred door early in the morning. I went first. I bade them both good-by. I didn't know where I was going or whether I would ever see them again. They took me to Mr. Whittaker's office, where he called my name.

"You're Mrs. Mary Nolan," said Whittaker.

"You're posted," said I.

"Are you willing to put on prison dress and go to the workroom?," said he.

I said, "No."

"Don't you know now that I am Mr. Whittaker, the superintendent?" he asked.

"Is there any age limit to your workhouse?" I said. "Would a woman of seventy-three or a child of two be sent here?"

I think I made him think. He motioned to the guard.

"Get a doctor to examine her," he said.

In the hospital cottage I was met by Mrs. Herndon and taken to a little room with two white beds and a hospital table.

"You can lie down if you want to," she said.

I took off my coat and hat. I just lay down on the bed and fell into a kind of stupor. It was nearly noon and I had had no food offered me since the sandwiches our friends brought us in the courtroom at noon the day before.

The doctor came and examined my heart. Then he examined my lame foot. It had a long blue bruise above the ankle, where they had knocked me as they took me across the night before. He asked me what caused the bruise. I said, "Those fiends when they dragged me to the cell last night." It was paining me. He asked if I wanted liniment and I said only hot water. They brought that, and I noticed they did not

lock the door. A negro trusty was there. I fell back again into the same stupor.

The next day they brought me some toast and a plate of food, the first I had been offered in over 36 hours. I just looked at the food and motioned it away. It made me sick . . . I was released on the sixth day and passed the dispensary as I came out. There were a group of my friends, Mrs. Brannan and Mrs. Morey and many others. They had on coarse striped dresses and big, grotesque, heavy shoes. I burst into tears as they led me away.

Mary I. Nolan, statement dictated upon her release from Occoquan workhouse, November 21, 1917, in Stevens, Jailed for Freedom, *196–199.*

Permit me to extend to you the deep appreciation of Organized Labor the country over for the stand you have taken in behalf of justice . . .

It is the duty of every citizen to awaken to the fact that not alone is America interested but the eyes of the world are focused upon the courts of California and it is really up to her noble womanhood whether the terrible stain that is cast upon them in the Mooney case shall remain unchallenged . . . Surely the women of California will not let this issue die.

I shall convey to Organized Labor the world over that the women of San Francisco, particularly the members of the W[omen's] C[hristian] T[emperance] U[nion] are the first to demand a revolution in our courts and your action I am sure will awaken other women of our nation.

Mary Harris "Mother" Jones, letter to Sara J. Dorr, president of the Women's Christian Temperance Union, December 16, 1917, in Steel, Correspondence of Mother Jones, *185–186.*

When I think of you I always think in italics. When I write to you I know there is danger of being over-effusive and I run up a little red flag of warning.

You see, there are so many things in you to admire and be grateful for that it is hard to be moderate in one's expression.

Stevenson said of certain people: "Their entrance into a room is as though another candle had been lighted." You never step into a room or out upon a platform that you do not carry this effect. Something cheery, illuminating, helpful, had been added.

As our Little General of the Suffrage Army of Brooklyn you have been not only loveable and lovely,

To War and Victory 345

mistress of yourself and of every situation, but so clear-headed, sensible, resourceful and untiring that Victory when it came seemed but your just reward.

For myself and for the district I represent I thank you for the effective work you have done and for the work you are to do during the coming year.

(Mrs. Earl H.) Maud Rittenhouse to Ethel Dreier, December 13, [1917], Ethel Eyre Valentine Dreier Papers, Sophia Smith Collection, Smith College.

This is a little letter to accompany the Christmas gift from the 5th A.D. [assembly district].

We sincerely wish you a Merry, Merry, Christmas and a very Happy New Year, for yourself and all your family.

I would like to be able to tell you how much we all love you and have admired your capable and wisely democratic leadership, during our campaign for "suffrage."

It was a delight to myself to watch you grow in capacity, poise and effectiveness, as you acted as chairman of our executive meetings, and last but by no means least, to see you grow in the love of us all, by your patience and kindly spirit.

The 5th Assembly District of the Woman Suffrage Party of Brooklyn again wishes you a Merry Christmas.

Annie [illegible] Roy (Mrs. R. H) to Ethel Dreier, December 19, 1917, Ethel Eyre Valentine Dreier Papers, Sophia Smith Collection, Smith College.

The 22nd A.D. joins with the other assembly Districts of Brooklyn in wishing you the best Christmas you have ever had.

The joy of service has been yours, and we who have been inspired by your untiring zeal in the great cause know that you feel now the joy of accomplishment.

We appreciate, admire and hold you in our hearts with loving thought, truly you have shown the Christmas spirit "good will to all".

May the wonderful season bring you full measure of happiness.

Edith L. Hart to Ethel Dreier, December 20, 1917, Ethel Eyre Valentine Dreier Papers, Sophia Smith Collection, Smith College.

It is rather difficult to put into words the deep feeling of gratitude which always comes to my thought, as I think of the work which you have done for Brook-

lyn. Not alone for the women of Brooklyn, but for all who live or shall live in the Borough, for you have helped to bring about a reform and a right that will last as long as our form of government continues.

I have felt that at this Christmas time I should like to have you know that personally I believe the one great secret of the success which has attended your work, has been your universal kindness. Your kindly manner has enabled you to meet the problems which have arisen in such a way as not to cause friction, but rather to bind the people who have been associated with you in a deeper sense of obligation to a common cause.

As one looks over the things which mean most in life, I believe we all agree that the ones which are lasting are only those which have helped others and made life better for them and in that way brought joy to us, so I feel that your children may always have the joy of knowing that the one whom they are privileged to call Mother, has brought into innumerable lives a new incentive and desire to do for others.

For myself, I shall always consider it an inspiration to have been associated with you and to have known of all the steps which have led to our great victory.

Ida L. Woolworth to Ethel Dreier, December 21, 1917, Ethel Eyre Valentine Dreier Papers, Sophia Smith Collection, Smith College.

This card is just to congratulate you on your wonderful leadership and courage in the past campaigns for suffrage.

You have won the love and admiration of all your workers with your untiring efforts and clear vision of the great cause.

Jane McKee to Ethel Dreier, December 23, [1917], Ethel Eyre Valentine Dreier Papers, Sophia Smith Collection, Smith College.

Christmas greetings to Mrs. Dreier with affectionate appreciation of the Seventeenth Assembly District for the splendid leadership which brought its women to the hoped for, longed for victory.

Unsigned note to Mrs. Dreier, [December 1917], Ethel Eyre Valentine Dreier Papers, Sophia Smith Collection, Smith College.

I have sat for half an hour, with my pen in my hand, trying to phrase in a few words what I want to tell you. Once again, I find how true it is that It is harder to express oneself in a few words, than in many—Yet, what I would say is what you surely know: that the source of your power is your absorption in the big meaning of everything you do. However practical and detailed may be the task in hand, to you it is always a part of the big thing—the ideal thing, never small, never unworthy.

All of which is only to say that you are really a big person; with a real belief in real democracy.

Halie[?] Loew Whitney[?] to Edith Dreier, December 23, 1917, Ethel Eyre Valentine Dreier Papers, Sophia Smith Collection, Smith College.

To Mrs. Dreier, personification of the highest ideals of womanhood:

We admire you for your gentleness and justice;
We respect you for your wisdom and ability;
We love you for your unselfishness and sacrifices.

From the women of the 20th assembly district to Ethel Eyre Valentine Dreier, [1917], Ethel Eyre Valentine Dreier Papers, Sophia Smith Collection, Smith College.

May I not take the liberty of expressing my earnest hope that Oklahoma will join the other suffrage States in ratifying the Federal Suffrage Amendment, thus demonstrating anew its sense of justice and retaining its place as a leader in Democracy.

President Wilson, telegram to legislature of Oklahoma in special session, February 27, 1919, in Catt and Shuler, Woman Suffrage, 392.

If they could get the suffrage amendment without enfranchising colored women, they would do it in a moment, all of them are mortally afraid of the South.

Walter White, letter to Mary Church Terrell, March 4, 1919, in Flexner, Century of Struggle, 316.

The situation in regard to the Federal Amendment has now reached its climax, and without that amendment there will not be universal woman suffrage in your lifetime. Until within a few years the Southern members of Congress have stood like a solid wall against it and have been sustained by the women of their States. Through reason, argument, logic and diplomacy every Southern State Suffrage Association now supports the Federal Amendment. With this backing *56* Southern Representatives voted for it when it was carried in the Lower House, Jan. 10,

Mary Church Terrell, writer, lecturer, educator *(Library of Congress)*

1917. In March, 1914, three Democratic Senators voted for it; in October, 1918, 12; in February, 1919, 13. These figures show the remarkable progress in Southern sentiment.

Such is the situation. Many of the Southern members are now willing to surrender their beloved doctrine of State's rights, and their only obstacle is fear of "the colored woman's vote" in the States where it is likely to equal or exceed the white women's vote . . . The opponents [of the amendment] are not leaving a stone unturned to defeat it and if the news is flashed throughout the Southern States at this most critical moment that the National American Association has just admitted an organization of 6,000 colored women, the enemies can cease from further effort—the defeat of the amendment will be assured.

Ida Husted Harper, letter written at Carrie Chapman Catt's request to Elizabeth C. Carter, president of the Northeastern Federation of Women's Clubs, to request that Carter withdraw her organization's request to join the National Woman Suffrage Association, March 18, 1919, in Kraditor, Ideas of the Woman Suffrage Movement, 214–215.

Our . . . Department of State, owing largely to the food conditions in Europe, has limited the number of passports to be issued to American women for attending the [International] Congress [of Women], to twelve . . .

May I ask you to telegraph me at Hull-House immediately as to the possibility of your going?

Upon receipt of the replies we will try to make out a list as fairly as possible, taking representation of organizations and geography into consideration . . .

As only twenty percent of the steamship space from Europe to the United States is being reserved for civilians, until all the soldiers and war workers shall have returned, we are told that it is quite possible that we may be obliged to stay for several months in Europe, even as late as October, owing to the difficulty of securing return passage.

Jane Addams, letter to women eligible to be U.S. delegates to the International Congress of Women, March 22, 1919, in the Carrie Chapman Catt Papers, Rare Books and Manuscripts Division, New York Public Library.

I join with you and all friends of the suffrage cause in rejoicing over the adoption of the suffrage amend-

Shown in an early 20th-century photograph, Jane Addams was the first president of the Women's International League for Peace and Freedom. *(Library of Congress)*

ment by the Congress. Please accept and convey to your association my warmest congratulations.

President Woodrow Wilson, from Paris, telegram to Carrie Chapman Catt, ca. June 4, 1919, in Catt and Shuler, Woman Suffrage, 342.

Ten State Legislatures now in session, or meeting in called session, are expected to ratify the Federal Suffrage Amendment. Four meeting January, 1920, are certain to do so. Would you be willing to agree to be one of twenty-two Governors to call a special session in order to complete ratification before Presidential election?

National American Woman Suffrage Association, telegram to 24 governors, June 9, 1919, in Catt and Shuler, Woman Suffrage, 344.

Why I Voted against Women Suff

I and my Wife agree on point I, a hous Wife belongs to home near her children and to keep hous, and not in open public Politic.

2ond. it is only for the city Women in larger Cities that want to vote and to get the controll of the Country vote. to Elect State officers and President of the U.S. because a Country Women wont not go to Vote they have all they wont to do to take care of their children and House Work garden and etc.

3th a Danger that the men will not go to the poles if the Women get Elected to any State Legislature. the big Danger will be that some hair pulling will going on if there will be Women Elected in the State Legislature they will be worse as the Attorneys at present.

State Senator Herman Bilgrien, of Wisconsin, handwritten explanation of his vote against ratification of the 19th Amendment, reproduced in the State Journal, June 12, 1919, in Catt and Shuler, Woman Suffrage, 345.

The services of women during this supreme crisis of the world's history have been of the most signal usefulness and distinction. The war could not have been fought without them, or its sacrifices endured. It is high time that some part of our debt of gratitude to them should be acknowledged and paid, and the only acknowledgement they ask is admission to the suffrage.

Woodrow Wilson, letter to Carrie Chapman Catt, with request that this message be conveyed to the members of the French Union for Women Suffrage, June 13, 1919, in the Carrie Chapman Catt Papers, Rare Books and Manuscripts Division, New York Public Library.

Within the short period of six months the resolution will come before the General Assembly in regular session and I believe there is no public necessity of calling a special session at this time or that the cause of woman suffrage will be in any way delayed or hindered by this course. Personally I am earnestly in favor of ratification.

> *Governor R. Livingston Beeckman, of Rhode Island, ca. June 27, 1919, in Catt and Shuler,* Woman Suffrage, *372.*

The plan of the antis is to find thirteen states which they can hold out against ratification. They have been good enough to give us the list of the states. They are the solid south states: Maryland, Virginia, North Carolina, South Carolina, Georgia, Alabama, Mississippi, Louisiana, Florida, Kentucky, Tennessee and Delaware. I do not think they would have very much trouble in holding all of these out. Now they will get their thirteenth state in New Jersey, Connecticut, Vermont or New Hampshire. They tell us so, and they have given up all the others.

> *Carrie Chapman Catt, letter to Marjorie Shuler, July 19, 1919, in Flexner,* Century of Struggle, *320.*

I'd rather see my daughter in her coffin than at the polls . . .

> *Arkansas legislator, during special session to consider Nineteenth Amendment, July 28, 1919, in Catt and Shuler,* Woman Suffrage, *354.*

The only reason that I got into this campaign as a candidate for the gubernatorial honors was that the State needed at least one man with the courage to stand four square against prohibition and woman suffrage.

> *Democratic James Nugent, explaining his (unsuccessful) candidacy for governor of New Jersey, August 1919, in Catt and Shuler,* Woman Suffrage, *387.*

The National American Woman Suffrage Association implores the Governors of the West . . . to find some ground of common agreement, so that the ratification of their Legislatures may be secured in the months of September or October and thus insure final ratification by February 1.

> *National American Woman Suffrage Association, message delivered by special envoys, to governors convened for annual conference in Salt Lake City, August 18–24, 1919, in Catt and Shuler,* Woman Suffrage, *352–353.*

Headquarters for the National Anti-suffrage Association *(Library of Congress)*

It is said that if I dare call the Legislature together, with the consent of the Council, they (the [liquor] ring) will flay me alive, kill every reform measure passed last winter, the trustee bill, the school bill and so on. This is silly. I will risk all dangers that may come to me. Let us come together briefly and keep our pledges to give women the ballot . . . No political or bodily fear will stop me for one second.

> *Governor John Henry Bartlett, of New Hampshire, writing prior to calling a special session of the legislature to consider the Nineteenth Amendment, September 9, 1919, in Catt and Shuler,* Woman Suffrage, *355–356.*

. . . you may not have kept pace with the progress of the woman suffrage movement in war-torn Europe. I beg, therefore, to call your attention to the fact that all the Allied Contries of Europe have now not only granted the suffrage, but the women have actually exercised the right, with the exception of France, Portugal, Montenegro and Greece. The last of these to extend the suffrage to women was Serbia. The Italian House of Deputies has passed the measure and the Italian women assure us that the Senate will do so soon.

All the enemy countries, with the exception of Turkey and Bulgaria, have extended the suffrage to women. All the neutral countries of Europe, except Spain and Switzerland, have now extended the vote to women, the last of these being Luxemburg, Holland and Sweden.

The suffrage for women in most of these countries has come as an act of revolution or, as in Serbia, as a ukase from the Government.

Meanwhile, Rhodesia and British East Africa, whose governments stand in comparison to the self-governing colonies of Great Britain much as the territories do to our own government, have extended suffrage to their women.

In the face of these amazing developments it comes as a very depressing humiliation to American women that the heavy, slow-moving machinery of our democracy has delayed so long this simple act of democratic justice.

It doubtless is impossible for you, who have lived all your life in a State where women have had equal suffrage with men and where no comment is made upon the fact, to realize the feelings of hundreds of thousands of American women who have borne the brunt of the struggle in this country for their own enfranchisement. Women have lived long lives and have died in advanced years and yet have given their very all during their lifetime to this struggle. Women still living look backward over more than a generation of continued service of education and pleading with the political parties of this country to do them justice. Now these women look across the ocean and see this act of democratic justice achieved as one of the results of the great world war, while we in this country are still questioning as to whether there may be some political advantage gained or lost by one party or the other.

I do beg of you in honor of our Nation, in respect to the history which is now being made the world around, to see that [your state], make its contribution of ratification in such time that posterity will not blush at the hesitancy of our country to put this amendment into the Constitution.

State auxiliary presidents of the National American Woman Suffrage Association and others, letter to the governors of Wyoming, Washington, Oregon, Oklahoma, North and South Dakota, New Mexico, Nevada, Idaho, Colorado, California, and Arizona, October 1919, in Catt and Shuler, Woman Suffrage, *357–358.*

We can perform a worthy and effective act if the Far Western Governors and Legislatures will present to the women of the West and of the nation a Thanksgiving present by ratifying the amendment. I am asking the Governors of Idaho, Nevada, Arizona, New Mexico, Wyoming, Oregon and Washington to join me in a group calling extra sessions before November 27, 1919. Will you call if the others will do so?

Governor William D. Stephens, of California, telegram to governors Carey of Wyoming, Campbell of Arizona, Lazzarola of New Mexico, Hart of Washington, Shoup of Colorado, and Boyle of Nevada, October 1919, in Catt and Shuler, Woman Suffrage, *359.*

California, Colorado and Nevada will have special sessions in November. Other Western States may also call. Will you not join with us to hasten the day that will give our nation the benefit of the vote of its women citizens? We realize how greatly the voting of the women has benefited California. We believe it will be of like value in the nation. I earnestly ask your cooperation.

Governor William D. Stephens, of California, telegram to 14 eastern and midwestern state governors, October 1919, in Catt and Shuler, Woman Suffrage, *359.*

The world moves and Maine will move with it.

The Kennebec Journal, *prior to Maine's ratification of the Nineteenth Amendment, November 5, 1919, in Catt and Shuler,* Woman Suffrage, *361.*

The women of Washington send greetings to the Victory Convention. We were a pioneer State, the fifth to be enfranchised. Therefore we resent the disgraceful humiliation put upon us by the stubborn refusal of our Governor to listen to our united demand for a special session to ratify the Suffrage Amendment.

Members of the Washington League of Women Voters, telegram to the Victory Convention, Chicago, February 1920, in Catt and Shuler, Woman Suffrage, *384.*

Washington is now the only enfranchised State which has taken no action toward ratification of the Federal Suffrage Amendment. Thirty-five ratifications are assured in the immediate future. The nation has been informed for many years that Washington approves woman suffrage. It therefore looks to you to call an immediate session of your Legislature and once more announce Washington's endorsement of woman suffrage by ratification of the Federal Amendment.

> *The Chicago Victory Convention, telegram to Governor Louis A. Hart, of Washington, ca. February 14, 1920, in Catt and Shuler,* Woman Suffrage, *384.*

May I not urge upon you the importance to the whole country of the prompt ratification of the Suffrage Amendment and express the hope that you will find it possible to lend your aid to this end.

> *President Woodrow Wilson, telegram to the senate of West Virginia, meeting in special session, February 27, 1920, in Catt and Shuler,* Woman Suffrage, *392.*

Our only hope lies in Washington. In Tennessee all swear by Woodrow Wilson. No one here believes he has clay feet. The Democratic State Convention on the 8th of June exhausted every adjective in our voluminous Southern vocabulary to approve, praise and glorify his every word and deed. If he will but speak, Tennessee must yield.

> *Chairperson of the Tennessee Ratification Committee, letter to the National American Woman Suffrage Association, June 1920, in Catt and Shuler,* Woman Suffrage, *426.*

It would be a real service to the party and to the nation if it is possible for you . . . to call a special session of the Legislature of Tennessee to consider the Suffrage Amendment. Allow me to urge this very earnestly.

> *President Woodrow Wilson, telegraph to Governor Roberts, of Tennessee, summer 1920, in Catt and Shuler,* Woman Suffrage, *427.*

A careful perusal of your proclamation refusing to call the Legislature of Vermont into special session impresses the most casual reader with the conviction that you have doubtless told the truth, but not the whole truth. In order that this generation of your fellowmen and posterity may not misunderstand your position, the National American Woman Suffrage Association urges you to supplement your proclamation with replies to the following questions: Do you acknowledge that the Federal Constitution is the supreme law of this land and supersedes all State Constitutions wherever the two are in conflict? Do you challenge this fact that has stood unchallenged for

131 years? Do you know that on January 10, 1791, Vermont ratified that Constitution, although she had one of her own, and by so doing accepted the precedence of the Federal Constitution over it and by that act was admitted into the Union as a member of the United States of America? If you do know these facts of common knowledge, why did you throw over your refusal to call a special session the camouflage of a dissertation about the alleged conflict between the Vermont and Federal Constitutions?

> *Carrie Chapman Catt, open letter to Governor Clement, of Vermont, following his proclamation of June 12, 1920, in Catt and Shuler,* Woman Suffrage, *406.*

During the evening groups of legislators under the escort of strange men had left the foyer and gone to a room on the eighth floor. As the evening grew late, legislators, both suffrage and anti-suffrage men, were reeling through the halls in a state of advanced intoxi-

Carrie Chapman Catt was a founder of the League of Women Voters. *(Library of Congress)*

cation—a sight no suffragist had before witnessed in the sixty years of suffrage struggle . . . Suffragists were plunged into helpless despair. Hour by hour suffrage men and women who went to the different hotels of the city to talk with the legislators, came back to the Hermitage headquarters to report. And every report told the same story—the Legislature was drunk! In agony of soul suffragists went to bed . . .

Carrie Chapman Catt, recalling the night of August 9, 1920, in Catt and Shuler, Woman Suffrage, *442.*

We now have 35½ states. We are up to the last half of the last state . . . The opposition of every sort is here fighting with no scruple, desperately. Women, including Kate Gordon and Laura Clay, are here, appealing to Negrophobia and every other cave man's prejudice. Men, lots of them, are here. What do they represent? God only knows.

We believe they are buying votes. We have a poll of the House showing victory, but they are trying to break a quorum, and God only knows the outcome. We are terribly worried, and so is the other side. We hope our fate is decided this week but God only knows that. I've been here a month. It's hot, muggy, nasty, and this last battle is desperate . . . We are low in our minds . . . Even if we win, we who have been here will never remember it with anything but a shudder.

Carrie Chapman Catt, from Tennessee, letter to M. G. Peck, August 15, 1920, in Flexner, Century of Struggle, *335–336.*

It will mean a great deal to you and your daughter in the future if this amendment is defeated.

Anti-suffragist male ("with tears in his eyes"), to his daughter, during Tennessee's consideration of the Nineteenth Amendment, August 1920, in Catt and Shuler, Woman Suffrage, *450.*

Mother and I would rather live in poverty all the rest of our lives than get money by treachery to our sex. We will not desert the suffragists and we are not proud of the work you are doing.

Response of the anti-suffragist's 17-year-old daughter, August 1920, in Catt and Shuler, Woman Suffrage, *450.*

Hurrah! And vote for suffrage and don't keep them in doubt. I notice some of the speeches against. They were very bitter. I have been watching to see how you stood, but have noticed nothing yet. Don't forget to be a good boy and help Mrs. Catt put 'Rat' in Ratification.

Mrs. J. L. Burn, letter to her son, Representative Harry Burn, during Tennessee's consideration of the Nineteenth Amendment, August 1920, in Flexner, Century of Struggle, *336.*

I desire to resent in the name of honesty and justice the veiled intimation and accusation regarding my vote on the Suffrage Amendment as indicated in certain statements, and it is my sincere belief that those responsible for their existence know there is not a scintilla of truth in them. I want to state that I changed my vote in favor of ratification first because I believe in full suffrage as a right; second, I believe we had a moral and legal right to ratify; third, I knew that a mother's advice is always safest for her boy to follow and my mother wanted me to vote for ratification; fourth, I appreciated the fact that an opportunity such as seldom comes to a mortal man to free seventeen million women from political slavery was mine; fifth, I desired that my party in both State and nation might say that it was a Republican from the East mountains of Tennessee, the purest Anglo-Saxon section in the world, who made national woman suffrage possible at this date, not for personal glory but for the glory of his party.

Congressman Harry Burn, to the House of Representatives of Tennessee, after his vote in support of the Nineteenth Amendment, August 1920, in Catt and Shuler, Woman Suffrage, *451.*

Woman was here to-day, claims to be wife of Governor of Louisiana, and secured an interview with me and tried by every means to get me to refute and say that the letter I sent to my son was false. The letter is authentic and was written by me and you can refute any statement that any party claims to have received from me. Any statement claiming to be from me is false. I stand squarely behind suffrage and request my son to stick to suffrage until the end. This woman was very insulting to me in my home, and I had a hard time to get her out of my home.

Mrs. J. L. Burn, telegram to the president of the League of Women Voters after Tennessee's ratification of the Nineteenth Amendment, August 1920, in Catt and Shuler, Woman Suffrage, *451.*

Will you take the opportunity to say to my fellow citizens that I deem it one of the greatest honors of my life that this great event, the ratification of this amendment, should have occurred during the period of my administration. Nothing has given me more pleasure than the privilege that has been mine to do what I could to advance the cause of ratification and to hasten the day when the womanhood of America would be recognized by the nation on the equal footing of citizenship that it deserves.

President Woodrow Wilson, letter to Carrie Chapman Catt, August 26, 1920, in History of Woman Suffrage, *Vol. 5, 652.*

Out here alone with my thoughts, I have kept Thanksgiving sacred to reflections upon the long trail behind us, and the triumph which was its inevitable conclusion. John Adams said long after the Revolution that only about one third of the people were for it, a third being against it, and the remaining third utterly indifferent. Perhaps this proportion applies to all movements. At least a third of the women were for our cause at the end . . . As I look back over the years . . . I realize that the greatest thing in the long campaign for us was not its crowning victory, but the discipline it gave us all . . . It was a great crusade, the world has seen none more wonderful . . . My admiration, love and reverence go out to that band which fought and won a revolution . . . with congratulations that we were permitted to establish a new and good thing in the world.

Carrie Chapman Catt, letter to members of her NAWSA office staff, Thanksgiving Day, 1920, in Peck, Carrie Chapman Catt, *352–353.*

EPILOGUE

It was 1923. American women had been enfranchised for nearly three years, and suffrage leaders were responding in various ways to the achievement of this goal.

In March 1919, Carrie Chapman Catt had founded the first chapters of the League of Women Voters in the 28 states which, by then, included women's suffrage in their constitutions. These organizations, Catt said, were to be, "non-partisan and non-sectarian and consecrated to . . . obtain[ing] the full enfranchisement of the women of every State . . . remov[ing] the remaining legal discriminations against women in the codes and constitutions of the several States . . . [and] mak[ing] our democracy so safe for the nation and so safe for the world that every citizen may feel secure and great men will acknowledge the worthiness of the American republic to lead."[1] Additional chapters were founded as additional states amended their constitutions. When the Nineteenth Amendment was finally ratified, the National American Woman Suffrage Association was resolved into the national League of Women Voters.

At this point, there had been lively debate among Catt's followers in the league about the manner in which women should wield their new political power. In her 1920 victory speech, Catt herself had predicted that the vote would not automatically move women into the policymaking center of the U.S. political system:

> . . . if you stay longer . . . and move around enough, keeping your eyes open, you will discover a little denser group, which we might call the umbra of the political party. You won't be so welcome there. Those are the people who are planning the platforms and picking out the candidates, and doing the work which you and the men voters will be expected to sanction at the polls. You won't be so welcome there, but that is the place to be. And if

Anna Lord Strauss, president of the National League of Women Voters, 1944–50 *(National Archives)*

353

you stay there long enough and are active enough, you will see something else—the real thing in the center, with the door locked tight, and you will have a long hard fight before you get behind that door, for there is the engine that moves the wheels of your party machinery. Nevertheless, it will be an interesting and thrilling struggle and well worth while. If you really want women's vote to count, make your way there.[2]

Although Catt was aware that women would not easily be integrated into the two-party system, she was sure that participation in that system was the clearest route to increased political power for women. When some in the league insisted that women should try to keep their political identity separate from men's, Catt was firm in her response: ". . . the only way to get things done is to get them done on the inside of a political party."[3] The parties Catt had in mind were the Democratic and Republican Parties, and league members would be encouraged to work within either one.

Alice Paul had taken a different approach. She did not advise her followers to become as integrated as possible into the existing political system. Instead, she dedicated the National Woman's Party to continued work for "the removal of all forms of the subjection of women."[4] As Crystal Eastman, one of the party's members, described Paul's goal, the National Woman's Party would find a way to "blot out of every law book in the land . . . sweep out of every dusty court-room . . . erase from every judge's mind that centuries-old precedent as to women's inferiority and dependence and need for protection; [and] substitute for it at one blow the simple new precedent of equality."[5]

Suffragists *(Library of Congress)*

That one blow, Paul had decided, would be struck by an equal rights amendment to the U.S. Constitution. The Declaration of Rights and Sentiments adopted in Seneca Falls had asked for much more than suffrage, Paul reminded her colleagues, and she insisted that her group would not "add to or subtract from 1848."[6] And so, in 1923, on the 75th anniversary of the Seneca Falls convention, Alice Paul brought her demands and her followers to Seneca Falls, New York. There, she reread the Declaration of Rights and Sentiments. Then she proposed a constitutional amendment that she hoped would become known as the Lucretia Mott amendment: "Men and women shall have equal rights throughout the United States and every place subject to its jurisdiction."[7]

The next phase of the women's rights movement had begun.

APPENDIX A
Documents

1. From "Appeal to the Christian Women of the South" by Angelina Grimké, September 1836
2. From *Society in America,* by Harriet Martineau, 1837
3. From a pastoral letter of "the General Association of Massachusetts (Orthodox) to the Churches under their care," 1837
4. From *American Notes for General Circulation,* by Charles Dickens, 1842
5. Commonwealth of Massachusetts Report, House of Representatives, March 12, 1845
6. Married Woman's Property Act, New York, 1848
7. Declaration of Rights and Sentiments, Seneca Falls, July 19–20, 1848
8. Editorial in the *North Star,* by Frederick Douglass, July 28, 1848
9. Debate of convention amending Indiana's constitution, 1850
10. Letter from Jeanne Deroine and Pauline Roland, Prison of St.-Lagare, Paris, June 15, 1851
11. Elizabeth Cady Stanton's address to the legislature of the state of New York, February 20, 1854
12. Appeal and petition circulated in the state of New York, 1859
13. Memorial [sent to every state legislature], May 12, 1859
14. Act concerning the rights and liabilities of husband and wife, March 20, 1860
15. Appeal to the women of New York, November 1860
16. Report No. 386 of the House of Representatives, Committee on Military Affairs (46th Congress, 3d Session), regarding Anna Ella Carroll and events of 1861, March 3, 1881
17. The emancipation address of the National Women's Loyal League, adopted May 15, 1863
18. Speech of Hon. Charles Sumner on the presentation of the first installment of the Emancipation Petition of the Woman's National Loyal League, February 9, 1864
19. Petition to Congress requesting women's suffrage, December 1865
20. Public Letter of Elizabeth Cady Stanton to the electors of the eighth congressional district, October 10, 1866
21. The Fourteenth Amendment to the Constitution, Sections 1, 2, 3, 5, July 28, 1868
22. Petition to Congress requesting the inclusion of women in the Fifteenth Amendment, December 1868
23. Constitution of the National Woman Suffrage Association, May 20, 1869

24. Constitution of the American Woman Suffrage Association, November 24–25, 1869
25. Resolutions of Francis Minor, Esq., 1869
26. The Fifteenth Amendment to the Constitution, March 30, 1870
27. Memorial of Victoria C. Woodhull, December 19, 1870
28. Victoria C. Woodhull's Address to the Judiciary Committee of the House of Representatives, January 11, 1871
29. Report No. 22 of the House of Representatives, Committee on the Judiciary (43d Congress, 3d Session), Regarding the Memorial of Victoria C. Woodhull, January 30, 1871
30. Virginia L. Minor's Petition, Submitted to the Circuit Court of St. Louis County, Missouri, December, 1872
31. Decision of the Supreme Court, *Bradwell v. Illinois,* 1873
32. Opinion of the Supreme Court, *Minor v. Happersett,* March 29, 1875
33. Declaration of Rights for Women, July 4, 1876
34. Joint Resolution Proposing an Amendment to the Constitution of the United States, January 10, 1878
35. Negative Report of the Committee on Privileges and Elections Regarding the Proposed Amendment, June 14, 1878
36. Constitution of the National American Woman Suffrage Association, 1890
37. "The Winning Policy," by Carrie Chapman Catt, 1916
38. Letter to the Commissioners of the District of Columbia Claiming Political Prisoner Status for Jailed Suffragists, 1917
39. Appeal of President Wilson to the U.S. Senate to Submit the Federal Amendment for Woman Suffrage, Delivered in Person, September 30, 1918
40. Nineteenth Amendment to the Constitution, 1920

1. From "Appeal to the Christian Women of the South" by Angelina Grimké, September 1836

I have thus, I think, clearly proved to you seven propositions, viz.: First, that slavery is contrary to the declaration of our independence. Second, that it is contrary to the first charter of human rights given to Adam, and renewed to Noah. Third, that the fact of slavery having been the subject of prophecy, furnishes *no* excuse whatever to slavedealers. Fourth, that no such system existed under the patriarchal dispensation. Fifth, that *slavery never* existed under the Jewish dispensation; but so far otherwise, that every servant was placed under the *protection of law,* and care taken not only to prevent all *involuntary* servitude, but all *voluntary perpetual* bondage. Sixth, that slavery in America reduces a *man* to a *thing,* a "chattel personal," *robs him* of *all* his rights as a *human being,* fetters both his mind and body, and protects the *master* in the most unnatural and unreasonable power, whilst it *throws him out* of the protection of law. Seventh, that slavery is contrary to the example and precepts of our holy and merciful Redeemer, and of his apostles.

But perhaps you will be ready to query, why appeal to *women* on this subject? *We* do not make the laws which perpetuate slavery. *No* legislative power is vested in *us; we* can do nothing to overthrow the system, even if we wished to do so. To this I reply, I know you do not make the laws, but I also know that *you are the wives and mothers, the sisters and daughters of those who do;* and if you really suppose *you* can do nothing to overthrow slavery, you are greatly mistaken. You can do much in every way: four things I will name. 1st. You can read on this subject. 2d. You can pray over this subject. 3d. You can speak on this subject. 4th. You can *act* on this subject. I have not placed reading before praying because I regard it more important, but because, in order to pray aright, we must understand what we are praying for; it is only then we can "pray with the understanding and the spirit also."

1. Read then on the subject of slavery. Search the Scriptures daily, whether the things I have told you are true. Other books and papers might be a great help to you in this investigation, but they are not necessary, and it is hardly probable that your Committees of Vigilance will allow you to have the other. The *Bible* then is the book I want you to read in the spirit of inquiry, and the spirit of prayer. Even the enemies of Abolitionists, acknowledged that their doctrines are drawn from it. In the great mob in Boston, last autumn, when the books and papers of the Anti-Slavery Society, were thrown out of the windows of their office, one individual laid hold of the Bible and was about tossing it out to the ground, when another reminded him that it was the Bible he had in his hand. *"O! 'tis all one,"* he replied, and out went the sacred volume, along with the rest. We thank him for the acknowledgment. Yes, *"it is all one,"* for our books and papers are mostly commentaries on the Bible, and the Declaration. Read the *Bible* then, it contains the words of Jesus, and they are spirit and life. Judge for yourselves whether *he sanctioned* such a system of oppression and crime.

2. Pray over this subject. When you have entered into your closets, and shut to the doors, then pray to your father, who seeth in secret, that he would open your eyes to see whether slavery is *sinful,* and if it is, that he would enable you to bear a faithful, open and unshrinking testimony against it, and to do whatsoever your hands find to do, leaving the consequences entirely to him, who still says to us whenever we try to reason away duty from the fear of consequences, *"What is that to thee, follow thou me."* Pray also for that poor slave, that he may be kept patient and submissive under his hard lot, until God is pleased to open the door of freedom to him without violence or bloodshed. Pray too for the master that his heart may be softened, and he made willing to acknowledge, as Joseph's brethren did, "Verily we are guilty concerning our brother," before he will be compelled to add in consequence of Divine judgment, "therefore is all this evil come upon us." Pray also for all your brethren and sisters who are laboring in the righteous cause of Emancipation in the Northern States, England and the world. There is great encouragement for prayer in these words of our Lord. "Whatsoever ye shall ask the Father *in my name,* he *will give* it to you"—Pray then without ceasing, in the closet and the social circle.

3. Speak on this subject. It is through the tongue, the pen, and the press, that truth is principally propagated. Speak then to your relatives, your friends, your acquaintances on the subject of slavery; be not afraid if you are conscientiously convinced it is *sinful,* to say so openly, but calmly, and to let your sentiments be known. If you are served by the slaves of others, try to ameliorate their condition as much as possible; never

aggravate their faults, and thus add fuel to the fire of anger already kindled, in a master and mistress's bosom; remember their extreme ignorance, and consider them as your Heavenly Father does the *less* culpable on this account, even when they do wrong things. Discountenance *all* cruelty to them, all starvation, all corporal chastisement; these may brutalize and *break* their spirits, but will never bend them to willing, cheerful obedience. If possible, see that they are comfortably and *seasonably* fed, whether in the house or the field; it is unreasonable and cruel to expect slaves to wait for their breakfast until eleven o'clock, when they rise at five or six. Do all you can, to induce their owners to clothe them well, and to allow them many little indulgences which would contribute to their comfort. Above all, try to persuade your husband, father, brothers and sons, that *slavery is a crime against God and man,* and that it is a great sin to keep *human beings* in such abject ignorance; to deny them the privilege of learning to read and write. The Catholics are universally condemned, for denying the Bible to the common people, but, *slaveholders must not* blame them, for *they* are doing the *very same thing,* and for the very same reason, neither of these systems can bear the light which bursts from the pages of that Holy Book. And lastly, endeavour to inculcate submission on the part of the slaves, but whilst doing this be faithful in pleading the cause of the oppressed.

> "Will you behold unheeding,
> Life's holiest feelings crushed,
> Where woman's heart is bleeding,
> Shall woman's voice be hushed?"

4. Act on this subject. Some of you *own* slaves yourselves. *If* you believe slavery is *sinful,* set them at liberty, "undo the heavy burdens and let the oppressed go free." If they wish to remain with you, pay them wages, if not let them leave you. Should they remain, teach them, and have them taught the common branches of an English education; they have minds and those minds, *ought to be improved.* So precious a talent as intellect, never was given to be wrapt in a napkin and buried in the earth. It is the *duty* of all, as far as they can, to improve their own mental faculties, because we are commanded to love God with *all our minds,* as well as with all our hearts, and we commit a great sin, if we *forbid or prevent* that cultivation of the mind in others, which would enable them to perform this duty. Teach your servants then to read &c, and

encourage them to believe it is their *duty* to learn, if it were only that they might read the Bible.

But some of you will say, we can neither free our slaves nor teach them to read, for the laws of our state forbid it. Be not surprised when I say such wicked laws *ought to be no barrier* in the way of your duty, and I appeal to the Bible to prove this position. What was the conduct of Shiphrah and Puah, when the king of Egypt issued his cruel mandate, with regard to the Hebrew children? "*They* feared *God,* and did *not* as the King of Egypt commanded them, but saved the men children alive." Did these *women* do right in disobeying that monarch? "*Therefore* (says the sacred text,) *God dealt well* with them, and made them houses" Ex. i. What was the conduct of Shadrach, Meshach, and Abednego, when Nebuchadnezzar set up a golden image in the plain of Dura, and commanded all people, nations, and languages to fall down and worship it? "Be it known, unto thee, (said these faithful *Jews*) O king, that *we will not* serve thy gods, nor worship the image which thou hast set up." Did these men *do right in disobeying the law* of their sovereign? Let their miraculous deliverance from the burning fiery furnace, answer; Dan. iii. . . . .

But some of you may say, if we do free our slaves, they will be taken up and sold, therefore there will be no use in doing it. Peter and John might just as well have said, we will not preach the gospel, for if we do, we shall be taken up and put in prison, therefore there will be no use in our preaching. *Consequences,* my friends, belong no more to *you,* than they did to these apostles. Duty is ours and events are God's. If you think slavery is sinful, all *you* have to do is to set your slaves at liberty, do all you can to protect them, and in humble faith and fervent prayer, commend them to your common Father. He can take care of them; but if for wise purposes he sees fit to allow them to be sold, this will afford you an opportunity of testifying openly, wherever you go, against the crime of *manstealing.* Such an act will be *clear robbery,* and if exposed, might, under the Divine direction, do the cause of Emancipation more good, than any thing that could happen, for, "He makes even the wrath of man to praise him, and the remainder of wrath he will restrain."

I know that this doctrine of obeying *God,* rather than man, will be considered as dangerous, and heretical by many, but I am not afraid openly to avow it, because it is the doctrine of the Bible; but I would not be understood to advocate resistance to any law however oppressive if, in obeying it, I was not obliged to commit *sin*. If for instance, there was a law, which imposed imprisonment or a fine upon me if I manumitted a slave, I would on no account resist that law, I would set the slave free, and then go to prison or pay the fine. If a law commands me to *sin I will break it;* if it calls me to *suffer,* I will let it take its course *unresistingly.* The doctrine of blind obedience and unqualified submission to *any human* power, whether civil or ecclesiastical, is the doctrine of despotism, and ought to have no place among Republicans and Christians.

But you will perhaps say, such a course of conduct would inevitably expose us to great suffering. Yes! my christian friends, I believe it would, but this will *not* excuse you or any one else for the neglect of *duty.* If Prophets and Apostles, Martyrs, and Reformers had not been willing to suffer for the truth's sake, where would the world have been now? If they had said, we cannot speak the truth, we cannot do what we believe is right, because the *laws of our country or public opinion are against us,* where would our holy religion have been now? ...

But you may say we are *women,* how can our hearts endure persecution? And why not? Have not women stood up in all the dignity and strength of moral courage to be the leaders of the people, and to bear a faithful testimony for the truth whenever the providence of God has called them to do so? Are there no *women* in that noble army of martyrs who are now singing the song of Moses and the Lamb? Who led out the women of Israel from the house of bondage, striking the timbrel, and singing the song of deliverance on the banks of that sea whose waters stood up like walls of crystal to open a passage for their escape? It was a *woman:* Miriam, the prophetess, the sister of Moses and Aaron. Who went up with Barak to Kadesh to fight against Jabin, King of Canaan, into whose hand Israel had been sold because of their iniquities? It was a *woman!* Deborah, the wife of Lapidoth, the judge, as well as the prophetess of that backsliding people; Judges iv, 9. Into whose hands was Sisera, the captain of Jabin's host delivered? Into the hands of a *woman.* Jael the wife of Heber! Judges vi, 21. Who dared to *speak the truth* concerning those judgments which were coming upon Judea, when Josiah, alarmed at finding that his people "had not kept the word of the Lord to do after all that was written in the book of the Law," sent to enquire of the Lord concerning these things? It was a *woman.*

Huldah the prophetess, the wife of Shallum; 2, Chron. xxxiv, 22. Who was chosen to deliver the whole Jewish nation from that murderous decree of Persia's King, which wicked Haman had obtained by calumny and fraud? It was a *woman;* Esther the Queen; yes, weak and trembling *woman* was the instrument appointed by God, to reverse the bloody mandate of the eastern monarch, and save the *whole visible church* from destruction. What human voice first proclaimed to Mary that she should be the mother of our Lord? It was a *woman!* Elizabeth, the wife of Zacharias; Luke i, 42, 43. Who united with the good old Simeon in giving thanks publicly in the temple, when the child, Jesus, was presented there by his parents, "and spake of him to all them that looked for redemption in Jerusalem?" It was a *woman!* Anna the prophetess. Who first proclaimed Christ as the true Messiah in the streets of Samaria, once the capital of the ten tribes? It was a *woman!* Who ministered to the Son of God whilst on earth, a despised and persecuted Reformer, in the humble garb of a carpenter? They were *women!* Who followed the rejected King of Israel, as his fainting footsteps trod the road to Calvary? "A great company of people and of *women;*" and it is remarkable that to *them alone,* he turned and addressed the pathetic language, "Daughters of Jerusalem, weep not for me, but weep for yourselves and your children." Ah! who sent unto the Roman Governor when he was set down on the judgment seat, saying unto him, "Have thou nothing to do with that just man, for I have suffered many things this day in a dream because of him?" It was a *woman!* the wife of Pilate. Although "*he knew* that for envy the Jews had delivered Christ," yet *he* consented to surrender the Son of God into the hands of a brutal soldiery, after having himself scourged his naked body. Had the *wife* of Pilate sat upon that judgment seat, what would have been the result of the trial of this "just person?" ...

And what, I would ask in conclusion, have *women* done for the great and glorious cause of Emancipation? Who wrote that pamphlet which moved the heart of Wilberforce to pray over the wrongs, and his tongue to plead the cause of the oppressed African? It was a *woman,* Elizabeth Heyrick. Who labored assiduously to keep the sufferings of the slave continually before the British public? They were *women.* And how did they do it? By their needles, paint brushes and pens, by speaking the truth, and petitioning

Parliament for the abolition of slavery. And what was the effect of their labors? Read it in the Emancipation bill of Great Britain. Read it, in the present state of her West India Colonies. Read it, in the impulse which has been given to the cause of freedom, in the United States of America. Have English women then done so much for the negro, and shall American women do nothing? Oh no! Already are there sixty female Anti-Slavery Societies in operation. These are doing just what the English women did, telling the story of the colored man's wrongs, praying for his deliverance, and presenting his kneeling image constantly before the public eye on bags and needle-books, card-racks, pen-wipers, pin-cushions, &c. Even the children of the north are inscribing on their handy work, "May the points of our needles prick the slaveholder's conscience." Some of the reports of these Societies exhibit not only considerable talent, but a deep sense of religious duty, and a determination to persevere through evil as well as good report, until every scourge, and every shackle, is buried under the feet of the manumitted slave.

The Ladies' Anti-Slavery Society of Boston was called last fall, to a severe trial of their faith and constancy. They were mobbed by "the gentlemen of property and standing," in that city at their anniversary meeting, and their lives were jeoparded by an infuriated crowd; but their conduct on that occasion did credit to our sex, and affords a full assurance that they will *never* abandon the cause of the slave. The pamphlet, Right and Wrong in Boston, issued by them in which a particular account is given of that "mob of broad cloth in broad day," does equal credit to the head and the heart of her who wrote it. I wish my Southern sisters could read it; they would then understand that the women of the North have engaged in this work from a sense of *religious duty,* and that nothing will ever induce them to take their hands from it until it is fully accomplished. They feel no hostility to you, no bitterness or wrath; they rather sympathize in your trials and difficulties; but they well know that the first thing to be done to help you, is to pour in the light of truth on your minds, to urge you to reflect on, and pray over the subject. This is all *they* can do for you, *you* must work out your own deliverance with fear and trembling, and with the direction and blessing of God, *you can do it.* Northern women may labor to produce a correct public opinion at the North, but if Southern women sit down in listless

indifference and criminal idleness, public opinion cannot be rectified and purified at the South. It is manifest to every reflecting mind, that slavery must be abolished; the era in which we live, and the light which is overspreading the whole world on this subject, clearly show that the time cannot be distant when it will be done. Now there are only two ways in which it can be effected, by moral power or physical force, and it is for *you* to choose which of these you prefer. Slavery always has, and always will produce insurrections wherever it exists, because it is a violation of the natural order of things, and no human power can much longer perpetuate it . . .

The *women of the South can overthrow* this horrible system of oppression and cruelty, licentiousness and wrong. Such appeals to your legislatures would be irresistible, for there is something in the heart of man which *will bend under moral suasion.* There is a swift witness for truth in his bosom, which *will respond to truth* when it is uttered with calmness and dignity. If you could obtain but six signatures to such a petition in only one state, I would say, send up that petition, and be not in the least discouraged by the scoffs and jeers of the heartless, or the resolution of the house to lay it on the table. It will be a great thing if the subject can be introduced into your legislatures in any way, even by *women,* and *they* will be the most likely to introduce it there in the best possible manner, as a matter of *morals* and *religion,* not of expediency or politics. You may petition, too, the different ecclesiastical bodies of the slave states. Slavery must be attacked with the whole power of truth and the sword of the spirit. You must take it up on *Christian* ground, and fight against it with Christian weapons, whilst your feet are shod with the preparation of the gospel of peace. And *you are now* loudly called upon by the cries of the widow and the orphan, to arise and gird yourselves for this great moral conflict, with the whole armour of righteousness upon the right hand and on the left.

2. FROM *SOCIETY IN AMERICA,* BY HARRIET MARTINEAU, 1837

. . . If a test of civilisation be sought, none can be so sure as the condition of that half of society over which the other half has power,—from the exercise of the right of the strongest. Tried by this test, the American civilisation appears to be of a lower order than might have been expected from some other symptoms of its social state. The Americans have, in the treatment of women, fallen below, not only their own democratic principles, but the practice of some parts of the Old World.

The unconsciousness of both parties as to the injuries suffered by women at the hands of those who hold the power is a sufficient proof of the low degree of civilisation in this important particular at which they rest. While women's intellect is confined, her morals crushed, her health ruined, her weaknesses encouraged, and her strength punished, she is told that her lot is cast in the paradise of women: and there is no country in the world where there is so much boasting of the "chivalrous" treatment she enjoys. That is to say,—she has the best place in stagecoaches: when there are not chairs enough for everybody, the gentlemen stand: she hears oratorical flourishes on public occasions about wives and home, and apostrophes to woman: her husband's hair stands on end at the idea of her working, and he toils to indulge her with money: she has liberty to get her brain turned by religious excitements, that her attention may be diverted from morals, politics, and philosophy; and, especially, her morals are guarded by the strictest observance of propriety in her presence. In short, indulgence is given her as a substitute for justice. Her case differs from that of the slave, as to the principle, just so far as this; that the indulgence is large and universal, instead of petty and capricious. In both cases, justice is denied on no better plea than the right of the strongest. In both cases, the acquiescence of the many, and the burning discontent of the few, of the oppressed, testify, the one to the actual degradation of the class, and the other to its fitness for the enjoyment of human rights.

The intellect of woman is confined by an unjustifiable restriction of both methods of education,—by express teaching, and by the discipline of circumstance. The former, though prior in the chronology of each individual, is a direct consequence of the latter, as regards the whole of the sex. As women have none of the objects in life for which an enlarged education is considered requisite, the education is not given. Female education in America is much what it is in England. There is a profession of some things being taught which are supposed necessary because everybody learns them. They serve to fill up time, to occupy attention harmlessly, to improve conversation, and

to make women something like companions to their husbands, and able to teach their children somewhat. But what is given is, for the most part, passively received; and what is obtained is, chiefly, by means of the memory. There is rarely or never a careful ordering of influences for the promotion of clear intellectual activity. Such activity, when it exceeds that which is necessary to make the work of the teacher easy, is feared and repressed. This is natural enough, as long as women are excluded from the objects for which men are trained. While there are natural rights which women may not use, just claims which are not to be listened to, large objects which may not be approached, even in imagination, intellectual activity is dangerous: or, as the phrase is, unfit. Accordingly, marriage is the only object left open to woman. Philosophy she may pursue only fancifully, and under pain of ridicule: science only as a pastime, and under a similar penalty. Art is declared to be left open: but the necessary learning, and, yet more, the indispensable experience of reality, are denied to her. Literature is also said to be permitted: but under what penalties and restrictions? Nothing is thus left for women but marriage.—Yes; Religion, is the reply.—Religion is a temper, not a pursuit. It is the moral atmosphere in which human beings are to live and move. Men do not live to breathe: they breathe to live.

The morals of women are crushed. If there be any human power and business and privilege which is absolutely universal, it is the discovery and adoption of the principle and laws of duty. As every individual, whether man or woman, has a reason and a conscience, this is a work which each is thereby authorised to do for him or herself. But it is not only virtually prohibited to beings who, like the American women, have scarcely any objects in life proposed to them; but the whole apparatus of opinion is brought to bear offensively upon individuals among women who exercise freedom of mind in deciding upon what duty is, and the methods by which it is to be pursued. There is nothing extraordinary to the disinterested observer in women being so grieved at the case of slaves,—slave wives and mothers, as well as spirit broken men,—as to wish to do what they could for their relief: there is nothing but what is natural in their being ashamed of the cowardice of such white slaves of the north as are deterred by intimidation from using their rights of speech and of the press, in behalf of the suffering race, and in their resolving not to do likewise: there is nothing but what is justifiable in their using their moral freedom, each for herself, in neglect of the threats of punishment: yet there were no bounds to the efforts made to crush the actions of women who thus used their human powers in the abolition question, and the convictions of those who looked on, and who might possibly be warmed into free action by the beauty of what they saw. It will be remembered that they were women who asserted the right of meeting and of discussion, on the day when Garrison was mobbed in Boston. Bills were posted about the city on this occasion, denouncing these women as casting off the refinement and delicacy of their sex: the newspapers, which laud the exertions of ladies in all other charities for the prosecution of which they are wont to meet and speak, teemed with the most disgusting reproaches and insinuations: and the pamphlets which related to the question all presumed to censure the act of duty which the women had performed in deciding upon their duty for themselves.—One lady, of high talents and character, whose books were very popular before she did a deed greater than that of writing any book, in acting upon an unusual conviction of duty, and becoming an abolitionist, has been almost excommunicated since. A family of ladies, whose talents and conscientiousness had placed them high in the estimation of society as teachers, have lost all their pupils since they declared their antislavery opinions. The reproach in all the many similar cases that I know is, not that the ladies hold antislavery opinions, but that they act upon them.

How fearfully the morals of woman are crushed, appears from the prevalent persuasion that there are virtues which are peculiarly masculine, and others which are peculiarly feminine. It is not only that masculine and feminine employments are supposed to be properly different. No one in the world, I believe, questions this. But it is actually supposed that what are called the hardy virtues are more appropriate to men, and the gentler to women. As all virtues nourish each other, and can no[t] otherwise be nourished, the consequence of the admitted fallacy is that men are, after all, not nearly so brave as they ought to be; nor women so gentle. But what is the manly character till it be gentle? The very word magnanimity cannot be thought of in relation to it till it becomes mild—Christ-like. Again, what can a woman be, or do, without bravery? While woman is human, men should

beware how they deprive her of any of the strength which is all needed for the strife and burden of humanity. Let them beware how they put her off her watch and defence, by promises which they cannot fulfil;—promises of a guardianship which can arise only from within; of support which can be derived only from the freest moral action,—from the self-reliance which can be generated by no other means.

But, it may be asked, how does society get on,—what does it do? for it acts on the supposition of there being masculine and feminine virtues,—upon the fallacy just exposed.

It does so; and the consequences are what might be looked for. Men are ungentle, tyrannical. They abuse the right of the strongest, however they may veil the abuse with indulgence. They want the magnanimity to discern woman's human rights; and they crush her morals rather than allow them. Women are, as might be anticipated, weak, ignorant and subservient, in as far as they exchange self-reliance on anything out of themselves. Those who will not submit to such a suspension of their moral functions, (for the work of self-perfection remains to be done, sooner or later,) have to suffer for their allegiance to duty. They have all the need of bravery that the few heroic men who assert the highest rights of women have of gentleness, to guard them from the encroachment to which power, custom, and education, incessantly conduce.

Such brave women and such just men there are in the United States, scattered among the multitude, whose false apprehension of rights leads to an enormous failure of duties. There are enough of such to commend the true understanding and practice to the simplest minds and most faithful hearts of the community, under whose testimony the right principle will spread and flourish. If it were not for the external prosperity of the country, the injured half of its society would probably obtain justice sooner than in any country of Europe. But the prosperity of America is a circumstance unfavourable to its women. It will be long before they are put to the proof as to what they are capable of thinking and doing: a proof to which hundreds, perhaps thousands of Englishwomen have been put by adversity, and the result of which is a remarkable improvement in their social condition, even within the space of ten years. Persecution for opinion, punishment for all manifestations of intellectual and moral strength, are still as common as women who have opinions and who manifest strength: but some things are easy, and many are possible of achievement, to women of ordinary powers, which it would have required genius to accomplish but a few years ago . . .

If there is any country on earth where the course of true love may be expected to run smooth, it is America. It is a country where all can marry early, where there need be no anxiety about a worldly provision, and where the troubles arising from conventional considerations of rank and connexion ought to be entirely absent. It is difficult for a stranger to imagine beforehand why all should not love and marry naturally and freely, to the prevention of vice out of the marriage state, and of the common causes of unhappiness within it. The anticipations of the stranger are not, however, fulfilled: and they never can be while the one sex overbears the other. Marriage is in America more nearly universal, more safe, more tranquil, more fortunate than in England: but it is still subject to the troubles which arise from the inequality of the parties in mind and in occupation. It is more nearly universal, from the entire prosperity of the country: it is safer, from the greater freedom of divorce, and consequent discouragement of swindling, and other vicious marriages: it is more tranquil and fortunate from the marriage vows being made absolutely reciprocal; from the arrangements about property being generally far more favorable to the wife than in England; and from her not being made, as in England, to all intents and purposes the property of her husband. The outward requisites to happiness are nearly complete, and the institution is purified from the grossest of the scandals which degrade it in the Old World: but it is still the imperfect institution which it must remain while women continue to be ill-educated, passive, and subservient: or well-educated, vigorous, and free only upon sufferance.

The institution presents a different aspect in the various parts of the country. I have spoken of the early marriages of silly children in the south and west, where, owing to the disproportion of numbers, every woman is married before she well knows how serious a matter human life is. She has an advantage which very few women elsewhere are allowed: she has her own property to manage. It would be a rare sight elsewhere to see a woman of twenty-one in her second widowhood, managing her own farm or plantation; and managing it well, because it had been in her

own hands during her marriage. In Louisiana, and also in Missouri, (and probably in other States,) a woman not only has half her husband's property by right at his death, but may always be considered as possessed of half his gains during his life; having at all times power to bequeath that amount. The husband interferes much less with his wife's property in the south, even through her voluntary relinquishment of it, than is at all usual where the cases of women having property during their marriage are rare. In the southern newspapers, advertisements may at any time be seen, running thus:—"Mrs. A, wife of Mr. A, will dispose of &c. &c." When Madame Lalaurie was mobbed in New Orleans, no one meddled with her husband or his possessions; as he was no more responsible for her management of her human property than anybody else. On the whole, the practice seems to be that the weakest and most ignorant women give up their property to their husbands; the husbands of such women being precisely the men most disposed to accept it: and that the strongest-minded and most conscientious women keep their property, and use their rights; the husbands of such women being precisely those who would refuse to deprive their wives of their social duties and privileges.

I have mentioned that divorce is more easily obtained in the United States than in England. In no country, I believe, are the marriage laws so iniquitous as in England, and the conjugal relation, in consequence, so impaired. Whatever may be thought of the principles which are to enter into laws of divorce, whether it be held that pleas for divorce should be one, (as narrow interpreters of the New Testament would have it;) or two, (as the law of England has it;) or several, (as the Continental and United States' laws in many instances allow,) nobody, I believe, defends the arrangement by which, in England, divorce is obtainable only by the very rich. It will be seen at a glance how such an arrangement tends to vitiate marriage: how it offers impunity to adventurers, and encouragement to every kind of mercenary marriages: how absolute is its oppression of the injured party: and how, by vitiating marriage, it originates and aggravates licentiousness to an incalculable extent. To England alone belongs the disgrace of such a method of legislation.

Of the American States, I believe New York approaches nearest to England in its laws of divorce. It is less rigid, in as far as that more is comprehended under the term "cruelty." The husband is supposed to be liable to cruelty from the wife, as well as the wife from the husband. There is no practical distinction made between rich and poor by the process being rendered expensive: and the cause is more easily resumable after a reconciliation of the parties. In Massachusetts, the term "cruelty" is made so comprehensive, and the mode of sustaining the plea is so considerately devised, that divorces are obtainable with peculiar ease. The natural consequence follows: such a thing is never heard of. A long-established and very eminent lawyer of Boston told me that he had known of only one in all his experience. Thus it is wherever the law is relaxed, and, *cæteris paribus,* in proportion to its relaxation: for the obvious reason, that the protection offered by law to the injured party causes marriages to be entered into with fewer risks, and the conjugal relation carried on with more equality. Retribution is known to impend over violations of conjugal duty. When I was in North Carolina, the wife of a gamester there obtained a divorce without the slightest difficulty. When she had brought evidence of the danger to herself and her children,—danger pecuniary and moral,—from her husband's gambling habits, the bill passed both Houses without a dissenting voice.

It is clear that the sole business which legislation has with marriage is with the arrangement of property; to guard the reciprocal rights of the children of the marriage and the community. There is no further pretence for the interference of the law, in any way. An advance towards the recognition of the true principle of legislative interference in marriage has been made in England, in the new law in which the agreement of marriage is made a civil contract, leaving the religious obligation to the conscience and taste of the parties. It will be probably next perceived that if the civil obligation is fulfilled, if the children of the marriage are legally and satisfactorily provided for by the parties, without the assistance of the legislature, the legislature has, in principle, nothing more to do with the matter.

It is assumed in America, particularly in New England, that the morals of society there are peculiarly pure. I am grieved to doubt the fact: but I do doubt it. Nothing like a comparison between one country and another in different circumstances can be instituted: nor would any one desire to enter upon such a comparison. The bottomless vice, the all-pervading corruption of European society cannot, by possibility,

be yet paralleled in America: but neither is it true that any outward prosperity, any arrangement of circumstances, can keep a society pure while there is corruption in its social methods, and among its principles of individual action. Even in America, where every young man may, if he chooses, marry at twenty-one, and appropriate all the best comforts of domestic life,—even here there is vice. Men do not choose to marry early, because they have learned to think other things of more importance than the best comforts of domestic life.

I was struck with the great number of New England women whom I saw married to men old enough to be their fathers. One instance which perplexed me exceedingly, on my entrance into the country, was explained very little to my satisfaction. The girl had been engaged to a young man whom she was attached to: her mother broke off the engagement, and married her to a rich old man. This story was a real shock to me; so persuaded had I been that in America, at least, one might escape from the disgusting spectacle of mercenary marriages. But I saw only too many instances afterwards. The practice was ascribed to the often-mentioned fact of the young men migrating westwards in large numbers, leaving those who should be their wives to marry widowers of double their age. The Auld Robin Gray story is a frequently enacted tragedy here.

The unavoidable consequence of such a mode of marrying is, that the sanctity of marriage is impaired, and that vice succeeds. Any one must see at a glance that if men and women marry those whom they do not love, they must love those whom they do not marry. There are sad tales in country villages, here and there, which attest this; and yet more in towns, in a rank of society where such things are seldom or never heard of in England. I rather think that married life is immeasurably purer in America than in England: but that there is not otherwise much superiority to boast of. I can only say, that I unavoidably knew of more cases of lapse in highly respectable families in one State than ever came to my knowledge at home; and that they were got over with a disgrace far more temporary and superficial than they could have been visited with in England.

The ultimate and very strong impression on the mind of a stranger, pondering the morals of society in America, is that human nature is much the same everywhere, whatever may be its environment of riches or poverty; and that it is justice to the human nature, and not improvement in fortunes, which must be looked to as the promise of a better time. Laws and customs may be creative of vice; and should be therefore perpetually under process of observation and correction: but laws and customs cannot be creative of virtue: they may encourage and help to preserve it; but they cannot originate it . . .

The greater number of American women have home and its affairs, wherewith to occupy themselves. Wifely and motherly occupation may be called the sole business of woman there. If she has not that, she has nothing. The only alternative, as I have said, is making an occupation of either religion or dissipation; neither of which is fit to be so used: the one being a state of mind; the other altogether a negation when not taken in alternation with business . . .

All American ladies should know how to clear-starch and iron: how to keep plate and glass: how to cook dainties: and, if they understand the making of bread and soup likewise, so much the better. The gentlemen usually charge themselves with the business of marketing; which is very fair . . .

As for the occupations with which American ladies fill up their leisure; what has been already said will show that there is no great weight or diversity of occupation. Many are largely engaged in charities, doing good or harm according to the enlightenment of mind which is carried to the work. In New England, a vast deal of time is spent in attending preachings, and other religious meetings: and in paying visits, for religious purposes, to the poor and sorrowful. The same results follow from this practice that may be witnessed wherever it is much pursued. In as far as sympathy is kept up, and acquaintanceship between different classes in society is occasioned, the practice is good. In as far as it unsettles the minds of the visitors, encourages a false craving for religious excitement, tempts to spiritual interference on the one hand, and cant on the other, and humours or oppresses those who need such offices least, while it alienates those who want them most, the practice is bad. I am disposed to think that much good is done, and much harm: and that, whenever women have a greater charge of indispensable business on their hands, so as to do good and reciprocate religious sympathy by laying hold of opportunities, instead of by making occupation, more than the present good will be done, without any of the harm.

All American ladies are more or less literary: and some are so to excellent purpose: to the saving of their minds from vacuity. Readers are plentiful: thinkers are rare. I met with more intellectual activity, more general power, among many ladies who gave little time to books, than among those who are distinguished as being literary. Natural philosophy is not pursued to any extent by women. There is some pretension to mental and moral philosophy; but the less that is said on that head the better.

This is a sad account of things. It may tempt some to ask 'what then are the American women?' They are better educated by Providence than by men. The lot of humanity is theirs: they have labour, probation, joy, and sorrow. They are good wives; and, under the teaching of nature, good mothers. They have, within the range of their activity, good sense, good temper, and good manners. Their beauty is very remarkable; and, I think, their wit no less. Their charity is overflowing, if it were but more enlightened: and it may be supposed that they could not exist without religion. It appears to superabound; but it is not usually of a healthy character. It may seem harsh to say this: but is it not the fact that religion emanates from the nature, from the moral state of the individual? Is it not therefore true that unless the nature be completely exercised, the moral state harmonised, the religion cannot be healthy?

One consequence, mournful and injurious, of the 'chivalrous' taste and temper of a country with regard to its women is that it is difficult, where it is not impossible, for women to earn their bread. Where it is a boast that women do not labour, the encouragement and rewards of labour are not provided. It is so in America. In some parts, there are now so many women dependent on their own exertions for a maintenance, that the evil will give way before the force of circumstances. In the meantime, the lot of poor women is sad. Before the opening of the factories, there were but three resources; teaching, needlework, and keeping boarding-houses or hotels. Now, there are the mills; and women are employed in printing-offices; as compositors, as well as folders and stitchers.

I dare not trust myself to do more than touch on this topic. There would be little use in dwelling upon it; for the mischief lies in the system by which women are depressed, so as to have the greater number of objects of pursuit placed beyond their reach, more than in any minor arrangements which might be rectified by an exposure of particular evils. I would only ask of philanthropists of all countries to inquire of physicians what is the state of health of sempstresses; and to judge thence whether it is not inconsistent with common humanity that women should depend for bread upon such employment. Let them inquire what is the recompense of this kind of labour, and then wonder if they can that the pleasures of the licentious are chiefly supplied from that class. Let them reverence the strength of such as keep their virtue, when the toil which they know is slowly and surely destroying them will barely afford them bread, while the wages of sin are luxury and idleness. During the present interval between the feudal age and the coming time, when life and its occupations will be freely thrown open to women as to men, the condition of the female working classes is such that if its sufferings were but made known, emotions of horror and shame would tremble through the whole of society.

For women who shrink from the lot of the needle-woman,—almost equally dreadful, from the fashionable milliner down to the humble stocking-darner,—for those who shrink through pride, or fear of sickness, poverty, or temptation, there is little resource but pretension to teach. Ladies who fully deserve the confidence of society may realise an independence in a few years by school-keeping in the north: but, on the whole, the scanty reward of female labour in America remains the reproach to the country which its philanthropists have for some years proclaimed it to be. I hope they will persevere in their proclamation, though special methods of charity will not avail to cure the evil. It lies deep; it lies in the subordination of the sex: and upon this the exposures and remonstrances of philanthropists may ultimately succeed in fixing the attention of society; particularly of women. The progression or emancipation of any class usually, if not always, takes place through the efforts of individuals of that class: and so it must be here. All women should inform themselves of the condition of their sex, and of their own position. It must necessarily follow that the noblest of them will, sooner or later, put forth a moral power which shall prostrate cant, and burst asunder the bonds, (silken to some, but cold iron to others,) of feudal prejudices and usages. In the meantime, is it to be understood that the principles of the Declaration of Independence bear no relation to half of the human race? If so, what is the ground of the limitation? If not so, how is the restricted and dependent state of women to be reconciled with the proclamation that "all are endowed by their Creator with certain inalienable rights; that among these are life, liberty, and the pursuit of happiness?" . . .

3. From a Pastoral Letter of "the General Association of Massachusetts (Orthodox) to the Churches under their care," 1837

III. We invite your attention to the dangers which at present seem to threaten the female character with wide-spread and permanent injury.

The appropriate duties and influence of woman are clearly stated in the New Testament. Those duties and that influence are unobtrusive and private, but the source of mighty power. When the mild, dependent, softening influence of woman upon the sternness of man's opinions is fully exercised, society feels the effects of it in a thousand forms. The power of woman is her dependence, flowing from the consciousness of that weakness which God has given her for her protection, (!) and which keeps her in those departments of life that form the character of individuals, and of the nation. There are social influences which females use in promoting piety and the great objects of Christian benevolence which we can not too highly commend.

We appreciate the unostentatious prayers and efforts of woman in advancing the cause of religion at home and abroad; in Sabbath-schools; in leading religious inquirers to the pastors (!) for instruction; and in all such associated effort as becomes the modesty of her sex: and earnestly hope that she may abound more and more in these labors of piety and love. But when she assumes the place and tone of man as a public reformer, our care and protection of her seem unnecessary; we put ourselves in self-defence (!) against her; she yields the power which God has given her for her protection, and her character becomes unnatural. If the vine, whose strength and beauty is to lean upon the trellis-work, and half conceal its clusters, thinks to assume the independence and the overshadowing nature of the elm, it will not only cease to bear fruit, but fall in shame and dishonor into the dust. We can not, therefore, but regret the mistaken conduct of those who encourage females to bear an obtrusive and ostentatious part in measures of reform, and countenance any of that sex who so far forget themselves as to itinerate in the character of public lecturers and teachers. We especially deplore the intimate acquaintance and promiscuous conversation of females with regard to things which ought not to be named; by which that modesty and delicacy which is the charm of domestic life, and which constitutes the true influence of woman in society, is consumed, and the way opened, as we apprehend, for degeneracy and ruin.

We say these things not to discourage proper influences against sin, but to secure such reformation (!) as we believe is Scriptural, and will be permanent.

4. FROM *AMERICAN NOTES FOR GENERAL CIRCULATION,* BY CHARLES DICKENS, 1842

. . . There are several factories in Lowell, each of which belongs to what we should term a Company of Proprietors, but what they call in America a Corporation. I went over several of these; such as a woollen factory, a carpet factory, and a cotton factory: examined them in every part; and saw them in their ordinary working aspect, with no preparation of any kind, or departure from their ordinary everyday proceedings. I may add that I am well acquainted with our manufacturing towns in England, and have visited many mills in Manchester and elsewhere in the same manner.

I happened to arrive at the first factory just as the dinner hour was over, and the girls were returning to their work; indeed the stairs of the mill were thronged with them as I ascended. They were all well dressed, but not to my thinking above their condition; for I like to see the humbler classes of society careful of their dress and appearance, and even, if they please, decorated with such little trinkets as come within the compass of their means. Supposing it confined within reasonable limits, I would always encourage this kind of pride, as a worthy element of self-respect, in any person I employed; and should no more be deterred from doing so, because some wretched female referred her fall to a love of dress, than I would allow my construction of the real intent and meaning of the Sabbath to be influenced by any warning to the well-disposed, founded on his backslidings on that particular day, which might emanate from the rather doubtful authority of a murderer in Newgate.

These girls, as I have said, were all well dressed: and that phrase necessarily includes extreme cleanliness. They had serviceable bonnets, good warm cloaks, and shawls; and were not above clogs and pattens. Moreover, there were places in the mill in which they could deposit these things without injury; and there were conveniences for washing. They were healthy in appearance, many of them remarkably so, and had the manners and deportment of young women: not of degraded brutes of burden. If I had seen in one of those mills (but I did not, though I looked for something of this kind with a sharp eye), the most lisping, mincing, affected, and ridiculous young creature that my imagination could suggest, I should have thought of the careless, moping, slatternly, degraded, dull reverse (I *have* seen that), and should have been still well pleased to look upon her.

The rooms in which they worked, were as well ordered as themselves. In the windows of some, there were green plants, which were trained to shade the glass; in all, there was as much fresh air, cleanliness, and comfort, as the nature of the occupation would possibly admit of. Out of so large a number of females, many of whom were only then just verging upon womanhood, it may be reasonably supposed that some were delicate and fragile in appearance: no doubt there were. But I solemnly declare, that from all the crowd I saw in the different factories that day, I cannot recall or separate one young face that gave me a painful impression; not one young girl whom, assuming it to be matter of necessity that she should gain her daily bread by the labour of her hands, I would have removed from those works if I had had the power.

They reside in various boarding-houses near at hand. The owners of the mills are particularly careful to allow no persons to enter upon the possession of these houses, whose characters have not undergone the most searching and thorough inquiry. Any complaint that is made against them, by the boarders, or by any one else, is fully investigated; and if good ground of complaint be shown to exist against them, they are removed, and their occupation is handed over to some more deserving person. There are a few children employed in these factories, but not many. The laws of the State forbid their working more than nine months in the year, and require that they be educated during the other three. For this purpose there are schools in Lowell; and there are churches and chapels of various persuasions, in which the young women may observe that form of Worship in which they have been educated.

At some distance from the factories, and on the highest and pleasantest ground in the neighbourhood, stands their hospital, or boarding-house for the sick: it is the best house in those parts, and was built by an eminent merchant for his own residence. Like that institution at Boston, which I have before described, it is not parcelled out into wards, but is divided into convenient chambers, each of which has all the comforts of a very comfortable home. The principal medical attendant resides under the same roof; and were the patients members of his own family, they could not be better cared for, or attended with greater gentleness and consideration. The weekly charge in this establishment for each female patient is three dollars, or twelve shillings English; but no girl employed by any of the corporations is ever excluded for want of the means of payment. That they do not very often want the means, may be gathered from the fact, that in July, 1841, no fewer than nine hundred and seventy-eight of these girls were depositors in the Lowell Savings Bank: the amount of whose joint savings was estimated at one hundred thousand dollars, or twenty thousand English pounds.

I am now going to state three facts, which will startle a large class of readers on this side of the Atlantic, very much.

Firstly, there is a joint-stock piano in a great many of the boarding-houses. Secondly, nearly all these young ladies subscribe to circulating libraries. Thirdly, they have got up among themselves a periodical called THE LOWELL OFFERING, "A repository of original articles, written exclusively by females actively employed in the mills,"—which is duly printed, published, and sold; and whereof I brought away from Lowell four hundred good solid pages, which I have read from beginning to end.

The large class of readers, startled by these facts, will exclaim, with one voice, "How very preposterous!" On my deferentially inquiring why, they will answer, "These things are above their station." In reply to that objection, I would beg to ask what their station is.

It is their station to work. And they *do* work. They labour in these mills, upon an average, twelve hours a day, which is unquestionably work, and pretty tight work too. Perhaps it is above their station to indulge

in such amusements, on any terms. Are we quite sure that we in England have not formed our ideas of the "station" of working people, from accustoming ourselves to the contemplation of that class as they are, and not as they might be? I think if we examine our own feelings, we shall find that the pianos, and the circulating libraries, and even the Lowell Offering, startle us by their novelty, and not by their bearing upon any abstract question of right or wrong.

For myself, I know no station in which, the occupation of to-day cheerfully done and the occupation of to-morrow cheerfully looked to, any one of these pursuits is not most humanising and laudable. I know no station which is rendered more endurable to the person in it, or more safe to the person out of it, by having ignorance for its associate. I know no station which has a right to monopolise the means of mutual instruction, improvement, and rational entertainment; or which has ever continued to be a station very long, after seeking to do so.

Of the merits of the Lowell Offering as a literary production, I will only observe, putting entirely out of sight the fact of the articles having been written by these girls after the arduous labours of the day, that it will compare advantageously with a great many English Annuals. It is pleasant to find that many of its Tales are of the Mills and of those who work in them; that they inculcate habits of self-denial and contentment, and teach good doctrines of enlarged benevolence. A strong feeling for the beauties of nature, as displayed in the solitudes the writers have left at home, breathes through its pages like wholesome village air; and though a circulating library is a favourable school for the study of such topics, it has very scant allusion to fine clothes, fine marriages, fine houses, or fine life. Some persons might object to the papers being signed occasionally with rather fine names, but this is an American fashion. One of the provinces of the state legislature of Massachusetts is to alter ugly names into pretty ones, as the children improve upon the tastes of their parents. These changes costing little or nothing, scores of Mary Annes are solemnly converted into Bevelinas every session.

It is said that on the occasion of a visit from General Jackson or General Harrison to this town (I forget which, but it is not to the purpose), he walked through three miles and a half of these young ladies all dressed out with parasols and silk stockings. But as

I am not aware that any worse consequence ensued, than a sudden looking-up of all the parasols and silk stockings in the market; and perhaps the bankruptcy of some speculative New Englander who bought them all up at any price, in expectation of a demand that never came; I set no great store by the circumstance.

In this brief account of Lowell, and inadequate expression of the gratification it yielded me, and cannot fail to afford to any foreigner to whom the condition of such people at home is a subject of interest and anxious speculation, I have carefully abstained from drawing a comparison between these factories and those of our own land. Many of the circumstances whose strong influence has been at work for years in our manufacturing towns have not arisen here; and there is no manufacturing population in Lowell, so to speak: for these girls (often the daughters of small farmers) come from other States, remain a few years in the mills, and then go home for good.

The contrast would be a strong one, for it would be between the Good and Evil, the living light and deepest shadow. I abstain from it, because I deem it just to do so. But I only the more earnestly adjure all those whose eyes may rest on these pages, to pause and reflect upon the difference between this town and those great haunts of desperate misery: to call to mind, if they can in the midst of party strife and squabble, the efforts that must be made to purge them of their suffering and danger: and last, and foremost, to remember how the precious Time is rushing by.

5. COMMONWEALTH OF MASSACHUSETTS REPORT, HOUSE OF REPRESENTATIVES, MARCH 12, 1845

The Special Committee to which was referred sundry petitions relating to the hours of labor, have considered the same and submit the following

Report:

The first petition which was referred to your committee, came from the city of Lowell and was signed by Mr. John Quincy Adams Thayer, and eight hundred and fifty others, "peaceable, industrious, hard working men and women of Lowell." The petitioners declare that they are confined to "from thirteen to fourteen hours per day in unhealthy apartments," and are thereby "hastening through pain, disease and pri-

vation, down to a premature grave." They therefore ask the Legislature "to pass a law providing that ten hours shall constitute a day's work," and that no corporation or private citizen "shall be allowed, except in cases of emergency, to employ one set of hands more than ten hours per day."

The second petition came from the town of Fall River, and is signed by John Gregory and four hundred and eighty-eight others. These petitions ask for the passage of a law to constitute "ten hours a day's work in *all corporations* created by the Legislature."

The third petition signed by Samuel W. Clark and five hundred others, citizens of Andover, is in precisely the same words as the one from Fall River.

The fourth petition is from Lowell, and is signed by James Carle and three hundred others. The petitioners ask for the enactment of a law making ten hours a day's work, where no specific agreement is entered into between the parties.

The whole number of names on the several petitions is 2,139, of which 1,151 are from Lowell. A very large proportion of the Lowell petitioners are females. Nearly one half of the Andover petitioners are females. The petition from Fall River is signed exclusively by males.

In view of the number and respectability of the petitioners who had brought their grievances before the Legislature, the Committee asked for and obtained leave of the House to send for "persons and papers," in order that they might enter into an examination of the matter, and report the result of their examination to the Legislature as a basis for legislative action, should any be deemed necessary.

On the 13th of February, the Committee held a session to hear the petitioners from the city of Lowell. Six of the female and three of the male petitioners were present, and gave in their testimony.

The first petitioner who testified was *Eliza R. Hemmingway.* She had worked 2 years and 9 months in the Lowell Factories; 2 years in the Middlesex, and 9 months in the Hamilton Corporations. Her employment is weaving,—works by the piece. The Hamilton Mill manufactures cotton fabrics. The Middlesex, woollen fabrics. She is now at work in the Middlesex Mills, and attends one loom. Her wages average from $16 to $23 a month exclusive of board. She complained of the hours for labor being too many, and the time for meals too limited. In the summer season, the work is commenced at 5 o'clock,

A.M., and continued till 7 o'clock, P.M., with half an hour for breakfast and three quarters of an hour for dinner. During eight months of the year, but half an hour is allowed for dinner. The air in the room she considered not to be wholesome. There were 293 small lamps and 61 large lamps lighted in the room in which she worked when evening work is required. These lamps are also lighted sometimes in the morning.—About 130 females, 11 men, and 12 children (between the ages of 11 and 14,) work in the room with her. She thought the children enjoyed about as good health as children generally do. The children work but 9 months out of 12. The other 3 months they must attend school. Thinks that there is no day when there are less than six of the females out of the mill from sickness. Has known as many as thirty. She, herself, is out quite often, on account of sickness. There was more sickness in the Summer than in Winter months; though in the Summer, lamps are not lighted. She thought there was a general desire among the females to work but ten hours, regardless of the pay. Most of the girls are from the country, who work in the Lowell Mills. The average time which they remain there is about three years. She knew one girl who had worked there 14 years. Her health was poor when she left. Miss Hemmingway said her health was better where she now worked, than it was when she worked on the Hamilton Corporation.

She knew of one girl who last winter went into the mill at half past 4 o'clock, A.M. and worked till half past 7 o'clock P.M. She did so to make more money. She earned from $25 to $30 per month. There is always a large number of girls at the gate wishing to get in before the bell rings. On the Middlesex Corporation one fourth part of the females go into the mill before they are obliged to. They do this to make more wages. A large number come to Lowell to make money to aid their parents who are poor. She knew of many cases where married women came to Lowell and worked in the mills to assist their husbands to pay for their farms. The moral character of the operatives is good. There was only one American female in the room with her who could not write her name.

Miss Sarah G. Bagley said she had worked in the Lowell Mills eight years and a half,—six years and a half on the Hamilton Corporation, and two years on the Middlesex. She is a weaver, and works by the piece. She worked in the mills three years before her health began to fail. She is a native of New Hamp-

shire, and went home six weeks during the summer. Last year she was out of the mill a third of the time. She thinks the health of the operatives is not so good as the health of females who do house-work or millinery business. The chief evil, so far as health is concerned, is the shortness of time allowed for meals. The next evil is the length of time employed—not giving them time to cultivate their minds. She spoke of the high moral and intellectual character of the girls. That many were engaged as teachers in the Sunday schools. That many attended the lectures of the Lowell Institute; and she thought, if more time was allowed, that more lectures would be given and more girls attend. She thought that the girls generally were favorable to the ten hour system. She had presented a petition, same as the one before the Committee, to 132 girls, most of whom said that they would prefer to work but ten hours. In a pecuniary point of view, it would be better, as their health would be improved. They would have more time for sewing. Their intellectual, moral and religious habits would also be benefited by the change.

Miss Bagley said, in addition to her labor in the mills, she had kept evening school during the winter months, for four years, and thought that this extra labor must have injured her health.

Miss Judith Payne testified that she came to Lowell 16 years ago, and worked a year and a half in the Merrimack Cotton Mills, left there on account of ill health, and remained out over seven years. She was sick most of the time she was out. Seven years ago she went to work in the Boott Mills, and has remained there ever since; works by the piece. She has lost, during the last seven years, about one year from ill health. She is a weaver, and attends three looms. Last pay-day she drew $14.66 for five weeks work; this was exclusive of board. She was absent during the five weeks but half a day. She says there is a very general feeling in favor of the ten hour system among the operatives. She attributes her ill health to the long hours of labor, the shortness of time for meals, and the bad air of the mills. She had never spoken to Mr. French, the agent, or to the overseer of her room, in relation to these matters. She could not say that more operatives died in Lowell than other people.

Miss Olive J. Clark.—She is employed on the Lawrence Corporation; has been there five years; makes about $1.62 1/2 per week, exclusive of board. She has been home to New Hampshire to school.

Her health never was good. The work is not laborious; can sit down about a quarter of the time. About fifty girls work in the spinning-room with her, three of whom signed the petition. She is in favor of the ten hour system, and thinks that the long hours had an effect upon her health. She is kindly treated by her employers. There is hardly a week in which there is not some one out on account of sickness. Thinks the air is bad, on account of the small particles of cotton which fly about. She has never spoken with the agent or overseer about working only ten hours.

Miss Celicia Phillips has worked four years in Lowell. Her testimony was similar to that given by Miss Clark.

Miss Elizabeth Rowe has worked in Lowell 16 months, all the time on the Lawrence Corporation, came from Maine, she is a weaver, works by the piece, runs four looms. "My health," she says, "has been very good indeed since I worked there, averaged three dollars a week since I have been there besides my board; have heard very little about the hours of labor being too long." She consented to have her name put on the petition because Miss Phillips asked her to. She would prefer to work only ten hours. Between 50 and 60 work in the room with her. Her room is better ventilated and more healthy than most others. Girls who wish to attend lectures can go out before the bell rings; my overseer lets them go, also Saturdays they go out before the bell rings. It was her wish to attend 4 looms. She has a sister who has worked in the mill 7 years. Her health is very good. Don't known that she has ever been out on account of sickness. The general health of the operatives is good. Have never spoken to my employers about the work being too hard, or the hours too long. Don't know any one who has been hastened to a premature grave by factory labor. I never attended any of the lectures in Lowell on the ten hour system. Nearly all the female operatives in Lowell work by the piece; and of the petitioners who appeared before the Committee, Miss Hemmingway, Miss Bagby, Miss Payne and Miss Rowe work by the piece, and Miss Clark and Miss Phillips by the week.

Mr. Gilman Gale, a member of the city council, and who keeps a provision store, testified that the short time allowed for meals he thought the greatest evil. He spoke highly of the character of the operatives and of the agents; also of the boarding houses and the public schools. He had two children in the mills who enjoyed good health. The mills are kept as clean and as well ventilated as it is possible for them to be.

Mr. Herman Abbott had worked in the Lawrence Corporation 13 years. Never heard much complaint among the girls about the long hours, never heard the subject spoken of in the mills. Does not think it would be satisfactory to the girls to work only ten hours, if their wages were to be reduced in proportion. Forty-two girls work in the room with him. The girls often get back to the gate before the bell rings.

Mr. John Quincy Adams Thayer, has lived in Lowell 4 years, "works at physical labor in the summer season, and mental labor in the winter." Has worked in the big machine shop 24 months, off and on; never worked in a cotton or woollen mill. Thinks that the mechanics in the machine shop are not so healthy as in other shops; nor so intelligent as the other classes in Lowell. He drafted the petition. Has heard many complain of the long hours.

Your Committee have not been able to give the petitions from the other towns in this State a hearing. We believed that the whole case was covered by the petition from Lowell, and to the consideration of that petition we have given our undivided attention, and we have come to the conclusion *unanimously,* that legislation is not necessary at the present time, and for the following reasons:—

1st. That a law limiting the hours of labor, if enacted at all, should be of a general nature. That it should apply to individuals or copartnerships as well as to corporations. Because, if it is wrong to labor more than ten hours in a corporation, it is also wrong when applied to individual employers, and your Committee are not aware that more complaint can justly be made against incorporated companies in regard to the hours of labor, than can be against individuals or copartnerships. But it will be said in reply to this, that corporations are the creatures of the Legislature, and therefore the Legislature can control them in this, as in other matters. This to a certain extent is true, but your Committee go farther than this, and say, that not only are corporations subject to the control of the Legislature but individuals are also, and if it should ever appear that the public morals, the physical condition, or the social well-being of society were endangered, from this cause or from any cause, then it would be in the power and would be the duty of the Legislature to interpose its prerogative to avert the evil.

2d. Your Committee believe that the factory system, as it is called, is not more injurious to health than other kinds of indoor labor. That a law which would compel all of the factories in Massachusetts to run their machinery but ten hours out of the 24, while those in Maine, New Hampshire, Rhode Island and other States in the Union, were not restricted at all, the effect would be to close the gate of every mill in the State. It would be the same as closing our mills one day in every week, and although Massachusetts capital, enterprise, and industry are willing to compete on fair terms with the same of other States, and, if needs be, with European nations, yet it is easy to perceive that we could not compete with our sister States, much less with foreign countries, if a restriction of this nature was put upon our manufactories.

3d. It would be impossible to legislate to restrict the hours of labor, without affecting very materially the question of wages; and that is a matter which experience has taught us can be much better regulated by the parties themselves than by the Legislature. Labor in Massachusetts is a very different commodity from what it is in foreign countries. Here labor is on an equality with capital, and indeed controls it, and so it ever will be while free education and free constitutions exist. And although we may find fault, and say, that labor works too many hours, and labor is too severely tasked, yet if we attempt by legislation to enter within its orbit and interfere with it plans, we will be told to keep clear and to mind our own business. Labor is intelligent enough to make its own bargains, and look out for its own interests without any interference from us; and your Committee want no better proof to convince them that Massachusetts men and Massachusetts women, are equal to this, and will take care of themselves better than we can take care of them, than we had from the intelligent and virtuous men and women who appeared in support of this petition, before the Committee.

4th. The Committee do not wish to be understood as conveying the impression, that there are no abuses in the present system of labor; we think there are abuses; we think that many improvements may be made, and we believe will be made, by which labor will not be so severely tasked as it now is. We think that it would be better if the hours for labor were less,—if more time was allowed for meals, if more attention was paid to ventilation and pure air in our manufactories, and work shops, and many other matters. We acknowledge all this, but we say, the remedy is not with us. We look for it in the progressive improvement in art and science, in a higher appreciation of man's destiny, in a less love for money, and a more ardent love for social happiness and intellectual superiority. Your Committee, therefore, while they agree with the petitioners in their desire to lessen the burthens imposed upon labor, differ only as is the means by which these burthens are sought to be removed.

It would be an interesting inquiry were we permitted to enter upon it, to give a brief history of the rise and progress of the factory system in Massachusetts, to speak of its small beginnings, and show its magnificent results. Labor has made it what it is, and labor will continue to improve upon it.

Your Committee, in conclusion, respectfully ask to be discharged from the further consideration of the matters referred to them, and that the petitions be referred to the next General Court.

For the Committee,
Wm. Schouler, Chairman

6. MARRIED WOMAN'S PROPERTY ACT, NEW YORK, 1848

The People of the State of New York, represented in Senate and Assembly, do enact as follows:

I The real and personal property of any female who may hereafter marry, and which she shall own at the time of her marriage, and the rents, issues and profits thereof, shall not be subject to the disposal of her husband nor be liable for his debts and shall continue her sole and separate property as if she were a single female.

II The real and personal property and the rents, issues and profits thereof of any female now married shall not be subject to the disposal of her husband; but shall be her sole and separate property as if she were a single female except so far as the same may be liable for the debts of her husband heretofore contracted.

III It shall be lawful for any married female to receive by gift, grant device or bequest, from any person other than her husband and to hold to her sole and separate use, as if she were a single female, real and personal property and the rents, issues and profits thereof, and the same shall not be subject to the disposal of her husband, nor be liable for his debts.

IV All contracts made between persons in contemplation of marriage shall remain in full force after such marriage takes place.

7. DECLARATION OF RIGHTS AND SENTIMENTS, SENECA FALLS, JULY 19–20, 1848

Declaration of Sentiments

WHEN, IN THE COURSE OF HUMAN EVENTS, it becomes necessary for one portion of the family of man to assume among the people of the earth a position different from that which they have hitherto occupied, but one to which the laws of nature and of nature's God entitle them, a decent respect to the opinions of mankind requires that they should declare the causes that impel them to such a course.

We hold these truths to be self-evident: that all men and women are created equal; that they are endowed by their Creator with certain inalienable rights; that among these are life, liberty, and the pursuit of happiness; that to secure these rights governments are instituted, deriving their just powers from the consent of the governed. Whenever any form of government becomes destructive of these ends, it is the right of those who suffer from it to refuse allegiance to it, and to insist upon the institution of a new government, laying its foundation on such principles and organizing its powers in such form, as to them shall seem most likely to effect their safety and happiness.

Prudence, indeed, will dictate that governments long established should not be changed for light and transient causes; and, accordingly, all experience has shown that mankind are more disposed to suffer, while evils are sufferable, than to right themselves by abolishing the forms to which they were accustomed. But when a long train of abuses and usurpations, pursuing invariably the same object, evinces a design to reduce them under absolute despotism, it is their duty to throw off such government and to provide new guards for their future security. Such has been the patient sufferance of the women under this government, and such is now the necessity which constrains them to demand the equal station to which they are entitled.

The history of mankind is a history of repeated injuries and usurpations on the part of man toward woman, having in direct object the establishment of an absolute tyranny over her. To prove this, let facts be submitted to a candid world.

He has never permitted her to exercise her inalienable right to the elective franchise.

He has compelled her to submit to laws in the formation of which she had no voice.

He has withheld from her rights which are given to the most ignorant and degraded men, both natives and foreigners.

Having deprived her of this first right of a citizen, the elective franchise, thereby leaving her without representation in the halls of legislation, he has oppressed her on all sides.

He has made her, if married, in the eye of the law, civilly dead.

He has taken from her all rights in property, even to the wages she earns.

He has made her, morally, an irresponsible being, as she can commit many crimes with impunity, provided they be done in the presence of her husband. In the covenant of marriage, she is compelled to promise obedience to her husband, he becoming, to all intents and purposes, her master—the law giving him power to deprive her of her liberty and to administer chastisement.

He has so framed the laws of divorce, as to what shall be the proper causes and, in case of separation, to whom the guardianship of the children shall be given, as to be wholly regardless of the happiness of women—the law, in all cases, going upon a false supposition of the supremacy of man and giving all power into his hands.

After depriving her of all rights as a married woman, if single and the owner of property, he has taxed her to support a government which recognizes her only when her property can be made profitable to it.

He has monopolized nearly all the profitable employments, and from those she is permitted to follow, she receives but a scanty remuneration. He closes against her all the avenues to wealth and distinction which he considers most honorable to himself. As a teacher of theology, medicine, or law, she is not known.

He has denied her the facilities for obtaining a thorough education, all colleges being closed against her.

He allows her in church, as well as state, but a subordinate position, claiming apostolic authority for her exclusion from the ministry, and, with some exceptions, from any public participation in the affairs of the church.

He has created a false public sentiment by giving to the world a different code of morals for men and women, by which moral delinquencies which exclude women from society are not only tolerated but deemed of little account in man.

He has usurped the prerogative of Jehovah himself, claiming it as his right to assign for her a sphere of action, when that belongs to her conscience and to her God.

He has endeavored, in every way that he could, to destroy her confidence in her own powers, to lessen her self-respect, and to make her willing to lead a dependent and abject life.

Now, in view of this entire disfranchisement of one-half the people of this country, their social and religious degradation, in view of the unjust laws above mentioned, and because women do feel themselves aggrieved, oppressed, and fraudulently deprived of their most sacred rights we insist that they have immediate admission to all the rights and privileges which belong to them as citizens of the United States.

In entering upon the great work before us, we anticipate no small amount of misconception, misrepresentation, and ridicule; but we shall use every instrumentality within our power to effect our object. We shall employ agents, circulate tracts, petition the state and national legislatures, and endeavor to enlist the pulpit and the press in our behalf. We hope this Convention will be followed by a series of conventions embracing every part of the country.

Resolutions

Whereas, the great precept of nature is conceded to be that "man shall pursue his own true and substantial happiness." Blackstone in his *Commentaries* remarks that this law of nature, being coeval with mankind and dictated by God himself, is, of course, superior in obligation to any other. It is binding over all the globe, in all countries and at all times; no human laws are of any validity if contrary to this, and such of them as are valid derive all their force, and all their validity, and all their authority, mediately and immediately, from this original; therefore,

Resolved, That such laws as conflict, in any way, with the true and substantial happiness of woman, are contrary to the great precept of nature and of no validity, for this is "superior in obligation to any other."

Resolved, that all laws which prevent woman from occupying such a station in society as her conscience shall dictate, or which place her in a position inferior to that of man, are contrary to the great precept of nature and therefore of no force or authority.

Resolved, that woman is man's equal, was intended to be so by the Creator, and the highest good of the race demands that she should be recognized as such.

Resolved, that the women of this country ought to be enlightened in regard to the laws under which they live, that they may no longer publish their degradation by declaring themselves satisfied with their present position, nor their ignorance, by asserting that they have all the rights they want.

Resolved, that inasmuch as man, while claiming for himself intellectual superiority, does accord to woman moral superiority, it is preeminently his duty to encourage her to speak and teach, as she has an opportunity, in all religious assemblies.

Resolved, that the same amount of virtue, delicacy, and refinement of behavior that is required of woman in the social state should also be required of man, and the same transgressions should be visited with equal severity on both man and woman.

Resolved, that the objection of indelicacy and impropriety, which is so often brought against woman when she addresses a public audience, comes with a very ill grace from those who encourage, by their attendance, her appearance on the stage, in the concert, or in feats of the circus.

Resolved, that woman has too long rested satisfied in the circumscribed limits which corrupt customs and a perverted application of the Scriptures have marked out for her, and that it is time she should move in the enlarged sphere which her great Creator has assigned her.

Resolved, that it is the duty of the women on this country to secure to themselves their sacred right to the elective franchise.

Resolved, that the equality of human rights results necessarily from the fact of the identity of the race in capabilities and responsibilities.

Resolved, that the speedy success of our cause depends upon the zealous and untiring efforts of both men and women for the overthrow of the monopoly of the pulpit, and for the securing to woman an equal participation with men in the various trades, professions, and commerce.

Resolved, therefore, that, being invested of the Creator with the same capabilities and the same consciousness of responsibility for their exercise, it is demonstrably the right and duty of woman, equally with man, to promote every righteous cause by every righteous means; and especially in regard to the great subjects of morals and religion, it is self-evidently her right to participate with her brother in teaching them, both in private and in public, by writing and by speaking, by any instrumentalities proper to be used, and in any assemblies proper to be held; and this being a self-evident truth growing out of the divinely implanted principles of human nature, any custom or authority adverse to it, whether modern or wearing the hoary sanction of antiquity, is to be regarded as a self-evident falsehood and at war with mankind.

8. EDITORIAL IN THE *NORTH STAR,* BY FREDERICK DOUGLASS, JULY 28, 1848

The Rights of Women.—One of the most interesting events of the past week, was the holding of what is technically styled a Woman's Rights Convention at Seneca Falls. The speaking, addresses, and resolutions of this extraordinary meeting were almost wholly conducted by women; and although they evidently felt themselves in a novel position, it is but simple justice to say that their whole proceedings were characterized by marked ability and dignity. No one present, we think, however much he might be disposed to differ from the views advanced by the leading speakers on that occasion, will fail to give them credit for brilliant talents and excellent dispositions. In this meeting, as in other deliberative assemblies, there were frequent differences of opinion and animated discussion; but in no case was there the slightest absence of good feeling and decorum. Several interesting documents setting forth the rights as well as grievances of women were read. Among these was a Declaration of Sentiments, to be regarded as the basis of a grand movement for attaining the civil, social, political, and religious rights of women. We should not do justice to our own convictions, or to the excellent persons connected with this infant movement, if we did not in this connection offer a few remarks on the general subject which the Convention met to consider and the objects they seek to attain. In doing so, we are not insensible that the bare mention of this truly important subject in any other than terms of contemptuous ridicule and scornful disfavor, is likely to excite against us the fury of bigotry and the folly of prejudice. A discussion of the rights of animals would be regarded with far more complacency by many of what are called the *wise* and the *good* of our land, than would be a discussion of the rights of women. It is, in their estimation, to be guilty of evil thoughts, to think that woman is entitled to equal rights with man. Many who have at last made the discovery that the negroes have some rights as well as other members of the human family, have yet to be convinced that women are entitled to any. Eight years ago a number of persons of this description actually abandoned the anti-slavery cause, lest by giving their influence in that direction they might possibly be giving countenance to the dangerous heresy that woman, in respect to rights, stands on an equal footing with man. In the judgment of such persons the American slave system, with all its concomitant horrors. is less to be deplored than this *wicked* idea. It is perhaps needless to say, that we cherish little sympathy for such sentiments or respect for such prejudices. Standing as we do upon the watch-tower of human freedom, we can not be deterred from an expression of our approbation of any movement, however humble, to improve and elevate the character of any members of the human family. While it is impossible for us to go into this subject at length, and dispose of the various objections which are often urged against such a doctrine as that of female equality, we are free to say that in respect to political rights, we hold woman to be justly entitled to all we claim for man. We go farther, and express our conviction that all political rights which it is expedient for man to exercise, it is equally so for woman. All that distinguishes man as an intelligent and accountable being, is equally true of woman; and if that government only is just which governs by the free consent of the governed, there can be no reason in the world for denying to woman the exercise of the elective franchise, or a hand in making and administering the laws of the land. Our doctrine is that "right is of no sex." We therefore bid the women engaged in this movement our humble Godspeed.

9. DEBATE OF CONVENTION AMENDING INDIANA'S CONSTITUTION, 1850

Mr. Owen: No subject of greater importance has come up since we met here, as next in estimation to the right of enjoying life and liberty, our Constitution enumerates the right of acquiring, possessing, protecting property. And these sections refer to the latter right, heretofore declared to be natural, inherent, inalienable, yet virtually withheld from one-half the citizens of our State. Women are not represented in our legislative halls; they have no voice in selecting those who make laws and constitutions for them; and one reason given for excluding women from the right of suffrage, is an expression of confident belief that their husbands and fathers will surely guard their interests. I should like, for the honor of my sex, to believe that the legal rights of women are, at all times, as zealously guarded as they would be if women had votes to give to those who watch over their interests.

Suffer me, sir, in defense of my skepticism on this point, to lay before you and this Convention, an item from my legislative recollection.

It will be thirteen years next winter, since I reported from a seat just over the way, a change in the then existing law of descent. At that time the widow of an intestate dying without children, was entitled, under ordinary circumstances, to dower in her husband's real estate, and one-third of his personal property. The change proposed was to give her one-third of the real estate of her husband absolutely, and two-thirds of his personal property—far too little, indeed; but yet as great an innovation as we thought we could carry. This law remained in force until 1841. How stands it now? The widow of an intestate, in case there be no children, and in case there be father, or mother, or brother, or sister of the husband, is heir to no part whatever of her deceased husband's real estate; she is entitled to dower only, of one-third of his estate. I ask you whether your hearts do not revolt at the idea, that when the husband is carried to his long home, his widow shall see snatched from her, by an inhuman law, the very property her watchful care had mainly contributed to increase and keep together.

Yet this idea, revolting as it is, is carried out in all its unmitigated rigor, by the statute to which I have just referred. Out of a yearly rental of a hundred and fifty dollars, the widow of an intestate rarely becomes entitled to more than fifty. The other hundred dollars goes—whither? To the husband's father or mother? Yes, if they survive! But if they are dead, what then? A brother-in-law or a sister-in-law takes it, or the husband's uncle, or his aunt, or his cousin! Do husbands toil through a life-time to support their aunts, and uncles, and cousins? If but a single cousin's child, a babe of six months, survive, to that infant goes a hundred dollars of the rental, and to the widow fifty. Can injustice go beyond this? What think you of a law like that, on the statute book of a civilized and a Christian land? When the husband's sustaining arm is laid in the grave, and the widow left without a husband to cherish, then comes the law more cruel than death, and decrees that poverty shall be added to desolation!

Say, delegates of the people of Indiana, answer and say whether you, whether those who sent you here are guiltless in this thing? Have you done justice? Have you loved mercy?

But let us turn to the question more immediately before us. Let us pass from the case of the widow and look to that of the wife: First, the husband becomes entitled, from the instant of marriage, to all the goods and chattels of his wife. His right is absolute, unconditional. Secondly, the husband acquires, in virtue of the marriage, the rents and profits (in all cases during her life) of his wife's real estate. The flagrant injustice of this has been somewhat modified by a statute barring the marital right to the rent of lands, but this protection does not extend to personal property. Is this as it should be? Are we meting out fair and equal justice? . . . There is a species of very silly sentimentalism which it is the fashion to put forth in after-dinner toasts and other equally veracious forms, about woman being the only tyrant in a free republic; about the chains she imposes on her willing slaves, etc.; it would be much more to our credit, if we would administer a little less flattery and a little more justice . . .

"I am of opinion that to adopt the proposition of the gentleman from Posey (Mr. Owen), will not ameliorate the conditions of married women."

"I can not see the propriety of establishing for women a distinct and separate interest, the consideration of which would, of necessity, withdraw their attention from that sacred duty which nature has, in its wisdom, assigned to their peculiar care. I think the law which unites in one common bond the pecuniary interests of husband and wife should remain. The sacred ordinance of marriage, and the relations growing out of it, should not be disturbed. The common law does seem to me to afford sufficient protection."

"If the law is changed, I believe that a most essential injury would result to the endearing relations of married life. Controversies would arise, husbands and wives would become armed against each other, to the utter destruction of true felicity in married life."

"To adopt it would be to throw a whole population morally and politically into confusion. Is it to explode a volcano under the foundation of the family union?"

"I object to the gentleman's proposition, because it is in contravention of one of the great fundamental principles of the Christian religion. The common law only embodies the divine law."

"Give to the wife a separate interest in law, and all those high motives to restrain the husband from wrong-doing will be, in a great degree, removed."

"I firmly believe that it would diminish, if it did not totally annihilate woman's influence."

"Woman's power comes through a self-sacrificing spirit, ready to offer up all her hopes upon the shrine of her husband's wishes."

"Sir, we have got along for eighteen hundred years, and shall we change now? Our fathers have for many generations maintained the principle of the common law in this regard, for some good and weighty reasons."

"The immortal Jefferson, writing in reference to the then state of society in France, and the debauched condition thereof, attributes the whole to the effects of the civil law then in force in France, permitting the wife to hold, acquire, and own property, separate and distinct from the husband."

"The females of this State are about as happy and contented with their present position in relation to this right (suffrage), as it is necessary they should be, and I do not favor the proposition (of Woman's Suffrage), which my friend from Posey, Mr. Owen, appears to countenance."

"It is not because I love justice less, but woman more, that I oppose this section."

"This doctrine of separate estate will stifle all the finer feelings, blast the brightest, fairest, happiest hopes of the human family, and go in direct contravention of that law which bears the everlasting impress of the Almighty Hand. Sir, I consider such a scheme not only as wild, but as wicked, if not in its intentions, at least in its results." . . .

Sir, I would that my principles on this, in contradistinction with those of the gentlemen from Posey, were written in characters of light across the noonday heavens, that all the world might read them. (Applause). I have in my drawer numerous other extracts from the writings of the gentleman from Posey, but am not allowed to read them; and, indeed, sir, under the circumstances, decency forbids their use. But if I were permitted to read them, and show their worse than damning influences upon society, in conjunction with this system of separate interests, I venture to aver that gentlemen would turn from them with disgust; aye, sir, they would shun them as they would shun man's worst enemy, and flee from them as from a poisonous reptile . . .

10. Letter from Jeanne Deroine and Pauline Roland, Prison of St.-Lagare, Paris, June 15, 1851

To the Convention of the Women of America:

Dear Sisters:—Your courageous declaration of Woman's Rights has resounded even to our prison, and has filled our souls with inexpressible joy.

In France the reaction has suppressed the cry of liberty of the women of the future. Deprived, like their brothers, of the Democracy, of the right to civil and political equality, and the fiscal laws which trammel the liberty of the press, hinder the propagation of those eternal truths which must regenerate humanity.

They wish the women of France to found a hospitable tribunal, which shall receive the cry of the oppressed and suffering, and vindicate in the name of humanity, solidarity, the social right for both sexes equally; and where woman, the mother of humanity, may claim in the name of her children, mutilated by tyranny, her right to true liberty, to the complete development and free exercise of all her faculties, and reveal that half of truth which is in her, and without which no social work can be complete.

The darkness of reaction has obscured the sun of 1848, which seemed to rise so radiantly. Why? Because the revolutionary tempest, in overturning at the same time the throne and the scaffold, in breaking the chain of the black slave, forgot to break the chain of the most oppressed of all of the pariahs of humanity.

"There shall be no more slaves," said our brethren. "We proclaim universal suffrage. All shall have the right to elect the agents who shall carry out the Constitution which should be based on the principles of liberty, equality, and fraternity. Let each one come and deposit his vote; the barrier of privilege is overturned; before the electoral urn there are no more oppressed, no more masters and slaves."

Woman, in listening to this appeal, rises and approaches the liberating arm to exercise her right of suffrage as a member of society. But the barrier of privilege rises also before her. "You must wait," they say. But by this claim alone woman affirms the right, not yet recognized, of the half of humanity—the right of woman to liberty, equality, and fraternity. She obliges man to verify the fatal attack which he makes on the integrity of his principles.

Soon, in fact during the wonderful days of June, 1848, liberty glides from her pedestal in the flood of the victims of the reaction; based on the "right of the strongest," she falls, overturned in the name of "the right of the strongest."

The Assembly kept silence in regard to the right of one-half of humanity, for which only one of its members raised his voice, but in vain. No mention was made of the right of woman in a Constitution framed in the name of Liberty, Equality, and Fraternity.

It is in the name of these principles that woman comes to claim her right to take part in the Legislative Assembly, and to help to form the laws which must govern society, of which she is a member.

She comes to demand of the electors the consecration of the principle of equality by the election of a woman, and by this act she obliges man to prove that the fundamental law which he has formed in the sole name of liberty, equality, and fraternity, is still based upon privilege, and soon privilege triumphs over this phantom of universal suffrage, which, being but half of itself, sinks on the 31st of May, 1850.

But while those selected by the half of the people—by men alone—evoke force to stifle liberty, and forge restrictive laws to establish order by compression, woman, guided by fraternity, foreseeing incessant struggles, and in the hope of putting an end to them, makes an appeal to the laborer to found liberty and equality on fraternal solidarity. The participation of woman gave to this work of enfranchisement an eminently pacific character, and the laborer recognizes the right of woman, his companion in labor.

The delegates of a hundred and four associations, united, without distinction of sex, elected two women, with several of their brethren, to participate equally with them in the administration of the interests of labor, and in the organization of the work of solidarity.

Fraternal associations were formed with the object of enfranchising the laborer from the yoke of spoliage and patronage, but, isolated in the midst of the Old World, their efforts could only produce a feeble amelioration for themselves.

The union of associations based on fraternal solidarity had for its end the organization of labor; that is to say, an equal division of labor, of instruments, and of the products of labor.

The means were, the union of labor, and of credit among the workers of all professions, in order to acquire the instruments of labor and the necessary materials, and to form a mutual guarantee for the education of their children, and to provide for the needs of the old, the sick, and the infirm.

In this organization all the workers, without distinction of sex or profession, having an equal right to election, and being eligible for all functions, and all having equally the initiative and the sovereign decision in the acts of common interests, they laid the foundation of a new society based on liberty, equality, and fraternity.

It is in the name of law framed by man only—by those elected by privilege—that the Old World, wishing to stifle in the term the holy work of pacific enfranchisement, has shut up within the walls of a prison those who had founded it—those elected by the laborers.

But the impulse has been given, a grand act has been accomplished. The right of woman has been recognized by the laborers, and they have consecrated that right by the election of those who had claimed it is vain for both sexes, before the electoral urn and before the electoral committees. They have received the true civil baptism, were elected by the laborers to accomplish the mission of enfranchisement, and after having shared their rights and their duties, they share to-day their captivity.

It is from the depths of their prison that they address to you the relation of these facts, which contain in themselves high instruction. It is by labor, it is by entering resolutely into the ranks of the working people, that women will conquer the civil and political equality on which depends the happiness of the world. As to moral equality, has she not conquered it by the power of sentiment? It is, therefore, by the sentiment of the love of humanity that the mother of humanity will find power to accomplish her high mission. It is when she shall have well comprehended the holy law of solidarity—which is not an obscure and mysterious dogma, but a living providential fact—that the kingdom of God promised by Jesus, and which is no other than the kingdom of equality and justice, shall be realized on earth.

Sisters of America! your socialist sisters of France are united with you in the vindication of the right of woman to civil and political equality. We have, moreover, the profound conviction that only by the power of association based on solidarity—by the union of the working-classes of both sexes to organize labor—can be acquired, completely and pacifically, the civil and political equality of woman, and the social right for all.

It is in this confidence that, from the depths of the jail which still imprison our bodies without reaching our hearts, we cry to you. Faith, Love, Hope, and send to you our sisterly salutations.

Jeanne Deroine,
Pauline Roland.

Paris, Prison of St. Lagare, *June* 15, 1851.

11. ELIZABETH CADY STANTON'S ADDRESS TO THE LEGISLATURE OF THE STATE OF NEW YORK, FEBRUARY 20, 1854

"The thinking minds of all nations call for change. There is a deep-lying struggle in the whole fabric of society; a boundless, grinding collision of the New with the Old."

The tyrant, Custom, has been summoned before the bar of Common-Sense. His majesty no longer awes the multitude—his sceptre is broken—his crown is trampled in the dust—the sentence of death is pronounced upon him. All nations, ranks, and classes have, in turn, questioned and repudiated his authority; and now, that the monster is chained and caged, timid woman, on tiptoe, comes to look him in the face, and to demand of her brave sires and sons, who have struck stout blows for liberty, if, in this change of dynasty, she, too, shall find relief. Yes, gentlemen, in republican America, in the nineteenth century, we, the

daughters of the revolutionary heroes of '76, demand at your hands the redress of our grievances—a revision of your State Constitution—a new code of laws. Permit us then, as briefly as possible, to call your attention to the legal disabilities under which we labor.

1st. Look at the position of woman as woman. It is not enough for us that by your laws we are permitted to live and breathe, to claim the necessaries of life from our legal protectors—to pay the penalty of our crimes; we demand the full recognition of all our rights as citizens of the Empire State. We are persons; native, free-born citizens; property-holders, tax-payers; yet are we denied the exercise of our right to the elective franchise. We support ourselves, and, in part, your schools, colleges, churches, your poorhouses, jails, prisons, the army, the navy, the whole machinery of government, and yet we have no voice in your councils. We have every qualification required by the Constitution, necessary to the legal voter, but the one of sex. We are moral, virtuous, and intelligent, and in all respects quite equal to the proud white man himself and yet by your laws we are classed with idiots, lunatics, and negroes; and though we do not feel honored by the place assigned us, yet, in fact, our legal position is lower than that of either; for the negro can be raised to the dignity of a voter if he possess himself of $250; the lunatic can vote in his moments of sanity, and the idiot, too, if he be a male one, and not more than nine-tenths a fool; but we, who have guided great movements of charity, established missions, edited journals, published works on history, economy, and statistics; who have governed nations, led armies, filled the professor's chair, taught philosophy and mathematics to the savants of our age, discovered planets, piloted ships across the sea, are denied the most sacred rights of citizens, because, forsooth, we came not into this republic crowned with the dignity of manhood! Woman is theoretically absolved from all allegiance to the laws of the State. Sec. 1, Bill of Rights, 2 R.S., 301, says that no authority can, on any pretence whatever, be exercised over the citizens of this State but such as is or shall be derived from, and granted by the people of this State.

Now, gentlemen, we would fain know by what authority you have disfranchised one-half the people of this State? You who have so boldly taken possession of the bulwarks of this republic, show us your credentials, and thus prove your exclusive right to govern, not only yourselves, but us. Judge Hurlburt, who has long occupied a high place at the bar in this State, and who recently retired with honor from the bench of the Supreme Court, in his profound work on Human Rights, has pronounced your present position rank usurpation. Can it be that here, where we acknowledge no royal blood, no apostolic descent, that you, who have declared that all men were created equal— that governments derive their just powers from the consent of the governed, would willingly build up an aristocracy that places the ignorant and vulgar above the educated and refined—the alien and the ditch-digger above the authors and poets of the day—an aristocracy that would raise the sons above the mothers that bore them? Would that the men who can sanction a Constitution so opposed to the genius of this government, who can enact and execute laws so degrading to womankind, had sprung, Minerva-like, from the brains of their fathers, that the matrons of this republic need not blush to own their sons!

Woman's position, under our free institutions, is much lower than under the monarchy of England. In England the idea of woman holding official station is not so strange as in the United States. The Countess of Pembroke, Dorset, and Montgomery held the office of hereditary sheriff of Westmoreland, and exercised it in person. At the assizes at Appleby, she sat with the judges on the bench. In a reported case, it is stated by counsel, and substantially assented to by the court, that a woman is capable of serving in almost all the offices of the kingdom, such as those of queen, marshal, great chamberlain and constable of England, the champion of England, commissioner of sewers, governor of work-house, sexton, keeper of the prison, of the gate-house of the dean and chapter of Westminster, returning officer for members of Parliament, and constable, the latter of which is in some respects judicial. The office of jailor is frequently exercised by a woman.

"In the United States a woman may administer on the effects of her deceased husband, and she has occasionally held a subordinate place in the postoffice department. She has therefore a sort of post mortem, post-mistress notoriety; but with the exception of handling letters of administration and letters mailed, she is the submissive creature of the old common law." True, the unmarried woman has a right to the property she inherits and the money she earns, but she is taxed without representation. And here again you place the negro, so unjustly degraded by you, in a superior position to your own wives and mothers; for colored males, if possessed of a certain amount of property and certain other qualifications, can vote, but if they do not have these qualifications they are not subject to direct taxation; wherein they have the advantage of woman, she being subject to taxation for whatever amount she may possess. (Constitution of New York, Article 2, Sec. 2). But, say you, are not all women sufficiently represented by their fathers, husbands, and brothers? Let your statute books answer the question.

Again we demand in criminal cases that most sacred of all rights, trial by a jury of our own peers. The establishment of trial by jury is of so early a date that its beginning is lost in antiquity; but the right of trial by a jury of one's own peers is a great progressive step of advanced civilization. No rank of men have ever been satisfied with being tried by jurors higher or lower in the civil or political scale than themselves; for jealousy on the one hand, and contempt on the other, has ever effectually blinded the eyes of justice. Hence, all along the pages of history, we find the king, the noble, the peasant, the cardinal, the priest, the layman, each in turn protesting against the authority of the tribunal before which they were summoned to appear. Charles the First refused to recognize the competency of the tribunal which condemned him: For how, said he, can subjects judge a king? The stern descendants of our Pilgrim Fathers refused to answer for their crimes before an English Parliament. For how, said they, can a king judge rebels? And shall woman here consent to be tried by her liege lord, who has dubbed himself law-maker, judge, juror, and sheriff too?—whose power, though sanctioned by Church and State, has no foundation in justice and equity, and is a bold assumption of our inalienable rights. In England a Parliament-lord could challenge a jury where a knight was not empanneled; an alien could demand a jury composed half of his own countrymen; or, in some special cases, juries were even constituted entirely of women. Having seen that man fails to do justice to woman in her best estate, to the virtuous, the noble, the true of our sex, should we trust to his tender mercies the weak, the ignorant, the morally insane? It is not to be denied that the interests of man and woman in the present undeveloped state of the race, and under the existing social arrangements, are and must be antagonistic. The nobleman can not make just laws for the peasant; the slaveholder for the slave; neither can man make and execute just laws for woman, because in each case, the one in power fails to apply the immutable principles of right to any grade but his own.

Shall an erring woman be dragged before a bar of grim-visaged judges, lawyers, and jurors, there to be grossly questioned in public on subjects which women scarce breathe in secret to one another? Shall the most sacred relations of life be called up and rudely scanned by men who, by their own admission, are so coarse that women could not meet them even at the polls without contamination? and yet shall she find there no woman's face or voice to pity and defend? Shall the frenzied mother, who, to save herself and child from exposure and disgrace, ended the life that had but just begun, be dragged before such a tribunal to answer for her crime? How can man enter into the feelings of that mother? How can he judge of the agonies of soul that impelled her to such an outrage of maternal instincts? How can he weigh the mountain of sorrow that crushed that mother's heart when she wildly tossed her helpless babe into the cold waters of the midnight sea? Where is he who by false vows thus blasted this trusting woman? Had that helpless child no claims on his protection? Ah, he is freely abroad in the dignity of manhood, in the pulpit, on the bench, in the professor's chair. The imprisonment of his victim and the death of his child, detract not a tithe from his standing and complacency. His peers made the law, and shall law-makers lay nets for those of their own rank? Shall laws which come from the logical brain of man take cognizance of violence done to the moral and affectional nature which predominates, as is said, in woman?

Statesmen of New York, whose daughters, guarded by your affection, and lapped amidst luxuries which your indulgence spreads, care more for their nodding plumes and velvet trains than for the statute laws by which their persons and properties are held—who, blinded by custom and prejudice to the degraded position which they and their sisters occupy in the civil scale, haughtily claim that they already have all the rights they want, how, think ye, you would feel to see a daughter summoned for such a crime—and remember these daughters are but human—before such a tribunal? Would it not, in that hour, be some consolation to see that she was surrounded by the wise and virtuous of her own sex; by those who had

known the depth of a mother's love and the misery of a lover's falsehood; to know that to these she could make her confession, and from them receive her sentence? If so, then listen to our just demands and make such a change in your laws as will secure to every woman tried in your courts, an impartial jury. At this moment among the hundreds of women who are shut up in prisons in this State, not one has enjoyed that most sacred of all rights—that right which you would die to defend for yourselves—trial by a jury of one's peers.

2d. Look at the position of woman as wife. Your laws relating to marriage—founded as they are on the old common law of England, a compound of barbarous usages, but partially modified by progressive civilization—are in open violation of our enlightened ideas of justice, and of the holiest feelings of our nature. If you take the highest view of marriage, as a Divine relation, which love alone can constitute and sanctify, then of course human legislation can only recognize it. Men can neither bind nor loose its ties, for that prerogative belongs to God alone, who makes man and woman, and the laws of attraction by which they are united. But if you regard marriage as a civil contract, then let it be subject to the same laws which control all other contracts. Do not make it a kind of half-human, half-divine institution, which you may build up, but can not regulate. Do not, by your special legislation for this one kind of contract, involve yourselves in the grossest absurdities and contradictions.

So long as by your laws no man can make a contract for a horse or piece of land until he is twenty-one years of age, and by which contract he is not bound if any deception has been practiced, or if the party contracting has not fulfilled his part of the agreement—so long as the parties in all mere civil contracts retain their identity and all the power and independence they had before contracting, with the full right to dissolve all partnerships and contracts for any reason, at the will and option of the parties themselves, upon what principle of civil jurisprudence do you permit the boy of fourteen and the girl of twelve, in violation of every natural law, to make a contract more momentous in importance than any other, and then hold them to it, come what may, the whole of their natural lives, in spite of disappointment, deception, and misery? Then, too, the signing of this contract is instant civil death to one of the parties. The woman who but yesterday was sued on bended knee, who stood so high in the scale of being as to make an agreement on equal terms with a proud Saxon man, to-day has no civil existence, no social freedom. The wife who inherits no property holds about the same legal position that does the slave on the Southern plantation. She can own nothing, sell nothing. She has no right even to the wages she earns; her person, her time, her services are the property of another. She can not testify, in many cases, against her husband. She can get no redress for wrongs in her own name in any court of justice. She can neither sue nor be sued. She is not held morally responsible for any crime committed in the presence of her husband, so completely is her very existence supposed by the law to be merged in that of another. Think of it; your wives may be thieves, libelers, burglars, incendiaries, and for crimes like these they are not held amenable to the laws of the land, if they but commit them in your dread presence. For them, alas! there is no higher law than the will of man. Herein behold the bloated conceit of these Petruchios of the law, who seem to say;

> "Nay, look not big, nor stamp, nor stare, nor fret,
> I will be master of what is mine own;
> She is my goods, my chattels; she is my house,
> My household stuff, my field, my barn,
> My horse, my ox, my ass, my anything;
> And here she stands, touch her whoever dare;
> I'll bring my action on the proudest he,
> That stops my way, in Padua."

How could man ever look thus on woman? She, at whose feet Socrates learned wisdom—she, who gave to the world a Saviour, and witnessed alike the adoration of the Magi and the agonies of the cross. How could such a being, so blessed and honored, ever become the ignoble, servile, cringing slave, with whom the fear of man could be paramount to the sacred dictates of conscience and the holy love of Heaven? By the common law of England, the spirit of which has been but too faithfully incorporated into our statute law, a husband has a right to whip his wife with a rod not larger than his thumb, to shut her up in a room, and administer whatever moderate chastisement he may deem necessary to insure obedience to his wishes, and for her healthful moral development! He can forbid all persons harboring or trusting her on his account. He can deprive her of all social intercourse with her nearest

and dearest friends. If by great economy she accumulates a small sum, which for future need she deposit, little by little, in a savings bank, the husband has a right to draw it out, at his option, to use it as he may see fit.

"Husband is entitled to wife's credit or business talents (whenever their intermarriage may have occurred); and goods purchased by her on her own credit, with his consent, while cohabiting with him, can be seized and sold in execution against him for his own debts, and this, though she carry on business in her own name."—7 *Howard's Practice Reports,* 105, *Lovett agt. Robinson and Whilbeck, sheriff, etc.*

"No letters of administration shall be granted to a person convicted of infamous crime; nor to any one incapable of law making a contract; nor to a person not a citizen of the United States, unless such person reside within this State; nor to any one who is under twenty-one years of age; nor to any person who shall be adjudged incompetent by the surrogate to execute duties of such trust, by reason of drunkenness, improvidence, or want of understanding, nor to any married woman; but where a married woman is entitled to administration, the same may be granted to her husband in her right and behalf."

There is nothing that an unruly wife might do against which the husband has not sufficient protection in the law. But not so with the wife. If she have a worthless husband, a confirmed drunkard, a villain, or a vagrant, he has still all the rights of a man, a husband, and a father. Though the whole support of the family be thrown upon the wife, if the wages she earns be paid to her by her employer, the husband can receive them again. If, by unwearied industry and perseverance, she can earn for herself and children a patch of ground and a shed to cover them, the husband can strip her of all her hard earnings, turn her and her little ones out in the cold northern blast, take the clothes from their backs, the bread from their mouths; all this by your laws may he do, and has he done, oft and again, to satisfy the rapacity of that monster in human form, the rum-seller.

But the wife who is so fortunate as to have inherited property, has, by the new law in this State, been redeemed from her lost condition. She is no longer a legal nonentity. This property law, if fairly construed, will overturn the whole code relating to woman and property. The right to property implies the right to buy and sell, to will and bequeath, and herein is the dawning of a civil existence for woman, for now the "femme covert" must have the right to make contracts. So, get ready, gentlemen; the "little justice" will be coming to you one day, deed in hand, for your acknowledgment. When he asks you "if you sign without fear or compulsion," say yes, boldly, as we do. Then, too, the right to will is ours. Now what becomes of the "tenant for life"? Shall he, the happy husband of a millionaire, who has lived in yonder princely mansion in the midst of plenty and elegance, be cut down in a day to the use of one-third of this estate and a few hundred a year, as long he remains her widower? And should he, in spite of this bounty on celibacy, impelled by his affections, marry again, choosing for a wife a woman as poor as himself, shall he be thrown penniless on the cold world—this child of fortune, enervated by ease and luxury, henceforth to be dependent wholly on his own resources? Poor man! He would be rich, though, in the sympathies of many women who have passed through just such an ordeal. But what is property without the right to protect that property by law? It is mockery to say a certain estate is mine, if, without my consent, you have the right to tax me when and how you please, while I have no voice in making the taxgatherer, the legislator, or the law. The right to property will, of necessity, compel us in due time to the exercise of our right to the elective franchise, and then naturally follows the right to hold office.

3d. Look at the position of woman as widow. Whenever we attempt to point out the wrongs of the wife, those who would have us believe that the laws can not be improved, point us to the privileges, powers, and claims of the widow. Let us look into these a little. Behold in yonder humble house a married pair, who, for long years, have lived together, childless and alone. Those few acres of welltilled land, with the small, white house that looks so cheerful through its vines and flowers, attest the honest thrift and simple taste of its owners. This man and woman, by their hard days' labor, have made this home their own. Here they live in peace and plenty, happy in the hope that they may dwell together securely under their own vine and fig-tree for the few years that remain to them, and that under the shadow of these trees, planted by their own hands, and in the midst of their household gods, so loved and familiar, they may make their last farewell of earth. But, alas for human hopes!

the husband dies, and without a will, and the stricken widow, at one fell blow, loses the companion of her youth, her house and home, and half the little sum she had in bank. For the law, which takes no cognizance of widows left with twelve children and not one cent, instantly spies out this widow, takes account of her effects, and announces to her the startling intelligence that but one-third of the house and lot, and one-half the personal property, are hers. The law has other favorites with whom she must share the hard-earned savings of years. In this dark hour of grief, the coarse minions of the law gather round the widow's hearthstone, and, in the name of justice, outrage all natural sense of right; mock at the sacredness of human love, and with cold familiarity proceed to place a moneyed value on the old arm-chair, in which, but a few brief hours since, she closed the eyes that had ever beamed on her with kindness and affection; on the solemn clock in the corner, that told the hour he passed away; on every garment with which his form and presence were associated, and on every article of comfort and convenience that the house contained, even down to the knives and forks and spoons—and the widow saw it all—and when the work was done, she gathered up what the law allowed her and went forth to seek another home! This is the much-talked-of-widow's dower. Behold the magnanimity of the law in allowing the widow to retain a life interest in one-third the landed estate, and one-half the personal property of her husband, and taking the lion's share to itself! Had she died first, the house and land would all have been the husband's still. No one would have dared to intrude upon the privacy of his home, or to molest him in his sacred retreat of sorrow. How, I ask you, can that be called justice, which makes such a distinction as this between man and woman?

By management, economy, and industry, our widow is able, in a few years, to redeem her house and home. But the law never loses sight of the purse, no matter how low in the scale of being its owner may be. It sends its officers round every year to gather in the harvest for the public crib, and no widow who owns a piece of land two feet square ever escapes this reckoning. Our widow, too, who has now twice earned her home, has her annual tax to pay also—a tribute of gratitude that she is permitted to breathe the free air of this republic, where "taxation without representation," by such worthies as John Hancock and Samuel Adams, has been declared "intolerable tyranny." Having glanced at the magnanimity of the law in its dealings with the widow, let us see how the individual man, under the influence of such laws, doles out justice to his helpmate. The husband has the absolute right to will away his property as he may see fit. If he has children, he can divide his property among them, leaving his wife her third only of the landed estate, thus making her a dependent on the bounty of her own children. A man with thirty thousand dollars in personal property, may leave his wife but a few hundred a year, as long as she remains his widow.

The cases are without number where women, who have lived in ease and elegance, at the death of their husbands have, by will, been reduced to the bare necessaries of life. The man who leaves his wife the sole guardian of his property and children is an exception to the general rule. Man has ever manifested a wish that the world should indeed be a blank to the companion whom he leaves behind him. The Hindoo makes that wish a law, and burns the widow on the funeral pyre of her husband; but the civilized man, impressed with a different view of the sacredness of life, takes a less summary mode of drawing his beloved partner after him; he does it by the deprivation and starvation of the flesh, and the humiliation and mortification of the spirit. In bequeathing to the wife just enough to keep soul and body together, man seems to lose sight of the fact that woman, like himself, takes great pleasure in acts of benevolence and charity. It is but just, therefore, that she should have it in her power to give during her life, and to will away at her death, as her benevolence or obligations might prompt her to do.

4th. Look at the position of woman as mother. There is no human love so strong and steadfast as that of the mother for her child; yet behold how ruthless are your laws touching this most sacred relation. Nature has clearly made the mother the guardian of the child; but man, in his inordinate love of power, does continually set nature and nature's laws at open defiance. The father may apprentice his child, bind him out to a trade, without the mother's consent— yes, in direct opposition to her most earnest entreaties, prayers and tears.

He may apprentice his son to a gamester or rum-seller, and thus cancel his debts of *honor.* By the abuse of this absolute power, he may bind his daughter to the owner of a brothel, and, by the degradation of his child, supply his daily wants: and such things, gentlemen, have been done in our very midst. Moreover, the father, about to die, may bind out all his children wherever and to whomsoever he may see fit, and thus, in fact, will away the guardianship of all his children from the mother. The Revised Statutes of New York provide that "every father, whether of full age or a minor, of a child to be born, or of any living child under the age of twenty-one years, and unmarried, may by his deed or last will, duly executed, dispose of the custody and tuition of such child during its minority, or for any less time, to any person or persons, in possession or remainder." 2 R. S., page 150, sec. 1. Thus, by your laws, the child is the absolute property of the father, wholly at his disposal in life or at death.

In case of separation, the law gives the children to the father; no matter what his character or condition. At this very time we can point you to noble, virtuous, well-educated mothers in this State, who have abandoned their husbands for their profligacy and confirmed drunkenness. All these have been robbed of their children, who are in the custody of the husband, under the care of his relatives, while the mothers are permitted to see them but at stated intervals. But, said one of these mothers, with a grandeur of attitude and manner worthy the noble Roman matron in the palmiest days of that republic, I would rather never see my child again, than be the medium to hand down the low animal nature of its father, to stamp degradation on the brow of another innocent being. It is enough that one child of his shall call me mother.

If you are far-sighted statesmen, and do wisely judge of the interests of this commonwealth, you will so shape your future laws as to encourage woman to take the high moral ground that the father of her children must be great and good. Instead of your present laws, which make the mother and her children the victims of vice and license, you might rather pass laws prohibiting to all drunkards, libertines, and fools, the rights of husbands and fathers. Do not the hundreds of laughing idiots that are crowding into our asylums, appeal to the wisdom of our statesmen for some new laws on marriage—to the mothers of this day for a higher, purer morality?

Again, as the condition of the child always follows that of the mother, and as by the sanction of your laws the father may beat the mother, so may he the child. What mother can not bear me witness to untold sufferings which cruel, vindictive fathers have visited upon their helpless children? Who ever saw a human being that would not abuse unlimited power? Base and ignoble must that man be who, let the provocation be what it may, would strike a woman: but he who would lacerate a trembling child is unworthy the name of man. A mother's love can be no protection to a child; she can not appeal to you to save it from a father's cruelty, for the laws take no cognizance of the mother's most grievous wrongs. Neither at home nor abroad can a mother protect her son. Look at the temptations that surround the paths of our youth at every step; look at the gambling and drinking saloons, the club rooms, the dens of infamy and abomination that infest all our villages and cities—slowly but surely sapping the very foundations of all virtue and strength.

By your laws, all these abominable resorts are permitted. It is folly to talk of a mother moulding the character of her son, when all mankind, backed up by law and public sentiment, conspire to destroy her influence. But when woman's moral power shall speak through the ballot-box, then shall her influence be seen and felt; then, in our legislative debates, such questions as the canal tolls on salt, the improvement of rivers and harbors, and the claims of Mr. Smith for damages against the State, would be secondary to the considerations of the legal existence of all these public resorts, which lure our youth on to excessive indulgence and destruction.

Many times and oft it has been asked us, with unaffected seriousness, "What do you women want? What are you aiming at?" Many have manifested a laudable curiosity to know what the wives and daughters could complain of in republican America, where their sires and sons have so bravely fought for freedom and gloriously secured their independence, trampling all tyranny, bigotry, and caste in the dust, and declaring to a waiting world the divine truth that all men are created equal. What can woman want under such a government? Admit a radical difference in sex, and you demand different spheres—water for fish, and air for birds.

It is impossible to make the Southern planter believe that his slave feels and reasons just as he does—that injustice and subjection are as galling as to him—that the degradation of living by the will of another, the mere dependent on his caprice, at the mercy of his passions, is as keenly felt by him as his master. If you can force on his unwilling vision a vivid picture of the negro's wrongs, and for a moment touch his soul, his logic brings him instant consolation. He says, the slave does not feel this as I would. Here, gentlemen, is our difficulty: When we plead our cause before the law-makers and savants of the republic, they can not take in the idea that men and women are alike; and so long as the mass rest in this delusion, the public mind will not be so much startled by the revelations made of the injustice and degradation of woman's position as by the fact that she should at length wake up to a sense of it.

If you, too, are thus deluded, what avails it that we show by your statute books that your laws are unjust—that woman is the victim of avarice and power? What avails it that we point out the wrongs of woman in social life; the victim of passion and lust? You scorn the thought that she has any natural love of freedom burning in her breast, any clear perception of justice urging her on to demand her rights.

Would to God you could know the burning indignation that fills woman's soul when she turns over the pages of your statute books, and sees there how like feudal barons you freemen hold your women. Would that you could know the humiliation she feels for sex, when she thinks of all the beardless boys in your law offices, learning these ideas of one-sided justice—taking their first lessons in contempt for all womankind—being indoctrinated into the incapacities of their mothers, and the lordly, absolute rights of man over all women, children, and property, and to know that these are to be our future presidents, judges, husbands, and fathers; in sorrow we exclaim, alas! for that nation whose sons bow not in loyalty to woman. The mother is the first object of the child's veneration and love, and they who root out this holy sentiment, dream not of the blighting effect it has on the boy and the man. The impression left on law students, fresh from your statute books, is most unfavorable to woman's influence; hence you see but few lawyers chivalrous and high-toned in their sentiments toward woman. They can not escape the legal view which, by constant reading, has become familiarized to their minds: *"Femme covert,"* "dower," "widow's claims," "protection," "incapacities," "incumbrance," is written on the brow of every woman they meet.

But if, gentlemen, you take the ground that the sexes are alike, and, therefore, you are our faithful representatives—then why all these special laws for woman? Would not one code answer for all of like needs and wants? Christ's golden rule is better than all the special legislation that the ingenuity of man can devise: "Do unto others as you would have others do unto you." This, men and brethren, is all we ask at your hands. We ask no better laws than those you have made for yourselves. We need no other protection than that which your present laws secure to you.

In conclusion, then, let us say, in behalf of the women of this State, we ask for all that you have asked for yourselves in the progress of your development, since the *Mayflower* cast anchor beside Plymouth rock; and simply on the ground that the rights of every human being are the same and identical. You may say that the mass of the women of this State do not make the demand; it comes from a few sour, disappointed old maids and childless women.

You are mistaken; the mass speak through us. A very large majority of the women of this State support themselves and their children, and many their husbands too. Go into any village you please, of three or four thousand inhabitants, and you will find as many as fifty men or more, whose only business is to discuss religion and politics, as they watch the trains come and go at the depot, or the passage of a canal boat through a lock; to laugh at the vagaries of some drunken brother, or the capers of a monkey dancing to the music of his master's organ. All these are supported by their mothers, wives, or sisters.

Now, do you candidly think these wives do not wish to control the wages they earn—to own the land they buy—the houses they build? to have at their disposal their own children, without being subject to the constant interference and tyranny of an idle, worthless profligate? Do you suppose that any woman is such a pattern of devotion and submission that she willingly stitches all day for the small sum of fifty cents, that she may enjoy the unspeakable privilege, in obedience to your laws, of paying for her husband's tobacco and rum? Think you the wife of the confirmed, beastly drunkard would consent to share with him her home and bed, if law and public sentiment would release her from such gross companionship? Verily, no! Think you the wife with whom endurance has ceased to be a virtue, who, through much suffering, has lost all faith in the justice of both heaven and earth, takes the law in her own hand, severs the unholy bond, and turns her back forever upon him

whom she once called husband, consents to the law that in such an hour tears her child from her—all that she has left on earth to love and cherish? The drunkards' wives speak through us, and they number 50,000. Think you that the woman who has worked hard all her days in helping her husband to accumulate a large property, consents to the law that places this wholly at his disposal? Would not the mother whose only child is bound out for a term of years against her expressed wish, deprive the father of this absolute power if she could?

For all these, then, we speak. If to this long list you add the laboring women who are loudly demanding remuneration for their unending toil; those women who teach in our seminaries, academies, and public schools for a miserable pittance; the widows who are taxed without mercy; the unfortunate ones in our work-houses, poor-houses, and prisons; who are they that we do not now represent? But a small class of the fashionable butterflies, who, through the short summer days, seek the sunshine and the flowers; but the cool breezes of autumn and the hoary frosts of winter will soon chase all these away; then they, too, will need and seek protection, and through other lips demand in their turn justice and equity at your hands.

12. Appeal and Petition Circulated in the State of New York, 1859

To the Women of the Empire State:

It is the desire and purpose of those interested in the Woman's Rights movement, to send up to our next Legislature an overwhelming petition, for the civil and political rights of woman. These rights must be secured just as soon as the majority of the women of the State make the demand. To this end, we have decided thoroughly to canvass our State before the close of the present year. We shall hold conventions in every county, distribute tracts and circulate petitions, in order, if possible, to arouse a proper self-respect in woman.

The want of funds has heretofore crippled all our efforts, but as large bequests have been made to our cause during the past year, we are now able to send out agents and to commence anew our work, which shall never end, until, in Church and State, and at the fireside, the equality of woman shall be fully recognized.

We hope much from our Republican legislators. Their well-known professions encourage us to believe that our task is by no means a hard one. We shall look for their hearty co-operation in every effort for the elevation of humanity. We have had bills before the Legislature for several years, on some of which, from time to time, have had most favorable reports. The property bill of '48 was passed by a large majority. The various bills of rights, to wages, children, suffrage, etc., have been respectfully considered. The bill presented at the last session, giving to married women their rights to make contracts, and to their wages, passed the House with only three dissenting votes, but owing to the pressure of business at the close of the session, it was never brought before the Senate.

Whilst man, by his legislation and generous donations, declares our cause righteous and just—whilst the very best men of the nation, those who stand first in Church and State, in literature, commerce, and the arts, are speaking for us such noble words and performing such God-like deeds—shall woman, herself, be indifferent to her own wrongs, insensible to all the responsibilities of her high and holy calling? No! No!! Let the women of the Empire State now speak out in deep and earnest tones that can not be misunderstood, demanding all those rights which are at the very foundation of Republicanism—a full and equal representation with man in the administration of our State and National Government.

Do you know, women of New York! that under our present laws married women have no right to the wages they earn? Think of the 40,000 drunkards' wives in this State—of the wives of men who are licentious—of gamblers—of the long line of those who do nothing; and is it no light matter that all these women who support themselves, their husbands and families, too, shall have no right to the disposition of their own earnings? Roll up, then, your petitions★ on this point, if no other, and secure to laboring women their wages at the coming session!

Now is the golden time to work! Before another Constitutional Convention be called, see to it that the public sentiment of this State shall demand suffrage for woman! Remember, "they who would be free, themselves must strike the blow!"

E. CADY STANTON,
Chairman Central Committee.

★Form of Petition.
To the Senate and Assembly of the State of New York:

The undersigned, citizens of——, New York, respectfully ask that you will take measures to submit to the people an amendment of the Constitution, allowing women to vote and hold office. And that you will enact laws securing to married women the full . . . [unfinished].

13. MEMORIAL [SENT TO EVERY STATE LEGISLATURE], MAY 12, 1859

To the Honorable the Legislature of the State of——

The National Woman's Rights Convention, held in New York City, May 12, 1859, appointed your memorialists a Committee to call your attention to the anomalous position of one-half the people of this Republic.

All republican constitutions set forth the great truth that every human being is endowed with certain inalienable rights—such as life, liberty, and the pursuit of happiness—and as a consequence, a right to the use of all those means necessary to secure these grand results.

1st.—A citizen can not be said to have a right to life, who may be deprived of it for the violation of laws to which she has never consented—who is denied the right of trial by a jury of her peers—who has no voice in the election of judges who are to decide her fate.

2d.—A citizen can not be said to have a right to liberty, when the custody of her person belongs to another; when she has no civil or political rights—no right even to the wages she earns; when she can make no contracts—neither buy nor sell, sue or be sued—and yet can be taxed without representation.

3d.—A citizen can not be said to have a right to happiness, when denied the right to person, property, children, and home; when the code of laws under which she is compelled to live is far more unjust and tyrannical than that which our fathers repudiated at the mouth of the cannon nearly one century ago.

Now, we would ask on what principle of republicanism, justice, or common humanity, a minority of the people of this Republic have monopolized to themselves all the rights of the whole? Where, under our Declaration of Independence, does the white Saxon man get his power to deprive all women and negroes of their inalienable rights?

The mothers of the Revolution bravely shared all dangers, persecutions, and death; and their daughters now claim an equal share in all the glories and triumphs of your success. Shall they stand before a body of American legislators and ask in vain for their right of suffrage—their right of property—their right to the wages they earn—their right to their children and their homes—their sacred right to personal liberty—to a trial by a jury of their peers?

In view of these high considerations, we demand, then, that you shall, by your future legislation, secure to women all those rights and privileges and immunities which in equity belong to every citizen of a republic.

And we demand that whenever you shall remodel the Constitution of the State in which you live, the word "male" shall be expurgated, and that henceforth you shall legislate for all citizens. There can be no privileged classes in a truly democratic government.

Elizabeth Cady Stanton, Martha C. Wright,
Wendell Phillips, Caroline M. Severance
Caroline H. Dall, Thomas W. Higginson,
Ernestine L. Rose, Susan B. Anthony,
Antoinette Brown Blackwell, *Committee.*

14. ACT CONCERNING THE RIGHTS AND LIABILITIES OF HUSBAND AND WIFE, MARCH 20, 1860

The People of the State of New York, represented in Senate and Assembly, do enact as follows:

Section 1. The property, both real and personal, which any married woman now owns, as her sole and separate property; that which comes to her by descent, devise, bequest, gift, or grant; that which she acquires by her trade, business, labor, or services, carried on or performed on her sole or separate account; that which a woman married in this State owns at the time of her marriage, and the rents, issues, and proceeds of all such property, shall notwithstanding her marriage, be and remain her sole and separate property, and may be used, collected, and invested by her in her own name, and shall not be subject to the interference or control of her husband, or liable for his debts, except such debts as may have been contracted for the support of herself or her children, by her as his agent.

§ 2. A married woman may bargain, sell, assign, and transfer her separate personal property, and carry on any trade or business, and perform any labor or services on her sole and separate account, and the earnings of any married woman from her trade, business, labor, or services shall be her sole and separate property, and may be used or invested by her in her own name.

§ 3. Any married woman possessed of real estate as her separate property may bargain, sell, and convey such property, and enter into any contract in reference to the same; but no such conveyance or contract shall be valid without the assent, in writing, of her husband, except as hereinafter provided.

§ 4. In case any married woman possessed of separate real property, as aforesaid, may desire to sell or convey the same, or to make any contract in relation thereto, and shall be unable to procure the assent of her husband as in the preceding section provided, in consequence of his refusal, absence, insanity, or other disability, such married woman may apply to the County Court in the county where she shall at the time reside, for leave to make such sale, conveyance, or contract, without the assent of her husband.

§ 5. Such application may be made by petition, verified by her, and setting forth the grounds of such application. If the husband be a resident of the county and not under disability from insanity or other cause, a copy of said petition shall be served upon him, with a notice of the time when the same will be presented to the said court, at least ten days before such application. In all other cases, the County Court to which such application shall be made, shall, in its discretion, determine whether any notice shall be given, and if any, the mode and manner of giving it.

§ 6. If it shall satisfactorily appear to such court upon application, that the husband of such applicant has willfully abandoned his said wife, and lives separate and apart from her, or that he is insane, or imprisoned as a convict in any state prison, or that he is an habitual drunkard, or that he is in any way disabled from making a contract, or that he refuses to give his consent without good cause therefor, then such court shall cause an order to be entered upon its records, authorizing such married woman to sell and convey her real estate, or contract in regard thereto without the assent of her husband, with the same effect as though such conveyance or contract had been made with his assent.

§ 7. Any married woman may, while married, sue and be sued in all matters having relation to her property, which may be her sole and separate property, or which may hereafter come to her by descent, devise, bequest, or the gift of any person except her husband, in the same manner as if she were sole. And any married woman may bring and maintain an action in her own name, for damages against any person or body corporate, for any injury to her person or character, the same as if she were sole; and the money received upon the settlement of any such action, or recovered upon a judgment, shall be her sole and separate property.

§ 8. No bargain or contract made by any married woman, in respect to her sole and separate property, or any property which may hereafter come to her by descent, devise, bequest, or gift of any person except her husband, and no bargain or contract entered into by any married woman in or about the carrying on of any trade or business under the statutes of this State, shall be binding upon her husband, or render him or his property in any way liable therefor.

§ 9. Every married woman is hereby constituted and declared to be the joint guardian of her children, with her husband, with equal powers, rights, and duties in regard to them, with the husband.

§ 10. At the decease of husband or wife, leaving no minor child or children, the survivor shall hold, possess, and enjoy a life estate in one-third of all the real estate of which the husband or wife died seized.

§ 11. At the decease of the husband or wife intestate, leaving minor child or children, the survivor shall hold, possess, and enjoy all the real estate of which the husband or wife died seized, and all the rents, issues, and profits thereof during the minority of the youngest child, and one-third thereof during his or her natural life.

On the final passage of the bill the following Senators, as *The Journal* shows, voted in favor of the measure, viz: Senators Abell, Bell, Colwin, Conally, Fiero, Goss, Hillhouse, Kelly, Lapham, Sessions, Manierre, Montgomery, Munroe, P. P. Murphy, Truman, Proser, Ramsey, Robertson, Rotch, Warner, William—21.

15. Appeal to the Women of New York, November 1860

Women of New York:—Once more we appeal to you to make renewed efforts for the elevation of our sex. In our marital laws we are now in advance of every State in the Union. Twelve years ago New York took the initiative step, and secured to married women their property, received by gift or inheritance. Our last Legislature passed a most liberal act, giving to married women their rights, to sue for damages of person or property, to their separate earnings and their children; and to the widow, the possession and control of the entire estate during the minority of the youngest child. Women of New York! You can no longer be insulted in the first days of your widowed grief by the coarse minions of the law at your fireside, coolly taking an inventory of your household gods, or robbing your children of their natural guardian.

While we rejoice in this progress made in our laws, we see also a change in the employment of women. They are coming down from the garrets and up from the cellars to occupy more profitable posts in every department of industry, literature, science, and art. In the church, too, behold the spirit of freedom at work. Within the past year, the very altar has been the scene of well-fought battles; women claiming and exercising their right to vote in church matters, in defiance of precedent, priest, or Paul.

Another evidence of the importance of our cause is seen in the deep interest men of wealth are manifesting in it. Three great bequests have been given to us in the past year. Five thousand dollars from an unknown hand, a share in the munificent fund left by that noble man of Boston, Charles F. Hovey, and four hundred thousand dollars by Mr. Vassar, of Poughkeepsie, to found a college for girls, equal in all respects to Yale and Harvard. Is it not strange that women of wealth are constantly giving large sums of money to endow professorships and colleges for boys exclusively—to churches and to the education of the ministry, and yet give no thought to their own sex—crushed in ignorance, poverty, and prostitution—the hopeless victims of custom, law, and Gospel, with few to offer a helping hand, while the whole world combine to aid the boy and glorify the man?

Our movement is already felt in the Old World. The nobility of England, with Lord Brougham at their head, have recently formed a "Society for Promoting the Employments of Women."

All this is the result of the agitation, technically called "Woman's Rights," through conventions, lectures, circulation of tracts and petitions, and by the faithful word uttered in the privacy of home. The few who stand forth to meet the world's cold gaze, its ridicule, its contumely, and its scorn, are urged onward by the prayers and tears, crushed hopes and withered hearts of the sad daughters of the race. The wretched will not let them falter; and they who seem to do the work, ever and anon draw fresh courage and inspiration from the noblest women of the age, who, from behind the scene, send forth good words of cheer and heartfelt thanks.

Six years hence, the men of New York purpose to revise our State Constitution. Among other changes demanded, is the right of suffrage for women—which right will surely be granted, if through all the intervening years every woman does her duty. Again do we appeal to each and all—to every class and condition— to inform themselves on this question, that woman may no longer publish her degradation by declaring herself satisfied in her present position, nor her ignorance by asserting that she has "all the rights she wants."

Any person who ponders the startling fact that there are four millions of African slaves in this republic, will instantly put the question to himself, "Why do these people submit to the cruel tyranny that our government exercises over them?" The answer is apparent—"simply because they are ignorant of their power." Should they rise *en masse*, assert and demand their rights, their freedom would be secure. It is the same with woman. Why is it that one-half the people of this nation are held in abject dependence—civilly, politically, socially, the slaves of man? Simply because woman knows not her power. To find out her natural rights, she must travel through such labyrinths of falsehood, that most minds stand appalled before the dark mysteries of life—the seeming contradictions in all laws, both human and divine. But, because woman can not solve the whole problem to her satisfaction, because she can not prove to a demonstration the rottenness and falsehood of our present customs, shall she, without protest, supinely endure evils she can not at once redress? The silkworm, in its many wrappings, knows not it yet shall fly. The woman, in her ignorance, her drapery, and her chains, knows not that in advancing civilization, she too must soon be free, to counsel with her conscience and her God.

The religion of our day teaches that in the most sacred relations of the race, the woman must ever be subject to the man; that in the husband centers all power and learning; that the difference in position between husband and wife is as vast as that between Christ and the church; and woman struggles to hold the noble impulses of her nature in abeyance to opinions uttered by a Jewish teacher, which, alas! the mass believe to be the will of God. Woman turns from what she is taught to believe are God's laws to the laws of man; and in his written codes she finds herself still a slave. No girl of fifteen could read the laws concerning woman, made, executed, and defended by those who are bound to her by every tie of affection, without a burst of righteous indignation. Few have ever read or heard of the barbarous laws that govern the mothers of this Christian republic, and fewer still care, until misfortune brings them into the iron grip of the law. It is the imperative duty of educated women to study the Constitution and statutes under which they live, that when they shall have a voice in the government, they may bring wisdom and not folly into its councils.

We now demand the ballot, trial by jury of our peers, and an equal right to the joint earnings of the marriage copartnership. And, until the Constitution be so changed as to give us a voice in the government, we demand that man shall make all his laws on property, marriage, and divorce, to bear equally on man and woman.

New York State Woman's Rights Committee.
November, 1860.
E. CADY STANTON, *President.*
LYDIA MOTT. *Sec. and Treas.*
ERNESTINE L. ROSE.
MARTHA C. WRIGHT.
SUSAN B. ANTHONY.

16. REPORT NO. 386 OF THE HOUSE OF REPRESENTATIVES, COMMITTEE ON MILITARY AFFAIRS (46TH CONGRESS, 3D SESSION), REGARDING ANNA ELLA CARROLL AND EVENTS OF 1861, MARCH 3, 1881

Committed to the Committee of the Whole House, and ordered to be printed.

Mr. Bragg, from the Committee on Military Affairs, submitted the following Report (to accompany bill H. R. 7,256):

The Committee on Military Affairs, to whom the memorial of Anna Ella Carroll was referred, asking national recognition and reward for services rendered the United States during the war between the States, after careful consideration of the same, submit the following:

In the autumn of 1861 the great question as to whether the Union could be saved, or whether it was hopelessly subverted, depended on the ability of the Government to open the Mississippi and deliver a fatal blow upon the resources of the Confederate power. The original plan was to reduce the formidable fortifications by descending this river, aided by the gun-boat fleet, then in preparation for that object.

President Lincoln had reserved to himself the special direction of this expedition, but before it was prepared to move he became convinced that the obstacles to be encountered were too grave and serious for the success which the exigencies of the crisis demanded, and the plan was then abandoned, and the armies diverted up the Tennessee River, and thence southward to the center of the Confederate power.

The evidence before this Committee completely establishes that Miss Anna Ella Carroll was the author of this change of plan, which involved a transfer of the National forces to their new base in North Mississippi and Alabama, in command of the Memphis and Charleston Railroad; that she devoted time and money in the autumn of 1861 to the investigation of its feasibility is established by the sworn testimony of L. D. Evans, Chief Justice of the Supreme Court of Texas, to the Military Committee of the United States Senate in the 42d Congress (see pp. 40, 41 of memorial); that after that investigation she submitted her plan in writing to the War Department at Washington, placing it in the hands of Thomas A. Scott, Assistant Secretary of War, as is confirmed by his statement (see p. 38 of memorial), also confirmed by the statement of Hon. B. F. Wade, Chairman of the Committee on the Conduct of the War, made to the same Committee (see p. 38), and of President Lincoln and Secretary Stanton (see p. 39 of memorial); also by Hon. O. H. Browning, of Illinois, Senator during the war, in confidential relations with President Lincoln and Secretary Stanton (see p. 39, memorial); also that of Hon. Elisha Whittlesey, Comptroller of the Treasury (see p. 41, memorial), also by Hon. Thomas H. Hicks, Governor of Maryland, and by Hon. Frederick Feckey's affidavit, Comptroller of the Public Works of Maryland (see p. 127 of memorial); by Hon. Reverdy Johnson (see pp. 26 and 41, memorial); Hon. George Vickers, United States Senator from Maryland (see p. 41, memorial); again by Hon. B. F. Wade (see p. 41, memorial); Hon. J. T. Headley (see p. 43, memorial); Rev. Dr. K. J. Breckinridge on services (see p. 47, memorial); Prof. Joseph Henry, Rev. Dr.

Hodge, of Theological Seminary at Princeton (see p. 30, memorial); remarkable interviews and correspondence of Judge B. F. Wade (see pp. 23–26 of memorial).

That this campaign prevented the recognition of Southern independence by its fatal effects on the Confederate States is shown by letters from Hon. C. M. Clay (see pp. 40–43 of memorial), and by his letters from St. Petersburgh; also those of Mr. Adams and Mr. Dayton from London and Paris (see pp. 100–102 of memorial).

That the campaign defeated National bankruptcy, then imminent, and opened the way for the system of finance to defend the Federal cause, is shown by the debates of the period in both Houses of Congress (see utterances of Mr. Spalding, Mr. Diven, Mr. Thaddeus Stevens, Mr. Roscoe Conkling, Mr. John Sherman, Mr. Henry Wilson, Mr. Fessenden, Mr. Trumbull, Mr. Foster, Mr. Garrett Davis, Mr. John J. Crittendon, etc., found for convenient reference in appendix to memorial, pp. 47–59. Also therein the opinion of the English press as to why the Union could not be restored).

The condition of the struggle can best be realized as depicted by the leading statesmen in Congress previous to the execution of these military movements (see synopsis of debates from *Congressional Globe,* pp. 21, 22 of memorial).

The effect of this campaign upon the country and the anxiety to find out and reward the author are evidenced by the resolution of Mr. Roscoe Conkling, in the House of Representatives 24th of February, 1862 (see debates on the origin of the campaign, pp. 39–63 of memorial). But it was deemed prudent to make no public claim as to authorship while the war lasted (see Colonel Scott's view, p. 32 of memorial).

The wisdom of the plan was proven, not only by the absolute advantages which resulted, giving the mastery of the conflict to the National arms and evermore assuring their success even against the powers of all Europe should they have combined, but it was likewise proven by the failures to open the Mississippi or win any decided success on the plan first devised by the Government.

It is further conclusively shown that no plan, order, letter, telegram, or suggestion of the Tennessee River as the line of invasion has ever been produced, except in the paper submitted by Miss Carroll on the 30th of November, 1861, and her subsequent letters to the Government as the campaign progressed.

It is further shown to this Committee that the able and patriotic publications of memorialist, in pamphlets and newspapers, with her high social influence, not only largely contributed to the cause of the Union in her own State, Maryland (see Governor Hicks' letters, p. 27, memorial), but exerted a wide and salutary influence on all the Border States (see Howard's report, p. 33 and p. 75 of memorial).

These publications were used by the Government as war measures, and the debate in Congress shows that she was the first writer on the war powers of the Government (see p. 45 of memorial). Leading statesmen and jurists bore testimony to their value, including President Lincoln, Secretaries Chase, Stanton, Seward, Welles, Smith, Attorney-General Bates, Senators Browning, Doolittle, Collamer, Cowan, Reverdy Johnson, and Hicks, Hon. Horace Binney, Hon. Benjamin H. Brewster, Hon. William M. Meredith, Hon. Robert J. Walker, Hon. Charles O'Conor, Hon. Edwards Pierrepont, Hon. Edward Everett, Hon. Thomas Corwin, Hon. Francis Thomas, of Maryland, and many others found in memorial.

The Military Committee, through Senator Howard, in the Forty-first Congress, third session, document No. 337, unanimously reported that Miss Carroll did cause the change of the military expedition from the Mississippi to the Tennessee River, etc.; and the aforesaid Committee, in the Forty-second Congress, second session, document No. 167, as found in memorial, reported, through the Hon. Henry Wilson, the evidence and bill in support of this claim.

Again, in the Forty-fourth Congress, the Military Committee of the House favorably considered this claim, and General A. S. Williams was prepared to report, and being prevented by want of time, placed on record that this claim is incontestably established, and that the country owes to Miss Carroll a large and honest compensation, both in money and honors, for her services in the National crisis.

In view of all the facts, this Committee believe that the thanks of the nation are due Miss Carroll, and that they are fully justified in recommending that she be placed on the pension rolls of the Government, as a partial measure of recognition for her public service, and report herewith a bill for such purpose and recommend its passage.

17. The Emancipation Address of the Women's National Loyal League, Adopted May 15, 1863

The Loyal Women of the Country to Abraham Lincoln, President of the United States.

Having heard many complaints of the want of enthusiasm among Northern women in the war, we deemed it fitting to call a National Convention. From every free State, we have received the most hearty responses of interest in each onward step of the Government as it approaches the idea of a true republic. From the letters received, and the numbers assembled here to-day, we can with confidence address you in the name of the loyal women of the North.

We come not to criticise or complain. Not for ourselves or our friends do we ask redress of specific grievances, or posts of honor or emolument. We speak from no considerations of mere material gain; but, inspired by true patriotism, in this dark hour of our nation's destiny, we come to pledge the loyal women of the Republic to freedom and our country. We come to strengthen you with earnest words of sympathy and encouragement. We come to thank you for your proclamation, in which the nineteenth century seems to echo back the Declaration of Seventy-six. Our fathers had a vision of the sublime idea of liberty, equality, and fraternity; but they failed to climb the heights that with anointed eyes they saw. To us, their children, belongs the work to build up the living reality of what they conceived and uttered.

It is not our mission to criticise the past. Nations, like individuals, must blunder and repent. It is not wise to waste one energy in vain regret, but from each failure rise up with renewed conscience and courage for nobler action. The follies and faults of yesterday we cast aside as the old garments we have outgrown. Born anew to freedom, slave creeds and codes and constitutions must now all pass away. "For men do not put new wine into old bottles, else the bottles break, and the wine runneth out, and the bottles perish; but they put new wine into new bottles, and both are preserved."

Our special thanks are due to you, that by your Proclamation two millions of women are freed from the foulest bondage humanity ever suffered. Slavery for man is bad enough, but the refinements of cruelty must ever fall on the mothers of the oppressed race, defrauded of all the rights of the family relation, and violated in the most holy instincts of their nature. A mother's life is bound up in that of her child. There center all her hopes and ambition. But the slavemother, in her degradation, rejoices not in the future promise of her daughter, for she knows by experience what her sad fate must be. No pen can describe the unutterable agony of that mother whose past, present, and future are all wrapped in darkness; who knows the crown of thorns she wears must press her daughter's brow: who knows that the wine-press she now treads, unwatched, those tender feet must tread alone. For, by the law of slavery, "the child follows the condition of the mother."

By your act, the family, that great conservator of national virtue and strength, has been restored to millions of humble homes, around whose altars coming generations shall magnify and bless the name of Abraham Lincoln. By a mere stroke of the pen you have emancipated millions from a condition of wholesale concubinage. We now ask you to finish the work by declaring that nowhere under our national flag shall the motherhood of any race plead in vain for justice and protection. So long as one slave breathes in this Republic, we drag the chain with him. God has so linked the race, man to man, that all must rise or fall together. Our history exemplifies this law. It was not enough that we at the North abolished slavery for ourselves, declared freedom of speech and the press, built up churches, colleges, and free schools, studied the science of morals, government, and economy, dignified labor, amassed wealth, whitened the sea with our commerce, and commanded the respect and admiration of the nations of the earth, so long as the South, by the natural proclivities of slavery, was sapping the very foundations of our national life . . .

You are the first President ever borne on the shoulders of freedom into the position you now fill. Your predecessors owed their elevation to the slave oligarchy, and in serving slavery they did but obey their masters. In your election, Northern freemen threw off the yoke. And with you rests the responsibility that our necks shall never bow again. At no time in the annals of the nation has there been a more auspicious moment to retrieve the one false step of the fathers in the concessions to slavery. The Constitution has been repudiated, and the compact broken by the Southern traitors now in arms. The firing of the first gun on Sumter released the North from all constitutional obligations to slavery. It left the Government, for the first time in our history, free to carry out the

Declaration of our Revolutionary fathers, and made us in fact what we have ever claimed to be, a nation of freemen.

"The Union as it was"—a compromise between barbarism and civilization—can never be restored, for the opposing principles of freedom and slavery can not exist together. Liberty is life, and every form of government yet tried proves that slavery is death. In obedience to this law, our Republic, divided and distracted by the collisions of caste and class, is tottering to its base, and can only be reconstructed on the sure foundations of impartial freedom to all men. The war in which we are involved is not the result of party or accident, but a forward step in the progress of the race never to be retraced. Revolution is no time for temporizing or diplomacy. In a radical upheaving, the people demand eternal principles to stand upon.

Northern power and loyalty can never be measured until the purpose of the war be liberty to man; for a lasting enthusiasm is ever based on a grand idea, and unity of action demands a definite end. At this time our greatest need is not in men or money, valiant generals or brilliant victories, but in a consistent policy, based on the principle that "all governments derive their just powers from the consent of the governed." And the nation waits for you to say that there is no power under our declaration of rights, nor under any laws, human or divine, by which *free* men can be made slaves; and therefore that your pledge to the slaves is irrevocable, and shall be redeemed.

It if be true, as it is said, that Northern women lack enthusiasm in this war, the fault rests with those who have confused and confounded its policy. The page of history glows with incidents of self-sacrifice by woman in the hour of her country's danger. Fear not that the daughters of this Republic will count any sacrifice too great to insure the triumph of freedom. Let the men who wield the nation's power be wise, brave, and magnanimous, and its women will be prompt to meet the duties of the hour with devotion and heroism.

When Fremont on the Western breeze proclaimed a day of jubilee to the bondmen within our gates, the women of the nation echoed back a loud Amen. When Hunter freed a million men, and gave them arms to fight our battles, justice and mercy crowned that act, and tyrants stood appalled. When Butler, in the chief city of the Southern despotism, hung a traitor, we felt a glow of pride; for that one act proved that we had a Government, and one man brave enough to administer its laws. And when Burnside would banish Vallandigham to the Dry Tortugas, let the sentence be approved, and the nation will ring with plaudits. Your Proclamation gives you immortality. Be just, and share your glory with men like these who wait to execute your will.

In behalf of the National Woman's Loyal League,
ELIZABETH CADY STANTON, *President.*
SUSAN B. ANTHONY, *Secretary.*

18. SPEECH OF HON. CHARLES SUMNER ON THE PRESENTATION OF THE FIRST INSTALLMENT OF THE EMANCIPATION PETITION OF THE NATIONAL WOMAN'S LOYAL LEAGUE, FEBRUARY 9, 1864

In the Senate of the United States . . .

Mr. Sumner.—Mr. President: I offer a petition which is now lying on the desk before me. It is too bulky for me to take up. I need not add that it is too bulky for any of the pages of this body to carry.

This petition marks a stage of public opinion in the history of slavery, and also in the suppression of the rebellion. As it is short I will read it:

> "To the Senate and House of Representatives of the United States:
>
> "The undersigned, women of the United States above the age of eighteen years, earnestly pray that your honorable body will pass at the earliest practicable day an act emancipating all persons of African descent held to involuntary service or labor in the United States."

There is also a duplicate of this petition signed by "men above the age of eighteen years."

It will be perceived that the petition is in rolls. Each roll represents a State.★ For instance, here is New York with a list of seventeen thousand seven hundred and six names; Illinois with fifteen thousand three hundred and eighty; and Massachusetts with eleven thousand six hundred and forty-one. These several petitions are consolidated into one petition, being another illustration of the motto on our coin— *E pluribus unum.*

This petition is signed by one hundred thousand men and women, who unite in this unparalleled number to support its prayer. They are from all parts of the country and from every condition of life. They are from the sea-board, fanned by the free airs of the ocean, and from the Mississippi and the prairies of the West, fanned by the free airs which fertilize that extensive region. They are from the families of the educated and uneducated, rich and poor, of every profession, business, and calling in life, representing every sentiment, thought, hope, passion, activity, intelligence which inspires, strengthens, and adorns our social system. Here they are, a mighty army, one hundred thousand strong, without arms or banners; the advance-guard of a yet larger army.

But though memorable for their numbers, these petitioners are more memorable still for the prayer in which they unite. They ask nothing less than universal emancipation; and this they ask directly at the hands of Congress. No reason is assigned. The prayer speaks for itself. It is simple, positive. So far as it proceeds from the women of the country, it is naturally a petition, and not an argument. But I need not remind the Senate that there is no reason so strong as the reason of the heart. Do not all great thoughts come from the heart?

It is not for me, on presenting this petition, to assign reasons which the army of petitioners has forborne to assign. But I may not improperly add that, naturally and obviously, they all feel in their hearts, what reason and knowledge confirm: not only that slavery *as a unit,* one and indivisible, is the guilty origin of the rebellion, but that its influence everywhere, even outside the rebel States, has been hostile to the Union, always impairing loyalty, and sometimes openly menacing the national government. It requires no difficult logic to conclude that such a monster, wherever it shows its head, is a *national enemy,* to be pursued and destroyed as such, or at least a nuisance to the national cause to be abated as such. The petitioners know well that Congress is the depository of those supreme powers by which the rebellion, alike in its root and in its distant offshoots, may be surely crushed, and by which unity and peace may be permanently secured. They know well that the action of Congress may be with the co-operation of the slave-masters, or even without the co-operation, under the overruling law of military necessity, or the commanding precept of the Constitution "to guarantee to every State a Republican form of government." Above all, they know well that to save the country from peril, especially to save the national life, there is no power, in the ample arsenal of self-defense, which Congress may not grasp; for to Congress, under the Constitution, belongs the prerogative of the Roman Dictator to see that the Republic receives no detriment. Therefore to Congress these petitioners now appeal. I ask the reference of the petition to the Select Committee on Slavery and Freedmen.

★State	Men	Women	Total
New York	6,519	11,187	17,706
Illinois	6,382	8,998	15,380
Massachusetts	4,248	7,392	11,641
Pennsylvania	2,259	6,366	8,625
Ohio	3,676	4,654	8,330
Michigan	1,741	4,441	6,182
Iowa	2,025	4,014	6,039
Maine	1,225	4,362	5,587
Wisconsin	1,639	2,391	4,030
Indiana	*1,075*	*2,591*	*3,666*
New Hampshire	*393*	*2,261*	*2,654*
New Jersey	824	1,709	2,533
Rhode Island	*827*	*1,451*	*2,278*
Vermont	375	1,183	1,558
Connecticut	393	1,162	1,555
Minnesota	396	1,094	1,490
West Virginia	82	100	182
Maryland	115	50	165
Kansas	84	74	158
Delaware	67	70	137
Nebraska	13	20	33
Kentucky	21		21
Louisiana (New Orleans)	14	14	
Citizens of the U.S. living in New Brunswick	19	17	36
	34,399	65,601	100,000

19. Petition to Congress Requesting Women's Suffrage, December 1865

Form of Petition.—*To the Senate and House of Representatives:*—The undersigned women of the United States, respectfully ask an amendment of the Constitution that shall prohibit the several States from disfranchising any of their citizens on the ground of sex.

In making our demand for Suffrage, we would call your attention to the fact that we represent fifteen million people—one-half the entire population of the country—intelligent, virtuous, native-born American citizens; and yet stand outside the pale of political recognition. The Constitution classes us as "free people," and counts us *whole* persons in the basis of representation; and yet are we governed without our consent, compelled to pay taxes without appeal, and punished for violations of law without choice of judge or juror. The experience of all ages, the Declarations of the Fathers, the Statute Laws of our own day, and the fearful revolution through which we have just passed, all prove the uncertain tenure of life, liberty, and property so long as the ballot—the only weapon of self-protection—is not in the hand of every citizen.

Therefore, as you are now amending the Constitution, and, in harmony with advancing civilization, placing new safeguards round the individual rights of four millions of emancipated slaves, we ask that you extend the right of Suffrage to Woman—the only remaining class of disfranchised citizens—and thus fulfill your constitutional obligation "to guarantee to every State in the Union a Republican form of Government." As all partial application of Republican principles must ever breed a complicated legislation as well as a discontented people, we would pray your Honorable Body, in order to simplify the machinery of Government and ensure domestic tranquillity, that you legislate hereafter for persons, citizens, tax-payers, and not for class or caste. For justice and equality your petitioners will ever pray.

20. Public Letter of Elizabeth Cady Stanton to the Electors of the Eighth Congressional District, October 10, 1866

Although, by the Constitution of the State of New York woman is denied the elective franchise, yet she is eligible to office; therefore, I present myself to you as a candidate for Representative to Congress. Belonging to a disfranchised class, I have no political antecedents to recommend me to your support,—but my creed is *free speech, free press, free men, and free trade,*—the cardinal points of democracy. Viewing all questions from the stand-point of principle rather than expediency, there is a fixed uniform law, as yet unrecognized by either of the leading parties, governing alike the social and political life of men and nations. The Republican party has occasionally a clear vision of personal rights, though in its protective policy it seems wholly blind to the rights of property and interests of commerce; while it recognizes the duty of benevolence between man and man, it teaches the narrowest selfishness in trade between nations. The Democrats, on the contrary, while holding sound and liberal principles on trade and commerce, have ever in their political affiliations maintained the idea of class and caste among men—an idea wholly at variance with the genius of our free institutions and fatal to high civilization. One party fails at one point and one at another.

In asking your suffrages—believing alike in free men and free trade—I could not represent either party as now constituted. Nevertheless, as an Independent Candidate, I desire an election at this time, as a rebuke to the dominant party for its retrogressive legislation in so amending the National Constitution as to make invidious distinctions on the ground of sex. That instrument recognizes as persons all citizens who obey the laws and support the State, and if the Constitutions of the several States were brought into harmony with the broad principles of the Federal Constitution, the women of the Nation would no longer be taxed without representation, or governed without their consent. Not one word should be added to that great charter of rights to the insult or injury of the humblest of our citizens. I would gladly have a voice and vote in the Fortieth Congress to demand *universal* suffrage, that thus a republican form of government might be secured to every State in the Union.

If the party now in the ascendency makes its demand for "Negro Suffrage" in good faith, on the ground of natural right, and because the highest good of the State demands that the republican idea be vindicated, on no principle of justice or safety can the women of the nation be ignored. In view of the fact that the Freedmen of the South and the millions of foreigners now crowding our shores, most of whom represent neither property, education, nor civilization, are all in the progress of events to be enfranchised, the best interests of the nation demand that we outweigh this incoming pauperism, ignorance, and degradation, with the wealth, education, and refinement of the women of the republic. On the high ground of safety to the Nation, and justice to citizens, I ask your support in the coming election.

New York, *Oct.* 10, 1866.

Elizabeth Cady Stanton.

21. THE FOURTEENTH AMENDMENT TO THE CONSTITUTION, SECTIONS 1, 2, 3, 5, JULY 28, 1868

Section 1. "All persons born or naturalized in the United States and subject to the jurisdiction thereof, are citizens of the United States and of the State wherein they reside. No State shall make or enforce any law which shall abridge the privileges or immunities of citizens of the United States; nor shall any State deprive any person of life, liberty, or property, without due process of law, nor deny to any person within its jurisdiction the equal protection of the laws."

Section 2. "Representatives shall be apportioned among the several States according to their respective numbers, counting the whole number of persons in each State, excluding Indians not taxed. But when the right to vote at any election for the choice of electors for President and Vice-President of the United States, Representatives in Congress, the Executive and Judicial officers of a State, or the members of the Legislature thereof, is denied to any of the male inhabitants of such State, being twenty-one years of age, and citizens of the United States, or in any way abridged, except for participation in rebellion or other crime, the basis of representation therein shall be reduced in the proportion which the number of such male citizens shall bear to the whole number of male citizens twenty-one years of age in such State."

Section 3. "No person shall be a Senator or Representative in Congress, or elector of President and Vice-President, or hold any office, civil or military, under the United States, or under any State, who, having previously taken an oath as a member of Congress, or as an officer of the United States, or as a member of any State Legislature, or as an Executive or Judicial officer of any State, to support the Constitution of the United States, shall have engaged in insurrection or rebellion against the same, or give aid or comfort to the enemies thereof. But Congress may, by a vote of two-thirds of each House, remove such disability."

. . . .

Section 5. "The Congress shall have power to enforce, by appropriate legislation, the provisions of this article."

22. PETITION TO CONGRESS REQUESTING THE INCLUSION OF WOMEN IN THE FIFTEENTH AMENDMENT, DECEMBER 1868

To the Senate and House of Representatives in Congress assembled:

The undersigned, citizens of the State of New York, earnestly but respectfully request, that in any change or amendment of the Constitution you may propose to extend or regulate suffrage, there shall be no distinctions made between men and women.

23. CONSTITUTION OF THE NATIONAL WOMAN SUFFRAGE ASSOCIATION, MAY 20, 1869

Constitution—Article 1. This organization shall be called the National Woman Suffrage Association.

Article 2. Its object shall be to secure the Ballot to the women of the nation on equal terms with men.

Article 3. Any citizen of the United States favoring this object, shall, by the payment of the sum of one dollar annually into the treasury, be considered a member of the Association, and no other shall be entitled to vote in its deliberations.

Article 4. The officers of the Association shall be a President, a Vice-President from each of the States and Territories, Corresponding and Recording Secretaries, Treasurer, an Executive Committee of not less than five nor more than nine members, located in New York City, and an Advisory Counsel of one person from each State and Territory, who shall be members of the National Executive Committee. The officers shall be chosen at each annual meeting of the Association.

Article 5. Any Woman's Suffrage Association may become auxiliary to the National Association by its officers becoming members of the Parent Association and sending an annual contribution of not less than twenty-five dollars.

24. CONSTITUTION OF THE AMERICAN WOMAN SUFFRAGE ASSOCIATION, NOVEMBER 24–25, 1869

Preamble: The undersigned, friends of woman suffrage, assembled in delegate Convention in Cleveland, Ohio, November 24th and 25th, 1869, in response to a call widely signed and after a public notice duly given, believing that a truly representative National organization is needed for the orderly and efficient prosecution of the suffrage movement in America, which shall embody the deliberate action of State and local organizations, and shall carry with it their united weight, do hereby form the American Woman Suffrage Association.

Article I.

Name: This Association shall be known as the American Woman Suffrage Association.

Article II.

Object: Its object shall be to concentrate the efforts of all the advocates of woman suffrage in the United States for National purposes only, viz:

Sec. 1. To form auxiliary State Associations in every State where none such now exist, and to cooperate with those already existing, which shall declare themselves auxillary before the first day of March next, the authority of the auxiliary Societies being recognized in their respective localities, and their plan being promoted by every means in our power.

Sec. 2. To hold an annual meeting of delegates for the transaction of business and the election of officers for the ensuing year; also, one or more national conventions for the advocacy of woman suffrage.

Sec. 3. To publish tracts, documents, and other matter for the supply of State and local societies and individuals at actual cost.

Sec. 4. To prepare and circulate petitions to State Legislatures, to Congress, or to constitutional conventions in behalf of the legal and political equality of woman; to employ lecturers and agents, and to take any measures the Executive Committee may think fit, to forward the objects of the Association.

Article III.—Organization.

Sec. 1. The officers of this Association shall be a President, eight Vice-Presidents at Large, Chairman of the Executive Committee, Foreign Corresponding Secretary, two Recording Secretaries, and a Treasurer, all of whom shall be *ex-officio* members of the Executive Committee from each State and Territory, and from the District of Columbia, as hereinafter provided.

Sec. 2. Every President of an auxiliary State society shall be *ex-officio* a vice-president of this Association.

Sec. 3. Every chairman of the Executive Committee of an auxiliary State society shall be *ex-officio* a member of the Executive Committee of this Association.

Sec. 4. In cases where no auxiliary State society exists, a suitable person may be selected by the annual meeting, by the Executive Committee, as Vice-President or member of the Executive Committee, to serve only until the organization of said State Association.

Sec. 5. The Executive Committee may fill all vacancies that may occur prior to the next annual meeting.

Sec. 6. All officers shall be elected annually at any annual meeting of delegates, on the basis of the Congressional representation of the respective States and Territories, except as above provided.

Sec. 7. No distinction on account of sex shall ever be made in the membership or in the selection of officers of this Society; but the general principle shall be that one half of the officers shall, as nearly as convenient, be men, and one half women.

Sec. 8. No money shall be paid by the Treasurer except under such restrictions as the Executive Committee may provide.

Sec. 9. Five members of the Executive Committee, when convened by the Chairman, after fifteen days written notice previously mailed to each of its members, shall constitute a quorum. But no action thus taken shall be final, until such proceedings shall have been ratified in writing by at least fifteen members of the Committee.

Sec. 10. The Chairman shall convene a meeting whenever requested to do so by five members of the Executive Committee.

Article IV.

This Association shall have a branch office in every State in connection with the office of the auxiliary State Society therein, and shall have a central office at such place as the Executive Committee may determine.

Article V.

This Constitution may be amended at any annual meeting, by a vote of three-fifths of the delegates present therein.

Article VI.

Any person may become a member of the American Woman Suffrage Association by signing the Constitution and paying the sum of $1 annually, or life members by paying the sum of $10, which membership shall entitle the individual to attend the business meetings of delegates and participate in their deliberations.

Article VII.

Honorary members may be appointed by the annual meeting or by the Executive Committee, in consideration of services rendered.

25. Resolutions of Francis Minor, Esq., 1869

WHEREAS, In the adjustment of the question of suffrage now before the people of this country for settlement, it is of the highest importance that the organic law of the land should be so framed and construed as to work injustice to none, but secure as far as possible perfect political equality among all classes of citizens; and,

WHEREAS, All persons born or naturalized in the United States, and subject to the jurisdiction thereof, are citizens of the United States, and of the State wherein they reside; be it

Resolved, 1. That the immunities and privileges of American citizenship, however defined, are National in character and paramount to all State authority.

2. That while the Constitution of the United States leaves the qualification of electors to the several States, it nowhere gives them the right to deprive any citizen of the elective franchise which is possessed by any other citizen—to regulate, not including the right to prohibit the franchise.

3. That, as the Constitution of the United States expressly declares that no State shall make or enforce any laws that shall abridge the privileges or immunities of citizens of the United States, those provisions of the several State Constitutions that exclude women from the franchise on account of sex, are violative alike of the spirit and letter of the Federal Constitution.

4. That, as the subject of naturalization is expressly withheld from the States, and as the States clearly would have no right to deprive of the franchise naturalized citizens, among whom women are expressly included, still more clearly have they no right to deprive native-born women citizens of this right.

5. That justice and equity can only be attained by having the same laws for men and women alike.

6. That having full faith and confidence in the truth and justice of these principles, we will never cease to urge the claims of women to a participation in the affairs of government equal with men.

26. THE FIFTEENTH AMENDMENT TO THE CONSTITUTION, MARCH 30, 1870

Section 1. "The right of citizens of the United to vote shall not be denied or abridged by the United States, or by any State, on account of race, color, or previous condition of servitude."

Section 2. "The Congress shall have power to enforce this article by appropriate legislation."

27. MEMORIAL OF VICTORIA C. WOODHULL, DECEMBER 19, 1870

To the Honorable the Senate and House of Representatives of the United States in Congress assembled, respectfully showeth:

That she was born in the State of Ohio, and is above the age of twenty-one years; that she has resided in the State of New York during the past three years; that she is still a resident thereof, and that she is a citizen of the United States, as declared by the XIV. Article of the Amendments to the Constitution of the United States.

That since the adoption of the XV. Article of the Amendments to the Constitution, neither the State of New York nor any other State, nor any Territory, has passed any law to abridge the right of any citizen of the United States to vote, as established by said article, neither on account of sex or otherwise. That, nevertheless, the right to vote is denied to women citizens of the United States by the operation of Election Laws in the several States and Territories, which laws were enacted prior to the adoption of the said XV. Article, and which are inconsistent with the Constitution as amended, and, therefore, are void and of no effect; but which, being still enforced by the said States and Territories, render the Constitution inoperative as regards the right of women citizens to vote:

And whereas, Article VI., Section 2, declares "That this Constitution and the laws of the United States which shall be made in pursuance thereof, and all treaties made, or which shall be made, under the authority of the United States, shall be the supreme law of the land; and all judges in every State shall be bound thereby, anything in the Constitution and laws of any State to the contrary, notwithstanding."

And whereas, no distinction between citizens is made in the Constitution of the United States on account of sex; but the XV. Article of Amendments to it provides that "No State shall make or enforce any law which shall abridge the privileges and immunities of citizens of the United States, nor deny to any person within its jurisdiction the equal protection of the laws."

And whereas, Congress has power to make laws which shall be necessary and proper for carrying into execution all powers vested by the Constitution in the Government of the United States; and to make or alter all regulations in relation to holding elections for senators or representatives, and especially to enforce, by appropriate legislation, the provisions of the said XIV. Article:

And whereas, the continuance of the enforcement of said local election laws, denying and abridging the right of citizens to vote on account of sex, is a grievance to your memorialist and to various other persons, citizens of the United States,

Therefore, your memorialist would most respectfully petition your honorable bodies to make such laws as in the wisdom of Congress shall be necessary and proper for carrying into execution the right vested by the Constitution in the citizens of the United States to vote, without regard to sex.

And your memorialist will ever pray.

Victoria C. Woodhull.

28. VICTORIA C. WOODHULL'S ADDRESS TO THE JUDICIARY COMMITTEE OF THE HOUSE OF REPRESENTATIVES, JANUARY 11, 1871

Having most respectfully memorialized Congress for the passage of such laws as in its wisdom shall seem necessary and proper to carry into effect the rights vested by the Constitution of the United States in the citizens to vote, without regard to sex, I beg leave to submit to your honorable body the following in favor of my prayer in said memorial which has been referred to your Committee.

The public law of the world is founded upon the conceded fact that sovereignty can not be forfeited or renounced. The sovereign power of this country is perpetually in the politically organized people of the

United States, and can neither be relinquished nor abandoned by any portion of them. The people in this republic who confer sovereignty are its citizens: in a monarchy the people are the subjects of sovereignty. All citizens of a republic by rightful act or implication confer sovereign power. All people of a monarchy are subjects who exist under its supreme shield and enjoy its immunities. The subject of a monarch takes municipal immunities from the sovereign as a gracious favor; but the woman citizen of this country has the inalienable "sovereign" right of self-government in her own proper person. Those who look upon woman's status by the dim light of the common law, which unfolded itself under the feudal and military institutions that establish right upon physical power, can not find any analogy in the status of the woman citizen of this country, where the broad sunshine of our Constitution has enfranchised all.

As sovereignty can not be forfeited, relinquished, or abandoned, those from whom it flows—the citizens—are equal in conferring the power, and should be equal in the enjoyment of its benefits and in the exercise of its rights and privileges. One portion of citizens have no power to deprive another portion of rights and privileges such as are possessed and exercised by themselves. The male citizen has no more right to deprive the female citizen of the free, public, political, expression of opinion than the female citizen has to deprive the male citizen thereof.

The sovereign will of the people is expressed in our written Constitution, which is the supreme law of the land. The Constitution makes no distinction of sex. The Constitution defines a woman born or naturalized in the United States, and subject to the jurisdiction thereof, to be a citizen. It recognizes the right of citizens to vote. It declares that the right of citizens of the United States to vote shall not be denied or abridged by the United States or by any State on account of "race, color, or previous condition of servitude."

Women, white and black, belong to races, although to different races. A race of people comprises all the people, male and female. The right to vote can not be denied on account of race. All people included in the term race have the right to vote, unless otherwise prohibited. Women of all races are white, black, or some intermediate color. Color comprises all people, of all races and both sexes. The right to vote can not be denied on account of color. All people included in the term color have the right to vote unless otherwise prohibited.

With the right to vote sex has nothing to do. Race and color include all people of both sexes. All people of both sexes have the right to vote, unless prohibited by special limited terms less comprehensive than race or color. No such limiting terms exist in the Constitution. Women, white and black, have from time immemorial groaned under what is properly termed in the Constitution "previous condition of servitude." Women are the equals of men before the law, and are equal in all their rights as citizens. Women are debarred from voting in some parts of the United States, although they are allowed to exercise that right elsewhere. Women were formerly permitted to vote in places where they are now debarred therefrom. The naturalization laws of the United States expressly provide for the naturalization of women. But the right to vote has only lately been definitely declared by the Constitution to be inalienable, under three distinct conditions—in all of which woman is clearly embraced.

The citizen who is taxed should also have a voice in the subject matter of taxation. "No taxation without representation" is a right which was fundamentally established at the very birth of our country's independence; and by what ethics does any free government impose taxes on women without giving them a voice upon the subject or a participation in the public declaration as to how and by whom these taxes shall be applied for common public use? Women are free to own and to control property, separate and free from males, and they are held responsible in their own proper persons, in every particular, as well as men, in and out of court. Women have the same inalienable right to life, liberty, and the pursuit of happiness that men have. Why have they not this right politically, as well as men?

Women constitute a majority of the people of this country—they hold vast portions of the nation's wealth and pay a proportionate share of the taxes. They are intrusted with the most vital responsibilities of society; they bear, rear, and educate men; they train and mould their characters; they inspire the noblest impulses in men; they often hold the accumulated fortunes of a man's life for the safety of the family and as guardians of the infants, and yet they are debarred from uttering any opinion by public vote, as to the management by public servants of these interests; they are the secret counselors, the best advisers, the most devoted aids in the most trying periods of men's lives, and yet men shrink from trusting them in the common questions of ordinary politics. Men trust women in the market, in the shop, on the highway and railroad, and in all other public places and assemblies, but when they propose to carry a slip of paper with a name upon it to the polls, they fear them. Nevertheless, as citizens, women have the right to vote; they are part and parcel of that great element in which the sovereign power of the land had birth; and it is by usurpation only that men debar them from this right. The American nation, in its march onward and upward, can not publicly choke the intellectual and political activity of half its citizens by narrow statutes. The will of the entire people is the true basis of republican government, and a free expression of that will by the public vote of all citizens, without distinctions of race, color, occupation, or sex, is the only means by which that will can be ascertained. As the world has advanced into civilization and culture; as mind has risen in its dominion over matter; as the principle of justice and moral right has gained sway, and merely physical organized power has yielded thereto; as the might of right has supplanted the right of might, so have the rights of women become more fully recognized, and that recognition is the result of the development of the minds of men, which through the ages she has polished, and thereby heightened the lustre of civilization.

It was reserved for our great country to recognize by constitutional enactment that political equality of all citizens which religion, affection, and common sense should have long since accorded; it was reserved for America to sweep away the mist of prejudice and ignorance, and that chivalric condescension of a darker age, for in the language of Holy Writ, "The night is far spent, the day is at hand, let us therefore cast off the work of darkness and let us put on the armor of light. Let us walk honestly as in the day." It may be argued against the proposition that there still remains upon the statute books of some States the word "male" to an exclusion; but as the Constitution, in its paramount character, can only be read by the light of the established principle, *ita lex Scripta est,* and as a subject of sex is not mentioned, and the Constitution is not limited either in terms or by necessary implication in the general rights of citizens to vote, this right can not be limited on account of anything in the spir-

it of inferior or previous enactments upon a subject which is not mentioned in the supreme law. A different construction would destroy a vested right in a portion of the citizens, and this no legislature has a right to do without compensation, and nothing can compensate a citizen for the loss of his or her suffrage—its value is equal to the value of life. Neither can it be presumed that women are to be kept from the polls as a mere police regulation: it is to be hoped, at least, that police regulations in their case need not be very active. The effect of the amendments to the Constitution must be to annul the power over this subject in the States, whether past, present, or future, which is contrary to the amendments. The amendments would even arrest the action of the Supreme Court in cases pending before it prior to their adoption, and operate as an absolute prohibition to the exercise of any other jurisdiction than merely to dismiss the suit. 8 Dall., 382: 6 Wheaton, 405; 9 ib., 868; 3d Circ. Pa., 1832.

And if the restrictions contained in the Constitution as to color, race or servitude, were designed to limit the State governments in reference to their own citizens, and were intended to operate also as restrictions on the federal power, and to prevent interference with the rights of the State and its citizens, how, then, can the State restrict citizens of the United States in the exercise of rights not mentioned in any restrictive clause in reference to actions on the part of those citizens having reference solely to the necessary functions of the General Government, such as the election of representatives and senators to Congress, whose election the Constitution expressly gives Congress the power to regulate? S. C., 1847: Fox vs. Ohio, 5 Howard, 410.

Your memorialist complains of the existence of State laws, and prays Congress, by appropriate legislation, to declare them, as they are, annulled, and to give vitality to the Constitution under its power to make and alter the regulations of the States contravening the same.

It may be urged in opposition that the courts have power, and should declare upon this subject. The Supreme Court has the power, and it would be its duty to declare the law: but the court will not do so unless a determination of such point as shall arise make it necessary to the determination of a controversy, and hence a case must be presented in which there can be no rational doubt. All this would subject the aggrieved parties to much dilatory, expensive and needless litigation, which your memorialist prays your honorable body to dispense with by appropriate legislation, as there can be no purpose in special arguments *"ad inconvenienti,"* enlarging or contracting the import of the language of the Constitution.

Therefore, Believing firmly in the right of citizens to freely approach those in whose hands their destiny is placed under the Providence of God, your memorialist has frankly, but humbly, appealed to you, and prays that the wisdom of Congress may be moved to action in this matter for the benefit and the increased happiness of our beloved country.

29. Report No. 22 of the House of Representatives, Committee on the Judiciary (43d Congress, 3d Session), Regarding the Memorial of Victoria C. Woodhull, January 30, 1871

The Memorialist asks the enactment of a law by Congress which shall secure to citizens of the United States in the several States the right to vote "without regard to sex." Since the adoption of the XIV. Amendment of the Constitution, there is no longer any reason to doubt that all persons, born or naturalized in the United States, and subject to the jurisdiction thereof, are citizens of the United States and of the State wherein they reside, for that is the express declaration of the amendment.

The clause of the XIV. Amendment, "No State shall make or enforce any law which shall abridge the privileges or immunities of citizens of the United States," does not, in the opinion of the Committee, refer to privileges and immunities of citizens of the United States other than those privileges and immunities embraced in the original text of the Constitution, article IV., section 2. The XIV. Amendment, it is believed, did not add to the privileges or immunities before mentioned, but was deemed necessary for their enforcement, as an express limitation upon the powers of the States. It has been judicially determined that the first eight articles of amendment of the Constitution were not limitations on the power of the States, and it was apprehended that the same might be held of the provision of section 2, article iv.

To remedy this defect of the Constitution, the express limitations upon the States contained in the first section of the XIV. Amendment, together with the grant of power in Congress to enforce them by legislation, were incorporated in the Constitution. The words "citizens of the United States," and "citizens of the States," as employed in the XIV. Amendment, did not change or modify the relations of citizens of the State and Nation as they existed under the original Constitution.

Attorney-General Bates gave the opinion that the Constitution uses the word "citizen," only to express the political quality of the individual in his relation to the Nation; to declare that he is a member of the body politic, and bound to it by the reciprocal obligation of allegiance on the one side and protection on the other. The phrase "a citizen of the United States," without addition or qualification, means neither more nor less than a member of the Nation. (Opinion of Attorney-General Bates on citizenship.)

The Supreme Court of the United States has ruled that, according to the express words and clear meaning of the section 2, article iv. of the Constitution, no privileges are secured by it except those which belong to citizenship. (Connor *et al. vs.* Elliott *et al.,* 18 Howard, 593). In Corfield *vs.* Coryell, 4 Washington Circuit Court Reports, 380, the Court say:

> The inquiry is, what are the privileges and immunities of citizens in the several States? We feel no hesitation in confining these expressions to those privileges and immunities which are in their nature fundamental; which belong of right to the citizens of all free governments; and which have at all times been enjoyed by the citizens of the several States which compose this Union, from the time of their becoming free, independent, and sovereign. What these fundamental principles are would, perhaps, be more tedious than difficult to enumerate. They may, however, be all comprehended under the following general heads: Protection by the Government; the enjoyment of life and liberty, with the right to acquire and possess property of every kind, and to pursue and obtain happiness and safety, subject, nevertheless, to such restraints as the Government may justly prescribe for the general good of the whole; the right of a citizen of one State to pass through or to reside in any other State, for the purpose of trade, agriculture, professional pursuits, or otherwise; to claim the benefit of the writ of *habeas corpus;* to institute and maintain actions of any kind in the courts of the State; to take, hold, and dispose of property,

either real or personal; and an exemption from higher taxes or impositions than are paid by the other citizens of the State, may be mentioned as some of the particular privileges and immunities of citizens which are clearly embraced by the general description of privileges deemed to be fundamental; to which may be added the elective franchise, as regulated and established by the laws or Constitution of the State in which it is to be exercised . . . But we can not accede to the proposition which was insisted on by the counsel, that under this provision of the Constitution, sec. 2, art. 4, the citizens of the several States are permitted to participate in all the rights which belong exclusively to the citizens of any other particular State.

The learned Justice Story declared that the intention of the clause—"the citizens of each State shall be entitled to all the privileges and immunities of citizens in the several States"—was to confer on the citizens of each State a general citizenship, and communicated all the privileges and immunities which a citizen of the same State would be entitled to under the circumstances. (Story on the Constitution, vol. 2, p. 605).

In the case of the Bank of the United States *vs.* Primrose, in the Supreme Court of the United States, Mr. Webster said:

> That this article in the Constitution (art. 4, sec. 2) does not confer on the citizens of each State political rights in every other State, is admitted. A citizen of Pennsylvania can not go into Virginia and vote at any election in that State, though when he has acquired a residence in Virginia, and is otherwise qualified, as required by the Constitution (of Virginia), he becomes, without formal adoption as a citizen of Virginia, a citizen of that State politically. (Webster's Works, vol. 6, p. 112).

It must be obvious that Mr. Webster was of opinion that the privileges and immunities of citizens, guaranteed to them in the several States, did not include the privilege of the elective franchise otherwise than as secured by the State Constitution. For, after making the statement above quoted, that a citizen of Pennsylvania can not go into Virginia and vote, Mr. Webster adds, "but for the purposes of trade, commerce, buying and selling, it is evidently not in the power of any State to impose any hindrance or embarrassment, etc., upon citizens of other States, or to place them, going there, upon a different footing

from her own citizens." (Ib.) The proposition is clear that no citizen of the United States can rightfully vote in any State of this Union who has not the qualifications required by the Constitution of the State in which the right is claimed to be exercised, except as to such conditions in the constitutions of such States as deny the right to vote to citizens resident therein "on account of race, color, or previous condition of servitude."

The adoption of the XV. Amendment to the Constitution imposing these three limitations upon the power to the several States, was by necessary implication, a declaration that the States had the power to regulate by a uniform rule the conditions upon which the elective franchise should be exercised by citizens of the United States resident therein. The limitations specified in the XV. Amendment exclude the conclusion that a State of this Union, having a government republican in form, may not prescribe conditions upon which alone citizens may vote other than those prohibited. It can hardly be said that a State law which excludes from voting women citizens, minor citizens, and non-resident citizens of the United States, on account of sex, minority, or domicil, is a denial of the right to vote on account of race, color, or previous condition of servitude.

It may be further added that the 2d section of the XIV. Amendment, by the provision that "when the right to vote at any election for the choice of electors of President and Vice-President of the United States, Representatives in Congress, or executive and judicial officers of the State, or the members of the Legislature thereof, is denied to any of the male inhabitants of such State, being twenty-one years of age, a citizen of the United States, or in any way abridged, except for participation in rebellion or other crime, the basis of representation therein shall be reduced in the proportion which the number of such male citizens shall bear to the whole number of male citizens twenty-one years of age in such State," implies that the several States may restrict the elective franchise as to other than male citizens. In disposing of this question effect must be given, if possible, to every provision of the Constitution. Article 1, section 2, of the Constitution provides:

> That the House of Representatives shall be composed of members chosen every second year by the people of the several States, and the electors in each State shall have the qualifications requisite for

electors of the most numerous branch of the State Legislature.

This provision has always been construed to vest in the several States the exclusive right to prescribe the qualifications of electors for the most numerous branch of the State Legislature, and therefore for Members of Congress. And this interpretation is supported by section 4, article 1, of the Constitution, which provides:

> That the time, places, and manner of holding elections for Senators and Representatives shall be prescribed in each State by the Legislature thereof; but the Congress may at any time by law make or alter such regulations except as to the place of choosing Senators.

Now it is submitted, if it had been intended that Congress should prescribe the qualifications of electors, that the grant would have read: The Congress may at any time by law make or alter such regulations, and also prescribe the qualifications of electors, etc. The power, on the contrary, is limited exclusively to the time, place, and manner, and does not extend to the qualification of the electors. This power to prescribe the qualification of electors in the several States has always been exercised, and is, to-day, by the several States of the Union; and we apprehend, until the Constitution shall be changed, will continue to be so exercised, subject only to express limitations imposed by the Constitution upon the several States, before noticed. We are of opinion, therefore, that it is not competent for the Congress of the United States to establish by law the right to vote without regard to sex in the several States of this Union, without the consent of the people of such States, and against their constitutions and laws; and that such legislation would be, in our judgment, a violation of the Constitution of the United States, and of the rights reserved to the States respectively by the Constitution. It is undoubtedly the right of the people of the several States so to reform their constitutions and laws as to secure the equal exercise of the right of suffrage at all elections held therein under the Constitution of the United States, to all citizens, without regard to sex; and as public opinion creates constitutions and governments in the several States, it is not to be doubted that whenever, in any State, the people are of opinion that such a reform is advisable, it will be made.

If however, as is claimed in the memorial referred to, the right to vote "is vested by the Constitution in the citizens of the United States without regard to sex," that right can be established in the courts without further legislation.

The suggestion is made that Congress, by a mere declaratory act, shall say that the construction claimed in the memorial is the true construction of the Constitution, or in other words, that by the Constitution of the United States the right to vote is vested in citizens of the United States "without regard to sex," anything in the constitution and laws of any State to the contrary notwithstanding. In the opinion of the Committee, such declaratory act is not authorized by the Constitution nor within the legislative power of Congress. We therefore recommend the adoption of the following resolution:

Resolved, That the prayer of the petitioner be not granted, that the memorial be laid on the table, and that the Committee on the Judiciary be discharged from the further consideration of the subject.

30. VIRGINIA L. MINOR'S PETITION, SUBMITTED TO THE CIRCUIT COURT OF ST. LOUIS COUNTY, MISSOURI, DECEMBER 1872

St. Louis County, ss.: Virginia L. Minor and Francis Minor, her husband, Plaintiffs, *vs.* Reese Happersett, Defendant.

The plaintiff, Virginia L. Minor (with whom is joined her husband, Francis Minor, as required by the law of Missouri), states, that under the Constitution and law of Missouri, all persons wishing to vote at any election, must previously have been registered in the manner pointed out by law, this being a condition precedent to the exercise of the elective franchise.

That on the fifteenth day of October, 1872 (one of the days fixed by law for the registration of voters), and long prior thereto, she was a native-born, free white citizen of the United States, and of the State of Missouri, and on the day last mentioned she was the age of twenty-one years.

That on said day, the plaintiff was a resident of the thirteenth election district of the city and county of St. Louis, in the State of Missouri, and had been so residing in said county and election district, for the entire period of twelve months and more, immediately preceding said fifteenth day of October, 1872, and for more than twenty years had been and is a tax-paying, lawabiding citizen of the county and State aforesaid.

That on said last mentioned day, the defendant, having been duly and legally appointed Registrar for said election district, and having accepted the said office of Registrar and entered upon the discharge of the duties thereof at the office of registration, to wit: No. 2004 Market Street, in said city and county of St. Louis, it became and was then and there his duty to register all citizens, resident in said district as aforesaid, entitled to the elective franchise, who might apply to him for that purpose.

The plaintiff further states, that wishing to exercise her privilege as a citizen of the United States, and vote for Electors for President and Vice-President of the United States, and for a Representative in Congress, and for other officers, at the General Election held in November, 1872: While said defendant was so acting as Registrar, on said 15th day of October, 1872, she appeared before him, at his office aforesaid, and then and there offered to take and subscribe the oath to support the Constitution of the United States and of the State of Missouri, as required by the registration law of said State, approved March 10, 1871, and respectfully applied to him to be registered as a lawful voter, which said defendant then and there refused to do.

The plaintiff further states, that the defendant, well knowing that she, as a citizen of the United States and of the State of Missouri, resident as aforesaid, was then and there entitled to all the privileges and immunities of citizenship, chief among which is the elective franchise, and as such, was entitled to be registered, in order to exercise said privilege: yet, unlawfully intending, contriving, and designing to deprive the plaintiff of said franchise or privilege, then and there knowingly, willfully, maliciously, and corruptly refused to place her name upon the list of registered voters, whereby she was deprived of her right to vote.

Defendant stated to plaintiff, that she was not entitled to be registered, or to vote, because she was not a "male" citizen, but a woman! That by the Constitution of Missouri, Art. II., Sec. 18, and by the aforesaid registration law of said State, approved March 10, 1871, it is provided and declared, that only

"male citizens" of the United States, etc., are entitled or permitted to vote.

But the plaintiff protests against such decision, and she declares and maintains that said provisions of the Constitution and registration law of Missouri aforesaid, are in conflict with, and repugnant to the Constitution of the United States, which is paramount to State authority; and that they are especially in conflict with the following articles and clauses of said Constitution of the United States, to wit:

Art. I. Sec. 9.—Which declares that no Bill of Attainder shall be passed.

Art. I. Sec. 10.—No State shall pass any Bill of Attainder, or grant any title of nobility.

Art. IV. Sec. 2.—The citizens of each State shall be entitled to all privileges and immunities of citizens in the several States.

Art. IV. Sec. 4.—The United States shall guarantee to every State a republican form of government.

Art. VI.—This Constitution and the laws of the United States which shall be made in pursuance thereof, shall be the supreme law of the land, anything in the Constitution or laws of any State to the contrary notwithstanding.

Amendments.

Art. V.—No person shall be . . . deprived of life, liberty, or property without due process of law.

Art. IX.—The enumeration in the Constitution of certain rights, shall not be construed to deny or disparage others retained by the people.

Art. XIV. Sec. 1.—All persons born or naturalized in the United States, and subject to the jurisdiction thereof, are citizens of the United States and of the State wherein they reside. No State shall make or enforce any law which shall abridge the privileges or immunities of citizens of the United States. Nor shall any State deprive any person of life, liberty, or property, without due process of law; nor deny to any person within its jurisdiction, the equal protection of the laws.

The plaintiff states, that by reason of the wrongful act of the defendant as aforesaid, she has been damaged in the sum of ten thousand dollars, for which she prays judgment.

John M. Krum,
Francis Minor,   } *Att'ys for Plffs.*
John B. Henderson,

31. DECISION OF THE SUPREME COURT, *BRADWELL V. ILLINOIS*, 1873

Mr. Justice Miller delivered the opinion of the court:

The claim that, under the 14th Amendment of the Constitution, which declares that no state shall make or enforce any law which shall abridge the privileges and immunities of citizens of the United States, and the statute law of Illinois, or the common law prevailing in that state, can no longer be set up as a barrier against the right of females to pursue any lawful employment for a livelihood (the practice of law included), assumes that it is one of the privileges and immunities of women as citizens to engage in any and every profession, occupation or employment in civil life.

It certainly cannot be affirmed, as a historical fact, that this has ever been established as one of the fundamental privileges and immunities of the sex. On the contrary, the civil law, as well as nature herself, has always recognized a wide difference in the respective spheres and destinies of man and woman. Man is, or should be woman's protector and defender. The natural and proper timidity and delicacy which belongs to the female sex evidently unfits it for many of the occupations of civil life. The constitution of the family organization, which is founded in the divine ordinance, as well as in the nature of things, indicates the domestic sphere as that which properly belongs to the domain and functions of womanhood. The harmony, not to say identity, of interests and views which belong or should belong to the family institution, is repugnant to the idea of a woman adopting a distinct and independent career from that of her husband. So firmly fixed was this sentiment in the founders of the common law that it became a maxim of that system of jurisprudence that a woman had no legal existence separate from her husband, who was regarded as her head and representative in the social state . . .

The paramount destiny and mission of woman are to fulfill the noble and benign offices of wife and mother. This is the law of the Creator. And the rules of civil society must be adapted to the general constitution of things, and cannot be based upon exceptional cases.

The humane movements of modern society, which have for their object the multiplication of avenues for woman's advancement, and of occupations adapted to her condition and sex, have my heartiest concurrence. But I am not prepared to say

that it is one of her fundamental rights and privileges to be admitted into every office and position, including those which require highly special qualifications and demanding special responsibilities. In the nature of things it is not every citizen of every age, sex, and condition that is qualified for every calling and position. It is the prerogative of the legislator to prescribe regulations founded on nature, reason, and experience for the due admission of qualified persons to professions and callings demanding special skill and confidence. This fairly belongs to the police power of the state; and, in my opinion, in view of the peculiar characteristics, destiny, and mission of woman, it is within the province of the legislature to ordain what offices, positions, and callings shall be filled and discharged by men, and shall receive the benefit of those energies and responsibilities, and that decision and firmness which are presumed to predominate in the sterner sex.

For these reasons I think that the laws of Illinois now complained of are not obnoxious to the charge of abridging any of the privileges and immunities of citizens of the United States.

32. OPINION OF THE SUPREME COURT, *MINOR V. HAPPERSETT*, MARCH 29, 1875

Supreme Court of the United States. No. 182.—October Term, 1874. Virginia L. Minor and Francis Minor, her husband, Plaintiffs in Error, *vs.* Reese Happersett. In error to the Supreme Court of the State of Missouri.

Mr. Chief Justice Waite delivered the opinion of the court.

The question is presented in this case, whether, since the adoption of the XIV. Amendment, a woman, who is a citizen of the United States and the State of Missouri, is a voter in that State, notwithstanding the provision of the Constitution and laws of the State, which confine the right of suffrage to men alone. We might perhaps decide the case upon other grounds, but this question is fairly made. From the opinion, we find that it was the only one decided in the court below, and it is the only one which has been argued here. The case was undoubtedly brought to this court for the sole purpose of having that question decided by us, and, in view of the evident propriety there is of having it settled, so far as it can be by such a decision, we have concluded to waive all other considerations and proceed at once to its determination.

It is contended that the provisions of the Constitution and laws of the State of Missouri, which confine the right of suffrage and registration therefore to men, are in violation of the Constitution of the United States, and therefore void. The argument is, that as a woman, born or naturalized in the United States and subject to the jurisdiction thereof, is a citizen of the United States and of the State in which she resides, she has the right of suffrage as one of the privileges and immunities of her citizenship, which the State can not by its laws or constitution abridge.

There is no doubt that women may be citizens. They are persons, and, by the XIV. Amendment, "all persons born or naturalized in the United States and subject to the jurisdiction thereof" are expressly declared to be "citizens of the United States and of the State wherein they reside." But, in our opinion, it did not need this Amendment to give them that position. Before its adoption, the Constitution of the United States did not in terms prescribe who should be citizens of the United States or of the several States, yet there were necessarily such citizens without such provision. There can not be a nation without a people. The very idea of a political community, such as a nation is, implies an association of persons for the promotion of their general welfare. Each one of the persons associated becomes a member of the nation formed by the association. He owes it allegiance, and is entitled to its protection. Allegiance and protection are, in this connection, reciprocal obligations. The one is a compensation for the other; allegiance for protection and protection for allegiance.

For convenience, it has been found necessary to give a name to this membership. The object is to designate by a title the person and the relation he bears to the nation. For this purpose the words "subject," "inhabitant," and "citizen" have been used, and the choice between them is sometimes made to depend upon the form of the government. Citizen is now more commonly employed, however, and as it has been considered better suited to the description of one living under a republican government, it was adopted by nearly all of the States upon their separation from Great Britain, and was afterward adopted in the articles of confederation and in the Constitution of the United States. When used in this sense, it is understood as conveying the idea of membership of a nation, and nothing more.

To determine, then, who were citizens of the United States before the adoption of the Amendment, it is necessary to ascertain what persons originally associated themselves together to form the nation, and what were afterward admitted to membership. Looking at the Constitution itself, we find that it was ordained and established by "the people of the United States" (Preamble, 1 Stat., 10), and then, going further back, we find that these were the people of the several States that had before dissolved the political bands which connected them with Great Britain and assumed a separate and equal station among the powers of the earth (Dec. of Ind., 1 Stat., 1), and that had by articles of confederation and perpetual union, in which they took the name of "the United States of America," entered into a firm league of friendship with each other for their common defense, the security of their liberties and their mutual and general welfare, binding themselves to assist each other against all force offered to or attack made upon them, or any of them, on account of religion, sovereignty, trade, or any other pretense whatever (Art. Confed., sec. 3, 1 Stat. 4).

Whoever then was one of the people of either of these States when the Constitution of the United States was adopted, became *ipso facto* a citizen—a member of the nation created by its adoption. He was one of the persons associating together to form the nation, and was, consequently, one of its original citizens. As to this there has never been a doubt. Disputes have arisen as to whether or not certain persons or certain classes of persons were part of the people at the time, but never as to their citizenship if they were.

Additions might always be made to the citizenship of the United States in two ways—first by birth and second by naturalization. This is apparent from the Constitution itself, for it provides (Art. 2, Sec. 1) that "no person except a natural born citizen, or a citizen of the United States at the time of the adoption of the Constitution, shall be eligible to the office of President," and (Art. 1, Sec. 8) that Congress shall have power "to establish a uniform rule of naturalization." Thus, new citizens may be born or they may be created by naturalization.

The Constitution does not in words say who shall be natural-born citizens. Resort must be had elsewhere to ascertain that. At common law, with the nomenclature of which the framers of the Constitution were familiar, it was never doubted that all children born in a country of parents who were its citizens became themselves upon their birth citizens also. These were natives, or natural-born citizens as distinguished from aliens or foreigners. Some authorities go further and include as citizens children born within the jurisdiction, without reference to the citizenship of their parents. As to this class there have been doubts, but never as to the first. For the purposes of this case it is not necessary to solve these doubts. It is sufficient for everything we have now to consider, that all children born of citizen parents within the jurisdiction are themselves citizens. The words "all children" are certainly as comprehensive when used in this connection as "all persons," and if females are included in the last, they must be in the first. That they are included in the last is not denied. In fact, the whole argument of the plaintiffs proceeds upon that idea.

Under the power to adopt a uniform system of naturalization, Congress as early as 1790 provided "that any alien, being a free white person," might be admitted as a citizen of the United States, and that the children of such persons so naturalized, dwelling within the United States, being under twenty-one years of age at the time of such naturalization, should also be considered citizens of the United States, and that the children of citizens of the United States that might be born beyond the sea, or out of the limits of the United States, should be considered as natural-born citizens (1 Stat. 103). These provisions thus enacted have, in substance, been retained in all the naturalization laws adopted since. In 1855, however, the last provision was somewhat extended, and all persons theretofore born or thereafter to be born out of the limits of the jurisdiction of the United States, whose fathers were, or should be at the time of their death, citizens of the United States, were declared to be citizens also (10 Stat. 604).

As early as 1804 it was enacted by Congress that when any alien, who had declared his intention to become a citizen in the manner provided by law, died before he was actually naturalized, his widow and children should be considered as citizens of the United States, and entitled to all rights and privileges as such upon taking the necessary oath (2 Stat., 293); and in 1855 it was further provided that any woman who might lawfully be naturalized under the existing laws, married, or who should be married to a citizen of the United States, should be deemed and taken to be a citizen (10 Stat., 604). From this it is apparent, that, from the commencement of the legislation upon this subject, alien women and alien minors could be made citizens by naturalization; and we think it will not be contended that this would have been done if it had not been supposed that native women and native minors were already citizens by birth.

But if more is necessary to show that women have always been considered as citizens the same as men, abundant proof is to be found in the legislative and judicial history of the country. Thus, by the Constitution, the judicial power of the United States is made to extend to controversies between citizens of different States. Under this it has been uniformly held, that the citizenship necessary to give the courts of the United States jurisdiction of a cause must be affirmatively shown on the record. Its existence as a fact may be put in issue and tried. If found not to exist, the case must be dismissed. Notwithstanding this, the records of the courts are full of cases in which the jurisdiction depends upon the citizenship of women, and not one can be found, we think, in which objection was made on that account. Certainly none can be found in which it has been held that women could not sue or be sued in the courts of the United States. Again, at the time of the adoption of the Constitution, in many of the States (and in some probably now) aliens could not inherit or transmit inheritance. There are a multitude of cases to be found in which the question has been presented whether a woman was or was not an alien, and as such capable or incapable of inheritance, but in no one has it been insisted that she was not a citizen because she was a woman. On the contrary, her right to citizenship has been in all cases assumed. The only question has been whether, in the particular case under consideration, she had availed herself of the right.

In the legislative department of the Government similar proof will be found. Thus, in the pre-emption laws (5 Stat., 455, sec. 10), a widow, "being a citizen of the United States," is allowed to make settlement on the public lands and purchase upon the terms specified, and women, "being citizens of the United States," are permitted to avail themselves of the benefit of the homestead law (12 Stat., 392).

Other proof of like character might be found, but certainly more can not be necessary to establish the fact that sex has never been made one of the elements of citizenship in the United States. In this respect men have never had an advantage over women. The same laws precisely apply to both. The XIV. Amendment did not affect the citizenship of women any more than it did of men. In this particular, therefore, the rights of Mrs. Minor do not depend upon the Amendment. She has always been a citizen from her birth, and entitled to all the privileges and immunities of citizenship. The Amendment prohibited the State, of which she is a citizen, from abridging any of her privileges and immunities as a citizen of the United States, but it did not confer citizenship on her; that she had before its adoption.

If the right of suffrage is one of the necessary privileges of a citizen of the United States, then the Constitution and laws of Missouri confining it to men are in violation of the Constitution of the United States as amended, and consequently void. The direct question is, therefore, presented whether all citizens are necessarily voters (p. 170, Wallace).

The Constitution does not define the privileges and immunities of citizens. For that definition we must look elsewhere. In this case we need not determine what they are, but only whether suffrage is necessarily one of them.

It certainly is nowhere made so in express terms. The United States has no voters in the States of its own creation. The elective officers of the United States are all elected directly or indirectly by State voters. The members of the House of Representatives are to be chosen by the people of the States, and the electors in each State must have the qualifications requisite for electors of the most numerous branch of the State Legislature (art. 1, sec. 2, Const.) Senators are to be chosen by the Legislatures of the States, and, necessarily, the members of the Legislature required to make the choice are elected by the voters of the State (art. 1, sec. 3). Each State must appoint, in such manner as the Legislature thereof may direct, the electors to elect the President and Vice-President (art. 2, sec. 2). The times, places, and manner of holding elections for Senators and Representatives are to be prescribed in each State by the Legislature thereof; but Congress may at any time by law make or alter such regulations, except as to the place of choosing Senators (art. 1, sec. 4). It is not necessary to inquire whether this power of supervision thus given to Congress is sufficient to authorize any interference with the State laws prescribing the qualifications of

voters, for no such interference has ever been attempted. The power of the State in this particular is certainly supreme until Congress acts.

The Amendment did not add to the privileges and immunities of a citizen. It simply furnished an additional guaranty for the protection of such as he already had. No new voters were necessarily made by it. Indirectly it may have had that effect, because it may have increased the number of citizens entitled to suffrage under the Constitution and laws of the States, but it operates for this purpose, if at all, through the States and the State laws, and not directly upon the citizen.

It is clear, therefore, we think, that the Constitution has not added the right of suffrage to the privileges and immunities of citizenship as they existed at the time it was adopted. This makes it proper to inquire whether suffrage was co-extensive with the citizenship of the States at the time of its adoption. If it was, then it may with force be argued that suffrage was one of the rights which belonged to citizenship, and in the enjoyment of which every citizen must be protected. But if it was not, the contrary may with propriety be assumed.

When the Constitution of the United States was adopted, all the several States, with the exception of Rhode Island, had constitutions of their own. Rhode Island continued to act under its charter from the Crown. Upon an examination of those constitutions, we find that in no State were all citizens permitted to vote. Each State determined for itself who should have that power.

Thus, in New Hampshire, "every male inhabitant of each town and parish, with town privileges and places unincorporated in the State, of twenty-one years of age and upwards, excepting paupers and persons excused from paying taxes at their own request," were its voters; in Massachusetts, "every male inhabitant of twenty-one years of age and upwards, having a freehold estate within the Commonwealth of the annual income of three pounds, or any estate of the value of sixty pounds"; in Rhode Island, "such as are admitted free of the company and society" of the colony; in Connecticut, such persons as had "maturity in years, quiet and peaceful behavior, a civil conversation, and forty shillings freehold or forty pounds personal estate," if so certified by the selectmen; in New York, "every male inhabitant of full age, who shall have personally resided within one of the counties of the State for six months immediately preceding the day of election . . . if during the time aforesaid he shall have been a freeholder, possessing a freehold of the value of twenty pounds within the country, or have rented a tenement therein of the yearly value of forty shillings, and been rated and actually paid taxes to the State"; in New Jersey, all inhabitants . . . "of full age, who are worth fifty pounds proclamation money, clear estate in the same, and have resided in the county in which they claim a vote for twelve months immediately preceding the election"; in Pennsylvania, "every freeman at the age of twenty-one years, having resided in the State two years next before the election, and within that time paid a State or county tax which shall have been assessed at least six months before the election"; in Delaware and Virginia, "as exercised by law at present"; in Maryland, "all freeman above twenty-one years of age, having a freehold of fifty acres of land in the county in which they offer to vote and residing therein, and all freeman having property in the State above the value of thirty pounds current money, and having resided in the county in which they offer to vote one whole year next preceding the election"; in North Carolina, for Senators, "all freemen of the age of twenty-one years, who have been inhabitants of any one county within the State twelve months immediately preceding the day of election, and possessed of a freehold within the same county of fifty acres of land for six months next before and at the day of election," and for members of the House of Commons, "all freemen of the age of twenty-one years, who have been inhabitants in any one county within the State twelve months immediately preceding the day of any election, and shall have paid public taxes"; in South Carolina, "every free white man of the age of twenty-one years, being a citizen of the State, and having resided therein two years previous to the day of election, and who hath a freehold of fifty acres of land, or a town lot of which he hath been legally seized and possessed at least six months before such election, or (not having such freehold or town lot), hath been a resident within the election district in which he offers to give his vote six months before said election, and hath paid a tax the preceding year of three shillings sterling toward the support of the Government"; and, in Georgia, such "citizens and inhabitants of the State as shall have attained to the age of twenty-one years, and shall have paid tax

for the year next preceding the election, and shall have resided six months within the county."

In this condition of the law in respect to suffrage in the several States, it can not for a moment be doubted that, if it had been intended to make all citizens of the United States voters, the framers of the Constitution would not have left it to implication. So important a change in the condition of citizenship as it actually existed, if intended, would have been expressly declared.

But if further proof is necessary to show that no such change was intended, it can easily be found both in and out of the Constitution. By article 4, section 2, it is provided that "the citizens of each State shall be entitled to all the privileges and immunities of citizens in the several States." If suffrage is necessarily a part of citizenship, then the citizens of each State must be entitled to vote in the several States precisely as their citizens are. This is more than asserting that they may change their residence and become citizens of the State and thus be voters. It goes to the extent of insisting that, while retaining their original citizenship, they may vote in any State. This, we think, has never been claimed. And again, by the very terms of the Amendment we have been considering (the XIV).

"Representatives shall be apportioned among the several States according to their respective numbers, counting the whole number of persons in each State, excluding Indians not taxed. But when the right to vote at any election for the choice of electors for President and Vice-President of the United States, Representatives in Congress, the Executive and Judicial officers of a State, or the Members of the Legislature thereof, is denied to any of the male inhabitants of such State, being twenty-one years of age and citizens of the United States, or in any way abridged, except for participation in the Rebellion or other crimes, the basis of representation therein shall be reduced in the proportion which the number of such male citizens shall bear to the whole number of male citizens twenty-one years of age in such State."

Why this, if it was not in the power of the Legislature to deny the right of suffrage to some male inhabitants? And if suffrage was necessarily one of the absolute rights of citizenship, why confine the operation of the limitation to male inhabitants? Women and children are, as we have seen, "persons." They are counted in the enumeration upon which the apportionment is to be made; but if they were necessarily voters because of their citizenship unless clearly excluded, why inflict the penalty for the exclusion of males alone? Clearly, no such form of words would have been selected to express the idea here indicated if suffrage was the absolute right of all citizens.

And still again, after the adoption of the XIV. Amendment, it was deemed necessary to adopt a XV., as follows: "The right of citizens of the United States to vote shall not be denied or abridged by the United States, or by any State, on account of race, color, or previous condition of servitude." The XIV. Amendment had already provided that no State should make or enforce any law which should abridge the privileges or immunities of citizens of the United States. If suffrage was one of these privileges or immunities, why amend the Constitution to prevent its being denied on account of race, etc.? Nothing is more evident than that the greater must include the less; and if all were already protected, why go through with the form of amending the Constitution to protect a part?

It is true that the United States guarantees to every State a republican form of government (art. 4, sec. 4). It is also true that no State can pass a bill of attainder (art. 1, section 10), and that no person can be deprived of life, liberty, or property, without due process of law (Amendment V). All these several provisions of the Constitution must be construed in connection with the other parts of the instrument, and in the light of the surrounding circumstances.

The guaranty is of a republican form of government. No particular government is designated as republican, neither is the exact form to be guaranteed, in any manner especially designated. Here, as in other parts of the instrument, we are compelled to resort elsewhere to ascertain what was intended. The guaranty necessarily implies a duty on the part of the States themselves to provide such a government. All the States had governments when the Constitution was adopted. In all, the people participated to some extent through their representatives elected in the manner specially provided. These governments the Constitution did not change. They were accepted precisely as they were, and it is therefore to be presumed that they were such as it was the duty of the States to provide. Thus, we have ummistakable evidence of what was republican in form, within the meaning of that term as employed in the Constitution. As has

been seen, all the citizens of the States were not invested with the right of suffrage. In all, save perhaps New Jersey, this right was only bestowed upon men, and not upon all of them. Under these circumstances, it is certainly now too late to contend that a Government is not republican within the meaning of this guaranty in the Constitution because women are not made voters.

The same may be said of the other provisions just quoted. Women were excluded from suffrage in nearly all the States by the express provision of their constitutions and laws. If that had been equivalent to a bill of attainder, certainly its abrogation would not have been left to implication. Nothing less than express language would have been employed to effect so radical a change. So also of the Amendment which declares that no person shall be deprived of life, liberty, or property, without due process of law; adopted as it was as early as 1791. If suffrage was intended to be included within its obligations, language better adapted to express that intent would most certainly have been employed. The right of suffrage, when granted, will be protected. He who has it can only be deprived of it by due process of law; but, in order to claim protection, he must first show that he has the right. But we have already sufficiently considered the proof found upon the inside of the Constitution. That upon the outside is equally effective.

The Constitution was submitted to the States for Adoption in 1787, and was ratified by nine States in 1788, and, finally, by the thirteen original States in 1790. Vermont was the first new State admitted to the Union, and it came in under a Constitution which conferred the right of suffrage only upon men of the full age of twenty-one years having resided in the State for the space of one whole year next before the election, and who were of quiet and peaceable behavior. This was in 1791. The next year (1792) Kentucky followed, with a Constitution confining the right of suffrage to free male citizens of the age of twenty-one years, who had resided in the State two years, or, in the county in which they offered to vote, one year next before the election. Then followed Tennessee in 1796, with voters of freemen of the age of twenty-one years and upward, possessing a freehold in the county wherein they may vote, and being inhabitants of the State or freemen being inhabitants of any one county in the State six months immediately preceding the day of election. But we need not particularize further. No new State has ever been admitted to the Union which has conferred the right of suffrage upon women, and this has never been considered a valid objection to her admission. On the contrary, as is claimed in the argument, the right of suffrage was withdrawn from women as early as 1807 in the State of New Jersey, with out any attempt to obtain the interference of the United States to prevent it. Since then the governments of the insurgent States have been reorganized under a requirement that, before their Representatives could be admitted to seats in Congress, they must have adopted new Constitutions, republican in form. In no one of these Constitutions was suffrage conferred upon women, and yet the States have all been restored to their original position as States in the Union.

Besides this, citizenship has not in all cases been made a condition precedent to the enjoyment of the right of suffrage. Thus, in Missouri, persons of foreign birth, who have declared their intention to become citizens of the United States, may under certain circumstances vote. The same provision is to be found in the Constitutions of Alabama, Arkansas, Florida, Georgia, Indiana, Kansas, Minnesota, and Texas. Certainly if the courts can consider any question settled, this is one. For near ninety years the people have acted upon the idea that the Constitution, when it conferred citizenship, did not necessarily confer the right of suffrage. If uniform practice long continued can settle the construction of so important an instrument as the Constitution of the United States confessedly is, most certainly it has been done here. Our province is to decide what the law is, not to declare what it should be.

We have given this case the careful consideration its importance demands. If the law is wrong it ought to be changed, but the power for that is not with us. The arguments addressed to us bearing upon such a view of the subject may perhaps be sufficient to induce those having the power to make the alteration, but they ought not to be permitted to influence our judgment in determining the present rights of the parties now litigating before us. No argument as to woman's need of suffrage can be considered. We can only act upon her rights as they exist. It is not for us to look at the hardship of withholding. Our duty is at an end, if we find it is within the power of a State to withhold.

Being unanimously of the opinion that the Constitution of the United States does not confer the right of suffrage upon any one, and that the Constitutions and laws of the several States which commit that important trust to men alone are not necessarily void, we affirm the judgment of the court below.

33. Declaration of Rights for Women, July 4, 1876

While the nation is buoyant with patriotism, and all hearts are attuned to praise, it is with sorrow we come to strike the one discordant note, on this one-hundredth anniversary of our country's birth. When subjects of kings, emperors, and czars, from the old world join in our national jubilee, shall the women of the republic refuse to lay their hands with benedictions on the nation's head? Surveying America's exposition, surpassing in magnificence those of London, Paris, and Vienna, shall we not rejoice at the success of the youngest rival among the nations of the earth? May not our hearts, in unison with all, swell with pride at our great achievements as a people; our free speech, free press, free schools, free church, and the rapid progress we have made in material wealth, trade, commerce and the inventive arts? And we do rejoice in the success, thus far, of our experiment of self-government. Our faith is firm and unwavering in the broad principles of human rights proclaimed in 1776, not only as abstract truths, but as the corner stones of a republic. Yet we cannot forget, even in this glad hour, that while all men of every race, and clime, and condition, have been invested with the full rights of citizenship under our hospitable flag, all women still suffer the degradation of disfranchisement.

The history of our country the past hundred years has been a series of assumptions and usurpations of power over woman, in direct opposition to the principles of just government, acknowledged by the United States as its foundation, which are:

First—The natural rights of each individual.

Second—The equality of these rights.

Third—That rights not delegated are retained by the individual.

Fourth—That no person can exercise the rights of others without delegated authority.

Fifth—That the non-use of rights does not destroy them.

And for the violation of these fundamental principles of our government, we arraign our rulers on this Fourth day of July, 1876,—and these are our articles of impeachment:

Bills of attainder have been passed by the introduction of the word "male" into all the State constitutions, denying to women the right of suffrage, and thereby making sex a crime—an exercise of power clearly forbidden in article 1, sections 9, 10, of the United States constitution.

The writ of habeas corpus, the only protection against *lettres de cachet* and all forms of unjust imprisonment, which the constitution declares "shall not be suspended, except when in cases of rebellion or invasion the public safety demands it," is held inoperative in every State of the Union, in case of a married woman against her husband—the marital rights of the husband being in all cases primary, and the rights of the wife secondary.

The right of trial by a jury of one's peers was so jealously guarded that States refused to ratify the original constitution until it was guaranteed by the sixth amendment. And yet the women of this nation have never been allowed a jury of their peers—being tried in all cases by men, native and foreign, educated and ignorant, virtuous and vicious. Young girls have been arraigned in our courts for the crime of infanticide; tried, convicted, hanged—victims, perchance, of judge, jurors, advocates—while no woman's voice could be heard in their defense. And not only are women denied a jury of their peers, but in some cases, jury trial altogether. During the war, a woman was tried and hanged by military law, in defiance of the fifth amendment, which specifically declares: "No person shall be held to answer for a capital or otherwise infamous crime, unless on a presentment or indictment of a grand jury, except in cases . . . of persons in actual service in time of war." During the last presidential campaign, a woman, arrested for voting, was denied the protection of a jury, tried, convicted, and sentenced to a fine and costs of prosecution, by the absolute power of a judge of the Supreme Court of the United States.

Taxation without representation, the immediate cause of the rebellion of the colonies against Great Britain, is one of the grievous wrongs the women of this country have suffered during the century. Deploring war, with all the demoralization that follows in its train, we have been taxed to support standing armies, with their waste of life and wealth. Believing in temperance, we have been taxed to support the vice, crime and pauperism of the liquor traffic. While we suffer its wrongs and abuses infinitely more than man, we have no power to protect our sons against this giant evil. During the temperance crusade, mothers were arrested, fined, imprisoned, for even praying and singing in the streets, while men blockade the sidewalks with impunity, even on Sunday, with their military parades and political processions. Believing in honesty, we are taxed to support a dangerous army of civilians, buying and selling the offices of government and sacrificing the best interests of the people. And, moreover, we are taxed to support the very legislators and judges who make laws, and render decisions adverse to woman. And for refusing to pay such unjust taxation, the houses, lands, bonds, and stock of women have been seized and sold within the present year, thus proving Lord Coke's assertion, that "The very act of taxing a man's property without his consent is, in effect, disfranchising him of every civil right."

Unequal codes for men and women. Held by law a perpetual minor, deemed incapable of self-protection, even in the industries of the world, woman is denied equality of rights. The fact of sex, not the quantity or quality of work, in most cases, decides the pay and position; and because of this injustice thousands of fatherless girls are compelled to choose between a life of shame and starvation. Laws catering to man's vices have created two codes of morals in which penalties are graded according to the political status of the offender. Under such laws, women are fined and imprisoned if found alone in the streets, or in public places of resort, at certain hours. Under the pretense of regulating public morals, police officers seizing the occupants of disreputable houses, march the women in platoons to prison, while the men, partners in their guilt, go free. While making a show of virtue in forbidding the importation of Chinese women on the Pacific coast for immoral purposes, our rulers, in many States, and even under the shadow of the national capitol, are now proposing to legalize the sale of American womanhood for the same vile purposes.

Special legislation for woman has placed us in a most anomalous position. Women invested with the rights of citizens in one section—voters, jurors, office-holders—crossing an imaginary line, are subjects in the next. In some States, a married woman may hold property and transact business in her own name; in others, her earnings belong to her husband. In some States, a woman may testify against her husband, sue and be sued in the courts; in others, she has no redress in case of damage to person, property, or character. In case of divorce on account of adultery in the husband, the innocent wife is held to possess no right to children or property, unless by special decree of the court. But in no State of the Union has the wife the right to her own person, or to any part of the joint earnings of the co-partnership during the life of her husband. In some States women may enter the law schools and practice in the courts; in others they are forbidden. In some universities girls enjoy equal educational advantages with boys, while many of the proudest institutions in the land deny them admittance, though the sons of China, Japan and Africa are welcomed there. But the privileges already granted in the several States are by no means secure. The right of suffrage once exercised by women in certain States and territories has been denied by subsequent legislation. A bill is now pending in congress to disfranchise the women of Utah, thus interfering to deprive United States citizens of the same rights which the Supreme Court has declared the national government powerless to protect anywhere. Laws passed after years of untiring effort, guaranteeing married women certain rights of property, and mothers the custody of their children, have been repealed in States where we supposed all was safe. Thus have our most sacred rights been made the football of legislative caprice, proving that a power which grants as a privilege what by nature is a right, may withhold the same as a penalty when deeming it necessary for its own perpetuation.

Representation of woman has had no place in the nation's thought. Since the incorporation of the thirteen original States, twenty-four have been admitted to the Union, not one of which has recognized woman's right of self-government. On this birthday of our national liberties, July Fourth, 1876, Colorado, like all her elder sisters, comes into the Union with the invidious word "male" in her constitution.

Universal manhood suffrage, by establishing an aristocracy of sex, imposes upon the women of this nation a more absolute and cruel depotism than monarchy; in that, woman finds a political master in her father, husband, brother, son. The aristocracies of the old world are based upon birth, wealth, refinement, education, nobility, brave deeds of chivalry; in this nation, on sex alone; exalting brute force above moral power, vice above virtue, ignorance above education, and the son above the mother who bore him.

The judiciary above the nation has proved itself out the echo of the party in power, by upholding and enforcing laws that are opposed to the spirit and letter of the constitution. When the slave power was dominant, the Supreme Court decided that a black man was not a citizen, because he had not the right to vote; and when the constitution was so amended as to make all persons citizens, the same high tribunal decided that a woman, though a citizen, had not the right to vote. Such vacillating interpretations of constitutional law unsettle our faith in judicial authority, and undermine the liberties of the whole people.

These articles of impeachment against our rulers we now submit to the impartial judgment of the people. To all these wrongs and oppressions woman has not submitted in silence and resignation. From the beginning of the century, when Abigail Adams, the wife of one president and mother of another, said, "We will not hold ourselves bound to obey laws in which we have no voice or representation," until now, woman's discontent has been steadily increasing, culminating nearly thirty years ago in a simultaneous movement among the women of the nation, demanding the right of suffrage. In making our just demands, a higher motive than the pride of sex inspires us; we feel that national safety and stability depend on the complete recognition of the broad principles of our government. Woman's degraded, helpless position is the weak point in our institutions to-day; a disturbing force everywhere, severing family ties, filling our asylums with the deaf, the dumb, the blind; our prisons with criminals, our cities with drunkenness and prostitution; our homes with disease and death. It was the boast of the founders of the republic, that the rights for which they contended were the rights of human nature. If these rights are ignored in the case of one-half the people, the nation is surely preparing for its downfall. Governments try themselves. The recognition of a governing and a governed class is incompatible with the first principles of freedom. Woman has not been a heedless spectator of the events of this century, nor a dull listener to the grand arguments for the equal rights of humanity. From the earliest history of our country woman has shown equal devotion with man to the cause of freedom, and has stood firmly by his side in its defense. Together, they have made this country what it is. Woman's wealth, thought and labor have cemented the stones of every monument man has reared to liberty.

And now, at the close of a hundred years, as the hour-hand of the great clock that marks the centuries points to 1876, we declare our faith in the principles of self-government; our full equality with man in natural rights; that woman was made first for her own happiness, with the absolute right to herself—to all the opportunities and advantages life affords for her complete development; and we deny that dogma of the centuries, incorporated in the codes of all nations—that woman was made for man—her best interests, in all cases, to be sacrificed to his will. We ask of our rulers, at this hour, no special favors, no special privileges, no special legislation. We ask justice, we ask equality, we ask that all the civil and political rights that belong to citizens of the United States, be guaranteed to us and our daughters forever.

[Signed by] Lucretia Mott, Elizabeth Cady Stanton, Paulina Wright Davis, Ernestine L. Rose, Clarina I. H. Nichols, Mary Ann McClintock, Mathilde Franceske Anneke, Sarah Pugh, Amy Post, Catharine A. F. Stebbins, Susan B. Anthony, Matilda Joslyn Gage, Clemence S. Lozier, Olympia Brown, Mathilde F. Wendt, Adeline Thomson, Ellen Clark Sargent, Virginia L. Minor, Catherine V. Waite, Elizabeth B. Schenck, Phoebe W. Couzins, Elizabeth Boynton Harbert, Laura DeForce Gordon, Sara Andrews Spencer, Lillie Devereux Blake, Jane Graham Jones, Abigail Scott Duniway, Belva A. Lockwood, Isabella Beecher Hooker, Sarah L. Williams, Abby P. Ela.

34. JOINT RESOLUTION PROPOSING AN AMENDMENT TO THE CONSTITUTION OF THE UNITED STATES, JANUARY 10, 1878

Resolved by the Senate and House of Representatives of the United States of America in congress assembled, two-thirds of each House concurring therein. That the following article be proposed to the legislatures of the several States as an amendment to the Constitution of the United States, which, when rati-

fied by three-fourths of the said legislatures, shall be valid as part of the said constitution, namely:

Article 16, Sec. 1.—The right of citizens of the United States to vote shall not be denied or abridged by the United States or by any State on account of sex.

Sec. 2.—Congress shall have power to enforce this article by appropriate legislation.

35. NEGATIVE REPORT OF THE COMMITTEE ON PRIVILEGES AND ELECTIONS REGARDING THE PROPOSED AMENDMENT, JUNE 14, 1878

The Committee on Privileges and Elections, to whom was referred the Resolution (S.Res.12) proposing an Amendment to the Constitution of the United States, and certain Petitions for and Remonstrances against the same, make the following Report:

This proposed amendment forbids the United States, or any State to deny or abridge the right to vote on account of sex. If adopted, it will make several millions of female voters, totally inexperienced in political affairs, quite generally dependent upon the other sex, all incapable of performing military duty and without the power to enforce the laws which their numerical strength may enable them to make, and comparatively very few of whom wish to assume the irksome and responsible political duties which this measure thrusts upon them. An experiment so novel, a change so great, should only be made slowly and in response to a general public demand, of the existence of which there is no evidence before your committee.

Petitions from various parts of the country, containing by estimate about 30,000 names, have been presented to congress asking for this legislation. They were procured through the efforts of woman suffrage societies, thoroughly organized, with active and zealous managers. The ease with which signatures may be procured to any petition is well known. The small number of petitioners, when compared with that of the intelligent women in the country, is striking evidence that there exists among them no general desire to take up the heavy burden of governing, which so many men seek to evade. It would be unjust, unwise and impolitic to impose that burden on the great mass of women throughout the country who do not wish for it, to gratify the comparatively few who do.

It has been strongly urged that without the right of suffrage, women are, and will be, subjected to great oppression and injustice.

But every one who has examined the subject at all knows that, without female suffrage, legislation for years has improved and is still improving the condition of woman. The disabilities imposed upon her by the common law have, one by one, been swept away, until in most of the States she has the full right to her property and all, or nearly all, the rights which can be granted without impairing or destroying the marriage relation. These changes have been wrought by the spirit of the age, and are not, generally at least, the result of any agitation by women in their own behalf.

Nor can women justly complain of any partiality in the administration of justice. They have the sympathy of judges and particularly of juries to an extent which would warrant loud complaint on the part of their adversaries of the sterner sex. Their appeals to legislatures against injustice are never unheeded, and there is no doubt that when any considerable part of the women of any State really wish for the right to vote, it will be granted without the intervention of congress.

Any State may grant the right of suffrage to women. Some of them have done so to a limited extent, and perhaps with good results. It is evident that in some States public opinion is much more strongly in favor of it than it is in others. Your committee regard it as unwise and inexpedient to enable three-fourths in number of the States, through an amendment to the national constitution, to force woman suffrage upon the other fourth in which the public opinion of both sexes may be strongly adverse to such a change.

For these reasons, your committee report back said resolution with a recommendation that it be indefinitely postponed.

36. CONSTITUTION OF THE NATIONAL AMERICAN WOMAN SUFFRAGE ASSOCIATION, 1890

This is the most democratic of organizations. Its sole object is to secure for women citizens protection in their right to vote. The general officers are nominated by an informal secret ballot, no one being put in nomination. The three persons receiving the highest number of votes are considered the nominees and the election is decided by secret ballot. Those entitled to vote are three delegates-at-large for each auxiliary State society and one delegate in addition for every one hundred members of each State auxiliary; the State presidents and State members of the National Executive Committee; the general officers of the association; the chairmen of standing committees. The delegates present from each State cast the full vote to which that State is entitled. The vote is taken in the same way upon any other question whenever the delegates present from five States request it. In other cases each delegate has one vote. Any State whose dues are unpaid on January 1 looses its vote in the convention for that year.

The two honorary presidents, president, vice-president-at-large, two secretaries, treasurer and two auditors constitute the Business Committee, which transacts the entire business of the association between the annual conventions.

The Executive Committee is composed of the Business Committee, the president of each State, and one member from each State, together with the chairmen of standing committees; fifteen make a quorum for the transaction of business. The decisions reached by the Executive Committee, which meets during the convention week, are presented in the form of recommendations at the business sessions of the convention.

The constitution may be amended by a two-thirds vote at any annual meeting, after one day's notice in the convention, notice of the proposed amendment having been previously given to the Business Committee, and by them published in the suffrage papers not less than three months in advance.

The association must hold an annual convention of regularly-elected delegates for the election of officers and the transaction of business. An annual meeting must be held in Washington, D.C., during the first session of each Congress.

The Committee on Resolutions must consist of one person from each State, elected by its delegation.

There are few changes in officers and the association is noted for the harmony of its meetings, although the delegates generally are of decided convictions and unusual force of character. Men are eligible to membership and a number belong, but the affairs of the organization are wholly in the hands of women.

Auxiliary State and Territorial associations exist in all but Wyoming, Idaho, Utah, Arkansas, Nevada and

Texas. Suffrage associations are not needed in the first three, as the women have the full franchise.

37. "THE WINNING POLICY," BY CARRIE CHAPMAN CATT, 1916

The following letter by Mrs. Catt was written in answer to an inquiry and is printed for the information of those who desire it.

Your letter requesting information as to

1. Why the Congressional Union came into existence
2. Why it advanced a policy contrary to that of the National American Woman Suffrage Association, and
3. What the differences are,

has been read with care. Your letter is one of many which have put similar questions. I will answer those questions as clearly as I am able.

1. In the year 1912 Arizona, Kansas and Oregon were won for suffrage, making a total of 12 suffrage states and in consequence a decided impetus was given to the Federal Suffrage Amendment which the National American Woman Suffrage Association had introduced long before and had always loyally supported. Miss Paul and Miss Burns whose zeal had been fired by work with the English Militants in Great Britain asked to be placed in charge of the congressional work in Washington and Miss Paul was made Chairman of the Congressional Committee of the National American Woman Suffrage Association and Miss Burns her chief assistant. While officially connected with the National Association they organized the Congressional Union after the plan of Mrs. Pankhurst's organization in Great Britain, the Women's Social and Political Union.

During the year they did much excellent work for which full and appreciative credit has been fully given them, but a break with the National occurred, because they refused to accede to certain established rules of the Association. One of these rules was that no National officer should enter any state to carry on National work without first consulting the State officers, nor should any work be done in a manner which conflicted with the policy of the state. This rule was frequently violated. Another rule was that every committee should render an itemized account of all receipts and disbursements to the National Board. This was never done, and when, at the Convention of 1913, Miss Paul was asked

why no such report had been rendered, she declared that it was impossible to separate the accounts of the Congressional Committee from those of the Congressional Union.

Since the funds received had been solicited from the National members and contributors and had usually been solicited on the National stationery in behalf of the Congressional Committee of the National American Woman Suffrage Association, this explanation was impossible of acceptance.

The National Board therefore decided that it was inadvisable to reappoint Miss Paul as Chairman of the Congressional Committee unless she resigned as Chairman of the Congressional Union. The constant confusion of the Committee of the National American Woman Suffrage Association with the Congressional Union, an organized society, made any other action impossible; but Miss Paul refused to accept these terms.

Subsequently, a financial report was rendered and included in the minutes of the National Association, although the separation of funds was not complete or satisfactory.

The Congressional Committee of the National American Woman Suffrage Association is a standing Committee and the work went on with renewed energy under the able chairmanship of Mrs. Medill McCormick. The Congressional Union also continued to work with Congress as an independent body, thus making two committees in Washington working for the same thing.

I was not a member of the National Board at the time of the break but I believe the above to be a correct statement of facts as to why the Congressional Union exists. In the action it took, the National Board was either right or wrong. If the National Board were right, its action should be upheld by every suffragist in the land; if it were wrong, there was still no need of secession since the democratic constitution of the National American Woman Suffrage Association provides for annual elections and any policy can be changed by a majority vote of the delegates at the annual meeting.

2. The Congressional Union soon announced that the only way to secure the submission of the Federal Amendment was to hold the "party in power responsible." This was Mrs. Pankhurst's policy. The National Association in various conferences afterwards discussed this policy and rejected it for two reasons:

a. It is contrary to the long established and tried policy of non-partisanship which neither endorses nor opposes a political party as such, holding men—not parties, responsible and

b. Because the same policy in Great Britain, after some years of trial, gave no promise of success but instead had produced acrimonious divisions among suffragists and antagonized many members of Parliament to the injury of the cause.

Upon the supposition that the Congressional Union is conscientiously wedded to its conviction that the anti-party policy is the only way and that the National American Woman Suffrage Association will continue to adhere to its non-partisan view, it is obvious that the division will continue. More, however tragic a division in our ranks may be, it is equally apparent that the line of separation of these opposing groups must be made definite and a clear statement of the reasons why rendered to the suffragists of the country.

3. The differences between these opposing policies and the reason why the National policy seems to many of us wiser, are as follows:

The constitution of the National American Woman Suffrage Association pledges the organization to "secure suffrage for women by appropriate national and state legislation." National legislation that always meant the Federal Suffrage Amendment which has been consistently supported for many years. State legislation has always meant suffrage within the state, statutory or referendum. The Congressional Union opposes state campaigns and would concentrate on the Federal Amendment exclusively, expecting the "party in power" to put it through. The National looks to both parties for support of the Federal Amendment and to intensive organization and vigorous activity within the states, to secure the ratification of the Federal Amendment; and the National would also secure the vote by suffrage referenda whenever possible.

The above is a fundamental difference based upon the constitution and history of the National American Woman Suffrage Association.

The following comments upon the fallacies of an anti-party policy and the wisdom of the established non-partisan policy are my own.

In this country, no party is ever in power in the sense that a party is "the government" in Great Britain. A party may control the National administration and Congress as the Democrats do now but the Republicans control many legislatures to which an appeal for the ratification of a Federal Amendment must be made. A policy which drives one party into an attitude of hostility toward the Federal Amendment, threatens to become a boomerang which will defeat the very purpose it has been invoked to serve.

Opposition to a party, as such, very naturally arouses resentment in that party since it is the character of humans to be persuaded and not forced. Unless the opposition is sufficiently powerful to make it clear that the party, to save its life, must adopt the idea in controversy, the party is set more firmly against the idea instead of being won to it. This is a psychological axiom so simple and universal as to need no amplification.

The Congressional Union, of course, hope to drive the Democrats, (now the party in control) to the point of believing that they must put the Federal Suffrage Amendment through or pay the penalty of loss of national power. In 1914, their representatives undertook to accomplish this end in the suffrage states where they hoped to mass the women voters against Democratic congressional candidates.

The theory had attractions to superficial observers and Republican suffragists of both sexes found the charge that Democrats had blocked the progress of suffrage, very seductive—just as Democratic suffragists, later on, may find the charge seductive that Republicans have delayed Federal Suffrage. So appealing was this phase that Republicans in several states gave "aid and comfort" to the Congressional Union workers and thus the plan seemed to succeed.

But what was the result? In the year 1913–14, the suffrage states sent 18 Democrats to Congress; in the year 1915–16 (when the Congressional Union campaigned against Democratic candidates) they sent 19 thus gaining one Democratic member despite the fact that it was said to be a Republican year. In Oregon, Senator Chamberlain, a long time consistent friend of suffrage, was the only Democrat elected on the National ticket. The women say they believed it to be more ethical to reward the man who had loyally stood by them in their state struggle than to punish him for what men from other states had failed to do. In Colorado, the Congressional Union campaigned against Senator Thomas. He had never failed the women, so the Colorado women took the same attitude as those of Oregon and rallied to his support. He was re-elected.

The Republican women voted against the Democratic candidates (as they would have done anyway) but apparently Democratic women did not desert their own candidates who had in their individual capacity been loyal to the suffrage cause. As one woman voter said: "We believe that it will be a poor inducement to men in the East to support suffrage, if they learn that men in the West who have done so were immediately turned down by women voters because other men in other states had been less progressive."

From the 12 suffrage states, no votes were gained for the Federal Amendment by the anti-party campaign but one will be lost. How did the campaign affect the vote from other states?

Southern Democrats who voted for the amendment in 1915 now declared that they will do so no more on account of suffrage opposition to their party. The hostility aroused is rapidly crystallizing the Democratic opposition to Federal action which did not exist before. It is clear that the Democrats have not been won to the Federal Amendment by a policy of threat and if returned at the coming election will support it in reduced numbers or perchance go against it as a party. If this condition should result, the Federal Amendment is blocked until another election. If further opposition to the Democrats should be shown, it would tend to strengthen their attitude of hostility rather than weaken it and, in consequence (so long as the Democrats remain in power), the amendment would be blocked.

Let us suppose that the Republicans are returned at the coming elections and that, to avoid suffrage opposition in their campaigns, they determine to put the Federal Amendment through as a party measure. *No party has controlled a two-thirds vote of Congress* since the days of the Reconstruction and the passage of the amendment requires that majority.

The difference between the majority which the Republicans could command and the two-thirds required must be solicited from Democrats. Would they give the necessary votes? Since the Republicans would get the chief credit and the probable reward of increased party loyalty among women voters, it would be the unusual man who would give his vote under the circumstances. It is quite possible that, under these conditions, the Democrats out of power would as effectually block the amendment as when in power.

Again, let us imagine that a sufficient number of Democrats would rise above their partnership to the exalted heights of being willing to serve a cause for its sake alone and that they would give the needed number of votes to make up the two-thirds majority. The amendment would then go to the legislature of the 48 states. It must be ratified by three-fourths of the states—that is 36. Leaving out the 12 Southern States, most solidly Democratic, every other state must be carried. Among them there will surely be Democratic legislatures. There the amendment would be blocked. One stubborn Democratic state might prevent the final ratification or a half-dozen stubborn legislators might postpone the final adoption for a generation.

It is claimed that, as the amendment would remain pending until the necessary three-fourths of the legislatures have been won, this need not matter since a concentrated effort could be made upon the r[e]calcitrant states. That sounds well but those of us who have seen a single man hold up a legislature do not feel so optimistic.

Why take all these risks? Why postpone the final victory? Men of both the dominant parties have given our cause splendid support. Even the submission of a state constitutional amendment to the voters has never passed a legislature by a party vote. It has always passed as a nonpartisan measure receiving the support of men of both parties. No amendment has been won at the polls without the support of both parties. Our cause has grown strong and popular with the passing years and the sacrificing devotion of many women, yet there remains a hard struggle ahead. The nonpartisan way is assuredly the line of least resistance; the safe, tried, sane way. All the suffrage won for women anywhere in the world was won by this method. Why not appeal to both parties not only for votes in Congress but for ratification in the legislatures afterwards.

The Congressional Union say theirs is the quick way. To my mind that plan for this country is "false in theory and pernicious in practice." The misfortunes which are not only possible but probable are these:
1. A division of workers aiming at the same object always spells inefficiency.
2. A division of funds always signifies lack of economy in expenditure.
3. A division of workers and funds lends to inevitable unrest, misunderstanding and acrimony which drives some workers out of the ranks and among those who remain diminishes the solidarity

and exalted spirit which puts "punch" into a movement.

4. A division of the forces within each state which must follow will reduce the efficiency of present state organizations and will prevent the further organization of the states to the point of thoroughness which will guarantee the ratification of the Federal Amendment when submitted.

5. The alienation of voters in state suffrage elections who belong to the party attacked. Although none of the results aimed at were attained in the anti-Democratic campaign in the West, the news reached Eastern campaign states and many a Democrat in New York (where I know conditions best) gave as his excuse for voting "no" that Western suffragists were being urged to vote against his party. To be sure, there was no logic in the excuse but had voters been guided by reason women would have been enfranchised long ago.

6. The anti-party policy is a threat, an effort at coercion; if the first step fails of effect the next must be taken "to save one's face" as the Chinese say, and if that fails, still another. This was the process which led the anti-party policy of Great Britain to the advanced stages of militancy which, when the war broke out, had so far discredited the cause in that country that there was no hope of favorable action by Parliament. The signs point to the development of that state of mind in this country quite as clearly as the same signs in England indicated it six years ago. That some women are working with the Congressional Union for the express purpose of developing such a movement in the United States, I know.

Among the Republicans in Congress there has been frequent and severe condemnation of the anti-party policy as being un-American. These men frankly point to our recent defeats as men's inevitable reaction against what they term the "degrading policy of the threat." They state that in their own affairs, men who threaten opponents no longer have weight; that that method was a part of the undesirable developments of politics among the lower class of politicians; that today intelligent men win campaigns by presenting facts and appealing to reason, not to fear and cowardice. Both Republicans and Democrats characterize the anti-party propaganda as a reversion to the basest form of politics and deplore the fact that any

women indulge in it. It causes them to question the sincerity and integrity of the suffragists.

7. Woman suffragists in the enfranchised states are trying to demonstrate women's capacity for good citizenship in such manner that their good works will redound to the credit of the entire sex and thus tend, still further, to break down the unreasoning prejudice which prevents the enfranchisement of women throughout the entire country. To attempt to mobilize women voters against a political party because of its failure to do the right thing in Washington is to intensify partisan feeling, to form new divisions, to arouse suspicions and criticisms which will be uncomfortable for women voters to bear at home and which will be positively detrimental to the movement at large.

8. In other words, the effect of an anti-party policy is throwing the proverbial "monkey wrench" into the machinery of suffrage evolution which is bound to put it out of order. Does it supply a new and more efficient machine to take its place? To my mind NO.

What, then, can be done to save the situation? Those who believe evolution is in the long run safer and surer than revolution should remain within the National fold. Select the best available women as leaders for State and National and together make a pull— a long pull and a strong pull toward a national victory. How can women voters help? By pressing the men of their parties in Washington to push the amendment, to fight for it, to make it a national issue. How can non-voting women help? By increasing the efficiency of education, agitation and organization within their own state in order to make certain that representatives in Congress will vote right on submitting the Federal Amendment and the Legislatures be prepared to ratify it when submitted. More, some of the energy and some of the money from the states must be devoted to the strengthening of weak states and weak places. What we need is a national campaign from the Atlantic to the Pacific, from Canada to the Gulf, with one constructive plan, with unity, will and never-give-up determination behind it.

The Federal Amendment route to enfranchisement is possible, but not under divided forces. Wellington, the great British General, once said: "A good army can be led to victory by a poor general, or a bad army may be led to victory by a good general, but no army can be led to victory under a debating society." The remark points to the weakness of a campaign following two policies and two organizations.

My appeal to all suffragists is to "get together," to cast out the non-essentials that the great Essential for which we labor may be established. Under what banner can that union be more effectively made that the one which has lifted the movement from ridicule to respect, from theory to the status of a political issue; the banner which has led to all the victories gained—that of the National American Woman Suffrage Association. What is the National American Woman Suffrage Association? A federation of state associations. Where they are strong, united, active, masterful, there the National American Woman Suffrage Association is strong. Where they are timorous, inactive, weak, the National American Woman Suffrage Association is weak. With unity all may be made strong and the strong shall conquer.

38. LETTER TO THE COMMISSIONERS OF THE DISTRICT OF COLUMBIA CLAIMING POLITICAL PRISONER STATUS FOR JAILED SUFFRAGISTS, 1917

To the Commissioners of the District of Columbia:

As political prisoners, we, the undersigned, refuse to work while in prison. We have taken this stand as a matter of principle after careful consideration, and from it we shall not recede.

This action is a necessary protest against an unjust sentence. In reminding President Wilson of his pre-election promises toward woman suffrage we were exercising the right of peaceful petition, guaranteed by the Constitution of the United States, which declares peaceful picketing is legal in the District of Columbia. That we are unjustly sentenced has been well recognized—when President Wilson pardoned the first group of suffragists who had been given sixty days in the workhouse, and again when Judge Mullowny suspended sentence for the last group of picketers. We wish to point out the inconsistency and injustice of our sentences—some of us have been given sixty days, a later group thirty days, and another group a suspended sentence for exactly the same action.

Conscious, therefore, of having acted in accordance with the highest standards of citizenship, we ask the Commissioners of the District to grant us the rights due political prisoners. We ask that we no longer be segregated and confined under locks and bars in small groups, but permitted to see each other, and that Miss Lucy Burns, who is in full sympathy with this letter, be released from solitary confinement in another building and given back to us.

We ask exemption from prison work, that our legal right to consult counsel be recognized, to have food sent to us from outside, to supply ourselves with writing material for as much correspondence as we may need, to receive books, letters, newspapers, our relatives and friends.

Our united demand for political treatment has been delayed, because on entering the workhouse we found conditions so very bad that before we could ask that the suffragists be treated as political prisoners, it was necessary to make a stand for the ordinary rights of human beings for all the inmates. Although this has not been accomplished we now wish to bring the important question of the status of political prisoners to the attention of the commissioners, who, we are informed, have full authority to make what regulations they please for the District prison and workhouse.

The Commissioners are requested to send us a written reply so that we may be sure this protest has reached them.

Signed by,

Mary Winsor, Lucy Branham, Ernestine Hara, Hilda Blumberg, Maud Malone, Pauline F. Adams, Eleanor A. Calnan, Edith Ainge, Annie Arneil, Dorothy J. Bartlett, Margaret Fotheringham.

39. APPEAL OF PRESIDENT WILSON TO THE U.S. SENATE TO SUBMIT THE FEDERAL AMENDMENT FOR WOMAN SUFFRAGE, DELIVERED IN PERSON, SEPTEMBER 30, 1918

Gentlemen of the Senate: The unusual circumstances of a World War in which we stand and are judged in the view not only of our own people and our own consciences but also in the view of all nations and peoples, will, I hope, justify in your thought, as it does in mine, the message I have come to bring you.

I regard the concurrence of the Senate in the constitutional amendment proposing the extension of the suffrage to women as vitally essential to the successful prosecution of the great war of humanity in which we are engaged. I have come to urge upon you the considerations which have led me to that conclusion. It is not only my privilege, it is also my duty to apprise you of every circumstance and element involved in this momentous struggle which seems to me to affect its very processes and its outcome. It is my duty to win the war and to ask you to remove every obstacle that stands in the way of winning it.

I had assumed that the Senate would concur in the amendment, because no disputable principle is involved but only a question of the method by which the suffrage is to be now extended to women. There is and can be no party issue involved in it. Both of our great national parties are pledged, explicitly pledged, to equality of suffrage for the women of the country.

Neither party, therefore, it seems to me, can justify hesitation as to the method of obtaining it, can rightfully hesitate to substitute Federal initiative for State initiative if the early adoption of this measure is necessary to the successful prosecution of the war, and if the method of State action proposed in the party platforms of 1916 is impracticable within any reasonable length of time, if practical at all. And its adoption is, in my judgment, clearly necessary to the successful prosecution of the war and the successful realization of the objects for which the war is being fought.

That judgment I take the liberty of urging upon you with solemn earnestness for reasons which I shall state very frankly and which I shall hope will seem as conclusive to you as they seem to me.

This is a people's war and the people's thinking constitutes its atmosphere and morale, not the predilections of the drawing room or the political considerations of the caucus. If we be indeed democrats and wish to lead the world to democracy, we can ask other peoples to accept in proof of our sincerity and our ability to lead them whither they wish to be led, nothing less persuasive and convincing than our actions.

Our professions will not suffice. Verification must be forthcoming when verification is asked for. And in this case verification is asked for—asked for in this particular matter. You ask by whom? Not through diplomatic channels; not by foreign ministers; not by the intimations of parliaments. It is asked for by the anxious, expectant, suffering peoples with whom we are dealing and who are willing to put their destinies in some measure in our hands, if they are sure that we wish the same things that they do.

I do not speak by conjecture. It is not alone that the voices of statesmen and of newspapers reach me, and that the voices of foolish and intemperate agitators do not reach me at all. Through many, many channels I have been made aware what the plain, struggling, workaday folk are thinking, upon whom the chief terror and suffering of this tragic war fall. They are looking to the great, powerful, famous democracy of the West to lead them to the new day for which they have so long waited; and they think, in their logical simplicity, that democracy means that women shall play their part in affairs alongside men and upon an equal footing with them.

If we reject measures like this, in ignorant defiance of what a new age has brought forth, of what they have seen but we have not, they will cease to believe in us; they will cease to follow or to trust us. They have seen their own governments accept this interpretation of democracy—seen old governments like that of Great Britain, which did not profess to be democratic, promise readily and as of course this justice to women, though they had before refused it; the strange revelations of this war having made many things new and plain to governments as well as to peoples.

Are we alone to refuse to learn the lesson? Are we alone to ask and take the utmost that our women can give—service and sacrifice of every kind—and still say we do not see what title that gives them to stand by our side in the guidance of the affairs of their nation and ours? We have made partners of the women in this war. Shall we admit them only to a partnership of suffering and sacrifice and toil and not to a partnership of privilege and right? This war could not have been fought, either by the other nations engaged or by America, if it had not been for the services of the women—services rendered in every sphere—not merely in the fields of efforts in which we have been accustomed to see them work but wherever men have worked and upon the very skirts and edges of the battle itself.

We shall not only be distrusted, but shall deserve to be distrusted if we do not enfranchise women with the fullest possible enfranchisement, as it is now certain that the other great free nations will enfranchise them. We cannot isolate our thought or action in such a matter from the thought of the rest of the world. We must either conform or deliberately reject what they approve and resign the leadership of liberal minds to others.

The women of America are too intelligent and too devoted to be slackers whether you give or withhold this thing that is mere justice; but I know the magic it will work in their thoughts and spirits if you give it to them. I propose it as I would propose to admit soldiers to the suffrage—the men fighting in the field of our liberties of the world—were they excluded.

The tasks of the women lie at the very heart of the war and I know how much stronger that heart will beat if you do this just thing and show our women that you trust them as much as you in fact and of necessity depend upon them.

I have said that the passage of this amendment is a vitally necessary war measure and do you need further proof? Do you stand in need of the trust of other peoples and of the trust of our own women? Is that trust an asset or is it not? I tell you plainly, as the commander-in-chief of our armies and of the gallant men in our fleets; as the present spokesman of this people in our dealings with the men and women throughout the world who are now our partners; as the responsible head of a great government which stands and is questioned day by day as to its purpose, its principles, its hope . . . I tell you plainly that this measure which I urge upon you is vital to the winning of the war and to the energies alike of preparation and of battle.

And not to the winning of the war only. It is vital to the right solution of the great problems which we must settle, and settle immediately, when the war is over. We shall need in our vision of affairs, as we have never needed them before, the sympathy and insight and clear moral instinct of the women of the world. The problems of that time will strike to the roots of many things that we have hitherto questioned, and I for one believe that our safety in those questioning days, as well as our comprehension of matters that touch society to the quick, will depend upon the direct and authoritative participation of women in our counsels. We shall need their moral sense to preserve what is right and fine and worthy in our system of life as well as to discover just what it is that ought to be purified and reformed. Without their counsellings we shall be only half wise.

That is my case. This is my appeal. Many may deny its validity, if they choose, but no one can brush aside or answer the arguments upon which it is based. The executive tasks of this war rest upon me. I ask that you lighten them and place in my hands instruments, spiritual instruments, which I have daily to apologize for not being able to employ.

40. NINETEENTH AMENDMENT TO THE CONSTITUTION, 1920
Adopted in 1920

The right of citizens of the United States to vote shall not be denied or abridged by the United States or by any State on account of sex.

The Congress shall have power to enforce this article by appropriate legislation.

APPENDIX B
Biographies of Major Personalities

Addams, Jane (September 6, 1860–May 21, 1935) *humanitarian, founder of Hull-House community center in Chicago*

In 1911 Addams became the first leader of the National Federation of Settlements. In January 1915 she was elected chairman of the U.S. Woman's Peace Party; in April 1915, president of the International Congress of Women at The Hague; and in 1919, the first president of the Women's International League for Peace and Freedom. A supporter of women's suffrage, she served as first vice president of the National American Woman Suffrage Association (1911–14). Addams was prominent at the International Woman Suffrage Alliance meeting in Budapest in 1913. She was also a hardworking supporter of the National Committee on the Cause and Cure of War, an organization founded in 1925 by Carrie Chapman Catt. Addams (as well as another recipient) was awarded the Nobel Peace Prize in 1931; she donated her share of the prize money to the Women's International League. Addams wrote many articles and books reflecting her strong views toward social reform, including: "Ethical Survivals in Municipal Corruption," published in the *International Journal of Ethics,* April 1898; *Democracy and Social Ethics,* a collection of lectures and articles published in 1902; *The Spirit of Youth and the City Streets* (1909); *Twenty Years at Hull-House* (1910); *A New Conscience and an Ancient Evil* (1912); and *The Second Twenty Years at Hull-House* (1930). She also wrote *Newer Ideals for Peace* (1907) and *Peace and Bread in Time of War* (1922), both of which reflected her pacifist views.

Anthony, Susan Brownell (February 15, 1820–March 13, 1906) *principal leader in the fight for women's suffrage*

In her early career Anthony was especially interested in women's labor issues but also worked for temperance and antislavery reform and in 1852 formed the Woman's New York State Temperance Society. From 1854 she organized petition drives for women's suffrage and the expansion of the Married Woman's Property Law. From 1856 she was William Lloyd Garrison's main New York representative for the American Anti-Slavery Society. A principal leader of the women's suffrage movement, she organized and led many reform organizations, often in partnership with Elizabeth Cady Stanton. These included the National Woman's Loyal League, which worked toward abolition, the American Equal Rights Association, the Working Woman's Association, and the National Woman Suffrage Association. Beginning in 1854, she solicited signatures to petition New York State for an expansion of the Married Woman's Property Law, passed in 1860. In 1866 she handed Congress petitions with thousands of signatures advocating the enfranchisement of women. She retired from the presidency of the National American Woman Suffrage Association at age 80; 20 years later the Nineteenth Amendment, which was named the Anthony Amendment in her honor, allowing women to vote, was adopted.

Avery, Rachel G. Foster (December 30, 1858–October 26, 1919) *suffrage worker*

Following a childhood spent in a household sympathetic to the cause of woman's rights and a private school education, Rachel Foster Avery became active at a young age in the Citizens' Suffrage Association. After attending the 1879 National Woman Suffrage Association convention, she devoted much of her energy to that cause. She was elected in 1880 as NWSA's corresponding secretary. In this capacity she directed the 1882 suffrage campaign in Nebraska. Avery became a close personal friend and confidante of Susan B. Anthony, and over the years Avery assumed many of Anthony's organizational responsibilities, including the planning of many state suffrage campaign strategies. She helped establish the International Council of Women and served as an officer from 1889 to 1893. She also served as secretary of the National Council of Women from 1891 to 1894 and on the Committee of the World's Congress of Representative Women in 1893. She supported the merger between the National Woman Suffrage Association and the American Woman Suffrage Association. She was secretary of the International Woman Suffrage Alliance from 1904 to 1909. Avery then served as first vice president of NAWSA from 1907 until her resignation in 1910. In 1908 she headed the Pennsylvania Woman Suffrage Association, and is credited with reinvigorating the cause of women's suffrage in that state. She died just 10 months prior to the adoption of the Nineteenth Amendment.

Bagley, Sarah G. (fl. 1835–1847) *early Massachusetts labor leader*
Bagley campaigned in the 1840s for a law that would limit the working day to 10 hours. In 1844 she founded and was the first president of the Lowell Female Labor Reform Association, which she later brought to several other Massachusetts and New Hampshire cities, and testified in the hearings of the first governmental investigation of labor conditions in the United States. Dissatisfied with deteriorating wages and working conditions, she criticized the corporation and attacked its magazine the *Lowell Offering* in an Independence Day address in 1845. In 1846 she attended the National Industrial Congress, an early New England labor organization. That year the Massachusetts senate turned down the mill workers' petition for the 10-hour day. Bagley's health failed her, but she found work as the country's first woman telegraph operator.

Barton, Clara (December 25, 1821–April 12, 1912) *nurse, founder of the American Red Cross, first woman to head a U.S. government bureau*
Clara Barton was born in Oxford, Massachusetts. Barton became a schoolteacher at age 15 and remained an educator for 18 years. In 1954 she became a clerk in the U.S. Patent Office in Washington, D.C. She began the Civil War work for which she is famous in 1861, advertising for the donation of nursing supplies and taking them with her to the front. It was the sol-

diers themselves who first called her the "Angel of the Battlefield," in gratitude for her tireless nursing of the fallen, even in the midst of battle. In 1865 Barton established an office to locate soldiers unaccounted for at the war's end. The federal government designated Barton's enterprise its Missing Soldier's Office, and Barton became the first woman to head a U.S. government bureau. The office located 22,000 missing soldiers between 1865 and 1868. Barton traveled to Europe in 1868, planning to recover her own taxed health. Instead, she joined the International Red Cross's relief efforts during the Franco-Prussian War and worked to improve conditions for poor women in Lyons and Strassburg. She was awarded the Gold Cross of Remembrance by the grand duke and duchess of Baden and the Iron Cross of Merit by the emperor and empress of Germany. Returning to the United States in 1873, she began a tireless campaign to persuade the United States to ratify the Geneva Convention and thus become a member of the International Red Cross. The treaty was finally signed in 1882. Barton thereafter directed the activities of an informally organized Red Cross. In 1900 the organization was reincorporated by an act of Congress as the American Red Cross, and Barton was named its first president. In response to complaints about her informal business management practices, she resigned in 1904.

Beecher, Catharine Esther (September 6, 1800–May 12, 1878) *author, educator*
Beecher established the Hartford Female Seminary in 1823, which trained girls in teaching and domestic science. Her lectures and writings, in particular "The Duty of American Women to Their Country," prompted Boston's Mount Vernon Church and Cleveland's Board of National Popular Education to place more than 500 female teachers in the western frontier region of the country. In 1852 Beecher founded the American Woman's Educational Association, which began schools in Milwaukee, Wisconsin; Dubuque, Iowa; and Quincy, Illinois. Beecher was concerned about women who were exploited factory workers or unhappy housewives and blamed women's lack of enthusiasm for their proper duties as happy and competent homemakers on the lack of sufficient education. In 1846 Beecher wrote a book discussing this problem: *The Evils Suffered by American Women and American Children: The Causes and the Remedy.* She

published several other books, including *An Essay on Slavery and Abolitionism, with Reference to the Duty of American Females* (1837). This publication was addressed to Angelina Grimké and argued that women belonged only in the domestic and social sphere. She also wrote *The Duty of American Women to Their Country* (1845), *A Treatise on Domestic Economy* (1841) and its sequel, *The Domestic Receipt Book* (1846).

Beecher, Henry Ward (June 24, 1813–March 8, 1887) *minister, antislavery activist*

Henry Ward Beecher was born in Litchfield, Connecticut, and was the brother of Harriet Beecher Stowe. Following his graduation from Amherst College (1834) and Lane Theological Seminary (1837), he was ordained a minister of the Presbyterian Church (New School) in 1837. He served in two Indiana parishes before becoming pastor of the newly established Plymouth Church in Brooklyn, New York, in 1847. Beecher was an extraordinarily gifted speaker. His sermons drew approximately 2,500 people to Plymouth Church each Sunday and were widely published in pamphlet form. An opponent of slavery, he used his pulpit to urge northerners to defy the Fugitive Slave Act and to move to Kansas and use force, if necessary, to make that state a "free-soil" state. He was also the editor of the *Independent* from 1861 to 1864 and of the *Christian Union* from 1870 to 1881. Victoria Woodhull made public accusations of adultery between Beecher and Elizabeth Tilton, a parishioner, in November 1872. Beecher's conduct was investigated and exonerated by a small committee of his church members and local laypersons, and by a subsequent investigation headed by the council of the Congregational churches. Theodore Tilton brought a civil lawsuit, but the jury failed to reach a unanimous verdict. Although the scandal was thereafter always attached to Beecher's name, he retained his popularity and his position as pastor of Plymouth Church until his death in 1887.

Belmont, Alva Erskine Smith Vanderbilt (January 17, 1853–January 26, 1933) *suffragist*

Born in Alabama and educated in private schools in France, Alva Smith returned to the United States and entered New York high society. She married William K. Vanderbilt in 1875, divorced 20 years later, and married Oliver Hazard Perry Belmont in 1896. It was not until her husband's death in 1908 that Alva Belmont entered the suffrage movement. She gave a large portion of her wealth, a militant enthusiasm, and the remainder of her life to the women's suffrage campaign. In 1909 she founded the Political Equality League, a suffrage organization in New York, and served as its president. In 1913 she served on the executive board of the Congressional Union, a radical organization led by Alice Paul and Lucy Burns. When the Congressional Union became the National Woman's Party, Belmont remained on the executive board; she was elected president of the National Woman's Party in 1921. At The Hague Conference on the Codification of International Law in 1930, Belmont represented the National Woman's Party and, in that capacity, argued unsuccessfully for the elimination of legal restrictions against women in international law.

Blackwell, Alice Stone (September 14, 1857–March 15, 1950) *editor, author*

Alice Stone Blackwell was reared to believe in the equality of men and women. Blackwell's mother, Lucy Stone, was a noted suffrage leader, her father, Henry Browne Blackwell, was a suffragist and reform enthusiast, her aunt Elizabeth Blackwell was the United States' first woman doctor, and her aunt Antoinette Brown Blackwell was the country's first ordained woman minister. All of these relatives provided strong, intelligent role models for Blackwell. In 1893 she became the sole editor of her mother's feminist publication, the *Woman's Journal*. Her influence helped merge the two rival suffrage organizations, the National Woman Suffrage Association and the American Woman Suffrage Association into the National American Woman Suffrage Association. Blackwell became recording secretary of that organization and held that position for almost 20 years. During her lifetime, she was a member of many organizations, including the Woman's Christian Temperance Union, the Women's Trade Union League, the National Association for the Advancement of Colored People, the American Peace Society, and the Anti-Vivisection Society. Blackwell published many articles, a biography of her mother, *Lucy Stone* (1930), several volumes of poetry translations, and *The Little Grandmother of the Russian Revolution: Reminiscences and Letters of Catherine Breshkovsky* (1917).

Blackwell, Antoinette Louisa Brown
(May 20, 1825–November 5, 1921) *author, lecturer, minister*

Blackwell traveled across the country preaching and lecturing on woman's rights, antislavery, and temperance. She was vice president of Julia Ward Howe's Association for the Advancement of Women. Despite opposition from her fellow clergy, Blackwell was ordained as minister of the First Congregational Church in Butler and Savannah, Wayne County, New York, on September 15, 1853, thus becoming the first ordained female minister of a mainstream U.S. denomination. She continued her intellectual pursuits while married to Samuel Blackwell and raising seven children. At the first congress of the Association for the Advancement of Women in 1873, she delivered a paper on her belief that women should maintain interests outside of their domestic lives and that paid part-time work outside of the home and domestic assistance from the husband were necessary means toward this end. In 1878 she supported Lucy Stone's leadership of the American Woman Suffrage Association. Blackwell wrote several books on the social implications of the new Darwinian theory of evolution and incorporated Darwin's ideas into her feminist beliefs. Blackwell died in 1921, a year after exercising her right to vote at the age of 95.

Blackwell, Elizabeth (February 3, 1821–
May 31, 1910) *physician, educator, suffragist*

Elizabeth Blackwell was born in Bristol, England, and immigrated to the United States with her parents and eight siblings in 1832. The family lived for six years in New York City and then relocated to Cincinnati, Ohio. Two of her younger siblings were Henry Blackwell, a political reformer, and Emily Blackwell, who also earned a medical degree. Women's rights leader Lucy Stone and minister Antionette Brown later became her sisters-in-law. Blackwell faced stiff resistance when she decided to apply to medical school, receiving rejections from almost two dozen institutions. At Geneva College in Geneva, New York (now Hobart and William Smith Colleges), the administration asked the all-male student body to vote whether to admit a female student. Treating the matter as a joke, the students unanimously approved her admission, and she began her studies in 1847. She graduated at the head of her class in 1849, becoming the first American woman to earn a medical degree. Blackwell traveled to Europe and received an additional six months' training in obstetrics at La Maternité in Paris and another year's experience at St. Bartholomew's Hospital in London before going to New York City. There, she founded the New York Dispensary for Poor Women and Children in 1854 and, with her sister Emily Blackwell, the New York Infirmary for Indigent Women and Children in 1857. In 1868 the sisters opened the Women's Medical College. In 1869 Elizabeth Blackwell returned to England, where she established a private practice and served as a professor of gynecology at the London School of Medicine for Women from 1875 to 1907. She was the first woman to have her name entered in the British Medical Register.

Blatch, Harriot Eaton Stanton (January 20, 1856–November 20, 1940) *author, suffrage organizer*

Harriot Stanton Blatch received a formal private education and, as the daughter of Elizabeth Cady Stanton, early exposure to the suffrage movement. She began her career helping her mother and Susan B. Anthony with the voluminous *History of Woman Suffrage*. In 1907, in an effort to revitalize the suffrage movement, she formed the Equality League of Self-Supporting Women, which would later become the Woman's Political Union. The organization's most influential members were its many women factory workers. It eventually merged with the more radical Congressional Union in 1917. Blatch was an effective organizer and a highly motivated and unrelenting lobbyist. After the United States entered World War I, she channeled her energies into the war effort as head of the Food Administration Speakers Bureau and director of the Woman's Land Army. Following the adoption of the Nineteenth Amendment, Blatch joined Alice Paul in her drive for an equal rights amendment. She wrote *Mobilizing Woman-Power* (1918), *A Woman's Point of View* (1920) and *Challenging Years* (with Alma Lutz, 1940) and edited with her brother, Theodore Stanton, *Elizabeth Cady Stanton: As Revealed in Her Letters, Diaries and Reminiscences* (1922).

Bloomer, Amelia Jenks (May 27, 1818–
December 30, 1894) *temperance and women's rights reformer, suffragist*

Bloomer lectured and wrote newspaper articles in support of her beliefs. She printed a temperance and woman's rights newspaper, the *Lily,* which grew in popularity when Bloomer's article defending Elizabeth Cady Stanton's attire of full Turkish pantaloons and a short skirt (first introduced by Gerrit Smith's daughter, Elizabeth Smith Miller) brought publicity to the paper and the outfit, making the "bloomer costume" a nationwide fad. Bloomer herself gave up the costume several years later after deciding that it drew attention away from more important feminist issues such as suffrage and women's property rights. In 1852 she spoke in favor of women divorcing their husbands on account of drunkenness. In 1853 she spoke in New York State with Susan B. Anthony and other suffrage leaders. In 1871 she became president of the Iowa Woman Suffrage Society.

Bradwell, Myra (February 12, 1831–
February 14, 1894) *lawyer, editor, Supreme Court plaintiff*
Myra Colby was born in Manchester, Vermont, to parents of Puritan descent. She was raised in Portage, New York, and Chicago, Illinois. Since most institutions of higher learning were still closed to women, Colby's formal education ended with her graduation from the Ladies Seminary at Elgin. She then worked as a schoolteacher. Within a few years of her 1852 marriage to lawyer James B. Bradwell, Myra Bradwell began the study of law. Her original intent was to better assist her husband in his office, but this was quickly replaced with a desire to practice law herself. She established the *Chicago Legal News* in 1868, which was considered so reliable a news source that the legislature issued a charter and passed an act declaring that Bradwell's publication of state law and legal opinions were adequate evidence that such laws existed and such decisions had been rendered. She passed the required legal examination in 1869 and applied to Illinois's supreme court for admission to the bar. The court declined, citing Bradwell's legal disabilities as a married woman. Bradwell appealed. The higher court upheld her exclusion and said that any woman—married or not—could be kept from the bar. Bradwell then appealed to the U.S. Supreme Court, arguing that Illinois's exclusion of women from the bar violated the Fourteenth Amendment. The Supreme Court disagreed, and ruled against her in *Bradwell v. Illinois* (1873). After the ruling, Bradwell worked to change Illinois law; in 1882 the legislature passed an act permitting entry into all professions without regard to gender. Although she did not reapply to the Illinois bar, she was admitted in 1885 on the basis or her original application. In 1892 she was

admitted to practice before the U.S. Supreme Court. Bradwell was the first female member of the Illinois Press Association and the Illinois State Bar Association. An active suffragist as well, she called the first woman's suffrage convention in Chicago in 1869 and drafted the 1869 Illinois law giving married women the right to their own earnings. She was also instrumental in organizing the American Woman Suffrage Association and was a member of the executive committee of the Illinois Woman Suffrage Association.

Brown, Hallie Quinn (March 10, 1850–
September 16, 1949) *educator, lecturer, organizer*
Hallie Q. Brown was educated in Pittsburgh, Pennsylvania, and Ontario, Canada, before entering Wilberforce University in Ohio. An African American, she moved south after her graduation in 1873 to help teach elementary school during the Reconstruction. During this time, she attended Chautauqua Lecture School and graduated in 1886. On returning to Ohio in 1887, she founded a school for African Americans from the south. She also traveled frequently as a noted elocutionist and lecturer. Once more moving south in 1892, Brown briefly held the position of principal of the Tuskegee Institute in Alabama. She then returned to Ohio as elocution professor at Wilberforce University. In association with the Wilberforce Concert Company, she made extensive trips abroad, lecturing on the subject of African-American life. Brown was a supporter of the U.S. Woman's Christian Temperance Union and traveled to England and Scotland to speak on behalf of the British Women's Temperance Association. She represented the United States at the meeting of the International Congress of Women held in England in 1899. Brown actively supported the African Methodist Episcopal Church and attended the World Conference on Missions in 1910. She founded the black women's Neighborhood Club at Wilberforce University, was president of the Ohio State Federation of Colored Women's Clubs for seven years (1905–12), helped found the Colored Woman's League of Washington, D.C. (a predecessor of the National Association of Colored Women) and served as president of the National Association of Colored Women from 1920 to 1924. Her political involvements included a term as vice president of the Ohio Council of Republican Women during the early 1920s. In 1924 she was named director of colored women's activities at the Republican Party's national

campaign headquarters in Chicago. She wrote several books, including *Homespun Heroines and Other Women of Distinction* (1926), *First Lessons in Public Speaking* (1920) and *A Choice Selection of Recitations* (1880).

Brown, Olympia (January 5, 1835–October 23, 1926) *suffragist, minister*

Olympia Brown was born in a log cabin in 1835 near Schoolcraft, Michigan. Her early education took place in a school her parents built on their land. She entered Mount Holyoke College in 1854, then transferred to Antioch College the following year and graduated in 1860. Brown received her theological training at the St. Lawrence Theological School in Canton, New York, the only such institution that accepted women. Upon her graduation, she was ordained a minister by the Northern Universalist Church. She became pastor of a Universalist church in Weymouth, Massachusetts, in 1864, and pastor of a Universalist church in Bridgeport, Connecticut, in 1869. In later life, she also presided over churches in Racine, Mukwonago, Neenah, and Columbus, Wisconsin. Brown became active in the suffragist movement in 1866, when she met Elizabeth Cady Stanton and Susan B. Anthony at a women's rights convention. She helped organize the American Equal Rights Association, formed to support women's suffrage as well as suffrage for African-American men. She gave a speech in favor of woman's suffrage before a congressional committee in Washington, D.C., in 1876 and, after her relocation to Wisconsin 1878, became president of the Wisconsin Woman Suffrage Association. She and others founded the Federal Suffrage Association in 1892. Of all the prominent early suffragists, only Antoinette Brown Blackwell and Olympia Brown lived to see victory. In 1913, in her late seventies, Brown joined the Congressional Union, which soon became the National Woman's Party. In 1917, then 82, Brown was among the National Woman's Party members marching through the streets to demand suffrage. When suffrage was won, she was among the women casting their first votes on November 2, 1920; she lived to vote for president again in 1924.

Burns, Lucy (July 28, 1879–December 22, 1966) *suffragist*

Lucy Burns was born in Brooklyn, New York, to parents of Irish descent. She graduated from the Packer Collegiate Institute in 1899 and from Vassar College in 1902. She then attended Yale University Graduate School (1902–03), where she studied etymology, and the Universities of Berlin (1906–08) and Bonn (1908–09), where she studied languages. Burns began work on her doctorate degree at Oxford University in 1909, but she abandoned it to join the British suffrage movement. While in England, Burns worked in the Women's Social and Political Union (WSPU) with Emmeline and Christabel Pankhurst, engaging in more militant tactics than were used in the United States. She was arrested on several occasions and took part in hunger strikes while incarcerated in 1909, ultimately receiving a medal of valor from the WSPU. Burns returned to the United States in 1912 and became vice chairman of the National American Woman Suffrage Association's (NAWSA) Congressional Committee. Alice Paul, whom Burns had met while in England, was the Congressional Committee's chairman; together, Paul and Burns organized the 1913 suffrage parade in Washington, D.C., and established the Congressional Union for Woman Suffrage to work exclusively toward a federal suffrage amendment. Disagreements between NAWSA and the Congressional Union led to Paul's removal and Burns's resignation from their Congressional Committee positions by the end of 1913 and a total separation of the Congressional Union and NAWSA. The Congressional Union became the National Woman's Party in 1916. Burns was at the forefront of the Congressional Union and National Woman's Party aggressive tactics to secure suffrage. Following through on the threat to hold the party in power responsible for Congress's failure to pass a federal suffrage amendment, Burns headed campaigns against Democrats in 1914 and 1916, in states where women had already won the vote. She was arrested several times in 1917 for picketing the White House with other National Woman's Party members; in prison she claimed political prisoner status and went on a 19-day hunger strike, which ended only when she was force fed. Burns retired from activism after women's suffrage was won.

Catt, Carrie Chapman (January 9, 1859–March 9, 1947) *administrator, organizer, and author*

Born in Wisconsin and educated in Iowa, Carrie Chapman Catt began her career as an educator and journalist. In 1887 she became a member of the Iowa Woman Suffrage Association. In 1890 she attended the first convention of the National American Woman Suffrage Association (NAWSA). A superior administrator and organizer, she served as chairman of the organization committee of NAWSA from 1895 to 1900. She was an excellent platform speaker and participated in 20 hearings before Congress on the proposed woman suffrage amendment. In 1900 Catt succeeded Susan B. Anthony as president of NAWSA. In 1902 she formed the International Woman Suffrage Alliance. In 1904 she resigned that NAWSA position due to her husband's poor health and, after her husband's death in 1905, devoted her energies to the alliance and to the local suffrage organizations in New York City and state. She served as president of the International Woman Suffrage Alliance from 1902 until 1923. In the United States she took control of the New York suffrage movement in 1912 and organized two major campaigns in 1913 and 1914. She was reelected to the presidency of NAWSA in 1915. She worked ceaselessly until the Nineteenth Amendment was finally adopted in 1920, due in large part to Catt's "Winning Plan." Anticipating victory in 1919, she founded the League of Women Voters to help educate the new voting force. Involved in the peace movement, Catt founded the National Committee on the Cause and Cure of War in 1925. She served as its chairman until 1932 and afterward as honorary chairman. She was also active in support of the League of Nations, national child-labor legislation, and relief of Jewish refugees from Germany. Her books include *Woman Suffrage and Politics* (1933) and *Why Wars Must Cease* (1935).

Chapman, Maria Weston (July 25, 1806–July 12, 1885) *abolitionist*

Chapman organized and became the leader of the Boston Anti-Slavery Society in 1832. The society distributed petitions for the abolition of slavery in the District of Columbia and favored the education of free African-American men and women in Boston. As William Lloyd Garrison's chief lieutenant, Chapman welcomed Sarah and Angelina Grimké to New England in 1837, as well as publicized their antislavery lectures. She spoke at antislavery meetings and conventions, and in May of 1838 she spoke at the Anti-Slavery Convention of American Women in Philadelphia while a mob (which later burned down the hall) raged outside. After the Emancipation Proclamation and the passage of the Thirteenth

Amendment, Chapman shared Garrison's opinion that it was time to disband the antislavery societies.

Child, Lydia Maria Francis (February 11, 1802–October 20, 1880) *author*

Child first gained fame for her romantic novels and light periodicals but eventually sacrificed her public standing when she began writing for the reform of slavery laws. A conservative woman until 1831, Child became an abolitionist when she met William Lloyd Garrison. In 1833 she published *An Appeal in Favor of That Class of Americans Called Africans,* a book describing the history and the evils of slavery, denouncing segregation and inequality of education and employment and rejecting colonization of the African continent as a solution to the abolitionist problem. Though the book won her nothing but ostracism and infamy in her own time, it gave Child historical importance. In 1840 Child was elected to the executive committee of the American Anti-Slavery Society, whose weekly periodical, the *National Anti-Slavery Standard,* she edited for three years, until she resigned in 1843 in response to abolitionist criticism of her mildness. When her attempt to attend to John Brown in prison after his raid on Harpers Ferry in 1859 was denounced by the wife of Senator James M. Mason of Virginia, the author of the Fugitive Slave Act, Child responded in a lengthy pamphlet condemning slavery, which was quickly circulated throughout the North. This pamphlet was followed by *The Duty of Disobedience to the Fugitive Slave Act, The Patriarchal Institution,* and *The Right Way, the Safe Way,* all published in 1860. In 1861 she edited *Incidents in the Life of a Slave Girl,* a book of the memories of former slave Harriet Jacobs, and published with her own money *The Freedmen's Book,* a collection of writings of former slaves. Though she did not write directly about women's issues or contribute to any women's organization, Child advocated greater equality between the sexes and used her talents to express her beliefs despite popular opinion.

Clay, Laura (February 9, 1849–June 29, 1941) *suffragist, states' rights supporter*

Born in Kentucky, Laura Clay was introduced to the women's suffrage movement when an older sister formed Kentucky's first suffrage club. In 1881 Clay was elected president of the newly organized Kentucky Woman Suffrage Association (which was later renamed the Kentucky Equal Rights Association). She served in this capacity until 1912. Under Clay's direction this organization was, by 1900, successful in overturning several statutes of Kentucky law that discriminated against women. In 1895 she joined the board of the National American Woman Suffrage Association as its first auditor and as chairman of its membership committee. During this time, she also served as a member of the Woman's Club of Central Kentucky. She began to separate herself from the national organization and in 1913 became vice president of the Southern States Woman Suffrage Conference. From 1915 to 1917 she was a member of the Woman's Peace Party. Throughout her life she was a strong supporter of the Woman's Christian Temperance Union. After resigning in June 1919 from both the National American Woman Suffrage Association and the State Equal Rights Association, she formed the Citizens' Committee for State Suffrage Amendment. A strong believer in states' rights, she continued to work toward state suffrage amendments and opposed a federal amendment to the constitution. She was disappointed when the Nineteenth Amendment was adopted. "Nothing but my religion has enabled me to stand it," she said.

Crandall, Prudence (September 3, 1803–January 28, 1890) *abolitionist*

Crandall opened the Canterbury Female Boarding School in Canterbury, Connecticut, in 1831. The first girls to enroll were white. She enjoyed community support until the daughter of a local black farmer was admitted. Crandall's decision to admit the girl caused public outrage. Having already been converted to the abolitionist cause by William Lloyd Garrison, Crandall closed the school and reopened it in April 1833 as a boarding school for the education of African-American girls. When attempts to force Crandall to close the school were unsuccessful, the people of Canterbury influenced the state legislature to pass a law that required the permission of town authorities before any school could be opened for out-of-state blacks. Crandall was consequently arrested, jailed, and tried under the conditions of the law, and her abolitionist supporters took advantage of the situation by allowing her to share a cell with a murderer for a night before they bailed her out. The event was then used as abolitionist propaganda; it was widely publicized in Garrison's *Liberator* and many other abolitionist periodicals. Crandall was convicted, but this decision was later reversed due to a technicality. However, Crandall was eventually forced to give up her school in September of 1834 when the townspeople set fire to the school. In 1886, after the death of her husband, the Connecticut legislature granted Crandall a small pension as restitution for its earlier decision.

Cutler, Hannah Maria Conant Tracy (December 25, 1815–February 11, 1896) *suffragist*

Cutler is known for her work toward the reform of married women's legal rights, in which she first took an interest while studying law with her first husband. An active participant in several reform movements, Cutler helped organize the Woman's Temperance Society in Rochester, New York, and was a delegate to the World's Peace Congress in London, August 1851, where she lectured on woman's rights and introduced the bloomer costume to the attendees. In 1852 she was elected president of the Ohio Woman's Association; she also served as president of the American Woman Suffrage Association from 1870 to 1871 after helping her friend Lucy Stone form the organization. Her most notable contribution to women's rights, however, resulted from canvassing for married women's legal rights in New York, Illinois, and Ohio in 1859 and 1860. These drives met with varied success: They achieved minimal changes in the laws of Illinois and Ohio, but in the state of New York won the right for married women to transfer personal property, the sole right to handle their personal earnings, and the joint guardianship over their children. In 1868 Cutler enrolled in the Women's Medical College in Cleveland, and she earned her medical degree in February of 1869. Cutler practiced medicine for the rest of her life and participated in her last women's suffrage campaign in 1873 when she canvassed Ohio.

Davis, Paulina Kellogg Wright (August 7, 1813–August 24, 1876) *antislavery, temperance, and women's suffrage reformer*

Davis's first memorable achievement was the organization of a Utica antislavery convention in October 1835, for which she suffered a mob attack on her home. In the 1830s she and Ernestine Rose joined forces in a petition to the New York legislature for a married women's property law. After 1850 Davis concentrated on woman's rights, helped organize the first National Woman's Rights Convention (held in

Worcester, Massachusetts), and published the second woman's rights periodical beginning in 1853, the *Una*. In 1868 she helped organize the New England Woman Suffrage Association as well as a Rhode Island association, of which she served as president until 1870. When the women's suffrage movement divided in 1869, Davis was one of the few New England women to side with Elizabeth Cady Stanton and Susan B. Anthony's National Woman Suffrage Association and made valuable contributions to its journal, *Revolution,* in 1869 and 1870.

Dickinson, Anna Elizabeth (October 28, 1842–October 22, 1932) *celebrated lecturer, playwright*

Dickinson was born in Philadelphia of Quaker ancestry. At the age of 17, she made her first speech before the Pennsylvania Anti-Slavery Society and quickly rose to fame as an eminent orator on political and social issues. Her speeches about abolition, the emancipation of women, prison reform, and help for the poor were delivered with intense emotion and described by both audiences and newspapers as "electrifying." Dickinson wrote two books—*What Answer* (1868) and *A Paying Investment* (1876). In spite of views sympathetic to the cause of woman suffrage and friendships with its leaders, she remained detached from involvement in the organized suffrage movement. When the field of public lecture no longer attracted audiences, Dickinson attempted a career in playwriting and acting. She made her acting debut in her play *A Crown of Thorns* in May 1876, but the reviews were not favorable. After many unsuccessful attempts, she wrote a play of reasonable success—*An American Girl.* A final attempt to regain status as a public speaker was made in 1888 for the Republican National Committee. The attempt failed, and Anna E. Dickinson resigned from public speaking.

Dix, Dorothea Lynde (April 4, 1802–July 18, 1887) *powerful campaigner for the reform of treatment of the mentally ill*

Dix opened her first school at age 14. In March 1841, Dix was asked to teach a Sunday school class for woman inmates of the East Cambridge jail, where she became aware of the horrible treatment and living conditions of the inmates, many of whom were not criminals but mentally ill. Dix brought her discoveries to the attention of the local court, which ultimately resulted in the renovation of the inmates' quarters.

Dix then embarked on eight months of research into the conditions in every jail, poorhouse, and house of correction in Massachusetts. Her address to the state legislature in January of 1843 regarding the cruelty, disease, and squalor she had seen convinced the legislature to fund an expansion of the Worcester facilities for the care of the mentally ill. Dix then surveyed the institutions of Rhode Island, New York, New Jersey, Kentucky, Pennsylvania, Maryland, Ohio, Illinois, Mississippi, Alabama, Tennessee, North Carolina, and other states, gradually soliciting improvements in the state facilities. In 1845 she wrote *Remarks on Prisons and Prison Discipline,* which pointed out the need for many reforms that were later made, such as the separation of different types of offenders. Through her international travels, Dix convinced a number of nations to improve the conditions in their asylums. During the Civil War, Dix became the superintendent of Union army nurses. She played a direct part in the founding of 32 state mental hospitals and indirectly caused the establishment of many more throughout the world.

Douglass, Frederick (ca. February 1817–February 20, 1895) *abolitionist, newspaper writer, public speaker*

Douglass was born to an enslaved woman and white father in Talbot County, Maryland. Shipped back and forth between owners in Baltimore and on the eastern shore, he knew little of his mother, Harriet, or his father. Self-taught, he was one of the 19th century's greatest orators. Originally named Frederick Augustus Washington Bailey, he escaped to freedom on September 3, 1838, and took the name Frederick Douglass from Walter Scott's "Lady of the Lake." In 1841 a speech he gave at the Massachusetts Anti-Slavery Society was so well received that he was named a lecturer for the society. He authored three autobiographies, including *Narrative of the Life of Frederick Douglass* in 1845, comparable in its impact to Harriet Beecher Stowe's novel *Uncle Tom's Cabin.* He also founded the abolitionist movement's most influential newspaper, the *North Star.* The paper supported women's suffrage and education for blacks. Douglass recruited regiments of black soldiers during the Civil War. Afterwards, he split with Elizabeth Cady Stanton and Susan B. Anthony over the Fifteenth Amendment. He held a variety of governmental jobs, including U.S. consul general to Haiti from 1889 to 1891.

Duniway, Abigail Jane Scott (October 22, 1834–October 11, 1915) *lecturer, author, newspaper publisher*
In 1852 Abigail Duniway's family left its native Illinois to resettle in the northwest territory of Oregon. In 1871 Abigail Duniway began to express her discontent with women's domestic servitude. In that year, she began the publication of a weekly newspaper, *New Northwest,* which prospered for 16 years. Before long, Duniway was lecturing throughout the Northwest for the suffrage cause. She founded and presided over the Oregon Equal Suffrage Association in 1873 and was, for many years, a constant presence at the Oregon legislature. Duniway was honorary president of the Oregon Federation of Women's Clubs and was elected president of the Portland Woman's Club. She was extremely instrumental in gaining women's suffrage in Washington territory and in Idaho, but her efforts repeatedly failed to secure suffrage for Oregon. This failure ultimately prompted the national suffrage leaders to assume control of the Oregon Equal Suffrage Association and effected the resignation of Duniway from that organization. When the Oregon campaign was finally successful, however, Abigail Duniway's early influence was fully recognized. She was asked to write the suffrage proclamation and was the first woman voter in the state of Oregon. She wrote several books, including *Captain Grey's Co.* (1859) and her autobiography, *Path Breaking* (1914).

Farley, Harriet (ca. February 18, 1813–November 12, 1907) *editor*
Farley was the editor of the *Lowell Offering* from 1842 to 1850, a periodical describing work in the Lowell Textile Mills as a liberating and positive experience. Her literary talent was first noticed in 1840 when her article defending the mill girls and mill owners was published in the *Lowell Offering.* As editor she excluded all controversial subject matter from the magazine, even during the 1840s when the battle was raging for shorter hours, higher wages, and better working conditions. This action resulted in the production of a polite periodical with declining popularity among the mill girls. In 1845 the *Lowell Offering* collapsed under competition with a radical new labor paper, but it returned in 1847 as the *New England Offering* with Farley as editor and publisher. However, the *New England Offering* was still not very popular, and it disappeared for good in 1850. Thanks to Farley's labors,

scholars have an invaluable collection of women's writings in the textile mills.

Forten, Sarah (Ada, Magawisca) (1814–1883) *writer, abolitionist, a founding member of the Philadelphia Female Anti-Slavery Society*
Sarah Forten was born into a wealthy family of free blacks in Philadelphia. In response to the segregation laws of the time and the inferior education generally available to blacks, Forten's parents joined with other wealthy free blacks to create a school for their children. Forten attended that school and also studied languages and music at home with a tutor. Forten's essays and poems were published in the *Abolitionist,* the *Liberator,* and other abolitionist publications, under the pseudonym "Ada." Many of her poems, including "The Grave of the Slave" (1831), "Past Joys" (1831), "The Slave Girl's Address to Her Mother" (1831), and "Prayer" (1831), deal with antislavery themes. In her poem "An Appeal to Women" (1834), Forten urges white women to "nobly dare to act a Christian's part" and recognize that "the fair and dark have equal birth." Her essay "The Abuse of Liberty" (1831) appeared under the name "Magawisca" and claims that only white men enjoyed the full range of human rights. In 1833 Forten was one of the signers of the Philadelphia Female Anti-Slavery Society's charter of incorporation. She served on its board of managers for two terms.

Foster, Abigail Kelley (January 15, 1810–January 14, 1887) *lecturer and agitator for temperance, women's rights, and abolition*
Recruited to the abolitionist cause by William Lloyd Garrison, she served as secretary of the Lynn Female Anti-Slavery Society in Massachusetts from 1835 to 1837 as well as acting as officer of the Lynn Female Peace Society. She was one of the first to support Garrison's radical nonviolent policy, helping him form the New England Non-Resistance Society in September of 1838. In May of the same year Foster had made her first public speech at the second woman's antislavery convention in Philadelphia's Pennsylvania Hall, which was burned down by a mob a day later, and met with so much success that she was begged to become an abolitionist lecturer. She began her lecturing career in Connecticut in May 1839. At this time there was dissension within the abolitionist movement over a number of issues, including the role of women, and Foster

played a part in the complete break that occurred at the 1840 convention of the American Anti-Slavery Society, when the conservatives in the movement so strongly objected to a female serving on the business committee (after Foster was elected to the committee by a majority) that they left the convention to form their own independent movement. As a traveling lecturer, Foster influenced many women to join the abolitionist and feminist causes.

Fowler, Lydia Folger (May 5, 1822– January 26, 1879) *medical doctor, activist*

Fowler began her career as a traveling lecturer to women on hygiene, physiology, and anatomy. In November 1849 she enrolled in the Central Medical College in Syracuse, New York, and in June of 1850 she was the second woman in the United States to receive a degree as doctor of medicine. In 1851 she became a professor of midwifery and diseases of women and children and addressed the New York State Eclectic Medical Society on these issues. In 1852 she moved to New York City, where she practiced medicine until 1860 while conducting private lectures to women at the Metropolitan Medical College and contributing to several reformist medical journals. Fowler was a strong believer in the need for woman physicians and believed that many modest women who needed medical care would not submit to an examination by a male physician. Fowler also contributed to several other movements; in January 1852 she served as delegate to the state Daughters of Temperance and was president of the women's temperance meeting in New York City. From 1860 to 1861 she went on a lecture tour of Europe with her husband and in 1863 moved with him to London, England where she served as honorary secretary of the Woman's British Temperance Society. Fowler published several books, among them *Familiar Lessons on Physiology, Familiar Lessons on Phrenology, Familiar Lessons on Astronomy, Nora, the Lost and Redeemed,* a novel, and finally a collection of her child-care lectures in 1865 entitled *The Pet of the Household and How to Save It.*

Fuller, Margaret (May 23, 1810–July 19, 1850) *critic, intellectual, member of the New England transcendentalist movement*

From 1839 to 1844 Fuller conducted her famed "conversations," group discussions with women on mythology, art, ethics, education and women's rights. In 1840 Fuller, Emerson, and others published the first issue of the transcendentalist journal, the *Dial,* of which Fuller served as editor until 1842. She helped establish Brook Farm, the transcendalist community in West Roxbury, Massachusetts, in 1841. She wrote two books between 1844 and 1845; the first, *Summer on the Lakes,* won her a position as literary critic for the New York *Tribune,* and the second, *Woman in the Nineteenth Century,* became a feminist classic with considerable influence on the Seneca Falls Conference on Woman's Rights in 1848. In 1846 Fuller became the *Tribune's* foreign correspondent and promptly left the United States for Europe. In Rome Fuller met Giovanni Angelo Marchese d'Ossoli, whom she married in 1849. In July 1849 Fuller moved to Florence, where she began work on a history of the Roman revolution. In May 1850 she sailed for America to publish her completed book in the United States, but she and her family were killed in a shipwreck.

Gage, Frances Dana Barker (October 12, 1808– November 10, 1884) *author, lecturer for women's equal rights, temperance, and abolition*

By 1850 Gage was writing for the *Ladies' Repository* of Cincinnati and the *Ohio Cultivator.* Her lecturing on reform issues gained her a place as a speaker at the second statewide woman's rights convention in Cleveland in 1851, after she had petitioned the state legislature to omit the words *white* and *male* from the constitution then being drafted. Soon her reform lectures took her out of state, where she made a name for herself as a public speaker. She moved to St. Louis, Missouri in 1853, but three fires, possibly sparked by her ill-received abolitionist activities in partnership with Elizabeth Cady Stanton and Susan B. Anthony, destroyed Gage's business and home in 1857, forcing Gage and her husband to return to Ohio. In Ohio Gage soon became associate editor of both the *Ohio Cultivator* and *Field Notes* but lost her job when the Civil War broke out. In 1862 Gage moved to South Carolina, where she and her children were the sole administrators for 500 freedmen on Parris Island. When she returned to New York in 1863 she lectured on freedmen's conditions in America and on temperance, particularly at the May 1866 meeting of the American Equal Rights Association. Gage published a temperance novel in 1867, *Elsie Magoon.*

Gage, Matilda Joslyn (March 25, 1826–March 18, 1898) *suffragist known for her writing and organizational abilities*

Gage was married at 18 to Henry H. Gage and was not related to Frances Gage. She initially joined the woman's rights movement as a speaker at the National Woman's Rights Convention in September 1852. She was critical of women's dependence upon men, and she urged equality in educational opportunity and legal status. In 1869 she actively entered the equal rights movement as a contributor to the National Woman Suffrage Association's newspaper, the *Revolution,* and as a member of NWSA's first advisory council. As an influential author and successful organizer, Gage served the NWSA as president for one year (1875–1876) and, subsequently, the New York State Woman Suffrage Association as president (1875). She was the editor of the *National Citizen and Ballot Box* (1878–81) during its lifetime. In 1890 she founded the Woman's National Liberal Union, which advocated separation of church and state. By this point in her career, Gage believed that religious teachings were responsible for the widespread belief of women's inferiority to men and that this was by far the greatest obstacle to women's emancipation. Her book *Woman, Church and State* (1893) reflected this conviction. She also wrote several pamphlets, *Woman as Inventor* (1870) and *Who Planned the Tennessee Campaign of 1862?* (1880) among them. Gage, along with Elizabeth Cady Stanton and Susan B. Anthony, produced the first three volumes of the *History of Woman Suffrage* (1881–86). Matilda Joslyn Gage was dedicated to the women's movement, and her contribution as a writer and organizer was of particular note. Her soft-spoken manner and stylish appearance also helped counterbalance the popular negative impression of feminists of that era.

Garrison, William Lloyd (December 10, 1805–May 24, 1879) *abolitionist*

Garrison founded the abolitionist paper the *Liberator* in Boston in 1831 and remained its editor until the last issue was published 35 years later. He was a founder of the New England Anti-Slavery Society in 1831 and the American Anti-Slavery Society in 1833. So uncompromising was his stand against slavery and so strong was northern resentment against slavery that an angry pro-slavery mob dragged Garrison through the streets of Boston on October 21, 1835, and he nearly lost his life. Garrison was allied with the women's suffrage movement and in 1840 quit the World Anti-Slavery Convention in London because of its refusal to honor the credentials of the American women delegates. In 1843 his leadership in the Massachusetts Anti-Slavery Society led that group to declare that the Constitution was "a covenant with death and an agreement with hell." On July 4, 1854, he burned the Constitution before a group in Framington, Massachusetts, declaring, "So perish all compromises with tyranny." Garrison supported Abraham Lincoln during the Civil War. After the war he allied himself with a number of progressive causes, including prohibition and women's suffrage.

Gordon, Kate M. (July 14, 1861–August 24, 1932) *social reform advocate*

Kate Gordon supported many social reforms but always believed that the emancipation of woman was the most direct route to any other desired reform. With the help of her sister, Jean Gordon, she founded the Equal Rights Association (known as the Era Club) in 1896 to work toward the goal of women's suffrage. The organization soon espoused many other eclectic reforms as well, resulting in the formation of satellite organizations such as the Woman's League for Sewerage and Drainage, of which Kate Gordon was president. Gordon entered the national suffrage movement in 1900 and was elected corresponding secretary of the National American Woman Suffrage Association in 1901. From 1904 to 1913 she led the Louisiana State Suffrage Association. A strong believer in states' rights, Gordon opposed the adoption of a federal amendment requiring the enfranchisement of women. In 1913 she founded the Southern States Woman Suffrage Conference to work for suffrage on a state-by-state basis. After ratification of the Nineteenth Amendment, Gordon's energies were devoted to the New Orleans Anti-Tuberculosis League, the Society for the Prevention of Cruelty to Animals and the Travelers Aid Society. She was also instrumental in the formation of New Orleans' first juvenile court and the New Orleans Hospital and Dispensary for Women and Children.

Greeley, Horace (February 3, 1811–November 29, 1872) *newspaper editor, reformer*

In 1841 he founded the *New York Tribune,* which published many of Elizabeth Cady Stanton's essays.

The newspaper championed women's rights, abolition, temperance and other reform issues. Greeley originated the slogan "Go west, young man" in support of the great western expansion. He was a founder of the Republican Party and supported Abraham Lincoln at the Chicago convention in 1860 but aligned himself during the Civil War with the radical faction of the antislavery movement. In 1872 he ran as the Liberal Republican candidate for president but lost to Ulysses S. Grant.

Griffing, Josephine S. (December 18, 1814–February 18, 1872) *abolitionist, suffragist, relief worker*
Josephine S. White was born in Hebron, Connecticut. Following her marriage in 1842, she moved with her husband to Litchfield, Ohio. The Griffings were active in the abolitionist movement, and their home was a stop on the Underground Railroad. Josephine Griffing served as an officer of the Western Anti-Slavery Society and wrote for the *Anti-Slavery Bugle* of Salem, Ohio. Griffing became active in the women's suffrage movement after the Ohio Women's Rights Convention of 1850, adding articles in favor of suffrage to the *Anti-Slavery Bugle* and becoming president of the Ohio Woman's Rights Association in 1853. She also supported the temperance movement. During the Civil War, Griffing was active in the National Woman's Loyal League, an organization created after the Emancipation Proclamation to lobby for the eradication of slavery in every state. After the war, she became the general agent of the National Freedman's Relief Association of the District of Columbia. Working to provide relief to the newly freed slaves, she established a vocational school for African-American women and persuaded the War Department to use empty barracks as temporary housing for black families. She was instrumental in persuading Congress to establish the Freedmen's Bureau, a federal agency to assist the formerly enslaved. She worked in various capacities in the Freedmen's Bureau and, when was it abolished in 1869, used her own home and resources to care for elderly former slaves. Griffing also resumed her women's suffrage work after the war. Between 1866 and her death in 1872, she served as a vice president of the American Equal Rights Association, president of the District of Columbia Woman Suffrage Association, and corresponding secretary of the National Woman Suffrage Association.

Grimké, Angelina Emily (February 20, 1805–October 26, 1879) *abolitionist, early defender of women's rights*
Angelina Grimké moved to Philadelphia from her home in Charleston, South Carolina, and joined the Philadelphia Female Anti-Slavery Society. In 1836 she published a pamphlet, *An Appeal to the Christian Women of the South,* after William Lloyd Garrison had brought fame to the Grimké name by printing Angelina's letter supporting the abolitionist cause in the *Liberator.* Though the pamphlet brought her threats from her hometown, it also earned her a job running meetings for small groups of New York women interested in the American Anti-Slavery Society. She also lectured in churches and in 1837 conducted a speaking tour of New York condemning slavery. She wrote her second pamphlet in 1837, *Appeal to the Women of the Nominally Free States.* Grimké's controversial practice of speaking to audiences of men and women aroused discussion about the rights of women. In July 1837 the Congregational Ministerial Association of Massachusetts distributed a pastoral letter condemning public behavior on the part of women like Angelina Grimké. Although urged not to, Grimké openly confronted the position of women in society in a series of letters to the *Liberator,* published in a pamphlet in 1838. Grimké's marriage to Theodore Weld in 1838 marked the end of her public activities; on May 16 she made her final public address at the Philadelphia antislavery convention, despite an angry mob outside that later burned down the hall. Weld and the Grimké sisters published a book in 1839, largely compiled from Southern newspaper clippings, entitled *American Slavery As It Is: Testimony of a Thousand Witnesses.*

Grimké, Sarah Moore (November 26, 1792–December 23, 1873) *abolitionist, feminist*
Grimké's first antislavery action was her conversion in 1821 from the Episcopal faith to the Society of Friends (Quakers) because of the Episcopalian position on slavery. She left the Quakers as well in August 1836, angered by their discriminatory practices, and moved to New York, where she joined her sister Angelina in antislavery efforts. She enrolled in the abolitionists' training course run by the famous orator Theodore Dwight Weld, following which she wrote her *Epistle to the Clergy of the Southern States,* denying the validity of the church's argument that the exis-

tence of slavery in biblical times justified its existence in the United States. In 1838 Sarah Grimké published *Letters on the Equality of the Sexes and the Condition of Woman,* a pamphlet written in response to the pastoral letter issued by the Congregational Ministerial Association of Massachusetts in July 1837. Sarah Grimké's active participation in the abolitionist movement came to an end when Angelina married Weld in 1838, although she helped Angelina and Weld write *American Slavery As It Is: Testimony of a Thousand Witnesses* in 1839.

Harper, Frances Watkins (September 24, 1825– February 22, 1911) *poet, abolitionist, suffragist*

Frances Watkins was born into a family of free blacks in Baltimore. Orphaned while quite young, she was raised by an abolitionist aunt and uncle and attended the William Watkins Academy for Free Negro Youth, a school founded by her uncle. She published her first book of poetry and prose, *Forest Leaves,* in about 1850. (No copy is known to survive.) By 1850, sentiment was rising against free blacks in Baltimore. Her relatives moved to Canada, and Frances moved first to Ohio and then to Pennsylvania, securing teaching positions in both states. Although she grew homesick for Baltimore, she dared not return: Maryland had passed legislation in 1853 that subjected free blacks to imprisonment or enslavement if they entered the state. When she learned of a free black man sold into slavery after returning to his native Maryland and his death following enslavement, she abandoned teaching and turned all her talents to the abolitionist cause. In 1854, she made her first anti-slavery speech in Bedford, Massachusetts, and published a collection of anti-slavery poems, *Poems on Miscellaneous Subjects.* She traveled throughout the North to demand abolition and published many poems in abolitionist newspapers. Her short story, "The Two Officers," was published in the *Anglo-African Magazine* in 1859 and is believed to be the first short story published by an African American. She married Ferton Harper in 1860. Frances Harper donated much of her literary income to the Underground Railroad. She was active in the women's suffrage movement, working with both the American Equal Rights Association and the American Woman Suffrage Association. A temperance supporter as well, she directed the National Woman's Christian Temperance Union's activities among African Americans from 1883 to 1890. She was an organizer of the National Association of Colored Women in 1896 and served as the organization's vice president that year. Harper published a number of works during her life, including three recently rediscovered novels: *Minnie's Sacrifice, Sowing and Reaping,* and *Trial and Triumph.*

Harper, Ida A. Husted (February 18, 1851– March 14, 1931) *journalist*

Born and educated in Indiana, Ida Husted Harper began her career in journalism in 1872 by contributing articles to the *Terre Haute Saturday Evening Mail,* initially under a male pseudonym. She continued to contribute articles and eventually wrote a column under her own name that appeared for approximately 12 years. From 1884 to 1893 she edited a section of the *Locomotive Firemen's Magazine,* and for a brief period in 1890 she held the position of editor-in-chief of the *Terre Haute Daily News.* Moving in that same year to Indianapolis, she joined the editorial staff of *Indianapolis News.* Harper was always a sympathizer of the women's movement but did not become actively involved in the suffrage movement until 1887 when she became secretary of an Indiana state suffrage society. Moving to California in 1896, Harper spearheaded a press campaign during California's attempt to secure a suffrage amendment to its constitution. In 1897 she moved to Rochester, New York, to write Susan B. Anthony's biography, a three-volume work entitled *Life and Work of Susan B. Anthony.* At this time she also began working with Anthony on volume four of *History of Woman Suffrage* (1902). After the passage of the Nineteenth Amendment, Harper worked on volumes five and six of the *History* (1922). Harper's journalistic talents were put to great use in the struggle for women's suffrage. She wrote numerous articles and letters to newspapers and journals across the United States in defense of the feminist cause. In 1916 she was asked to act as head of national publicity for the Leslie Bureau of Suffrage Education. Prior to her death, she lived in Washington, D.C., at the headquarters of the American Association of University Women.

Holley, Sallie (February 17, 1818–January 12, 1893) *abolitionist, lecturer, teacher of southern freedmen*

Holley began her career as a lecturer for the American Anti-Slavery Society after graduation from Oberlin College in 1851 and continued until emancipation.

Holley's accounts of her lecture experiences were printed in William Lloyd Garrison's periodical, the *Liberator.* From 1863 to 1870 she lectured for black suffrage and simultaneously collected clothes for freedmen and funds for the American Anti-Slavery Society. The society died in 1870 despite her efforts, however, and Holley moved to Virginia where she spent the rest of her life running the Holley School for southern freedmen with her friend Caroline Putnam; they taught blacks housekeeping, gardening, reading, writing, and politics. Holley also attended several women's rights conventions in the 1850s.

Hooker, Isabelle Beecher (February 22, 1822– January 25, 1907) *women's rights supporter*

Beecher was converted to the women's rights movement upon reading John Stuart Mill's *The Subjection of Women.* In 1868 she helped found the New England Woman Suffrage Association and in 1869 arranged the convention in Hartford that resulted in the formation of the Connecticut Woman Suffrage Association, of which Hooker was president until 1905. In 1868 she wrote "A Mother's Letters to a Daughter on Woman's Suffrage," which was eventually published under her name in an 1870 treatise on suffrage. With her support, a married woman's property bill was passed by the Connecticut legislature in 1877. Hooker first came to the attention of national suffrage leaders when she spoke at the second convention of the National Woman Suffrage Association (NWSA) in 1870. She spent much of her time in Washington, D.C., rallying the support of its citizens and of Congress for a suffrage amendment to the Constitution. Hooker played an active part in the NWSA, speaking at its conventions and at congressional hearings.

Howe, Julia Ward (May 27, 1819– October 17, 1910) *author of "Battle Hymn of the Republic," leader of many women's clubs and suffrage associations*

Howe's famous poem, "Battle Hymn of the Republic," was published in February 1862. Howe volunteered for the women's department of the New England Sanitary Commission and was elected director and vice president of the American Peace Society. After the Civil War she discovered the women's movement and in 1868 founded the New England Women's Club and joined Lucy Stone and others in forming the New England Woman Suffrage Association. In 1869, when the women's suffrage movement divided into two factions, Howe became president of the American Woman Suffrage Association; she was also a member of the board that negotiated the reunion of the suffrage movement in 1889. She served as president of the Massachusetts Woman Suffrage Association from 1870 to 1878 and from 1891 to 1893 and of the New England Woman Suffrage Association from 1868 to 1877 and from 1893 to 1910. In 1870 she was a founder of the *Woman's Journal,* which she helped edit and contributed to for 20 years. She edited *Sex and Education* in 1874 and in 1883 published a biography of Margaret Fuller. She helped found the Association for the Advancement of Women and aided in the establishment of the General Federation of Women's Clubs in 1890. She was also the first to direct the Massachusetts Federation of Women's Clubs, started in 1893. In 1900 she published her book, *Reminiscences.* In 1908 Howe was the first woman elected to the American Academy of Arts and Letters.

Jones, Jane Elizabeth Hitchcock (March 13, 1813–January 13, 1896) *antislavery and women's rights lecturer*

Jones spoke throughout New England and eastern Pennsylvania. In 1845 she moved with a group of antislavery lecturers to Salem, Ohio, which was then a hotbed of abolitionism. In September of that year, Jones became coeditor of the new *Anti-Slavery Bugle,* a post she continued to occupy until 1849. Jones managed an antislavery book agency and in 1848 published a children's book, *The Young Abolitionists.* Jones also worked for women's rights, speaking at the first convention of Ohio women in Salem in April 1850. Jones began a successful career lecturing on health and hygiene in May 1850 but returned to an abolitionist focus after 1856. She was a member of the Western Anti-Slavery Society and the Ohio Woman's Rights Association. Jones also made a valuable contribution toward gaining property rights and custodial rights of children for women by lecturing and campaigning in many states and finally delivering a speech that was published by the state of Ohio as *Address to the Woman's Rights Committee of the Ohio Legislature* in 1861. The speech helped facilitate the passage of a married women's property law in that state.

Keckley, Elizabeth (ca. 1818–May 26, 1907)
founder of the Contraband Relief Association
Elizabeth Keckley was born enslaved in Dinwiddie, Virginia, in about 1818. When her owner, Mr. Garland, proposed renting out Keckley's elderly mother, Keckley prevented their separation by establishing a sewing business, the proceeds of which belonged to Garland. After Garland's death, Keckley's sewing clients lent her the funds to purchase her freedom. Relocating to Washington, D.C., Keckley quickly developed a clientele among the capital's notables; when the Lincolns arrived in Washington, D.C., in early 1861, Keckley was hired as Mary Todd Lincoln's seamstress. In 1862 Keckley established the Contraband Relief Association, intending that African Americans assist the "unfortunate freedmen." Mary Todd Lincoln made the first donation, but the majority of funds were donated by African Americans in Boston, New York, and Washington, D.C. In her later life, Keckley's autobiography, *Behind the Scenes: Thirty Years in the White House,* was published; scholars disagree as to whether she wrote it entirely on her own, but it is certain that the book's inclusion of personal family details caused a breach between Keckley and the Lincoln family. She died in the Washington, D.C., Home for Destitute Women and Children, which she had helped to establish.

Larcom, Lucy (May 5, 1824–April 17, 1893) *poet, author, teacher, editor*
Larcom spent 10 years of her youth working in the Lowell textile mills, an experience she described in several of her books, including *An Idyl of Work* and the book for which she is best known today, *A New England Girlhood,* published in 1889. Her sentiments about mill life were mostly ones of gratitude; she had no sympathy for the activism for improved working conditions. She first contributed her writing, both prose and verse, to the *Lowell Offering,* and as early as 1849 she was included in Rufus W. Griswold's *Female Poets of America.* Her teaching career began in 1846 at a school in Illinois. After her college education, at the Montessori Seminary between 1849 and 1852, she taught at the Wheaton Seminary in Massachusetts, where she remained for nearly eight years. In 1862 she resigned, however, and earned a living for the rest of her life by contributing creative writing to magazines and by editing the periodical, *Our Young Folks.*

Livermore, Mary (December 19, 1820–May 23, 1905) *suffragist, temperance worker, editor, author*
Mary Ashton Rice was born in Boston, Massachusetts. At 14 she graduated from the Hancock Grammar School and entered the Female Seminary of Charlestown, where she was both a student and a teacher. Following her graduation, she continued to teach for a time at the school and then accepted an invitation to teach in Virginia. She returned to Massachusetts and met the Rev. Daniel Parker Livermore, whom she married in 1845. The couple ultimately settled in Chicago. Livermore assisted her husband with church study groups and charity work, and she served an as associate editor to the *New Covenant,* a church periodical edited by her husband. In this capacity, she covered the convention at which Abraham Lincoln was nominated. During the Civil War, she was active in the Northwestern Branch of the U.S. Sanitary Commission. It was this experience that convinced her that women needed the vote in order to help direct national affairs. She gave the opening address at Chicago's first woman suffrage convention and served as president of the Illinois Woman's Suffrage Association. She founded the suffrage newspaper the *Agitator* in 1869; when it was merged with the *Woman's Journal* later that year, Livermore moved to Boston and became one of the *Journal's* editor. There, she also served as president of the Massachusetts Woman's Suffrage Association and as president of the Massachusetts Women's Christian Temperance Union. Livermore's *My Story of the War: A Woman's Narrative of Four Years Personal Experience* was published in 1888 and her *The Story of My Life, or, The Sunshine and Shadow of Seventy Years,* in 1897. She was a coeditor, with Frances E. Willard, of *A Woman of the Century,* a collection of biographical essays about prominent women of the era.

Lockwood, Belva (October 24, 1830–May 19, 1917) *suffragist, lawyer, first woman admitted to practice before the U.S. Supreme Court*
Belva Lockwood was born in Royalton in Niagara County, New York. Her early career was in teaching. She began the study of law following the Civil War, graduating from the National University Law School in 1873 when she was 43. She was admitted to the Washington bar in 1873 and to practice before the U.S. Supreme Court in 1879, the latter after some opposition. In 1880 she was the sponsor of Samuel

R. Lowery, the first African American from the South to be admitted to practice before the Supreme Court. In 1906 she successfully argued a case on behalf of the Eastern Cherokee Indians before the Supreme Court, winning the tribe a $5 million award. Lockwood was active in the women's rights movement, volunteering her legal talents and serving as an officer in the National Woman Suffrage Association, the National American Woman Suffrage Association, and the League of Women Voters. She accepted the presidential nomination of the informally organized Equal Rights Party in 1884. Although the national suffrage leaders feared an ineffective spectacle and kept their distance from Lockwood's campaign, she addressed the needs of women, blacks, and Native Americans, ultimately winning 4,149 votes. She ran again for president in 1888, earning fewer votes. Also active in the world peace movement, Lockwood attended the International Peace Congress of 1889 and participated in the International Council of Women.

Lyon, Mary (February 28, 1797–March 5, 1849)
educator

Lyon founded the Mount Holyoke Female Seminary (Mount Holyoke College) in 1836, the first institution for the higher education of girls that was both permanent and nonprofit. The seminary opened in November 1837 with a student body of 80 girls aged 17 and over and grew rapidly, with the curriculum increasing the length of the program from three to four years in 1861. Before the founding of her institution, Lyon taught at various schools, particularly the Ipswich Female Seminary, the Adams Female Academy and the Buckland Female Academy, which she founded for young ladies in 1824 but which closed soon after her departure in 1828. She also played a major part in the planning of the Wheaton Female Seminary.

Martin, Anne (September 30, 1875–April 15, 1951)
suffragist, first woman to run for election to the U.S. Senate, women's rights activist

Anne Martin was born in Empire City, Nevada. She received her first B.A. degree from the University of Nevada in 1894 and a second B.A. and a master's degree from Stanford University in 1896. She established the University of Nevada's history department in 1897 and served as its head until 1901. Martin trav-

eled to England in 1909; while there, she participated in the British suffrage movement under Emmeline Pankhurst's leadership and was arrested with other demonstrators in 1910. Once back in the United States, Martin served as president of the Nevada Equal Franchise Society in 1914, leading the successful fight for ratification of a woman's suffrage amendment to the state constitution.

Focusing next on a federal amendment, Martin became an executive member of the National American Woman Suffrage Association and the Congressional Union. When the National Woman's Party was organized in 1916, Martin was its first vice chairman. Arrested with other National Woman's Party members for picketing the White House in July 1917, she was sentenced to time in the Occoquan workhouse. She ran for election to the U.S. Senate in both 1918 and 1920, failing to win the office but garnering at least 20 percent of the vote in each election. Martin was also active in the peace movement, serving as a national board member of the Women's International League for Peace and Freedom from 1926 to 1936 and serving as the organization's delegate to several international conventions.

Merrick, Caroline Elizabeth Thomas
(November 24, 1825–March 29, 1908) *Louisiana women's suffrage and temperance reform leader*

Merrick petitioned the Louisiana constitutional convention in 1878, at age 52, demanding the removal of women's legal disabilities and the granting of at least partial suffrage rights to women. She became president of the national Woman's Christian Temperance Union in 1882, and she formed a Louisiana chapter in 1883 and served as its president for 10 years. In 1892 she organized the Portia Club, a society devoted to studying politics and in particular the legal rights of women and children. In 1896 the Portia Club merged with the Era Club to form a state suffrage association, which gained the right to vote for woman taxpayers when tax issues were referred to the electorate in 1898. Merrick also attended several conventions of the National American Woman Suffrage Association and in 1888 testified for suffrage before a Senate committee at the first meeting of the International Council of Women in Washington. Merrick also published an autobiography, *Old Times in Dixie Land: A Southern Matron's Memories,* in 1901.

Miller, Elizabeth Smith (September 20, 1822–May 22, 1911) *designer of the bloomer costume*
Miller created what became known as "bloomers" after losing patience with the clumsiness of her long skirts in the garden. The bloomer costume consisted of a dress that hung about four inches below the knee and baggy "Turkish" pantaloons. Miller wore the outfit to visit her cousin Elizabeth Cady Stanton in Seneca Falls, whereupon both Stanton and Amelia Bloomer adopted the costume, pleased with its practicality. When Bloomer defended the costume in her periodical, the *Lily*, the dress became known by her name. Miller also gave financial support to both national and New York suffrage groups and served as honorary president of the Geneva Political Equality Club until her death.

Minor, Virginia Louisa (March 27, 1824–August 14, 1894) *suffrage supporter*
Born and educated in the state of Virginia, Virginia Minor moved to St. Louis, Missouri, after her marriage to Francis Minor, a distant cousin. Despite her southern background, she was a member of the St. Louis Ladies Union Aid Society, founded in 1861 to help Union soldiers and their families during the Civil War. This society later became a branch of the Western Sanitary Commission. Mrs. Minor's energies were redirected to the rights of women in 1865 when the St. Louis Ladies Union Aid was dissolved. Minor believed that women, as well as African-American males, deserved the right to vote. Minor is said to be the first woman to speak out for woman's rights in Missouri. In 1867 she petitioned the Missouri state legislature to include women in a proposed constitutional amendment to enfranchise black males. Minor helped form the Woman Suffrage Association of Missouri (1867). She was elected president and subsequently reelected for five consecutive yearly terms. When in 1871 this organization voted to join the American Woman Suffrage Association, Minor resigned her position due to her ties with the National Woman Suffrage Association (NWSA). She later became president of the St. Louis branch of the NWSA. In 1890, when the two national organizations united, Virginia Minor was elected president of the Missouri branch of the new organization. Minor's most significant contribution to the women's movement, however, was her and her husband's unsuccessful support of a legal interpretation of the U.S.

Constitution that would have given women the right to vote as citizens of the United States. This interpretation was presented by Francis Minor for the first time in 1869 at a convention of the Woman Suffrage Association of Missouri, of which Virginia Minor was president. Minor herself tried to vote and, when her ballot was refused, sued the registrar. The case, *Minor v. Happersett,* reached the Supreme Court, which, in 1874, found that women had no right to suffrage under the U.S. Constitution.

Mott, Lucretia Coffin (January 3, 1793–November 11, 1880) *liberal Quaker minister, radical abolitionist, women's rights pioneer*
After the Society of Friends divided into two sects, Mott joined the Hicksite group: Both her religious attitudes and her feelings about slavery were greatly influenced by Elias Hicks. (From 1825 until emancipation, Mott followed Hicks's policy of boycotting products created by slave labor.) In 1833 Mott attended the convention called by William Lloyd Garrison where the American Anti-Slavery Society was organized, and when women were denied admission to this organization, she helped create the Philadelphia Female Anti-Slavery Society. Later, when admission in the national society was opened to women, Mott became an active member and served on the executive committee of its Pennsylvania branch. She was among the women who organized the Anti-Slavery Convention of American Women, which took place at Pennsylvania Hall in Philadelphia on May 15, 1838. When the meeting was interrupted by the ragings of a proslavery mob, Mott encouraged the women to keep calm. Two days later, she calmly waited in her home when the mob, after burning Pennsylvania Hall to the ground, headed toward the Mott household, but the mob was diverted. In March 1840 she was elected to serve as delegate from the American Anti-Slavery Society to the British and Foreign (World) Anti-Slavery Convention in London but was denied recognition there, along with the other women. This event prompted Mott and Elizabeth Cady Stanton to take up the cause of woman's rights in 1848, when the first woman's rights convention was held in Seneca Falls, New York. In 1852 Mott was elected president of the convention in Syracuse, New York. She was president of the American Equal Rights Association in 1866. When the women's movement split in 1869, she

sought a reconciliation. Mott was active until the end of her life, dying at age 87.

Nichols, Clarina Irene Howard (January 25, 1810–January 11, 1885) *women's rights leader, writer, editor*

Nichols wrote for the *Windham County Democrat* of Brattleboro, Vermont, of which she eventually became editor. Under her editorship, the paper grew in popularity as it became more radical, advocating abolitionism, prohibition and other reforms. She became active in the women's rights movement in 1847 by writing articles on the need for reform in women's legal and property rights. Her pressure led to the passage of a married woman's property law by the Vermont state legislature in 1847. In 1852 Nichols petitioned the Vermont legislature for women's right to vote in school meetings. She lectured for lyceums and committees in Vermont and New Hampshire and spoke at the women's rights conventions at Worcester, Massachusetts, in 1850, Syracuse, New York, in 1852, West Chester, Pennsylvania, in 1852 and New York City in 1853. She moved to Kansas in 1853, canvassing for the Kansas Woman's Rights Association. Her activities prompted the delegates of the Kansas constitutional convention to assure women equal rights to education in state schools, votes on school issues, and custodial rights over their children.

Nichols, Mary Sargeant Neal Grove (August 10, 1810–May 30, 1884) *feminist, health reformer*

Nichols believed that improved health was the key to greater freedom for women. In 1837 she opened a school for girls in Lynn, Massachusetts. Soon afterward she began lecturing women on anatomy, physiology, and hygiene and was possibly the first of her sex to do so. In 1838 she began a course of lectures to the Ladies Physiological Society in Boston. In 1840 she edited the *Health Journal and Advocate of Physiological Reform* and in 1842 published her own book, *Lectures to Ladies on Anatomy and Physiology*. She established the *Health Journal and Independent Magazine* in 1843, but it ceased publication after just one issue. In 1848 Nichols divorced Hiram Grove to marry Thomas Low Nichols, a writer who supported equal rights for women. Nichols wrote stories for *Godey's Ladies Book* and several novels: *Uncle John: or, "It Is Too Much Trouble"*, *Agnes Morris: or, the Heroine of Domestic Life*, *The Two Loves: or, Eros and Anteros*, *Uncle Agnes* and *Jerry: A Novel of Yankee American Life*.

O'Reilly, Leonora (February 16, 1870–April 3, 1927) *labor leader, reformer, a founder of the National Association for the Advancement of Colored People*

Leonora O'Reilly was born in New York City to parents arrived from Ireland. Her father died in 1871, and her mother, a garment worker, became the family's sole support. O'Reilly's early education ended when she entered the garment trades at age 11. O'Reilly and her mother attended labor meetings together, and Leonora joined the Knights of Labor in 1886, when she was 16. That same year, she established the Working Woman's Society. She joined the Social Reform club in 1894 and was elected its vice president in 1897. By then a forewoman working 10-hour days in a shirtwaist factory, O'Reilly established a woman's local of the United Garment Workers of America. Throughout the years, she also worked to advance her education, joining a sociological theory study group in 1888 and entering the Pratt Institute in Brooklyn in 1898. Upon her graduation from Pratt in 1900, she was qualified to instruct those who wished to teach sewing in New York City's high schools, but failed to find such employment. She taught in a Brooklyn settlement house and a charitable organization's summer sewing program until she was hired by the Manhattan Trade School for Girls in 1902. She taught there for seven years and was a lifelong supporter of vocational training. O'Reilly was a board member of the National Women's Trade Union League, founded in 1903, and she was actively involved in the New York garment workers' strike that took place during the winter of 1909–10. Following the Triangle Shirtwaist fire in March 1911, O'Reilly led the National Trade Union League's investigation of work environments and safety laws. She was active in the women's suffrage movement and served as the New York City Woman's Suffrage Party's chairman of the industrial committee. O'Reilly was also a founder of the National Association for the Advancement of Colored People and a member of its first General Committee. An opponent of America's entry into World War I, she was the Trade Union League's delegate to the 1915 International Congress of Women at The Hague; after the war's end, she participated in the Trade Union League's committee on social and industrial reconstruction. In weakened health near the end of her life, she nonetheless taught labor movement theory to students at the New School for Social Research in 1925–26.

Pankhurst, Emmeline (July 14, 1858– June 14, 1928) *suffragist*

Born and raised in Manchester, England, Emmeline Pankhurst was 14 when she attended her first suffrage meeting. After her marriage in 1879, she and her husband worked for the Married Women's Property Committee and the Manchester Woman's Suffrage Committee. They also joined the Fabian Society and, in 1893, the Independent Labour Party. In 1903 Pankhurst and her daughter formed the militant Women's Social and Political Union (WSPU). Pankhurst led many marches and recruitment drives in her pursuit for woman suffrage. She was arrested on numerous occasions and responded with hunger and thirst strikes. The activities of the WSPU were suspended during World War I, and it was then that Pankhurst threw herself into conscription propaganda. In 1917 Pankhurst founded the Woman's Party with her daughter Christabel; this organization collapsed in 1918 after an unsuccessful campaign for elected office by Christabel. Pankhurst's interest in the cause waned after this defeat. Her energies were then directed toward the welfare of several illegitimate children whom she fostered, then adopted, during the war.

Paul, Alice (January 11, 1885–July 9, 1977) *militant suffragist, Equal Rights Amendment supporter*

Alice Paul was born into a Quaker family and educated in private schools. She entered Swarthmore College in, 1905, received her M.A. in 1907 and her Ph.D. in 1912 from the University of Pennsylvania. Part of her postgraduate work was done in England during a three-year stay, between 1907 and 1909, and it was there she became involved in suffrage demonstrations and was imprisoned several times. Paul served as chairman of the congressional committee of the National American Woman Suffrage Association in 1912, and in 1913 she led a group of militant suffragists in secession from that organization. The Congressional Union for Woman Suffrage was founded, and Paul served as national chairman until 1917. This organization merged in 1917 with the Woman's Party to form the National Woman's Party. From 1917 to 1921 Alice Paul served as chairman of the national

executive committee of the National Woman's Party. She introduced militant methods into the U.S. suffrage campaign and was again imprisoned. After the passage of the Nineteenth Amendment, Paul earned several law degrees. Beginning in 1923, she campaigned for the Equal Rights Amendment to the Constitution, which was defeated in 1983. She also advocated an international equal rights treaty. From 1927 to 1937, Alice Paul served as chairman of the Woman's Research Foundation and from 1930 to 1933 as a member of the Nationality Committee of the Inter-American Commission of Women. She was a member of the Women's Consultative Committee on Nationality of the League of Nations. She helped found the World Woman's Party and was instrumental in having a reference to sex equality included in the preamble to the United Nations charter.

Pugh, Sarah (October 6, 1800–August 1, 1884) *anti-slavery advocate, schoolteacher*

Pugh first took up the radical Garrisonian abolitionist cause after hearing George Thompson speak in 1835. She joined the Philadelphia Female Anti-Slavery Society, of which she was presiding officer for many years, and the American Anti-Slavery Society. When a mob burned down Pennsylvania Hall on May 17, 1838, the Anti-Slavery Convention of American Women continued its business in Sarah Pugh's schoolhouse. In 1840 Pugh resigned from her school to travel with Lucretia Mott, Mary Grew, and others to the meeting of the British and Foreign (World) Anti-Slavery Society in London. When the women were denied participation in the meeting, it was Pugh who wrote the protest. She returned to America after a tour of the British Isles and continued to canvass her neighborhood and attend antislavery conventions and meetings. After her mother's death in 1851, Pugh returned to England, where she lectured to the British about American antislavery goals and participated in the abolitionist movement there. Back in Philadelphia, Pugh worked for the improvement of the freedmen's situation and for women's rights after the Civil War.

Rankin, Jeannette (June 11, 1880–May 18, 1973) *politician, suffragist*

Jeannette Rankin was born in Montana Territory. She attended Montana's public schools and, in 1902, graduated from the University of Montana. Rankin's early career was as a social worker. She became active in the suffrage movement in 1911 and was appointed a field secretary for the National American Woman Suffrage Association in 1913. In that capacity, she traveled to 15 states, including what was by then the state of Montana, to work for woman's suffrage. Montana's women won suffrage in 1914. Rankin ran for election to Congress in 1916, specifically seeking the women's vote. She won the election and became the first woman to serve in the U.S. Congress on April 1, 1917. Five days later, she was one of 57 representatives to vote against U.S. entry into World War I. During this first time, she was an advocate for a federal woman's suffrage amendment. While Rankin returned to private life in 1919, she did not put aside her public concerns. She worked with the National Consumers' League and the Women's International League for Peace and Freedom, and she was part of the 1919 Second International Congress of Women in Zurich. Reelected to Congress in 1940, she quicky caused controversy by casting the House of Representatives' only vote against U.S. entry into World War II. Returning once again to private life, she continued to advocate on peace issues and women's rights until old age. In 1968, at age 88, she led the Jeannette Rankin Brigade in an anti–Vietnam War protest in Washington, D.C.

Rose, Ernestine Louise Siismondi Potowski
(January 13, 1810–August 4, 1892) *utopian socialist, feminist*

Rose rejected her father's male-dominated Jewish faith when only 16. She took her father to court in Poland to protest his intention to marry her off and give her inheritance from her deceased mother to her new husband as a dowry. When she came to New York, Rose found a similar cause to work for in the married women's property bill that had been introduced to the state legislature; Rose circulated petitions for the bill and spoke before a legislative committee in Albany, in partnership with Elizabeth Cady Stanton and Paulina Wright. She contributed to the periodical the *Boston Investigator* for 50 years. In the 1850s she concentrated her energies on women's rights and attended the first national women's rights convention at Worcester, Massachusetts, in 1850. Rose also lectured at many conventions throughout the country to deliver her message on women's rights, temperance, antislavery, and freedom of thought. Dur-

ing the Civil War she worked with Elizabeth Cady Stanton and Susan B. Anthony in the National Woman's Loyal League and after the war in the American Equal Rights Association. In 1869 Rose helped transform the Equal Rights Association into the National Woman Suffrage Association.

Shaw, Anna Howard (February 14, 1847– July 2, 1919) *minister, doctor, women's rights activist*

Shaw had little formal education during her frontier childhood, but nonetheless became the first ordained woman minister in the Methodist Protestant Church in 1880. In 1885 Shaw entered the women's suffrage cause by joining the Massachusetts Woman Suffrage Association in the capacity of lecturer and organizer, a position she held for two years. She graduated in 1886 from Boston University's medical school. From 1888 to 1892 she held the position of superintendent of the franchise department of the National Woman's Christian Temperance Union. Shaw was active in both the American Woman Suffrage Association and the National Woman Suffrage Association even before the merger of the two groups in 1890. In 1891 she held the position of national lecturer of the National American Woman Suffrage Association (NAWSA). She was the organization's vice president from 1892 until 1904. Women's suffrage became her life's work. She attended numerous conventions and congressional hearings and traveled around the country to work in the various campaigns for state suffrage. She traveled extensively and spoke eloquently, always on behalf of NAWSA. She became president of NAWSA in 1904 and presided for 11 years. She served as chairman of the woman's committee of the U.S. Council of National Defense and in 1919 received the Distinguished Service Medal for services performed during World War I.

Smith, Abby Hadassah (June 1, 1797– July 23, 1878) *Connecticut suffragist*

Smith and her sister Julia invited William Lloyd Garrison, then unwelcome in all Hartford churches, to hold his abolitionist meetings in front of their house. Julia was at this time the distributor of the antislavery newspaper the *Charter Oak*. In 1869 the Smiths attended their first women's suffrage meeting in Hartford and were rallied to the cause. In 1873 Julia traveled to New York to attend the first meeting of the Association for the Advancement of Women. In

November of the same year, the Smiths began their activities in support of women's suffrage. They willfully faced a meeting of men to deny the justice of a property tax demanded of women. When Abby was granted permission to speak at the first hearing, she protested taxation without representation. When denied permission to speak five months later at the second hearing, Abby stood on a wagon parked outside of the building and delivered her speech from there. After these experiences, the Smiths refused to pay any taxes, and their land and their cows (called the "Glastonbury Cows") were seized in payment by the state. The sisters sued and eventually won the right to buy back part of their property. Accounts of their case were collected and published in a pamphlet in 1877, *Abby Smith and Her Cows, with a Report of the Law Case Decided Contrary to Law.*

Smith, Gerrit (March 6, 1797–December 28, 1874) *social reformer*

Smith was born in Utica, New York. A cousin of Elizabeth Cady Stanton, he inspired her with his reform ideas. He managed the family fortune and dispensed much of it to various philanthropies for the poor. He supported the temperance, women's rights, and abolitionist causes. In 1840 he helped start the Anti-Slavery Liberal Party and was its candidate for governor of New York that year. In 1853 he was elected to the U.S. House of Representatives on an abolitionist ticket. Beginning in 1858 he gave financial support to John Brown and may have known about the raid on the federal arsenal at Harpers Ferry, West Virginia, in 1859. During the Civil War, Smith turned Republican and supported Lincoln for reelection in 1864. In 1872 he was a delegate to the Republican national convention.

Smith, Hannah Whitall (February 7, 1832– May 1, 1911) *religious reformer, evangelist, temperance reformer*

In 1874 Smith went to England where she preached in the interdenominational "Higher Life" movement—a form of revivalism—that was popular there from 1873 to 1875. She wrote *The Record of a Happy Life* in 1872, *The Christian's Secret of a Happy Life* in 1875, and many other books. After 1875 she spoke at many women's suffrage conventions, advocating the right of girls to a college education. She helped found the Woman's Christian Temperance Union and was an important liaison between the English and American temperance movements. In 1891 she accompanied Lady Henry Somerset, England's temperance leader, to the United States for the first World Woman's Christian Temperance Union meeting.

Smith, Sophia (August 27, 1796–June 12, 1870) *founder of Smith College, the first American woman to found a college*

At the age of 65 Smith inherited a large family fortune, which she used to found a women's college equal in quality and academic expectations to men's colleges. Her donation of $393,105 funded Smith College, which was chartered in 1871 and opened in 1875.

Stanton, Elizabeth Cady (November 12, 1815– October 26, 1902) *women's rights leader*

Stanton first became interested in the reform of women's legal rights in early childhood. Later she witnessed the exclusion of women delegates from the British and Foreign (World) Anti-Slavery Convention in London in 1840. She petitioned for the bill passed by the New York State legislature in March 1848 granting married women the right to hold real estate. She and Lucretia Mott organized the women's rights convention at Seneca Falls in 1848, and Stanton wrote the Declaration of Sentiments based on the Declaration of Independence. Stanton contributed to many magazines and newspapers, including Horace Greeley's *New York Tribune* and the *Lily*. In 1854 she addressed the New York state legislature on the need for an expanded married woman's property law, a law passed in 1860, giving women the right to their wages and to the custody of their children. Stanton created a sensation that year when she endorsed divorce reform at a national women's rights convention. In May 1863 Stanton formed the National Woman's Loyal League, which petitioned for immediate abolition of slavery by constitutional amendment. In 1868 Stanton proposed a 16th amendment that would grant suffrage regardless of color, race, or sex; though ignored at the time, the amendment was finally made part of the Constitution in 1920. She was president of the National Woman Suffrage Association from 1869 to 1870, and when the two factions of the woman's movement reunited in 1890, she served as president of the National American Woman Suffrage Association during its early years. She also lectured for the New York Lyceum Bureau for 12 years, starting in 1869. In 1895 she published her controversial *The Woman's Bible,* which challenged the clergy's limiting of women's sphere on the basis of scripture by reanalyzing the Bible's references to women. The second volume of *The Woman's Bible* was published in 1898, along with Stanton's reminiscences, *Eighty Years and More.*

Stewart, Maria W. (1803–December 17, 1879)
women's rights advocate, abolitionist

Maria Stewart was born in Hartford, Connecticut. She was reared by a local clergyman after her parents died and, while she received no formal education, she learned to read and was given free access to the clergyman's library. At a time when only Frances Wright had dared to speak in public, Stewart made four public speeches. In 1832 she implored her audience of fellow free African-American women to secure an education for themselves and their children. In an 1833 speech she criticized the colonization movement's plan to expatriate African Americans to Liberia. Like Wright, Stewart was ridiculed and criticized for stepping outside women's sphere. On September 21, 1833, she made her farewell address and retired from public life. Her speeches were then collected by abolitionist William Lloyd Garrison and published in 1835 as the *Productions of Mrs. Maria W. Stewart.*

Stone, Lucy (August 13, 1818–October 18, 1893)
women's rights reformer, abolitionist

Stone studied at the Mount Holyoke Female Seminary and in 1847 became the first Massachusetts woman to earn a college degree when she graduated with honors from Oberlin College. She began a lecturing career for the Garrisonian American Anti-Slavery Society, lecturing on women's rights during the week and on abolitionism on weekends. In 1850 she helped call the first national convention on women's rights in Worcester, Massachusetts. On May 1, 1855, she married Henry Browne Blackwell but kept her maiden name. She presided over the National Woman's Rights Convention in New York. Stone became less active in the movement following the birth of her daughter but resumed her women's rights career after the Civil War. In 1866 she organized the American Equal Rights Association and served on the executive committee. She was president of the New Jersey Woman Suffrage Association and helped found the New England Woman Suffrage Association in 1868. In 1867 a conflict over whether or not to support the Fifteenth Amendment, which granted suffrage regardless of race, color, or previous condition of servitude with no reference to women, caused the national suffrage movement to separate into two factions, the American Woman Suffrage Association, founded by Stone, and the National Woman Suffrage Association, founded by Stanton and Anthony. Stone also founded the weekly paper the *Woman's Journal,* of which she was editor after 1872. When the two factions reunited in 1890 to form the National American Woman Suffrage Association, Stone was chairman of the group's executive committee. Stone gave her last public address at the World's Columbian Exposition in Chicago in 1893.

Stowe, Harriet Beecher (June 14, 1811– July 1, 1896) *author*

Harriet Beecher began teaching at her sister Catharine's school at age 16 and continued to teach until her marriage to Calvin Ellis Stowe on January 6, 1836. She wrote to help pay the expenses of her large family but decided to make a more serious literary effort when a collection of her stories, *The Mayflower,* published by Harper & Brothers in 1843, met with great success. Her readings acquainted her with the cruelties and abuse of slavery, and her novel *Uncle Tom's Cabin* was designed to enlighten Americans to the sin of slavery and lead people to more holy Christian lives. *Uncle Tom's Cabin* was printed in 1851 by the publisher of a Washington, D.C., antislavery newspaper, *National Era.* Instantly popular, the book brought sudden fame and prosperity to Stowe, although it also aroused much controversy. Stowe responded with *A Key to Uncle Tom's Cabin* in 1853, which provided much evidence for the abuse depicted in her first novel. Upon her return from a voyage to Europe, where she befriended Lady Byron, Stowe published *Sunny Memories of Foreign Lands* in 1854. Another, less hopeful antislavery novel, *Dred,* appeared in 1856. Stowe was a prolific writer; several of her other novels were *The Minister's Wooing, The Pearls of Orr's Island, Oldtown Folks* and *Poganuc People,* many of which drew upon her memories of childhood in New England.

Swisshelm, Jane Grey Cannon
December 6, 1815–July 22, 1884) *journalist, reformer*

Swisshelm was deeply affected by her encounters with slavery while living in Louisville, Kentucky; they prompted her to avidly support the antislavery cause.

In 1848 she began an antislavery paper, the *Saturday Visiter,* and for 10 years published articles advocating abolitionism and women's rights. Her editorials expressed the need for reform in married women's property rights and may have influenced the governor of Pennsylvania in his decision to support a reform bill, which was passed in 1848. When she abandoned her paper and moved with her husband to Minnesota in 1857, the *Visiter* had attained national circulation. She became editor of the *St. Cloud Visiter* in Minnesota, but the hatred and consequent lawsuit her reformist ideas incited from the leader of the state Democratic Party brought an end to the paper. Swisshelm immediately formed the *St. Cloud Democrat* and began lecturing throughout the state, preaching reform. After the Civil War, in 1867, she started the *Reconstructionist* but lost her job due to her criticism of President Andrew Johnson. She continued to work for reform and was a delegate to the National Prohibition Party convention in 1872. Her autobiography, *Half a Century,* was published in 1880.

Thomas, Mary Frame Myers

(October 28, 1816–August 19, 1888) *medical doctor, reformer*

Thomas was first inspired to the women's rights cause by Lucretia Mott's address to the Friends Yearly Meeting in 1845. In 1849 she began studying medicine with her husband in Indiana, earning an M.D. degree from the Penn Medical University in Philadelphia in 1854. She opened a medical practice in Richmond, Indiana, and was an army contract surgeon and a member of the Sanitary Commission during the Civil War. From 1880 on she worked to get women hired at the state institution for the insane. In 1855 she became vice president of the Indiana Woman's Rights Society, petitioning the Indiana General Assembly for a married women's property law and a women's suffrage amendment to the constitution. She edited two suffrage papers, the *Lily* and the *Mayflower.* In 1869, after the Civil War, she helped reorganize the women's movement by forming an Indiana branch of Lucy Stone's American Woman Suffrage Association, also serving as president of both the state and the national organizations.

Truth, Sojourner (ca. 1797–November 26, 1883)

abolitionist, orator

She was born Isabella Baumfree into slavery in New York State. From 1810 to 1827 she lived in New Paltz, where she gave birth to five children. Two of her daughters were sold to other families. In 1827 she ran away and was taken in by Isaac and Maria Van Wagener, whose last name she adopted. Around 1829 she moved to New York City, where she worked as a domestic servant, joined a religious cult called the Retrenchment Society and preached to prostitutes. In 1833 she joined Robert Matthews' "Zion Hill" spiritual community in Sing Sing, New York. In 1843 Truth's mystic visions inspired her to take on the name Sojourner Truth and travel the country preaching the love of God. That winter Truth became a member of a communal farm, the Northampton Association of Education and Industry, founded by George W. Benson, the brother-in-law of William Lloyd Garrison. Truth quickly took up the cause of abolitionism, embarking on a tour of the country speaking out against slavery. She was a popular speaker at women's rights conventions as well. Truth was counselor to the Freedmen's Relief Association, which petitioned President Grant for the formation of an African-American state on the western public lands. Her autobiography, *Narrative of Sojourner Truth,* written with Olive Gilbert, was published in 1850. In 1870 she petitioned President Ulysses Grant to give freed slaves western lands on which to live. The migration of many freed men and women to Kansas and Missouri resulted from her efforts.

Tubman, Harriet (ca. 1820–March 10, 1913)

liberator of enslaved people, Civil War nurse

Tubman was born on a Maryland plantation and married a freed African American, John Tubman, in 1844. Between 1847 and 1849 she worked for Anthony Thompson, and when he died she decided to run away. Once free, she began her practice of freeing the enslaved through the Underground Railroad, making about 19 trips to Maryland from her home in New York and rescuing between 60 and 100. Her name was known among abolitionists and also among the slaveholders; they offered a $40,000 reward for her capture. For three years during the Civil War she served the federal forces as a scout and a spy, extracting information from African Americans on the Confederate side, and as a nurse. After the war she began the Harriet Tubman Home for Indigent Old Negroes on her New York farm, which continued for several years after her death. In 1869 Sarah Bradford published *Harriet Tubman: The Moses of Her People,* which widened Tubman's fame.

Turner, Eliza L. Sproat Randolph (1826–
June 20, 1903) *author, social reformer*
Turner was a member of the Philadelphia Female Anti-Slavery Society before the Civil War and afterwards turned her attention to improving the situation of women. In December 1869 she helped form the Pennsylvania Woman Suffrage Association. She was its corresponding secretary and wrote a tract, *Four Quite New Reasons Why You Should Wish Your Wife to Vote* (1875). She edited and contributed to the newspaper, *New Century for Women.* She was chairman of a committee organizing evening classes for working women and girls.

Upton, Harriet Taylor (December 17, 1853–
November 2, 1945) *suffrage and political activist, author*
The daughter of a politician, Upton grew up in an intellectually stimulating household. In her early years she served as secretary of the Woman's Christian Temperance Union but was a strong opponent of women's suffrage. When she started to do research for an antisuffrage article, however, her viewpoint changed. Upton then joined the National American Woman Suffrage Association (NAWSA) in 1890. In 1894 she was elected treasurer of NAWSA, and she served in that capacity until 1910. From 1902 until 1910 she edited the suffrage monthly *Progress.* She was a seemingly inexhaustible part of the suffrage movement. She appeared before congressional committees, prepared reports of conventions, traveled extensively, organized annual conventions for the Ohio Woman Suffrage Association, ran two unsuccessful state suffrage campaigns, and directed a successful 1916 campaign to secure municipal suffrage for Ohio's women. She was also president of the Ohio Woman Suffrage Association for 18 years. After ratification of the Nineteenth Amendment, Upton continued to stay close to politics. In 1920 she became the first woman to hold the position of vice chairman of the Republican National Executive Committee, an office she held until 1924. Her last appointment was as liaison officer between the Ohio Department of Public Welfare and the Ohio governor, Myers Y. Cooper. Upton wrote numerous political articles for newspapers and magazines that emphasized women's roles in American history. She also published a children's book and two historical works, *A Twentieth Century History of Trum-* bull County, Ohio (1909) and *History of the Western Reserve* (1910).

Wallace, Zerelda Gray Sanders
(August 6, 1817–March 19, 1901) *temperance and women's suffrage reformer*
A former first lady of Indiana (1837–41), Wallace in 1874 traveled to Cleveland where 17 state delegates formed the National Woman's Christian Temperance Union (WCTU). Wallace became a prominent member of the union, and she organized an Indiana branch of the WCTU, of which she served as president in 1877 and later from 1879 to 1883. In 1875 she offered a resolution before the national convention of WCTU stating that women's suffrage was essential to the temperance movement, which was approved. In 1878 she helped May Wright Sewall launch the Indianapolis Equal Suffrage Association. She also founded the Indiana Woman Suffrage association after the example of Susan B. Anthony's National Woman Suffrage Association.

Warren, Mercy Otis (September 14, 1728–
October 29, 1814) *historian, poet, playwright, Revolutionary War patriot*
Mercy Otis Warren was born in Barnstable, Massachusetts. She received no formal education but listened to her brothers' lessons and enjoyed access to her uncle's library. Warren's husband, James Warren, was a member of the Massachusetts legislature; this, along with Warren's ties to her friend Abigail Adams and her brother James Otis, a leader of the colonies' resistance to the Stamp Act of 1765, gave Warren an inside look at Revolutionary politics. She began her three-volume *History of the Rise, Progress, and Termination of the American Revolution* near the end of the 1770s; it was published in 1805. Warren's plays include *The Adulterer* (1772), *The Defeat* (1773), and *The Group* (1775). Under the pseudonym "A Columbian Patriot," she wrote a critical analysis of the U.S. Constitution, *Observations on the New Constitution, and on Federal Conventions* (1788). Her *Poems, Dramatic, and Miscellaneous* was published in 1790.

Weld, Theodore Dwight (November 23, 1803–
February 3, 1895) *abolitionist, supporter of women's suffrage*
Weld was born in Hampton, Connecticut. He prepared for the ministry at Oneida Institute in Whitesboro, New York. As a student there, he worked in

support of temperance and became one of its most powerful advocates. In 1834 Weld trained agents for the American Anti-Slavery Society. By 1836 the success of these agents was so great that the American Anti-Slavery Society abandoned its pamphlet campaign and devoted all its resources to the speakers, whose numbers had now reached 70. One of these new speakers was Angelina Grimké, whom Weld married on March 14, 1838. Weld lobbied for abolition in Washington and assisted John Quincy Adams in his campaign against slavery in the House of Representatives. Weld's most famous publication was *American Slavery As It Is: Testimony of a Thousand Witnesses* (1839), prepared with his wife, Angelina, and her sister, Sarah Grimké.

Wells-Barnett, Ida Bell (July 16, 1862– March 25, 1931) *journalist, teacher, organizer*
Born of enslaved parents in Holly Springs, Mississippi, and educated in a local freedmen's school, Wells-Barnett began her career in teaching. Moving to Memphis in 1884, she continued to teach and to further her own education at Fisk University and Lemoyne Institute. While riding on the Chesapeake & Ohio Railroad she was forcibly removed from a car reserved for whites. Wells-Barnett filed a lawsuit against the railroad and wrote an article about the incident. She then began writing for black newspapers under the pen name "Iola." Due to her criticisms of the disparate educations offered to black and white children, she lost her teaching job in 1891. She then directed all her energy toward a career in journalism. During this time Wells-Barnett purchased an interest in the *Memphis Free Speech* newspaper. In 1892, in response to the lynching of three friends who had been accused of raping a white woman, Wells-Barnett began a crusade against lynching. She toured the United States and England lecturing on this subject. She founded antilynching societies and African-American women's clubs wherever she visited. Her statistical study of lynchings during a three-year period, entitled *A Red Record,* was published in 1895. In the years to come she would help establish the National Association of Colored Women and the National Association for the Advancement of Colored People and sit as chairman of the Chicago Equal Rights League. As Chicago's black population increased, she organized a black women's organization to initiate long-term projects for that community. In

1910 she founded the Negro Fellowship League and, with her salary as a court probation officer, helped fund such projects as a community shelter and a recreation and employment center. She also organized the first black women's suffrage association, the Alpha Suffrage Club.

Willard, Frances E. (September 28, 1839– February 18, 1898) *orator, suffrage and temperance activist*
Following her graduation from North Western Female College in 1859, Frances Willard began teaching. After working at a succession of schools, she became president of the Evanston College for Ladies in 1871, the year of its founding. When the college became part of Northwestern University in 1873, Willard became the university's dean of women. In 1874 she resigned her position at Northwestern and joined the growing crusade against liquor by becoming the corresponding secretary of the National Woman's Christian Temperance Union. In 1879 she became its president, holding this position until her death. She was a powerful speaker who was able to bring about effective political action on behalf of the temperance and women suffrage movements. Many women who had never before been politically active joined her crusade and then became suffragists as well. She became very influential in the Prohibition Party and also in the Populist Party but was disappointed in her wish to merge these two parties into a national reform party. In 1883 she organized the World's Woman's Christian Temperance Union and became its first president. She was elected president of the National Council of Women in 1888. She wrote many articles and several books, including: *Woman and Temperance* (1883), the autobiographical *Glimpses of Fifty Years* (1889), *How to Win* (1886), and *A Great Mother* (1894). She coedited *A Woman of the Century* (1893) with Mary Livermore.

Woodhull, Victoria Claflin (September 23, 1838– June 10, 1927) *reformer, orator*
A woman of diverse talents, Woodhull utilized her oratory acumen—and methods viewed as quite unconventional—to campaign against Victorian American sexual standards. Woodhull and her sister, Tennessee Celeste Claflin (1845–1923), were spiritualists, the proprietors of a successful brokerage house, and the owners of a weekly publication. Influenced by Stephen Paul Andrews, a proponent of Pantarchy (a belief that an

ideal government would be characterized by "free love," common property, and the shared care of children), Woodhull published *Origins, Tendencies and Principles of Government* in series form in 1870 and as a book in 1871. Its success was instrumental in her decision to declare herself a candidate for the U.S. presidency in 1870. This failed candidacy brought to her attention the cause of women's suffrage. She immediately seized upon the resolutions drawn up by Francis Minor, which stated that women, as citizens, already had their rights—including the right of suffrage—guaranteed under the Fourteenth Amendment. Her speech to the House of Representatives judiciary committee urging congressional recognition of this position catapulted her dramatically, but briefly, into the organized woman's movement. In 1870 Woodhull began *Woodhull & Claflin's Weekly;* she maintained publication for six years, with several interruptions, and used the newspaper to amplify her views and interests. Woodhull's waning popularity and mounting financial problems were increased when she again made headlines by revealing the Beecher-Tilton adultery case in a speech before the National Association of Spiritualists in 1872. The small part she played in this scandal by publicly revealing it speedily concluded her career in the United States. Woodhull moved to England in 1877. There she married her third husband, resumed lecturing, and published a journal, the *Humanitarian,* devoted to eugenics, from 1892 to 1901.

Wright, Frances (September 6, 1795–December 13, 1852) *abolitionist, author*

Wright's first successful book, *Views of Society and Manners in America,* was published in 1821 upon her return to Great Britain from a tour of the United States. When she witnessed slavery in Mississippi in 1825, she published *A Plan for the Gradual Abolition of Slavery Without Danger of Loss to the Citizens of the South,* which offered Congress a proposal to use public lands for slave labor but credit profits toward the purchase of slaves' freedom. When the proposal was ignored, Wright established a model community in Tennessee, a plantation she named Nashoba, and bought several slaves and put them to work toward their emancipation. Opposing religion in 1829, Wright bought a church on Broome Street in New York City that she converted into a "hall of science" where she conducted regular lectures on numerous issues, including the legal rights of women. Wright became an important figure in the working-class political movement in New York. She won a seat in the legislature for the state elections, as a member of the working-class "Fanny Wright party." Wright began lecturing in Cincinnati, speaking for the Democratic ticket in the presidential election of 1836 and for the midterm elections in New York in 1838. Her last book, *England, the Civilizer,* was published in 1848.

Wright, Martha Coffin Pelham
(December 25, 1806–January 4, 1875) *suffragist*

Wright's reform activities began in 1848 when she joined her sister Lucretia Mott and Elizabeth Cady Stanton in organizing the first national women's rights convention at Seneca Falls. She was secretary of the woman's rights convention at Syracuse in 1852, vice president of the Philadelphia convention in 1854, and in 1855 served as president of conventions in Cincinnati, Saratoga, and Albany. She was an important member of the New York State Woman's Rights Committee and served as president of its convention in New York City in 1860. She was a chief adviser of Susan B Anthony and Elizabeth Cady Stanton and advocated a gradual approach to women's rights, beginning on a state level and moving up toward national suffrage. In 1866 she joined Anthony and Stanton in forming the American Equal Rights Association. In 1869 she helped establish the National Woman Suffrage Association. In 1874 she was elected president of the National Woman Suffrage Association.

APPENDIX C
Maps

1. American women enfranchised at the time of the Seneca Falls Convention, 1848
2. States and territories extending suffrage to women by the 50th anniversary of the Seneca Falls Convention, 1898
3. States and territories extending suffrage to women prior to the adoption of the Nineteenth Amendment, August 26, 1920
4. States and territories ratifying the Nineteenth Amendment to the U.S. Constitution prior to its adoption, August 26, 1920
5. States and territories ratifying the Nineteenth Amendment to the U.S. Constitution, September 1920–1984
6. Key sites of the Women's Suffrage Movement, 1807–1917

American Women Enfranchised at the Time of the Seneca Falls Convention, 1848

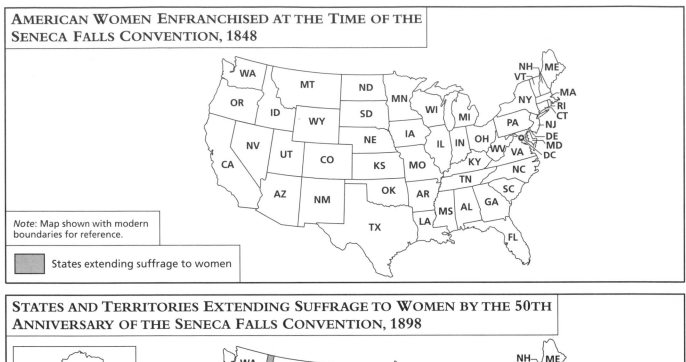

Note: Map shown with modern boundaries for reference.

☐ States extending suffrage to women

States and Territories Extending Suffrage to Women by the 50th Anniversary of the Seneca Falls Convention, 1898

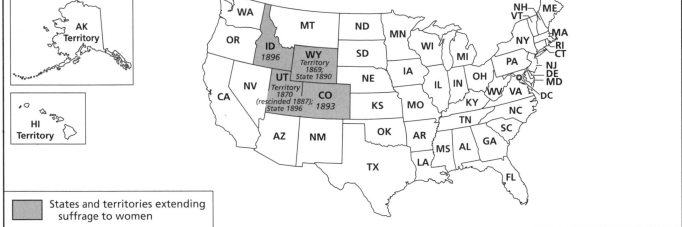

AK Territory

HI Territory

WA

MT

OR

ID *1896*

WY Territory *1869*; State *1890*

ND

MN

NH VT

ME

NV

UT Territory *1870* (rescinded *1887*); State *1896*

CO *1893*

SD

WI

NY

MA RI CT

CA

NE

IA

MI

PA

NJ DE MD

IL

IN

OH

WV VA

DC

KS

MO

KY

NC

AZ

NM

OK

AR

TN

SC

TX

MS

AL

GA

LA

FL

☐ States and territories extending suffrage to women

States and Territories Extending Suffrage to Women Prior to the Adoption of the Nineteenth Amendment, August 26, 1920

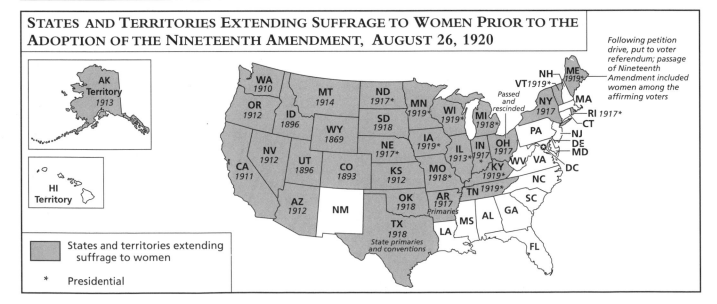

Following petition drive, put to voter referendum; passage of Nineteenth Amendment included women among the affirming voters

AK Territory *1913*

HI Territory

WA *1910*

MT *1914*

ND *1917**

MN *1919**

WI *1919**

MI *1918**

NH

VT *1919**

ME *1919**

OR *1912*

ID *1896*

WY *1869*

SD *1918*

IA *1919**

IL *1913**

IN *1917**

OH *1917*

Passed and rescinded

NY *1917*

MA

RI *1917**

CT

NV *1912*

UT *1896*

CO *1893*

NE *1917**

MO *1918**

KY *1919**

PA

NJ DE MD

WV VA

DC

CA *1911*

KS *1912*

AR *1917 Primaries*

TN *1919**

NC

AZ *1912*

NM

OK *1918*

SC

TX *1918 State primaries and conventions*

LA

MS

AL

GA

FL

☐ States and territories extending suffrage to women

* Presidential

STATES AND TERRITORIES RATIFYING THE NINETEENTH AMENDMENT TO THE U.S. CONSTITUTION PRIOR TO ITS ADOPTION, AUGUST 26, 1920

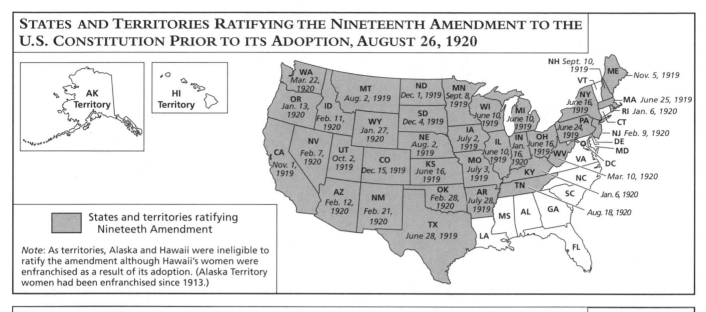

States and territories ratifying Nineteeth Amendment

Note: As territories, Alaska and Hawaii were ineligible to ratify the amendment although Hawaii's women were enfranchised as a result of its adoption. (Alaska Territory women had been enfranchised since 1913.)

STATES AND TERRITORIES RATIFYING THE NINETEENTH AMENDMENT TO THE U.S. CONSTITUTION, SEPTEMBER 1920–1984

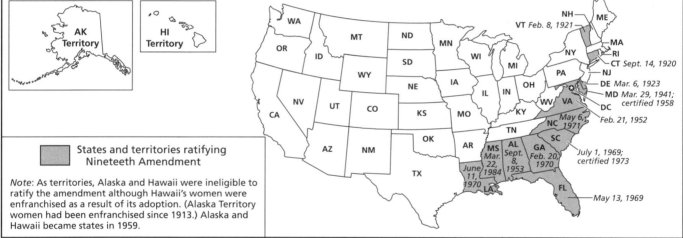

States and territories ratifying Nineteeth Amendment

Note: As territories, Alaska and Hawaii were ineligible to ratify the amendment although Hawaii's women were enfranchised as a result of its adoption. (Alaska Territory women had been enfranchised since 1913.) Alaska and Hawaii became states in 1959.

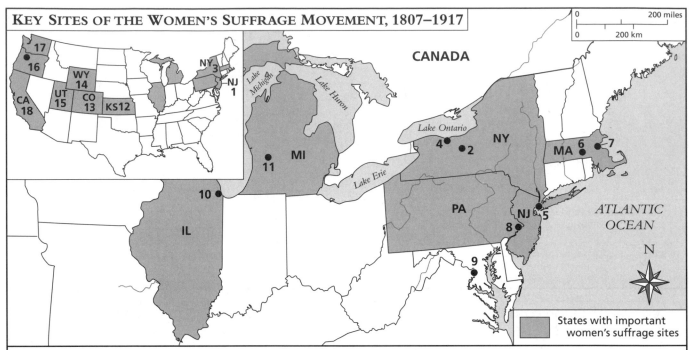

KEY SITES OF THE WOMEN'S SUFFRAGE MOVEMENT, 1807–1917

States with important women's suffrage sites

1. **New Jersey (State of), 1807:** New Jersey passes a bill denying women the vote. Women had been voting in that state since 1787.

2. **Seneca Falls, New York, 1848:** A women's rights convention is led by Elizabeth Cady Stanton, Lucretia Mott, and Lucy Stone and produces "Declaration of Rights and Sentiments."

3. **New York (State of), 1867:** Lucy Stone, Susan B. Anthony, and Elizabeth Cady Stanton address the Constitutional Convention requesting that the revised constitution include women's suffrage, but their efforts fail.

4. **Rochester, New York, 1872:** Fourteen women successfully vote in the presidential elections, including Susan B. Anthony, who casts her ballot for Ulysses S. Grant. She is arrested several days later and fined $100 (which she refuses to pay) during her 1873 trial.

5. **New York, New York, 1910, 1912, 1915:** The first suffrage parade in New York City is organized by the Women's Political Union in 1910. In 1912, 20,000 suffrage supporters join a parade; by 1915, 40,000 march in a suffrage parade.

6. **Worcester, Massachusetts, 1850:** The first national women's rights convention attracts more than 1,000 participants. Annual conferences are held through 1860 (except 1857).

7. **Boston, Massachusetts, 1869:** After Congress adopts the Fifteenth Amendment to the U.S. Constitution, which guarantees voting rights to every male citizen regardless of race, the women's rights movement splits into factions due to disagreements over the amendment. Elizabeth Cady Stanton and Susan B. Anthony believe it should be scrapped in favor of universal suffrage, and they form the National American Woman Suffrage Association (NWSA) in New York. Lucy Stone, Henry Blackwell, and Julia Ward Howe support suffrage for black men first and organize the American Woman Suffrage Association (AWSA) in Boston.

8. **Philadelphia, Pennsylvania, 1876:** NWSA members write a document entitled "Declaration and Protest of the Women of the July 4 United States" to be read at the centennial celebration in Philadelphia. When the request to present the declaration is denied, Susan B. Anthony and four other women charge the speakers' rostrum and thrust the document into the hands of Vice President Thomas W. Ferry.

9. **Washington, D.C., 1913 and 1917:** Alice Paul and Lucy Burns form the Congressional Union (later the National Women's Party) and organize a parade of more than 5,000 suffragists. Though marchers are mobbed by abusive crowds along the way, the parade successfully draws attention away from newly elected president Woodrow Wilson's arrival in the city. While peacefully picketing for suffrage in front of the White House, Alice Paul and 96 other members of the National Woman's Party are arrested for "obstructing traffic."

10. **Chicago, Illinois, 1913:** Ida B. Wells-Barnett founds the Alpha Suffrage Club, the first black women's suffrage association in Illinois, through which she presses for integration of the National American Woman Suffrage Association.

11. **Grand Rapids, Michigan, 1872:** Sojourner Truth is turned away from a polling booth.

12. **Kansas (State of), 1867:** Lucy Stone, Susan B. Anthony, and Elizabeth Cady Stanton traverse the state speaking in favor of a state referendum to enfranchise blacks and women, but suffrage is voted down.

13. **Colorado (State of), 1893:** Colorado becomes the first state to adopt an amendment enfranchising women.

14. **Wyoming (Territory of), 1869 and 1890:** In 1869, the Wyoming Territory grants women the right to vote and hold office, becoming the first area in the world to do so. In 1890, Wyoming joins the union as the first state with voting rights for women.

15. **Utah (Territory of), 1870:** Utah Territory grants suffrage to women.

16. **Portland, Oregon, 1871:** Abigail Scott Duniway begins publishing a weekly newspaper, *New Northwest*, dedicated to women's rights and suffrage.

17. **Washington (State of), 1910:** Women win the vote in Washington State.

18. **California (State of), 1911:** The most elaborate campaign ever mounted for suffrage succeeds in California by 3,587 votes, an average of one in every precinct.

NOTES

1. WHAT DO WOMEN WANT? 1800–1834

1. *The Lawes Resolutions of Womens Rights; or The Lawes Provision for Women* (London, 1632), pp. 124–125, as quoted in Flexner, *Century of Struggle*, 7–8. See also Hymowitz and Weissman, *History of Women in America*, 22.
2. McPherson, *Battle Cry of Freedom*, 33.
3. Ehrenreich and English, *For Her Own Good*, 142.
4. Robinson, *Massachusetts Bureau of Statistics of Labor, 14th Annual Report, 1883*, in *Feminism*, ed. Miriam Schneir, 55.
5. Dubois, *Feminism and Suffrage*, 45.
6. Flexner, *Century of Struggle*, 63.
7. Clinton, *Other Civil War*, 8.
8. Flexner, *Century of Struggle*, 9, 63.
9. "Old Records Reveal Clara Barton's Role as a Sleuth," *New York Times*, December 2, 1997.
10. Robinson, *Massachusetts Statistics of Labor, 14th Annual Report*, in Schneir's *Feminism*, 55.
11. Clinton, *Other Civil War*, 14–16.
12. Cott, *The Bonds of Womanhood*, 108–109. See also Evans, *Born for Liberty*, 70.
13. Flexner, *Century of Struggle*, 21.
14. Conway et al., *Female Experience*, 58.
15. Foner, *Factory Girls*, xvii.
16. Clinton, *Other Civil War*, 22. See also Flexner, *Century of Struggle*, 52.
17. Foner, *Factory Girls*, xix.
18. Conway et al., *Female Experience*, 82.
19. Evans, *Born for Liberty*, 88.
20. Sterling, *We Are Your Sisters*, 105, 107.
21. Ibid.
22. Clinton, *Other Civil War*, 58.

2. SLAVERY AND SUFFRAGE: 1835–1839

1. Lerner, *Grimké Sisters*, 7.
2. Griffith, *In Her Own Right*, 15.
3. Lerner, *Grimké Sisters*, 271.
4. Flexner, *Century of Struggle*, 42.
5. Berkin and Norton, *Women of America*, 179–181.
6. Clinton, *Other Civil War*, 46.
7. Evans, *Born for Liberty*, 76.
8. Ibid.
9. Conway et al., *Female Experience*, 40.
10. Evans, *Born for Liberty*, 78.
11. Lerner, *Grimké Sisters*, 11.

3. WOMEN OVERSEAS—THE WORLD ANTI-SLAVERY CONVENTION: 1840–1847

1. Tolles, *Slavery and "The Woman Question,"* 1.
2. *History of Woman Suffrage*, vol. 1, 408.
3. Tolles, *Slavery and "The Woman Question,"* 1.
4. Griffith, *In Her Own Right*, 23.
5. Stanton, Elizabeth Cady, letter to John Greenleaf Whittier, July 11, 1840, cited in Griffith, *In Her Own Right*, 6.
6. Stanton, *Eighty Years and More*, 20.
7. Stanton, Elizabeth Cady, letter to John Greenleaf Whittier, July 11, 1840, cited in Griffith, *In Her Own Right*, 6.
8. Tolles, *Slavery and "The Woman Question,"* 8.
9. *History of Woman Suffrage*, vol. 1, 420.
10. Tolles, *Slavery and "The Woman Question,"* 9.
11. *History of Woman Suffrage*, vol. 1, 55–59.
12. Gurko, *Ladies of Seneca Falls*, 50.
13. Stanton, *Eighty Years and More*, 3.
14. Ibid., 147–148.
15. Schlissel, Gibbens and Hampsten, *Far from Home*, 5–13.
16. Evans, *Born for Liberty*, 72.
17. Stanton, *Eighty Years and More*, 145–147.

4. WOMEN OF SENECA FALLS: 1848–1849

1. *History of Woman Suffrage,* vol. 1, 68.
2. Ibid., 68–73.
3. Ibid., 69.
4. Gurko, *Ladies of Seneca Falls,* 103.
5. *History of Woman Suffrage,* vol. 1, 73.
6. Ibid., 76.
7. Ibid., 76, 809. See also Barry, *Susan B. Anthony,* 62.

5. A WAVE OF AGITATION: 1850–1854

1. Harper, *Susan B. Anthony,* vol. 1, 59. See also Gurko, *Ladies of Seneca Falls,* 114.
2. Flexner, *Century of Struggle,* 78.
3. Gurko, *Ladies of Seneca Falls,* 137.
4. Ibid., 123.
5. Ibid., 123–127.
6. Harper, *Susan B. Anthony,* vol. 1, 65.
7. Gurko, *Ladies of Seneca Falls,* 109.
8. *History of Woman Suffrage,* vol. 1, 115.

6. A WHIFF OF SCANDAL—DIVORCE AND REFORM: 1855–1860

1. Harper, *Susan B. Anthony,* vol. 1, 123.
2. Ibid., 140–141.
3. *Shaw v. Shaw* 17 Day Conn. 189, 189–196.
4. Stanton, *Eighty Years and More,* 20.

7. CIVIL WARS: 1861–1865

1. *History of Woman Suffrage,* vol. 2, 883.
2. *History of Woman Suffrage,* vol. 2, 886.
3. *History of Woman Suffrage,* vol. 2, 883.
4. *History of Woman Suffrage,* vol. 2, 882.
5. *History of Woman Suffrage,* vol. 2, 882.
6. Stanton, *Eighty Years and More,* 254. See also Susan B. Anthony to Lydia Mott, cited in Barry, *Susan B. Anthony,* 149.
7. Benton, "What Women Did," 10–11. See also Livermore, *My Story,* 128–130; *History of Woman Suffrage,* vol. 2, 13–17.
8. Benton, "What Women Did," 9. See also Guernsey and Alden, *Pictorial History,* 792.
9. For accounts of homes turned into hospitals, see Chesnut, *Mary Chesnut's Civil War;* for an account of a southern woman going north to nurse Confederate soldiers, see Andrews, *War-Time Journal,* 50.
10. John G. B. Adams, in his introduction to Holland, *Our Army Nurses,* 13.
11. "Old Records Reveal Clara Barton's Role as a Sleuth," *New York Times,* December 2, 1997, 22.
12. Guernsey and Alden, *Pictorial History,* 792.
13. Benton, "What The War Did," 12–13.
14. Guernsey and Alden, *Pictorial History,* 792. Flexner, *Century of Struggle,* gives a figure of $50 million for the Sanitary Commission alone, while Benton, in "What The War Did," gives $54 million and *History of Woman Suffrage,* vol. 3, 17, gives $92 million as the Sanitary Commission's debt to women.
15. "Old Records Reveal Clara Barton's Role as a Sleuth," *New York Times,* December 2, 1997, 22.
16. Avary, *Virginia Girl,* 52. See also Chesnut, *Mary Chestnut's Civil War.*
17. Brock, *Richmond During the War,* 85–86.
18. Livermore, *My Story,* 137–139.
19. Anderson, *Brokenburn,* 100–101.
20. Ross, *Rebel Rose: Life of Rose O'Neal Greenhow, Confederate Spy,* 3, 113–116, 135–149, 192–119, 237.
21. Sigaud, Louis A. *Belle Boyd: Confederate Spy,* 1, 23–25, 35–51, 68–77, 123–139.
22. Sterling, Dorothy, 257–251.
23. Clinton, *Other Civil War,* 85.
24. *History of Woman Suffrage,* vol. 2, 18–23. See also Moore, *Women of the War,* 529–535 and Clinton, *Other Civil War,* 85.
25. Ibid.
26. *History of Woman Suffrage,* vol. 2, 284.
27. For supporting accounts, see *History of Woman Suffrage,* vol. 2, 3–13 and 863–869; Blackwell, *Military Genius,* vol. 1. For an overview of questions about these accounts, see James, James, and Boyer, *Notable Women,* vol. 1, 289–292.
28. The *National Citizen,* September 1881, cited in *History of Woman Suffrage,* vol. 2, 868–869.
29. *History of Woman Suffrage,* vol. 2, 27–39 and 869–875.
30. Sterling *We Are Your Sisters,* 249–251.
31. See Sterling, *We Are Your Sisters,* 261–300 for a general discussion, 265–266 for quote.
32. Griffith, *In Her Own Right,* 112.
33. *History of Woman Suffrage,* vol. 2, 50–69 and 894–895; Stanton, *Eighty Years and More,* 234–242; and Griffith, *In Her Own Right,* 112.
34. Griffith, *In Her Own Right,* 112.

35. *History of Woman Suffrage,* vol. 2, 78–80, and Flexner, *Century of Struggle,* 110–112.
36. *History of Woman Suffrage,* vol. 2, 40–50.
37. See letters sent to Elizabeth Cady Stanton and Susan B. Anthony in connection with the National Woman's Loyal League cited in *History of Woman Suffrage,* vol. 2, 875–888.
38. Miriam Fish to Susan B. Anthony, May 8, 1863, cited in *History of Woman Suffrage,* vol. 2, 884–885.

8. BITTER DEFEATS: 1865–1869

1. Stanton, *Eighty Years and More,* 242.
2. Flexner, *Century of Struggle,* 146–147.
3. Harper, *Susan B. Anthony,* vol. 1, 252; Barry, *Susan B. Anthony,* 164–165; and *History of Woman Suffrage,* vol. 2, 92.
4. Griffith, *In Her Own Right,* 123.
5. Wendell Phillips to Elizabeth Cady Stanton, May 10, 1865, cited in Stanton and Blatch, *Elizabeth Cady Stanton,* vol. 2, 104. See also Griffith, *In Her Own Right,* 123.
6. Elizabeth Cady Stanton to Wendell Phillips, May 25, 1865, cited in Stanton and Blatch, *Elizabeth Cady Stanton,* vol. 2, 104–105. See also Griffith, *In Her Own Right,* 123.
7. *History of Woman Suffrage,* vol. 2, 91–92.
8. Stanton, *Eighty Years and More,* 254.
9. Regarding difficulty in obtaining *any* signatures, see Elizabeth Cady Stanton to Martha C. Wright, January 6, 1866, cited in Stanton and Blatch, *Elizabeth Cady Stanton,* vol. 2, 111–112. See also *History of Woman Suffrage,* vol. 2, 93–97.
10. Flexner, *Century of Struggle,* 147–148.
11. Barry, *Susan B. Anthony,* 168–169.
12. Elizabeth Cady Stanton to Martha C. Wright, January 20, 1866, cited in Stanton and Blatch, *Elizabeth Cady Stanton,* vol. 2, 112–113.
13. Flexner, *Century of Struggle,* 146–147.
14. Barry, *Susan B. Anthony,* 172.
15. Elizabeth Cady Stanton to Martha C. Wright, January 20, 1866, cited in Stanton and Blatch, *Elizabeth Cady Stanton,* vol. 2, 112.
16. *History of Woman Suffrage,* vol. 2, 92.
17. Ibid., 152–153.
18. Ibid., 910–919.
19. F. Ellen Burr to Susan B. Anthony, April 22, 1866, cited in *History of Woman Suffrage,* vol. 2, 912.
20. *History of Woman Suffrage,* vol. 2, 153–173.
21. Ibid., 171–172.
22. Ibid., 173.
23. Ibid., 174.
24. Griffith, *In Her Own Right,* 125; *History of Woman Suffrage,* vol. 2, 178.
25. Barry, *Susan B. Anthony,* 170. See also letters of Lucy Stone complaining of sudden lack of press for women's suffrage issue, cited Wheeler, *Loving Warriors,* 215–217, 219.
26. *History of Woman Suffrage,* vol. 2, 180–181; Stanton and Blatch, *Elizabeth Cady Stanton,* vol. 2, 114–115.
27. *History of Woman Suffrage,* vol. 2, 102; Flexner, *Century of Struggle,* 151–152; Griffith, *In Her Own Right,* 126.
28. *History of Woman Suffrage,* vol. 2, 270–284.
29. Ibid., 286–287.
30. See Sterling, *We Are Your Sisters,* 332–344, for quote, 332.
31. *History of Woman Suffrage,* vol. 2, 919.
32. Ibid., 200.
33. Ibid., 194.
34. Henry Blackwell to Elizabeth Cady Stanton and Susan B. Anthony, cited in *History of Woman Suffrage,* vol. 2, 235.
35. *History of Woman Suffrage,* vol. 2, 238.
36. Barry, *Susan B. Anthony,* 178.
37. Ibid., 182.
38. Ibid.
39. Ibid., 180–182.
40. Ibid., 384.
41. Flexner, *Century of Struggle,* 151.
42. Elizabeth Cady Stanton to Lucretia Mott, January 21, 1869, cited in Stanton and Blatch, *Elizabeth Cady Stanton,* vol. 2, 121–122.
43. See Lucy Stone to the Reverend James Freeman Clarke, October 6, 1869, cited in Wheeler, *Loving Warriors,* 228–229.
44. The young woman was Hester Vaughan. See Barry, *Susan B. Anthony,* 216–217.
45. Lucy Stone to Elizabeth Cady Stanton, October 19, 1869, cited in Wheeler, *Loving Warriors,* 229.

9. SEPARATE PATHS TO SUFFRAGE: 1870–1879

1. *History of Woman Suffrage,* vol. 2, 400.
2. Griffith, *In Her Own Right,* 142.

3. Flexner, *Century of Struggle,* 156. See also Henry Blackwell to the Reverend Freeman Clark, November 17, 1870, cited in Wheeler, *Loving Warriors,* 237–238.

4. Flexner, *Century of Struggle,* 154.

5. Barry, *Susan B. Anthony,* 221–223; Griffith, *In Her Own Right,* 145.

6. Barry, *Susan B. Anthony,* 223.

7. Elizabeth Cady Stanton to Martha C. Wright, March 21, 1871, cited in Stanton and Blatch, *Elizabeth Cady Stanton,* 130–131.

8. Lucy Stone to Mrs. Campbell, June 13, 1874, cited in Wheeler, *Loving Warriors,* 250.

9. Elizabeth Cady Stanton to Susan B. Anthony, June 27, 1870, cited in Stanton and Blatch, *Elizabeth Cady Stanton,* vol. 2, 127.

10. Griffith, *In Her Own Right,* 161.

11. Flexner, *Century of Struggle,* 163.

12. *History of Woman Suffrage,* vol. 2, 731.

13. The *New York Times,* November 21, 1871, and December 21, 1871.

14. Letter of Eliza B. Snow and six other women to their "Dearly Beloved Sisters," dated June 21, 1871, in the *New York Times,* July 6, 1871.

15. Flexner, *Century of Struggle,* 165–166.

16. Victoria Woodhull to the editor of the *New York Times,* May 20, 1871, published in that newspaper May 22, 1871.

17. Flexner, *Century of Struggle,* 171–172; Griffith, *In Her Own Right,* 184.

18. *History of Woman Suffrage,* vol. 2, 443–458.

19. Isabella Beecher Hooker to Mary Rice Livermore, March 15, 1871, cited in Boydston, Kelley, and Margolis, *The Limits of Sisterhood,* 309–310.

20. *History of Woman Suffrage,* vol. 2, 461–464.

21. Flexner, *Century of Struggle,* 168.

22. *History of Woman Suffrage,* vol. 2, 934–935, 647–689; Flexner, *Century of Struggle,* 168–171.

23. *History of Woman Suffrage,* vol. 2, 630–632.

24. Ibid., 687–689.

25. Ibid.

26. Flexner, *Century of Struggle,* 172–173.

27. *History of Woman Suffrage,* vol. 2, 98.

28. *History of Woman Suffrage,* vol. 3, 42–43.

29. Lucy Stone to Elizabeth Cady Stanton, August 3, 1876, cited in Wheeler, *Loving Warriors,* 255–256.

30. Griffith, *In Her Own Right,* 156–157.

31. See Victoria Woodhull to the editor of the *New York Times,* May 20, 1871, published in that newspaper May 21, 1871.

32. Flexner, *Century of Struggle,* 176.

33. *History of Woman Suffrage,* vol. 3, 93; Flexner, *Century of Struggle,* 176.

34. Flexner, *Century of Struggle,* 177.

35. Cullen-DuPont, *Encyclopedia of Women's History in America,* 167–168, 190, 233; Flexner, 124–129.

36. *History of Woman Suffrage,* vol. 3, 119.

10. UNITED ONCE MORE: 1880–1892

1. DuBois, *Elizabeth Cady Stanton/Susan B. Anthony,* 201–207. See also *History of Woman Suffrage,* vol. 3, 179.

2. *History of Woman Suffrage,* vol. 4, 40.

3. Flexner, *Century of Struggle,* 176.

4. *History of Woman Suffrage,* vol. 4, 40.

5. See, for example, Lucy Stone to Alice Stone Blackwell, September 24, 1880, cited in Wheeler, *Loving Warriors,* 283.

6. See Henry Blackwell to Alice Stone Blackwell, September 24, 1880, cited in Wheeler, *Loving Warriors,* 282–283, and Zerelda G. Wallace to Susan B. Anthony, January 21, 1882, cited in *History of Woman Suffrage,* vol. 3, 257–258.

7. Flexner, *Century of Struggle,* 176.

8. *History of Woman Suffrage,* vol. 4, 967–970.

9. Ibid., 40.

10. Stevens, *Jailed for Freedom,* 348.

11. For full discussion of the debate, see *History of Woman Suffrage,* vol. 4, 85–111.

12. *History of Woman Suffrage,* vol. 4, 983–940.

13. Flexner, *Century of Struggle,* 180.

14. *History of Woman Suffrage,* vol. 4, 460.

15. Ibid.

16. Ibid.

17. Ibid., 992.

18. Ibid., 866.

19. *Willard, Frances.* "Address of Frances E. Willard, President of the Woman's National Council of the United States, (Founded in 1888,) at its First Triennial Meeting, Albaugh's Opera House, Washington, D.C., February 22–25, 1891. Available online. URL: http://prohibition.history.ohio-state.edu/Willard/willard.htm.

20. Cullen-DuPont, Encyclopedia of Women's History, 270, 272; Flexner, *Century of Struggle,* 187.

21. Flexner, *Century of Struggle,* 177.

22. Stanton and Blatch, *Elizabeth Cady Stanton,* vol. 2, 188.

23. Ibid.

24. *History of Woman Suffrage,* vol. 4, 994–998.

25. Ibid., 999.

26. Ibid.

27. Ibid., 1000.

28. Ibid., 1003.

29. Ibid., 135–136.

30. Ibid., 174.

11. END OF AN ERA: 1893–1906

1. *History of Woman Suffrage,* vol. 4, xiii–ix.

2. Ibid., xxx.

3. Ibid.

4. Ibid., xxiii.

5. Ibid., xxx.

6. Ibid., 455.

7. Ibid., 458.

8. Ibid.

9. Ibid.

10. Ibid., 461.

11. Stanton and Blatch, *Elizabeth Cady Stanton,* vol. 2, 302.

12. *History of Woman Suffrage,* vol. 5, 59.

13. Ibid.

14. Ibid.

15. Ibid.

16. Ibid., 59–60.

17. Ibid, 59.

18. Susan B. Anthony to Isabel Howland, signed "Susan B. Anthony (Per A.)" in another's handwriting, October 5, 1897, and Anna Howard Shaw to Isabel Howland, September 26, 1905, both in the Isabel Howland Papers, Sophia Smith Collection, Smith College, and both included in the Eyewitness Testimony section of this chapter.

19. Ibid., 253–254.

20. Griffith, *In Her Own Right,* 205.

21. Ibid.

22. Stanton, *The Woman's Bible,* 214.

23. Barry, *Susan B. Anthony,* 308.

24. Ibid.

25. Harper, *Susan B. Anthony,* vol. 3, 1163–1172.

26. Barry, *Susan B. Anthony,* 355.

12. ON STRIKE AND ON PARADE: 1907–1916

1. Elizabeth Cady Stanton, "Solitude of Self," in DuBois, *Elizabeth Cady Stanton/Susan B. Anthony,* 247.

2. Scott, "Miss Melinda Scott, Hat Trimmer."

3. Wertheimer, *We Were There,* 294–295.

4. Ibid., 275.

5. Ibid., 301.

6. Flexner, *Century of Struggle,* 252.

7. Kenneally, *Women and American Trade Unions,* 51.

8. Ibid., 63.

9. *History of Woman Suffrage,* vol. 4, 113.

10. Wertheimer, *We Were There,* 309–315.

11. Ibid., 278.

12. Kraditor, *Ideas of the Women Suffrage Movement,* 213.

13. U.S. Congress, "Suffrage Parade Hearings," 6.

14. Ibid., 27.

15. Flexner, *Century of Struggle,* 289–292. Flexner notes on page 386 that the original "Winning Plan" document has not been located. The "Winning Policy" included in the documents section of this book is a separate document that explains Catt's rejection of the confrontational methods used by the Congressional Union and, later, by the National Women's Party.

13. TO WAR AND VICTORY: 1917–1920

1. Blatch and Lutz, *Challenging Years,* 278.

2. Frost-Knappman and Cullen-DuPont, *Women's Rights on Trial,* 25–28; Flexner, *Century of Struggle,* 294–295.

3. See Stevens, *Jailed for Freedom,* 177.

4. Frost-Knappman and Cullen-DuPont, *Women's Rights on Trial,* 25–28; Flexner, *Century of Struggle,* 297.

5. Ibid., Flexner, 317.

6. Kraditor, *Ideas of the Woman Suffrage Movement,* 188–190, Flexner 317.

7. Kraditor, 213–215.

8. Ethel Eyre Valentine Dreier Papers, Sophia Smith Archives, Smith College; many of these letters are included in the Eyewitness Testimony section of this chapter.
9. See Carrie Chapman Catt Papers, New York Public Library.
10. Flexner, *Century of Struggle,* 322.
11. United Nations. *The World's Women,* 39–43.

Epilogue

1. *History of Woman Suffrage,* vol. 5, 684.
2. Flexner, *Century of Struggle,* 340.
3. Chafe, *The American Woman,* 34.
4. Evans, *Born for Liberty,* 187.
5. Brown, *American Women in the 1920s,* 60.
6. Ibid.
7. Ibid., 62.

BIBLIOGRAPHY

Alcott, Louisa May. *Hospital Sketches.* Bedford, Mass.: A BLS Publication/Applewood Books, 1993.

Anthony, Katherine. *Susan B. Anthony: Her Personal Story and Her Era,* Garden City, N.Y.: Doubleday & Company, 1954.

Ames, Mary. *From a New England Woman's Diary in Dixie.* Norwood, Mass.: Plimpton Press, 1906.

Anderson, John Q. *Brokenburn: The Journal of Kate Stone, 1861–1868.* Baton Rouge: Louisiana State University Press, 1955.

Andrews, Eliza Frances. *The War-Time Journal of a Georgia Girl, 1864–1865.* New York: D. Appleton, 1908.

Aptheker, Herbert. *A Documentary History of the Negro People in the United States.* Vol. 1. New York: A Citadel Press Book/Carol Publishing Group, 1951.

Avary, Myrta Lockett. *A Virginia Girl in the Civil War, 1861–1865.* New York: D. Appleton, 1903.

Bacon, Margaret Hope. *Valiant Friend: The Life of Lucretia Mott.* New York: Walker, 1980.

Baer, Judith A. *Women in American Law: The Struggle for Equality from the New Deal to the Present.* New York: Holmes & Meier, 1991.

Ballou, Patricia K. *Women: A Bibliography of Bibliographies.* Boston: Hall, 1980.

Bank, Mirra. *Anonymous Was a Woman: A Celebration in Words and Images of Traditional American Art—and the Women Who Made It.* New York: St. Martin's Press, 1979.

Barnes, Gilbert H., and Dwight L. Dumond, eds. *Letters of Theodore Dwight Weld, Angelina Grimké Weld and Sarah Grimké, 1822–1844.* Gloucester, Mass.: Peter Smith/American Historical Association, 1965.

Barry, Kathleen. *Susan B. Anthony: A Biography of a Singular Feminist.* New York: New York University Press, 1988.

Barton, Clara. *The Red Cross: A History of This Remarkable Movement in the Interest of Humanity.* Washington, D.C.: American National Red Cross, 1898.

Baxandall, Rosalyn, Linda Gordon, and Susan Reverby. *America's Working Women.* New York: Random House, 1976.

Benton, Josiah H., Jr. "What Women Did for the War, and What the War Did for Women." Memorial Day speech before the Soldier's Club, Wellesley, Mass., May 30, 1894. Woodbridge, Conn.: Research Publications, 1977. Microfilm.

Berkin, Carol. *First Generations: Women in Colonial America.* New York: Hill and Wang, 1996.

Berkin, Carol Ruth, and Mary Beth Norton. *Women of America: A History.* Boston: Houghton Mifflin, 1979.

Blackwell, Alice Stone. *Lucy Stone: Pioneer of Woman's Rights.* Boston: Little, Brown, 1930. Reprint, Detroit: Grand River Books, 1971.

Blackwell, Elizabeth. *Pioneer Work in Opening the Medical Profession to Women.* Hastings, U.K.: K. Barry, 1895.

Blackwell, Sarah Ellen. *A Military Genius: Life of Anna Ella Carroll of Maryland.* 2 vols. Washington, D.C.: Judd Detweiler, 1891–95. Reprint, Woodbridge, Conn.: Research Publications, 1983. Microfilm.

Blatch, Harriot Stanton, and Alma Lutz. *Challenging Years: The Memoirs of Harriot Stanton Blatch.* New York: Putnam, 1940.

Blom, Benjamin. *New York Photographs, 1850–1950.* New York: Dutton, 1982.

Bowne, Eliza Southgate. *A Girl's Life Eighty Years Ago.* Women In America Series. New York: Arno Press, 1974.

Boydston, Jeanne, Mary Kelley, and Anne Margolis. *The Limits of Sisterhood: The Beecher Sisters on Women's Rights and Women's Sphere.* Chapel Hill: University of North Carolina Press, 1988.

Brock, Sallie. *Richmond During the War; Four Years of Personal Observation. By a Richmond Lady.* New York: G. W. Carleton & Co., 1867. Reprint, Alexandria, Va.: Time-Life Books, 1983.

Brown, Dorothy M. *American Women in the 1920s: Setting a Course.* Boston: Twayne Publishers, 1987.

Buel, Joy Day, and Richard Buel, Jr. *The Way of Duty: A Woman and Her Family in Revolutionary America.* New York: W. W. Norton, 1984.

Burnett-Smith, A. *As Others See Her: An Englishwoman's Impressions of the American Woman in War Time.* Boston: Houghton Mifflin, 1919.

Butterfield, L. H., Marc Friedlander, and Mary-Jo Kline, eds. *The Book of Abigail and John: Selected Letters of the Adams Family 1762–1782.* Cambridge, Mass.: Harvard University Press, 1975.

Caroli, Betty Boyd. *First Ladies.* New York: Oxford University Press, 1987.

Catt, Carrie Chapman. Papers. Manuscript and Archives Division, New York Public Library.

————. "The Winning Policy." New York: National American Woman Suffrage Association, 1916. Microfilm.

Catt, Carrie Chapman, and Nettie Rogers Shuler. *Woman Suffrage and Politics.* New York: Scribner, 1923.

Chafe, William Henry. *The American Woman: Her Changing Social, Economic, and Political Roles, 1920–1970.* New York: Oxford University Press, 1972.

Chesnut, Mary. *Mary Chesnut's Civil War.* Edited by C. Vann Woodward. New Haven, Conn.: Yale University Press, 1981.

Child, Lydia Maria. *Letters of Lydia Maria Child.* Biographical introduction by John G. Whittier and appendix by Wendell Phillips. Boston: Houghton Mifflin, 1883. Reprint, New York: Negro University Press, 1969.

————. *Selected Letters, 1817–1880.* Edited by Milton Meltzer and Patricia G. Holland. Amherst: University of Massachusetts Press, 1982.

Civil War: Clippings from Various Newspapers, 1860–1863. New York Public Library.

Clinton, Catherine. *The Other Civil War: American Women in the Nineteenth Century.* New York: Hill and Wang, 1984.

Conway, Jill K., et al. *The Female Experience in Eighteenth and Nineteenth Century America: A Guide to the History of American Women.* Princeton, N.J.: Princeton University Press, 1985.

Cott, Nancy F. *The Bonds of Womanhood: "Woman's Sphere" in New England, 1780–1835.* New Haven, Conn.: Yale University Press, 1977.

————. *The Grounding of Modern Feminism.* New Haven: Yale University Press, 1987.

————. *Roots of Bitterness: Documents of the Social History of American Women.* New York: Dutton, 1972.

Crawford, Anne, et al. *The Europa Biographical Dictionary of British Women: Over 1,000 Notable Women from Britain's Past.* Detroit: Europa Publications, 1983.

Cullen-DuPont, Kathryn. *American Women Activists' Writings: An Anthology, 1637–2002.* New York: Cooper Square Press, 2002.

————. *The Encyclopedia of Women's History in America,* 2d ed. New York: Facts On File, 2000.

Culley, Margo. *A Day at a Time: The Diary Literature of American Women From 1764 to the Present.* New York: Feminist Press, 1985.

Dann, John C., ed. *The Revolution Remembered: Eyewitness Accounts of the War for Independence.* Chicago, Ill.: University of Chicago Press, 1980.

Davis, Allen F. *American Heroine—The Life & Legend—Jane Addams.* New York: Oxford University Press, 1973.

De Pauw, Linda Grant. *Founding Mothers: Women in America in the Revolutionary Era.* Boston: Houghton Mifflin Company, 1975.

Dexter, Elizabeth Anthony. *Colonial Women of Affairs: A Study of Women in Business and the Professions in America before 1776.* Boston: Houghton Mifflin, 1924.

Dickens, Charles. *American Notes For General Circulation.* New York: Wilson & Company, 1842. Reprint, Penguin Books, 1989.

Diner, Hasia R. *Erin's Daughters in America: Irish Immigrant Women in the Nineteenth Century.* Baltimore, Md.: Johns Hopkins University Press, 1983.

Douglass, Frederick. *Life and Times of Frederick Douglass.* New York: Collier Books/Macmillan Publishing Company, 1962.

Dublin, Thomas. *Farm to Factory: Women's Letters, 1830–1860.* New York: Columbia University Press, 1981.

DuBois, Ellen Carol. *Elizabeth Cady Stanton/Susan B. Anthony: Correspondence, Writings, Speeches.* New York: Schocken, 1981.

————. *Feminism and Suffrage: The Emergence of an Independent Women's Movement in America, 1848–1869.* Ithaca, N.Y.: Cornell University Press, 1978.

Duniway, Abigail Scott. *Path Breaking: An Autobiographical History of the Equal Suffrage Movement in Pacific Coast States.* Portland, Oreg.: James, Kerbs & Abbot, 1914.

Earle, Alice Morse. *Home Life in Colonial Days.* Stockbridge, Mass.: Berkshire House Publishers, 1993.

Ehrenreich, Barbara, and Deidre English. *For Her Own Good: 150 Years of the Experts' Advice to Women.* New York: Doubleday, 1989.

Eisler, Benita. *The Lowell Offering: Writings by New England Mill Women (1840–1845).* New York: Lippincott, 1977.

Elshtain, Jean Bethke. *Women and War.* New York: Basil Books, 1987.

Ethel Eyre Valentine Dreier Papers, Sophia Smith Collection, Smith College, Northampton, Mass.

Evans, Sara M. *Born for Liberty: A History of Women in America.* New York: Free Press, 1989.

Female Labor Reform Movement Association. *Factory Life As It Is by an Operative. Factory Tracts 1 and 2.* Lowell, Mass.: Lowell Publishing Company, 1845.

Finch, Jessica Garretson. *How the Ballot Would Help the Working Woman.* New York: The Equal Franchise Society of New York City, 1909.

Flexner, Eleanor. *Century of Struggle: The Women's Rights Movement in the United States.* Rev. ed. Cambridge, Mass.: Harvard University Press, 1975.

Foner, Philip S. *Frederick Douglass on Women's Rights.* Westport, Conn.: Greenwood Press, 1976.

———. *Women and the American Labor Movement: From Colonial Times to the Eve of World War I.* New York: Free Press, 1979.

Foner, Philip S., ed., *The Factory Girls.* Chicago: University of Illinois Press, 1977.

Foote, Katherine, *88 Bis and V.I.H.: Letters from Two Hospitals, by an American V.A.D.* Boston: Atlantic Monthly Press, 1919.

Fox-Genovese, Elizabeth. *Within the Plantation Household: Black and White Women of the Old South.* Chapel Hill: University of North Carolina Press, 1988.

Friedman, Jane M. *America's First Woman Lawyer: The Biography of Myra Bradwell.* New York: Prometheus, 1993.

Frost-Knappman, Elizabeth, and Kathryn Cullen-DuPont. *Women's Rights on Trial: 101 Historic Trials from Anne Hutchinson to the Virginia Military Institute Cadets.* Detroit: Gale, 1997.

Fuller, Margaret. *Woman in the Nineteenth Century*. New York: W. W. Norton, 1971.

Garrison, Wendell Phillips, and Francis Jackson Garrison. *William Lloyd Garrison 1805–1879*. Vol. 2. New York: Arno Press, 1969.

Gates, Henry Louis, Jr., gen. ed. *Six Women's Slave Narratives*. Introduction by William L. Andrews. The Schomburg Library of Nineteenth-Century Black Women Writers. New York: Oxford University Press, 1988.

Genovese, Eugene D. *Roll, Jordan, Roll: The World the Slaves Made*. New York: Vintage Books, 1976.

Goldstein, Leslie Friedman. *The Constitutional Rights of Women: Cases in Law and Social Change*. Madison: University of Wisconsin Press, 1989.

Goldsmith, Barbara. *Other Powers: The Age of Suffrage, Spiritualism, and the Scandalous Victoria Woodhull*. New York: Alfred Knopf, 1998.

Greenwood, John Ormerod. *Henry Hodgkin: The Road to Pendle Hill*. Lebanon: Pendle Hill, 1980.

Grew, Mary. *Dairy, 1840*. Woodbridge, Conn.: Research Publications, 1983. Microfilm.

Griffith, Elisabeth. *In Her Own Right: The Life of Elizabeth Cady Stanton*. New York: Oxford University Press, 1984.

Guernsey, Alfred H., and Henry M. Alden, eds. *Harper's Pictorial History of the Civil War*. New York: Fairfax Press, 1866.

Gurko, Miriam. *The Ladies of Seneca Falls: The Birth of the Women's Rights Movement*. New York: Schocken Books, 1974.

Harper, Francis Watkins. *Poems on Miscellaneous Subjects*. Philadelphia: Herrihew and Thompson, 1857.

Harper, Ida Husted. *The Life and Work of Susan B. Anthony*. Vols. 1–3. Indianapolis, Ind.: Hollenbeck Press, 1898.

Hendrick, Joan D. *Harriet Beecher Stowe: A Life*. New York: Oxford University Press, 1994.

Herr, Pamela. *Jessie Benton Frémont: A Biography*. New York: Franklin Watts, 1987.

Hertell, Judge. Remarks comprising in substance Judge Hertell's argument in the House of Assembly of the State of New York, in the Session of 1837, in support of the Bill to restore to married women "The Right of Property," as guaranteed by the Constitution of this State. New York: H. Durell, 1839.

Hill, Marilyn Wood. *Their Sister's Keepers: Prostitution in New York City, 1830–1870*. Berkeley: University of California Press, 1993.

History of Woman Suffrage. Vol. 1 (1881), vol. 2 (1882), vol. 3 (1886), eds. Elizabeth Cady Stanton, Susan B. Anthony, and Matilda Joslyn Gage; vol. 4 (1902), eds. Susan B. Anthony and Ida Husted Harper; vols. 5 and 6 (1922), ed. Ida Husted Harper. Reprints, Salem, New Hampshire: Ayer, 1985.

Hoff, Joan. *Law, Gender, and Injustice: A Legal History of U.S. Women*. New York: New York University Press, 1991.

Hoffer, Peter Charles. *Law and People in Colonial America*. Baltimore: Johns Hopkins University Press, 1992.

Hoffman, Ronald, and Peter J. Albert, eds. *Women in the Age of the American Revolution*. Charlottsville: University Press of Virginia, 1992.

Holland, Mary A. Gardner, ed. *Our Army Nurses. Interesting Sketches, Addresses, and Photographs of Nearly One Hundred of the Noble Women Who Served in Hospitals and on Battlefields During our Civil War*. Introduction by John G. B. Adams. Boston: Wilkins, 1895.

Hymowitz, Carol, and Michaele Weissman. *History of Women in America*. New York: Bantam, 1978.

Isabel Howland Papers, Sophia Smith Collection, Smith College, Northampton, Mass.

James, Edward T., Janet Wilson James, and Paul S. Boyer, eds. *Notable American Women, 1607–1950: A Biographical Dictionary*. Vols. 1–3. Cambridge, Mass.: Belknap Press of Harvard University, 1971.

Jeffrey, Julie Roy. *Frontier Women: The Trans-Mississippi West 1840–1880*. New York: Hill and Wang, 1979.

Jones, Jacqueline. *Labor of Love, Labor of Sorrow: Black Women, Work, and the Family from Slavery to the Present*. New York: Vintage Books, 1985.

Keckley, Elizabeth. *Behind the Scenes: Thirty Years a Slave and Four Years in the White House*. New York: G. W. Carleton & Co., 1868. Reprint, New York: Arno Press and *The New York Times,* 1968.

Kelley, Florence. "Woman Suffrage: Its Relation to Working Women and Children." Political Equality Series, vol. 4, no. 23, n.d. Woodbridge, Conn.: Research Publications, 1977. Microfilm.

Kemble, Frances Anne. *Journal of a Residence on a Georgian Plantation in 1838–1839*. Edited by John A. Scott. Athens: University of Georgia Press, 1984.

Kenneally, James J. *Women and American Trade Unions.* St. Albans, Vt.: Eden Press Women's Publications, 1979.

Kerber, Linda K. *No Constitutional Right to Be Ladies: Women and the Obligations of Citizenship.* New York: Hill and Wang, 1998.

———. *Women of the Republic: Intellect and Ideology in Revolutionary America.* New York: W. W. Norton, 1980.

Kerr, Andrea Moore. *Lucy Stone: Speaking Out for Equality.* New Brunswick, N.J.: Rutgers University Press, 1992.

Kimmel, Michael S., and Thomas E. Mosmiller. *Against the Tide; Pro-Feminist Men in the United States, 1776–1990.* Boston: Beacon Press, 1992.

Kleiman, Dana. "Alice Paul, a Leader for Suffrage and Women's Rights, Dies at 92." *New York Times,* July 10, 1977, 42.

Knight, Sarah Kemble. *The Journal of Madam Knight.* Boston: Small, Maynard & Company, 1920.

Kraditor, Aileen S. *The Ideas of the Woman Suffrage Movement, 1890–1920.* New York: Norton, 1981.

Lansing, Marian. *Mary Lyon through Her Letters.* Boston: Books, 1937.

Larcom, Lucy. *A New England Girlhood.* Boston: Houghton Mifflin, 1889. Reprint, Boston: Northeastern University Press, 1986.

Lasser, Carol, and Marlene Deahl Merrill, eds. *Friends and Sisters: Letters between Lucy Stone and Antoinette Brown Blackwell, 1846–93.* Urbana: University of Illinois Press, 1987.

Leonard, Elizabeth D. *Yankee Women: Gender Battles in the Civil War.* New York: W. W. Norton, 1994.

Lerner, Gerda. *Black Women in White America: A Documentary History.* New York: Pantheon Books, 1972.

———. *The Grimké Sisters from South Carolina: Pioneers for Women's Rights and Abolition.* New York: Schocken Books, 1967.

Livermore, Mary A. *My Story of the War: A Woman's Narrative of Four Years Personal Experience As Nurse in the Union Army, and in Relief Work at Home, in Hospitals, Camps, and at the Front, during the War of the Rebellion.* Hartford, Conn.: Worthington & Company, 1887. Reprint, Williamstown, Mass.: Corner House, 1978.

Lockridge, Kenneth A. *Literacy in Colonial New England: An Enquiry into the Social Context of Literacy in the Early Modern West.* New York: W. W. Norton, 1974.

McCreesh, Carolyn Daniel. *Women in the Campaign to Organize Garment Workers, 1880–1917.* New York: Garland, 1985.

McFeely, William S. *Frederick Douglass.* New York: W. W. Norton, 1991.

McPhee, Carol, and Ann Fitzgerald. *Feminist Quotations: Voices of Rebels, Reformers, and Visionaries.* New York: Crowell, 1979.

McPherson, James M. *Battle Cry of Freedom: The Civil War Era.* New York: Oxford University Press, 1988.

"Mademoiselle Miss," Letters from an American Girl Serving with the Rank of Lieutenant in a French Army Hospital at the Front. Boston: Butterfield, 1916.

Martineau, Harriet. *Society in America.* New York: Saunders and Otley, 1837. Reprint, edited by Seymour Martin Lipset. New Brunswick, N.J.: Transaction Books, 1981.

Massachusetts Supreme Judicial Court. "Brief for Alice Stone Blackwell, et al., Petitioners Under Bill, House No. 797, in Support of the Constitutionality of Said Bill, June 1917." Woodbridge, Conn.: Research Publications, 1977. Microfilm.

Meltzer, Milton, Patricia G. Holland, and Francine Krasno, eds. *Lydia Maria Child: Selected Letters, 1817–1880.* Amherst: University of Massachusetts, 1982.

Moffar, MaryJane, and Charlotte Painter, eds. *Revelations: Diaries of Women.* New York: Vintage Books, 1975.

Moore, Frank. *Women of the War: Their Heroism and Self-Sacrifice.* Hartford, Conn.: Scranton, 1866.

Moritz, Charles, ed. *Current Biography Who's News and Why 1977.* New York: Wilson, 1978.

Muccigrosso, Robert, ed. *Research Guide to American Historical Biography.* Vols. 1–3. Washington, D.C.: Beacham, 1988.

Norton, Mary Beth. *Liberty's Daughters: The Revolutionary Experience of American Women, 1750–1800.* New York: HarperCollins, 1980.

"Old Records Reveal Clara Barton's Role as a Sleuth," *New York Times,* December 2, 1997, p. 22.

O'Neill, William L. *Everyone Was Brave: A History of Feminism in America.* Quadrangle, 1971.

Osborn, Thomas Ward. *The Fiery Trail: A Union Officer's Account of Sherman's Last Campaigns.* Edited by Richard Harwell and Philip N. Racine. Knoxville: University of Tennessee Press, 1986.

Ossoli, Margaret Fuller, *Woman in the Nineteenth Century, and Kindred Papers Relating to the Sphere, Condition and Duties of Woman.* Boston: J. P. Jewett & Company, 1855. Reprint, New York: Books for Libraries Press, 1972.

Paul, Susan. *Memoir of James Jackson: The Attentive and Obedient Scholar, Who Died in Boston, October 31, 1833, Aged Six Years and Eleven Months.* Edited by Lois Brown. Cambridge, Mass.: Harvard University Press, 2000.

Payne, Elizabeth Anne. *Reform, Labor, and Feminism: Margaret Dreier Robins and the Women's Trade Union League.* Urbana: University of Illinois Press, 1988.

Payne, Karen. *Between Ourselves: Letters between Mothers and Daughters 1750–1982.* Boston: Houghton Mifflin, 1983.

Pease, Jane H., and William H. *Ladies, Women & Wenches; Choice and Constraint in Antebellum Charleston & Boston.* Chapel Hill: University of North Carolina Press, 1990.

Peavy, Linda, and Ursula Smith. *Women in Waiting in the Westward Movement: Life on the Home Frontier.* Norman: University of Oklahoma Press, 1994.

Peck, Mary Gray. *Carrie Chapman Catt: A Biography.* New York: H. W. Wilson Company, 1944.

Peckford v. Peckford, 1 Paige's Chancery Reports 275 (N.Y., 1828), pp. 274–275.

Phillips, Catherine Coffin. *Jessie Benton Frémont: A Woman Who Made History.* Lincoln: University of Nebraska Press, 1995.

Rankin, Jeannette. *Activist for World Peace, Women's Rights, and Democratic Government.* Typescript of an oral history conducted in 1972 by Malca Chall and Hannah Josephson, Regional Oral History Office, the Bancroft Library, University of California, Berkeley, 1974.

Richardson, Dorothy. *The Long Day: The Story of a New York Working Girl As Told by Herself.* New York: Century, 1905.

Robinson, Harriet. *Loom and Spindle: Or Life Among the Early Mill Girls.* New York: Crowell, 1898. Reprint, Kailua, Hawaii: Press Pacifica, 1976.

Roe, Elizabeth A., *Recollections of Frontier Life.* New York: Arno Press, 1980; first published, 1885.

Ross, Ishbel. *Rebel Rose: Life of Rose O'Neal Greenhow, Confederate Spy.* New York: Harper & Brothers, 1954.

Research Publications, History of Women, Guide to the Microfilm Collection. Woodbridge, Conn.: 1983.

Rossi, Alice S., ed. *The Feminist Papers.* Boston: Northeastern University Press, 1973.

Rothe, Anna, ed. *Current Biography Who's News and Why 1947.* New York: Wilson, 1948.

Rozier, John, ed. *The Granite Farm Letters: The Civil War Correspondence of Edgeworth & Sallie Bird.* Athens: University of Georgia Press, 1988.

Salmon, Marylynn. *Women and the Law of Property in Early America.* Chapel Hill: University of North Carolina Press, 1986.

Schlesinger, Arthur M. *The Almanac of American History.* New York: Putnam, 1983.

———. *The Birth of a Nation.* Boston: Houghton Mifflin, 1968.

Schlissel, Lillian. *Women's Diaries of the Westward Journey.* New York: Schocken Books, 1982.

Schlissel, Lillian, Byrd Gibbens, and Elizabeth Hampsten. *Far from Home: Families of the Westward Journey.* New York: Schocken Books, 1989.

Schneiderman, Rose. *Miss Rose Schneiderman, Cap Maker, Replies to New York Senator.* New York: Wage Earners' Suffrage League, n.d. Reprint, Woodbridge, Conn.: Research Publications, 1977. Microfilm.

Schneir, Miriam, ed. *Feminism: The Essential Historical Writings.* New York: Vintage Books, 1972.

Scott, Melinda. *Miss Melinda Scott, Hat Trimmer, Replies to New York Senator.* New York: Wage Earners' Suffrage League, n.d. Reprint, Woodbridge, Conn.: Research Publications, 1977. Microfilm.

Shaw v. Shaw 17 Day Conn. 189 (1845).

Shaw, Anna Howard. "What the War Meant to Women." Speech delivered during 1919. New York: League to Enforce Peace, 1919.

Sheppard, Alice. *Cartooning for Suffrage.* Albuquerque: University of New Mexico Press, 1994.

Sigaud, Louis. *Belle Boyd: Confederate Spy.* Richmond, Va.: Dietz Press, 1944.

Sklar, Kathryn Kish. *Catharine Beecher: A Study in American Domesticity.* New Haven, Conn.: Yale University Press, 1973.

Smith, Ethan. *Memoirs of Mrs. Abigail Bailey.* Boston: Samuel T. Armstrong, 1815. Reprint, New York: Arno Press, 1980.

Smith Family Papers. Manuscript and Archives Division, New York Public Library.

Spruill, Julia Cherry. *Women's Life and Work in the Southern Colonies.* New York: W. W. Norton, 1972.

Stanton, Elizabeth Cady. *Eighty Years and More: Reminiscences 1815–1897.* New York: European Publishing Co., 1898. Reprint, Schocken Books, 1971.

———. *The Woman's Bible.* New York: European Publishing Co., 1895. Reprint, Salem, N.H.: Ayer, 1988.

Stanton, Theodore, and Harriot Stanton Blatch. *Elizabeth Cady Stanton: As Revealed in Her Letters, Diary and Reminiscences.* Vols. 1 and 2. New York: Harper and Brothers, 1922. Reprint, New York: Arno Press and the *New York Times,* 1969.

Starkey, Marion L. *The Devil in Massachusetts: A Modern Inquiry into the Salem Witch Trials.* New York: Anchor Books, 1949.

Steel, Edward M., ed. *The Correspondence of Mother Jones.* Pittsburgh, Pa.: University of Pittsburgh Press, 1985.

Sterling, Dorothy. *Black Foremothers—Three Lives.* New York: Feminist Press and McGraw-Hill, 1973.

———. *We Are Your Sisters: Black Women in the Nineteenth Century.* New York: Norton, 1984.

Stern, Madeleine B. *We the Women: Career Firsts of Nineteenth-Century America.* New York: Schulte, 1963.

Stevens, Doris. *Jailed for Freedom.* New York: Boni and Liveright, 1920.

Stevenson, Brenda, ed. *The Journals of Charlotte Forten Grimké.* New York: Oxford University Press, 1988.

Stewart, Maria W. *Maria W. Stewart, America's First Black Woman Political Writer: Essays and Speeches.* Edited by Marilyn Richardson. Bloomington and Indianapolis: Indiana University Press, 1987.

Stimson, Julia C. *Finding Themselves: The Letters of an American Army Chief Nurse in a British Hospital in France.* New York: Macmillan, 1918. Reprint, Woodbridge, Conn.: Research Publications, 1983. Microfilm.

Strane, Susan, *A Whole-Souled Woman: Prudence Crandall and the Education of Black Women*. New York: W. W. Norton, 1990.

Stratton, Joanna L. *Pioneer Women: Voices from the Kansas Frontier*. New York: Touchstone, 1981.

Suhl, Yuri. *Ernestine L. Rose: Women's Rights Pioneer*. New York: Biblio Press, 1959.

Tingley, Elizabeth, and Donald Tingley. *Women and Feminism in American History: A Guide to Information Sources*. American Government And History Informational Guide Series, vol. 12. Detroit, Mich.: Gale Research, 1981.

Tocqueville, Alexis de. *Democracy in America*. Vol. 2. New York: Anchor Books, 1955.

Tolles, Frederick B., ed. *Slavery and "the Woman Question": Lucretia Mott's Diary on Her Visit to Great Britain to Attend the World's Anti-Slavery Convention of 1840*. Supplement no. 23 to the journal of the Friends' Historical Society. Haverford, Pa.: Friends' Historical Association, 1952.

Tomalin, Claire. *The Life and Death of Mary Wollstonecraft*. New York: New American Library, 1974.

Trollope, Frances Milton. *Domestic Manners of the Americans*. London: Whittakes, Treacher and Co., 1832. Reprint, Suffolk: England: Oxford University Press, 1984.

Uglow, Jennifer S., ed. *The Continuum Dictionary of Women's Biography*. New York: Continuum, 1989.

———. *International Dictionary of Women's Biographies*. New York: Continuum, 1982.

Ulrich, Laurel Thatcher. *Good Wives: Image and Reality in the Lives of Women in Northern New England, 1650–1750*. New York: Vintage Books, 1982.

———. *The Life of Martha Ballard, Based on Her Diary, 1785–1812*. New York: Alfred A. Knopf, 1991.

United Nations. *The World's Women 1970–1990: Trends and Statistics*. New York: United Nations, 1991.

U.S. Congress, Senate, Subcommittee of the Committee on the District of Columbia. *Suffrage Parade Hearings*. 63d Cong., special sess. Washington, D.C.: Government Printing Office, 1913. Reprint, Woodbridge, Conn.: Research Publications, 1977, Microfilm.

Van Doren, Charles, ed. *Webster's American Biographies*. Springfield, Mass.: Merriam, 1974.

Warren, Mercy Otis. *History of the Rise, Progress and Termination of the American Revolution.* Vols. 1 and 2. Indianapolis, Liberty Classics, 1988.

Weatherford, Doris. *Foreign and Female: Immigrant Women in America, 1840–1930.* New York: Schocken Books, 1986.

———. *Milestones: A Chronology of American Women's History.* New York: Facts On File, 1997.

Welch, Marvis Olive. *Prudence Crandall: A Biography.* Manchester, Conn.: Jason Publishers, 1983.

Weld, Timothy Dwight. *American Slavery As It Is.* Salem, N.H.: Ayer Company, 1991.

Wertheimer, Barbara Mayer. *We Were There: The Story of Working Women in America.* New York: Pantheon Books, 1977.

Wheeler, Leslie, ed. *Loving Warriors: Selected Letters of Lucy Stone and Henry B. Blackwell, 1853 to 1893.* New York: Dial Press, 1981.

White, Deborah Gray. *Ar'n't I a Woman? Females in the Plantation South.* New York: W. W. Norton, 1985.

Whittick, Arnold. *Woman into Citizen.* Santa Barbara, Calif.: ABC-Clio, 1979.

Who's Who in American History—Historical Volume 1607–1967. Rev. ed. Wilmette, Ill.: Marquis Publications, 1967.

Willard, Frances. Address of Frances E. Willard, President of the Woman's National Council of the United States, (Founded in 1888,) at its First Triennial Meeting, Albaugh's Opera House, Washington, D.C., February 22–25, 1891, np. Available online. URL: http://prohibition.history.ohio-state.edu/Willard/willard.htm. Downloaded June 1, 2004.

———. *Glimpses of Fifty Years: The Autobiography of an American Woman.* Chicago: National Women's Christian Temperance Union, 1889.

Wolf, Stephanie Grauman. *As Various as Their Land: The Everyday Lives of Eighteenth-Century Americans.* New York: HarperPerennial, 1993.

Wollstonecraft, Mary. *A Vindication of the Rights of Women.* Edited by Carol H. Poston. New York: W. W. Norton, 1975.

Wortman, Marlene Stein, ed. *Women in American Law.* Vols. 1 and 2. New York: Holmes & Meier Publishers, 1985.

Wright, Frances. *Views of Society and Manners In America.* London: Longman et al., 1821. Reprint, edited by Paul K. Baker. Cambridge, Mass.: Belknap Press of Harvard University, 1963.

Yale University Debating Association. *A Discussion of Woman Suffrage By the Yale University Debating Teams, in the 1914 Triangular Debate with Harvard and Princeton.* New Haven, Conn.: Yale Co-operative Corporation, 1914.

INDEX

Locators in *italics* indicate illustrations. Locators in **boldface** indicate biographical entries.
Locators followed by *m* indicate maps. Locators followed by *c* indicate chronology entries.

A

abandonment (grounds for divorce) 119
Abbot, Emma 210*c*
Abbot Academy 9*c*
Abbott, Grace 329*c*
abolition and abolitionists. *See also* slavery
American and Foreign Anti-Slavery Society 50–52, 55*c*
American Anti-Slavery Society 10*c*, 23, 50, 51, 55*c*, 119, 122*c*, 123*c*, 140
American Anti-Slavery Women 28*c*
Boston Female Anti-Slavery Society 10*c*
Lydia Maria Francis Child 24
William Lloyd Garrison 22, 23, 50
Angelina Grimké 21–23, *23*
Sarah Grimké 22, 23, 28*c*
men 165–166
Lucretia Coffin Mott 10*c*, 28*c*
National Anti-Slavery Society Convention 28*c*
National Female Anti-Slavery Society 28*c*
National Woman's Anti-Slavery Convention 25
petitions for 141
Philadelphia Anti-Slavery Society 51, *98*

Philadelphia Female Anti-Slavery Society 10*c*, 22
Republican Party 119, 120, 141, 144*c*, 145*c*
Maria W. Stewart 22
and women's rights activists 135, 202
World Anti-Slavery Convention 49–52, 55*c*
abortion 120
Abramowitz, Bessie 299*c*
Act Concerning the Rights and Liabilities of Husband and Wife, 1860 390–391
An Act for the Protection and Preservation of the Rights of Property of Married Women 30
Ada. *See* Forten, Sarah
Adair Act 91*c*
Adams, Abigail 1, 8*c*, 11
Adams, Annette Abbott 303*c*, 332*c*
Adams, F. G. 256
Adams, John 11, 136
Adams, John Quincy 28*c*–29*c*, 43
Adams Academy for Girls 9*c*
Addams, Jane 123*c*, *347*, **426**
ACLU 332*c*
books of 274*c*, 298*c*–300*c*
eyewitness account 347
Hull-House 243*c*, 271*c*, 272*c*, 298*c*
Woman's Peace Party 304*c*, 331*c*

adultery 8*c*, 119, 207, 211*c*
AERA. *See* American Equal Rights Association
African Americans *70*, 210*c*, 303*c*. *See also* abolition and abolitionists; slavery; *specific headings*
black male suffrage 166, 170, 171
Canterbury Female Boarding School 10*c*
Mary Ann Shadd Cary 91*c*
citizenship 121
disenfranchisement 267
Frederick Douglass. *See* Douglass, Frederick
education 4, 10*c*, 25
employment 27
factory workers *286*
field work 27
Fifteenth Amendment 209*c*
former slaves 140–141
Charlotte Forten 28*c*, 122*c*, 145*c*
Sarah Forten 33, **435**
Fourteenth Amendment 173*c*
Frances E. Watkins Harper 169, 196, **439**
mutual aid societies 5–6
NAACP 298*c*, 331*c*
National Association of Colored Nurses 298*c*
National Association of Colored Women 271*c*
NAWSA 326

newly freed women 169
nurses 330*c*
Mary Jane Patterson 143*c*
as property 169
Maria W. Stewart 10*c*, 22, 24, **448**
suffrage for 165, 170–171
teachers 24, 90*c*, 122*c*
Sojourner Truth. *See* Truth, Sojourner
Harriet Tubman. *See* Tubman, Harriet
Maggie Lena Walker 274*c*
Ida B. Wells-Barnett 144*c*, 296, 301*c*, **451**
women's organization 273*c*
African Female Benevolent Society of Newport 6
African Methodist Episcopal Church 173*c*
Agassiz, Elizabeth Cabot 9*c*, 241*c*, 298*c*
"age of protection" 237–238, 242*c*, 271*c*, 330*c*
Ahern, Mary Eileen 271*c*, 272*c*
Ahmanson, Caroline Leonetti 330*c*
aid societies 5–6, 27, 140–141
Akron convention 88–89, 91*c*, *94*
Alabama 301*c*
Alaska 273*c*, 300*c*, 304*c*
Albany convention 91*c*, 122*c*, 136, 143*c*
alcohol. *See* liquor

Alcott, Louisa May 144*c*, 173*c*, 209*c*, 227, 242*c*
Alden, Henry M. 154
alimony 56*c*
Allen, Florence Ellinswood 331*c*, 332*c*
"allies" 293
Allyn, Abba 11
Alpha Suffrage Club 296, 301*c*
Alphonsa, Mary Lathrop 273*c*
AMA (American Medical Association) 211*c*
American Academy of Arts and Letters 298*c*
American and Foreign Anti-Slavery Society 50–52, 55*c*
American Anti-Slavery Society 10*c*, 23, 50, 51, 55*c*, 119, 122*c*, 123*c*, 140
American Anti-Slavery Women 28*c*
American Association of University Women 241*c*
American Bar Association 329*c*, 330*c*
American Civil Liberties Union 332*c*
American Equal Rights Association (AERA) 166, 167, 171, 173*c*, 202
American Federation of Labor 243*c*, 244*c*
American Medical Association (AMA) 211*c*
American Medical Women's Association (AMWA) 304*c*
American Missionary Association 141
American Notes for General Circulation (Charles Dickens) 369–371
American Nursing Association 298*c*
American Psychological Association (APA) 274*c*
American Red Cross. *See* Red Cross

American Society of Civil Engineers (ASCE) 274*c*
American Woman's Educational Association 174*c*
The American Woman's Home (Catherine Beecher) 55*c*, 173*c*
American Woman Suffrage Association 172, 174*c*, 202, 235, 240, 243*c*
America's Working Woman (Rosalyn Baxandall, Linda Gordon, and Susan Reverby) 15
Ames, Mary 160, 161
AMWA (American Medical Women's Association) 304*c*
"An Act Concerning the Rights and Liabilities of Husband and Wife" 123*c*
Anderson, John Q. 150, 156, 158
Anderson, Manervia 192
Anderson, Margaret 303*c*
Anderson, Mary 332*c*
Andersonville Confederate prison camp 137, 145*c*
Andrews, Eliza Frances 158, 160–162
Anneke, Mathilde 56*c*, 75*c*
Anonymous Was a Woman (Mirra Bank) 12
Anthony, Lucy E. 289
Anthony, Mary S. 291
Anthony, Susan Brownell 8*c*, 89, 237, 240, **426**
on 25th anniversary of suffrage movement 225–226
on 50th anniversary of Seneca Falls Convention 279–280
on abolition 157
and AERA 167
arrest of 205, 210*c*
on being fined for voting 225
bequest to 241*c*

on Harriot Stanton Blatch 293
and Amelia Jenks Bloomer 88
censor of Stanton by 268
and Civil War 121, 135, 136, 142, 165
and coeducation 118
Daughters of Temperance 75*c*
deathbed words 289
death of 270, 274*c*
at Democratic Convention 173*c*
description of 88
diary excerpt 175
and divorce reform 120
on Elizabeth Cady Stanton 263
and emancipation 141
exchange with Frederick Douglass 195
eyewitness account 277
and federal amendment 274*c*
final years of 268–269, *269*
and first women's rights convention 86–87
Fourteenth Amendment 165, 204
The History of Woman Suffrage 241*c*, 242*c*, 274*c*
illegal voting of 205, 210*c*
International Council of Women 240
on length of suffrage battle 285
letter to James A. Garfield on importance of suffrage 248
Married Woman's Property Act 91*c*, 117, 122*c*, 123*c*
at national women's rights convention 167
NAWSA 243*c*, 244*c*, 269, 272*c*
and New York state legislature 89, 122*c*, 123*c*, 168

on not addressing civil rights issues 280
on parallels between American Revolution and suffrage movement 131
and party platforms 235
petitions of 122*c*
predictions of success for suffrage 191
on preparations for International Council of Women 258–259
on presidency of NAWSA 262
on proposal of Sixteenth Amendment 247
on protection of civil rights 227
public speaking 118
and racism 171
on receiving annuity 275–276
on religion 277, 278–279
resignation of 269
resignation speech 281–282
and *Revolution* 202–203
and slavery 119–121
and Southern suffragists 267
and Elizabeth Cady Stanton 90*c*, *278*
and state-by-state approach 235–236
on suffrage meetings/lectures in New York State 124–127
on suffrage tracts 187, 188
on Syracuse convention 264
on temperance law 101
temperance movement 87–88, 90*c*
travels in New York State 117–118
trial of 205–206, 211*c*
at U.S. centennial 206–207

Anthony, Susan Brownell
(continued)
    on votes for submitting
        suffrage amendment
        275
    voting by 205, 210c
    on voting in 1872 225
    on westward migration 85
    on women's subjugation in
        marriage 131
Anthony amendment 303c.
    See also Sixteenth
    Amendment, proposed;
    Susan B. Anthony
    amendment
Anti-Female Suffrage
    Committee 170
Antioch College 208
Anti-Slavery Convention of
    American Women 28c
Anti-Slavery Standard 167,
    168
APA (American
    Psychological
    Association) 274c
Appeal and Petition
    Circulated in the State of
    New York, 1859
    388–389
Appeal of President Wilson
    to the U.S. Senate to
    Submit the Federal
    Amendment for Woman
    Suffrage, 1918 423–425
"Appeal to the Christian
    Women of the South"
    (Angelina Grimké)
    22–23, 28c, 359–362
Appeal to the Women of
    New York, 1860
    391–392
Aptheker, A. 14–15
Arizona 300c
Arkansas 329c, 330c
Arkon convention 90c
Armstrong, Mother 123c
Army, U.S. 272c, 273c, 332c
Arneil, Annie 339
Arnold, Virginia 339
arrest 329c
Arthur, T. S. 62

ASCE (American Society of
    Civil Engineers) 274c
assassination 145c
attorney general, assistant
    332c
"Aunt Susan" 270. See also
    Anthony, Susan Brownell
Avary, Myrta Lockett
    148–149
Avery, Rachel G. Foster
    284, 426–427
The Awakening (Kate
    Chopin) 272c
Ayers, Mary 10c

B
Babb, Arabella Mansfield
    174c
Bagley, Sarah G. 27, 53, 56c,
    427
Bank, Mirra 12
banks 274c, 329c–331c
bar, admission to 174c, 206,
    212c, 213, 298c
Barker, Frances Dana 75c
Barnard College 299c
Barnes, Gilbert H. 31,
    33–35, 38–47, 57, 60,
    61–62
Barrett, Rose Tyler 332c
Barry, Kathleen 170,
    180–181, 191–193,
    198–199, 201, 262, 277,
    278, 289
Barry, Leonora 242c
Bartlett, John Henry 348
Barton, Clara 9c, 136–137,
    143c, 145c, 164, 213,
    241c, 427
Bary, Francis 114
Bash, Elizabeth 188
"Battle Hymn of the
    Republic" 143c, 210
Baxandall, Rosalyn 15
Beard, Charles 321–322
Beaumont, Mrs. A. 247
Beauregard, Pierre G. T.
    138, 139
Beckley, Lucy 12
Beecher, Catharine Ester
    7c, 34, 55c, 211c, 427–428

American Woman's
    Educational Association
    90c
American Woman's Home
    173c
    on education 56c, 90c
    eyewitness accounts 14,
        34, 67, 215, 222, 223
    Angelina Grimké 24
    Hartford Female Seminary
        9c, 25–26
Beecher, Henry Ward 207,
    211c, 428
Beecher, Lyman 14
Beeckman, R. Livingston
    348
Bellanca, Dorothy Jacobs
    329c
Bellemy, Mary 298c
Bellows, Henry 93
Belmont, Alva Erskine
    Smith Vanderbilt 293,
    299c, 304c, 428
benevolent societies 27
Benjamin, Judah P. 139
bequests, to women's
    movement 239, 241c,
    272c, 304c
Berkin, Carol Ruth 11–14,
    32, 33, 70
Between Ourselves (Karen
    Payne) 67, 319
Bible 23
Bickerdyke, Mary Ann 144c
Biggs, Caroline A. 251
Bilgrien, Herman 347
Birbeck v. Ackroyd 211c
Bird, Edgeworth 158
Birney, James 50
birth control 211c, 302c,
    304c, 305c, 330c
Bissell, Emily Perkins 298c
Black, Winifred Sweet
    Bonfils 274c
black male suffrage 166,
    170, 171
Blackwell, Alice Stone 117,
    122c, 209, 240, 243c,
    254, 263–264, 278, 428
Blackwell, Antoinette L.
    Brown 9c, 132, 141,

211c, 225, 227–228, 230,
    256, 429
Blackwell, Elizabeth 9c, 75c,
    122c, 143c, 267, 429
Blackwell, Emily 242c
Blackwell, Henry B.
    on 1872 Republican
        Convention 224
    on Cleveland convention
        199, 216
    on Colorado suffrage
        campaign 275
    on combining black
        suffrage and woman
        suffrage issues 182,
        183
    on Kansas campaign 201
    lobbies for suffrage 241c
    on Nebraska suffrage
        campaign 251
    on prohibition 261
    Republican Party 207,
        241c
    on Rhode Island suffrage
        campaign 257–258
    Lucy Stone 117, 122c, 268
    on suffrage campaign in
        Kansas 190
    on women's rights in
        marriage 115–116
Blackwell, Samuel 117,
    122c
Blair, Henry W. 252
Blake, Ann M. 63
Blake, Lillie Devereux 273c
Blanck, Max 295
Blatch, Harriot Eaton
    Stanton 293, 311, 429
    Susan Brownell Anthony
        293
    Challenging Years 306–318,
        321–322, 333–334, 336
    Elizabeth Cady Stanton. See
        Elizabeth Cady Stanton
    Equality League of Self-
        Supporting Women
        293–294, 298c
    eyewitness accounts 312,
        313, 315–317, 334, 336
    Mobilizing Woman Power
        330c

National Woman's Party 325

return to United States 274c

Women's Political Union 294, 298c

Blatch, Nora Stanton 274c

blockades 138

Bloomer, Amelia Jenks 8c, 75c, 88, *88*, 91c, *96*, 135, **429–430**

Bloomer outfits 84, 88, 90c, 91c, *96*

Bly, Nellie 242c

The Bonds of Womanhood (Nancy F. Cott) 11–16, 19, 62

Bonham, Mary T. 156

The Book of Abigail and John: Selected Letters of the Adams Family (L. H. Butterfield, Marc Friedlander, and Mary-Jo Kline) 11

Bordon, Hannah 8c

Boston Female Anti-Slavery Society 10c

Boston Manufacturing Co. 7c

Boston, Massachusetts 456m

Boston University 174c, 208, 210c, 211c

Boyd, Belle 139

Boydston, Jeanne 14, 217, 220–224, 230, 260–262, 284

Boyle, Emmet D. 301c

Bradford, George 51

Bradford Academy 10c

Bradley, Amy M. 148, 150–151

Bradwell, Myra 10c, 173c, 174c, 206, 211c, 271c, **430**

Bradwell v. Illinois 211c, 408

Brahany, T. W. 340

Breckenridge, John C. 143c

Breckinridge, Margaret 143c

Brewster, Mary 271c

brickyard workers *84*

Brock, Sallie 149, 154–156

Brodie, Alexander O. 273c

Brokenburn (John Q. Anderson) 150, 156, 158

Brooklyn Association of Relief 137

Brown, Antoinette L. Blackwell 85, 86, 90c, 91c, 102, 117, 122c

Brown, Beriah 220–221

Brown, Hallie Quinn **430–431**

Brown, John 123c

Brown, Joseph A. 257

Brown, Mary Olney 199–200, 250

Brown, M. C. 253

Brown, Olympia 28c, 144c, 190–191, 244c, **431**

Brownell, Kady 143c

Bryan, William Jennings 273c, 303c

Bryant, Alice Gertrude 303c

Bryn Mawr College 241c, 242c, 298c

Buckminster, Joseph 11

Bullard, Laura Curtis 203

Burleigh, Celia 197

Burn, Ethel 305c

Burn, Harry 328, 351

Burn, Mrs. J. L. 351

Burnett, Mr. 111

Burnham, Carrie S. 210c

Burns, Lucy 300c–302c, 326, 342, 343, **431**

Burr, Frances Ellen 109, 178, 227

Burroughs, Nanny Helen 273c

Bush, Abigail 74

Butler, Benjamin F. 151

Butterfield, L. H. 11

C

Cady, Daniel 123c

California 299c, 456m

Calkins, Mary Whiton 274c

Callor, Mrs. 246–247

Campbell, John Allen 203

Camp Fire Girls 299c

Canterbury, Connecticut 25

Canterbury Female Boarding School 10c

Carrie Chapman Catt (Mary Gray Peck) 352

Carrie Chapman Catt Papers 311, 320–322, 324, 333–335, 337–340, 347

Carroll, Anna Ella 140, 143c

Cary, Mary Ann Shadd 91c

cash economy 6

Catharine Beecher: A Study in American Domesticity (Kathryn Kish Sklar) 34, 43

Cather, Willa 300c, 302c

Catt, Carrie Chapman *283, 350*, **431–432**. *See also* Carrie Chapman Catt Papers

bequest to 304c

eyewitness accounts 276–278, 282, 317, 320–324, 348, 350–352

League of Women Voters 353

NAWSA 269, 270, 272c, 274c, 297, 299c, 305c

Nineteenth Amendment 353, 354

on power of vote 353, 354

Senate Committee on Woman Suffrage 273c, 330c

and Southern suffragists 326

strategies of 297, 326

wartime approach of 326, 329c

"Winning Plan/Policy" 297, 326, 419–423

Woman Suffrage 346–351

Woodrow Wilson 305c

census 241c

Centennial Tea Party 211c

Century of Struggle (Eleanor Flexner) 12, 15, 17, 20, 60, 62, 63, 67, 77,

322–323, 335–336, 346, 348, 351

Chace, Elizabeth B. 254, 255

Challenging Years (Harriot Stanton Blatch and Alma Lutz) 306–318, 321–322, 333–334, 336

Chamberlain, George E. 301c

Chapman, Maria Weston 7c, 34, **432**

Chenoweth, Alice 332c

Chesnut, Mary Boykin 146–147, 242c

Chicago, Illinois 456m

Child, Lydia Maria Francis 7c, *46*, 143c, 145c, 241c, **432**

as abolitionist 24

eyewitness accounts 17, 44, 46–47, 159, 161, 178

children

"age of protection" 237–238, 242c, 271c, 330c

"best interest" of 8c

custody of. *See* custody rights

labor of 271c, 305c, 329c

support of 56c

Children's Bureau 300c, 329c

Chopin, Kate 272c

Christian Scientists 211c

Christmas seal 298c

churches 5, 23, 209c

"civil death" 2

civil disobedience 122c

Civil Service Act 241c

Civil Service Commission 332c

Civil War **135–164**

aid to former slaves in 140–141

Susan B. Anthony 121, 135, 136, 142, 165

approach to 135–136, 325

battlefield *146*

care of wounded 136

Civil War *(continued)*
  and Anna Ella Carroll
    140
  fund-raising 137–138
  nursing 136–137
  plans in 140
  spies 138, 139, 142, 145*c*
  Elizabeth Cady Stanton
    135, 136, 165
  and voting 142
  women's contributions
    142
  women soldiers 139–140,
    142
Civil War: Clippings 148, 151
Claflin, Tennessee "Tinnie"
  207, *207,* 211*c*
Clark, Clarence D. 277
Clark, Frank 318–319
Clay, Laura 75*c,* 273*c,* 326,
  327, **432–433**
Clayson, Esther Pohl 298*c*
clergymen 23, 88, 89
Cleveland, Grover 271*c*
Clinton, Catherine 11
Clinton, DeWitt 8*c*
Cochrane, Elizabeth 242*c*
coeducation, need for 118
Cohn, Elizabeth 273*c*
Colby, Clara Bewick 75*c*
Colby College 208, 209*c*
Cole, Mrs. E. 193
Colfax, Schuyler 141
college president 210*c*
Collins, Emily 83
colonial America 1–3
Colorado 266, 271*c,* 273*c,*
  331*c,* 456*m*
Coly, Miriam M. 227
commitment laws 145*c*
common law 1, 8*c,* 26, 75*c,*
  123*c*
"Common Sense Applied to
  Woman Suffrage" (Mary
  Putnam-Jacobi) 271*c*
Commonwealth of
  Massachusetts Report,
  1845 (House of
  Representatives)
  371–374
Compton, Elizabeth 139

Comstock, Ada 300*c*
Comstock Act 210*c*
Confederacy (U.S. Civil
  War) 136–141
Congregationalist Church
  22, 28*c*
Congress, U.S.
  debates women's suffrage
    173*c*
  federal amendment 301*c,*
    329*c*
  first women candidate for
    167–168
  Jeannette Rankin 305*c,*
    329*c, 330,* 330*c,*
    445–446
  Elizabeth Cady Stanton
    167–168, 173*c*
  and women's suffrage
    committees 238, 241*c*
  Victoria C. Woodhull
    204–205, 210*c*
Congressional Committee
  of NAWSA 301*c,* 302*c*
Congressional Medal of
  Honor 145*c*
Congressional Union for
  Woman Suffrage
  301*c*–305*c*
Conley, Lyda Burton 298*c*
Connecticut 10*c,* 119–120
Constitution, Indiana
  378–379
Constitution, U.S. *See also
  under individual
  amendments*
  states ratifying the
    Nineteenth Amendment
    of 455*m*
  states subsequent
    ratification of the
    Nineteenth Amendment
    to the 455*m*
  use of gender in 165, 166
constitutional conventions
  Kansas 123*c*
  New York 168–170, 173*c*
Constitution of the
  American Woman
  Suffrage Association,
  1869 399–400

Constitution of the
  National American
  Woman Suffrage
  Association, 1890
  418–419
Constitution of the
  National Woman
  Suffrage Association,
  1869 399
consumers 1, 24
Contraband Relief
  Association 140–141,
  144*c*
"contrabands" 140
contraception. *See* birth
  control
contracts 73
conventions. *See specific
  conventions*
Cook, Eliza 92–93, 111
Cornell University 208,
  211*c*
*Correspondence of Mother
  Jones* (Edward M. Steel)
  306, 316, 324, 344
Cott, Nancy F. 12–17, 19,
  62
cotton, burning of 138
court decisions xv
Coutts v. Greenhoe 7*c*
Couzins, Phoebe W. 29*c,*
  174*c,* 231
coverture, law of 10*c*
Cowan, Thomas 168
Crandall, Prudence 7*c,* 10*c,*
  25, **433**
Crewdson, W. D. 58
Crocker, Hannah Mather
  8*c,* 12
Crocket, Jean A. 330*c*
Croly, Jennie C. 173*c*
cruelty (grounds for
  divorce) 119, 120, 123*c*
Cullom Bill 203, 204
Culter, George Younglove
  13
Curtis, George William
  168, 187
Cushman, Pauline 144*c*
Custis, Martha Dandridge
  242*c*

custody rights 89, 91*c,*
  117, 123*c,* 142, 143*c,*
  212*c*
  child's "best interest" 8*c*
  in colonial America 2–3
  and drunkeness 87
  married woman 8*c*
  protected in Kansas 123*c*
  sole 266
  Lucy Stone on 169
Cutler, Hannah Maria
  Conant Tracy **433**

D

Daffin, S. L. 162
Dahlgren, Madeline Victor
  222
Dana, Emily W. 144*c*
Daniels, Josephus 305*c*
Dartt, Justus 252
Daughters of St. Crispin
  174*c,* 209*c*
Daughters of Temperance
  75*c*
Davidson, Josephine 139
Davies (professor)
  109–110
Davis, Jefferson 139
Davis, Paulina Kellogg
  Wright 8*c,* 85, *86,* 91*c,*
  433–434
Day, Lucie Stanton
  157–158
dean 241*c*
Dean, Mary 153
Dean, Phebe B. 154
Debate of Convention
  Amending Indiana's
  Constitution, 1850
  378–379
debt, of husband 26
Declaration of
  Independence 72, 206,
  292
Declaration of Rights and
  Sentiments, Seneca Falls,
  1848 72–73, 75*c,* 265,
  355, 375–377
Declaration of Rights for
  Women, 1876 206, 211*c,*
  414–417

delegates, women *216,*
    273*c*
  to White House 300*c,*
    302*c*
  World Anti-Slavery
    Convention 51–52, 55*c*
Democracy in America (Alexis
    de Tocqueville) 17
Democratic National
    Convention 273*c*
Democratic Party
  and League of Woman
    Voters 354
  platform of 235, 298*c,* 303*c*
demonstrations and protests
    206, 210*c,* 300*c,* 303*c,*
    304*c. See also* parades,
    suffragists'
Dennett, Mary Ware 313
dentistry 173*c,* 211*c*
Department of Labor 332*c*
deportation 302*c*
depression, economic 28*c*
Deroine, Jeanne 97
desertion (grounds for
    divorce) 123*c*
Dewey Decimal System
    272*c*
Dickens, Charles 369–371
Dickinson, Anna Elizabeth
    142, *142,* 144*c,* **434**
  eyewitness accounts
    156–157
  oration of 141, 143*c*–145*c*
Dickinson, Emily 10*c,* 242*c*
Dillon, Halle T. 263
Diner, Hasia R. 217, 222,
    225
Distinguished Service
    Medal 331*c*
divorce
  in colonial America 2–3
  and custody 89, 91*c,* 117
  difficulty obtaining 26
  and drunkenness 87, 91*c,*
    119, 123*c*
  "easy" 301*c*
  grounds for 119, 120, 123*c*
  incompatibility 120
  legislative reform attempts
    117–121

New York State bill on
    123*c*
  property rights 2–3, 75*c*
  reform 119, 120, 122*c,*
    123*c,* 202
  Elizabeth Cady Stanton on
    119, 120, 122*c,* 123*c*
  Lucy Stone on 120, 202
Dix, Dorothea Lynde 7*c,*
    28*c,* 53, 55*c,* 56*c,* 75*c,*
    136, 143*c,* 242*c,* **434**
Dix, John A. 75*c*
Dock, Lavinia 339
doctors 75*c*
"doctrine of intentions"
    8*c*
*A Documentary History of the
    Negro People in the United
    States* (A. Aptheker)
    14–15
Dodge, Grace 241*c*
"domestic bondage" 119
*Domestic Manners of the
    Americans* 16–17
domestic servant 266
Donlon, Mary H. 331*c*
Doroine, Jeanne 379–381
Dorsett, Olive B. 275
Douglas, Henry Kyd 139
Douglass, Frederick *79,*
    144*c,* 177, 377, **434**
  eyewitness accounts
    78–79, 94, 110–111,
    177, 195
  Seneca Falls Convention
    73
  on woman's suffrage 171
dower rights 2, 3
draft registration 298*c*
Dred Scott decision 119
Dreier, Ethel 320, 323, 326,
    341
Dresser, Horace 229–230
Drier, Mary Elizabeth 274*c,*
    299*c*
drunkenness
  custody rights 87
  and divorce 87, 91*c,* 119,
    123*c*
  of legislators 327–328
Dublin, Thomas 63, 65–67

DuBois, Ellen Carol
    245–247
Duckering, Florence West
    303*c*
Duffy, Mary 306, 307
Dumond, Dwight L. 31,
    33–35, 38–47, 57, 60–62
Dunbar, Matilda 160
Duniway, Abigail Jane Scott
    10*c,* 130–131, 253, *254,*
    435
Dunning, Emily (Barringer)
    274*c*

E
Eastman, Crystal 299*c,* 354
Eastman, Max 299*c*
"easy divorce" law 301*c*
Eddy, Eliza 23, 241*c*
Eddy, Mary Baker 211*c*
Edmunds-Tucker Bill 204,
    237, 242*c*
education 9*c,* 56*c*
  African Americans 4, 10*c,*
    25
  Catharine Beecher 25–26,
    56*c,* 90*c*
  colonial America 3
  Declaration of Sentiments
    73
  female seminary 8*c*
  graduate school 293
  housewives 26
  increasing opportunities in
    208, 239, 266, 271*c*
  land grant colleges 143*c*
  need for 25
  nursing 210*c*
  schools for women 25–26
Eighteenth Amendment
    331*c*
88 Bis and V.I.H. (Katherine
    Foote) 333–335, 341
Eighty Years and More
    (Elizabeth Cady Stanton)
    59, 175
Election Day *314*
Electoral College 329*c*
Elizabeth Cady Stanton's
    Address to the
    Legislature of the State of

New York, 1854
    381–388
*Elizabeth Cady
    Stanton/Susan B. Anthony*
    (Ellen Carol DuBois)
    245–247
*Elizabeth Cady Stanton, Vol.
    2* (Theodore Stanton and
    Harriot Stanton Blatch)
    64, 67, 71, 76, 81–83, 93,
    96–98, 100–101,
    103–105, 110, 124, 125,
    127, 129–131, 134,
    175–177, 187–188,
    191–194, 200–201, 215,
    217, 219, 223–225, 228,
    233–234, 245, 249, 253,
    259–264, 275, 276, 280,
    281, 285–287
Elliot, Maude Howe 304*c*
Elliott, Sarah Barnwell 75*c*
Elmendorf, Theresa West
    299*c*
Emancipation Address of
    the Women's National
    Loyal League, 1863
    394–396
emancipation of slaves 119,
    121, 141, 142
Emancipation Proclamation
    141, 144*c*
Emerson, Joseph 8*c,* 14
Emerson, Ralph Waldo 55*c*
employment *266,* 329*c*
  brickyard workers *84*
  of children 271*c,* 305*c,*
    329*c*
  as citizenship right 206
  factory work 52–53, *63,*
    85, *85, 286,* 292–293
  garment workers
    292–293, 295, 298*c,*
    301*c*
  manufacturing 27, 85, 266
  mill work 4–5, 7*c*–8*c,* 10*c,*
    25–27, 53, 56*c*
  opportunities in 266
  protective labor laws 173*c*
  protests 210*c*
  working conditions 292,
    295

enfranchisement of women.
   See also voting
   by 50th anniversary of
      Seneca Falls
      Convention, 1898
      454*m*
   immediately prior to
      ratification of
      Nineteenth
      Amendment, July 1920
      454*m*
   at time of Seneca Falls
      Convention, 1848
      454*m*
enlistment 329*c*
*Epistle to the Clergy of
   Southern States* (Sarah
   Grimké) 23, 28*c*
Equality League of Self-
   Supporting Women
   293–294, 298*c*
equal pay for equal work
   173*c*, 209*c*, 210*c*
equal rights amendment
   355
Equal Rights Association
   242*c*
Equal Rights Party 210*c*,
   241*c*, 242*c*
Equal Suffrage Party 304*c*
equal treatment under law
   72
Era Club 272*c*
Erin's Daughters in America
   (Hasia R. Diner) 217,
   222, 225
escort, male 298*c*
Ethel Eyre Valentine Dreier
   Papers 318–320, 323,
   341, 344–346
Evans, Matilda A. 307
Evanston College for Ladies
   210*c*
Ewing v. Smith 7*c*

F
The Factory Girls (Philip S.
   Foner) 62, 64, 66–70
factory work 52–53, *63*,
   85, *85, 286,* 292–293
Fall River, Massachusetts 8*c*

Farley, Harriet 8*c,* 27, 53,
   56*c,* **435**
Farm to Factory (Thomas
   Dublin) 63, 65–67
fathers
   and custody 266
   guardianship 274*c*
Federal Reserve bank 330*c*
federal women's suffrage
   amendment 241*c*–244*c*,
   271*c*, 297, 301*c*–304*c*. *See
   also* Sixteenth
   Amendment, proposed;
   Nineteenth Amendment
   Carrie Chapman Catt on
      299*c*
   House on 330*c*, 331*c*
   opposition to 327–328
   Senate on 331*c*
   and states' rights 326
   Woodrow Wilson on
      326–327, 330*c*, 331*c*
Female Medical College
   173*c*
female seminary 8*c*
Feminism (Miriam Schneir)
   18, 35, 38, 41
The Feminist Papers (Rossi,
   Alice S., ed.) 32
Ferber, Edna 304*c*
Ferrin, Mary Upton 75*c*
Field, Jessie Shambaugh
   274*c*
Field, Sara B. 304*c*
The Fiery Trail (Thomas
   Ward Osborn) 159
Fifteenth Amendment
   171–172, 209*c*, 401
Filley, Mary A. P. 252
Finding Themselves (Julia C.
   Stimson) 334–336,
   339–341
Finnery, Charles Grandison
   10*c*
fire, at Triangle Shirtwaist
   Company 295,
   299*c*–300*c*
Fish, Miriam H. 154
Fish, Sarah D. 73
Fisher, Chief Justice
   251–252

Fiske, Catherine 8*c*
Flexner, Eleanor 12, 15, 17,
   20, 60, 62, 63, 67, 77,
   322–323, 335–336, 346,
   348, 351
Flynn, Elizabeth Gurley
   313
Foeking, Emilie 211*c*
Folger, Charles 168
Foner, Philip S. 62, 64,
   66–70, 79, 93, 94,
   110–111, 114
Foote, Katherine 333–335,
   341
Foote, Samuel G. 118, 126
force feeding 325
Forten, Charlotte L. 28*c*,
   122*c*, 145*c*
Forten, Sarah (Ada,
   Magawisca) 33, **435**
Foster, Abigail Kelley 7*c*,
   85, **435–436**
Fourteenth Amendment
   165–166, 171, 173*c*,
   398
   Susan B. Anthony 165,
      204
   Francis Minor and 204,
      209*c*
   Elizabeth Cady Stanton
      204
   voting under 206, 210*c*,
      211*c*
   women's inclusion in 206
   Victoria C. Woodhull
      204–205
Fowler, Fannie Holden 75*c*,
   254
Fowler, Lydia Folger 9*c*,
   436
Fox, William Henry 318
Frank, Leslie 23
"Frank Miller" (Frances
   Hook) 139
Frederick Douglass (Philip S.
   Foner) 79, 93, 94,
   110–111, 114
Freedman's Industrial
   Society *177*
Freedmen's Bureau 140,
   145*c*, 169

Freeman, Rose 180
Friedlander, Marc 11
Friends and Sisters (Carol
   Lasser and Marlene
   Deahl Merrill) 199, 213,
   225, 227–228, 230–231,
   256, 259
Friends' Associations 141
*From a New England Woman's
   Diary* (Mary Ames) 160,
   161
Frothingham, Octavius B.
   262–263
Frusch, M. Alice 146
Fugitive Slave Law 121
Fuller, Margaret 7*c*, 29*c*,
   55*c*, 56*c*, **436**
fund-raising 137–138, 142
funeral parade 295
Furman, Virginia 331*c*

G
Gage, Frances Dana Barker
   7*c*, 87–89, *95*, **436**
   eyewitness accounts
      94–96, 186–187
   on former slaves 169
Gage, Matilda Joslyn *76*,
   211*c*, **437**
   eyewitness accounts 222,
      225–226
   *The History of Woman
      Suffrage* 241*c*, 242*c*
   at U.S. centennial
      206–207
Gage, Portia 227
Galusha, Eben 59
Gardener, Helen Hamilton
   332*c*, 337–339
Gardner, Gilson 333
Gardner, Nannette B. 210*c*
Garfield, James A. 241*c*,
   247–248
Garlick, Mr. 26
Garlick, Mrs. 26
Garlick v. Strong 10*c*
garment workers 292–293,
   295, 298*c*, 301*c*
Garmo, Rhoda De 74
Garrison, Francis Jackson
   46, 57, 58, 61

Garrison, Wendell Phillips 46, 57–59, 61

Garrison, William Lloyd *59, 107,* **437**
  as abolitionist 22, 23, 50
  American Anti-Slavery Association 55*c*
  eyewitness accounts 46, 57, 61, 177, 191
  on women's rights 23
  World Anti-Slavery Convention 52

Gaynor, William J. 295

Geddes, George 76–77

gender restriction, in Constitution 165

General Federation of Women's Clubs 272*c,* 274*c*

Geneva Convention 137

Georgia 331*c*
  age of consent 330*c*
  age of protection 271*c*
  women's suffrage in 272*c*

Gibson, Justice 12–13

Gildersleeve, Virginia Crocheron 299*c*

Gillespie, Mabel Edna 331*c*

Gilman, Caroline 30

Gilman, Charlotte Perkins 244*c,* 272*c,* 300*c*

Girl Scouts 300*c*

Gleason, Kate 329*c*

Glimpses of Fifty Years (Frances Willard) 259–260

Goldman, Emma 305*c*

Goodridge, Ellen 139

Gordon, Daisy 300*c*

Gordon, Kate M. 300*c,* 326, 327, **437**

Gordon, Linda 15

Gougar, Helen M. 253

graduate school 293

Grand Rapids, Michigan 456*m*

The Granite Farm Letters 158

Grant, Ulysses 209*c*

Grant, Zilpah 9*c*

grassroots activism 84–89

Graves, S. H. *220*

Gray, Mary Tenney 123*c*

Greeley, Horace 87, 118, 120, **437–438**
  eyewitness accounts 102, 105, 109, 128, 187
  on suffrage subcommittee 168–169

Greeley, Mrs. Horace 168–169

Greenhow, Rose O'Neal 138, 139

Gregory v. Paul 8*c*

Grew, Henry 58

Grier, Eliza Anna 284

Griffing, Josephine S. 140, 145*c,* 152, **438**

Griffith, Elisabeth 93–94, 191

Grimké, Angelina Emily 7*c,* 9*c,* 28*c,* **438**
  as abolitionist 21–23, *23*
  "Appeal to the Christian Women of the South" 359–362
  eyewitness accounts 32–35, 38–40, 42–44
  at first national women's convention 85
  National Woman's Loyal League 141
  public speaking 21–24, 27, 28*c*

Grimké, Sarah Moore 9*c,* *22,* **438–439**
  as abolitionist 22, 23, 28*c*
  eyewitness accounts 33–38, 41–43, 46, 61–62
  public speaking 22

The Grimké Sisters from South Carolina (Gerda Lerner) 15, 32, 38, 40, 44, 45

Griswold, Mrs. H. 246

Gruening, Martha 310

guardianship 8*c,* 73, 123*c,* 143*c,* 266, 271*c,* 274*c*

Guernsey, Alfred H. 154

Gulick, Charlotte Vetter 299*c*

Gulick, Luther H. 299*c*

Gurko, Miriam 23

gynecology 122*c*

H

Hale, Horace M. 283–284

Hale, Sarah Josepha 9*c*

Haley, Margaret 273*c*

Hall, Mary 241*c*

Hallowell, Mary H. 73

Hamilton, Alice 331*c*

Hamlin, Hannibal 156

Happersett, Reese 210*c*

Harper, Frances Watkins 169, 196, **439**

Harper, Ida A. Husted 274*c,* 346, **439.** *See also The Life and Work of Susan B. Anthony*

Harpers Ferry, raid on 123*c*

Harper's Pictorial History (Alfred H. Guernsey and Henry M. Alden) 154

Harris, Isaac 295

Harris, Mrs. John 150

Hart, Edith L. 345

Hartford Female Seminary 9*c,* 25–26

Harvard Medical School 271*c,* 331*c*

Hawley, Harriet W. F. 161

Hays, S. H. 284

hay wagon *313*

Haywood, Bill 313–314

Hazeltine, Father L. 126–127

Hazle, Ann Maria *125*

Healey, Mary 8*c*

health, board of 298*c*

Heflin, Thomas J. 303*c*

Helms v. Fanciscus 8*c*

Henry, Alice 299*c*

Henry Street Settlement 271*c*

Hertell, Thomas 30

Hierst, H. Houston 313

Higginson, Thomas Wentworth 115

Highgate, Edmonia G. 176–177

Hillman, Bessie Abramowitz 303*c*

Hills, Florence Bayard 333–334, 339

Hinchey, Margaret 317

Hinkley, Frederick A. 255–256

History of Woman Suffrage, Vol. 1 19, 30, 35, 57–60, 76–81, 83, 92–103, 105–116, 126, 128–129

History of Woman Suffrage, Vol. 2 147–148, 151–154, 156–158, 162–163, 178, 180–191, 193–198, 213, 215, 222, 225–227, 229–230

History of Woman Suffrage, Vol. 3 199–200, 214, 231, 233, 245, 247–256, 261

History of Woman Suffrage, Vol. 4 251–253, 274*c,* 277, 282–285

History of Woman Suffrage, Vol. 5 285, 287, 352

History of Woman Suffrage, Vol. 6 319

History of Women, Guide to the Microfilm Collection 30, 92–93

Hobbs, Lucy B. 173*c*

Hoge, A. H. 143*c*

Holland, Mary A. Gardner 146, 152, 153, 157–159

Holland, Patricia G. 47

Holley, Sallie **439–440**

home-based producers 1

home sewing 138, *138*

Homestead Law 143*c*

Hook, Frances 139

Hooker, Isabelle Beecher 170, 171, 201, 217, 221, 224, 260–262, 284, **440**

"Hooligan woman" 297. *See also* Pankhurst, Emmeline

Hooper, Jessie J. 335–336

Hope, Rody Ann 180

Hornsby, Mrs. Richard 297, 305*c*

Hosford, Mary 55*c*

hospital(s) 143c, 272c
  homes as 136
  ward for 129
  women's 122c
hours, working 53, 56c, 292, 298c
House of Representatives, U.S. 303c
  Mary Bellemy 298c
  on federal amendment 241c–243c, 271c, 303c–304c, 329c–331c
  Federal Woman Suffrage Amendment 327
  Nineteenth Amendment 331c
  Jeannette Rankin 305c, 329c, 330, 330c, 445–446
  Select Committees on Woman Suffrage 238, 241c, 330c
housewives 26
Howard, Jacob M. 140
Howe, Church 250
Howe, Judge 214
Howe, Julia Ward 8c, 143c, 173c, 210, 211c, 241c, 298c, 304c, 440
Howe, Marie Jenny 300c
Howitt, William 60
Hoyt, Mary F. 241c
Huber, Alice 273c
Hudson Street Presbyterian Church 87
Hulett, Alta 209c
Hull-House 243c, 271c, 272c, 298c
Human Rights platform, of Seneca Falls Convention 167
Hunt, Jane 75c
Hunt, Mary H. 237
Hunt, Ward 205, 211c
Huntington, Susan Mansfield 11
Husband, Mary Morris 144c
Hussey, Cornelia Collins 252
Hutchinson Family Singers 185

Hyatt, James L. 272c
Hyde, Ida 271c

I
Idaho 266
The Ideas of the Woman Suffrage Movement (Aileen S. Kraditor) 262–263, 279, 313, 317–319, 346
ILGWU. *See* International Ladies Garment Workers' Union
Illinois 244c, 301c
Illinois Equal Suffrage Association 174c
immoral acts 299c
"immoral use" 211c
inauguration parade 301c
incompatibility (grounds for divorce) 120
Indiana 329c, 378–379
Indiana University 123c
infanticide 120
inheritance 123c, 142
  bequests to women's movement 239, 241c, 272c, 304c
  in colonial America 2
  married women 8c
In Her Own Right (Elisabeth Griffith) 93–94, 191
insane asylums 28c, 75c
institutionalization 145c
International Council of Women 240, 240, 242c, 271c
International Ladies Garment Workers' Union (ILGWU) 273c, 295, 330c
International Red Cross 137
Iowa 300c, 331c
Isabel Howland Papers 263–264, 276–281, 287–288

J
Jackson, E. Garrison 155
Jackson, Kate 200

Jackson, Mercy B. 183–184
Jackson, Stonewall 139
Jacksonian equality 26
Jacobs, Harriet 143c, 151
Jailed for Freedom (Doris Stevens) 333, 336–344
Jamison, Maud 339
Jane, Mary 64
Jennings, Janet 289
Jewish women, assembly of 271c
job discrimination 303c
Johns Hopkins University 243c, 273c
Johnson, Eliza 16
Johnson, Opha May 331c
Johnson v. Thompson 8c
joint property 2
Joint Resolution I 301c, 302c
Joint Resolution Proposing an Amendment to the Constitution of the United States, 1878 417
Jones, Jane Elizabeth Hitchcock 440
Jones, Mary Harris "Mother" 294, 300c, 306, 316, 344
Jones, Wesley M. 302c
Jourdan v. Jourdan 14
Journal of a Residence on a Georgian Plantation (Frances Anne Kemble) 47–48
Joyce, James 303c
judgeship 332c
Judiciary Committee 205, 216, 237, 303c
jurors 203, 209c, 241c
juvenile court 272c, 330c

K
Kaiser, Lucy L. C. 153
Kansas 456m
  black suffrage in 170, 171
  constitution of 123c
  municipal voting 267
  women's suffrage in 170, 171, 173c, 271c, 300c
Kearney, Leonora 75c

Keckley, Elizabeth 140, 144c, 152–153, 441
Keen, Dora 300c
Keene, Laura 91c
Kehew, Mary Kimball 274c
Keller, Helen 301c, 319
Kelley, Abby 55c
Kelley, Florence 272c
Kelley, Mary 14, 217, 220–224, 230, 260–262, 284
Kemble, Francis Anne 47–48, 96, 144c
Kempe, Grace 7c
Kenneally, James J. 308
Kenney, Mary O'Sullivan 244c, 272c
Kenny v. Udall 9c
Kent, Elizabeth 299c
Kentucky 242c, 303c
Kepley, Ada 209c
Kerber, Linda K. 12
key sites of the women's suffrage movement 456m
Kline, Mary-Jo 11
Knights of Labor 173c, 241c, 242c
Kraditor, Aileen S. 262–263, 279, 313, 317–319, 346
Krasno, Francine 47

L
labor movement **292–295, 306–324**
labor organization 9c
labor unions. *See* unions
La Follete, Belle 303c
land grant colleges 143c
Lane, Gertrude Battles 300c
Larcom, Lucy 9c, 17, 18, 18, 43, 64–65, 441
Lasser, Carol 199, 213, 225, 227–228, 230–231, 256, 259
Lathrop, Julia Clifford 300c, 315, 316
Lathrop, Mary Frances 329c
Laurie, Annie 274c
law, practice of 209c–211c

law review 331c
law school 174c
Lawson, Maggie 160
lawyers 174c
Lease, Mary Elizabeth 258
Lee, Joseph 8c
Lee, J. S. 178
Lee, Mary W. 144c
legal aid, free 173c
LeGallienne, Richard 314
Lerner, Gerda 15, 32, 38, 40, 44, 45
Leslie, Frank 304c
Lesse v. Kennedy 7c
Letter from Jeanne Doroine and Pauline Roland, Prison of St-Lagare, Paris, 1851 379–381
Letters of Lydia Maria Child (Lydia Maria Child) 44
Letters of Theodore Dwight Weld, Angelina Grimké Weld and Sarah Grimké (Gilbert H. Barnes and Dwight L. Dumond, eds.) 31, 33–35, 38–47, 57, 60, 61–62
Letter to the Commissioners of the District of Columbia Claiming Political Prisoner Status for Jailed Suffragists, 1917 423
Lewis, Mrs. Lawrence 342
Liberator (newspaper) 107
libraries and librarians 53, 271c–273c, 299c
The Life and Work of Susan B. Anthony (Ida Husted Harper) 102, 104, 105, 124–128, 130–133, 175, 178–179, 181, 191, 194–196, 200, 220–221, 257, 258, 260, 275, 277, 280–283, 289–291
Lily (feminist journal) 88, 88, 91c
The Limits of Sisterhood (Jeanne Boydston, Mary Kelley, and Anne Margolis) 14, 217,

221–224, 230, 260–262, 284
Lincoln, Abraham 120, 121, 123c, 136, 140, 143c–145c, 144
Lincoln, Mary Todd 140, 141, 145c
Lindbergh, Charles A. 336
liquor
    prohibition of 75c, 91c, 331c
    voting on matters of 212c
liquor interests 327–328
literacy rate 25
Livermore, Mary A. 123c, 173c, 184, 194, 196, 196, 441
Lizzie (slave) 160
Lobetkin, Esther 310
Locher v. the United States 274c
Lockwood, Belva 10c, 212c, 213, 241c, 242c, 329c, 441–442
Long, John D. 237, 245
Longfellow, Samuel 120
Longshore, Hannah E. Meyers 90c
loom 8c, 45
Loom and Spindle 17–20, 30–31
Loomis, Mary A. 146
Louisiana 330c
Loving Warriors (Leslie Wheeler, ed.) 182, 183, 190, 194, 195, 198, 199, 216–218, 221, 223, 224, 228–229, 231–233, 245, 248, 251, 253, 256–258, 260, 261, 263, 275
Low, Juliette 300c
Lowell, Francis Cabot 4, 7c
Lowell Female Labor Reform Association 53, 56c
Lowell, Massachusetts 4–5, 10c, 20, 27, 42, 52, 56c
Lowell Offering (magazine) 52–53, 55c, 56c
Lowry v. Tierman and Williamson 9c

Lucretia Mott amendment 355
"Lucy Stoner" 122c
Luhring, Marie 332c
Lutz, Alma 306–318, 321–322, 333–334, 336
Lydia Maria Child, Selected Letters (Milton Meltzer, Patricia G. Holland and Francine Krasno) 47
Lyon, Mary 9c, 10c, 25, 28c, 32, 32, 33, 442

M
Magawisca. See Forten, Sara
Magill, Helen White 211c
maiden name 122c
Maine 329c
Malkiel, Theresa 310
Malone, Dudley Field 340
Mann Act 299c
manufacturing 27, 85, 266
maps 454m–456m
Margolis, Anne 14, 217, 220–224, 260–262, 284
Marine Corps, U.S. 331c
market economy 26
Marot, Helen 309, 312
Married Woman's Property Act, New York, 1848 7c, 28c, 75c, 88, 89, 91c, 117, 123c, 374–375
    Susan B. Anthony 91c, 117, 122c, 123c
    expanded 123c
    New York state legislature 52
    sections repealed in 142, 143c
    Elizabeth Cady Stanton 52, 122c
married women. See also divorce
    admission to bar of 174c
    custody rights 8c, 89
    dower rights 3
    freedoms of 2
    inheritance rights 8c
    institutionalization of 145c
    and practice of law 211c

property rights 8c–10c, 24, 26, 29c, 30, 55c, 56c, 75c, 123c, 211c, 266
    rights of 2
    wages 3, 89, 117, 174c, 266
Marshall, Florence M. 274c
Marshall, John 7c
Martin, Anne Henrietta 330c, 338–339, 442
Martin, James 11
Martin, John A. 190
Martine, Senator 318
Martineau, Harriet 10c, 28c, 362–368
Martin v. Commonwealth of Massachusetts 7c, 11
Mary Chesnut's Civil War (Mary Chesnut) 146–147
Massachusetts 7c
    guardianship 274c
    legislature 28c, 173c
    school suffrage 237
    on women's suffrage 304c
Massachusetts Anti-Slavery Society 86
Massachusetts Institute of Technology 210c
maximum-hour law 298c
mayor 242c, 301c
McCauley, Mary Ludwig Hays 9c
McClintock, Mary Ann
    Rochester convention 72–73
    Seneca Falls Convention 72–73, 75c
McCreesh, Carolyn Daniel 310
McCulloch, Catharine W. 304c
McDowell, Anne E. 9c, 122c
McDowell, Madeline 242c
McDowell, Mary 243, 243c, 271c
McGee, Anita Newcomb 272c
McKay, Charlotte 143c

McKee, Jane 345
McKim v. McKim 212c
medical associations 136
medical degree 75c, 242c
medical research 271c, 273c
medical school 75c, 243c
medical societies 211c
Melinda Scott, Hat Trimmer
    307
Meltzer, Milton 47
Memorial of Victoria C.
    Woodhull, 1870 401
Memorial (sent to every
    state legislature), 1859
    389–390
Men's League for Woman
    Suffrage 299c
mental illness 55c
Meriwether, Elizabeth Avery
    261
Merrick, Caroline Elizabeth
    Thomas **442**
Merrill, Marlene Deahl
    199, 213, 225, 227–228,
    230–231, 256, 259
Methodist Episcopal
    Church 174c
Meyer, Annie Nathan 314
Michigan 211c, 329c, 330c
Michigan University 209c
Middlebury Female
    Seminary *4, 8c*
midwives 299c, 300c
migration, westward 53
militancy 293, 297, 299c,
    300c
military pension 9c
Millar, Rabina Craig 13,
    14
Miller, Elizabeth Smith 90c,
    91c, 199, 267, *276,* **443**
Miller, Helen Guthrie 333
Miller, Mary 274c
mills and mill work 4–5,
    7c–8c, 10c, 25–27, 53,
    56c, 75c
Mindell, Fania 305c
minimum wage 274c
minister, first woman 86,
    91c, 144c, 241c
"mink brigade" 293

Minor, Francis 400–401
    and Fourteenth
        Amendment 173c, 204,
        209c
    lawsuit by 206, 210c
Minor, Virginia Louisa
    204, 206, 210c, 406–407,
    443
Minor v. Happersett 211c,
    229, 408–414
Missing Soldier's Office
    137, 145c
Mississippi 29c
Mississippi Industrial
    Institute and College
    241c
Missouri 206, 302c, 331c
Missouri Compromise 119
Mitchell, Maria 8c, 75c,
    243c
Mondell, Frank 301c
Mondell Resolution 303c
Montana 302c, 332c
Montgomery, James 139
monument 271c
Moore, Anna Carroll 273c
Moore, Frank 148–151,
    156, 160, 161
Morey, Katherine 336, 339
Morgan, Anne 293
Morgenthau, Mrs. Henry
    293
Mormon Church 204
Morrill Act 143c
Morrill Land Grant colleges
    208
Morris, Esther 203, 209c
Morrison, Reverend 59
Morrison, Sarah Parke 123c
mortgage 9c, 10c
mother and child welfare
    bill 330c
motherhood, effect on
    leadership 117, 118
Mott, James 73, *98*
Mott, Lucretia Coffin 77,
    233, **443–444**
    as abolitionist 10c, 28c
    AERA 167, 173c
    death of 241c
    early years 49

eyewitness accounts
    57–60, 76, 180–181,
    233
Philadelphia Anti-Slavery
    Society *98*
Philadelphia Female Anti-
    Slavery Society 10c
Rochester convention
    72–73
Seneca Falls Convention
    72–73, 75c, 207
Elizabeth Cady Stanton
    49, 52, 54, 87
Worcester convention 85
World Anti-Slavery
    Convention 49, 51, 52,
    55c
Mott, Lydia 87, 142
Mount Holyoke Female
    Seminary 25, 28c, *32*
"muckraker" 274c
Muller v. Oregon 298c
Mullowny, Alexander 339
Muncy Act 300c
"municipal suffrage" 237
municipal voting 267
Munson, Clara 301c
Murphy, Eliza 272c
mutual aid societies 5–6

N
NAACP. *See* National
    Association for the
    Advancement of Colored
    People
Nation, Carrie 273c
National American Woman
    Suffrage Association
    (NAWSA) 244c, 273c,
    293, 299c
    campaign against
        legislators 327
    Carrie Chapman Catt
        269, 270, 274c, 297,
        299c, 305c
    conflict in 302c, 303c
    Congressional Committee
        301c, 302c
    delegation to White House
        300c, 302c
    formation of 240

League of Women Voters
    353
    and militancy 300c
    petition of 298c
    racism 267, 326
    resignation of Susan B.
        Anthony 272c
    Anna Howard Shaw 269,
        270, 274c
    and Southern suffragists
        326
    and Elizabeth Cady
        Stanton 268
    wartime approach of 329c
    and Ida B. Wells-Barnett
        296
    and *The Woman's Bible*
        268, 269, 272c
National Antislavery
    Convention 28c
National Anti-suffrage
    Association *348*
National Association for the
    Advancement of Colored
    People (NAACP) 298c,
    331c
National Association of
    Colored Nurses 298c
National Association of
    Colored Women 271c
National Birth Control
    League 303c, 304c
National Consumer's
    League 272c
National Education
    Association 273c
National Federation of
    Settlements 299c
National Female Anti-
    Slavery Society 28c
National Freedman's Relief
    Association of the
    District of Columbia
    140
National Labor Union
    173c
National League of Women
    Voters *273,* 331c, 353,
    .354
National Legislative League
    273c

National Woman's Anti-Slavery Convention 25
National Woman's Loyal League 141, 144c, 145c, 165
National Woman's Party 305c, 354
  protest at White House 325, 329c
  wartime approach of 236, 325
National Woman Suffrage Association (NWSA) 171, 203, 211c
  and federal women's suffrage 236–237
  membership in 202
  merger of 240, 243c
  and U.S. centennial 206
  and Victoria C. Woodhull 205
National Women's Rights Convention
  first 85–87, 90c
  second 90c
  third 91c
  fourth 91c
  fifth 91c
  sixth 122c
  seventh 118, 119, 122c
  eighth 119, 122c
  10th 120, 123c
  11th 166–167, 173c
Native Americans 298c
"natural rights" argument 292, 298c
Navy, U.S. 272c, 329c
Navy Nurse Corps 298c
Navy Reserve Act 305c
NAWSA. See National American Woman Suffrage Association
Neblett, A. Viola 272c
Nebraska 236, 302c, 329c, 332c
Negative Report of the Committee on Privileges and Elections Regarding the Proposed Amendment, 1878 417–418

Nevada 301c, 302c
New England 4, 24, 25
A New England Girlhood (Lucy Larcom) 17, 18, 43, 64–65
New England Hospital for Women and Children 210c
New England Women's Club 173c, 189
New England women's rights convention 123c
New Hampshire 209c, 274c
New Jersey 456m
  school suffrage 272c
  voting 3, 3, 7c
  on women's suffrage 304c
Newman, Pauline M. 307–308, 309, 330c
New Mexico 299c
newspaper, first women's 122c
news reporter 123c, 274c
New York City 22, 294, 295–296, 298c, 299c, 316, 320, 326
New York reform campaign of 1853–54 89
New York State 456m
  age of protection 237
  constitution 271c
  property rights 212c
  school suffrage 237
  suffrage amendment 301c
  on women's suffrage 304c
  women's suffrage in 330c
New York state legislature 10c
  constitutional convention 168–169
  Married Woman's Property Act 52
  petitions to 89
  Elizabeth Cady Stanton's address to 381–388
New York Trade Union League 295
New York University Infirmary for Women and Children 122c

New York v. Sanger 330c
New York Women's Central Association of Relief 137
Nichols, Clarina Irene Howard 7c, 56c, 90c, 98–100, 102, 106, 115, 122c, 123c, 153–154, 158, 444
Nichols, Mary Sargeant Neal Grove 444
Nineteenth Amendment 142, 165, 236, 305c, 327, 331c, 353–355, 425
  adoption of 332c
  Carrie Chapman Catt 353, 354
  ratification 327, 328, 331c, 332c
  states ratifying 455m
  states subsequently ratifying 455m
  suffrage to women immediately prior to ratification of 454m
No Constitutional Right to Be Ladies (Linda K. Kerber) 12
Nolan, Mary I. 343–344
North Carolina 272c
North Dakota 302c, 329c
The North Star editorial (Frederick Douglass) 377
Norton, Mary Beth 11–14, 32, 33, 70
notaries public 300c
Noyes, Clara Dutton 299c
Nugent, James 348
nursing and nurses 137, 142, 143c–145c, 159, 265, 300c, 330c
  American Nurses Association 272c
  associations 298c
  Clara Barton 136–137, 143c
  in Civil War 136–137
  Navy Nurse Corps 298c
  school for 210c

Spanish-American War 272c, 273c
  Harriet Tubman 139
  in U.S. Army 332c
  visiting nurses 271c
  in World War I 325
NWSA. See National Woman Suffrage Association
Nye, James W. 188–189

O
Oates, William C. 239
Oberlin College 10c, 25, 55c, 56c, 75c, 86, 90c, 125, 143c, 208, 241c
obscenity 210c, 304c
"obstructing traffic" 325
Octavia 62
Odenheimer, Cordelia Powell 315
Ogden, John Cosens 3
Ohio 271c, 302c, 329c
Oklahoma 330c, 331c
Oliver, Anna 250
Olmsted, Willard 310
Oregon 236, 241c, 274c, 298c
O'Reilly, John Boyle 217
O'Reilly, Leonora 295, 444–445
organized labor. See labor movement
Orlady, Mary 321
Ormand, John J. 132–133
Osborn, Thomas Ward 159
The Other Civil War (Catherine Clinton) 11
Our Army Nurses (Mary A. Gardner Holland) 146, 152, 153, 157–159
Ovington, Mary White 331c
Owen, Robert Dale 19, 92, 119, 165
Owen, Sarah C. 73

P
Packard, Elizabeth Ware 145c
Packard v. Packard 145c

Pankhurst, Emmeline 297,
    299c, 302c, 303c,
    308–309, *309*, **445**
parades, funeral 295
parades, suffragists'
    Chicago *323*
    Georgia 304c
    "Homemakers" *296*
    Illinois 303c
    inauguration 301c
    New York City *294,
    295–296*, 298c, 299c,
    316, 320, 326
    Washington, D.C. *295,
    296*, 301c, *317, 318*
Parent-Teachers Association
    272c
Park, Maud Wood 272c,
    273, 273c
"parlour talks" 23
Parson, Theopolis 11
Pastoral Letter of "the
    General Association of
    Massachusetts
    (Orthodox) to the
    Churches under their
    care" 23, 28c, 35,
    368–369
Path Breaking 130–131
Patsy (freedwoman) 180
Patten, Mary Ann 122c
Patterson, Mary Jane 143c
Patterson, Thomas M. 285
Paul, Alice 299c, 300c,
    304c, 326, *326, 342,*
    445
    arrest of 325, 330c
    Congressional Union for
        Woman Suffrage 302c,
        303c
    equal rights amendment
        355
    inauguration parade 301c
    and militancy 300c
    NAWSA 302c, 303c
    Nineteenth Amendment
        354, 355
    The Suffragist 302c
Paul, Mary S. 65–67
Payne, Elizabeth Anne 310
Payne, Karen 67, 319

Peabody, George Foster
    299c
Peck, Annie Smith 298c
Peck, Mary Gray 352
Peckford, Mrs. 2–3, 9c
Peckford v. Peckford 3, 9c
Pennsylvania 304c
Pennsylvania Avenue 296
Pennsylvania v. Addicks 8c
pension, army 241c
petition(s)
    abolitionist 141
    and constitutional
        amendment 166
    on federal amendment
        301c, 304c
    of Mary Upton Ferrin 75c
    NAWSA 298c
    to New York state
        legislature 89, 91c, 117,
        118, 122c
    for outlawing slavery 141
    right of 28c
    on suffrage 238
    for vote on liquor 212c
Petition to Congress
    Requesting the Inclusion
    of Women in the
    Fifteenth Amendment,
    1868 399
Petition to Congress
    Requesting Women's
    Suffrage, 1865 397
Philadelphia, Pennsylvania
    22, 456m
Philadelphia Anti-Slavery
    Society 51, *98*
Philadelphia Female Anti-
    Slavery Society 10c, 22
Phillips, Mrs. George 341
Phillips, Wendell 51, 119,
    120, 131–132, 167, 175,
    176
Phillis Wheatley Club 267
physical danger, wife in
    119–120
picketing, White House
    325, 326, 329c, *334*
pickets 330c
Pierce, D. J. 215
Pierpont, John 108–109

Pillsbury, Parker 171
Pitcher, Molly 9c
police and police brutality
    293, 296, 297, 299c, 301c
Political Prisoner
    Commission (War
    Department) 139
political prisoner status 325
polygamy 203, 204, 237,
    242c
Pool, Mrs. L. M. R. 246
Porter, Eleanor H. 300c
Portland, Oregon 456m
Post, Amy 73, 74, 207
postcards 235
posters 302c
Powell, Aaron Macy 242c
Prall, Elizabeth Smith 55c
preachers, convention of
    211c
Preston, Ann 101–102,
    173c
Prince v. Prince 56c
prisoners and prison 28c,
    56c, 205–206, 300c
professions 73, 266
Progressive Party 300c
property rights 7c, 143c
    in colonial America 2
    Declaration of Sentiments
        73
    divorce 2–3, 75c
    married women 8c–10c,
        24, 26, 29c, 30, 55c, 56c,
        75c, 123c, 211c, 266
    New York State 212c
    protected in Kansas 123c
prosecutor 331c
protection, age of. *See* "age
    of protection"
"protective legislation"
    298c
protests. *See* demonstrations
    and protests
Pryor, Live 245–246
psychic healer 204
Public Letter of Elizabeth
    Cady Stanton to the
    Electors of the Eighth
    Congressional District,
    1866 397–398

public speaking
    Susan B. Anthony 118
    Declaration of Sentiments
        72
    Anna E. Dickinson 141,
        143c–145c
    Angelina Grimké 21–24,
        27, 28c
    Sarah Grimké 22, 23
    Rochester convention 74
    Elizabeth Cady Stanton
        73, 89
    Maria Stewart 24
    Lucy Stone 86
    Sojourner Truth 88–89
Pugh, Sara **445**
Pulitzer Prize 304c
Pure Food and Drug Act
    274c
Purvis, Robert 178–179
Putnam-Jacobi, Mary 145c,
    271c

Q
Quakers 24, 49, 77, 88
Quimby, Harriet 300c
Quong v. Oregon 300c
Qvam, F. M. 311

R
racism xv, 25, 170, 171,
    267, 296
Radcliffe College 9c, 241c,
    271c, 272c, 298c
radicalism 119
Rankin, Jeannette 305c,
    329c, *330*, 330c, **445–446**
Raoul, Eleanor 304c
rape 120, 237–238
Rathbun, Alzina 247
"ration-houses" 140
Ray, Charlotte 210c
Reagon, John 239
Red Cross 9c, 137, 241c,
    325–326, 330c
The Red Cross (Clara
    Barton) 164
Reed, Dorothy Mendenhall
    272c
Reeds, Ester 272c
Reed v. Reed 206

Reform, Labor, and Feminism (Elizabeth Anne Payne) 310
religion 5
Report No. 22 of the House of Representatives, Committee on the Judiciary, Regarding the Memorial of Victoria C. Woodhull, 1871 404–406
Report No. 386 of the House of Representatives, Committee on Military Affairs, Regarding Anna Ella Carroll and Events of 1861 392–394
Republican National Convention 120, 123*c*, 354
Republican Party
  and AERA 170
  platform of 207, 235
  and slavery 119, 120, 141, 144*c*, 145*c*
Resolutions of Francis Minor Esq., 1869 400–401
Reverby, Susan 15
Revolution (newspaper) 171, 172, 173*c*, 195, 199, 202–204
Reynolds, Belle 143*c*, 149
Rhode Island 143*c*, 242*c*, 329*c*
  child custody 212*c*
  suffrage in 236
Richards, Ellen Swallow 210*c*
Richards, Laura Howe 304*c*
Richardson, Joseph 19
Richman, Julia 242*c*
Richmond During the War (Sallie Brock) 149, 154–156
Ricker, Marilla M. 209*c*, 210*c*
rights
  dower 2

enumerated 72
of married women 2
Rinehart, Mary Roberts 304*c*
Ripley, Sarah Bradford 11
Rittenhouse, Maud 344–345
Robb, Isabel Hamptom 272*c*
Robbins, Elizabeth 298*c*
Robins, Margaret Dreier 274*c*
Robinson, Harriet 1, 9*c*, 17–20, 30–31
Robinson, Helen Ring 300*c*
Robinson, Mary Jane 19
Rochester, New York 456*m*
Rochester convention 73–74, 75*c*
Rochester Daughters of Temperance 87
Rogers, Harriet Burbank 173*c*
Rogers, Mrs. John, Jr. 338
Roland, Pauline 97, 379–381
Roosevelt, Theodore 300*c*, 311, 330*c*
Root, H. K. 105–106
Roots of Bitterness (Nancy F. Cott) 17
Rose, Ada 310
Rose, Ernestine Louise Siismondi Potowski 7*c*, 24, *27*, 28*c*, 30, 55*c*, 85, 87, 120, 141, 194, **446**
Rosencrantz v. Washington 241*c*
Rossi, Alice S. 32
Roy, Annie 345
Rudd, Caroline Mary 55*c*
Ruffin, Josphine St. Pierre 271*c*, 272*c*
Russell, Lucinda 249

S
Sabin, Florence R. 273*c*
Sacagawea (Sacajawea) 274*c*

Sage College 208, 211*c*
St. Lawrence University 173*c*
St. Louis Law School 174*c*
Salem, Ohio 85
Salmon, Marylynn 26
Salter, Suzanna Madora 242*c*
Samarodin, Vera 341–342
Sanborn, Jemima 63
Sanger, Margaret 302*c*–305*c*, 330*c*
Sanitary Commission 136, *137*, 138, 143*c*
"sanitary fairs" 138
Sargent, A. A. 207, 211*c*
Saulsbury, Willard, Jr. 327
Schmidt, Katherine L. 324
Schneiderman, Rose 274*c*, *306*
Schneir, Miriam 18, 35, 38, 41
school, public girls' 9*c*
school suffrage 143*c*, 237, 241*c*, 267, 271*c*, 272*c*, 299*c*, 303*c*
school voting 90*c*
Schreiner, Olive 318
Scott, Charlotte 271*c*
Scott, Francis M. 275
Scott, Melinda 292, 303*c*, 307
Scott, Thomas A. 140
scouts 138, 139
Sears, Eleonora R. 299*c*
Secret Service 144*c*
"Secret Six" 123*c*
Seelye, Sarah Edmonds 241*c*
Select Committees on Woman Suffrage 238, 241*c*
Selected Letters (Lydia Maria Child) 159, 161
Sellers, Kathryn 330*c*
Senate, U.S.
  on federal amendment 241*c*, 242*c*, 244*c*, 301*c*–303*c*, 327, 331*c*
  Anne Henrietta Martin 330*c*

Nineteenth Amendment 331*c*
Helen Ring Robinson 300*c*
Select Committees on Woman Suffrage 238, 241*c*, 273*c*, 330*c*
Seneca Falls Convention **72–83**, 75*c*
  30th anniversary of 207, 211*c*
  40th anniversary of 240
  Declaration of Rights and Sentiments 72–73, 75*c*, 265, 355, 375–377
  enfranchisement of women at time of 454*m*
  enfranchisement of women by the 50th anniversary of 454*m*
Seneca Falls, New York 53–54, 56*c*, 456*m*
Seton, Elizabeth Ann Bayley 7*c*
Severance, Caroline M. 173*c*, *189*
Severance, T. C. 188
Sewall, May Wright 250–251
Seward, William H. 145*c*
sewing *286*
Shaforth-Palmer Amendment 303*c*
"Shake Hands" (Lily M. Spencer) *116*
Shakers 27
Shapiro, Anne 299*c*
Shattuck, Harriet R. 252–253
Shaw, Anna Howard 56*c*, 241*c*, 242*c*, 267, 272*c*, *289*, 302*c*, 331*c*, **446**
  Distinguished Service Medal 331*c*
  eyewitness accounts 288
  NAWSA 269, 270, 274*c*
Shaw, Daniel 119–120
Shaw, Emeline 119–120
Shaw, Sarah B. 168
Shaw v. Shaw 119–120

Sherman-Ricker, Marcena 289

Shuler, Nettie Rogers 346–351

Silver, Clara 306

Simmons College 274*c*

Singer company *133*

single women 2, 143*c*

Sinnotte, Ruth Helena 152

Sixteenth Amendment, proposed 172, 174*c*, 207, 211*c*, 327. *See also* federal women's suffrage amendment

Skinner, Deborah 8*c*

skirts 300*c*

Sklar, Kathryn Kish 34, 43

slavery 75*c. See also* abolition and abolitionists
aid to former slaves 140–141
Civil War 135
emancipation 119, 121, 141, 142, 144*c*
extension into territories 119
eyewitness accounts 30–48
Freedmen's Bureau 140
movement against 119
in new territories 85
outlawing 141, 145*c*
and Republican Party 120
and voting 142
and women's suffrage **21–48**

Slavery and "The Woman Question" (Frederick B. Tolles) 57–61

slaves, former 140, 209*c*

Slocumb, C. B. 250

slotting fuses *85*

Smith, Abby Hadassah 206, 210*c*, **446–447**

Smith, Gerrit 9*c, 56,* 119, 123*c*, 128, 167, 193, 226, **447**

Smith, Hannah Whitall **447**

Smith, Julia 206, 210*c*, 233

Smith, Sophia 209*c*, **447**

Smith College 208, 209*c*, 298*c*, 300*c*

Smith Family Papers 199, 227, 258–259, 263, 275–276, 279, 280, 284, 285, 287–289, 291

smoking *297,* 298*c*

Snow, Eliza B. 219–220

Sobers, Jane E. 246

social work 123*c*, 298*c*–300*c*, 329*c*

Society for the Collegiate Instruction of Women 241*c*

Society in America (Harriet Martineau) 362–368

Society of Collegiate Alumnae 239

soldiers
care for 136
death rate of 136
missing 137, 145*c*
Union *159*
women 139–140, 142
wounded 136

soldier's aid societies 136–138, 143*c*

"sole custody" 266

Solomon, Hannah Greenbaum 271*c*

Sons of Temperance 87, 90*c*

Sorosis (women's club) 173*c*

Soule, Caroline White 210*c*

South Carolina 56*c*

South Dakota 236, 243*c*, 302*c*, 330*c*

southern suffragists 267, 296, 326

southern women 22–23

Spanish-American War *265, 272c, 273c*

Speech of Hon. Charles Sumner on the Presentation of the First Installment of the Emancipation Petition of the National Woman's Loyal League, 1864 396–397

Spencer, Lily M. *116*

Spencer, Sara Andrews 210*c*

spies (in Civil War) 138, 139, 142, 145*c*

Spinks, Mrs. 329*c*

Stanley, Sara G. 157

Stanton, Edwin M. 140

Stanton, Elizabeth Cady 8*c*–10*c*, 29*c*, 30, 56, 122, *237, 240, 278,* **447–448**
on abolition 157
address to New York state legislature 381–388
address to younger women of 208
and AERA 167
and Susan B. Anthony 88, *278*
on Beecher-Tilton scandal 228
on black suffrage and woman suffrage 175–176, 193–194
as candidate for Congress 167–168, 173*c*
on childbearing 103
and Civil War 135, 136, 165
and coeducation 118
as congressional candidate 180
correspondence with John Greenleaf Whittier 64, 67
on Paulina Wright Davis 116
on death of Lucretia Mott 249
on divisions in suffrage movement 198–199, 215
on divorce law 253
and divorce reform 119, 120, 122*c*, 123*c*
on domestic responsibilities 127, 131, 134
on duration of suffrage movement 275
on earliest meeting with Susan B. Anthony 93–94
early years 49–50
education of 266
Eighty Years and More 59, 175
and emancipation 141
on Fifteenth Amendment 198, 217
on "Foremothers' Day" 264
Fourteenth Amendment 165, 166, 204, 209*c*
on future of voting 267
and Horace Greeley 187–188
on her 80th birthday 276
on her domestic responsibilities 104–105, 110
on her failing faculties 280
The History of Woman Suffrage 241*c*, 242*c*
illness/death of 268, 274*c*
inheritance 123*c*
International Council of Women 240
on Johnstown school elections 253
as lecture circuit speaker 203
letter to electors of 397–398
letter to Theodore Roosevelt on suffrage 285–287
on male leadership of woman suffrage organizations 261–262
on marriage 103–104, 129–130
Married Woman's Property Act 52, 122*c*
on militancy 293
motherhood of 117
and Lucretia Mott 49, 52, 54, 87
on nagging 83
National Legislative League 273*c*
NAWSA 243*c*, 244*c*, 272*c*
on New York politics 96

and New York reform
    campaign of 1853–54
    89
and New York state
    legislature 122c, 123c,
    168
on not changing the name
    of the *Revolution*
    200–201
on Ohio campaign 260
on petitions 238
on Philadelphia plank
    224–225
on proposal of Sixteenth
    Amendment 172, 194
protest of murder
    conviction 173c
racism 171
Republican Party 121
resolutions for 1900
    meeting of NAWSA
    281
Revolution 171, 202
Rochester convention
    72–73
in Seneca Falls 53–54, 56c
Seneca Falls Convention
    72–73, 75c
on Seneca Falls
    Convention editorials
    81–82
on Sixteenth Amendment
    233–234
on specific skills of women
    81
Henry B. Stanton 55, 55c
and Lucy Stone 88
on struggle for women's
    rights 125
on taxation without
    representation 102
and temperance
    movement 87, 90c, 91c
on temperance movement
    259
on the temperance
    movement 100–101
on union of suffrage forces
    245
and U.S. centennial 206
in Utah 219

voting of 242c
and Frances Willard 238
The Woman's Bible 268,
    268, 269, 271c, 272c,
    278–279
on women's clothing 64,
    96–98
on women's married
    names 71
on Victoria Claflin
    Woodhull 223–224
World Anti-Slavery
    Convention 49, 51, 52,
    57–60
Stanton, Harriet Eaton 117
Stanton, Henry Brewster
    50–53, *55,* 55c, 56c,
    72–73, 121, 141
Starr, Ellen 243c
state-by-state approach
    235–236
state colleges and
    universities 208
states
    extending suffrage to
        women 454m
    ratification of Nineteenth
        Amendment 455m
    suffrage amendments 326
states' rights 326
Steel, Edward M. 306, 316,
    324, 344
Stephens, Ann
    Winterbotham 29c
Stephens, William D. 349
Sterling 180
Sterling, Dorothy 16, 151,
    152–153, 155, 157–158,
    160–162, 176–177, 188,
    191–193, 220, 256, 257,
    263, 284, 307
Stevens, Alzina Parsons
    211c
Stevens, Doris 333,
    336–344
Stevens, Nathaniel 28c
Stevenson, Sarah 211c
Stewart, Eliza Daniel 210c
Stewart, Maria W. 10c, 22,
    24, **448**
Stewart, Samuel V. 332c

Stimson, Julia C. 334–336,
    339–341
stockbroker 204
Stone, Kate 150, 158
Stone, Lucy 5, *8, 8c, 28,*
    75c, 87, 88, 141, *170,*
    173c, 241c, 243c, **448**
American Woman Suffrage
    Association 172, 198,
    235
bequests to 241c
on black suffrage and
    woman suffrage
    182–185, 194, 195–196
on Henry Blackwell 124
on child custody 169
civil disobedience of 122c
on Cleveland convention
    199
on Colorado suffrage
    campaign 229
on consolidation of AWSA
    and NWSA 213
and Declaration of Rights
    for Women 207
on divisions in AWSA
    217–218
and divorce reform 120
on domestic
    responsibilities
    232–233
earns degree 56c
education of 266
and Fifteenth Amendment
    171
at first national convention
    85–86
illness/death of 267–268,
    271c
on Indiana campaign 253
International Council of
    Women 240
on lack of rights 128
on lack of support for her
    work 77
on marriage 102,
    115–116
marriage of 117, 122c
on Michigan suffrage
    campaign 228
motherhood of 117

on Nebraska campaign
    248, 251
on New Jersey suffrage
    campaign 230–231
and Republican Party
    207
on speaking for Anti-
    Slavery Society 67
on split with Elizabeth
    Cady Stanton 256–257
on Elizabeth Cady Stanton
    203
tax protest of 122c
on Elizabeth Tilton 228
on union of AWSA and
    NWSA 258–260
on women as public
    speakers 109
on Victoria Claflin
    Woodhull 221
on writing of history of
    suffrage movement
    231–232
Stout, C. 59
Stowe, Harriet Beecher 7c,
    34, 90, 90c, 173c, 230,
    448
Strauss, Anna Lord *353*
strike(s) 9c, 56c, 75c, 272c,
    292–293, 299c, 301c. *See
    also* labor movement
first 5
in Northeast 27
textile workers 300c
at Triangle Shirtwaist
    Company 292, 295,
    298c, 299c
Sturge, Joseph 61
suffrage movement
    key sites of 456m
    states extending suffrage
    454m
Suffrage Parade 315, 316
"suffrage quilts" 239
suffrage resolution 72–74
suffrage subcommittee,
    New York state
    legislature 168
The Suffragist 302c
suffragists *354*
Sullivan Ordinance 298c

Sumner, Charles 141, 396–397
Sumner, Helen L. 20
Sumner, Mary Brown 310
Sunderland, Byron 103
support (by husband) 119–120
Supreme Court, Connecticut 241c
Supreme Court, Massachusetts 8c
Supreme Court, U.S. 212c, 213
  Bradwell v. Illinois 211c, 408
  and employment 206
  Fourteenth Amendment 206
  Locher v. the United States 274c
  Minor v. Happersett 211c, 229, 408–414
  Muller v. Oregon 298c
  Quong v. Oregon 300c
surgeon 144c, 147, 209c, 303c
surgeon general 272c
Surratt, Mary E. Jenkins 145c
"Susan B. Anthony amendment" 142c, 242c, 271c. See also Anthony amendment; Sixteenth Amendment, proposed
Susan B. Anthony (Kathleen Barry) 180–181, 191–193, 198–199, 201, 262, 277, 278, 289
Swarthmore College 145c, 208
Swartz, Vesta M. 159
swimsuit 239
Swisshelm, Jane Grey Cannon 8c, 75c, 448–449

T
Taft, Helen 293
Tappan, Lewis 57
Tappan, Mary J. 154
Tarbell, Ida 274c

Tarbox, Walter Scott 70
taxation without representation 206
tax protest 122c, 210c
teachers and teaching
  African American 24, 90c, 122c
  Civil War 141, 142
  Prudence Crandall 25
  of deaf 173c
  in Massachusetts 25
  single women as 53
  Maria Stewart 24
temperance movement xv, 6, 15, 29c, 212c, 242c, 273c
  Susan Brownell Anthony 87–88, 90c
  first league 210c
  Lydia Mott 87
  Elizabeth Cady Stanton 87, 90c, 91c
  and suffrage movement 238
Tennessee 328, 332c
Tennessee River 140
Tenney, R. S. 190
Terrell, Mary Church 291, 346
Texas 330c–332c
textile industry 4, 7c–10c, 25, 27, 28c, 138, 292–293, 300c. See also mills and mill work
Thirteenth Amendment 145c
Thomas, Mary Carey 122c, 241c
Thomas, Mary Frame Myers 135, 136, 449
Thome, J. A. 45, 46
Thompson, Frank 241c
Thompson, Gertrude Hickman 271c
Thompson, Mary Harris 209c
Thompson, Sophia 139
Thurber, Jeannette 244c
Tiernan v. Poor 9c
Tillman, Juliann Jane 70
Tilton, Elizabeth 207

Tilton, Theodore 166, 202, 203, 207
Tocqueville, Alexis de 17
Tolles, Frederick B. 57–61
Torbet v. Twining 11
Tracy, Hannah Conant 75c
Trader, Ella 143c
trades 73, 266
trade school 274c
Train, George Francis 170, 171, 191, 202
transportation of women 299c
Travis, Mary 247
"trial by her peers" 173c
Triangle Shirtwaist Company 292–293, 295, 298c–300c
Trilling, Blanche 329c
Trollope, Frances Milton 16–17
Troy Female Seminary 3–4, 9c, 10c, 50
Truth, Sojourner 85, 449
  at Akron convention 88–89, 90c, 94
  and enfranchisement of women 169
  eyewitness accounts 162, 186
  petition to President Grant 209c
Tubman, Harriet 8c, 75c, 82, 139, 301c, 449–450
"Turkish dress." See Bloomer outfits
Turner, Eliza L. Sproat Randolph 450
two-party system 354
Tyler, Mrs. W. C. 329c

U
Uncle Tom's Cabin (Harriet Beecher Stowe) 90, 90c
Underground Railroad 75c, 87
Union (U.S. Civil War) 135–137, 142, 143c
  slaves in 141
  spies for 139
  troops 144c

women soldiers 139
wounded 136–137
unions 27, 174c, 209c, 211c, 242c, 303c
  cigar makers 173c
  and fire 295
  Union soldiers 159
U.S. centennial 206
United Tailoresses Society of New York 9c
universal emancipation 141
universal suffrage 166–167, 170
universities 208
University of Chicago Settlement 271c
University of Kansas 244c
Upton, Harriet Taylor 450
Ursuline College 208, 209c
Usher, Rebecca R. 160
Utah 456m
  disfranchisement in 204, 242c
  women's suffrage in 174c, 203–204, 209c, 237, 266, 271c

V
Van Blarcom, Carolyn C. 300c
Van Cott, Margaret 174c
Van Dyck, Henry H. 130
Van Hoosen, Bertha 304c
Van Valkenburg, Ellen Rand 210c
Vassar Female College 143c, 208
Vaughan, Mary 87, 173c
Velesh, Eva MacDonald 308
Vermont 56c, 237
Vernon, Mabel 339
Vest, George G. 239
Victoria C. Woodhull's Address to the Judiciary Committee of the House of Representatives, 1871 401–404
Views of Society and Manners in America 13–14
violence 22

A Virginia Girl (Myrta Lockett Avary) 148–149
Virginia L. Minor's Petition, submitted to the Circuit Court of St. Louis County, Missouri, 1872 406–407
visiting nurses 271*c*
Voice of Industry (magazine) 53
voting 255. *See also* enfranchisement of women
    attempts 209*c*, 211*c*
    Chicago 337, 338
    Declaration of Sentiments 72–73
    on liquor matters 212*c*
    New Jersey 7*c*
    petition to New York state legislature 89, 91*c*, 117
    school 90*c*
    and slavery 142

W
Wade, Benjamin F. 147–148
Wadleigh, Senator 207
wages 74, 292
    factory 27
    low 27
    married women 3, 89, 117, 174*c*, 266
    minimum 274*c*
    for teachers 141
Waite, Catharine W. 210*c*
Wald, Lillian D. 271*c*, 300*c*
Walker, Maggie Lena 274*c*
Walker, Mary 144*c*, 145*c*, 147, 156
Wallace, Zerelda Gray Sanders 249, 251, **450**
Walsh, Loretta 329*c*
Walsh, Reverend Father 279
Waltham, Massachusetts 8*c*
Wanchope, Captain 59
Warner, Susan 90*c*
Warren, Mercy Otis 7*c*, **450**
The War-Time Journal (Eliza Frances Andrews) 158, 160–162

Washington, D.C. 295, 296, 301*c*, 317, 318, 456*m*
Washington, George 242*c*
Washington, Joseph E. 238
Washington, Martha Ball 271*c*, 274*c*
Washington State 236, 241*c*, 242*c*, 299*c*, 456*m*
Watson v. Bailey 7*c*
Watson v. Mercer 12–13
Wattles, Susan E. 190
We Are Your Sisters (Dorothy Sterling) 16, 151–153, 155, 157–158, 160–162, 176–177, 180, 188, 192, 193, 220, 256, 257, 263, 284, 307
Webster, Sarah E. 210*c*
Weed, Thurlow 87
Weeks, John W. 327
Weld, Theodore Dwight 23–24, 31, 33–34, 38–41, 44–45, 61–62, **450–451**
Wellesley College 208, 209*c*
Wells, Alice Stebins 299*c*
Wells, Herbert M. 285
Wells-Barnett, Ida Bell 144*c*, 296, 301*c*, **451**
Wertheimer, Barbara Mayer 307–310, 312–314
Western Anti-Slavery Society 140
Weston, Modenia R. McColl 157
West Virginia 304*c*
We Were There (Barbara Mayer Wertheimer) 307–310, 312–314
Wheaton Female Seminary 10*c*
White, Mrs. John Jay 303*c*
White, Walter 346
Whitehouse, Mrs. Norman deR. 319
White House, protest at 325, 326, 329*c*
White Slave Trade Act 299*c*
white supremacy 267
Whittelsey, Abigail Goodrich 10*c*

Whittier, John Greenleaf 23, 38
widows 26, 142, 143*c*, 169, 174*c*
Wilkinson, E. M. 135
Willard, Emma Hart 3, 4, 8*c*–10*c*, 50
Willard, Frances Elizabeth 29*c*, 210*c*, 212*c*, 238, 259–260, 271*c*, 272, 272*c*, 327, **451**
William Lloyd Garrison (Wendell Phillips Garrison and Francis Jackson Garrison) 46, 57, 58, 61
Williams, Justice 120
Williams, Sylvanie 267
Williamson, Paulina Lyons 256, 257
wills 239, 266
Wilson, Edith Galt 305*c*
Wilson, Woodrow 295, 297, 301*c*–305*c*, 326, 329*c*, 332*c*
    on addressing NAWSA 322
    on delaying suffrage debate in Congress 334
    on federal amendment 326–327, 330*c*, 331*c*
    on Oklahoma suffrage vote 346
    on passage of suffrage amendment 347, 352
    pressure on 326, 327
    on Russian women's rights 334–335
    on suffrage plank 321
    on Tennessee suffrage vote 350
"Winning Plan" 297, 305*c*, 326
"The Winning Policy" (Carrie Chapman Catt) 419–423
Winslow, Rose 342
Winters, Sallie 8*c*
Wisconsin 237, 242*c*
Wittenmeyer, Anne 238
Woman's Advocate 9*c*

The Woman's Bible (Elizabeth Cady Stanton) 268, 268, 269, 271*c*, 272*c*, 278–279
Woman's Journal (newspaper) 203, 209, 209*c*
Woman's Peace Party 304*c*, 331*c*
"woman's sphere" 24
Woman's State Temperance Convention 87
Woman's Temperance League 210*c*
Woman's Temperance Society 90*c*
Woman Suffrage (Carrie Chapman Catt and Nettie Rogers Shuler) 346–351
Woman Suffrage Convention (Washington, D.C.) 173*c*
woman suffrage headquarters, Cleveland, Ohio 321
Woman Suffrage Party 298*c*
Women and American Trade Unions (James J. Kenneally) 308
Women in America (Carol Ruth Berkin and Mary Beth Norton) 11–14
Women in the Campaign (Carolyn Daniel McCreesh) 310
Women of America (Carol Ruth Berkin and Mary Beth Norton) 32, 33, 70
Women of the War (Frank Moore) 148–151, 156, 160, 161
Women's Bureau 332*c*
Women's Centenary Association 209*c*, 210*c*
Women's Central Association of Relief 136
Women's Christian Temperance Union 211*c*, 237, 238, 242*c*–244*c*, 267, 271*c*, 327, 331*c*

Women's Convention 273c
Women's Hospital 122c
women's movement. *See also
    individual women's
    movement organizations*
and antislavery fight 119
bequests to 239, 241c,
    272c, 304c
scandal in 207
split in 170–172, 202, 240,
    243c
Women's Political Union
    294, 298c, 299c
women's rights 50, 51, 55c,
    72, 192
women's studies 244c
Women's Trade Union
    League (WTUL) 293
Wood, Sam 170

Woodhull, Victoria Claflin
    204, 401–404, **451–452**
address to Congress
    204–205, 210c
and Beecher affair 207
eyewitness accounts 218,
    219
move to England 211c
as presidential candidate
    210c
Woolworth, Ida L. 345
Worcester, Massachusetts
    85, 90c, 456m
worker's compensation
    299c
working conditions 292,
    295
Working Girls' Club 239,
    241c

Working Girls' Societies
    242c
working hours 53, 56c, 292,
    298c
Working Women's
    Protective Union 173c
World Anti-Slavery
    Convention **49–71,** 55c
World War I 304c, 325,
    329c, 331c, 333–341
worldwide enfranchisement
    327
wounded, care of 136–137
Wright, Elizur 32
Wright, Frances C. 3, 9c,
    13–14, 24, 87, **452**
Wright, Martha Coffin
    Pelham 7c, 72, 73, 75c,
    166, 188, **452**

WTUL (Women's Trade
    Union League) 293
Wylie, Mrs. 329c
Wyoming 243c, 456m
jurors in 209c
statehood of 238–239
women's suffrage in 174c,
    203, *203,* 238–239,
    266

Y
The Yellow Wallpaper
    (Charlotte Perkins
    Gilman) 244c
Young Women's Christian
    Association 242c
Young Women's Hebrew
    Association 242c